THE PRACTICE OF PSYCHOLOGICAL ASSESSMENT

Norman Tallent

Prentice Hall, Upper Saddle River, New Jersey 07458

Library of Congress Cataloging-in-Publication Data

Tallent, Norman, (date)
    The practice of psychological assessment / Norman Tallent.
      p. cm.
    Includes bibliographical references and index.
    ISBN 0-13-678111-X
    1. Psychometrics.   2. Psychological tests.   3. Psychodiagnostics.
  I. Title.
BF176.T34   1992
150'.28'7--dc20   91-9776
                                                                          CIP

Acquisition Editor: SUSAN FINNEMORE
Editor-in-Chief: CHARLYCE JONES OWEN
Production Editor: ELIZABETH BEST
Copy Editor: KATHRYN M. BECK
Cover Designer: CAROL CERALDI
Prepress Buyer: KELLY BEHR
Manufacturing Buyer: MARY ANNE GLORIANDE
Page Makeup: JOH LISA

© 1992 by Prentice-Hall, Inc.
A Pearson Education Company
Upper Saddle River, NJ 07458

All rights reserved. No part of this book may be
reproduced, in any form or by any means,
without permission in writing from the publisher.

Printed in the United States of America
10 9 8 7 6 5 4 3 2 1

0-13-678111-X

Prentice-Hall International (UK) Limited, London
Prentice-Hall of Australia Pty. Limited, Sydney
Prentice-Hall Canada Inc., Toronto
Prentice-Hall Hispanoamericana, S.A., Mexico
Prentice-Hall of India Private Limited, New Delhi
Prentice-Hall of Japan, Inc., Tokyo
Pearson Education Asia Pte. Ltd., Singapore
Editoria Prentice-Hall do Brasil, Ltda., Rio De Janeiro

To Shirley, Marc, Robert, and Anne–
who make it all meaningful.

CONTENTS

Preface   ix

Part I: Fundamentals of Psychological Assessment

Chapter 1:
PSYCHOLOGICAL ASSESSMENT: *Meaning and Issues*   1

    The Roots of Psychological Assessment, *1*
    The Current Scope of Psychological Assessment, *3*
    Psychological Assessment: What Is It? *4*
    Confusion of Assessment with Testing, *6*
    Psychological Assessment: Science and/or Art? *8*
    From Testing to Assessment, *9*
    The Modern Matrix of Psychological Assessment, *14*
    The Influence of Practical Settings, *17*
    The Teaching and Application of Psychological Assessment...
       and the Outlook, *19*

Chapter 2:
THE PSYCHOLOGICAL ASSESSOR 24

>Judging Others: Gordon Allport, *25*
>Personality Type as a Factor in Judging Others: Henry A. Murray, *26*
>Orientations to Clinical Judgment, *28*
>The Practical Use of Psychological Assessment, *34*
>The Psychological Assessor: Role-Related Issues, *36*
>Perceptions of the Role of Psychological Assessor, *36*
>Ethical Orientation to Psychological Assessment, *45*

Chapter 3:
THE CONTEXT OF PSYCHOLOGICAL ASSESSMENT 47

>The Changing *Zeitgeist*, *47*
>New Orientations to Assessment, *48*
>Philosophical/Scientific Underpinnings of Assessment, *50*
>Changing Orientations to Personality and Psychopathology, *50*
>Assessment and Classification, *53*
>The Information-Gathering Tools of Psychological Assessment, *61*
>Reliability/Validity: How Good Is Psychological Assessment? *62*
>Some Technical Problems with Psychometric Testing, *65*
>Validity of Computer Testing, *67*
>Clinical versus Statistical Prediction: Focus on The Validity of Two Approaches to Psychological Evaluation, *69*
>The Economics of Psychological Assessment, *73*
>The Social Context of Psychological Assessment, *75*

Chapter 4:
THE MEASUREMENT TRADITION 77

>The Psychometric Concept, *77*
>The Practice of Psychometric Testing, *81*
>The Psychometric Cafeteria, *82*
>Some Special Problems with Psychometric Testing, *86*
>Computer Testing, *92*

Chapter 5:
THE CLINICAL TRADITION 98

>The Measurement Tradition and the Clinical Tradition: Differences and Similarities, *99*
>When Is a Test Not a Test? *104*

The Clinical Tradition: The Modern Phase, *107*
Schafer on the Rapaport-Schafer Tradition, *114*
Holt on Rapaport-Schafer, *116*
The Current Status of the Clinical Tradition, *119*

Part II: The Tools of Psychological Assessment

Chapter 6:
PSYCHOLOGICAL TESTING: *Intellectual and Neuropsychological Evaluation* — 121

Intelligence Testing, *121*
Neuropsychological Assessment, *133*

Chapter 7:
PSYCHOLOGICAL TESTING: *Personality Inventories and Projective Techniques* — 145

Personality Inventories, *145*
Projective Techniques, *156*

Chapter 8:
ADDITIONAL TOOLS OF PSYCHOLOGICAL ASSESSMENT: *Observing and Interviewing, and a System of Classification* — 170

Observing and Interviewing, *170*
The Diagnostic and Statistical Manual, *177*

Part III: Applications of Psychological Assessment

Chapter 9:
THE ASSESSMENT PROCESS — 186

Conceptualizing an Assessment Schema, *186*
A Schema to Present the Basic Concepts of This Book, *196*
Approaches to Case Formulation, *202*
Exemplification of Case Formulation, *210*

Chapter 10:
THE ASSESSMENT PROCESS, CONTINUED: *Responsible and Effective Psychological Report Writing* — 220

Content of the Psychological Report, *220*
The Common Content Categories in "Traditional" Psychological Reports: A Critique, *224*
Responsibility and Effectiveness, *229*
"Quickie" Reports, *244*
The Perennial Pitfalls in Writing Psychological Reports, *246*

Chapter 11:
ASSESSMENT FOR TREATMENT — 262

Questioning the Assumption, *263*
Reconceptualizing the Relationship of Psychological Assessment to Therapy, *270*
The Current Status of Psychological Assessment in the Practice of Psychotherapy, *273*
The Road Map Concept of Psychological Therapeutics, *285*

Chapter 12:
THE CASE WORKUP — 290

Selecting a Battery, *290*
Gathering Necessary Data, *291*
The Role of Scoring, *293*
Interpretive Strategies, *294*
A Brief Discourse on Rationale in Psychological Interpretation, *300*
Illustrative Case Workup, *309*

Chapter 13:
VARIATIONS AND TRENDS IN PSYCHOLOGICAL ASSESSMENT — 323

"Creative Variations" in Psychological Assessment, *324*
Further Approaches for Enhancing the Productivity of the Assessment Process, *330*
The Role of the Psychological Technician in Assessment, *343*
Technician-Level versus Assessor-Level Functions, *346*
Psychological Assessment as a Transaction, *347*

References — 351

Author Index — 385

Subject Index — 393

PREFACE

This book is about psychological assessment and psychological assessors, an indissoluble combination in the professional enterprise of understanding individuals for defined and useful purposes. Psychological assessment is a conceptual, flexible, problem-solving *process* for reaching this objective. It should not be exclusively identified with tools, like tests and formulas; or with methods and techniques, though all of these are important to that process and are addressed here.

So too is the judgment that the assessor must exercise. Whether in the continuous ongoing of psychotherapy or in the formal consultation that typically leads to a comprehensive report, each case for assessment presents a unique challenge. Step-by-step rules therefore cannot be prescribed. What is offered on the following pages is more in the way of an examination of assessment tools and the setting forth of principles and guidelines to practice, approaches, and strategies.

The thrust of this work is *practice*...Particularly in clinical, counseling, and school settings. It is oriented to where the action is. In addition to mastering the nitty-gritty of tests and testing, observing and interviewing, the psychological assessor requires additional grounding in the basics of the practice. These include a comfortable familiarity with the theory of tests and measurement, personality theory, and classification and systems for ordering data on personality and psychopathology, together with ways of applying these in generating, selecting, and formulating meaningful psychological information.

Psychological assessment is a rather new term, but the *practice* of psychological assessment extends back multiple millennia. Modern assessment theory and practices build on a number of disciplines, such as school and clinical testing, psychotherapy, behavior therapy, and psychiatry. Among the pioneers of assessment are Thorndike, Witmer, Freud, Binet, Wechsler, and Murray, and contributions to the advancement of theory and practice continue to be well represented in current publications.

I would like to thank the following Prentice-Hall reviewers: Timothy Baker, University of Wisconsin, John J. Burke Ph.D., East Central University, James F. Calhoun Ph.D., The University of Georgia, Juris G. Draguns, Pennsylvania State University, Robert B. Hampson Ph.D., Associate Professor of Psychology, Southern Methodist University, and Barry L. Mallinger Ph.D., Radford University.

Part I The Fundamentals of Psychological Assessment

1

PSYCHOLOGICAL ASSESSMENT:
Meaning and Issues

Psychological assessment, like so many of our concepts, such as neurosis, normality, intelligence, validity, love, and life itself, defies adequate definition. We can, nevertheless, describe, discuss, teach, research, and improve upon the practices that relate to this concept—one that extends backward to antiquity and has acquired an ever-expanding role in today's world.

THE ROOTS OF PSYCHOLOGICAL ASSESSMENT

Today's practice of psychological assessment stems from roots in antiquity. Ancient peoples recognized, just as we currently do, the need to understand oneself and one's associates (Boring, 1950), particularly their dispositions, proficiencies, or ways of living that are problematic. From the beginning, psychological assessment has pursued goals that are practical and that foster the understanding we need to relate to one another and to ourselves.

Assessment techniques in the service of practical needs are referred to in the Old Testament, a number of examples being found in Judges. To select soldiers for a forthcoming battle, "The Lord said to Gideon, 'The people are still too many; take them to the water and I will *test* them for you there'" (Judg. 7:4) (emphasis added). And when the men of Gilead, in combat with the men of E'phraim, seized the fords of the Jordan, thus blocking escape of the enemy, a number of E'phraimites sought to get away by posing as Gileadites. But the Gileadites proved too clever for their foe. When any of the fugitives sought permission to cross the stream they were queried, "'Are you an E'phraimite?' When he said, 'No' they said to him, 'Then say Shibboleth,' and he said 'Sibboleth,' for he could not pronounce it right; then they seized him and slew him at the fords of the Jordan." (Judg. 12:5–6) To this day *Shibboleth* means *test*, though the consequences of failing generally are not so serious as once they were.

McReynolds (1975, 1986) discusses a number of ancient approaches to personality assessment. These include the humoral psychology of Hippocrates and the related methods of physiognomy, hepatoscopy ("the minute examination of the liver of a sacrificed animal in order to ascertain the presence or absence of particular signs which, when properly interpreted, would give some clue to the future."), and astrology—perhaps the oldest scheme for delineating the personality and predicting the future. DuBois (1966) notes the beginning of civil service testing about 2200 B.C., and the initiation of a formal system of examinations, including a sampling of job proficiency, during the Chan dynasty in 1115 B.C. Plato noted an even earlier approach to vocational assessment in Greece (Doyle, 1974).

Thus we see a continuity between ancient concepts and methods, and those of the present day—skill testing, job sampling, identification of significant variables, personality description, prediction, and interpretation. Astrology, systematically studied by the ancients, and its many "insights," continues largely unchanged into the present period—its influence reaching even into the White House of the 1980s (Reagan, 1989; Quigley, 1990). Snyder (1974), in his study, "Why Horoscopes Are True" helps to explain why:

> All Ss were given an identical general horoscope interpretation, but were assigned randomly to one of three specificity conditions (N = 21 per condition) in which they were told the interpretation was (1) "generally true of people," (2) derived for them on the basis of the year and month of their birth, or (3) derived for them on the basis of the year, month, and day of their birth. Results significantly showed that the more specific birth time referent the S ascribed to the astrological interpretation, the more the interpretation was accepted as an accurate description of the S's personality.

Additionally, "horoscopes may achieve 'verification' or acceptance because of situation factors alone, rather than any actual relationship between astrological interpretations and one's observed personality." The seriousness of this observation relates to the fact, as Snyder reminds us, "that individuals readily accept general personality interpretations supposedly based upon information derived from psychological tests as accurate descriptions of their personalities." Such "validation" of personality descriptions that rest on general or stereotyped psychological reporting is a serious issue and is dealt with further in Chapter 10 in a discussion of "Barnum" and "Aunt Fanny" statements.

The era of modern psychological assessment grows from the late nineteenth century work of Sir Francis Galton, a biologist with an abiding interest in heredity. In order to study the transmission of human characteristics it was first necessary that he have some measure of these characteristics—reaction time, muscle strength, vision and hearing, for example. Techniques that he employed, that variously had application to the measurement of physical and psychological characteristics, included free association, questionnaires, and rating scales. Most significant for its application to psychological assessment was his adaptation of statistical methods to his work.

James McKeen Cattell was influenced by Galton, and his subsequent work, in large measure, was an extension of the latter's approach. Cattell amassed a sizable store of data through the annual administration of a battery of tests to entering freshmen at Columbia University, measures similar to those used by Galton—such as tests of memory, sensory function, and muscle strength. He coined the term *mental test* in an 1890 article.

Moving toward a now familiar format of the mental test was the Binet-Simon test of 1905, an instrument designed to identify slow learners who could not profit from ordinary classroom instruction. Through a series of revisions in France and the United States the Binet continues in contemporary use.

Following the introduction of this instrument the testing movement took off like a skyrocket. Large-scale group testing made its debut in World War I with the introduction of the Army Alpha and the nonlanguage Army Beta. Tests of interest, aptitude, and achievement took their place in the armamentarium of testers, particularly in such settings as schools and counselors' offices.

Assessment in the modern era, particularly by clinical, counseling, school, and research psychologists, rests heavily on instruments whose origins extend back a half-century or more, and the leaders among these have enjoyed steady popularity for decades (Sundberg, 1961; Jackson & Wohl, 1966; Thelen, Varble, & Johnson, 1968; Thelen & Ewing, 1970; Lubin, Wallis, & Paine, 1971; Levy & Fox, 1975; Brown & McGuire, 1976; Reynolds & Sundberg, 1976; Wade & Baker, 1977; Wade, Baker, Morton, & Baker, 1978; Piotrowski & Keller, 1978, 1984a,b, 1989a,b; Sell & Torres-Henry, 1979; Tuma & Pratt, 1982; Piotrowski, 1984, 1985; Lubin, Larsen, & Matarazzo, 1984; Lubin, Larsen, Matarazzo, & Seever, 1985; Piotrowski, Sherry, & Keller, 1985; Pruitt, Smith, Thelen, & Lubin, 1985; Ritzler & Alter, 1986; Durand, Blanchard, & Mindell, 1988; Watkins & Campbell, 1989; Craig & Horowitz, 1990). The series of Wechsler scales, the MMPI, and the TAT had their beginnings in the late 1930s. The Rorschach stands proud among numerous psychological assessors—as measured by its widespread clinical usage and application to research as it goes into its eighth decade. Compared with these venerable instruments, widely accepted behavioral assessment is a relatively new development.

THE CURRENT SCOPE OF PSYCHOLOGICAL ASSESSMENT

The need to understand ourselves and others in everyday life is as great as ever. As I write these words I reflect on a recent presidential campaign and recollect that the attention given to the personalities of the candidates often seemed to overshadow the issues. Observations were freely made, by citizens and press, on such topics as the candidates' intelligence, knowledgeableness, honesty and sincerity, ability to use language effectively, warmth, likability, spontaneity, quality of interpersonal relations, performance skills, optimism or pessimism, social stimulus value, stage presence, energy level, ability to cope with stressful situations, mental health, and sexual proclivities—indeed, a veritable lexicon of traits. A need to assess the candidates in some dependable manner was also recognized, and some of the concepts informing this goal were borrowed from chemistry. There was much talk of the "acid test" and the "litmus test." For example, how a candidate voted or commented on some particular issue was said to establish his or her position on the political spectrum.

At a time when the use of assessment methods is at an all-time high, the assessment *Zeitgeist* is reflected in a statement by the American Psychological Association (1970):

> The nature of man and of society makes it necessary that we attempt to assess psychological characteristics. Individual human beings differ from one another in a variety of ways; society requires a variety of diverse contributions from its members. The more accurately we can judge each person's suitability for potential roles consistent with his interests, the more successfully a society will function. Accurate assessment brings benefits to the individual as well by enabling him to locate the particular kinds of situations in which he can function most effectively as he seeks education, employment, medical and psychological services, and fuller personal development. In attempting to understand others and to predict how they will function under various circumstances, all of us utilize a great variety of assessment methods—observations, careful or casual, interviews, formal or informal, and comments and recommendations based on varying degrees of acquaintance with the person being judged. Specialized psychological assessment techniques have been developed as refinements on these general methods or as supplements to them. What such specialized techniques add is some indication of the validity and usefulness of the information. They also provide some degree of *standardization of conditions* under which observations are made or samples of behavior obtained and, where possible, some *quantification* of the findings. This makes possible systematic comparisons of the individual's characteristics with those of reference or norm groups. But the psychological procedures are similar in many ways to the more informal appraisals of people that constantly go on.

PSYCHOLOGICAL ASSESSMENT: WHAT IS IT?

A basic point of agreement on psychological assessment (or personality assessment, intellectual assessment, and so on) is that it is a *process* and not a set of tools or rules. Thus, Maloney and Ward (1976) observe that psychological assessment is "an extremely complex...*process of solving problems (answering questions)* in which psychological tests are often used as *one* of the methods of collecting relevant data." Further, "psychological assessment is a variable process, depending on the question asked, the person involved, time commitments, and myriad other factors. As such, it cannot be reduced to a finite set of specific rules or steps." This understanding of assessment will be evident throughout this book.

In his APA presidential address, Matarazzo (1990) makes a case for the valid role of tests in buttressing clinical opinions and indicates, further, the limitations of objectivity:

> Even in our nation's most advanced centers for psychological assessment, the measurement of intelligence (or personality, memory, or other psychological functions) is not, even today, a totally objective, completely science-based activity. Rather, in common with much of medical diagnosis, experience in our nation's courtrooms is forcefully making clear...that the assessment of intelligence, personality, or type or level of impairment is a highly complex operation that involves extracting diagnostic meaning from an individual's personal history and objectively recorded test scores. Rather than being totally objective, assessment involves a subjective component.

And, consistent with Maloney and Ward:

> Competent practitioners in psychology learn from clinician role models during apprenticeship training and from their own subsequent experiences that, objective psychological *testing* and clinically sanctioned and licensed psychological *assessment* are vastly different even though assessment usually includes testing.

Sloves, Docherty, and Schneider (1979) similarly view psychological assessment "as a variable process of problem solving, decision making, and evaluation procedures." A formula for carrying out this process clearly is not at hand. An assessment schema identifying key features of the process can be formulated, however (see Chapter 9).

Maloney and Ward (1976) identify three components of the assessment process. These are: (1) specification of the problem to be solved, (2) data collection, and (3) interpreting the data (answering the question asked). Sloves, Docherty, and Schneider (1979) present their problem-solving model in six steps: (1) problem clarification, (2) planning, (3) development, (4) implementation, (5) outcome determination, and (6) dissemination. Howe's (1981) approach to problem solving adds to the usual concern for understanding the client's need to understand the treatment context. Thus the unique situation in which an assessment takes place and the orientation of the assessor and the therapist are among the "myriad other factors" to which Maloney and Ward refer.

This author (Tallent, 1988) conceptualizes a schema that recognizes the assessment process as one of multiple and complex interaction, an integrative task with the focus on the client (see Chapter 9). Specifically, the task of the psychological assessor is to relate to four key areas of information, and to those who provide and use the information (the referral source or the client, for example). The four key areas of information are: (1) the reason for assessment, (2) the raw data, (3) a frame—or frames—of reference, and (4) interpretation, case conceptualization, and the psychological report. The implementation of this assessment schema is spelled out in Chapters 9 and 10.

Korchin and Schuldberg (1981) discuss assessment in terms of what the process *is* and its *purpose*:

> Stated broadly, "clinical assessment is the process by which clinicians gain understanding of the patient necessary for making informed decisions" (Korchin, 1976, p. 124). Clinical diagnosis, in the restricted sense, may be included, but more usually the intent is description and prediction toward the ends of planning, executing, and evaluating therapeutic intervention and predicting future behavior. Any of numerous techniques can be used, singly or in combination, depending on the orientation of the clinician and the specific questions for which answers are sought. Thus, interviews with the client or with others; observations in natural or contrived situations; or the use of tests of different functions, varying in breadth, objectivity, psychometric refinement, and inference might all be included. The immediate goal may be the relatively precise measurement of a particular psychological function or the construction of a "working image or model of the person" (Sundberg & Tyler, 1962).

CONFUSION OF ASSESSMENT WITH TESTING

Commonly, but erroneously (in terms of the discussion on the last several pages), the expressions *psychological assessment* and *psychological testing* are used synonymously or interchangeably. Wechsler (1975), whose name is on a number of intelligence tests, exemplifies that there is, in fact, a distinction between the two.

Intelligence tests, he asserts, do not measure the variables they are generally thought to measure. In their best use, intelligence tests do not focus on the measurement of discrete skills, but on the individual's intelligence as it may be available in everyday functioning:

> What we measure with tests is not what tests measure—not information, not spatial perception, not reasoning ability. These are only means to an end. What intelligence tests measure, what we hope they measure, is something much more important: the capacity of an individual to understand the world about him and his resourcefulness to cope with its challenges.

To appraise these qualities, Wechsler advises, we must take into consideration (1) the *nonintellective factors of intelligence*, and (2) the *autonomous factors of intelligence*. He includes among the nonintellective factors drive, persistence, and goal awareness. The latter

> relate to an individual's potential to perceive and respond to social, moral, and aesthetic values. These factors involve not so much knowledge or skills as a capacity to assess excellence and worthwhileness of human aims and performance. They relate to underlying motivations, particular attitudes, and certain impacts, recognizable when present though not always nor everywhere equally esteemed.

Testing is psychometric, a physicalistic (mechanical, formula-following) procedure (Rosenwald, 1965), and follows an actuarial paradigm. Psychological assessment and psychological testing are different processes, and they yield different products. Nevertheless, the reaching of conclusions through the use of psychometrics often is mislabeled as "assessment," as, for example, in "computer assessment" (Tallent, 1987; see Chapter 4). Similarly, reflecting a lack of historical distinction between testing and assessment, many who in fact practice assessment have considered themselves to be testers. One recollects Molière's character, Monsieur Jourdain, who was struck with the insight: "For more than forty years I have been talking prose without knowing it."

Sloves, Docherty, and Schneider (1979) make the following distinction between assessment and testing:

> Psychological testing is defined as a set of skills, tactics, and strategies subsumed under the heading of psychological methods. In this view, methods represent the technical skills used as a means of carrying out a psychological assessment. Psychological assessment is systems and problem oriented, dynamic, and conceptual; whereas psychological testing is methods and measurement oriented, descriptive and technical.

The authors then point out the consequence of not attending to this distinction, and suggest a remedy:

> The failure by many practitioners and trainers in professional psychology to distinguish between assessment and testing has led to a tendency for the profession to focus its attention on the mechanistic and technical aspects of test administration and to ignore or slight the conceptual basis of the assessment process. Bardon and Bennett (1967) have proposed as a solution to this problem that practice and training, not just in assessment but in all areas of psychological services, shift away from its current emphasis on knowledge and technical expertise and toward a conceptual approach to professional psychology that trains psychologists to *think like psychologists* (emphasis added).

Such close linking of tests to assessment does not accurately reflect today's practices. Even psychologists who are well trained in testing may choose to limit, or not use at all, the psychological instruments available to them, the decision to test or not to test being based on their judgment in the individual case. Among those professionals who do not have expertise in testing are many competent practitioners who are skilled in the art of psychological assessment.

That a distinction between assessment and testing is of the greatest importance will become clearer yet as the different products yielded by these different procedures are examined in the unfolding thesis of this book. At the same time we note that testing is extensively employed in conducting psychological assessments (pp. 4–6)—which fact may contribute to the confusion between assessment and testing. As pointed out, however, testing is but one of a number of means of acquiring data in the assessment process. Testing skills are but one of the skills that may be demanded of the psychological assessor. And they are important skills, which is the rationale for the extensive discussion of major personality, intelligence, and neuropsychological tests in Part II.

PSYCHOLOGICAL ASSESSMENT: SCIENCE AND/OR ART?

As a variable process involving myriad factors, psychological assessment does not—cannot—meticulously follow a scientific model. Assessment is not systematic, or carried out in accordance with laws. The subjective factor, including the personality make-up of the assessor, looms large and is valued. The subjective operations of the process are still inadequately defined and understood, hence they cannot readily be taught, except by imitation, as Holt (1968) and Polanyi (1958) point out. Assessors are likely to reach somewhat different conclusions when evaluating the same person, and some assessors are recognized to be more skilled than others.

Holt (1968) views assessment in these terms:

> We are forced to improvise, to create hypotheses where someday it may be possible simply to invoke established laws. Each new subject for testing might be compared to an unsolved problem in theory for another science: different experts will approach it differently, drawing on their intuition, hunches, purely heuristic rules of thumb, anything to make possible some start; and they may end up with different solutions, sometimes partly, sometimes equally plausible but unrelated to one another.

Assessment clearly is an art—and the practitioner of assessment is an artisan (Matarazzo, 1990). At the same time we must recognize that assessment does follow scientific principles, such as empiricism; and some assessment procedures, such as testing, bear various trappings of science. Such considerations led Holt to characterize psychological assessment as a "scientific art."

All psychologists, however, are not comfortable with the fact that art plays a role in interpretation. Levy's (1963) point of view is representative of this contrary position. He notes, correctly, that some clinical workers, particularly beginners, are inclined to be "too tolerant of patient behavior." That is, they commonly overlook pathology—they *underinterpret* their data. Others veer in the opposite direction. They overpathologize their data—they *overinterpret*. Levy contends that to the extent that interpretive rules are not entirely explicit, "interpretation does remain an art; to the same extent it is fraught with error and confusion."

However, at the conclusion of his book he dilutes this judgment:

> The fact that I have denied psychological interpretation any special status among the arts and have attempted to lay bare the logic underlying this process does not mean that I believe that anyone understanding this logic can be assured of success in its application. At various points in this book I have pointed out the demands made upon the clinician's personality by psychological interpretation and the ways in which his personality may affect his practice. This undoubtedly represents one of the major uncontrolled sources of variation in psychological interpretation, and an extremely subtle one as well. But beyond this, although I have maintained an avowedly—perhaps even aggressively—positivistic viewpoint with regard to psychological interpretation in this book, I should like to conclude by conceding that there is still another type of personal element which probably no amount of abstract knowledge of the interpretive process can seriously alter, and which

may, in the final analysis, differentiate between the successful and the unsuccessful, the mediocre and the brilliant, application of interpretation. This is *style*. In interpretation, as in diplomacy, it is quite likely that style may often count for as much as, if not more than, content in making the difference between success and failure.

FROM TESTING TO ASSESSMENT

Testing

The modern practice of psychological assessment, as practiced by most psychologists, builds on the foundation of psychological testing. Starting with Binet testing, the testing concept continues strong. Rapaport (Rapaport, Gill, & Schafer, 1945, 1946), the father of a widely practiced current approach to psychological assessment labels his procedure *diagnostic psychological testing*, and other leading psychologist assessors, such as Schafer (1989), Rosenwald (1963), Holt (1968), and Appelbaum (1970) have retained in their writings expressions like *testing* and *tester*. Psychological instruments such as the Rorschach, the TAT, and the Bender Gestalt, commonly employed as nonpsychometric tools, nevertheless are generally identified as *tests*.

In the Binet tradition of testing, the goal is to determine a subject's level of mental functioning, and hence educability or the need for educational remediation. This limited purpose of testing ultimately gave way to a broader range of educational diagnoses and remedial implications in the schools, and to diagnosis and treatment planning in the mental health and counseling fields.

Paralleling an emphasis on measurement and formal classification has been an emphasis on generating *test results*. These might include scores, score patterns, or responses to test items, with a view to translating such data into educational or clinical diagnoses, or to various other kinds of useful information. Frequently, however, we hear the complaint that such an emphasis detracts from the goal of understanding the client in favor of an eager interest in tests and test performance, a situation known as *test centrism*.

Case Formulation/Problem Solving

The making of formal clinical diagnoses is a basic in psychiatric practice, the fundamentals of which are entrenched in the *Diagnostic and Statistical Manual* (DSM) series of the American Psychiatric Association (1952, 1968, 1980, 1987). In practice, however, *case formulation* exists along with the making of diagnoses. Indeed, "Making a DSM-III-R diagnosis represents only an initial step in a comprehensive evaluation." (American Psychiatric Association, 1987). Just as test centrism detracts from knowing your client, so can an overemphasis on formal diagnosis: "Establishing the diagnosis is often done at the expense of curiosity about the patient" (Cooper & Michels, 1988).

Perry, Cooper, and Michels (1987) clarify the similarities and differences in a clinical diagnosis and a (psychodynamic) case formulation:

> In many respects a dynamic formulation and a clinical diagnosis share a common purpose. Although both hold intellectual, didactic, and research interests, their primary function is to provide a succinct conceptualization of the case and thereby guide a treatment plan. Like a psychiatric diagnosis, a psychodynamic formulation is specific, brief, focused, and therefore limited in its intent, scope, and wisdom. It concisely and incisively clarifies the central issues and conflicts, differentiating what the therapist sees as essential from what is secondary. Also like the diagnosis, additional information and changes over time may lead to modification of the patient's dynamics and how they are formulated, with corresponding alterations in treatment. Again, like the diagnosis, the psychodynamic understanding of a patient serves as a stabilizing force in conducting any form of therapy; its general effect is conservative, discouraging a change in tack with every slight shift of the wind.

It is the impression of many clinicians that diagnosis, particularly among psychiatrists, is overemphasized and misunderstood. Cohen (1990) observes "a state of mind in which the categories and criteria of DSM-III-R has become reified and codified."

Simon (1990), in agreement with Cohen, amplifies on this very serious problem in contemporary psychiatry. He suggests that "The labels we attach to phenomena are being treated as if they were the phenomena." Further, "for roughly 15 years, APA [American Psychiatric Association] has been preoccupied with classifying and reclassifying. This was not always the case. We always had a classification system, but it had not been the major concern that it has now become at the expense, one fears, of more basic considerations. All too often, to follow the direction of Dr. Cohen's thoughts, it has frozen rather than liberated our thinking. We study the diagnostic rule book instead of the patient.

This classification zeal has not been justified by a major breakthrough in our knowledge that would oblige us to revolutionize our diagnostic categories. Indeed, the changes that have been made are not revolutionary. On the contrary, they seem to be seeking a refinement that impresses some of us as excessive."

Case formulation, whether dynamic or otherwise, behavioral, for example, is the end statement, or report, that the assessment process produces. The essential concept of this view of the case formulation is *focus*, and a *case-focused report* (Tallent, 1988) is the hallmark of a meaningful assessment. Thus, a psychological examiner may focus on a child's presenting problem, namely loss of interest in studies, with a view to understanding the child's difficulty and making recommendations for remediation. The assessor's task, then, as Maloney and Ward (1976), Sloves, Docherty, and Schneider (1979), Howe (1981), and numerous other contemporary writers, (as reviewed by Lovitt, 1988) suggest is problem solving. Test data, "test results," or a diagnosis can be nothing more than part of the means to the end of solving a presenting problem.

Role of the Psychological Assessor

From the discussion thus far, and particularly the understanding that the purpose of assessment is problem solving, the assessor is viewed as central, more important than tests or other sources of data that may contribute to the problem-solving process. The centrality of the psychological assessor to problem solving is graphically shown on page 197. Thus postulated, so far as the psychological assessor is concerned, she or he is something much more than a "tester," and the role of her or his tests is decreased. Clinical wisdom holds that it is most important to establish the validity of the psychological assessor, the crucial tool in the assessment process.

Hunt (1946) was perhaps the first to propose this role for the psychological assessor:

> We should consider the individual clinician as a clinical instrument, and study and evaluate his performance exactly as we study and evaluate a test.

In a later paper (Hunt, 1951) he developed the idea further:

> The justification of a good clinician depends not upon his success with any single case, but upon his overall batting average over a period of time and with a number of cases.

Matarazzo (1990) frames the current status of Holt's position thus:

> As some of our psychologist colleague-critics and federal and state legislators and judges have recently made clear, psychological assessment techniques, in common with most tools, can be used for many purposes, some harmful and some helpful, and their use cannot be separated from their validity and from the training, competence, and ethical values of the psychologist using them. In the hands of a good clinician, the results of an examination of intelligence or personality, correlated with information from the person's history, are as useful as analogous information would be in the hands of a good surgeon, internist, accountant, or plumber. In the hands of a fool—whether psychologist, physician, physicist, elementary school teacher, college admissions officer, surgeon, or plumber—such data are tools for potential harm.

Put in terms of a long ongoing controversy, the issue is *clinical judgment*, which is discussed in several contexts in this book. The problem has been approached by a number of investigators who sought to determine whether some psychological assessors are better judges of clinical variables than are others. More specifically, the hypothesis considers that training and experience make for better, that is, more valid judgments. However, the data favoring the prowess of the well-trained assessor over the neophyte psychologist, or even over untrained persons, are not abundant, and some of the data are variously interpreted. Only a weak-to-modest relationship between training and experience, and quality of clinical judgment is reported by Giedt (1955), Oskamp (1962, 1965), Lehman, Ban, and Donaldson (1965), Goldberg (1968), and in a summary article by Wiggins (1973).

Clashing reviews of Rock, Bransford, Morey, and Maisto (1988), and Garb (1988, 1989) document this state of affairs. Nevertheless, studies such as that of Goldberg (1959) may be instructive. Overall, Goldberg's findings were negative with respect to the diagnostic powers of psychologists and psychology trainees to differentiate patients with organic brain damage from nonorganics with the aid of the Bender Gestalt. In this respect their performance did not exceed that of nonprofessionals:

> The most striking finding of this study is the complete overlap between groups of judges on diagnostic accuracy. And in general the results indicate that diagnostic accuracy... does *not* depend on experience or training in psychology (unless, perhaps, that training includes years of intensive work with the instrument in question). If he is not a real expert in the use of the Bender, a clinician will find that his secretary can probably do this particular job of differential diagnosis as well as himself.

Support for the possibly greater diagnostic power of the expert stems from the highly superior performance of one of Goldberg's judges, Max Hutt, "one of the country's foremost authorities on the Bender test." Obviously, much more evidence is needed to support the general superiority of the expert assessor, but a tentative finding to this effect has since been reported (Lambert & Wertheimer, 1988): "A robust relationship between accuracy of diagnostic categorization and both relevant education and experience can indeed be demonstrated."

Also tentative is the earlier report of Chambers and Hamlin (1957) who found large differences in the ability of psychologists to classify patients into one of five known diagnostic groups on the basis of blind Rorschach analysis....

Of the twenty judges in the study, five succeeded in identifying correctly all five protocols submitted to them. Four judges missed in all, or all but one, of the choices they made.

However, the authors caution that "the study does not justify any firm conclusions as to the consistent differential ability of various judges."

The above findings are of interest, and form a basis for further investigation. It remains a challenge to demonstrate convincingly that some (indeed many) assessors are clearly superior to others, particularly those who are minimally trained or are deficient in their aptitude for assessment. This is a widespread impression among assessors and their colleagues.

Another approach to the study of diagnostic judgement focuses on the inferential processes that have been observed in clinical work (therapy, counseling, assessment). Dumont and Lecomte (1987) have identified common errors that detract from the quality of inference making and the faulty case formulations that result. These are labeled and explained by the authors as follows:

1. The Availability Heuristic
    When one is searching for an explanation of a troubling clinical event, certain ideas inevitably present themselves before others. One idea may spring to mind as a function of the vividness with which one experienced it in the past; another asserts

itself fresh from a reading of a journal article that touches on the clinical issue; or a comment made in passing during lunch by a friend or a colleague sticks in one's mind. This random factor gets built into our diagnoses, as we are prone to use the first available idea or set of ideas that provide us with an adequate explanation of a puzzling effect.

2. The Vividness Criterion in Assessment

   Enzle, Hansen, and Lowe...demonstrated that the level of imagery in the information that we receive determines the level of impact that the information will have on our inferences, regardless of the intrinsic usefulness of that information. The datum that proves to be a "red herring" gets folded into our analysis as a function of the degree to which it reeks.

3. Theories as Procrustean Beds

   Explanations are usually conceptualized in terms of the theoretical system or school in which the therapists have been trained. Even if they should not be using any formal theory, they have some prejudices of a theoretical nature that profoundly shape their inference making. That system allows them to formulate a global explanation rather than list an assortment of disparate, unconnected causes. Therapists who choose to work within a single, closed system are prone, almost by definition, to overlook a multitude of contingencies—physical, social, medical, genetic, educational, or recreational—that might have significantly contributed to the core problem of their clients and, in any event, contribute perhaps to aggravate their condition.

4. Theories and Simple-Cause Etiologies

   There is a further complication that arises from a narrow purist approach to developing a diagnosis of a disorder. It is related to the medical penchant (quite justifiable in most cases in that context) to seek a single disease entity to explain a symptom or a complex of symptoms. The pitfall here is for therapists to stop their exploration of a problem when they have satisfied themselves that the cause that has emerged will adequately explain the pernicious effect that the client wishes to eradicate...This is fine if there are not several independent, or even interacting, causes underlying the client's problems.

5. Dispositional Versus Situational Factors

   It is a dispositional frame of reference rather than a situational frame of reference that psychologically-minded clinicians tend to adopt in working with others...Batson (1975) found that a professional "is more likely to attribute problems to and direct help toward changing the person in need rather than the social situation, even if the needy person is clearly seeking the opposite...Because counselors and therapists see themselves in the mind-shaping business rather than the casework business, it should not be surprising that graduate clinical students develop skills rather quickly in shifting themselves into the perspectives, attitudes, moods, aspirations, fears, perceptual biases, and knowledge structures of their clients. But they seem less adept (and perhaps less willing) to plunge into the pressing, concrete, pungent, unforgiving, and brutal reality of the context in which these clients are tormented.

Some clinicians have a contrary bias, however, and favor external formulations at the expense of overlooking dispositional factors. Thus, for example,

It is not uncommon for those who work with junkies and other types of street folk to conceptualize the client's problem primarily in terms of social pressure or peer pressure.

THE MODERN MATRIX OF PSYCHOLOGICAL ASSESSMENT

The "Four Cultures of Psychology"

Korchin and Schuldberg (1981) identify four models, orientations, or basic approaches to clinical assessment, all of them "manifestations of ideological conflicts among the 'four cultures of psychology', reflecting profound differences in their conceptions of human nature, psychological distress, and the conditions for effecting therapeutic change." These several ideologies are also associated with profound variations in the assessment process, including the instruments used and the ways of using them—or in some cases, with the downplaying of assessment or the eschewal of psychological assessment instruments.

The oldest model—the psychometric—continues strong, and indeed, is expanding, and is the entire subject matter of Chapter 4. Measurement, by testing, is the cornerstone of this model. Statistical prediction of traits is the goal, which requires that the tests used be valid and reliable. Test items ideally are well structured and normed, as are entire scales. The objectivity of the test items must be approached by the objectivity of the examiner. In modern usage, however, judgment and inference have taken on a sanctioned role (American Psychological Association, *Standards for educational and psychological testing*, 1985).

What Korchin and Schuldberg call *psychodiagnosis* is identified in this book as the *clinical tradition*, and constitutes the subject matter of Chapter 5. The clinical tradition sets the tone for the view of assessment developed in this book; it is, according to Korchin and Schuldberg, "the dominant model of clinical assessment." The clinical assessor may (and typically does) utilize psychometric techniques, but in contrast to the psychometric goal of delineating traits of the individual, the assessor in the clinical tradition focuses on character or personality description embracing multiple areas and levels of functioning. The clinical assessor, functioning in accordance with the clinical tradition, emphasizes the use of judgment, inference, and subjectivity—such as recognizing the value of countertransference (Sugarman, 1981). Symbolism and the content of responses (e.g., Gold, 1987) coexist with an interest in scores.

Korchin and Schuldberg (1981) succinctly define the assessor's role in psychodiagnosis:

> Above all, the psychodiagnostic orientation puts the clinician rather than the test at the center of the assessment process. The clinician has to organize and conceptualize the question to be answered, the techniques to use, and finally integrate diverse findings into a coherent whole. At all points, clinical judgment and inference are required, and the value of the assessment findings ultimately depends heavily on the skill and knowledge of the interpreting clinician.

Behavior assessment, a third "culture," differs sharply from both the psychometric model and the clinical tradition, in concept and in practice. Behavior assessors shun dispositional or trait conceptions of personality; they reject the notion that personality relates to what an individual *is* or *has*, but rather to what the individual *does*. The situation or context of behavior is accorded a key position as a determiner of behavior and the role of testing is minimized inasmuch as the use of instruments is largely inconsistent with behavior theory and therapy: "Psychometric criteria are largely incompatible with behavioral assumptions." (Nelson, 1983) The outcome of operating under this assumption is a functional, case-focused approach in the service of contemplated therapy.

Goldfried and Sprafkin (1976) conceptualize behavior assessment in terms of the acronym SORC: Stimulus-Organism-Response-Consequences. S stands for the stimulus that acts on the organism-O—that in turn leads to a response—R. C refers to the consequences of the response, that is, to the maladaptive behavior that is targeted for modification.

While emphasizing differences between behavior assessment and other approaches, Barrios and Hartmann (1986) point out that behavior assessment does not stand totally apart from other areas of psychology and long established techniques:

> Neither traditional assessment nor behavioral assessment are monolithic, homogeneous edifices. Indeed, while differing "on average" both are highly fractionated and sometimes contradictory approaches. Traditional assessment, as used here, includes psychodynamic and trait-oriented approaches to assessment. Behavioral assessment has even more diverse constituents. It includes conceptual aspects of the applied behavioral, neobehavioristic mediational stimulus-response, cognitive-behavioral, and social learning models. Behavioral assessment also includes strategic aspects of behavioral-analytic, criterion-referenced, norm-based, as well as various idiographic approaches to assessment.

The fourth "culture," humanistic psychology, is surrounded by controversy over the practice of assessment, many in the humanistic movement being largely or totally negative to assessment. Rogers (1942) has been particularly influential in his opposition, a major point of his emphasis being that an authoritative stance to the client is counterproductive:

> The place of tests in counseling treatment is not nearly so clearcut. The disadvantage of using tests at the outset of a series of therapeutic contacts are the same as the disadvantages of taking a complete case history. If the psychologist begins his work with a complete battery of tests, this fact carries with it the implication that he will provide the solution to the client's problems. The point of view consistently maintained throughout this book is that such "solutions" are not genuine and do not deeply help the individual, but tend to make him either resentful or overdependent.

Amplifying on this theme, Rogers (1951) holds that it is the client, not the therapist, who must be the "diagnostician." Insights developed by the therapist are of no value; the client must gain his own insights. He must not believe that an "expert" knows him better than he knows himself. Such a belief can lead to a surrender of personhood. In a later paper, Rogers (1955) observes, "insofar as I see him only as an object, the client will tend to become only an object."

An effective means of helping the client to gain insight through the use of assessment has been described by Fischer (1970). In this approach the client functions as a co-evaluator of the assessment protocol. [In order to better] "understand his past behavior, predict his future behavior, or identify feasible possibilities, the client's perspectives must be understood." Mosak and Gushurst (1972) and Craddick (1972, 1975) follow a similar procedure. These authors also involve their clients in the assessment process by sharing the psychological report with them.

May (1958) and Bugental (1963, 1964) view assessment as a dehumanizing experience. They complain that assessment is *about* rather than *of* the person. They assert that it is too impersonal, too detached, too dispassionate, too deindividualizing, too dependency-fostering. They further state that it does not aid the client in the search for meaning. The product of assessment, Bugental proposes, is "part function" information. This complaint is also made by Brown (1972) who asserts that "to proceed psychometrically violates the major tenets of humanistic psychology, violating "the *image of man*, and the image of human relationships." Craddick (1972) counters that the "separation of man into parts is antithetical to *both* the humanistic tradition *and* to personality assessment" (emphasis added).

These arguments aside, many humanistically oriented therapists *do* engage in (or make use of) psychological assessment, even some of those who have expressed negative views about the process and its outcomes. Thus, "Nothing we are saying here in the slightest deprecates the importance of gathering and studying seriously all the specific data we can get about the given person." (May, 1958) Bugental resorts to testing on occasion, such as when either the therapist or the client must reach a decision on whether psychotherapy is indicated, or whether some other service should be considered. Rogers (1942) also considers that assessment *does* have a role:

> With some individuals...handicapped in fundamental ways by their own inadequacies or the destructive quality of their environment...In such cases to initiate psychotherapy without a diagnostic study may only plunge the client further into hopelessness as his own lacks are brought into greater prominence by his increasing insight. Consequently, even though the diagnostic study may interfere somewhat with a counseling process, it is definitely advisable here.

Sugarman (1978) examined five extant allegations to the effect that psychological assessment is not humanistic. They are:

Assessment is reductionistic
Assessment is artificial
Assessment does not pay attention to the examiner-patient relationship
Assessment judges the patient
Assessment is too intellectual

His conclusion:

> An emphatic yes is the only logical response to "Is Psychodiagnostic Assessment Humanistic?" That is, if the assessment process and philosophy follow the model proposed herein, then it is incomprehensible to state that it is not humanistic.

THE INFLUENCE OF PRACTICAL SETTINGS

Psychological assessment takes place in a variety of settings. Each setting has a typical mission and a characteristic ambiance: objectives, values, perceptions, procedures. And within professional cultures of the setting we find subcultures based on membership in a discipline. Thus, Tallent and Reiss (1959a,b,c) report discrepancies among psychologists, psychiatrists, and social workers regarding such matters as preferences for the content and style of psychological reports. Tallent and Rafi (1965) report comparable differences among clinicians across national cultures. Most striking in the latter study was the tendency of British psychiatrists, more so than their American counterparts, to regard the psychologist's responsibilities and consultative role as more limited than that of psychologists in the United States. A number of the British psychiatrists tended to view psychologists as somewhat akin to technicians.

The mission and/or ambiance of the practice setting help to determine how psychologists use particular instruments. In a clinic where a psychoanalytic orientation prevails, the Rorschach examiner might search the protocol for material bearing on such factors as defenses, ego strength, dynamics, conflicts, and fixations. In a psychiatric clinic where treatment is closely linked to DSM diagnoses, the Rorschach examiner is likely to focus on diagnostic indicators and prominent features that contribute to formulating diagnoses, such as the quality of reality testing, indicators of anxiety, depression, mood instability, quality of impulse control, and neuropsychological deficits. Or, consider how differently an age-appropriate Wechsler scale might be used in different settings. In a school, the Wechsler can be valuable in helping the school psychologist to delineate learning problems. In a mental health clinic, the typical contribution of the Wechsler is to aid in making a formal diagnosis (and, increasingly, case formulation), as early on described by Gilliland (1941), Rapaport, Gill, and Schafer (1945, 1946), (Schafer, 1967), and many authors since. In a head-injury center, the Wechsler is typically a key instrument in a neuropsychological battery.

In contrast to an orientation to a specific purpose, when psychological examiners lack a focus the product of assessment is likely to be stereotyped content that readily betrays its source in some particular test. It is almost certain when an assessor reports on a client's fund of information, vocabulary level, conceptual ability, knowledge of cultural precepts, or visual-motor skills that his or her conclusions on these topics were derived from the Wechsler. Equally likely, when the examiner reports that the client has good respect for reality, constricted affect, poverty of fantasy, or a rich inner life, reference is being made to the Rorschach. The assessor who lacks focus, and who uses these instruments in a routine manner, routinely reports such variables. The instrument is allowed to dictate the product. If you are a hammer you treat everything like a nail.

The "medical model" (or "disease model") has long been influential in various psychiatric settings and also among many nonmedical professionals, such as psychologists, social workers, and attorneys. This is a model that stresses the classification of dysfunctional or distressing states—symptoms—and attempts to link carefully described categories of disorder with their causes and cures.

Many psychological assessors oppose portions of the medical model, and particularly the basic concept of mental illness. Szasz (1960, 1961) labels mental illness a myth, and the view that mental illness is a metaphor, a flawed analogy with bodily illness, is widespread. Sarbin (1967) supplies history that is relevant to this point:

> The 16th Century witnessed the beginnings of a reaction against the excesses of the Inquisition. The beginnings of humanistic philosophy, the discovery and serious study of Galen and other classical writers, the renunciation of scholasticism—the whole thrust of the Renaissance was opposite that of the Inquisition. In this atmosphere, Teresa of Avila, an outstanding figure of the Counter-Reformation, contributed to the shift from demons to "illness" as the cause of conduct disturbances. A group of nuns was exhibiting conduct which at a later date would have been called hysteria. By declaring these women to be infirm or ill, Teresa was able to fend off the Inquisition. However, the appeal that a diagnosis should be changed from witchcraft to illness required some cognitive elaboration. She invoked the notion of natural causes. Among the natural causes were (a) melancholy (Galenic humoral pathology), (b) weak imagination, and (c) drowsiness. If a person's conduct could be accounted for by such natural causes, it was to be regarded not as evil, but comas enfermas, *as if sick*. By employing the metaphor "as if sick," she implied that practitioners of physic rather than clergymen should be the responsible social specialists. Eventually, the "as if" fell out of usage, leaving the concept of sickness to stand by itself.

Despite the dissemination of anti-mental illness views, the extent to which the medical model is entrenched among nonmedical clinical personnel may be gauged by their vocabulary. Not to exhaust the list, consider the extent to which these medical terms are used today: *diagnosis, prognosis, etiology, psychopathology, pathognomonic sign, patient, onset, symptom, syndrome, course, treatment, therapy,* and *remission*.

A further indicator of the influence of the medical model on nonmedical assessors is the assessors' extensive use of the DSM, which is increasingly coordinated with the International Classification of Diseases (ICD) (American Psychiatric Association, 1987). Perhaps more significant, the American Psychological Association is reported to be considering the creation of its own diagnostic manual (Landers, 1986). This, it is anticipated, would be a more scientific version of the extant DSM, resting additionally on information drawn from the ICD. It is said that imitation is the sincerest flattery.

THE TEACHING AND APPLICATION OF PSYCHOLOGICAL ASSESSMENT...AND THE OUTLOOK

Longstanding issues, such as the statistical/clinical controversy (introduced on page 69), are associated with tensions between practitioners and their more empirically oriented colleagues. This has been particularly true when questions concerning the use of the Rorschach and other projective techniques arose. Weiner (1972), concerned with the question, "does psychodiagnosis have a future?" reviewed the problems facing the psychodiagnostic enterprise a generation ago:

> In 1971 I was invited to give a colloquium at a major university with a highly regarded clinical psychology program. The faculty in the program were concerned about their students' lack of interest in learning about psychological testing, and my task was to present the positive case for psychodiagnostic assessment. This was to include dispelling doubts about the worth and propriety of psychodiagnosis and explaining why clinicians should strive to become competent psychodiagnosticians.
>
> This was not an easy task in 1971, which was a low point in the history of psychodiagnosis. Psychodiagnosis can be defined as the clinical use of psychological tests to facilitate personality assessment. As such, it was under heavy attack when the 1960s drew to a close. The emergence of behavioral approaches to psychology had seriously questioned the value of personality assessment. Mischel (1968) and Peterson (1968) had argued in influential books that clinicians who want to predict behavior reliably should stop trying to infer personality characteristics from test responses and instead concentrate on constructing test situations that provide representative samples of the behavior to be predicted.

In addition to the impact of the behavioral revolution, Weiner also cites in his paper the negative influence of humanistic psychology on personality assessment.

A number of surveys at the time were consistent with Weiner's appraisal of psychological assessment at its low point. McCully's (1965) survey found that while psychology faculties tended to support training in projective techniques, they discouraged the use of these instruments in research. Jackson and Wohl (1966), focusing on the Rorschach technique, found the teaching of its use in assessment slighted: "While Rorschach is clearly the most emphasized diagnostic technique, in many departments instruction is being conducted at an introductory level." And, "Students often appear to reflect derogatory attitudes toward testing which stem from their university instruction." Thelen, Varble, and Johnson (1968) similarly reported a decline among clinical faculty in acceptance of projective techniques as a result of the belief that their use was not supported by research. And a survey some 15 years later (Pruitt, Smith, Thelen, & Lubin, 1985) documented a further decline in the acceptance of projective techniques over that noted by Thelen et al.: "More of the 1983 respondents than the 1968 respondents expressed negative attitudes toward specific projectives such as the Rorschach. Negative attitudes toward projectives were particularly prominent among the younger respondents in the 1983 survey." Alexander and Basowitz (1965) summarized the negative attitude to assessment characteristic of the time:

> Without question, the clinical student of today is less concerned than the student of 10 years ago with the problems of diagnosis, less skilled in the use of fantasy material for personality assessment, but more conversant with objective, machine-scored measures used for this purpose.

Numerous publications of that era bemoaned an impression of severe problems with assessment, particularly with respect to projective techniques, the Rorschach often being singled out for special attention. A sampling of conclusions is instructive: Holt (1967) reported diagnostic testing to be "in a funk." Hertz (1970) spoke of a "crisis." Ivnik (1977) wrote of "the uncertain status of psychological tests in clinical psychology." Smith and Allen (1984), and Lewandowski and Saccuzzo (1970) viewed the situation as one of "decline," and Cleveland (1976) listed a number of reasons for "the rise and fall of psychodiagnosis."

In contrast to the above, many viewers of the contemporary scene report that the situation in psychological assessment is much more upbeat. Either there has been a resurgence of assessment activities, or matters never really were as bad as had been reported. For all the while that assessment was being flayed, the practice of assessment in applied settings was a hardy enterprise.

The only sour note in the field of applied work was the inability to recruit enough assessors. Levy and Fox (1975) denied that the practice of assessment had fallen on hard times—"Psychological Testing Is Alive and Well"—is the title of their paper, and they reported that skilled assessors were greatly in demand. Fein (1979) despaired that the problem with assessment was not in the process, but in a shortage of qualified personnel to contribute, through assessment, to the mental health needs of the community.

> In the context of these chaotic social trends directors of mental health delivery agencies discovered that the post-doctoral applicants for staff positions in psychology lacked even minimal skills in psychodiagnostic testing and personality assessment. In dismay these employers warned of the incipient demise of psychodiagnostic testing and personality assessment skills in training programs at the universities, a trend that was creating an ever widening gap between the needs of mental health delivery systems and graduate training in psychological measurements.

The widely-reported disjunction between town and gown is further documented by Durand, Blanchard, and Mindell (1988): "Directors of internship programs appeared to value projective techniques more than did directors of doctoral programs, and they expected students to have more experience with these techniques than is typically provided in doctoral programs." Wade, Baker, Morton, and Baker (1978) "determined that both objective and projective tests were used with great frequency"—with particular enthusiasm for projective techniques. Behavior therapists, however, were less favorable to these instruments, as were clinicians engaged in substantial teaching and research. Piotrowski (1984, 1985); Piotrowski, Sherry, and Keller (1985); and Piotrowski and Keller (1978, 1989a,b) found that practicing clinicians viewed psychological assessment, in general, and projective techniques in particular, with favor. An exception was provided by psychologists in the clinical academic setting (Piotrowski, 1984; Piotrowski and Keller, 1984a). A further exception to this rule, reported by Piotrowski and Keller (1984b), was observed in a survey of members of the Association for Advancement of Behavior Therapy.

What sustains the psychological assessment enterprise in the face of so many negatives? In some instances the answer is as simple as looking at the other side of the coin, or consulting more recent research. Thus, a survey by Ritzler and Alter (1986) carried out at approximately the same time as the Pruitt et al. study, but addressed both to faculty attitudes and actual teaching practices, leads to quite a different view concerning the acceptance of projective techniques, and particularly of the Rorschach. Eighty-eight percent of the programs surveyed "place major emphasis on the Rorschach in at least one assessment course." And, concerning attitudes, in apparent contradiction to the findings reported by Thelen et al. (1968), Pruitt et al. (1985), and others, according to the data of Ritzler and Alter, academics tend to look on the Rorschach as a valuable clinical tool and teaching aid, but are wary of using the blots as a research tool. They add, "Recent developments in the application of the Rorschach technique (e.g., Exner, 1974, 1978, 1984) seem to be having an impact on instructor attitudes."

With respect to test use specifically among counseling psychologists, data are sparse. In a survey conducted by Fee, Elkins, and Boyd (1982), it was reported that 35.9 percent of the clients of counseling psychologists had been given objective tests and 11.4 percent were tested with projective instruments, the latter being used primarily for the purpose of defining the personality structure of clients. In a replication and extension of this study, Watkins and Campbell (1989) surveyed 1,000 members of the Division of Counseling Psychology of the American Psychological Association. From the results of their survey, in combination with those of Fee et al., Watkins and Campbell conclude:

> First, counseling psychologists appear to use a variety of tests in their assessment efforts, including both objective and projective personality instruments. Second, counseling psychologists are using many tests that seemingly have not been and still are not covered in the counseling psychology literature. One would be hard pressed to find a recent (or not so recent) publication on the MMPI, sentence completion methods, DAP, Rorschach, or TAT in any major counseling psychology publication. Yet these instruments are being used, with varying frequency, by counseling psychologists across various work settings.

Watkins and Campbell are of the opinion that "the unique perspective of counseling psychology and how it applies to tests largely remains elusive and ill-defined." They further believe that personality assessment and its place in counseling psychology is at a crossroads: "Counseling psychology has much to offer in the area of personality assessment. Unfortunately, we do not believe the richness of the specialty has been fully mined."

In a related study focusing on the use of the MMPI, Watkins, Campbell, McGregor, and Godin (1989) conclude:

> It was found that the MMPI (a) was taught in one or more courses in virtually all programs; (b) was viewed as useful by most respondents; and (c) was included, with some variability, in practicum training and on doctoral qualifying examinations. As in clinical psychology programs, the MMPI appeared to occupy a place of importance in the assessment training of counseling psychologists.

Millon (1984) reports on a "renaissance" or a "resurrection" of both personality assessment and personality theory—with advances in personality theory playing a central role in breathing new life into assessment. Specifically, he makes reference to "the refurbishing of analytic, interpersonal, and learning theories of personality." Particularly original is Millon's conceptualization of the role of personality and the personality disorders as defined in terms of sets of criteria (e.g., cognitive style, affective expression, and self-perception) against which the various recognized disorders may be compared.

> I see not only bright prospects ahead in personality assessment but, perhaps more fundamentally, in its scientific foundations. The psychometric developments among holistic and psychodynamic inventories, the revival and refinements in personality theory, the specification of parallel explicit criteria for the personality disorders, and the recognition that personality serves both as core and context for understanding other psychopathologies, all bode extremely well for us as professionals and, more importantly, for the patients we serve.

The "bright prospects" for personality assessment appear to be well documented in the minutes of the Society for Personality Assessment:

> Our increasing membership continues to hold and the rate of almost 200 new applications for the last several 6-month periods is virtually fourfold of similar periods in the past (Lerner, 1988).

At the same time as scientific advances in assessment are made and published, personal factors of the assessor also play a prominent role, as Wade and Baker (1977) report:

> Clinicians indicated that personal clinical experience with a test was more important in their test-use decisions than pragmatic or psychometric considerations.

Reynolds and Sundberg (1976) summarize a similar finding:

> Based on a survey of psychologists' judgments of test quality, the authors concluded that "good psychometric properties do not test leaders make."

In a later study, Reynolds (1979) quantifies this impression:

> Although a statistically significant relationship was found between test quality and usage, only 1/3 of the test variance in test usage was accounted for by test quality, indicating that test usage is not primarily a function of test quality.

The personal equation of the psychological assessor is the theme of the next chapter. If assessment is indeed partly an art, as proposed earlier in this chapter, and if the psychological assessor is indeed the key instrument in the assessment process, as many have long maintained, then we must attend to this human factor if we are to understand the process.

2
THE PSYCHOLOGICAL ASSESSOR

The concept of the *personal equation* has a long history in physical science and medicine, and in more recent years has been employed in psychology. Originally, the term recognized that there were individual differences among observers in the recording of astronomical observations, and that these differences were due to human factors: the scientific data they gathered were in part objective and in part subjective. The subjective element in psychological assessment sometimes is identified as *art*. More frequently, assessment skills are considered to be aspects of *clinical judgment*, a complex variable that might give up its secrets more readily than art.

With each assessor bringing personal resources to the task, we must expect that different assessors will not evaluate the same person uniformly, and such is typically the case. For example, in diagnosing a child as suffering from separation anxiety disorder related to the recent onset of a life-threatening illness in his mother, several assessors may be in full agreement. But with respect to other factors, such as nuances of the child's disorder, predisposing factors, or approaches to intervention in the case, the input of different assessors likely will show variations.

Is this bad? Not necessarily. One can—and it may be desirable to—approach human issues from various angles. A person with a problem can be helped in more than one way, and when different assessments are melded the results can be particularly advantageous. We see this situation routinely in clinical case conferences when various team members, for example, a teacher, a psychologist, a nurse, and a social worker each contributes a different assessment of a child's problems and needs. A seminar of mental health workers may generate almost as many ideas about a client as there are participants, yet, as a result, each may emerge from the meeting with a clearer or broader conceptualization of the client.

JUDGING OTHERS: GORDON ALLPORT

What makes a person adept at reaching an understanding of others? It has long been common understanding that some people are keener observers of their fellows than others; that their conclusions about people are more accurate and trustworthy. This impression has found its way into the German language in the term *Menschenkenner*, which is defined as a *knower of people*—or as a *psychologist*.

In two books, Allport (1937, 1961) explored this question, specifically seeking to tease out the characteristics of the "good judge" of personality. In the latter work he listed nine attributes of the hypothetical good judge on the basis of the then extant literature. Such a person is hypothetical because Allport considered that "the ability is not completely 'across the board.'"

Experience One cannot make an accurate appraisal of that which is not familiar. When you want a diamond appraised, you go to a gemologist, not a plumber, who in turn is more competent than the gemologist to judge the condition of the pipes in your home. An American may have difficulty understanding the meaning of certain momentous life events to a person who comes from another country, and a psychologist without experience in working with members of street gangs cannot competently assess a youthful offender from that subculture.

Similarity When you are similar to another person you presumably have had a number of similar experiences. A sincere and intelligent man may understand certain experiences of a woman less well than another woman can. This widely accepted view has given rise to the old saw "It takes one to know one." At least it can help.

Intelligence In general, Allport finds a relationship between intelligence and the ability to judge others. "The positive correlation holds even within the narrow range of high intelligence that characterizes the selected judges used in most experiments"—a finding that suggests that even among professional assessors, those with the highest IQs will be the most effective.

Cognitive complexity "As a rule, people cannot comprehend others who are more complex and subtle than they." By way of extrapolation from this observation, Allport suggests that those of complex personality make-up who work in a psychopathological context are best situated to grasp the "intricate mental tangles" of their clients. He further suggests that such complexity may include having neurotic problems—provided they are well managed.

Self-insight Allport seems to believe that he is on shaky ground in attempting to relate this variable to the ability to judge people. Perhaps he is overly cautious. Presumably those who can look deeply into themselves in an abiding search for self-knowledge can also brush aside second-hand stereotyped and overly conventional ways of thinking that commonly distort judgments of others. This issue is approached again in this chapter in the discussion of *psychological-mindedness*.

Social skill and adjustment A number of positive attributes are commonly associated with those who are good judges of people: social skill, leadership qualities, popularity, outgoingness, nurturance, a take-charge attitude, emotional stability, and freedom from neurosis—although, as noted above, there may be an exception.

Detachment The good judge of people is sufficiently independent to maintain objectivity and not permit self-needs to color his or her assessments. They do not, for example, have a need to see all people as "good" people. In clinical terms we would say that their assessments are not burdened by non-insightful countertransference.

Esthetic attitude Allport ranks an esthetic attitude as a major asset in the ability to judge people. An esthetic attitude uncovers an often overlooked, but very real, dimension of humanity. Dorr's psychological report to "John and Mary" (pp. 335–343) is instructive.

Intraceptiveness This characteristic, first discussed by Murray (1938), is a major asset in judging people. A tendency to understand oneself and others in a psychological frame of reference is a key feature of *psychological-mindedness*.

PERSONALITY TYPE AS A FACTOR IN JUDGING OTHERS: HENRY A. MURRAY

In his monumental contribution, *Explorations in Personality*, Murray (1938) identifies the personality modes of *intraception* and *extraception*, major elements of the personal equation that enter the process of assessment.

On reading the spectrum of literature on psychological assessment, and making personal observations on how assessment is done, it appears that some assessors are intraceptors and some are extraceptors, and that some assessors use intraceptive *and* extraceptive means of understanding their clients. Murray holds that the same person can be both intraceptive and extraceptive—they show an *ambitendency*, as he calls it. The present thesis is that assessments based on both of these modes of achieving understanding gain in focus and balance.

Murray observes that the thinking of the intraceptor prominently involves "the disposition to be determined by diffuse personal feelings and inclinations (intangible subjective facts), fantasies, and wishful creations or imaginative reconstructions of external happenings." The thinking of the extraceptor, by contrast, "is dominated by the disposition to bring ideas into accord with observed facts or the need to further some particular aim."

Lists of adjectives spell out additional distinctions. The intraceptor is: "subjective, imaginative (fanciful), somewhat inaccurate, personal in his dealings, impractical, connotative in speech, metaphysical, partial in his opinions, warm and passionate, 'unreasonable' in action, sensitive, egocentric, individualistic, tender-minded, deductive, intuitive in his observations, artistic or religious, psychologically penetrating, idealistic, dynamistic, monistic or dualistic."

The extraceptor is commonly characterized by several of the following adjectives: "objective, factual, accurate, impersonal, practical, denotative in speech, empirical, utilitarian, impartial, cool and phlegmatic, reasonable in action, insensitive, sociocentric, conforming, tough-minded, inductive, systematic in observations, scientific, psychologically superficial, materialistic, mechanistic, pluralistic."

Further observations by Murray also are obviously applicable to situations involving clinical judgment:

> Extraceptive perception and apperception are marked by the exclusion of everything except bare sense facts (objective facts): tangible objects and their physical relations and the outward behavior of other people. It is usually orderly, systematic, and conventional. Intraceptive perception and apperception on the other hand are characterized by the intrusion of affections and images evoked by the facts: sentiments, imaginal elaborations, symbolic meanings, interpretations of the feelings and motives of other people. It is selective; emphasizing and elaborating upon one or more details to the exclusion of others.

Overlap with the concept of intraception/extraception is seen in Murray's division of psychologists into two large, but heterogeneous, classes holding opposite dispositions. These he calls *centralists* and *peripheralists*, the first being comparable to the intraceptors, the second to the extraceptors. When we consider how centralists and peripheralists differ, as Murray understands it, we can see how basic orientation may influence clinical judgment and the assessment product.

Thus, the peripheralist has objective inclinations, is disposed to be a positivist, and to favor mechanistic or physiological explanations. Consonant with John B. Watson, the peripheralist endorses the position that "personality is the sum total of the habitual responses," and tends to define personality in terms of action *qua* action, to focus on elements rather than on a unity, to emphasize external stimuli over internal promptings as the origin of behavior, and to give prominence to physical patterns of overt behavior.

The centralists tend to be "conceptualists" rather than positivists, subjective, and concerned with feelings, desires, and intentions. They also tend to be empathic intuitivists who seek "to know the inner nature of other persons as they know their own." Much of their focus is on intangibles knowable only by inference. They "stress the directions or ends of behavior, underlying instinctual forces, inherited dispositions, maturation and inner transformations, distortions of perception by wish and fantasy, emotion, irrational or semi-conscious mental processes, repressed sentiments and the objects of erotic interest."

The (subjectively oriented) intraceptor tends more to the clinical approach and the (objective, positivistic) extraceptor more to the statistical position (pp. 100–103). We might consider, then, how these personality orientations are likely to affect the assessment process and product. We should at the same time bear in mind Murray's position that there is an overlap between the two: "the differences among extraceptors or among intraceptors (due to other factors) being as great as the differences between extraceptors and intraceptors."

Nevertheless, Murray identifies some prominent characteristics of intraceptors and extraceptors as their modes of observation and thinking pertain to the assessment process. Thus, the intraceptor is tender-minded and psychologically penetrating, but somewhat inaccurate. Indeed,

> The intraceptive mode of perception seems to be basic to an intuitive understanding of other people. It may be largely unconscious and inarticulate; and it is certainly liable to err grossly, but there is no other way of immediately apprehending the primary tendencies which explain the multiplicity of superficially dissimilar phenomena.

Murray believes, however, that the weaknesses of the intraceptor's assessment process and product are not beyond redemption:

> The intraceptive person who becomes conscious and critical of his own psychology may learn to correct for the projections which commonly occur, and by constant practice his interpretations of others may become reasonably reliable.

Extraception, on the other hand, "leads to an emphasis upon overt behavior and observable traits," and the tendency to deal with data in an orderly and systematic manner. Murray indicates, however, that there is also a downside to this orientation:

> He [the extraceptor] may be confused by complex emotional situations, and he will be deficient in his interpretations of the more irrational phases of human experience: dreams, fantasies, the play and perversities of children, the erotic impulses of adolescents, the religious practices of savages, the poetical and metaphysical utterances of adults, the vagaries of neurotic and psychotic patients.

ORIENTATIONS TO CLINICAL JUDGMENT

As a process of problem solving and decision making, psychological assessment is a human activity, as opposed to merely a set of mechanical, formula following, or purely mathematical procedures. Much of what the assessor does to solve problems involves a complex of behaviors subsumed under the heading of *clinical judgment*. How we understand clinical judgment–what it *is* and how we *use* it–is crucial to the understanding of the assessment process itself.

However we understand it, the need to use judgment in understanding people is beyond dispute and transcends personal and professional orientations (see, for example, American Psychological Association, *Standards for educational and psychological testing*, 1985, and *Guidelines for computer-based tests and interpretations*, 1986). This maxim holds equally for those who are centralists/intraceptors, peripheralists/extraceptors, and those who have an ambitendency with respect to these dispositions.

Much of the judgment of centralists/intraceptors has been equated with psychological-mindedness (pp. 32–33)—a way of looking at and understanding people that unabashedly calls on such subjective modes as feel, fantasy, hunches, sympathy, and empathy. Peripheralist/extraceptors, on the other hand, are objectively oriented. They look for meaning in facts and figures, and tend to be more comfortable than the psychological-minded with norms and regression equations. Yet in the interest of performing competently and ethically, they recognize that statistics alone do not automatically bring understanding of another person; they must also use judgment. And those who have an ambitendency to the above two dispositions would be expected to hold an eclectic position—such as the "sophisticated clinical method" of Holt (p. 72).

The Role of Intuition in Clinical Judgment

Hunt (1959), in formulating a position on clinical judgment, makes two basic points: (1) the role of *intuition* in judgment has long been recognized, and (2) clinical judgment is a variant of psychophysical judgment. He traces support for the intuitive position to the historians Dilthey and Spengler, and to Spranger, the latter using the concept of intuition in his *psychology of understanding* (*Verstehen*). He also presents his own data and arguments to link clinical and psychophysical judgment:

> At every point where we even approach the exactitude of specificity and control of stimulus, judgmental setting, and categories of report which are typical of experimental psychophysics, communalities appear in our clinical data, and the uniformity and sequential repetitiveness necessary for statistical prediction begins to show itself, There is both logic and data... to support my position that the clinical judgment is qualitatively related to the psychophysical judgment, that the differences are ones of quantity rather than kind, that they are contrasting in amount rather than conflicting in nature, and that the clinical judgment is a culturally handicapped country cousin of the psychophysical judgment, and not a different species of being.

Thorne (1961) is in close agreement with Hunt, but generally, among students of the assessment process, consensus is lacking. The existence of clinical judgment is generally acknowledged, but there is disagreement over how effective a tool it is. Some regard intuition as frivolous or liken it to superstition; while other, equally respected observers, view intuition as fundamental and vital to human existence. Westcott (1968) cites the need for a term to recognize the widely accepted fact that "some people 'get the point' more quickly than others do."

Anecdotal accounts of intuition, such as the tour de force reported by Reik (1948), are frequently cited by those who present the case for the reality of intuition, at least among highly sensitive observers:

> Our session at this time took the following course. After a few sentences about the uneventful day, the patient fell into a long silence. She assured me that nothing was in her thoughts. Silence from me. After many minutes she complained about a toothache. She told me that she had been to the dentist yesterday. He had given her an injection and pulled a wisdom tooth. The spot was hurting again. New and longer silence. She pointed to my bookcase in the corner and said, "There's a book standing on its head." Without the slightest hesitation and in a reproachful voice I said, "But why did you not tell me that you had had an abortion?"

Sarbin, Taft, and Bailey (1960) deny that there is a phenomenon of intuition that plays a useful role in assessment. What some call intuition they regard as inference, and they believe that proponents of intuition endow the process of intuition with an aura of mystery simply because we do not understand it well. To these authors, intuition is a superfluous concept, and suspect.

The fact that elements of the process called intuition are inaccessible is generally acknowledged, but this is not daunting to those who are comfortable in calling on the role of the unconscious as an explanation for actions whose source is not evident. Berne (1949) writes, "Intuition is knowledge based on experience and acquired through sensory contact with the subject without the 'intuiter' being able to formulate to himself or others exactly how he came to his conclusions." Board's (1958) definition is similar: "Intuition is a concept composed of a relation structure some of whose empirical observations and symbols are unconscious or otherwise unavailable for conscious delineation." Hunt (1951) summarizes the argument in long-term perspective:

> Despite all our evidence that inference can go on at an unconscious level, despite the fact that Helmholtz years ago gave us a name for it (*unbewusste Schluss*), many of us still cling to intuition as a mystical process of revelation in its own right. We speak of intuition as a means of knowledge peculiar to the clinical situation, thereby opposing it to the usual processes of rational, empirical evaluation common to the other sciences.

Westcott's (1968) basic statement on intuition, that "Some people 'get the point' more quickly than others do" is in harmony with the common view that intuitive knowledge is gained *directly, immediately*. But, to call on Hunt (1951) once more, we find that the immediacy of intuition is possible only after the groundwork for such immediacy is first put in place over an extended period of time.

Intuition can never be divorced from its empirical backgrounds. This immediate act of knowledge is permitted to physicians, but only after many years of medical school and postgraduate residence. It is permitted to the clinical psychologist in interpreting his test results, but only after he has experienced the same testing situation with many subjects. In the field of personality interpretation it is perhaps most famous in the work of Spranger and his method of understanding (*Verstehen*). To Spranger, understanding is immediate while science is mediate. Yet when one reads Spranger one finds that the act of understanding can come only after a background of empirical knowledge has been acquired. One can only understand people after one has noted the books they read, the pictures they hang on their walls, the diversions they seek, and the company they keep. Here, certainly, is no mystical process but an orderly formula for the acquisition of knowledge which may later form the basis for a rational judgment, albeit the particular and extensive bases for that judgment may not be present in consciousness at the moment the judgment is made.

The training of psychological assessors is predicated in large part on the cultivation of knowledge, skills, and sensitivities as a basis for making clinical judgments, and thus would appear to fly in the face of those studies, such as those reported on pp. 11–12, that fail to support the notion that professional training leads to an improved assessment product. For example, topics that the student psychological assessor must learn, in both classroom and practicum settings, include:

Observational skills, cue sensitivity

Effective interviewing and interactive techniques

Recognizing and using knowledge of such concepts as halo effect, transference, and countertransference

Conceptualizing assessment problems

Effective descriptive skills

Formulating focused, meaningful reports

Effective interaction with colleagues, and understanding their roles and needs

Knowledge of personality, psychopathology, and treatment methods

Understanding and application of ethical standards

This list might be extended to accommodate particular orientations and practices (see also Shakow, 1976; Russ, 1978). We should also recognize that everyday life experiences, particularly those from which we learn about people, how to relate, and knowledge of the world play a role in the development of intuition. Effectively making use of intuition, some people develop a sophisticated complex of abilities, including psychological-assessment skills.

There is appreciable consensus that intuition is real. There is room, however, for differences of opinion on how much this understudied way of understanding can contribute to psychological assessment. Clearly, there is no justification for employing intuitive approaches to the neglect of approaches that are better validated and consonant with a theory that enjoys appreciable acceptance.

Psychological-Mindedness

Together, the well-researched articles of Appelbaum (1973) and Farber (1985) are a gold mine of information and ideas on psychological-mindedness that contribute to an understanding of how this psychological quality may enhance the assessment process. Farber traces the roots of psychological-mindedness to childhood family dynamics and also to early cultural influences. The outcome "may be considered a trait which has at its core the disposition to reflect upon the meaning and motivation of behavior, thoughts, and feelings in oneself and others." Or, as put succinctly by Appelbaum, "Those inclined this way wonder what makes people tick..."An introspective mode is central; the psychologically minded person is given to introspection, seeking insight or self-awareness, and to understanding the inner processes of others by using the self as a diagnostic tool. Empathy and sympathy are means of getting to know others, as is use of self-analogue: the psychologically minded person compares others with the self, becoming aware of similarities and differences.

Psychological-mindedness is a complex quality. Indeed, following Levinson, Sharaf, and Gilbert (1966), Farber discusses two kinds of psychological-mindedness. Experientially, in relating to others there is "the capacity to grasp the implicit language of emotional communication, to be in touch with and share another's feelings...Intellectual knowing, on the other hand, is more logical and linear...[It] is essentially uninfused with a personal, 'feeling' component. As Levinson *et al.* point out, this form of psychological-mindedness produces 'knowledge *about* psychological matters rather than knowledge *of* such matters.'"

Psychological-mindedness is a complex quality, involving, as it does, intuitive, cognitive, and affective qualities. While Farber notes of certain therapists that "their capacity for psychological-mindedness is more fully developed and fluently expressed in intellectual rather than experiential terms," Appelbaum espouses Loewenstein's (1967) position that "It [psychological-mindedness] 'is undoubtedly influenced by factors from all psychic structures...'"

The relation of psychological-mindedness to psychological assessment involves some complex questions. Perhaps the use of this "gift," as Farber regards psychological-mindedness, can be overused or misused: "Emotional awareness may occur at the expense of cognitive objectivity." Certainly there is a caveat here. The feeling component may be very useful, but it must be controlled. Appelbaum deals with this issue through relating *psychological thinking* (the thinking mode of psychologically-minded persons) to Kris's (1952) concept of "regression in the service of the ego," a cognitive-affective experience that can be helpful in professional work as it is in art and in adapting to life:

> A rough two-step model for psychological thinking would include: (1) a 'passive-regressive' phase of allowing unconscious and preconscious ideas into consciousness such as in free associations. The psychologically-minded person must be able to negotiate this aspect of the basic rule as a necessary, but insufficient, condition. He must also be

able to negotiate the next step. (2) The 'active-progressive' phase of listening and trying to make new sense out of 'what comes to mind.' Though Step 2 is often only an implicit codicil to the basic rule, it constitutes the fullest, most useful fulfillment of the basic rule.

"Can a person be trained to become psychologically-minded?", Appelbaum asks. He answers his own question thus: "Probably not, to the extent that it is dependent upon constitutional or other early developmental structures, just as high musical proficiency cannot be taught to those without basic musical abilities." Farber argues that early tendencies can be enhanced, and suggests that such happens in mental-health training programs: "What is clear...is that whatever tendencies toward psychological-mindedness a student brings with him or her to a training program are markedly intensified by a lengthy period of professional socialization during which years are spent as a psychotherapist, supervisee, patient, and student."

Objectivity in Psychological Understanding

Compared to psychological-mindedness, more objective approaches to psychological assessment are less inscrutable. In sharp contrast to the role of psychological-mindedness is the seeking of understanding that rests on evident facts and on logical propositions that can be spelled out, communicated, and taught. When using psychological tests, psychometric theory and the characteristics and technical qualities of specific instruments (e.g., reliability, validity, standardization samples) are basic to reaching conclusions. A less technical, or at least less statistical, logic may be applied to construing data when approaches such as interviewing (pp. 171–174) or the Mental Status Examination (pp. 175–177) are employed.

The accepted goal of (relatively) objective approaches to personality assessment is to contribute to the competent and ethical development and use of psychological information (see also American Psychological Association, *Standards for educational and psychological testing*, 1985; and American Psychological Association, 1981, 1986). Tests, or other assessment tools, do not provide automatic answers to real problems. To say "Test results indicate..." is to abdicate the responsibility that is incumbent on the psychological assessor. What test results mean in any given case is a human judgment. This is particularly true when computers are used as aids in psychological testing:

> There must be a clinician between the computer and the client. Even the very best reports, whether generated by clinician or by computer, are of little value in the hands of an incompetent, poorly trained clinician who cannot put the results into the context of the patient's life. Computer-based interpretative reports are "generic" interpretations. They describe the characteristics of a "typical patient" with the particular test scores observed. A well-designed interpretation system based on a well-validated test can provide a useful source of hypotheses for the clinician whose task it is to examine those hypotheses in the light of the clinical history and behavioral observations. The problems associated with

the CBTI [Computer-based Test Interpretation] are not inherent in the technology but in the training of the professionals who will use it (Fowler & Butcher, 1986).

The psychological assessor should not employ unfamiliar techniques, or techniques that he or she is not fully competent to use. Thus, "Psychologists responsible for decisions involving individuals or policies based on test results have an understanding of psychological or educational measurement, validation problems, and test research." (American Psychological Association, "Ethical Principles of Psychologists," Principle 2e, 1981).

There are several other ethical injunctions that require judgment pertaining to the use of psychological instruments. Assessment tools should always be selected in terms of how appropriate they are judged to be to contribute to answers to the problem under consideration. The Rorschach, for example, may be the instrument of choice to delineate lapses in the reality contact of a patient, but not particularly effective as a predictor of adjustment to military and combat flying (Holtzman & Sells, 1954). Thus the test-using assessor must be well read in the research that is pertinent to the instruments being considered for use. Are there shortcomings, or a lack of relevance, in any given context? Good judgment was particularly lacking when, according to a horror story circulating during World War II, military recruits were tested at all hours of the day and night, often after arriving at a reception center following an arduous train ride.

THE PRACTICAL USE OF PSYCHOLOGICAL ASSESSMENT

We see from much of the above that there are vastly different approaches to psychological assessment. They are not easily comparable, however, since they commonly are applied by differently trained and oriented assessors to more or less different situations. But they can be compatible and complimentary.

In addition to the personal disposition of the assessor, the nature of the problem being dealt with is an important factor. Are we concerned with overt behaviors or with psychodynamics; with academic or performance skills, with personal adjustment issues; with normative matters, or with idiosyncratic intrapsychic issues?

Thus, it is a matter of judgment as to which approach is most appropriate to a given case, which in turn rests on personal disposition relating to developmental experiences and life orientation, on training and subsequent professional growth and experience, and on the problem and the assessment context.

Applying these observations to real assessment tasks, we find myriad occasions where clinical judgments, based on either objective or subjective considerations, or both, should be made. Assessment is a problem-solving process, as earlier indicated, and the first challenge facing the assessor is to define the problem that is to be solved. Commonly, the reason for doing an assessment is not clear, perhaps even to the colleague who requests an assessment, perhaps to the assessor. Does a clinician really need to establish a diagnosis in order to initiate treatment, or would a case formulation be more to the point? Is delineating a client's symptom picture the issue, or is predicting the interaction between client and therapist likely to have a better payoff? The definition of a meaningful problem to be solved through assessment may come about through studying and reflecting on a case and/or through discussion with a colleague.

Cohen (1980) suggests that "there is a manifest and a latent content to many testing referrals." In this Freudian orientation, Cohen postulates that the latent content may pertain to interpersonal factors among clinic personnel, and he illustrates with a personal anecdote. The real issue in Cohen's case (the latent content) stemmed from a disagreement between a psychiatrist and his patient over the patient's diagnosis. Thus the "need" to establish a diagnosis was the manifest content, and the need that led to the making of a referral was the psychiatrist's need for an ally. Berg (1988) has made similar observations regarding referrals.

Judgment over how to deal with colleagues is a continuous requirement of the assessor, even though situations such as the above probably are rare. The making of technical judgments is also a continuous requirement. How shall a particular case be approached? Is psychological testing indicated, and, if so, which tests might prove most helpful? Is each instrument under consideration appropriate to its contemplated use and to the individual client? What is the significance of scores, score patterns, or verbalizations *in this case*?

Continuing in this vein, would the use of any particular instrument be too time-consuming in terms of the helpful information that might be derived from its use? Might needed information be obtained more economically from, for example, an interview, a discussion with colleagues or members of the client's family, or perusal of the client's case folder—or some combination of these? Might one or two tests suffice in place of a battery that the assessor has found to be useful with *most* clients?

The need to exercise sound judgment is particularly strong when data are being molded into a useful communication—a case formulation or a psychological report. The crowning achievement of a psychological assessment is proficiency in making interpretations that are accurate and pertinent to the reason for carrying out the assessment, in the ability to focus this information, and in presenting it in an understandable and meaningful manner. The latter consideration may particularly prove to be a challenge when the outcome of an assessment is communicated to a client or another layperson. The need for human judgment is particularly increased in this age of automation; judgment cannot be automated, and the human must monitor the machine:

> Computer-generated interpretive reports should be used only in conjunction with professional judgment. The user should judge for each test taker the validity of the computerized test report based on the user's professional knowledge of the total context of testing and the test taker's performance and characteristics.

Further spelling out this guideline to the use of computers as an assessment aid—

It is imperative that the final decision be made by a qualified professional who takes responsibility for overseeing both the process of testing and judging the applicability of the interpretive report for individual test takers, consistent with legal, ethical, and professional requirements. In some circumstances, professional providers may need to edit or amend the computer report to take into account their own observations and judgments and to ensure that the report is comprehensible, free of jargon, and true to the person evaluated (American Psychological Association, 1986).

THE PSYCHOLOGICAL ASSESSOR: ROLE-RELATED ISSUES

Human factors, largely subjective, enter the assessment process. These include the assessor's perception of his or her role, and the possible role-related conflicts that may affect both the assessment process and product. Problems arising from these sources may become particularly evident in the assessor's relations with colleagues.

PERCEPTIONS OF THE ROLE OF PSYCHOLOGICAL ASSESSOR

It is little wonder that psychological assessment, particularly when carried out by psychologists, has long been mired in ambiguity. Definitions of the role of the psychological assessor lack consensus, for in fact the psychological assessor has three roles, and they all have practical consequences. There is the role as defined by the assessor's own perception of his or her duties, the role as understood by the assessor's colleagues, and the role that is defined by what the assessor actually does. These three roles may not be, and often are not, in agreement.

The resultant confusion experienced by the assessor is not unlike that experienced by the adolescent in the fifth stage of Erikson's (1959) sequence of personality development: identity versus identity diffusion (or role confusion). In the case of the adolescent, difficulties at this stage are accompanied by negative self-views, impairment in relations, and ineffectual performance ("work paralysis"). The psychological assessor who does not have a meaningful and satisfying definition of his or her role has comparable personal and professional problems.

The Role of Tester Versus the Role of Assessor

The confusion of testing with assessment, as summarized in Chapter 1, is paralleled by confusion of the tester with the assessor. Even the modern assessor, whose primary concern may be with unquantifiable psychodynamics, may be mislabeled as a tester. This error may be due to inertia, habit, or cultural fixation—an evident holdover from the era of *mental testers* and *IQ testers*. Schafer (1989) and Appelbaum (1970), for example, who did yeoman work in the development of assessment theory and methods, continued to refer to "testers" long after the practices they advanced were well established.

The classical role of tester stems from the classical function of testing—the generation of accurate scores, such as an IQ. In this role the tester (or *examiner*) must make a number of judgments with respect to the instruments to be selected to ensure that the obtained scores will be valid. He or she must make decisions regarding the appropriateness of a particular test for a particular person (the WAIS-R, for example, would not be used with a 15-year old because the scale is not normed at this level). The testing procedure must be monitored: Is the client cooperative, adequately motivated, understanding of the requirements of testing, apparently free of incapacitating psychological or physical distress, such as might accompany a bad cold? Is the room too stuffy, the temperature too warm, the light too glaring? An overall judgment might be made as to whether the obtained test score(s) is (are) representative of the client's performance, and optimal.

Compared with the assessor, who is active and interactive (e.g., pp. 103, 264, 334–335), the tester's is a relatively passive role. Rosenwald (1963) characterizes the passive tester thus:

> The tester does little. He speaks to the patient merely instrumentally—to induce him to talk more. He depends on his test material... The tester is ideally seen but not heard.

Current testing practices show a meaningful shift from this approach in the direction of incorporating *some* of the practices of assessment. Greater responsibility (than is exercised by the traditional tester—see following discussion) is thus mandated to the highly trained *test user*, the term that has replaced *tester*, particularly in official publications (e.g., American Psychological Association, 1985, 1986, 1988). The *Standards for Educational and Psychological Testing* (1985) provides that "test users should have a sound technical *and professional* basis for their actions" (emphasis added).

A high level of responsibility is particularly in evidence when the psychological assessor sets out to develop an independent opinion at the behest of another professional. In this capacity he or she functions as a consultant, a role that diverges sharply from that of tester or technician:

> The laboratory technician functions in a limited, circumscribed role for which the formal and practical preparation is much less lengthy and rigorous than that required for full professional functioning at the Ph.D., Psy.D., Ed.D., or M.D. level, for example. The training of the technician is always in accordance with the principles and needs of a professional group, and the parent group, through various direct and indirect means, influences the training program: The students are trained explicitly to serve the group. The technician is asked to make a particular determination; the procedure will be the same regardless of the purpose. The technician does not interpret findings, make a judgment on which findings are relevant and which are not, or make recommendations. The technician is not sought out by the person who made the referral to discuss possible

implications of findings or the need for additional tests or subsequent retests. It is sufficient that the technician gives results along with some indication of their reliability. The report of a psychological technician may contain such material as an IQ, various other requested scores, ratios, profiles, psychographs, or whatever raw responses might be requested by a supervisor.

The consultant, by contrast, is a product of advanced scientific and professional education designed to prepare an individual for high level, responsible functioning. The consultant must have a grasp of both broad and specific knowledge and the ability to reach decisions that may be of major importance. Such training is under the sponsorship and the direction of the discipline of the consultant, who claims a unique role.

Thus, the psychologist is thoroughly familiar with concepts of human personality, carries out psychological techniques with expertise, and works from a background of relevant research orientation. He or she must be familiar with the nature and the background of the problem at hand and the alternative decisions that might be influenced by the psychological report. On this basis the consultant must then decide on what kind(s) of data to seek, which findings have relevance, and how these can be most effectively presented (Tallent, 1988).

Kingsbury (1987), writing from the standpoint of one who has been through an American Psychological Association-approved clinical psychology program, and who also had experience with an American Psychiatric Association-approved psychiatric residency, suggests that it is the training of psychiatrists that leads them to view psychologists as testers who are not qualified to be consultants.

> One surprise in medical school and residency was how rarely clinical psychology was mentioned. There were two lectures in my four years of medical school (one by a psychologist) about psychological testing in which it was briefly mentioned that this was a skill of psychologists. Also, related health professionals were occasionally mentioned, usually in a list—chiropractors, optometrists, psychologists, midwives, and so forth. It would be relatively easy to finish medical school and a decent portion of some psychiatric residencies without a clear idea of what psychologists do beyond testing. Although I had been prepared to defend psychology, the almost complete ignoring of psychology surprised me.
>
> It is not surprising, then, that when psychologists strive for equity in responsibility, psychiatrists may view them as overreaching beyond their testing responsibilities. Or psychiatrists may be confused and wonder why a paramedical professional would think of trying to take medical responsibility, equating it with the trend for nurses to seek greater clinical responsibilities. On the other hand, clinical psychologists may wonder how their years of training can be "ignored" and may feel resentful.

Meyer, Fink, and Carey (1988) make a similar point on the basis of a survey of internists and family practitioners: "many of the difficulties that appear in practice between physicians and psychologists appear to have originated in medical school training. Medical students have little contact with contemporary psychology during medical training." Further, "the most common instructor for behavioral sciences was a psychiatrist." As a consequence, "many medical students develop a myopic view of the role and the purpose of the psychologist."

Overvaluation and Undervaluation of the Assessor's Role and Contributions

Thus misperceived as a "tester," the role and value of the psychological assessor's contribution is further misperceived according to the views held of tests and testing at any given time. These, generally, are unrealistic. Psychological instruments and the outcome of their use have, by and large over the years, been both vastly overrated and underrated.

In the early days of personality assessment the practice was surrounded with an aura of mystery, myth, and magic, the "tester" being regarded as omniscient, omnipotent—a charismatic figure. Schafer (1984) was perhaps the first of many to point out that psychological testers wore the mantle of an oracle, an exalted position to which projective tools contributed in no small measure. This state of affairs was pithily documented in Appelbaum's (1976) recollection of the way in which psychological assessment was regarded at the Menninger Clinic of an earlier time: "In the Rapaport period no member of the psychiatric team was allowed to see the test report prior to its ceremonial unveiling at a case conference."

Such a reputation accorded the psychological assessor and psychological instruments, built on bubbles as it was, had to collapse when confronted by reality or by well-articulated challenges of varying degrees of merit. Replacing the fanciful terms of the previous paragraph were expressions of disillusionment and disenchantment, with a nihilistic outlook on assessment displacing an oversold faith in the powers of psychological assessment.

Challenges to psychological instruments and to the practice of psychological assessment have come from a variety of sources. These include psychological colleagues—academics and clinician researchers, psychiatrists, and attorneys. Each group, or subgroup, of critics tends to emphasize a reason for its opposition peculiar to its own orientation or needs. Having access to the same data and theories, on the basis of personal factors (including the assimilation of the views of mentors and associates) those involved with psychological assessment hold varying outlooks on a number of issues. (How personal factors lead us to identify with theorists, and how, in turn, the personality and experiences of theorists shape their theories is explored by Stolorow and Atwood [1979]—who stress the role of subjectivity in personality theory, and Mindess [1988]—whose thesis is the "personal factor" that may be found in the major theorists and their theories. Neither assessment theory nor practice is oriented to absolute, immutable reference points.)

Thus, many humanistic psychologists believe that psychological assessment is nonhumanistic (pp. 16–17) and behavior therapists may have a problem with tests that rest on trait theory and do not tap the all-important (according to behavior theory) environmental determiners of behavior (e.g., Nelson, 1983; Nelson & Hayes, 1979). One of the most searing appraisals of psychological (and psychiatric) assessment reflects the position of Jay Ziskin (1981), a psychologist and a lawyer:

It is the aim of this book to demonstrate that despite the ever increasing utilization of psychiatric and psychological evidence in the legal process, such evidence frequently does not meet reasonable criteria of admissibility and should not be admitted to a court of law and, if admitted, should be given little or no weight.

Studies that are frequently cited as demonstrating that psychological instruments (or psychologists using these instruments) are ineffectual at various diagnostic tasks are not hard to come by, particularly for those instruments that involve appreciable subjectivity in their interpretation. Just a few illustrations will suffice at this point.

Thus, Goldberg's (1959) study of the Bender-Gestalt as a diagnostic instrument to identify patients with organic brain damage (p. 12) would seem to suggest that this instrument is not suitable for such a purpose, both trained and untrained judges evidencing low success rates. The Holtzman and Sells (1954) study that reported the inability of the Rorschach to predict adjustment to military and combat flying is commonly chalked up as another classical failure of projective techniques. And in the Albert, Fox, and Kahn (1980) study, which more closely resembled a clinical situation, expert judges were unable to detect faked Rorschach protocols.

Such studies, however, have by no means disposed of the validity question, with which we deal further in the next chapter. Similarly, the evidence that has been advanced in the clinical versus statistical controversy (pp. 69–72) has not settled matters for many who have followed the arguments. Practicing clinicians, rather, have been inclined to be skeptical, if not flatly rejecting or deprecating, of the victory claimed by those favoring the actuarial position.

You may readily observe the personal equation in action, both in performing and interpreting validity research, from McArthur's (1968) comments on a grade-predicting study carried out by Donivan Watley (1966a,b; 1968a,b; Watley & Vance, 1964):

> What bothered this reader is why anyone would want to do it... To predict grades is scarcely a brainworthy assignment, nor is it part of the guidance man's job. What duffer in the trade doesn't answer that question by turning to his handy-dandy experience table? Why study experimentally a task nobody performs?
>
> One reason Watley studied a task nobody performs is that he was under the illusion that this monkey trick was "clinical prediction!" Nor is Watley alone in this strange view: Meehl, Taft, Sarbin, and a host of others seem to share it. To them, "clinical" seems to mean "anything not computerized." In this era, when hardware determines what we are allowed to think about, we can anticipate a still more wide spread of such usage—and more of such studies as Watley's, that label a nonclinical straw man "clinical prediction," then knock him down. For that is what Watley does. He is wise enough to call the reader's attention to the other better morals of his experiment, but he keeps using the "clinical versus actuarial" jargon, so that one suspects the original grant to have been given on this pretext and one wonders if that august grant-giving body also misunderstands what clinical prediction is all about! Watley keeps pointing out that the human prophets did well to approach the accuracy of the regression equation as an asymptote in his set piece. He seems to think that this observation has some kind of "actuarial is better" moral. The

real moral is "actuarial is better when the question is trivial." Machines have the world's best multiple-choice minds.

Such studies beg the question of their results by their choice of criteria and predictor variables. Over and over we are showing that man is a poor to adequate substitute for the mindless machine at performing mindless tasks. Long ago I suggested that clinician and actuary be given freedom to choose the data of their choice, the methods of their choice, and the criteria of their choice if they are ever to be compared on even terms... What Watley proved is that, set the task of emulating the machine, men can come close to that goal, especially if they, too, are programmed.

Watley's (1968) reply to McArthur is also informative, also hard hitting, but less colorful.

While validity issues thus loom large where the assessor's role is undervalued, in many instances psychological assessment is downgraded because it appears to fall short of expectations and an impasse is created between assessor and consumer. "Why won't they listen to me?" Shectman (1979) asks plaintively, and he answers his question by pointing out a number of misunderstandings and problems of communication between assessors and consumers. These are among the perennial "pitfalls" in psychological report writing (see Chapter 10, and also Tallent, 1988). The inevitable result is a far less than optimal effectiveness of the assessment process.

Shectman approaches this issue from several angles. First he urges that the problem is not with our instruments; it is with *ourselves*. And further, communication is a "people process," not a language process. Taking a Freudian stance, he likens the impasse between assessors and consumers to the resistance that Freud discovered as a feature of the therapist-patient relationship. Also following Freud, he believes such resistance must be analyzed and dealt with, not regarded as a nuisance.

Also concerned with assessor shortcomings, Schafer (1989) presents a dynamic point of view in delineating a number of noncognitive factors that may enter the assessment process and which must be recognized by the assessor in order to minimize harmful effects in the form of a product quite different from the outcome of careful psychological thinking. In this vein, he discusses the consequences of the tester's personality when insight is lacking.

Thus, the "rigidly intellectualistic tester" is inclined to "use his findings in a provocatively 'informed' manner to complicate the case unnecessarily; he will interpret everything in sight, and substitute quantity for quality, doubt for responsibility, and overabstractions for descriptions." The "sadistic tester" may distort his client's personality in a different direction: "Testing may become a means of ferreting out the 'weak,' 'debasing,' 'humiliating' aspects of the lives of the hated Others." Still other misrepresentations of clients may be created by assessors who are masochistic, who have "an uncertain sense of personal identity," who are socially inhibited or withdrawn, who have a dependent orientation or "rigid defenses against dependent needs," or "rigid defenses against hostility"—that may lead to an attitude of "saintliness" to the point of becoming "a powerful sadistic weapon."

The assessor must attend to the needs of the consumer, not necessarily to the question the consumer raises. As pointed out earlier (p. 35), there often is a latent question, as well as the manifest question the consumer asks. Volumes of data typically do not meet the consumer's need. *Information overload* is a common problem in the consultation, and "more is not better," Shectman cautions. Only selected information, targeted to the consumer's needs, personal as well as strictly professional, should be offered.

If a surfeit of data does not meet the consumer's needs, neither does a curt *yes* or *no* adequately or responsibly answer many questions that may be asked (e.g., Is this patient suicidal?). Such questions commonly relate to personality and to personal and environmental contingencies and as much pertinent information as can be gained should be set forth in a joint effort of assessor and consumer to look at the client's situation in a practical and constructive manner.

Continuing in a dynamic frame of reference, Shectman stresses an interpersonal frame of reference in the consultation. The psychological assessor in the consultation must (inoffensively) play the role of the psychologist. He or she must not only understand his or her colleagues' needs, but also work with them to reach a better understanding of their clients' needs.

This goal is best achieved when the assessor shuns the false and threatening role of oracle, but also realistically helps to develop in his colleagues an appreciation of the capabilities of assessment. The assessor must recognize that it may be difficult for a colleague to accept psychological findings that he or she cannot "see" (e.g., deep pathological trends), and to trust instead what can be "seen." Here the assessor must find a way to bridge the gap between what is obvious and what is not. It may be pointed out to colleagues, for example, that there is a logical relation between overt conduct and unobservable inner states that might account for these surface behaviors.

The acceptability of the psychological report (and the report writer) can therefore be enhanced by attending to a number of principles of report writing *and* interpersonal attitudes and relations. We must be aware of what makes sense to our colleagues. The psychological report is more likely to be accepted, for example, when the client is presented in a manner that makes him or her "come alive," as opposed to presenting scores, ratios, responses, and so on. "Client-centered" reports are generally to be preferred to "test-centered" reports. These and other principles and issues pertaining to the effective presentation of psychological information are the concern of Chapter 10. In the meantime, we should bear in mind that there are things we can do to make "them" listen to us.

The definition of the role of the psychological assessor can have great impact on the person who exercises that role, which in turn can very much affect how he or she carries out assessment duties and the quality of the resultant assessment product. How the role of psychological assessor is defined and understood can, and frequently does, determine the psychologist's job satisfaction and self-esteem, and whether he or she will choose to assume this role, or to abandon it after trying it out.

The role of psychological assessor is to an extent self-defined, but it is also largely defined by what the assessor actually does or is expected to do. Colleagues can also be quite influential in defining the role. When the assessor is fully recognized as a high-level, responsible consultant, with valued and unique skills to offer, the impact can only be positive on the assessor *and* colleagues. William C. Menninger (1950) early spelled out how such a role for the psychological assessor can contribute to the clinical process.

> I expect to receive a diagnostic appraisal of a total personality, with discussion of the nature of the illness, character structure, strengths or weaknesses of ego defenses, characteristic modes of adaptation, likely course of the illness and amenability to treatment. True, that I have opinions about most, if not all of these, myself, but I conceive of the psychologist's function as being to render an additional professional opinion which can hardly be fulfilled by merely requesting that he give some tests. This, it seems to me, is the difference between laboratory "prescription testing" and diagnostic consultation.

The "Less Of A Test" Concept

To relate effectively to such questions might require that we reconceptualize the nature of our psychological instruments so that we may use them to do what they can do best. This task was perhaps first accomplished by Zubin, Eron, and Schumer (1965) who advocated that the Rorschach is not adequate as a psychometric tool, but is most profitably employed as a clinical interview, a position embraced by Reznikoff (1972) and by Singer (1968, 1977b), who called this use of the instrument a "transaction." In the "consensus Rorschach" method (pp. 326–328), transactions are the source of the essentially qualitative data the clinician or researcher seeks. When we depart from the scoring and quantifying of responses that have been basic to the Rorschach method since its inception, we may, with Korchin and Schuldberg (1981) speak of the instrument as *less of a test*. When an instrument becomes less of a test, the person of the assessor looms larger. And there is, of course, less need to validate the instrument in the ways that tests have long been validated.

Such a view, assigning to the assessor a role more important than that of tester, has long been heresy in some quarters.

Psychodiagnostics and Its Discontents

In many settings, however, regardless of actual practice, testing and its principles are considered to be the proper approach to gaining psychological information. Assessment psychologists are widely regarded as "testers," psychometricians, or technicians, and therefore often in a subordinate role, particularly in psychiatric settings. Thus perceived, the assessor tends to perceive himself or herself similarly.

In a searching commentary, Rosenwald (1963) has aptly grasped the psychological assessor's plight in titling his paper *Psychodiagnostics and Its Discontents*. Chained to a testing role (by others' perceptions, if not in fact), the consumers of the psychological assessor's efforts often expect "miracles" and a (physicalistic) scientific product—both of these at the same time—and have disdain for the assessor whose approach to the development of a case formulation entails artistry.

Implicitly or explicitly, such conflicts betray the personal equation in both the psychological assessor *and* the consumer, and questions of validity are entwined in these personal equations. How useful is the information the psychological assessor provides? Rosenwald commonsensically observes:

> Under close scrutiny, it becomes apparent that the application of tests to a diagnostic problem has little in common with laboratory science. The utility of a test report to its consumer depends less on the observance of scientific procedures than on some sort of emergent meaningfulness and truth. A test report is, after all, a service from a professional consumer, and, as is true of any service, cannot be validated or invalidated absolutely. It depends on the skill of the individual practitioner. What is more, it depends on the personal equation of the consumer. Anxious testers often assume that the therapist knows all there is to know about psychotherapy, and that his help to the patient hinges crucially on receiving the complete and perfect test report. The fact is that many therapists have only a foggy notion of how to utilize a good report. It follows that to be successful a diagnostician must produce a report compatible with the needs of its reader.

But–

> The consumer's personal equation is not usually kept in mind in conventional studies of test validity. Generally speaking, significant research into the *clinical* usefulness of tests cannot be performed until clearer formulations are made of what is expected of and by therapists.

Vying to be the chief source of discontent among psychodiagnosticians is the validity research of psychologists—such as the studies mentioned on pages 65–66. The clinical versus statistical controversy (pp. 69–72) has cast a chronic pall over the psychodiagnostic enterprise, and, particularly, the choice words in one of Meehl's (1956) mid-fifties bombshells (his call for a "good cookbook") have done little to raise the comfort level of numerous practitioners of the art:

> What are the pragmatic implications of the preceding analysis? [the argument favoring the cookbook] Putting it bluntly, it suggests that for a rather wide range of clinical problems involving personality description from tests, the clinical interpreter is a costly middleman who might better be eliminated. An initial layout of research time could result in a cookbook whose recipes would encompass the great majority of psychometric configurations seen in daily work. I am fully aware of the prospect of a "clinical clerk" simply looking up Rorschach pattern number 73 J 10–5 or Multiphasic curve "Halbower Verzeichnis 626" seems very odd and even dangerous. I reassure myself by recalling that the number of phenotypic and genotypic attributes is, after all, finite; and that the number which are often found attributed or denied even in an extensive sample of psychological reports on patients is actually very limited...I invite you to consider the possibility that the emotional block we all experience in connection with the cookbook approach could

be dissolved simply by trying it out until our daily successes finally get us accustomed to the idea.

Admittedly this would take some of the "fun" out of psychodiagnostic activity. But I suspect that most of the clinicians who put a high value on this kind of fun would have even more fun doing intensive psychotherapy. The great personnel needs today, and for the next generation or more, are for psychotherapists and researchers. (If you don't believe much in the efficacy of therapy, this is the more reason for research.)

The case for research is well taken, and applies to both diagnostics and therapy—as Meehl indicates. But one cannot simply note the shortcomings of assessment and suggest, therefore, that practitioners abandon assessment in favor of becoming therapists—which seems to be the message many psychologists have received. Rosenwald (1963) implies an impetus for psychologists to become therapists in view of the acceptance of this activity "by some observers outside the field who yet remain staunch opponents of testing."

Commonalities of Assessment and Psychotherapy

There is a great all-around similarity between psychological assessment and therapy, and commonality in validation objectives. Allen (1981), particularly, has noted great overlap and identical features in the assessment and therapeutic enterprises. For example, in one situation we must establish a therapeutic alliance; in the other a diagnostic alliance. "All the concepts that are employed to understand the therapeutic relationship (e.g., alliance, transference, countertransference) are central to the testing process." Psychological assessment, again in Allen's words, is "treatment in microcosm"—"for it is a systematic investigation of the nature and meaning of the patient's psychological problems." To be a good diagnostician, Allen suggests, one must be a good therapist. The reverse would also appear to be true. Assessment and therapy employ very much the same approach to helping people. "One can view the interaction between the patient and the clinician as a *diagnostic* process or a *treatment* process depending upon one's purpose in making the discrimination" (Schlesinger, 1973).

ETHICAL ORIENTATION TO PSYCHOLOGICAL ASSESSMENT

The promotion of human welfare is a basic purpose of the American Psychological Association (American Psychological Association, 1985a). Deriving from this premise, psychological ethics, generally, and the ethics of psychological assessment are broadly humanistic. The "Ethical Principles of Psychologists" (American Psychological Association, 1981) calls on the practitioner to "promote the welfare and respect the dignity and worth of the individual, and strive to preserve and protect fundamental human rights." Key concepts in the application of the "Ethical Principles" stress the psychologist's responsibility, competence, and concern for the best interests of the client.

Several other American Psychological Association publications, variously addressed to problems of testing and assessment, have reference to the "Ethical Principles." These are: *Standards for Educational and Psychological Testing* (1985), *Guidelines for Computer-Based Tests and Interpretations* (1986), and *Standards for Providers of Psychological Services* (1977). In a number of instances, these publications interpret or amplify on the "Ethical Principles." This added information is most welcome, particularly as it has reference to relatively new applications of testing or assessment, such as computer testing.

3
THE CONTEXT OF PSYCHOLOGICAL ASSESSMENT

Psychological assessment hinges on a number of personal and social issues among the individuals involved in the process, as we saw in the last chapter. Particularly important are such matters as the traditions, beliefs, assumptions, and attitudes of assessors and of the consumers of the assessment product. We must attend also to the tools available to do the job, both the conceptual tools and the materials of the craft.

THE CHANGING *ZEITGEIST*

From the time of Witmer, psychological assessment has been linked to distinct orientations (Tallent, 1969). Currently, this fact is most evident in the measurement tradition, the topic of Chapter 4, and in the clinical tradition, the topic of Chapter 5. Technically, the conduct of assessment relates closely to methods that have gained acceptance as capable of efficiently generating valid data, but the practical purpose for which these data are sought also is a major factor in applied work. Thus, we recollect from Korchin and Schuldberg (1981) that the usual intent of clinical assessment is "description and prediction toward the ends of planning, executing, and evaluating therapeutic interactions and predicting future behavior."

Along with this role for assessment has been the assumption of a practical role for theory. Therapists generally have subscribed to the view that when intervention in a case is contemplated, the therapist must be guided by the personality theory that underlies the intervention. Such an intimate relationship between assessment goals and theory-dictated therapeutic approaches is noted in the case of behavior therapy, as discussed on page 15 and in numerous other places; for example, in Nelson and Hayes (1986). Holt (1968), in the ego-psychology tradition of Rapaport, Gill, and Schafer (1945, 1946), advises that the purpose of assessment is to produce a description that will "emphasize the *structure* of personality, its enduring principles of organization such as defenses, abilities, and styles of adaptation, with only secondary concern for so-called dynamics, by which is usually meant hypothetical reconstructions of genetic sequences such as the fate of the oedipus complex, and statements about the relative strength of various motives."

NEW ORIENTATIONS TO ASSESSMENT

For many years, orientations to psychotherapy have differed, sometimes being poles apart. Psychoanalytic therapies and behavior therapies, in particular, have stood opposed to one another, both in theory and in practice. Psychoanalytically oriented therapists would (and many still do) engage in heated polemics "at the drop of a hat."

In current *practice*, however, the dictates of personality theory are "more honored in the breech." Messer (1986), for example, finds a "confluence of attitudes" among practitioners of analytically oriented therapies and behavior therapists, with therapists from both camps "inclined to incorporate perspectives or attitudes of the other." Both of these therapies, in turn, "surely owe a debt to humanistic therapies like those of Maslow and Rogers, particularly in conceptualizing the nature of the client-therapist relationship."

As an outcome of his study of therapists' perspectives, Messer advocates a number of heresies to both behavior therapists and psychoanalytic therapists. Thus, for "behavior therapists inclined to incorporate psychoanalytically toned interventions, the following (suggestions) can be made":

> In discerning schemas or core organizing principles and giving feedback to clients about them, behavior therapists should be attuned to their possible (a) unconscious character, (b) childhood origins, and (c) base in conflicting feelings, typically hostility, love, and dependency. In other words, behavior therapists may want to try to elaborate their clients' unconscious fantasies before choosing the point of entry for the behavioral modification.

And, "for psychoanalytic therapists inclined to be influenced by the attitudes of behavior therapists," the following is one of six points of advice:

> The ability of clients to control their affect, both its inhibition and its expression, should be given more credence. Stated differently, clients can be viewed somewhat less as passive reactors to unconscious forces, and somewhat more as conscious creators or maintainers of their current pathological situation, including their cognition, affect, and behavior.

Beitman, Goldfried, and Norcross (1989), in an overview of current therapeutic approaches, also identify a convergence, which they define as "the tendency to grow alike, to develop similarities in form." Numerous arguments are cited. In terms of outcomes among therapies, no one approach commands a lead: "With few exceptions, there is little compelling evidence to recommend the use of one form of psychotherapy over another in the treatment of specific problems." They note Beutler's (1983) suggestion that "different therapeutic orientations probably do not dictate the specific orientations used so much as they determine the therapeutic goals to pursue." Experience in the conduct of therapy seems to lead therapists away from rigid commitment to specific theories: "Today's psychodynamic therapists have begun to recognize the importance of conscious thoughts, action, and environmental factors, and behavior therapists' recognition of cognitive factors has led them to accept the importance of 'implicit' thoughts."

Continuing with data garnered by Beitman, Goldfried, and Norcross, we may conclude that embracing one point of view is the mark of the neophyte therapist:

> The existing research has not delineated any consistent differences between those psychotherapists who identify themselves as eclectic and those who identify themselves as noneclectic, with the exception of clinical experience. This research has indicated that clinicians ascribing to eclecticism tend to be older and more experienced. Conversely, inexperienced therapists are more likely to endorse exclusive theoretical orientations. Reliance on one theory and a few techniques may be the product of inexperience; put another way, with experience comes diversity and flexibility.

Summarizing their argument, Beitman, Goldfried, and Norcross conclude: "The integrative movement appears to be gaining momentum and is likely to be the *Zeitgeist* of the next several decades of psychotherapy research and practice." Their definition of *integration* is germane:

> Although "eclecticism" is certainly one component of the integration of psychotherapy in that it integrates clinical methods from diverse sources, the term "integration" has come to acquire a more therapeutic meaning. "Integration" commonly denotes the conceptual synthesis of diverse theoretical systems. "Eclecticism," by contrast, is theoretical but empirical in pragmatically applying what already exists. "Integration" is more theoretical than empirical in creating something "new": a superordinate umbrella, coherent theoretical gestalt, metatheoretical framework, or conceptually superior therapy.

All of this is directly pertinent to the practice of psychological assessment, as it pertains to providing service to psychotherapists. Primarily, assessment efforts directed to theoretical personality variables, whether to such matters as theory-linked techniques or to theory-defined developmental phases and experiences, are largely misplaced. Beitman, Goldfried, and Norcross, abstracting pertinent research, conclude that "only 10%–12% of outcome variance is generally accounted for by technique variables." *A delineation of client variables is much more to the point.*

much to the point are orientations to the concept of the functioning
[no]rmal and abnormal—how we think about this central topic of
psy[chological a]ssessment of personality is a companion topic, and various theoretical issues underlie its practice.

PHILOSOPHICAL/SCIENTIFIC UNDERPINNINGS OF ASSESSMENT

Quite different understandings of science and the application of science to assessment coexist. One has its roots in the philosophical tenet of positivism. Stemming from this orientation are empiricism, objectivity, stimulus-response psychology, and operationism—all fundamental to the psychometric approach, also called in this book the *measurement tradition*. The other dominant position in assessment has significant ties to phenomenology.

Some psychological instruments—intelligence tests, for example—are basically psychometric tools, while other instruments—sentence completions, for example—yield the richest data when interpreted in the light of the client's phenomenology. Still other instruments may be used dominantly either psychometrically or in a phenomenological frame of reference.

The Rorschach furnishes a prime example of an instrument with polymorphous potential. Here is a tool long used to tap the individual's experiences of the world, partly through the interpretation of qualitative data, while gaining other personality information through interpretation of scores and score patterns—in the manner that Rorschach first used his test. In recent years, Exner (1985) has vastly refined the psychometric approach to the Rorschach in his microcomputer program known as the *Rorschach Interpretation Assistance Program* (RIAP). Both approaches to the Rorschach are currently popular, leading Korchin and Schuldberg (1981) to the "more of a test, less of a test" concept, "test" being a psychometric instrument.

Blatt's (1986) view of the Rorschach is that its best, and certainly its trendiest, use is as "less of a test." He sees a new theoretical emphasis in psychology, "a view of psychology as a science of the construction of meaning as well as a behavioral science, [that] has been reflected in personality assessment."

> The Rorschach is increasingly being used, not so much as a test, but as an experimental procedure to study the relationship between cognitive constructions or mental representations and personality organization. It is this new emphasis on cognitive constructions and representational processes in psychological theory and science that will also be expressed increasingly in personality assessment as we approach the 21st century.

CHANGING ORIENTATIONS TO PERSONALITY AND PSYCHOPATHOLOGY

Psychological assessment is in the service of producing useful statements about people—commonly as an aspect of initiating psychotherapy or other intervention.

This would be a difficult, not to say invalid, approach to engaging in a helping relationship with people if the personality features we identify in our assessment were evanescent and disjointed, having no lasting existence across situations or meaningful connectedness to one another.

Yet this is precisely the view of personality held by a number of influential members of the psychological community, particularly during the 1960s and 1970s. Mischel (e.g., 1969, 1976) took a leadership role in advocating this position, which Bem and Allen (1974) captured in the words of Abraham Lincoln. Consistent behavior, they suggested, characterizes only "some of the people some of the time." Millon (1984) sums up the situation thus:

> What were once the splendidly astute and discriminating clinical portrayals by Freud, Horney, Fromm, and Sullivan, each of whom stirred our curiosities and inspired us to further our desire to know, were now outdated curiosities, grandiose speculations to be replaced by tightly focused and empirically anchored constructs. The conceptual models and cogent insights of Lewin, Murray, and Murphy resonated with our early, personally more prosaic efforts to penetrate and give order to the mysteries of our patients' psychic worlds, *but* they were too out of vogue, skillfully rent by what I term the anticoherency and anticonsistency movements.

In more recent years, this anticoherency, anticonsistency position has shifted, and holistic views of personality are more widely accepted. Mischel's (1984) modified outlook recognizes greater consistency of personality than did his earlier views. Thus, in a delay-of-gratification paradigm, he reports that "convergent experimental and correlational results indicate the nature of the competence basic for this ability and identify both coherence over time and cross-situational discriminativeness in self-control."

Mischel notes here one line of research that "investigated how psychological situations and the specific *mental representations* of the rewards in the delay-of-gratification paradigm...systematically influence the developing child's ability to defer immediate gratification for larger delayed consequences" (emphasis added). These results do not negate that behavior is the outcome of person x situation. It is simply that the subjects of such studies have demonstrated that they carry around with them, through mental representations, the environmental contingencies that are relevant to their behavior. He eschews "a preemptive dichotomy between the person and the situation...what a situation does to people depends on just how they think about it, on their ideation more than on what they are actually facing."

A number of additional studies suggest the stability of personality. Epstein (1979) thus telegraphs in the title of his paper conclusions that are at sharp variance to those of Bem and Allen (1974): "On Predicting Most of the People Much of the Time."

In a later paper, Epstein (1980) proposes that reported failures to demonstrate stability were the result of methodological shortcomings and proposed the following hypothesis and a corollary:

> Hypothesis: Stability can be demonstrated over a wide range of variables so long as the behavior in question is averaged over a sufficient number of occurrences. Corollary: Reliable relationships can be demonstrated between ratings by others and self-ratings, including standard personality inventories, on the one hand, and objective behavior, on the other, so long as the objective behavior is sampled over an appropriate level of generality and averaged over a sufficient number of occurrences.

These he tested in a series of four studies, leading to the following conclusions:

> The findings from these four studies support the conclusion that the reason previous attempts failed to establish the existence of traits when the criterion consisted of objective behavior measured in the laboratory may simply be that inadequate samples of behavior were obtained in the laboratory. As a result, the laboratory behavior itself was unreliable and therefore incapable of establishing strong relationships. Behavior observed on a single occasion, whether in the laboratory or elsewhere, is apt to be so situationally unique as to be incapable of establishing reliable generalizations that hold over even the most minor variations in the situation. To the extent that this is true, it follows that the laboratory study as normally conducted is often unreplicable.

Costa and McCrae (1986) also present impressive evidence for stability:

> Over the past decade, a series of longitudinal studies have demonstrated that personality traits are stable in adulthood. There are no age-related shifts in mean levels, and individuals maintain very similar rank ordering on traits after intervals of up to 30 years.

In a manner similar to that of Epstein, these authors point up a methodological weakness of many studies of stability and find strength in the pooling of data:

> No single strategy—not even longitudinal studies— can give unequivocal evidence, but a pattern of findings from a variety of study designs can lead to some assurance about conclusions. For this reason, it is important to note that, on the whole, retrospective and cross-sectional studies are consistent with the position of stability in personality.

It is important to establish the stability of personality because stability contributes to the meaningfulness of psychological assessment. Psychological conclusions about a person obviously would be of little value if they were prone to change overnight. The establishment of the stability of personality—of the existence of (long-term) traits, or dispositions–also lends support to the creation of a category of personality disorders. As Costa and McCrae point out, there are "important similarities between normal personality and personality disorders, [and] in some respects, personality disorders appear to be simply certain combinations of personality traits that are disturbing to the individual or to society."

Millon (1984), in defining a role for the concept of personality disorders, proposes that the position these disorders now occupy in the psychopathological scheme of things is of great significance for clinicians. From the following passage, *clinicians* would appear to have reference to both psychological assessors and therapists:

> Personality can serve usefully as a dynamic substrate from which clinicians can better grasp the significance and meaning of their patients' transient and florid disorders. In the DSM-III, then, personality disorders not only attained a nosological status of prominence in their own right, but were assigned a contextual role that made them fundamental to the understanding and interpretation of other psychopathologies.

Everly (1986) amplifies on this point. Generally, he suggests, it is the personality styles of clients that provide the most meaningful target behaviors for therapy, and, as above, they also provide context in which to understand other pathology. Pathological personality styles are not only dysfunctional in their own right, "Axis I clinical syndromes [having reference to the *Diagnostic and Statistical Manual of Mental Disorders* (American Psychiatric Association, 1980; 1987, pp. 177–185)] are best understood as pathological extensions of dysfunctional personality styles." Thus, "the real target of intermediate and long-term psychotherapeutic efforts becomes the personality dysfunction." Further, "there is evidence that personality styles and dysfunctions serve not only to predispose, but to differentially affect psychotherapeutic and/or psychopharmacologic outcome."

ASSESSMENT AND CLASSIFICATION

"To classify is to know," taught da Vinci, and the classification of psychological characteristics extends back further than we know. The Bible is concerned with such human assets and shortcomings as *wisdom, foolishness, pridefulness, stubbornness, rebelliousness*, and being *sick at heart*. Over the long years of astrological influence, we have picked up terms like *lunatic, mercurial, jovial*, and *saturnine*. From Hippocrates, we have expressions pertaining to temperament, like *sanguine, phlegmatic, choleric*, and *melancholic*. When our concern centers on intelligence, or, really, the lack of it, we find terms like *idiot* and *imbecile*, which are hundreds of years old. All of these terms continue to have some use, though not particularly in psychology, while some relatively more modern coinages, like Bleuler's *moral idiot* and *moral imbecile* have faded from use.

The classical study of Allport and Odbert (1936) extracted from the dictionary 17,953 terms characterizing behavior and personality. From Jung, we have polarities like *introversion* and *extraversion* (originally seventeenth century terms); from James, *tough-minded* and *tender-minded*; and from Leary (1957), *competitive-narcissistic* and *docile-dependent* (there are many others). Freud, of course, contributed *oral, anal*, and *phallic*, all of which may have application to the description of both normal and abnormal personality. Robert Burton, a contemporary of Shakespeare, also developed a vocabulary applicable to both normals and those with psychopathological problems (see Dell & Jordan-Smith, 1927;

Evans, 1972). And, like a number of current classifications, Burton's included a listing of etiological factors. These included God, the devil, witches, faulty diet, and waste retention and elimination.

The classification of what is now widely called *mental disorder* has been practiced for a long time. The purpose of classifying abnormal mental conditions may be subdivided into three objectives, all conceptualized as "*C* words": *Communication* (among scientists and professionals), *Control* (by way of prevention and alleviation), and *Comprehension* (understanding in the interest of knowing what causes and maintains mental conditions, the better to treat them) (Spitzer & Williams, 1985).

In the 1840 United States census (which incorporated "the first official system for tabulating mental disorder in the United States"—Spitzer & Williams, 1985), there was but one category, consisting of "idiocy" and "insanity." Recognition for inaugurating the modern era of classification is usually accorded to Emil Kraeplin, who at the end of the nineteenth century classified the two major psychoses that he then recognized into the broad categories of *dementia praecox* and *manic-depressive psychosis*.

The Diagnostic and Statistical Manuals

Subsequent classification of mental disorder as disease entities continues to be spoken of as "Kraeplinian"—often with pejorative connotation—by those who adhere to a psychodynamic orientation. During World War II, William Menninger developed for military use a considerably more elaborate system of classification that was later adopted, with minor changes, by the Veterans Administration.

Still later, with additional minor revision, this classification was published as the *Diagnostic and Statistical Manual of Mental Disorders* (American Psychiatric Association, 1952). This document became popularly known as the DSM, and many years later as DSM-I to distinguish it from the DSMs that followed. A decade-and-a-half after the publication of DSM-I appeared a second edition, DSM-II (American Psychiatric Association, 1968) to better reflect international consensus on disease. Additionally, the manual had as an objective a closer unity of psychiatry with medical concepts and practices: "The rapid integration of psychiatry with the rest of medicine also helped create a need to have psychiatric classification closely integrated with those of other medical practitioners" (American Psychiatric Association, 1968).

This spirit continued with the better researched, much expanded and more detailed third edition—DSM-III (American Psychiatric Association, 1980), and its revised version—DSM-III-R (American Psychiatric Association, 1987). A fuller history of the DSM is available in Millon (1986a). Because it is a basic tool that is used by many psychological assessors, its structure and use are more fully explicated in Chapter 8.

DSM-III is a highly successful venture in terms of sales and the widespread acceptance it has achieved by the medical profession and the legal system (more lawyers than psychiatrists are said to own a copy of the manual), as well as by psychiatry. Privately practicing psychotherapists overwhelmingly report diagnoses of their clients to insurance companies in accord with DSM categories. The proverbial "intelligent layman" is likely to be aware of the work. DSM-III has also had an impact outside of the United States. Nevertheless, it attracts considerable scrutiny and critique, and DSM bashing has become a popular sport.

The DSM and the psychodynamic orientation Mental health workers who subscribe fully to a psychodynamic orientation are likely to regard the DSM approach as beside the point. In the DSM frame of reference—designed to be "atheoretical"—though only partially successful in meeting this objective (Faust & Miner, 1986; Frances et al., 1990)—psychodynamically oriented clinicians do not find the syndromes listed in the manual to contribute to what, to them, would be meaningful case formulations and guidelines to treatment. Rather than focusing on the largely surface behaviors that are the substance of the manual, psychodynamic clinicians deal with matters that are often more inferential than objective, such as developmental level, conflicts, defenses, representations, and modes of adaptation. Possibly the suggestion of Karasu and Skodol (1980) to add a new "axis" to provide for psychodynamic evaluation might attenuate some objections, but little support for the proposal is evident so far. "An axis describing mechanisms of defense which might have helped to focus on enduring characteristics of the personality was aborted during the early consultations on DSM-III-R" (Cooper & Michels, 1988). Nevertheless, these authors envision a DSM that is more influenced by clinical findings and an interest in psychological processes.

A contrary psychiatric view of the DSM Chodoff (1986) presents a psychiatric viewpoint on the DSM-III and psychotherapy, particularly with respect to "psychodynamically oriented psychiatrists in private practice and residents with a similar orientation"—who tend to evaluate the DSM-III negatively (Jampala, Sierles, & Taylor, 1986). His position is that the DSM-III is more appropriate as an aid to formulating treatment—whether behavioral, psychotherapeutic, or chemotherapeutic—for clinical syndromes (Axis I disorders) than they are for coming to grips with the personality disorders that are listed on Axis II. (The DSM-III system of classification by Axis is discussed in Chapter 8, pp. 177–185.) And, treating personality disorders makes up a sizable portion of the practice of psychotherapists and psychoanalysts.

Chodoff summarizes and underscores his position in the following statement:

> Faced with these inadequacies of DSM-III in guiding paychotherapeutic treatment planning, psychotherapists tend to ignore the manual and to continue to rely on the individual psychodynamic formulation of a case to guide their treatment. But, of course, a formulation is not a diagnosis. This is not always fully realized, and some unjustified criticism of DSM-III comes from a failure to distinguish between the two concepts. To make the difference explicit, the goal of medical diagnosis, which is the model for DSM-III, is to make class distinctions based on the commonalities among the conditions

being studied and then to apply diagnoses on the basis of these class distinctions. A formulation, on the other hand, is an assessment of a patient's individual psychodynamics, those aspects of life history and functioning that make him or her different from, rather than like, other patients. Although class diagnoses offer some guidance in choosing between drug, behavioral, psychotherapeutic, or other approaches, particularly with Axis I cases, such diagnoses are less useful for these purposes with Axis II cases. This constitutes still another reason why psychotherapists derive limited benefits from the DSM-III diagnostic scheme.

A psychological view of the DSM Smith and Kraft (1983) indicate widespread discontent with DSM-III on the part of psychologists. The following passage from their article captures a number of the reasons they feel this way:

> The position of the American Psychological Association (APA) during the development of DSM-III could be described conservatively as cautious. Overall reservations about DSM-III were strong enough that in January 1977, the Council of Representatives of APA created the Task Force on Descriptive Behavioral Classification to assess the need for an alternative diagnostic system, identify minimal criteria for the development and use of classification systems, and demonstrate the feasibility of developing a behaviorally oriented approach that avoids some of the inadequacies inherent in the DSMs. The task force (1977) concluded that the approach in DSM-III is an unsatisfactory method of classification because (1) its disease-based model is used inappropriately to describe problems in living; (2) its specific categories show consistently high levels of unreliability; (3) it is a mixed model that bases the groupings variously on symptom clusters, antisocial behaviors, theoretical considerations, or developmental influences; (4) categories have been either created or deleted on committee vote rather than on hard scientific data; (5) the labels have assumed strong judgmental qualities that frequently result in bias and social injustice; and (6) it offers low capability for indicating treatment modality or predicting clinical outcome.

Another matter that should be considered here is the relation of psychological diagnostic methods to DSM diagnoses. Tests, including tests of sleep architecture, neuroendocrine challenge, imaging, and psychological testing generally have not been found to be of value for this purpose: "It is controversial which, if any, of the tests currently used in psychiatry...have demonstrated sufficient ability to discriminate patients with particular disorders from the wide variety of comparison groups that require differential diagnosis" (Frances et al., 1990). Possible exceptions, according to these authors, include organic disorders, mental retardation, and learning disabilities.

This view is consistent with a long history of generally unsatisfactory attempts to validate the psychometric diagnosis of psychiatric disorders. These, in the DSM system, are diagnosed on the basis of such factors as history (including duration of "illness" and age at onset), presence or absence of other disorders, current behaviors, behavioral and cultural norms, complaints, bodily symptoms, verbalizations, and social values—all specific criteria falling under these rubrics being offered as guidelines rather than as firm prescriptions. It is hard to imagine why the various ingredients that enter the psychiatric diagnostic process would relate systematically to psychological test scores with the obvious exception in the case of such disorders as mental retardation or when the documentation of neuropsychological deficit contributes to a diagnosis of dementia.

Psychological *assessment*, however, can *contribute* to a DSM diagnosis. Assessment, in addition to offering findings pertinent to a diagnosis, may serve as an independent opinion gained with psychological tools that can help to identify clinically relevant variables. Emerging from the process is a case formulation holding information on such matters as etiology, prognosis, and recommendations regarding intervention. Additionally, assessment may reveal other valuable data, such as thought disorder, tendencies to anxiety, depression, dissociation, or regressive fantasies that may or may not be gained clinically or from history.

In a chapter on factitious disorders, Sussman (1989) discusses information pertinent to this disorder that may be elucidated with psychological tools. He notes, specifically, underlying pathology, a normal or above average IQ, absence of formal thought disorder, a poor sense of identity, including confusion over sexual identity, poor sexual adjustment, low frustration tolerance, strong dependency needs, and narcissism.

Weiss (1989) is critical of the extant practice of diagnosing disorders on the basis of the symptom pictures they present. "Symptom-based diagnoses," he points out, rest on multidetermined symptoms, hence detract from the ability of a diagnosis to fulfill its purpose: "A diagnosis is powerful to the extent that it predicts and describes symptoms, course, process, and etiology." Thus, in the case of schizophrenia, he reasons that to address the underlying cognitive, attentional, and arousal dysfunctions [features that are accessible with psychological instruments] is more meaningful than listing a patient's presenting symptoms.

A behavior therapy view of the DSM Nelson (1987), from the standpoint of a psychologist and a behavior therapist, elaborates on the above, and offers a few of her own criticisms. Overall, she is ambivalent to the DSM and cites both pros and cons. We are, in effect, "stuck" with the classification, a feeling shared by many psychologists. But it would be too great a task and too expensive to develop a more acceptable system (existing alternatives have found little acceptance among behavior therapists). Nevertheless, DSM-III has communication value, particularly when communicating with insurance companies.

Nelson summarizes from her presentation other assets and liabilities that are pertinent to the practice of behavior therapy:

> Main deterrents from [a behavioral perspective] are: the historical emphasis by behaviorists on singular target behaviors; the inferential nature of a diagnostic system of mental disorders; the nomothetic nature of diagnosis; and the structural nature of diagnosis. Main attractions are: increasing recognition by behaviorists of response covariation and of diagnosis-based treatment efficacy; lack of an acceptable alternative to DSM-III; and several positive features of DSM-III itself. Regarding the goals of behavioral assessment, DSM-III was judged as offering useful suggestions in identifying target behaviors, selecting treatment, and evaluating treatment outcome, but as not replacing behavioral assessment in fulfilling these goals.

Turner and Turkat (1988) contrast the use of a DSM-III diagnosis and case formulation in the conduct of behavior therapy. While pointing out that the use of diagnosis among behavior therapists is widespread, these authors suggest that behavior therapists also plan their treatment on the basis of their own behavior analytic strategies. To illustrate the advantage of case formulation over diagnosis, they present material on two patients taken from Turkat and Maisto (1983). Though each carried a diagnosis of narcissistic personality disorder, case formulations clearly dictated different treatments. While one manifested a primary impulse-control deficit and 13 different problems were identified, the second had an empathy deficit with eight identified problem areas.

Pervasive Controversies Bearing on Classification

We see, then, that criticisms come from a number of directions. Two of the most pervasive, overlapping issues may be singled out for special attention. These are: (1) the *empirical* versus *theoretical* controversy, and (2) the *categorical* versus *dimensional* controversy.

DSM-III was conceived with a specific rationale concerning theory:

> The major justification for the generally atheoretical approach taken in DSM-III with regard to etiology is that the inclusion of etiological theories would be an obstacle to use of the manual by clinicians of varying theoretical orientations, since it would not be possible to present all reasonable etiological theories for each disorder. For example, Phobic Disorders are believed by many to represent a displacement of anxiety resulting from the breakdown of defensive operations for keeping internal conflict out of consciousness. Other investigators explain phobias on the basis of learned avoidance responses to conditioned anxiety. Still others believe that certain phobias result from a dysregulation of basic biological systems mediating separation anxiety. In any case, as the field trials have demonstrated, clinicians can agree on the identification of mental disorders on the basis of their clinical manifestations without agreeing on how the disturbances came about (American Psychiatric Association, 1980).

Epstein (1987), however, points out with a culinary metaphor the downside of this approach. Diagnoses are made not unlike the way one orders from a Chinese menu: One from Appetizers, one from Soup, and so on. Looking at an example of how one may go about diagnosing post-traumatic stress disorder, he also recognizes the same redeeming features that the framers of DSM-III proposed, namely that the diagnostic process is shielded from the theoretical bias of the diagnostician:

> The symptoms are listed in a manner comparable to the listing of the ingredients in a cooking recipe: One requires one of these, one of those, and two of these. If certain ingredients are unavailable, others can be substituted. One hyperalertness is equal to one guilt over survival is equal to one memory impairment. Using such procedures, an individual can make a diagnosis without understanding anything about traumatic neurosis, presumably much like an individual can bake a cake without knowing anything about

organic chemistry. Thus, an obviously positive feature of the system is that it can be applied mindlessly, and therefore is not susceptible to the influence of the theoretical bias of the diagnostician. Given different theoretical biases by different diagnosticians, this is obviously a virtue, as it permits a uniform standard to be established, which is a second virtue. The obvious disadvantage to the diagnostic recipe is that it lacks elegance, coherence, and therefore conviction. Why two out of six and not three or four out of six? Why are some very different symptoms treated as equivalents? And, most important, how does the whole thing work? So long as the symptoms appear to be atheoretically selected and to lack coherence, what assurance can one have that other equally important symptoms were not omitted because no one knew where to look?

Salzinger (1986) makes a similar point.

A basic problem with the *categorical* approach to diagnosis is illustrated above by the two cases of narcissistic personality disorder discussed by Turner and Turkat (1988) and by Epstein's (1987) exposition of how to diagnose post-traumatic stress disorder. Clearly, the narcissistic-personality-disorder patient presented with a primary impulse control deficit is differently constituted psychologically than the patient who carries the same diagnosis but has an empathy deficit. What are the implications for treatment of a patient who qualifies for a diagnosis of post-traumatic stress disorder, in part by virtue of his hyperalertness, versus the patient who is assigned this diagnosis because of his complaint of survivor guilt?

The Special Diagnostic Problems of the Personality Disorders

The diagnosis of DSM-III and DSM-III-R personality disorders tends to be of low reliability, and "the *coverage* of the personality disorders is seen as too narrow, which results in a large number of patients receiving 'mixed' or 'atypical' personality disorder diagnoses, which have little meaning." (Morey, 1988). This is a position also documented by Gartner et al. (1989). How "mixed" a personality-disorder can be is evident from Millon's (1981) observations of the behavioral features, self-descriptions and complaints, inferred intrapsychic processes, and interpersonal coping styles of clients who carry the diagnosis borderline personality disorder, which indicate a number of clinical syndromes and prominent features of other personality disorders that may be associated with the borderline picture:

a.
Axis I Disorders That May Be Associated with Borderline Personality Disorders
Obsessive-Compulsive Disorders
Somatoform Disorders
Dissociative Disorders
Affective Disorders
Schizoaffective Disorders

b.
Axis II Disorders That May Be "Mixed" with Borderline Personality Disorders
Dependent Personality Disorder
Histrionic Personality Disorder
Compulsive Personality Disorder
Passive-Aggressive Personality Disorder

Tyrer's (1988) pessimistic review of the state of the personality disorders—one of several such reviews, e.g., Frances (1980), Frances and Widiger (1986), Widiger and Kelso (1983), Widiger and Frances (1985)—finds that the operational criteria approach to defining DSM-III mental states does not work well for the personality disorders: "The aim of identifying mutually exclusive personality disorder categories...seems to be a mirage."

There is now a widespread call for replacing the traditional categorical classification of mental disorders, particularly of personality disorders. A *dimensional* approach, whereby personality variables are assigned values along continua and assembled as profiles that may serve as a basis for making diagnoses, is gaining favor.

Tyrer's (1988) position is that:

> The dimensional approach has many advantages. If, as many argue, personality disorders are regarded as the extremes of a continuum in which various degrees of personality difficulty grade toward normal personality variation, then it is obviously more appropriate to record the abnormality in dimensional terms. By doing this one avoids the Procrustean distinction of a cutoff between normal, and allegedly healthy, personality functioning and the extreme category of personality disorder. It also allows examination of the relative importance of different types of personality disorder.

Widiger and Kelso (1983) contrast *dimensional* and *categorical* classification:

> Dimensional systems of classification are recognized as presenting more flexible, specific, and comprehensive information, while categorical systems tend to be procrustean, lose information, and result in many classificatory dilemmas when patients do not meet the criteria for any category or meet the criteria for two or more mutually exclusive categories. Because patients typically do not fall into discrete categories, with homogeneous membership and distinct boundaries, diagnostic taxonomy is typically faced with the dilemma of defining very restrictive diagnoses in order to increase homogeneity of membership (e.g., the DSM-III schizophrenic diagnosis), but then requiring the addition of a number of "wastebasket" categories to cover the large number of patients who are unable to meet these restrictive criteria (e.g. atypical psychosis and schizoaffective disorders).

The Reconceptualization of Classification Systems

Clearly, assessment suffers from a severe crisis of approaches to classification, and new systems of classification are actively being explored. Two books currently given over to this problem are Millon and Klerman (1986) and Last and Hersen (1987). McReynolds (1989) reminds us that "DSM-III-R is not the only game in town":

> At present there is no viable taxonomic alternative—on the criteria of breadth of coverage and detailed exposition—to DSM-III-R. This is not to say that broad alternatives to DSM-III-R cannot or will not be developed, or that more limited psychopathological taxonomies do not exist. Further, it needs to be emphasized that many clinicians, while they may utilize the DSM-III-R taxonomy for practical and legal reasons, will continue,

in their everyday clinical work as well as in their research, to follow those paradigms they have already found useful—the psychodynamic, the social-learning, the behavioral, the psychometric, and so on. Nor is such a double accounting to be decried; indeed there is reason to believe that it is by such a mixing of metaphors that science most typically advances.

Among the developing approaches to classification is that of DeNelsky and Boat (1986), proposed by the authors as an alternative to DSM-III. They suggest that medically oriented diagnoses are of limited value in guiding intervention, a deficiency they propose can be dealt with through use of their Coping Skills Model (CSM), which focuses on the client's adaptability in significant aspects of living.

Psychometric contributions to classification are of particular interest, as reflected in recent activity centering about some of the older dimensional approaches, such as Leary's (1957) interpersonal circumplex and Millon's (1969, 1981) three-dimensional scheme (active-passive, self-other, pleasure-pain). Sharing attention with these is the five-factor model (Costa & McCrae, 1985; McCrae & Costa, 1986, 1990; John, 1990), proposed as a "universal and comprehensive framework for the description of individual differences in personality" (McCrae & Costa, 1986). The five factors, recoverable from the *NEO Personality Inventory* (Costa & McCrae, 1985), and also from adjective check lists, questionnaires, and Q-sorts (Block, 1961, 1981) are: *Neuroticism, Extraversion, Openness, Agreeableness,* and *Conscientiousness.* Although there are many adherents to the five-factor approach, Waller and Ben-Porath (1987) find that the evidence for reliability exceeds that for validity, that a number of scales that contribute to the five-factor solution were "selected to tap the five factors." They thus challenge the comprehensiveness claimed for the paradigm, and suggest that the model should be regarded as heuristic.

THE INFORMATION-GATHERING TOOLS OF PSYCHOLOGICAL ASSESSMENT

The Role of Tests

In the practice of testing (as distinguished from assessment), tests, quite naturally, occupy center stage. All of the trappings of tests (discussed more fully in the next chapter)—such as standardization, validity, and reliability—take top billing. If sufficient attention is paid to the hallmarks of good testing, the obtained numbers may yield the information for which testing was done. The illogical extreme of this orientation provides the topic of a little story told by Meehl (1956), a tale of a young man in need of vocational counseling whose time budget didn't allow for him to commit 14 hours to take a prescribed battery. No need to despair:

> "Oh, well," said the great psychologist reassuringly, "don't worry about *that*. If you're too busy, you can arrange to have my assistant take these tests *for* you. I don't care who takes them, just so long as they come out in quantitative form."

Quite a different view is taken by Hadley (1972), who cautions that, in the assessment situation, "the test is not the thing.":

> It should be no secret to most thinking psychologists that there is no magic in psychological tests *per se*. A test result is exactly that—a test result. It is difficult to conceptualize what value there is to knowing how a person behaves on a particular test unless there was a reason for giving the test. The reason should be that there is a definable question which needs an answer and a particular test is assumed to provide the best approximation of the answer. Psychologists have, however, for many years encouraged the belief that tests provide a shortcut to understanding the person. Psychologists have asked for the role of "testers." They have developed tests of many psychological variables and have expounded at length on the characteristics of the individual who performed in a particular fashion on the test. They have acted as if they have forgotten that a test result is only a sample of behavior in a particular situation.

Other Information-Gathering Methods in the Assessment Context

The assessment armamentarium is broader than the testing armamentarium. It includes information assembled by others (such as teachers, psychiatrists, social workers, lawyers) before the assessor meets the client, personal and family history, and identification of the problem to which assessment might contribute a solution. The assessor, as a matter of routine, observes and interviews clients, probing various background features–such as personal history (including interpersonal relations, education, development, sex, and so on), family history, medical history, and psychological functioning. Particularly when the format for gathering these classes of information more or less follows an outline, we may describe the procedure as a *mental status examination* (see, for example, Ginsberg, 1985b). The mental status examination is presented in Chapter 8.

RELIABILITY/VALIDITY: HOW GOOD IS PSYCHOLOGICAL ASSESSMENT?

Historically, the related issues of validity and reliability have, quite properly, been basic technical and ethical concerns when psychological characteristics are evaluated. These are concepts that have to do with the soundness of the conclusions reached by the psychological assessor, or the psychological tester—which typically have reference to quite different matters. Attitudes to psychological testing and psychological assessment, and decisions to use or not to use psychological evaluation techniques, have long centered about the issues of reliability and validity.

Reliability

Reliability refers to consistency or stability of measurement. The logic is straightforward. To the extent that measurement is erratic, its value as a basis for reaching conclusions is reduced. What can we say of the intelligence of an individual who scores 120 on an instrument designed to measure intelligence, but scores 85 a week later, and 132 a month after that? On the other hand, a number of personality variables are not stable, as a matter of observation. Mood, for example, changes. Depression, we know, can go into remission, and when a person seeks therapy for depression, it is with the recognition of the possibility that it will.

Several ways to measure reliability are in common use. These are *test-retest reliability, alternate form reliability, interjudge reliability,* and *split-half reliability.*

Test-retest reliability This concept rests on the notion that personality is consistent, as demonstrated in summaries by Epstein (1980) and Costa and McCrae (1986, 1990). But as just noted, all personality features are not stable. A number of time-limited personality *states* have been proposed; for example, an *anger state* (Spielberger, Jacobs, Russel, & Crane, 1983).

Alternate-form reliability This method is computed by correlating one form of an instrument (Form I or Form A, for example) with an alternate form of that instrument (Form II or Form B, for example). If both forms measure the same variable, the correlation should be high.

Interjudge reliability This is a way of checking that the human factor does not significantly influence scores. Thus, the ratings of two or more raters may be compared. Similarly, when judgment is required in scoring test responses—such as on a number of Wechsler scales, the Rorschach, and the TAT—interjudge reliability should be established.

Split-half reliability This method is used to establish internal consistency of an instrument. It may be computed by correlating the first half of the instrument with the second half, or by correlating the odd-numbered items with the even-numbered items—*odd-even reliability.*

Validity

The early understanding of *validity* (the degree to which a test measures what it purports to measure) has enjoyed long and uncritical acceptance, and continues to be offered as a basic definition of the concept (e.g., Anastasi, 1988). This fundamental view has subsequently been expanded and refined to include several classes of validity: *content-related evidence of validity, construct-related evidence of validity,* and *criterion-related evidence* of validity (American Psychological Association, *Standards for educational and psychological testing,* 1985).

Content-related evidence of validity This type of validity is based on the extent to which test content faithfully samples the content domain that is to be measured with the test. Thus, if social adjustment is to be measured, the items included must have to do with social functioning; and conversely, items that do not relate to social functioning—mathematical ability, for example—are excluded. Whether this criterion is met may be a matter of expert opinion, or of logical and empirical methods.

Criterion-related evidence of validity This class of validity exists when test scores can be shown to relate to an external criterion measure. Thus, a test of school aptitude can be validated by correlating test scores with grade-point averages. A test designed to classify mental disorders may be validated by determining the extent to which the classifications agree with the diagnoses of clinicians. In the first instance, since the test is concerned with future outcomes, we recognize a subtype of criterion-related validity called *predictive validity*. In the clinical example, where test information is related to a current situation, we have another subtype of criterion validity, *concurrent validity*.

Construct-related evidence of validity This type of validity is gained through measurement of a theoretical construction—a concept. Any number of traits can be thus considered—anxiety, mechanical aptitude, or verbal-reasoning ability. A variety of strategies may be used to establish such validity. These include the identification of traits through the method of factor analysis; the demonstration of increasing scores with age (during the childhood years) on a test of intelligence, since theory calls for such increases; and by showing a relationship of a test with acceptable ways of identifying a characteristic. For example, we could demonstrate construct validity for a test of "popularity" if scores on this test correlated well with peer ratings of "popularity." Calling on the related concepts of *convergent validation* and *discriminant validation* (Campbell & Fiske, 1959; Campbell, 1960) in order to show construct validity, a test should correlate highly with tests which presumably measure similar variables and fail to correlate significantly with tests that do not measure these variables. Thus, a test of mathematical reasoning should correlate well with scores on a math test, but not with ratings of performance in physical education. Consistency of measurement, as shown, for example, through intercorrelation of items is also a valuable way to show that the various items tend to measure the same construct.

There continue to be, however, serious conceptual and technical concerns over the classical approach to validity (e.g., Ebel, 1961; Maloney & Ward, 1976; Weiner, 1977a; Cronbach, 1980; Messick, 1980; Atkinson, Quarrington, Alp, & Cyr, 1986; and Mitchell, 1986). In addition to allegations of flawed conceptualization, other concerns about the adoption of instruments, procedures, theories of personality, and assessment goals not in existence when the "established ideas on validity" (Mitchell, 1986) were formulated contribute to extant challenges. The Rorschach is a prime example of an instrument that was not anticipated as a common staple of assessment batteries when the validity principle was introduced. Equally unanticipated was the computer and the role it was destined to play in psychological evaluation.

Amid concurrent protest and acquiescence, a nascent paradigm shift, from psychometric (test) validity to assessment validity is underway in the assessment context. But the testing model continues dominant. The efforts of researchers to apply earlier concepts to later situations has become a "square-peg, round-hole" state of affairs, and vindication of an evolving technology has risen and fallen on the ability to establish modest correlations that might suggest psychometric validity.

Any number of issues contributes to the problem of how we shall conceptualize and provide evidence of validity. Is the person, for example, a bagful of traits, or is the situation relatively more important as a determiner of behavior in the person-situation interaction? (See, for example, Hogan, DeSoto, & Solano, 1977.) What is the purpose of assessment, what are its personal and social consequences? Is a nomothetic, individual-differences approach likely to yield the most useful information, or is an idiothetic approach the best way of knowing an individual? Shall we emphasize measurement and prediction, or is gathering data that will help us to understand and explain a person's behavior more germane?

SOME TECHNICAL PROBLEMS WITH PSYCHOMETRIC TESTING

The house of psychometrics is not in good order. In a critical review, Mitchell (1986) looks at four key areas of the enterprise and decries the current status of both its fundamentals and applications. This review covers issues in (1) validity, (2) computer-based test interpretation (CBTI), (3) "the joys and pitfalls of the psychologist as entrepreneur and of the entrepreneur as practicing psychologist," and (4) "the plight of the test user in the struggle to obtain consumer knowledge." His position is abstracted below, with the exception of his views on CBTI, which are incorporated in the next section.

Crisis of Validity

Validity, as noted earlier, is a hallmark of psychometrics. Thus, the observations of Mitchell, incorporating the views of a number of psychometricians, including Cronbach (1980, 1983), Ebel (1983), Guion (1977), Messick (1975, 1980, 1981), Tenopyr (1977), Fitzpatrick (1983), Flanagan (1983), and Gardner (1983), add up to a distressing situation for test developers and practitioners of psychological testing and assessment:

> ...I, like Cronbach (1980), believe that the field of measurement is in a "crisis" with respect to the established ideas on validity, and I believe further that this crisis is now having an increased effect on test development and validation efforts and the messages that are sent to the test user.
>
> ...the present "crisis" and confusion about validity demand a total effort to provide greater conceptual clarity and consensus and to reduce uncertainty in practice. Although the holy trinity of validity concepts–content, criterion-related, and construct validity–is taught with fervent conviction in measurement classes, none of these has escaped

controversy and criticism, sometimes heated. Ebel was certainly not averse to serving in the role of iconoclast on occasion, but he did so in a way that was constructive in terms of alerting psychologists to looming or existing discrepancies between what they profess in psychometric theory and what they can reasonably expect to implement in practice. In this article Ebel [1983] challenged just about all of the conventional measurement wisdom. He disposed of criterion-related validity by contending that "few of the widely used tests of ability have been supported with impressive evidence of criterion-related validity" (p. 9) and then persuasively urged why this should be so, citing some of the reasons outlined earlier. He then confronted construct validity and disposed of it with such statements as "This is a neat conception in the abstract, but it has turned out not to be very practical" (p. 10). "The process of construct validation is intriguing. The product is seldom decisive." (p. 10), and "For educators and other practitioners whose main interest is in measuring abilities, construct validation has little to offer." (p. 10) All of this is asserted despite the very evident fact that many of the leading figures in the field of measurement are now contending that all forms of validation procedures and validity evidence are properly subsumable under the umbrella rubric of construct validation (Guion, 1977; Messick, 1975, 1980; Tenopyr, 1977).

Mitchell captures "the confusion and uncertainty that presently plague the entire validation enterprise" in down-to-earth language:

> I strongly contend that this lack of consensus about validity issues of such major importance, combined with the gap that often exists between psychometric aspirations for validity and the practical possibilities for implementing them, is creating the kind of situation in which test authors and publishers must feel that they are required to play the game without being sure of what the rules really are. As a result, some statements about validity in test manuals represent a strange new genre of escapist literature... Even politicians could learn something from these statements about how to appear to be saying something important without saying anything at all.

Entrepreneurship and Psychology

The situation does not get better as discussion focuses on the application of psychometrics. Added to the current weaknesses of validation is the deliberate abuse of the validity concept. This problem thrives in an ambiance of commercialism and hucksterism. The ideals of science, psychology, ethics, and commitment to humanity fall by the wayside in the more compelling commitment to the need to turn a profit.

Mitchell cites Adair's (1978) position here, with particular emphasis on what the latter identifies as a dichotomy between the professional psychologist and the entrepreneurial psychologist:

> The dilemma of whether to uphold professional ethics or to make a profit is seen most vividly in the promotional literature of the several services [scoring services]...The literature of promotion takes on a Madison Avenue-like quality where caveats are included in the fine print. (p. 940)

Mitchell clearly is not happy that

the "name of the game" often becomes that of exerting every conceivable effort to make the product look good, however accomplished, and then conducting a kind of defensive validation exercise that will serve reasonably well to keep one out of trouble with one's professional peers.

The "Plight" of the Test User

The American Psychological Association is concerned with the impact of testing on the individual and society (see its publication, *Standards for educational and psychological testing*, 1985.). Judgment and informed decision making are therefore integral to the testing process. Considerations of validity loom large, inasmuch as *Standards* points out that "validity is the most important consideration in test evaluation," and "refers to the appropriateness, meaningfulness, and usefulness of the specific inferences made from test scores."
Further,

> In selecting a test, a potential user should depend heavily upon the developer's research documentation that is clearly related to the intended application. Although the test developer should supply the needed information, the ultimate responsibility for appropriate test use lies with the user.

So far, so good. The problem is (1) the questionable validation procedures, noted above, the details of which may not be readily available to the test user; (2) proprietary or political interests that make for the withholding of this and other information; and (3) the technical and esoteric nature of much basic data about tests. Mitchell presents the following as the current factual state of affairs:

> Many of the recent developments in measurement, although admirable in their own right, have served to create wider knowledge gaps between test developers and typical test users, and the result is that the latter increasingly lack an adequate foundation for making judicious choices about tests and their interpretation and implications. As measurement has become more sophisticated and even esoteric, the knowledge base and understanding of the typical test user has been left further behind. *More and more has to be accepted on faith* (emphasis added).

To remedy this obviously unacceptable situation, Mitchell proposes "a test-consumer-protection movement directed toward finding more effective ways of disseminating complex information to test consumers in understandable ways, and also exploring and reducing obstacles to open and effective dissemination."

VALIDITY OF COMPUTER TESTING

With computers, we have all of the old validity problems of psychometric testing, plus some new ones peculiar to the use of this technology. As a first consideration, the equivalence of conventional tests and their computerized versions must be established. However, "At present, there is no extensive evidence about the validities of computerized versions of conventional tests" (American Psychological Association, 1986). Similarly, there are such issues as whether validity coefficients established for booklet administration of the MMPI apply when data are generated at a computer console (e.g, Hofer & Green, 1985).

Subjective input by software authors in the development of algorithms adds to the validity problem. The validity of subjective interpretation by clinicians has long drawn fire as an invalid procedure, or at least as a procedure whose validity has not been established. The fact that subjective interpretations are processed by high tech equipment does not improve their validity. Thus, Matarazzo (1983) is impressed that "to date, there is no evidence published in peer reviewed journals that one full page of the narrative descriptions is valid."

Indeed, the barrier to validation becomes insurmountable when interpretations stem from algorithms developed with proprietary information that is not made available to independent investigators. Butcher (1978) complains about one of the widely used computer services: "One of the biggest points of concern in the reports from Behaviordyne is the inclusion of numerous interpretations that are outside of the MMPI clinical and research literature."

In a more general critique of the validity of computer testing, Butcher (1987b) chides test publishers who put on the market a product for use in computer testing that shortchanges professional consumers (and their clients) and the testing enterprise itself:

> Test publishers who follow APA standards for psychological testing assume some responsibility for ensuring that only valid tests are marketed and made commercially available through a test-scoring service. However, these standards appear to have been eroded in recent years. With more psychological tests being computerized, there is a greater demand for new and specialized measures of psychological attributes. To meet this demand some publishers have rushed to make available various computer versions of tests, sometimes without sufficient test validation studies. The unwary test-scoring service customer may well find that the new, flashy test to measure trait y or psychological characteristic x may not have been cross-validated or even initially validated sufficiently to meet minimum test publication standards. This problem has increased in recent years and may, in the long run, prove detrimental to the psychological testing field.

Moreland (1985) presents a further shocking observation that underlines the need for the American Psychological Association's *Guidelines*:

> Gone...are the days when the tremendous investment necessary to develop and market CBTIs virtually guaranteed that they had been developed by experts whose interpretations stayed as close as possible to the empirical data available for thoroughly investigated instruments. Many CBTIs are now developed by individuals who have no special qualifications. They have never published a scholarly article on either the test in question or on the CBTI nor do they have any credentials (e.g., a diploma from the American

Board of Examiners in Professional Psychology) that indicate any expertise as practitioners. The CBTIs by such authors often stray far from available empirical data, with some employing idiosyncratic scoring procedures or interpretive algorithms. Perhaps even worse, highly detailed, well-written, empirical sounding CBTIs are available for tests for which validity data are practically nonexistent. Indeed, some of these poorly validated tests cannot be purchased apart from their CBTIs.

A further validity consideration is that the consumer of the computer's output, in effect, further interprets the data; the information that is applied to problems is not necessarily the same as what issues from the computer, but rather the consumer's understanding of that information. For this reason Rodgers (1972), with special reference to the MMPI, is wary of the use of computerized interpretations: "I regard them as basically dangerous except in the hands of a person who is sufficiently expert with the MMPI that he probably will not utilize the computer printout."

Similarly, Eichman (1972) is alarmed over use of the computer printout by persons who are not, in the expression of *Guidelines*, qualified professionals. He warns that a physician who does not meet this standard might use computer-supplied information as a "substitute for clinical judgment rather than as a supplement to it. Armed with such a report," the physician "is likely to feel that he knows much more than is actually the case and proceed with radical treatment procedures." Unfortunately, consumers of computer reports cover a broad spectrum that includes "employers, physicians, psychologists, social workers, counselors, nurse practitioners, and other licensed health care providers" (Matarazzo, 1983), many of whom, no doubt, do not meet the APA standard of being qualified professionals as test users.

Mitchell (1986) finds himself in agreement with Matarazzo and others who hold similar critical positions. While he considers that computer testing has potential, in the meantime he is troubled by three "major concerns":

(a) the secrecy often surrounding the algorithms and decision rules that govern the inferential narrative statements that make up a CBTI report,
(b) the conspicuous lack of validation for most of these CBTI systems, and
(c) the magnitude of the problems inherent in any effort to provide adequate validity evidence for such systems.

CLINICAL VERSUS STATISTICAL PREDICTION: FOCUS ON THE VALIDITY OF TWO APPROACHES TO PSYCHOLOGICAL EVALUATION

More than a third of a century ago, Meehl (1954) published a "disturbing little book" (Meehl, 1986) of 149 pages bearing the title *Clinical versus Statistical Prediction*. Since that bombshell was hurled, a forest's worth of paper has carried heated arguments relative to Meehl's position—pro, con, and in-between.

Meehl's thesis is simply stated: Actuarial (statistical) formulas are better predictors of human behavior than are the clinician. Prediction, in turn, is understood to mean either the ability to foretell future events (such as whether a person will have a successful marriage, or function well as a clinical psychologist) or to make accurate statements about ongoing or past events that have not been observed by the predictor (such as the extent to which a person is hostile, or the nature of a person's infantile trauma).

This simple thesis is far-reaching in its implications, and, indeed, the evidence that supports it figures prominently in the presentation in Chapter 4 ("The Measurement Tradition") and Chapter 5 ("The Clinical Tradition"). If Meehl is correct in his conclusion that formulas, in demonstrated fact, are superior to the judgment of clinicians, then the evidence may be used to challenge the validity of assessment in general, and hence of clinical psychology, since assessment is a basic method in clinical psychology. The title of Holt's (1970) paper, "Yet Another Look at Clinical and Statistical Prediction: Or, Is Clinical Psychology Worthwhile?"— recognizes this threat:

Meehl, however, seeks to attenuate the perception of threat. In an American Psychological Association symposium (Meehl, 1959, 1967), he voices a now familiar theme:

> I am puzzled by the extent to which both statisticians and clinicians perceive the book as an attack upon the clinician. On the contrary, my position was, and is, that the clinician performs certain unique, important, and unduplicable functions, in some of which he has literally no competition. I think the book states this very clearly.

And:

> My position is not, therefore, one of being "for" or "against" the clinician, or proposing to eliminate him. I cannot understand, for example, how my friend Bill Hunt could possibly read me as viewing "the exercise of clinical judgment as a necessary evil," as he states in the Bass and Berg (1959) volume, rather than, as for him, "a fascinating phenomenon with a genuine predictive potential." Two full chapters of my book, and portions of two others, were devoted to analyzing (and defending!) the clinician's nonformalized judging and hypothesizing behavior, and I should have thought that my own fascination with the phenomenon was quite apparent.

Elsewhere, Meehl (1965) reports on a study "which demonstrates a clear superiority of the clinical judge over formalized (actuarial) methods of data combination." And in another publication (Meehl, 1957) he examines the question of *when* it is appropriate to "use our heads instead of the formula," and concludes that the extreme answers of "Always" and "Never" are equally unacceptable. But, "mostly we will use our heads, because there just isn't any formula."

Kleinmuntz's (1990) more recent opinion, based on an extensive review of the pertinent literature, is consonant with Meehl's position on heads versus formulas.

The answer as to why people still use their heads, flawed as they may be, instead of formulas, is that for many decisions, inferences, choices, and problems there are as yet no available formulas. When formulas are available, their evaluation is not feasible, when used either alone or in combination with intuition.

Coming full circle, he shares "the recognition that people may have to use their heads *instead* of, or *together* with, formulas while awaiting new decision support developments." He concludes with "a note of cautious optimism regarding the formula's future role as a decision aid."

These views exist alongside Meehl's earlier (and later) conclusions that precipitated the statistical-versus-clinical controversy:

> Review and reflection indicate that no more than 5% of what was written in the 1954 book entitled *Clinical versus Statistical Prediction* (Meehl, 1954) needs to be retracted 30 years later. If anything, these retractions would result in the book's being more actuarial than it was. Seven factors appear to account for the failure of mental health professionals to apply in practice the strong and clearly supported empirical generalizations demonstrating the superiority of actuarial over clinical prediction (Meehl, 1986).

Holt's (1970) review (he calls it a "counterattack") of the issue carries the banner for the clinical position. He critiques several key studies and commentaries, blasting both research and researchers who support the actuarial position. Thus, in critiquing Sawyer's (1966) widely quoted conclusions gleaned from 45 studies, which are presented as support for the actuarial method, Holt observes, "Aside from...deficiencies in the studies themselves, several of the procedures Sawyer used in presenting, summarizing, and tabulating the evidence are biased in favor of mechanical measurement and prediction." In contrast to Sawyer's publication, Holt quotes the study of Korman (1968), the results of which support the position that clinical prediction is superior.

In this manner, a number of Holt's criticisms of those who advance the actuarial method are rather sweeping. He thus considers that the generalizations and implications drawn from data often involve "little regard for elementary standards of scientific reasoning." Regarding the work of Meehl, Holt charges that he "greatly overgeneralized the results of the research on clinical and statistical prediction, and overlooked some of the data..." Along with other observers, Holt charges that *the clinical predictions that were studied do not reflect what clinicians actually do....* Thus he reports that Sawyer "included only a dozen papers in which the criteria are of the kinds clinicians are ordinarily concerned with": the tests of statistical-versus-clinical prediction were not fair comparisons. And he notes that Meehl indicates that "the researches he collated 'all involve the prediction of somewhat heterogeneous, crude, socially defined behavior outcome'" In a similar vein, Holt approvingly cites Gough (1963): "No fully adequate study of the clinician's forecasting skills has been carried out." This observation clearly is also pertinent to the earlier discussion (p. 11–12) of the difficulty in establishing that some psychological assessors are better judges of clinical variables than are others.

At another fundamental level, Holt, in downgrading the role of prediction in assessment, is in agreement with Zubin (1956a) who suggests "the dilemma to be nonexistent," and anticipates his later position on the controversy (Holt, 1986): "I feel it necessary to decenter as vigorously as I can." The issue is fundamental to how one conceptualizes the role of prediction in science:

> Several authors (e.g. Gough, 1963; Sawyer, 1966) have traced the importance of deciding whether clinical or statistical predictions are more accurate to the allegedly fundamental role of prediction in science. According to Sawyer, "It underlies explanation." As I see it (following Polanyi, 1964), the aim of science is explanation through understanding. Though prediction may be the best way to verify that your understanding is valid and not self-deceptive, it is a means and not an end in itself. It is perfectly possible to predict and control without understanding, a state of affairs that leads to empiricism rather than science.

The dust kicked up by the statistical/clinical topic shows signs of settling. Like Zubin (1956), psychological assessors increasingly view the controversy as a nonissue, and dismiss the box-score method of accounting to establish what is the *best* approach to evaluating personality as irrelevant. A broader perspective now tempers the perennial argument in many quarters. The issue becomes how we can best use, individually and in combination, both approaches; and under what circumstances each may be most appropriate.

Sarbin (1943; see also Sarbin, Taft, & Bailey [1960]) who submitted that the clinician functions as an actuary—albeit a very crude actuary—four decades later (Sarbin, 1986) believes that the controversy over clinical and statistical prediction "has faded into the shadows." His latter-day view of "the issues of which prediction method should be preferred involves choosing between a quest for *historical* truth (that is, correspondence demonstrated by statistical methods) and a quest for *narrative* truth (coherence achieved by clinical formulations).

Holt (1958) earlier promulgated a scheme that, rather than opposing clinical and statistical methods, proposed that they are best used together. In the "sophisticated clinical method," "naive clinical" data—data that are "primarily qualitative with no attempt at objectification," are combined with "pure actuarial"—objective data, statistically processed:

> Qualitative data from such sources as interviews, life histories, and projective techniques are used as well as objective facts and scores, but as much as possible of objectivity, organization, and scientific method are introduced into the planning, the gathering of the data, and their analysis. All the refinements of design that the actuarial tradition has furnished are employed, including job analysis, and successive cross-validations. Quantification and statistics are used wherever helpful, but the clinician himself is retained as one of the prime instruments, with an effort to make him as reliable a valid data-processor as possible; and he makes the final organization of the data to yield a set of predictions *tailored to each individual case* (emphasis added).

THE ECONOMICS OF PSYCHOLOGICAL ASSESSMENT

Psychological assessment is not just a technical matter. The cost of assessment enters into how assessment is done, and whether it is done at all.

The Unhurried Days of Assessment

In the far-gone days that preceded our present cost-conscious era, psychological assessment could be characterized as deliberate, methodical, and unhurried. For a psychologist, especially a trainee, to spend two—or more—days in testing, being supervised, writing a report, and revising the report, was not unusual. And if the report was to be presented at a staff conference, its gestation period might have been even longer.

Even highly experienced psychological assessors seemed to require a large allotment of hours to do their work. Thus, to do a Rorschach (administration, scoring, interpreting, and writing a report), "The consensus is that the average test requires a little more than four hours, but...the total time required will sometimes be less than two hours, and at other times over eight hours." (Odom, 1950) From the same source we learn that even Samuel Beck, a Rorschach pioneer, spent "on the average from three and one half hours at the minimum to about nine hours at the maximum in completing a Rorschach test."

This was a time when psychologists were new to the clinical scene, out to validate themselves and feeling defensive, not uncommonly, for good reasons. The psychological report was an obvious place to demonstrate one's skills, even to attempt to establish superiority in the assessment enterprise. Reports typically were lengthy, prolix; the emphasis was on how much information you could "get." Thus the "shotgun report" which features something about every possible area of the client's life became common, whether all of the various components commented upon were integrated or not, and whether or not all such information was responsive to the problem for which assessment was carried out. All of this was fluffed out with impressive-sounding jargon and observations that were recondite, though not pertinent. In addition to consuming too many hours to produce too many words, and thus being overly costly, reports that matched this description were commonly experienced by psychologists as tedious and odious to write.

Economic Reality

The above practices are as much out of harmony with today's economic climate as they are with sound assessment practice. Budgets are tight and staff is short. We must do with less resources, but, fortunately, not with less quality—or quantity. Indeed, attentiveness to sound principles of assessment can only result in a product that is superior and less costly. Since the preparation of psychological reports typically takes a large share of the time required to carry out assessments, reports that are prepared in accordance with a well-conceived rationale can contribute impressively to cost-effectiveness.

The money squeeze is likely to get worse, not better, economists tell us. In private practice, cost-conscious therapists might decide against having a consultation for psychological assessment out of consideration for the client's wallet. In institutional practice, comptrollers maintain a tight rein on the budget, which means that appropriations to fund assessments likely are restricted. On the other hand, cost-cutting measures, like the system of DRGs (Diagnosis-Related Groups) to regulate the length of a patient's stay, on the basis of his or her diagnosis, logically calls for the quick establishment of a diagnosis and the early initiation of rational and effective treatment. The need, clearly, is for accurate and timely diagnoses and case formulations. Such considerations rule out the unhurried pace of psychological assessment characteristic of an earlier time.

More (and Better) Assessment

Consultation for psychological assessment frequently starts with a referral. This may be in the form of an "order," for example, "Do psychological testing." Or, the referral may be in the form of a request that is somewhat more helpful than the preceding in helping to structure the assessor's task: "please help to establish a diagnosis;" "differential diagnosis between borderline personality disorder and histrionic personality disorder." Following is an example of a referral *statement* that makes it clear to the assessor what the question is. It contains a brief history and a description of current concerns:

> Jeb, age 11 1/2, has until recently been an A/B student, pleasant, sociable, and well liked. On returning to school this fall he presented an entirely different picture. He has no interest in schoolwork and his effort is half-hearted at best. He is poorly responsive to me and his peers, and appears to be daydreaming much of the time. He is in danger of failing. His mother (there is no father in the home) refuses to come to school for a conference, claiming she is "too busy." Contacted by phone she insists there is nothing wrong with Jeb. Please clarify Jeb's problem and make recommendations for dealing with it.

Here is a problem to which the assessor can respond; the task is focused; she or he knows how to proceed, and what diagnostic techniques are most likely to lead to rewarding information. A face-to-face discussion between the assessor and teacher, enriched by a few to-the-point questions, will further sharpen the assessor's ability to efficiently "zero in" on the problem. Unlike the practice of "ordering" an assessment, assessment is most productive when it is a collaborative effort.

A case-focused assessment starts with a focused reason for doing an assessment. Calling once again on Shectman's (1979) slogan, "More Is Not Better," we note that excess length of the psychological report is "not better" not only from a clinical standpoint, but for economic reasons as well. Piling unneeded information on paper is too demanding of the assessor's time. The surfeit of ink is also demanding of the report reader's time and patience—if indeed he or she reads the entire report.

Case-focused reports are quicker to write and to read–and easier to understand. The strategy for conceptualizing such reports is set forth in Chapter 9. In Chapter 10 is discussed the use of "quickie reports," very short, hard-hitting reports that at times can serve well—or better than—the more usual, lengthy clinical documents.

Any discussion of the economics of assessment would be incomplete without considering the role of the computer. Computers, of course, are remarkably efficient in recording and processing data, and in spewing out information, A computer report, however, is not an assessment report. And the economic advantages of computers must be balanced against the technical qualities of computer reports (Tallent, 1987, 1988; Chapter 4).

THE SOCIAL CONTEXT OF PSYCHOLOGICAL ASSESSMENT

Many of the above issues are best understood in the context of the interprofessional relations in which they occur. Particularly, the relations between psychological assessors and psychiatrists have been most extensively discussed in the literature. Kingsbury (1987) emphasizes communication problems as a basic difference between members of the psychological and psychiatric professions, ascribing these differences to dissimilarities in training experiences:

> Differences in perspective about psychopathology and its treatment may create many of the difficulties in communication between clinical psychologists and psychiatrists. These differences, engendered by different training experiences, include how the professions view science, diagnosis, clinical experience, other disciplines, and the hierarchical nature of organizations.

Berg (1988) holds a similar position, and also explores how interdisciplinary friction develops in the assessment situation. Faulty psychological reporting, in particular, creates problems (see the section, "The Perennial Pitfalls in Writing Psychological Reports," Chapter 10; also Tallent, 1988, Chapter 2). Thus, Berg chides those psychologists who submit "a poorly written report that offers information irrelevant to the practical needs of the psychiatrist or virtuoso displays of jargon suitable for framing but little else."

These pitfalls can be overcome in the interest of building a "diagnostic alliance between psychiatrist and psychologist." A conference between clinicians, centering on the psychological report as a basis for understanding the patient, is a key strategy in forging such an alliance. Another strategy, discussed elsewhere (Berg, 1984b) involves teaching the fundamentals of psychological testing to psychiatric residents "to help them become sophisticated consumers of the psychologist's consultative service."

Probably working against reducing distance between professional groups is the current trend to biologizing and remedicalizing psychiatry. Diagnosing patients on the basis of their complaints, surface behaviors, and laboratory tests, in an "atheoretical" frame of reference, and emphasizing chemical and physical treatments, tends to obviate the need for careful case formulations. The other side of the issue is that large numbers of psychiatrists are not in sympathy with this trend.

Not all disharmony between professions stems from differing technical positions, however. It is an open secret that very human matters are also of great importance. Conflicts over turf, money, power, position, privileges, and prestige are also involved. There also appears to be conflict among some members of the older profession over seeking help from members of a newer and nonmedical profession. Perhaps this problem helps to explain why, as Appelbaum (1977) notes, psychiatrists are prone to ignore psychological findings when these findings are at variance with their own impressions, even though psychologists' predictions have been demonstrated to be more accurate than their own. Also,

> Consumers [i.e. psychiatrists who consult with a psychological assessor] are apt to experience too much gloom and perhaps feelings of nihilism when a patient's...difficulties are so amply portrayed by assessment reports...[and] are so unexpected and disconcerting in their implications. They may then protect themselves against this sense of hopelessness by ignoring the test report, especially if in their work with the patient they see little of the severity of illness (Shectman, 1979).

Whatever the reasons, there will always be differences between psychologists and psychiatrists, at least to the extent that people, in general, differ in their perceptions of events. This trite observation illuminates a situation that is not necessarily bad. Berg (1988), in an interesting variation on clinical practice, suggests a diagnostic approach to analyzing the group processes in the triadic system consisting of psychologist, psychiatrist, and patient. How the patient differentially impacts on psychologist and psychiatrist, perhaps culminating in an irritable exchange between the two, can be a rich source of information leading to a search for new insights from the patient's behavior and test data:

> Both professionals were able to contain their annoyance with the patient, but it inadvertently spilled over into their conversations about the patient. Their irritability *toward each other* also caught their attention because they typically worked well together. Observing this interpersonal strain enabled the clinicians to trace its causes to the patient's subtle provocations, which covertly induced others to guiltily deny their anger, thus impeding recognition of the patient's own hostility. At this point the patient's passive-aggressive behavior was more clearly identified and became the focus of diagnostic understanding. In turn, this recognition of the patient's suppressed anger led the psychologist to tune in to subtle manifestations of hostility in the projective test data. These indications, camouflaged beneath compliant conventionality, had previously escaped notice.

4
THE MEASUREMENT TRADITION

> If we take in our hand any volume—let us ask, *Does it contain any abstract reasoning concerning quantity or number?* No. *Does it contain any experimental reasoning concerning matter of fact and existence?* No. Commit it then to the flames: for it can contain nothing but sophistry and illusion!
> —David Hume

> When you can measure what you are speaking about and express it in numbers, you know something about it; but when you cannot measure it, when you cannot express it in numbers, your knowledge is of a meager and unsatisfactory kind: it may be the beginning of knowledge, but you have scarcely, in your thoughts, advanced to the stage of science.
> —William Thomson, Lord Kelvin

THE PSYCHOMETRIC CONCEPT

Psychometrics and Its Relation to Physical and Biological Science

Measurement served Lord Kelvin, physicist, electrical genius, and discoverer of the second law of thermodynamics, very well. It is understandable that he should praise it so highly. Galton, who studied physiological variables, also found measurement to be highly useful, and James McKeen Cattell, continuing Galton's work, extended measurement to some of the psychological variables that are closely identified with physiological processes.

The basic statement of the role of measurement in psychology is that of Thorndike:

If a thing exists, it exists in some amount.

And,

If it exists in some amount, it can be measured.

This is the position of *physicalism*. In developing this concept as central to psychometrics, Rosenwald (1965) calls attention to the application of the language of physical science to psychodiagnostic tasks. Thorndike's language, that is, "a thing," and "it," used in an inanimate sense, are in this mode. Traits, which are what we measure, also have a physicalistic ring. They parallel the physical concept of "properties"—the enduring chemical and physical characteristics of matter—like hardness, melting point, and boiling point—all of which, of course, can be measured, and the magnitude of these characteristics of one thing compared with those of others. And, just as the dimensions of physical characteristics may be arranged on a scale (e.g., a scale of hardness), so may a person's degree of psychological characteristics be established with the aid of a psychometric scale (e.g., the Wechsler Intelligence Scale for Children).

Such *psychometric* scales are defined as *tests* in the measurement tradition. (Other assessment instruments, also called tests by laypersons and many psychologists, alike, are not tests in this sense.) As above, their purpose is to help to understand *testees* in terms of how their scores compare with those of other people. This goal may be achieved when *norms*—the typical level of test performance for some group—have been established: eight-year-old boys, or "normal adults," for example. The scores used must have some basis of comparison, such as points of IQ, as these have reference to some particular scale; or be standard scores, such as T-scores. This is the common method of *norm-referenced testing*. In another form of comparison, *criterion-referenced testing*, the score is compared with a standard or criterion; for example, to determine the extent to which a student has mastered the subject matter of a course.

> These several usages rest on the assumption that we know what abilities are being assessed, that abilities and knowledge can be represented by a numerical score, and that a particular score means the same thing for any individual taking the test (Miller-Jones, 1989).

A Critique of Physicalism

The physicalistic proposition never has set well with many psychologists and philosophers, being seen as doing violence to the "nature of man." Humanistic psychologists are particularly likely to be opposed to physicalism. The clinical pioneer Witmer (1925; Tallent, 1969), for example, was unequivocally hostile to physicalism ("a dynamic system called mechanism") and quantification. When confronted with statistical evidence or the "finality" of an IQ, he felt a need to "pray for all the guidance necessary."

A more modern objection to physicalism is captured by the word "mechanomorphic" (Waters, 1948), referring to "the ascription of mechanical characteristics to the human individual, and the interpretation of human behavior in terms of concepts and processes characteristic of machines." Others hold that you just cannot assign numbers to some of the more human experiences, such as love or meaning.

May (1958), presenting an existential point of view, decries the fragmentation of the person, which is how the study of part processes, such as traits, may be described. It is a "delusion that reality can be comprehended in an abstracted, detached way." Knowledge *about* the individual, the typical outcome of case studies, is well worth knowing, he assures us, but overarching knowledge is *of* the person, the knowledge that may be gained only through direct encounter with the person, a matter of the observer's experience.

Rosenwald (1965) attacks physicalism on three philosophical fronts. These are (1) *disjunctivism*, (2) *quantification*, and (3) *oligotomy*. Each of these, in Rosenwald's thesis, contributes to an inferior diagnostic product and a disheartening effect on the diagnostic practitioner and the consumer of his or her contribution.

(1) *Disjunctivism.* Rosenwald discusses under disjunctivism two propositions, each of which is logically seductive, yet flies in the face of clinical experience and even everyday observations. The first, *the law of the excluded middle*, insists that for every psychological characteristic you can think of you should be able, if you have valid powers of observation, to declare whether any given subject has that particular characteristic, or the extent to which it is present. The Q-sort method, which may require that a person be rated on hundreds of trait items, rests on such presumption. Overlooked is the fact that many such items may be irrelevant in any case under consideration. Rosenwald points to the low base rates in the population of some characteristics, and further suggests, by way of illustrating the law of the excluded middle, that "if we attempt to Q-sort a patient on 1,000 items, 950 of these might be objectively irrelevant or inapplicable to his personality, and of the 50 which apply, only 25 might be indicated in the tests."

The second aspect of disjunctivism, the *law of contradiction*, overlooks the fact that people are a mass of contradictions. Especially in clinical work do we find abundant evidence of ambivalence, conflicts, contrary tendencies, and coexisting impulses and defenses against them. What the person ardently desires in the unconscious, or perhaps even in consciousness, may be roundly condemned—socially, or within the self. Not just clinical experience, but also life experience, argues that it (psychological disposition) doesn't have to be "this or that."

(2) *Quantification.* Rosenwald views the quantitative approach to understanding personality as superficial and specious, and like many observers, disparages the ability of psychologists to put into numbers the fundamentals of their stock in trade, psychoanalytic variables, for example. These, he contends, "are neither exhaustively charted or even crudely conceptualized or interrelated as yet," and assigning numbers cannot add to our understanding of them. Like disjunctivism, quantification in psychology has a powerful appeal, modeled as it is on the "exact sciences," which psychologists might wish to emulate:

> Some psychologists feel that their field of interest must be subjected to strict metric mathematization in order to take its place among the sciences.

Rosenwald carries his position beyond how psychologists may *feel*; they may also be impressed (or impress others) with the way quantification *looks*. He chooses as an example to show how "appealing scientific" quantification may appear to be when applied to a battery that includes one of our psychometrically less-advanced techniques:

The diagnostician couches some of his communication in numbers, and letter symbols. He performs a few impressive calculations. He appraises the significance of percentages and ratios. He is busy with such counting and tallying, and he does not go out of his way to minimize the public appeal of these measurements. Especially if he feels embarrassed about his intuitive inferences, he will gain respite in the IQ, the F+%, or in the M : C ratio.

Further, he observes:

Psychodiagnostic methods look superficially more objective, rigorous and explicit than they are. Many diagnosticians vindictively underscore these scientific aspects to make their work more acceptable to their experimental challengers and to their own scientific consciences.

Yet another criticism of quantification is that it is too inflexible, and particularly, that it lacks the flexibility to which written language lends itself. He contends that quantification leads to squeezing too much information into a few numbers. Written language, on the other hand, can be used to bring out the richness, functional interrelatedness, and subtlety of a person's life, and permit the psychological assessor to assign appropriate emphasis to personality trends. Using language in this way is discussed in Chapter 10.

(3) *Oligotomy.* This "Greekism" is adapted by Rosenwald to mean "division into few categories," specifically, too few categories. The complaint here was spelled out in the discussion of disjunctiveness; namely, the necessity to eliminate low base-rate items, though these might be important in conceptualizing individual descriptions of personality. The (nonquantitatively oriented) diagnostician, by contrast, enjoys an "unlimited descriptive domain."

A second shortcoming of oligotomy is that of *reduction*—reduction of the descriptive terminology available to the diagnostician. In a quantitative system, scores are equated to discontinuous, nonconfigural personality characteristics; whereas the (nonquantitatively oriented) diagnostician, attending to context and individuality, may integrate discrete data units into a novel, unique, more lifelike description. Rosenwald points out that "there are more traits we can attach to people than there are dimensions we can isolate on the tests themselves."

Conclusion on Physicalism and Psychometrics

Criticisms of both a theoretical and a practical nature, such as those of Rosenwald, cannot be easily dismissed. The other side of the coin is that physicalism has an established track record. Psychometrics is of heuristic value and plays a key role in numerous areas of research. Psychometric tools have proven themselves to be up to the task, from predicting academic achievement to predicting performance of aircrew personnel. It is also of significance that psychometrics continues to hold a strong position in clinical psychological assessment, from whence come the most outspoken critics of physicalism and psychometrics, such as Rosenwald. Rapaport and Schafer (Rapaport, Gill, & Schafer, 1945, 1946), who in their role in developing the clinical tradition in psychological assessment (Chapter 5), relied to a significant extent on psychometrics in the diagnosis of mental disorders, though they introduced significant departures from basic psychometric usage. Neuropsychologists rely heavily on tests in the assessment of organic deficit. Physicalism is alive and well, and psychometrics flourishes.

Hallmarks of Psychometrics

Reliability and validity These concepts (pp. 62–65) are fundamentals in psychological testing. Without the ability to demonstrate these, the psychometric enterprise would have no basis for acceptance.

Objectivity This is a requirement of psychometric instruments, or at least a goal which should be approximated. An objective test is so designed that (barring clerical errors—such as recording the answer "A" when the testee actually answers "B") different testers will obtain the same score. True-False and multiple-choice tests are ideal in this respect. We could show this is true by correlating the scores of two examiners scoring the same test forms: the correlation coefficient would be very high. But within the limits of acceptability are tests such as the Wechsler scales, where open-ended responses given to test questions are scored by comparing them with sample answers furnished by the test author. Training in the use of these samples improves objectivity.

Standardization This aspect of psychometrics is another key requirement of psychometric instruments. Tests vary in the degree to which they meet standardization criteria. Some of the best standardized tests are those that are distributed on a national scale and have won widespread acceptance. Presumably, to gain such acceptance, standardized tests must meet three criteria: First, adequate validity must be demonstrated for the test. Second, the test must be well normed, with a sufficiently large, appropriately sampled standardization group. When this requirement is met, it will be a meaningful exercise to compare a testee's scores with standardization group norms. Finally, with respect to administration, standardized tests must carry precise instructions so they may be administered in precisely the same way to all who take the test. Time limits must be strictly adhered to.

THE PRACTICE OF PSYCHOMETRIC TESTING

A Little Historical Background

Although James McKeen Cattell laid the foundation for mental measurement, intelligence testing and the *testing movement* stem from the creative bent of Alfred Binet. It was in 1904 that he was approached by the French Committee of Public Instruction to serve on, what today we would call a task force, to tackle the problem of "backward" children. This effort culminated with the publication in 1905, with

Theodore Simon as a collaborator, of an intelligence scale composed of heterogeneous test items grouped by age level on the basis of empirical trials. With the establishment of norms, it was then possible to determine the "mental age" of children, based on points earned for the age-graded subtests they passed. The initial approach was revised in 1908 and 1911, and in 1912 Wilhelm Stern in Germany devised the well-known intelligence quotient as a means of expressing Binet intelligence levels.

The Binet-Simon test now has numerous descendants, including the entire psychometric approach to appraising intelligence and personality. Frederick Kuhlmann produced a revision in 1912, and Lewis Terman (with the long-time collaboration of Maud Merrill) presided over a number of (Stanford-Binet) revisions and restandardizations carried out over more than a half-century.

Other prominent instruments followed, including the Army Alpha and the Army Beta (the latter designed for illiterate recruits), used to test millions of American soldiers in World War I. The Wechsler-Bellevue scale of 1939 was a descendant of the Binet, though some of its premises differed (see Chapter 6). Following the success of the Wechsler-Bellevue, came the Wechsler Adult Intelligence Scale (WAIS), a revision of this scale (WAIS-R), the Wechsler Intelligence Scale for Children (WISC), also followed by a revision (WISC-R), itself subsequently revised in a third edition, the WISC-III, and the Wechsler Preschool and Primary Scale of Intelligence (WPPSI) and its revision (WPPSI-R).

What the Binet test did for the measurement of intelligence, the Minnesota Multiphasic Personality Inventory (MMPI) did for the measurement of personality. Following an inauspicious birthing involving multiple rejections by publishers and eventual publication by the University of Minnesota Press (Hathaway, 1960), the MMPI has become the most widely used objective personality test in the United States. The revised, restandardized MMPI-2, appearing on its golden anniversary, arrived with the prediction that "we can be assured of at least another 50 years of MMPI research literature, with the development of new scales and their corresponding emotional and behavioral correlates." (Friedman, Webb, & Lewak, 1989). A century!

THE PSYCHOMETRIC CAFETERIA

Tests of early vintage in the psychometric era—or at least their descendants in the form of revisions, modifications, and restandardizations (e.g., the Binet, the Wechsler scales, and the MMPI) continue to be widely accepted and heavily used. At the same time the development of new tests is proliferating (more than 20,000 cognitive and behavioral tests each year according to the office of communications of the American Psychological Association, few of these developed and tested for reliability and validity). APA briefly (Hausburg, J., 1991). As I glance at the heap of test catalogs in front of me, I am impressed with the size and the scope of today's testing industry. Nevertheless, psychologists seem to depend heavily on their "old faithful" instruments. Piotrowski and Keller (1989a) observe: "Apparently clinicians rely on traditional tests despite the proliferation of new assessment instruments [overwhelmingly psychometric] in the clinical literature."

Table 4–1 from Piotrowski and Keller (1989) lists the most frequently used instruments in outpatient mental health facilities.

TABLE 4–1 Rank Order by Weighted Score for the 30 Most Frequently Used Tests[1]

Test Instrument	Total Mentions	Weighted Score	Weighted Score Rank
MMPI	394	1,024	1
WAIS-R	400	909	2
Bender-Gestalt	377	833	3
WISC-R/WPPSI	365	823	4
Human Figure Drawings	366	800	5
Sentence Completion (all kinds)	356	714	6
House-Tree-Person	338	677	7
Rorschach	353	621	8
Thematic Apperception Test	362	596	9
Wide Range Achievement Test	316	588	10
Peabody Picture Vocabulary Test	268	397	11
Beck Depression Inventory	249	394	12
Wechsler Memory Scale	251	388	13
Children's Apperception Test	261	387	14
Vineland Social Maturity Scale	267	377	15
Stanford-Binet Intelligence Scale	230	307	16
Strong-Campbell Interest Inventory	189	239	17
16 PF Questionnaire	157	225	18
MCMI/MCMI-II	108	198	19
Personality Inventory for Children	124	191	20
Benton Visual Retention Test	134	180	21
Halstead-Reitan Neuropsychological Battery	122	166	22
Graham-Kendall Memory-for-Designs Test	130	165	23
Luria-Nebraska Neuropsychological Battery	115	138	24
California Psychological Inventory	99	116	25
Interview for Recent Life Events	83	110	26
Millon Behavioral Health Inventory	68	88	27
Taylor Manifest Anxiety Scale	69	79	28
SCL-90/SCL-90-R	39	76	29
Children's Depression Inventory	55	73	30

[1]From Chris Piotrowski and John W. Keller, "Psychological Testing in Outpatient Mental Health Facilities: A National Study," *Professional Psychology: Research and Practice*, 20 (1989), 423–425. Reproduced by permission of the authors and the American Psychological Association.

Note: $N = 413$. MMPI = Minnesota Multiphasic Personality Inventory; WAIS-R = Wechsler Adult Intelligence Scale-Revised; WISC-R = Wechsler Intelligence Scale for Children-Revised; WPPSI = Wechsler Preschool and Primary Scale of Intelligence; 16 PF = Sixteen Personality Factor Questionnaire; MCMI = Millon Clinical Multiaxial Inventory; SCL = Symptom Checklist-90 (R = Revised).

I am impressed also with how difficult it is to pull together all of the psychometric instruments on the market into a tight, nonarbitrary classification. No matter how classified, the categories will overlap.

In terms of what is measured, instruments are concerned with areas such as:

School subject matter (e.g., Algebra, French)

Intelligence, ability, cognition (level of intellectual functioning, areas of intellectual strengths and weaknesses, aptitudes)

Personality (global personality, specific traits, psychopathology, prognosis, recommendations for intervention)

Neuropsychological status (presence or absence of brain damage, nature of lesion, lateralization and localization of insult, extent or pattern of loss, organic basis for mental disorder, prognosis, recommendations for retraining)

Aptitude (potential for achievement)

Achievement (current functioning, generally after a period of training)

Interests (likes, dislikes, attitudes associated with kinds of occupations)

Development (achievement in language, motor skills, perception, social skills, etc.)

Identified as classes of instruments in terms of how the test taker is to respond are such devices as:

Verbal tests (require verbal responses to items)

Nonverbal and performance tests (require nonverbal responses, such as drawing or manipulating materials)

Inventories (lists of questions or statements to which the subject responds to provide information on personality, vocational interests, etc.)

Objective tests (tests yielding responses to which scorers demonstrate high interjudge reliability)

Structured tests (composed of unambiguous items or tasks)

Unstructured tests (composed of ambiguous items or tasks)

In terms of manner of administration, we have:

Individual tests (for administration to one testee at a time)

Group tests (may be administered to a number of testees simultaneously)

Computer-administered tests

Tests may be designated as:

Single-variable tests (measure one variable, e.g., anxiety, hostility)

Multiple-variable tests (measure a number of variables, e.g., global intelligence, global personality)

Global Tests

Many human characteristics of widespread interest are complexities or aggregates of interacting elements. Such a conception of intelligence is basic in the design of a number of intelligence tests and is emphasized in Wechsler's scales (Wechsler, 1944, 1958). These are conceived as yielding a global statement that reflects the pattern formed by a variety of elements of intelligent behavior, including nonintellective factors of intelligence.

In a similar sense, the MMPI is a global measure of personality, ranging far and wide as it does over the spectrum of personality functions. To be sure, the instrument consists of a fairly small number of scales, but each scale measures more than a discrete or homogeneous entity. Thus, Graham (1987) identifies no fewer than 42 descriptors that may apply to high-scorers on the hypomanic scale, and 14 that may characterize low-scorers. A high-scorer, for example, may be having a manic episode, be poised and self-confident; or, if a male, he may possibly be concerned about homosexual impulses. A few scores, therefore, can be assembled into a complex personality picture.

The Millon Clinical Multiaxial Inventory-II (MCMI-II) also covers a very broad territory, measuring 22 personality disorders and clinical syndromes that coordinate with DSM-III-R diagnoses (American Psychiatric Association, 1987). Each of these categories, in turn, is based on a pattern of personality characteristics.

Yet another global measure commanding interest is the NEO Personality Inventory (NEO-PI, Costa & McCrae, 1985). Purporting to measure "all domains of personality," as established by rational and factor analytic methods, the instrument yields scores for Neuroticism, Extraversion, Openness to Experience, Agreeableness, and Conscientiousness. In turn, each of these domains is divided into a number of "facet scales."

Single-Variable Tests

In contrast to instruments that seek to measure such broad areas of intelligence or personality, are instruments with a narrower focus. Corcoran and Fischer (1987) have compiled a list of numerous instruments of this sort. These include, for example, a scale of clinical anxiety, a state-trait anger scale, sexual behavior inventories, and a scale of impulsivity.

Latitude in Test Use

Standards for Educational and Psychological Testing (1985), is the outgrowth of years of experience with psychometric tools and reflection and codification of principles, policies, and ethics. How testing *should* be carried out, it is clear from *Standards*, is more in the spirit of the flexibility that characterizes a cafeteria than with the rigidity that goes with excessive prescription and proscription. It is also clear, however, that the need for making decisions and the taking into consideration of practical constraints must not compromise the premises of psychometrics:

In applying standards to test use, as opposed to test development, more flexibility and use of professional judgment are required. The appropriateness of specific test uses cannot be evaluated in the abstract but only in the context of the larger assessment process. The principle questions to be asked in evaluating test use are whether or not the test is appropriate (valid) for its specific role in the larger assessment process and whether or not the test user has accurately described the extent to which the score supports any decision made or administrative action taken.

Although it is not appropriate to tell a test user that particular levels of predictive validity and reliability need to be met, it is appropriate to ask the user to ascertain that procedures result in adequately valid predictions or reliable classifications for the purposes of the testing. Cost-benefit compromises become as necessary in test use as they do in test development. However, as with standards for test development, when test standards are not met in test use, reasons should be available. Here again, the criteria of impact on test takers applies. The greater the potential impact, the greater the need to satisfy relevant standards (p. 41).

Latitude in test use may be exercised in various ways. It is particularly in clinical testing that rigid psychometric precepts are commonly inapplicable. The following excerpt from *Standards* is in harmony with long-standing clinical practice:

Projective techniques and many interview and behavioral observation techniques are often used as aids in clinical assessment and treatment selection. Each of these methods yields multiple hypotheses regarding the behavior of the subject in various situations as they arise, with each hypothesis modifiable on the basis of further information. When one of these measures is so used, interpretations are judged by its total contribution to the clinical understanding of an individual rather than by the validity of each hypothesis (p.45).

Similar considerations apply in other clinical situations, such as when standardized instruments are applied in nonstandardized ways. This is the state of affairs often present when testing is done with deviant populations. Sensory limitations, confusion, and thought disorder, for example, can create problems. It is obviously a meaningless exercise to seek to compare intelligence test results of a disturbed psychotic patient with a normal standardization group; the published norms are just not applicable. Nevertheless, useful conclusions and hypotheses may be generated from the patient's performance.

Other hypotheses relate more closely to psychometric premises. The Rorschach Interpretation Assistance Program (RIAP; Exner, 1985) is a prime example. A computer program, the RIAP yields hypotheses, which, though presented as a report, is not a final product in the absence of human judgment and further human interpretation, which involves consideration of variables that are in addition to the insights based on this use of the Rorschach.

SOME SPECIAL PROBLEMS WITH PSYCHOMETRIC TESTING

As pointed out in the discussion of ethics in Chapter 2, the bylaws of the American Psychological Association set forth as an object the advancement of psychology as a means of promoting human welfare. Segments of the public, however, do not see the outcome of certain psychological practices—such as testing—as consonant with this goal. There is abundant testimony to this effect in a spate of publications starting in the 1950s.

Book titles and newspaper heads bearing on psychological testing were often graphic and carried poignant messages. William H. Whyte, Jr. (1956), in his book *The Organization Man*, viewed tests as a means to help force people into a pattern of conformity, and to be resisted. In what he regards as a public service, he presents an Appendix, "How To Cheat on Personality Tests." The victimized test taker "must" cheat, he advises. *The Brain Watchers*, by Martin L. Gross (1962), also professes to be in the public interest in its dedication to the "50,000,000 hapless Americans" who as students and workers are subjected to the scrutiny of "the brain watchers." From a scholarly background, Banesh Hoffman (1962), in *The Tyranny of Testing*, builds a case that "objective tests" (his quotes) fall short of their intended purpose and, in fact, are counterproductive of this purpose.

A few years later, *American Psychologist* (Amrine, 1965) published a thick special issue on testing and public policy. The occasion, in part, was the investigation of testing by both houses of Congress. In an atmosphere of near "hysteria," pickets paraded in front of APA headquarters, handing out leaflets and bearing placards with such messages as *Don't Be Brainwashed by Some Ph.D.*, *See Your Clergyman or Doctor*, *Help Stop Psychological Sex Tests*, and *Write Your Congressman*. Headlines screamed antitesting messages such as "Psychological Tests Assailed; UW Professor Asks for Probe" (*The Milwaukee Journal*), "Civil Service Bans Use of Personality Testing" (*The Washington Post*), and "Personality X-Rays or Peeping Toms?" (*The Washington Post*). A cartoon by HERBLOCK in *The Washington Post* shows a stern, finger-pointing figure labeled "Congress," berating a small, cowering figure identified as "Government Employment Questionnaires": "You've Been Deciding Who's All Right and Who Isn't."

These antitesting positions are concerned with one or more of three issues: (1) validity, (2) bias, and (3) privacy. The latter issue, in turn, centers about the invasion of privacy and/or breaches of confidentiality.

Validity

Validity in the present context embraces validity in the technical sense and also from the point of view of social considerations of effectiveness. Hoffman (1962), for example, has done his homework and discusses the technical status of validity, "warts" and all—in fact, mostly the warts. Similarly, Gross (1962), plumbs such authoritative sources as the Mental Measurements Yearbooks and a number of other authorities as well. In addition to accumulating opinions to the effect that technical validity leaves much to be desired, he gathers support in opposition to the practice of using personality tests to screen applicants for employment. Thus, from George K. Bennett, then president of The Psychological Corporation: "Personality tests are of little, if any, value in employment." To call once more upon Whyte's

(1956) slant on testing as a search for conformists, the social value of testing is questioned from another angle.

Many lay commentators—Whyte and Gross are but two examples—pay much attention to test items, and from a logical point of view find them wanting. Items having to do with sex practices, especially, come in for a good deal of attention. In addition to identifying an apparent lack of face validity in terms of the purpose of testing—employment screening, for example—these reviewers find offensive the use of items with sex content—which they believe are possibly harmful to children.

Gross establishes as the central concept of his book "the argument against personality testing as one of modern morality." This argument is paired with the companion themes of low test validity ("Many doubt the existence of any valid prediction by personality testers, even on a broad group basis."), and the dimensions of the economic structure of the testing enterprise captured in his expression "the personality colossus." We have already noted (pp. 66–67) Mitchell's (1986) view of how commercialism can adversely affect proper concern for validity. Had Mitchell's paper been available when Gross wrote his book he no doubt would have prominently cited it.

Bias

The topic of bias in testing pertains to the widely discussed test-taking disadvantages among people whose origin is in a culture different from that in which the test was developed. Here the concept of culture includes subculture, inasmuch as economic and social deprivation in certain subcultures have been linked to being disadvantaged as a test taker. In turn, such test-takers may be misclassified or their potential underestimated, with the consequence that they may be denied employment or educational opportunities, or suffer such inequities as being improperly placed in special-education programs designed for the educable mentally retarded (EMR).

The use of tests that bring about this sort of result is, of course, patently unjust and has long been the subject of debate and challenge. Two well-publicized California cases having to do with the overrepresentation of minority children in EMR special-education classes, allegedly on the basis of test scores, are *Diana* v. *Board of Education*, C70-37 RFP (N.D. Cal. June 18, 1973), and *Larry P.* v. *Riles*, 343 F. Supp. 1306 (N.D. Cal. 1972)...and subsequent litigation.

Early in the history of large-scale testing there was hope that *culture-free* tests would be developed. The pursuit of such a goal proved to be unfeasible, however—inevitably a test reflects the culture of its origin—as reviewers agree was the case with Cattell's (1933) culture-free intelligence test. The subsequent concept of *culture-fair* tests reflected Cattell's agreement with the updated consensus concerning the possibility of culture-free measures, and his (1959) culture-fair test of intelligence emerged as a test of Spearman's g. Other terms in the culture-fair vein are *culture-common* and *cross-cultural*.

To be considered fair, especially for achievement tests, Miller-Jones (1989) suggests that "the content sampled by items needs to reflect the kind of coverage of subject matter likely to be encountered by most students." Hence, when a testee from a deprived background does poorly on a test when content relates to the sort of real-life situation—for example, academic, vocational—that he or she will encounter, can we say the test is unfair? Or would it be more accurate to say that the test documents the consequences of growing up in an unfair situation, that it reflects the unfairness of the culture?

Green (1978) suggests that "there is no difference in the meaning of test scores for blacks and whites. On the average, a black student with a score of 500 on a college entrance exam does just about as well academically as a white student with a score of 500." It is his impression that "large ethnic differences in average test scores are probably not the result of test bias, but probably indicate the extent of educational disadvantage experienced by minorities."

Shall we condemn the test because it yields such results? Well, we do not, like kings of old, execute the messenger who brings bad news. It is important, in fact, to know of the weaknesses that the test discloses. This information can form the basis for a remediation plan. It would not be the best use of a test, nor in the best interest of the test-taker or society, to merely note low test scores and predict failure, and perhaps to use these scores as the sole basis to make decisions that will help to insure failure. A more meaningful and socially responsible use of test data is to predict the outcome following indicated intervention. To deal with data this way calls for the exercise of clinical judgment.

The approach of Mercer and Lewis (1978) uses as a basis for prediction and placement what we might call "adjusted" or "compensated" scores, scores that take into account the background of deprived children. Thus, the "bottom line" of the System of Multicultural Pluralistic Assessment (SOMPA) is arrived at on the basis of actual credits earned, to which is added points to reflect various kinds of deprivation—for example, living in poverty or growing up in the absence of a father in the home.

Lambert (1981), on the other hand, challenges the basic premise of unfairness. On the basis of her analysis of the relevant literature, she concludes that "individual intelligence tests provide a fair assessment of minority children," and, "there is no evidence that the tests are biased."

While most of the concern with test bias pertains to tests of intelligence, ability, aptitude, and achievement, Dana (1988) calls our attention to an "unintentional bias" in the interpretation of the MMPI. Thus, members of minority groups who have experiences that are out of the cultural mainstream show "consistent group differences in item responding." Current interpretation of the MMPI, however, tends to overlook these group differences, and, in addition, the instrument itself does not adequately come to grips with them:

> Interpretation of item differences for Afro-Americans should include the contribution of world view to belief in external control and experiences that require continuous and conspicuous attention to social inconsistencies, social injustice, and feelings of personal impotence...Afro-Americans share some symptoms of alienation from mainstream American culture, but they also share with one another an identity formation process and

a variety of culturally appropriate coping styles that are not going to be discerned from the MMPI profile because the instrument does not tap the collective cultural consciousness of groups that differ from the original standardization group. These ingredients are absent from the profile...An understanding of the cultural variance involved in measurement of Afro-American psychopathology is obscured because there has been no opportunity for measurement of unique sources of personal strength contained in the dimension of meaningfulness, or Afro-American identity.

Sex bias can also be a factor in testing (Tittle & Zytowski, 1978; Tittle, 1982; Zytowski & Borgen, 1983), and such unfairness may also be unintentional. Consider the case of interest inventories that compare the subject's general life-interests with those who are established in various fields. The logic is sound, except when a field is dominated by one sex or the other. Such is true in work areas like construction or engineering. Consequently, a woman who well might find appealing the sort of work that construction people or engineers do, probably would be steered away from these occupations because her general interests are different from those of men. Interestingly, sex bias has been demonstrated even when the explicit descriptive statements of DSM are used in making a diagnosis. (Ford & Widiger, 1989)

Privacy

The issue of privacy is basic to the testing enterprise across all situations where testing is done. This includes clinical, educational, industrial, governmental, and research applications. Special attention to the latter is found in Ruebhausen and Brim (1966) and *Privacy and Behavioral Research* (1967). It is discussed in *Standards* under the heading "Protecting the Rights of Test Takers." Privacy is a matter of psychological ethics, and guidelines to practice are spelled out in Principle I, Part B, Confidentiality, of the "Ethical Principles of Psychologists" (American Psychological Association, 1981). Privacy, as it pertains to testing, also is a legal matter that is addressed in a number of statutes.

Basic to the testing process is the *informed consent* of the test-taker, as set forth in Standard 16.1 of *Standards*. Exceptions to this general rule reflect variations in the application of the privacy concept across different situations:

> Informed consent should be obtained from test takers or their legal representatives before testing is done except (a) when testing without consent is mandated by law or governmental regulation (e.g., statewide testing programs); (b) when testing is conducted as a regular part of school activities (e.g., schoolwide testing programs and participation by schools in norming and research studies); or (c) when consent is clearly implied (e.g., application for employment or educational admissions). When consent is not required, test takers should be informed concerning the testing process.

Comment accompanying this standard holds that test-takers, or their representatives (e.g., parents, guardians), should have explained to them, in everyday language, the sort of tests they will be given, their purpose, what use will be made of the information gained with the use of the test, who will have access to the material, and with what consequences. With appropriate consideration for their limitations, children as young as two or three or mentally retarded test-takers should be similarly informed.

The privacy of the individual also must be considered when tests are selected. These should be relevant to the purpose for which testing is done. Applicants for employment have frequently been critical of test items such as some of those that appear on the MMPI. They fail to see that whether or not a person believes a minister can cure disease by touching a person's head pertains to one's work potential. They particularly resent items that query sex practices, regarding them as irrelevant to employee selection and therefore a totally unwarranted invasion of privacy.

Adequate explanation, per the guidelines set forth in *Standards*, and with particular attention to offensive and seemingly irrelevant items, can forestall resistance and large-scale opposition to testing. Explanation, in the context of rapport, can also be most helpful in securing cooperation and avoiding the unnecessary anxiety that may result when the test taker reacts to testing as a mysterious probing that could result in the unwitting disclosure of that which he or she would prefer to keep private. Post-testing feedback, in situations where it is feasible, can also help to overcome this problem. Such indeed, is good clinical and humane practice, a fact not overlooked in a number of statutes, such as the Privacy Act of 1974, the "Buckley Amendment," and the Education for All Handicapped Children Act of 1975 (Public Law 94–142).

Psychologists should assure confidentiality in the storage and disposal of their records. This injunction may be implemented by ascertaining that there is a secure lock on the door or the file cabinet, and by prohibiting the access of unauthorized persons to areas where confidential records are kept. Further, obsolete material should be removed from client's files to preclude its use in a manner inappropriate to changed situations. For example, increased maturity or therapy may have significantly altered personality factors that prompted a client to seek psychological help at an earlier phase of life.

A new dimension of concern with confidentiality came into being with the introduction of the computer to psychometrics. Noting the widespread popularity of this tool, Bongar's (1988) review of the confidentiality issue raised by computer use centers on a discussion of "the ease and rapidity with which the microcomputer's magnetic media can be duplicated, damaged, or destroyed." He approaches the problem of wrongful access to magnetically-held information from direct desk-top invasion of privacy to invasion over the telephone lines. He suggests ways of safeguarding confidential material, including locks and other antitheft devices, the removal of disks for storage in locked file cabinets, and encryption, that is, coding by use of a mathematical formula, or algorithm. He would require psychology students to be trained in computer literacy, which would include training covering security issues.

Nevertheless, attempts to protect confidentiality cannot be foolproof. Bongar points out that "security procedures can be complicated by the use of multiple microcomputer input stations, multiple networks of computers, and patients taking psychological tests on-line." Those who take a professional role in the generation of information, and therefore are responsible for safeguarding it, may not always have the ability to do so. Consider further the case when clinical findings are made available to insurance companies, and stored in their mainframes, or when research data are shared with other investigators in various locations. And, as news stories remind us from time to time, few, if any, systems are immune to being penetrated by resourceful "hackers." Bongar would extend the application of the principle of informed consent to include the requirement that clients who are asked to give consent be made aware that there are risks that confidentiality may be broached when their personal data are entrusted to the computer.

"The IQ Controversy"

Controversy over testing thus continues to be very much alive. Focusing on "The IQ controversy," Snyderman and Rothman (1987, 1988) note that intelligence tests have been under attack virtually since their inception. Among the key survey-based conclusions of these authors is the distinct impression that there is a disjunction of views on intelligence testing between experts—psychologists, educators, and sociologists, on the one hand, and the media and the informed public on the other. The professionals tended to the opinion that intelligence tests are valid and useful, while 20 percent of the media were found to be biased and, for the most part, antitesting.

COMPUTER TESTING

The use of computers in psychological testing was initiated well over a quarter century ago (Fowler, 1985). The rate of growth of computer testing is remarkable (Butcher, 1987a). Meehl (1987) adds perspective to this state of affairs: "It would be strange, and embarrassing, if clinical psychologists, supposedly sophisticated methodologically and quantitatively trained, were to lag behind internal medicine, investment analysis, and factory operation control in accepting the computer revolution."

Participants In The Computer-Testing Enterprise

Guidelines for Computer-Based Tests and Interpretations (American Psychological Association, 1986)—subsequently referred to as *Guidelines*—provides a small glossary covering the roles and responsibilities of those involved with computer testing. Familiarity with these terms can avoid potential confusion, such as mistaking the *test user* for the *test taker*.

Test Developer The test developer may be an individual or an agency. *Guidelines* focuses on the test *author*, the *software author*, and the *test or software publisher*. Thus, David Wechsler, who developed the Wechsler series of intelligence scales, and Theodore Millon, who constructed the Millon Clinical Multiaxial Inventory, are test authors. Software authors create algorithms for test administration, scoring, and interpretation. Software publishers market computer software.

Test User The test user employs tests as a basis for reaching decisions, or passes along test information to a second party–a school administrator or a probation officer, perhaps–who needs test data that will be helpful in making decisions. The test user is a professional who meets the high standards of a *qualified professional* as set forth in *Guidelines*:

> The test user should be a qualified professional with (a) knowledge of psychological measurement; (b) background in the history of the tests or inventories being used; (c) experience in the use and familiarity with the research on the tests or inventories, including gender, age, and cultural differences if applicable; and (d) knowledge of the area of intended application. For example, in the case of personality inventories, the user should have knowledge of psychopathology or personality theory.

Test Taker The test taker is the test subject, the person who takes the test, the testee. But under certain conditions the test taker may also be the test user. This situation may come about when the test taker is the ultimate consumer of interpreted test data, which is the case, for example, when the instrument is a vocational interest inventory. In this case, the test taker/test user (obviously not a professional) must still understand the test results sufficiently well to be able to make intelligent decisions.

Test Administrator The test administrator, who is not necessarily the test user, is in charge of actual test administration. The administrator holds responsibility for the proper conduct of testing, though immediate supervision of testing may be delegated to a proctor or technician. The administrator is ultimately responsible for ascertaining that the test taker is familiar with the computer equipment on which testing is done, that test items displayed on the screen are legible and free from glare, and that the testing room is quiet, comfortable, and free of distraction.

Rationale, Scope, and Status of Computer Testing

Technically, computer testing has its origin in physicalism and psychometrics, and the computer applied to psychological testing may be considered a *psychometric machine*. (Tallent, 1987) The philosophy is that of statistical—or actuarial—prediction, Meehl's (1956) ideal of the "good cookbook." Support for application of the cookbook method derives from the *Clinical versus Statistical Controversy* precipitated by Meehl's (1954) bombshell. The basic thesis is that test scores may be empirically linked to nontest behaviors of test takers. Such interpretation—translation of scores to conclusions—is the rationale of the old MMPI *Atlas* (Hathaway & Meehl, 1951), of which computer interpretation may be considered an updated, electronic version.

The role the computer was destined to play in psychological testing, related ethical issues, and concerns with the quality of the computer-testing product were addressed early on by the American Psychological Association (Newman, 1966), and continued to be addressed in subsequent publications (*Standards for educational and psychological testing*, American Psychological Association, American

Educational Research Association, & National Council on Measurement in Education, 1974; *Guidelines for computer-based tests and interpretations*, American Psychological Association, 1986; and in numerous APA Journal articles).

The computer is a versatile tool, as evidenced in its widespread applications and variations of use. It has been found useful in such diverse information-gathering approaches as observation, interviewing, history taking, checklists and rating scales, personality evaluation with inventories, and projective instruments; and with cognitive, ability, and neuropsychological tests. Programs are available for administering, scoring, profiling, interpretation, and report writing for old tests, and for new instruments designed specifically for computer analysis. Creative variations have appeared. In *adaptive testing* (Weiss, 1985), for example, items presented to the test taker are contingent on his or her earlier responses, similar to Binet testing, where tests at a given age-level are administered only if at least one subtest has been passed at the immediately lower year-level.

Tests for computer interpretation may be administered in the old-fashioned clinical way, such as is typical with the Rorschach, and the scores then entered into the computer for processing. Or, testing may be *interactive*, that is, the test taker responds on the computer keyboard to test items presented on the screen.

The versatility of the computer is seen in the multiple processing modes listed by Fowler (1985) in a "taxonomy of computer-based psychological software":

a. *Remote* The computer is located away from the site of administration, and data are mailed or transmitted by telephone; the testing is not interactive.

b. *Dial-in (teleprocessing)* The test is administered in the usual way and transmitted by data terminal to a mainframe computer for processing.

c. *Punch-in* The test is administered in the usual clinical or paper-and-pencil manner, and the responses are entered in an on-site computer for processing.

d. *On-line* The test is administered, scored, and the report generated by computer.

Basic to the process of computer interpretation of test scores is the use of algorithms (a partly Greek term honoring the ninth century Arab mathematician al-Khuwārizmi), which are mechanical rules for making decisions. For example, on the basis of empirical correlates, when MMPI Scale 6 is above a T-score of 75, we may expect that the test taker will show disturbed thinking, have delusions of persecution and/or grandeur, ideas of reference, feel mistreated, picked on, be angry and resentful, harbor grudges, and rely heavily on projection as a defense mechanism. A likely diagnosis of the test taker would be paranoid schizophrenia or paranoid state (Graham, 1987). On the basis of such established relations between scores and symptom pictures, characteristics that are commonly found with particular score elevations and patterns may be fashioned into statements, stored in a statement library, and called back whenever a test taker registers the scores that have been shown to empirically relate to these statements.

However, in practice, the statements that eventually issue from the computer are not derived entirely by blind adherence to this scheme. The algorithms additionally incorporate the experience of their author, and are not free of clinical lore, theoretical bias, clinical flavoring, intuition, and personally held insights.

While computer testing was inspired by the actuarial/cookbook concept, it is fact that

> At this time no purely actuarial computerized narrative interpretive systems exist. The necessary developmental research is prohibitive; the amount of empirical data required by such a system increases geometrically with the number of variables and score levels to be interpreted by the program. Existing actuarial systems such as the MMPI "cookbooks"...either leave a large percentage of examinees unclassified or use such broad categories that fine interpretive discriminations are impossible. As a result, the interpretive systems written for even the most popular and well-researched psychological tests are actually a mixture of rules based on actuarially validated relationships and other rules culled from established clinical lore or from the expert author's personal experience with the test (Vale & Keller, 1987; cf. Carson, 1990).

Early beliefs that the computer would eliminate the need for skilled diagnostic clinicians has not materialized. Errors, inconsistencies, and misleading statements are always a possibility. When computer-derived information is to be employed by a person who does not have sufficient psychological background to use the material responsibly, it falls upon a psychologist to interpret to that person the computer interpretation. To repeat an earlier point (pp. 33–34), "There must be a clinician between the computer and the client." (Fowler & Butcher, 1986).

Clinical judgment, far from being obsolete in the computer age, takes on a new role and a new importance. *Guidelines* counsels:

> Computer-generated interpretive reports should be used only in conjunction with professional judgment. The user should judge for each test taker the validity of the computerized test report based on the user's professional knowledge of the total context of testing and the test taker's performance and characteristics.

Commenting to clarify this position, and taking into consideration the clinical-versus-statistical-prediction literature, *Guidelines* spells out further the relationship between psychologist and computer, together with a proviso: "The final decision must be that of a qualified provider with sensitivity for nuances of test administration and interpretation. Altering the interpretation should not be done routinely, but only for good and compelling reasons.":

> It is imperative that the final decision be made by a qualified professional who takes responsibility for overseeing both the process of testing and judging the applicability of the interpretive report for individual test takers, consistent with legal, ethical, and professional requirements. In some circumstances, professional providers may need to edit or amend the computer report to take into account their own observations and judgments and to ensure that the report is comprehensible, free of jargon, and true to the person evaluated.

Carson (1990) holds an aggressive position with respect to the role of the assessor:

Perhaps the most general and telling observation that can be made here is to point to the manifest deficiencies of the printouts that are the normal outcome of a CBTI assessment. It is impossible for me to believe that a practitioner, even one protected by guild-inspired laws and regulations designed to limit access to the product, could long remain in business as a mere passive way station between the CBTI system and the ultimate consumer. In fact, the more professionally responsible authors/sponsors of CBTI systems, such as my good friend and sometime co-author James Butcher, have from the beginning insisted that these printouts be considered only as aids to an otherwise well-qualified clinician user and that they are not designed for unfiltered transmission to end-users. And indeed they are not, as perusal of a sample of them from the most professional of the available CBTI services will amply confirm. In my experience, making sense out of them is a major clinical undertaking, even without regard to their necessary integration with the presenting client problem and its background history.

Manner of Presenting Information

The canned locutions that make up statement libraries, particularly those of the early days of computer testing, could be described as hackneyed, stereotyped, and impersonal. One only has to look at a number of MMPI interpretations based on a 278 or 49 code-type, or a "Conversion V" pattern, processed by the same algorithm, to conclude that sections of a number of reports are interchangeable. If you see enough reports from certain populations, like Vietnam veterans who carry a diagnosis of post-traumatic stress disorder, with each report the feeling of déjà vu is likely to be particularly strong.

Another common problem has been emphasis on volume rather than focus. Matarazzo (1983) has seen reports holding "up to 50 pages of valid sounding statements" and Butcher (1978) has reviewed computer printouts that report on "everything you could possibly tell about a person from the test." To call on Shectman (1979) just once more, "more is not better," and we must be wary of "information overload": "Diagnosticians typically know more about the patients than they should include in their communications to the referring colleagues. In fact, part of the task of all psychologists is to choose just what needs to be communicated out of the wealth of material at their disposal."

A number of computer reports show evolution. Increasing the number of statements in the library, and tailoring them more closely to variations in scale elevations, can make them more accurate and less monotonous. Nonpersonalized statements, like "Individuals with this pattern...," or *"They* may..." (emphasis added) perhaps no longer appear in a number of current reports that instead suggest specific reference to the person being evaluated (though, in truth, the statements pertain to group trends rather than to the individual who supposedly is described in the report). Add to these refinements improved syntax and the impression may be created that the canned comments were custom-written about the person who was tested. These changes may improve acceptability, or "customer satisfaction" (Lanyon, 1984) of reports, but not necessarily their validity (pp. 68–69).

Using Computer Reports

There are several ways in which the test user can appropriate the statements provided by computerized reports. She or he may use the report "as is," within the constraints of *Guidelines*. Or, the hypotheses that constitute the computer report may be considered along with data from other sources. As a collection of statements, some or all of which may be valid, they should be considered in the process of case formulation. The computer report may also serve as a "second opinion"—to be compared with the impressions of a psychological assessor.

5

THE CLINICAL TRADITION

Psychological assessment in the clinical tradition is firmly rooted in the contributions of Lightner Witmer, who is generally credited with the founding of the field of clinical psychology in 1896. The "clinical method in psychology" was his designation for this departure from what was then the mainstream of his science. Of particular interest, at a time when psychometrics and psychological assessment were both in their early developmental stages, was Witmer's attitude to tests and the manner in which he used them. Watson (1951) indicates that Witmer's position was "to use tests when they are indicated, but not to be bound by them." Such practice is evident in Witmer's (1925) writing which clearly identifies the psychological assessor as superordinate to tests:

> Every performance must...be critically examined and judicially interpreted, by one who has insight and experience enough to give his interpretation the weight of authority. The ascertained results of observation, test and measurement, constitute the problem of clinical diagnosis. The judgment of the diagnostician in clinical psychology begins to operate at the very point where psychometrists and group testers cease to function.
>
> Experience also led me to believe in the inefficacy of the quantified result of a test, as for example the Binet test. If someone reports to me that a fifteen year old child has a Binet age of twelve, I do not consider this fact as having by itself diagnostic value. It is an interesting statement, which however I would not risk making anything of, until I further examined the child. I do not know of any single test on which I can rely for diagnostic purposes.

The inauguration of the modern era of psychological assessment was in 1945. The basic approach was set forth in two volumes entitled *Diagnostic Psychological*

Testing: The Theory, Statistical Evaluation, and Diagnostic Application of a Battery of Tests (Rapaport, Gill, & Schafer, 1945, 1946). The Rapaport-Schafer approach is also referred to as the Menninger tradition, after the setting in which the basic development took place, or the Menninger-Riggs tradition in recognition of the role of the Austen Riggs Foundation where Rapaport and Schafer continued their work after leaving Menninger. The tradition continues strong and serves as a base on which to build further advances in psychological assessment theory and methods.

From the beginning, the clinical tradition in psychology has represented a commitment to improving the lot of those who are, in a manner of speaking, sick (Greek: klinikos—a [sick] bed). Watson (1951) observes: "The clinical method has as its one invariant, omnipresent aim the assistance of an individual in distress regardless of the field in which the difficulty occurs." For many years clinical psychological assessment was practiced (and developed) largely in hospitals and clinics with the goal of helping persons who, in today's terminology, were suffering with various mental disorders. Currently, however, assessment in the clinical tradition has a broader outlook, with foci such as modifying troubling behaviors in the schools and in the community, personnel selection, forensic evaluation, and research in myriad areas.

THE MEASUREMENT TRADITION AND THE CLINICAL TRADITION: DIFFERENCES AND SIMILARITIES

Moving from the measurement tradition to the clinical tradition entails a decided paradigm shift, such as noted in the above material from Witmer. What makes psychometric sense does not necessarily make clinical sense, and vice versa. But there is overlap, convergence, and cross-fertilization between the two approaches; functioning in the clinical tradition may involve the use of psychometrics—indeed, there was a time when to many the practice of psychometrics was synonymous with the entire field of clinical psychology (Loutitt, 1939)—and the enlightened and ethical use of psychometric tools incorporates features that are basic to the clinical tradition; most notably, judgment, interpretation (including the use of clinically fortified algorithms for computer interpretation (p. 95), the consideration of personal and demographic nontest variables, and the need to make sense of apparently conflicting or contradictory data. While the differences between the two approaches are extensive and far reaching in their theoretical and practical ramifications, the commonalities and similarities must not be overlooked.

In some instances the differences between the two traditions is a difference in emphasis. Algorithms that incorporate clinical experience and insights, for example, nevertheless are constructed basically from empirical relationships between test performance and behaviors. Actual practices are not uniform in either tradition, however—each practitioner has his or her personal approach. Exner and Exner (1972), on the basis of a large-scale survey of clinicians, suggest that "the formal and informal modifications of those systems [the extant Rorschach systems] make for almost as many different approaches to the Rorschach as there are Rorschachers." Practices also vary with the setting and with the *Zeitgeist*. Witmer's early emphasis on "doing something for the child, and those who are responsible for his welfare" differed considerably from Rapaport's (Rapaport, Gill, & Schafer, 1945, 1946) ego-psychology approach, with its accent on personality structure, and from the later concern of numerous assessors with object-relations phenomena—self-representations, object representations, and ego states. The clinical tradition is more flexible than the measurement tradition in its applications because it is less constrained by the scientific and theoretical precepts that instruct those who adhere to the latter.

Philosophy/Basic Understandings/Orientation/Goals

Following Witmer, the clinical tradition is closely associated with helping people by contributing solutions to their psychological problems through the application of assessment methods.

In assigning to the assessor the central role in the assessment process—a role that overshadows that of the armamentarium of instruments—scientific credibility is diminished among those who promote the position of a rigorous, quantitative science, for the professional functioning of the assessor has not been—cannot be—studied with the mathematical precision with which the statistical qualities of tests are scrutinized. While those who seek to help people in the clinical tradition believe that their focus on people issues is superior to the measurement tradition as a means of promoting human welfare, adherents of the measurement tradition are convinced that their method of understanding people is more accurate, and therefore better suited to promote human welfare.

In the clinical tradition, the time-honored commitment to prediction of variously defined behaviors is of less concern than it is to those who subscribe to the measurement tradition. Greater emphasis is placed on understanding—the clinician's insight into the client's problems based on a formulation of relations between these difficulties and the factors that precipitated and sustain them.

More generally, the Longman *Dictionary of Psychology and Psychiatry* (1984) notes that "understanding may refer to the process of discerning the network of relationships existing between a client's behavior and his environment, history, aptitudes, motivation, ideas, feelings, relationships, and modes of expression." Understanding may not be a goal in itself; it may be of greater value as a basis for formulating solutions to the client's problems. Additionally, understanding may make for more effective prediction (Martin, 1967). Holt (1967), however, views understanding from another angle. He suggests that "an empathic sharing, an imaginative penetration into the inner life of another person is at the heart of what we *mean* when we speak of understanding him, far more so than the ability to predict his behavior."

In this orientation, the focus is on the individual. While group norms and how the individual compares with others is of some importance in the data mix that leads to understanding her or him, the clinical tradition emphasizes the *idiographic* (Allport, 1961) or *idiothetic* method (Lamiell, 1981) as a credible scientific alternative to seeking understanding by noting how an individual is different from other individuals (the *nomothetic* method). Lamiell considers that "the problem for a science of personality is that of empirically describing the personalities of individuals, that is, identifying those qualities, attributes, or characteristics which are manifested by individuals at certain levels with some degree of regularity or consistency over time and across situations."

The orientation of the clinical tradition stresses psychological-mindedness and psychological thinking (pp. 32–33). Schafer (1949) pioneered an approach that assigned a lessened role to the statistical basis of diagnosis and to scores, and elevated psychological thinking and interpretation on a case-by-case basis:

> The psychological significance of any one score depends on the context of scores and verbalizations in which it occurs...Scores are not meant to replace psychological thinking; they are designed to facilitate it, and as such they can be relegated to the background when this is warranted by the logic of the problem...The alternative to considering the score the adequate meaningful micro-unit is considering the interpretation the meaningful unit. This approach recognizes that the same score can have different meanings and that the same meaning can be conveyed by different scores. It also recognizes the fact that scores in general do not adequately convey all the implications of a response or a set of responses. This viewpoint, reflecting clinical experience and insights, is applied to building a case against "score-oriented research."
>
> Interpretations rather than scores are the proper units for research. An interpretation may be defined as a prediction from test results that a certain pattern of behavior, thought and feeling will characterize the patient in his everyday life. This prediction can be checked against careful clinical personality examination. If, and only if, the principles of interpretation used are set forth in detail, with thorough elaboration of contexts which indicate this or that personality characteristic—if the cloud of intuition is lifted from the interpretive procedure—then the validity of our procedures can be established.

In the clinical tradition, the subjectivity of the examiner—as well as of the client—is highly valued. Intuition and hunches are recognized by many—not all—clinicians to be of importance in developing case formulations. But attending to personal impressions gained of the client is only part of the process, and these impressions in their raw state cannot be responsibly offered as conclusions. However, impressions gained from observation and interview may profitably be integrated with test data: "Psychological testing and interview techniques complement each other in the assessment of a patient's situation" (Seime, McCauley, & Madsen, 1977).

Sugarman (1981) discusses the use of countertransference as a diagnostic handle. "Why do I feel as I do toward the client?" may be a useful question to ask in the search for diagnostic understanding. Sugarman considers "The examiner's subjective emotional response to the patient" as a valuable data source. Further,

> By integrating the test response paradigm with his own response to the patient...the examiner is more likely to validate the therapist's countertransference. Consequently the therapist will be able to use his countertransference in a therapeutic fashion.

Content (data) goals in the clinical tradition, in general, differ appreciably from the goals of the measurement tradition. Over the years, measurement has tended to focus on relatively circumscribed traits (generally more circumscribed in definition than in behavior)—intelligence, aptitudes, skills, personality characteristics, diagnoses. The clinical tradition commonly is concerned with broader, less sharply, less operationally defined characteristics, such as psychoanalytic or existential concepts: unconscious processes, inner conflicts, ego states, self and object representations, defenses, and personality structure. Latter-day psychometrics, however, most recently computer algorithms, may incorporate aspects of the psychoanalytic domain.

The clinical tradition has tended to be concerned with complexities as opposed to, for example, a relatively simple patterning of trait levels. In the clinical tradition, personality is conceived in terms of a multilevel patterning, multiply and situationally interactive. The goal stemming from this view is the construction of a "working image or model of the person." (Sundberg & Tyler, 1962) The implementation of such a goal is illustrated in the case-focused psychological reports presented in Chapters 9, 10, and 11.

The experiences of the client come in for a good deal of attention among many assessors in the clinical tradition. Lyons (1967) puts forth the proposition that "clinical data consist of...the communication of experiences." Schachtel (1966, 1967) has written extensively on the experiential qualities of the Rorschach:

> It has seemed to me that *experiential data* are at the very center of what we study when we try to understand and interpret a Rorschach record. I believe that this is so whether the clinician interpreting a test is aware of it or not. The nature of the test data can be described as consisting primarily of experiences of the testee while taking the test and of his reactions to these experiences. As you know, Rorschach...wrote that from his test, specifically from the experience type, one could see, not *what*, but *how* a person experiences. If we acknowledge any validity to this claim, we must assume that the test data and the abstractions from these data as represented by the score and the psychogram are based on certain qualities of the testee's way of experiencing. I believe, indeed, that not only the experience type in the technical sense of this term, that is, the relation of the movement to the color responses, but the entire test shows us something of the way in which the testee approaches, avoids or limits and in which he handles his experience of the ink blots in the context of the test task (Schachtel, 1967).

Blatt (1986), looking back over 50 years of personality assessment, emphasizes a shift away from a stimulus-response orientation and the role of perceptual processes, particularly in Rorschach psychology. The study of cognitive processes now occupies center stage. How the individual constructs meaning and reality as a basis for living has become a dominant issue in assessment:

> Interests have begun to center on constructive or representational cognitive processes and how cognitive schemes influence the way individuals conduct their lives and establish relationships...These cognitive schemes express the basic structures through which individuals organize their lives...[their] construction of meaning and their unique interpretations about themselves and their interpersonal and physical world...Psychology has begun to shift from the view that reality is well defined and that we must understand how individuals come to perceive this reality veridically, to a view that reality is constructed

by each individual based on his relative position and assumptions...The task for psychology is to appreciate the individual's constructions of reality and especially the assumptions on which the individual comes to create a conception of reality and construct meaning.

The Practice of Assessment

Activity and flexibility   Just as the outlook of the assessor differs from that of the tester, so does the practice of assessment call for a role different from that taken by the tester in the measurement tradition. The role of the tester is one of constraint, a role prescribed to ensure standardized testing conditions. As noted earlier (p. 37), "the tester does little" (Rosenwald, 1963). The tester's function vis-à-vis the client is largely to present standard stimuli, record responses, and in some situations (such as individual testing), to facilitate or clarify them when necessary. Complementing this essentially passive role, the test taker accepts the task of responding to the stimuli that are presented.

The clinical tradition requires that the psychological assessor, and the client, exercise a more active and flexible role. The assessor may ignore the constraints of standardized testing when the situation requires it, leading to wider latitude in the use of instruments and interaction with the client. The assessor is ruled at least as much by the need to pursue assessment goals individualized to each case, and to follow leads and insights that develop as examination of the client progresses, as he or she is guided by instructions for administration in test manuals. These might be altered at the sacrifice of some accuracy in quantitative data—an IQ, for example—if other information that can be elicited with the use of test stimuli are potentially more meaningful to the purpose of the examination in the opinion of the assessor.

At times, however, such a goal can be pursued without violating standard administration procedures, as when an *inquiry* or *testing the limits* follows usual administration procedures. These strategies are discussed in subsequent contexts. The use and development of *interactive testing* is considered in Chapter 13, where this approach is viewed as a productive supplement or alternative to routine testing.

Recognizing nontest factors   In the test and score emphasis that characterizes the measurement tradition, nontest factors that influence scores are considered an extraneous and unwanted source of variance—influences that lead us astray and contaminate our conclusions. Ziskin (1981), writing from a legal position advises lawyers:

> The point should be hammered home as forcefully as possible that *unless and until adequate methods are provided to control for variation due to examiner and situation effects, the data of the clinical examination are absolutely worthless* (emphasis original).

In the clinical tradition, by contrast, these factors are organic to assessment. Recognizing and interpreting them provide valuable information about the client.

The *process* of responding to test items may be of greater diagnostic value than the responses. Furth and Milgram (1965) illustrate this point through a study of verbal factors in performance on the Similarities subtest of the Wechsler Intelligence Scale for Children. The findings indicate that this subtest is "not an adequate measure of verbal conceptual level in children"—as inspection of the component items would appear to suggest. Rather, the verbal response factor was found to be of "overwhelming importance." Weiner (1957) also showed the influence of response style on intelligence test items. Focusing on an attitude of distrust among test takers responding to Similarities items, it can readily be shown that responses such as "They're not alike" may reflect this attitude more than they are indicators of poor abstract ability.

Masling (1960) reports at length on the influence of situational and interpersonal variables in projective testing. Topics covered include the influence of the method of analysis, the influence of the testing situation, the influence of the examiner, and the influence of the subject. The latter, an understudied area of clinical interaction, has been shown to be a nontest factor that affects the assessor's interpretations (Masling, 1957).

Masling's (1960) conclusion holds far-reaching implications for the practice of psychological assessment:

> The procedure that many clinicians hoped would serve as an X ray proves, on close examination, to function also as a mirror, reflecting impartially S, E, the situation and their interactions. This need not be a cause for despair, except for those who feel that E and situational influences contaminate a protocol. These influences are not sources of error, however, but indications of adaptation to the task. One reason for the poor record of blind analysis as a procedure for validating projective devices is that this method can utilize only a fraction of the material available in a protocol. Instead of trying to eliminate interpersonal and situational influence E might better make a more thorough search of his own attitudes and of S's attitudes toward the test and the situation (Leventhal, Rosenblatt, Gluck, & Slepian, 1958). The interpersonal situation "is not an evil. It should not be striven against. As in psychoanalytic technique, this relationship must be regarded as inevitable, as a particularly significant influence on the patient's productions, and as a possible gold mine of material for interpretation" (Schafer, 1954, p. 6).

WHEN IS A TEST NOT A TEST?

Observations such as those of Masling (1960) and Furth and Milgram (1965) suggest that in addition to, or instead of, measuring what they purport to measure, psychological instruments may contribute to the assessment of factors they do not purport to measure. We cannot take on faith that a test of X measures X or only X. The test may deliberately be used to assess dimensions other than X. Singer (1977b), for example, reports on the use of interaction testing with the Rorschach as a transaction for exploring aspects of interpersonal verbal communication. Singer (1968) and Klopfer (1984a) describe a *consensus Rorschach* as a diagnostic approach to the assessment of interpersonal transactions. Other innovative test uses are presented in Chapter 13.

There are numerous examples of using tests in the "less of a test" mode (Korchin & Schuldberg, 1981). Employing the Rorschach as an interview is probably the most prevalent application of the alternative use of a psychological instrument—alternative in the sense of departing from what once was the only accepted approach to its use. Zubin, Eron, and Schumer (1965) are closely identified with advocating that the only justified use of the Rorschach is as an interview method and not as a psychometric instrument. The Rorschach, to these authors, is "an interview—an interview under the veil of inkblots." Those who use the Rorschach this way sometimes refer to their practice as a qualitative approach, as focusing on content, as application of clinical judgment, or as following an idiographic route to understanding personality.

Zubin, Eron, and Schumer explain their advocacy not only on psychometric limitations of the Rorschach, but also on the power of the interview method:

> New developments in the interview itself are fast turning it into a scientific tool, and since the interview in the last analysis is still the basis for personality evaluation, no test today can rise above it. If we obtain objective criteria via the interview for classification and evaluation of personality, perhaps such criteria may serve as a basis for the validation of tests. But without an anchored interview, we float aimlessly in the sea of personality without compass or rudder.

Capitalizing on the strength of the Rorschach as an interview,

> its correct evaluation, like the correct evaluation of any interview, depends on its content and the characteristic ways of thinking which it reveals. If we provide scales for analyzing this content, we shall be well on the way toward clarifying many of the present-day contradictions, and obtain a better perspective on personality.

Aronow and Reznikoff (1973), in a summarization of numerous book reviews pertinent to the Rorschach, reach conclusions consistent with the above. Focusing on attitudes expressed about the instrument and to aspects of its use, these authors reported as a widespread belief that there is too much emphasis on scoring. With Zubin et al., they suggest that the future utilization of the Rorschach will be as a standardized interview.

In a later paper, Aronow, Reznikoff, and Rauchway (1979) conclude that the Rorschach yields poor psychometric data: "The Rorschach provides both poor psychometric data as seen by the researcher and rich idiographic data as seen by the clinician." They propose attending to its nomothetic properties, perhaps along the line of doing research with psychometric instruments such as the Holtzman Inkblot Technique (HIT) (Holtzman, Thorpe, Swartz, & Herron, 1961) as one possible way of enhancing the Rorschach product. They also view as promising Exner's (1974, 1978, 1986) *Comprehensive System* approach to the Rorschach.

A second course of action considers making improvements to the current prevalent idiographic use of the Rorschach, which Aronow et al. present as follows:

> It is our belief that clinicians use the Rorschach test primarily for the idiographic information that it provides, as evidenced by the fact that the HIT, clearly a superior psychometric inkblot test, has not by any means supplanted the Rorschach in the clinician's test battery. Consistent with this proposition, Potkay (1971), Powers and

Hamlin (1957), and Symonds (1955) have found that clinicians rely primarily on the raw verbalizations of Rorschach responses in arriving at interpretations. The findings of Wade and Baker (1977) that clinicians rely on "personalized evaluation procedures" when interpreting projective tests and that high projective test users consider testing an "insightful diagnostic process" rather than an objective technical skill would also be consistent with our view of the primacy of idiographic data in Rorschach testing. This would make more understandable such reports as that of Wade and Baker (1977) on the relative indifference of clinicians to the accumulated negative findings on the (nomothetically based) reliability and validity of inkblot and other projective test scales.

The results of a survey by Exner and Exner (1972) are consistent with the impressions of others who have noted that the dominant approach to Rorschach interpretation is clinical—or at least that it does not follow good psychometric practice. Approximately one out of five Rorschachers who responded to the survey reported that they do not score responses, while most of the remainder of the sample—four out of five—indicated that they "personalize" their scoring. Further, "about 19% indicate they weigh quantitative data most heavily in interpretation. Twenty-five per cent weigh content most heavily in interpretation and 56% indicate that they weigh both equally in their interpretive approach." Sound norms, if available, would have diminished utility when brought to bear under the circumstances revealed by this survey.

A number of our instruments, the Rorschach included, have long been known as *techniques—projective techniques*—in preference to *tests*. Murstein (1968) stresses the importance of the distinction. A *technique*, he notes, "is an aid in arriving at information...and its keynote is flexibility." While some, particularly research-oriented clinical psychologists, may consider projective instruments to be tests, this conception goes contrary to the raison d'être of projective techniques:

> When we consider projective techniques as *tests*, we cause some of our projective forefathers to experience a dyspeptic moment or two because the original *cause celebre* of projective techniques was to free psychology from its preoccupation with numbers and have it instead embrace the whole individual.

The Rapaportian position (Rapaport, Gill, & Schafer (1946)—set forth below—anticipated much of the "less of a test" concept of the Rorschach, and particularly of its use as an interview technique. Along with the use of quantification, great stress was also placed on qualitative features and verbalizations, along with the suggestion that scoring can lend itself to misuse:

> It is to a large extent inevitable that further refinements of scoring lead the tester, and especially the novice, to the "dream-book" type of interpretation. These refinements also obscure the fact that scoring categories are merely aids to facilitate an appraisal of what has happened in the course of the test, and that a "correct" set of scores is not an end in itself.

Exner (1986) clarifies for his readers the psychometric characteristics of the Rorschach, while addressing specifically the criticisms of Zubin et al., and others who regard the Rorschach similarly:

To some extent, critics such as Zubin have been correct in the assumption that all Rorschach "scores" do not meet some of the psychometric characteristics that are common in most psychological tests. For instance, many scores are not normally distributed, making the application of parametric statistics at best, difficult. Others are valid but not temporally consistent, and some have levels of temporal consistency or reliability that account for less than one-half of the variance. Moreover, the test is open-ended; that is, all protocols are not of the same length. Even when the total number of responses is the same for two records, it is highly unlikely that the distribution of codes or scores to each of the 10 cards will be the same. This is both an asset and a liability for the test. It is a liability because it restricts the full usefulness of normative comparisons and thus makes for greater difficulty in establishing useful normative data (Cronbach, 1949). Holtzman, et al. (1961) pointed out, "Providing a subject with only ten inkblots and permitting him to give as many or as few responses as he wishes characteristically results in a set of unreliable scores with sharply skewed distributions." The Cronbach-Holtzman criticism concerning the variability of the number of responses cannot be denied, but they erred in suggesting that this makes the test psychometrically unapproachable. It is quite true that this composite of *measurement* problems constitutes a difficult problem for the statistician, and a virtual nightmare for the psychometric purist, but none have been unresolvable in the context of contemporary statistical methods plus the use of reasonably large samples of data.

Exner further points out that a misunderstanding of the Rorschach rests on how the instrument is basically conceptualized, and also by "misunderstanding and overgeneralization of the term *score*." *Coding* would be a more appropriate term in "a special Rorschach language," "like a system of shorthand." He considers that "The Rorschach scores that are crucial to interpretation are the frequency scores for each of the codes and the numerous percentages, ratios, and other metrically useful derivations that are calculated from them. Collectively, they represent the *Structural Summary* of the record."

THE CLINICAL TRADITION: THE MODERN PHASE

Although Witmer was the founder of the clinical tradition in psychology, we must agree with Holt (1968) that clinical psychology prior to the end of World War II had little impact that can be recalled; how it was practiced, for the most part, is difficult to reconstruct:

> (Clinical psychology) was in a real sense a prehistoric era. Our science and profession might fairly be said to have had its true beginning after the war [World War II]; surely the numbers of clinical psychologists were very small and their influence slight before the heroic efforts to expand training that began in the 1940's.

The Rapaport-Schafer, or Menninger-Riggs tradition goes far, far beyond Witmer, with an emphasis on personality issues, advances in assessment practices linked to instruments not available to Witmer, to extant and developing personality theory, and the creation of test theory that made this new approach possible.

The Clinical Tradition and the Role of Statistics

The clinical tradition is built on tests, albeit most of those used in the Rapaport-Schafer research (Rapaport, Gill, & Schafer, 1945, 1946), and by subsequent generations of clinicians (Sweeney, Clarkin, & Fitzgibbon, 1987), cannot boast strong psychometric properties (the Rorschach, for example, or the TAT, or the Sorting Test). At the very beginning of the Rapaport, Gill, and Schafer work, the following basic departures from the measurement tradition were stressed:

> In all tests, we indicated not a mechanically standard procedure of administration, but one which creates optimal conditions for the patient...
>
> No attempt was made to proceed with the testing of all patients in the same manner. The requirement of "identity of conditions of testing" was interpreted to be a requirement for the tester to adapt himself to the specific characteristics of the patient.

The general attitude to statistics reads:

> We...did not hesitate to call on experience and reasoning not supported by statistics...we felt it better to present what experience teaches than to by-pass it for lack of statistical evidence.

In another passage, the authors indicate some respect for statistics, but suggest that there are limitations to the method:

> We did not take the usual attitude that...statistical work is useless and unnecessary. We applied statistical procedures because we believe that they put clinically discovered relationships into easily communicable and reasonably convincing form. We did not, however take the stand that what one cannot prove statistically is not significant or not true.

All of the above is incorporated in the view that the assessor is the principal diagnostic instrument in the clinical armamentarium (pp. 11, 197). Holt (1968) summarizes the attitude to tests and testers, and the relation between them, by those who adhere to the clinical tradition: "Neither testing nor interviewing is any better or more valid than the interpretive intelligence through which the resulting data are filtered."

Hallmarks of the Clinical Tradition

Rational underpinnings and test rationale Departure from strict psychometric principles and procedures, a prominent feature of the clinical tradition, is but one of its defining parameters. Test rationale, test administration, scoring, and interpretation all differ significantly from psychometric doctrine. We must not dwell, however, on what the clinical tradition is not, but on its innovative approaches that give it a distinct identity. These are spelled out in a number of works, particularly Rapaport, Gill, and Schafer (1945, 1946), Schafer (1967, 1989), Rapaport (1950), and Holt (1968).

The clinical tradition rests on clinical rather than statistical propositions. First to be noted is an emphasis on theory–personality theory (particularly psychoanalytic ego-psychology) and test theory. Together these converge to form *clinical assessment theory*, a set of understandings, principles, guidelines, and procedures.

Clinical assessment theory is closely identified with Freud and developments in the Freudian tradition, especially with Freud's later structural theory (the id, ego, superego conceptualization). The Rapaport-Schafer approach accents ego-psychological functioning, thought processes (together with inferences about personality organization), and impulse-defense configurations. Dynamic formulation is assigned a secondary role by Rapaport and Schafer, although individual assessors may be intrigued by this component of personality.

Rationale of tests and test responses Test theory is extensively set forth in *rationales* for testing; that is, "a systematic linkage of the test-responding process (and its products) to a theory of personality, thought organization, and psychopathology" (Holt, 1968). In this orientation, the value to be gained from understanding the psychological processes that give rise to responses exceeds that of the responses themselves and the scores that may be attached to them. Rapaport developed rationales for tests as a whole, for segments of tests—such as Wechsler subtests, and for response categories—Whole Rorschach responses or the Human Movement Rorschach response, for example. A key element of rationale is the role of the *projective hypothesis*, the axiom that every response made by a client to the test stimuli or to the assessor is a reflection, or projection of his or her private world. The projective hypothesis is a versatile concept that can be employed both with projective instruments and with what were designed as psychometric tools, the Wechsler intelligence scales, for example. The latter, however, tend to be weak as projective instruments since they are highly structured and tend to elicit conventional or stereotyped responses.

To follow the development of a rationale for various subtests can be instructive and provides a background for developing insights based on clients' test performance. Consider the Information subtest of the Wechsler. After reading the Rapaport, Gill, and Schafer (1945) account of the development of a rationale for this subtest, it is difficult to consider Information as simply a measure of how much a person knows. People are conceived in the Rapaportian rationale as having a natural intellectual endowment, which, in interaction with an "educational environment," schooling, and cultural factors, leads quite naturally to the acquisition of information. Opposing this tendency may be various impeding factors, setbacks, and the onset of deterioration (since the ability to respond correctly to Information items is dependent on memory). Severe anxiety may have the effect of the individual being unable to recollect information—a situation called "temporary inefficiency," and repression can also put information beyond retrieval in the test situation. Or, psychotic distortion of reality can lead to inferior responses with a score value of zero. In considering these various possibilities, the assessor is able to develop hypotheses concerning the client's intellect, personality, and pathology, if this is a factor.

All diagnostic hypotheses growing out of the Rapaport-Schafer research have not been supported by subsequent investigation. Piedmont, Sokolove, and Fleming (1989), in a test of 12 Rapaportian hypotheses based on the relation of Wechsler subtest scores to one another, found support for only two of these. Hypotheses based on Wechsler patterns, then, are not suitable for developing valid algorithms or decision rules. The point is well taken. However, these hypotheses were not established as a basis for developing decision rules. They were meant to be clinical hypotheses in battery interpretations, to be considered in combination with other data (p. 114).

The viability of Rapaportian hypotheses is analagous to the present status of Freud. Numerous Freudian hypotheses lack support or have encountered withering critiques, and Freudianism has been extensively modified. Nevertheless, Freud continues as a central force in psychology, and as a reference point for alternate theories and hypotheses. Similarly, the Rapaport tradition occupies a secure position in the assessment enterprise.

The development of a rationale for Rorschach responses in the Rapaport-Schafer tradition can be an elaborate process. The formulation of a rationale for the Form (F) response, for example, is worth noting. In addition to clinical experience regarding the meaning of F, the Rapaport, Gill, and Schafer text (1946) unfolds a rationale stemming from a consideration of cultural influences in bringing about this response and theoretical (ego-psychological) principles as they have implications for its meaning. Empirical findings that are consistent with the rationale thus created are also presented. Elements of Rorschach test theory complete the rationale of the Form response. These have to do with the interrelated roles—"cogwheeling" was Rapaport's term—of association and perceptual organization, processes that seek explanation in psychoanalytic theory and Gestalt psychology, respectively:

> The form level of a response indicates the extent to which there has been a balanced interplay or cogwheeling of the perceptual and associative processes. The subject's mode of functioning should allow for the delay necessary for a perceptual articulation of the inkblot, for an initiation of associative processes on the basis of the initial perceptual impressions, for a consequent reorganization of the perceptual material to obtain a congruence with the possibilities offered by the associative processes, and finally for a critical appraisal of the response which came forth; otherwise the form-level of the response will be poor (Rapaport, Gill, & Schafer, 1946).

Concerning cultural influences, the Rapaport, Gill, and Schafer work suggests that the primitive and childlike mode of perception is undifferentiated and that formal and affective features are fused. Further, their responses are determined by affective features and appraisal of the usefulness of what they perceive. Culture alters this basic perceptual mode in terms of the formal and the objective. We come to guide our lives on a shared understanding of what the world is about, less on the basis of highly personal understandings, feelings, and needs. The consensual F response is an indicator of a shared approach to understanding the world.

The F response may be further understood from an ego-psychological point of view. The reasoning behind this conclusion invokes Hartmann's concept of a conflict-free sphere of the ego—secondary process—a sphere free of intrusions from the unconscious and disrupting affects. F responses, then, represent a freedom of conscious intellectual expression ("This looks like a bear *because* it is shaped like a bear."), an autonomy of perceptual and thought processes. The fact of a significant number of responses based on Form perception, then, is evidence of control over unwanted impulse expression, the ability to inhibit impulses and to delay gratification. Conversely, few Fs in a record may be an indication that the subject is impulsive and will have difficulty in delaying gratification. Rapaport, Gill, and Schafer (1946) present data in support of such a relationship, with subjects who show especially good Form responses also showing the greatest capacity for impulse delay.

In addition to scores, the assessment tradition recognizes context, client verbalizations and other behaviors, assessor-client interactions, and test content as assessment data. Masling's (1960) position (p. 104) on the role—the influence and value—of situational and interpersonal variables in assessment nicely exemplifies a pervasive attitude of those who function in the clinical tradition. An early statement by Schafer (1989) on the interpersonal relationship in testing and on the "real test situation" indicates how broad is the scope of variables that provide raw data—other than test scores—for psychological interpretation:

> Analyzing the interpersonal relationship and the real test situation may take us out to, or beyond, the borders of "objective" test interpretation—in the narrow and, I believe, superficial sense of "objective" test interpretation. But if we mean, as we should, to track down the origins and vicissitudes of the patient's test responses, we must deal with the total situation in which the responses occur. The inkblot alone, the digit span sequence alone, the picture of a boy and a violin alone, do not totally define the stimulus situation existing at any moment. There are many other more or less uncontrolled but more or less identifiable stimuli in the situation. There are larger situational and interpersonal meanings that surround and invade the simple test stimuli.

The clinical behavior of clients has, of course, long been recognized by clinicians to be a valuable source of data. In the Mental Status Examination, the mainstay of psychological examination in psychiatry, the examiner capitalizes on what he or she can learn from observing such variables as appearance, manner, speech, and interpersonal exchanges with the client. These observations may reveal such characteristics of clinical interest as hostility, submissiveness, manipulativeness, repression, or passive-aggressiveness, and often do so more efficiently than tests alone, and in a more lifelike stance. For years, many psychologists have (some still do), in the manner of a tester, dutifully and conscientiously presented their clinical observations in the psychological report—to be interpreted by others to whom these data are secondhand and who are not in a position to interpret them in conjunction with test data. This is the function of the psychological assessor in the clinical tradition.

In the clinical tradition, nonpsychometric data are coaxed (or "milked") to give up much more information than was ever envisioned by the tests' authors. Rapaport, Gill, and Schafer (1946), for example, identify 14 categories of "deviant verbalizations" on the Rorschach, many of them typical of schizophrenic patients or of persons suffering with various other disorders. Thus, the response "A rabbit's head with snakes coming out of its eyes" given to Card X, D10 (Exner, 1986) is a "fabulized combination" and probably was offered by a schizophrenic person. "Two people, one male, one female" given to the identical D2 areas of Card VII is a "peculiar verbalization" observed in a hysteric patient. Holt (1977), in a chapter on primary process manifestations, presents a classification of both primary process and secondary process variables.

The method of *Inquiry* is a powerful tool when skillfully used. In psychometrics, inquiry is used to elicit sufficient additional information, beyond that originally offered by the client, to permit accurate scoring of the response. This is true for the Rorschach in psychometric usage (e.g., Exner, 1986) when the examiner must seek to determine (for example) whether a response should be scored color-primary/form-secondary (CF), or whether a response should be scored pure form (F) or as animal movement (FM)—a determination that often must be made when the client sees the familiar bat on Card I. Similarly, with tests such as those in the Wechsler group, clients may be asked to explain their responses. On the WAIS-R, for example, a client may indicate, to a Comprehension item, that people who are born deaf usually can't talk because they can't hear. Many who respond this way do not really understand the connection between deafness and inability to speak and merit zero credit for this response, while others do, in fact, understand the relation. Hence the issue may be resolved by a query such as "How do you mean?"

In the clinical tradition, by contrast, a major purpose of *Inquiry* is to elicit substantive information concerning the client. It is a process that demands flexibility, good judgment, alertness, and sometimes ingenuity. Commonly, inquiry is indicated to better understand a client's responses, but often it is used to follow up leads and elicit more information. The client may simply be asked to clarify. Or the assessor may request, "Can you tell me more about that?" The client may be gently prodded to give more information with such statements as "You're doing fine," or, as to a TAT story, "How does it turn out?" or "How does she feel about that?" Or, queries may drop all pretense of disguise—as having the client speak through a TAT character—and ask such questions as "Have you ever had a similar experience?," or, "Do you know anyone like that?" But at times the client will beat you to the punch: "This is me," or "This is the story of my life!"

Open-ended items can lead to rich payoffs, even with minimum inquiry. Responses to sentence completion roots can be the springboard for helping a client to reveal information. "Can you explain that?," or, "Can you tell me more about that?" may be all that is necessary. Inquiry (query) in the following examples is indicated by a "?":

> My sex life...is terrible. ? I've never been with a woman. I wouldn't know what to do.
> My greatest fault is...my experiences. ? My mother seducing me.
> Most of my friends don't know that I am afraid of...me. ? The voices. They keep telling me to kill myself. And I will.

Inquiry is also profitably applied to responses to structured test items—such as MMPI items. A number of these have been designated as "Critical Items" (see Koss & Butcher, 1973; Graham, 1987 for listings of such items). "Inquiry Items" might be a more suitable term, since significant data might be extracted from following up on items such as:

At times I feel I am no good at all.
There is something wrong with my mind.
If people had not had it in for me I would have been much more successful.
Someone has it in for me.[1]

It is my impression that *students do not inquire enough,* and that as a result much valuable diagnostic ore goes unmined.

Content that is elicited in the form of symbols and themes can be of greater diagnostic value than clear-cut, readily scored responses. Thus, reacting primarily to the Dl2 area of Rorschach Card VI (Exner, 1986), sometimes identified as a vagina, a visibly disturbed male client blurts out, "This is something that scares a man!" He cannot explain further and the assessor tactfully backs off. Another client, a 24-year-old male who spontaneously volunteers that he is a homosexual, looks at the same area on Card VI and complains, "I want to look at this bottom part, but my eyes keep going to the top," indicating D6 (an area that frequently elicits phallic references). He perhaps is not as fully accepting of his homosexuality as he proclaims.

The Dd26 and associated detail in the general "female genital area" (clinical jargon) of Card VII can also give rise to some interesting responses. Consider three of them offered by male clients. The first sees "a dark, mysterious, forbidding cave." Here is a sex conflict that perhaps should be worked through in therapy. The second client also is conflicted about sex, but the situation is somewhat different. He also reports a cave, this one blocked by huge icicles. The frustration of the third client, responding to the vertical lines and surrounding gray of the Dd27 area, again, is qualitatively different from that of the other two. It is sad to hear the response, in the context of a personal reference: "These are the gates of heaven. They are locked. I can't get in."

All five of these examples can contribute to more focused interpretations than can generally be gained from test scores or patterns. Each of them can lead to more specific conclusions than, say, "sex conflicts," "poor gender-identity," "inadequate sense of maleness," or "poor heterosexual relations." There is much grist for the therapist's mill in the clients' responses.

The Rapaport-Schafer tradition contributes another diagnostically valuable qualitative approach to evaluating test responses in the companion notions of decreased distance and increased distance in manner of responding. When distance is lost, the client reacts to test stimuli—an inkblot, for example—as something much more than the test stimulus that it is. The subject may evidence various emotional reactions such as visible or reported anger, fright, euphoria, sexual excitement, or there

---

[1]Minnesota Multiphasic Personality Inventory. Copyright © the University of Minnesota 1942, 1943 (renewed 1990). Reprinted by permission of the University of Minnesota Press.

may be an alteration in the subject's mode of responding to the Rorschach (for example, significant change in response time, in an increase or decrease in number of responses, and so on) as noted in *shock*. The client (mentioned previously), for example, who was frightened by an inkblot, obviously was reacting to the stimulus as something more than an inkblot. He evidently perceived the stimulus (unconsciously) as a female genital, which in turn activated deep-seated conflicts. Increase in distance, by contrast, occurs when connection between the stimulus and response is not evident. The response "a bunch of fish" given to Rorschach Card VII obviously gives little indication that the test subject was attending to the blot that was presented.

Another major contribution of the Rapaport-Schafer tradition is the establishment of the centrality of the battery approach. Holt (1968) considers the routine use of a battery of tests as "the second most distinctive contribution to diagnostic testing"—secondary to the role in testing that Rapaport assigned to theory. The use of a battery has the advantage over single tests in that batteries have the potential to tap various personality components in the distinctive idioms of the instruments employed.

Holt (1968) presents the essence of the battery approach thus:

(a) No single test proves to yield a diagnosis in all cases, or to be in all cases correct in the diagnosis it indicates.
(b) Psychological maladjustment, whether severe or mild, may encroach on any of several of the functions tapped by these tests, leaving other functions absolutely or relatively unimpaired.

He further makes a case for the battery approach in terms of some basics of probability and validity:

> Every diagnostic conclusion is a hypothesis...and it behooves the tester to test all hypotheses that occur to him as he goes over his data, buttressing his final conclusions as well as possible by a multiplicity of converging probabilities. If the content of one TAT story suggests a hypothesis, only weak confirmation is supplied by the emergence of similar content in another story, because there is little independence of approach to the construct in question. If the subject's test behaviors, or formal aspects of his stories, lead to the same hypothesis, the probability that it is correct is more usefully enhanced; while convergence of interpretations arising from different tests and different types of interpretive principles is the soundest basis of all for the tester's having enough confidence in his point to include it in his report.

SCHAFER ON THE RAPAPORT-SCHAFER TRADITION

Originally scheduled as a third volume in the Rapaport, Gill, and Schafer (1945, 1946) set, Schafer (1967) published as a sequel to the earlier works *The Clinical Application of Psychological Tests*. In addition to the major portion of the book consisting of a discussion of personality characteristics and pathological tendencies, and how to assess them with tests, Schafer presents a review of "the sources and implications of test responses, and with the nature of the process of diagnostic reasoning from test results."

Thus focused, Schafer sets forth seven propositions as organic to the clinical tradition:

First Proposition *Clinical psychological testing starts with the proposition that a person's distinctive style of thinking is indicative of ingrained features of his character make-up.* There are three components to this proposition. In addition to the central role of an individual's *thinking* in understanding the client's personality, we must look particularly to the person's thinking as it may reveal those enduring modes of personality functioning we call *character*, with emphasis on the *defenses* that do so much to define individuality. Schafer mentions in this context such commonly observed defenses as repression, denial, projection, and intellectualization. "The selective responses to stimulation," Schafer suggests, "is the attempt to guarantee that life situations will be so perceived or organized as to preclude the entrance into consciousness of especially disturbing material."

Second Proposition *Responses to the various test items...are, almost entirely, verbalized end-products of thought processes initiated by these items.* Scores are accorded an appreciably lower position than they hold in psychometrics. Scores are abstractions that permit the making of interindividual and intraindividual comparisons. But to rely on scores does "violence to the nature of the raw material." Further, "The scores do not communicate the responses in full," a conclusion Schafer readily establishes by showing how two vastly different responses to the same test item may earn the same score. Test responses may disclose not only more than the individual wishes to reveal but also more than can be accommodated by a score. Further, when only scores are available the assessor does not have access to the verbalizations that are expressions of the client's thinking.

Third Proposition *The subject must be made to think in a variety of problem situations to enable the examiner to distinguish the pervasive, fundamental or pathological aspects of his characteristic adjustment efforts.* This proposition asserts the central role of the battery approach, as discussed in various contexts, particularly on pp. 110, and 114.

Fourth Proposition *Two general aspects of thinking must be studied intensively; first, thinking that primarily reflects past achievements and second, thinking that primarily reflects creative applications of assets and liabilities to new problems.* Typically, there is linkage between past and present performance, though different emphases in approach over time may indicate different adjustment problems. Radical discontinuity, when observed, may reflect the acquisition of a pathological adjustment mode. Schafer offers here the example of the schizophrenic who premorbidly relied on such defenses as repression and obsessive thinking. He suggests also how various tests may be approached in terms of what they reveal about the past or present. The responses given to the Rorschach typically have reference to past achievements, but are also valued as a source of information on a subject's "creative application of assets and liabilities to new problems." These in combination with Wechsler data can define intellectual-emotional adjustment patterns that effectively point up such pathological styles as those that characterize hysterics and obsessives.

Fifth Proposition *Certain aspects of the test results indicate the effectiveness of the characteristic efforts at adjustment.* In this proposition Schafer cites various forms of maladaptive test performance—such as emotional lability and rigid approach—as failures of adjustment efforts and as indicators of pathologies that are characteristic of the failure of the person's defenses.

Sixth Proposition *Often the formal test indications of the same characteristics vary in different cases, and often the same formal patterns have different implications in different contexts.* Context is the key term here. Scores vary not only inasmuch as they might reflect pathological trends, for example, but also as a result of a number of intellectual, personality, and situational variables. We will go astray if we assert that all patients in a particular diagnostic category will score high or low on some test, scale, or score variable. Single responses, such as the Rorschach response "a church built on a butterfly" can have strong diagnostic implications, but in general, the assessor must look at a larger picture, and be attentive to diagnostic indicators as these converge toward increasingly obvious conclusions. The better the clinical judgment brought to bear in this approach, the more justifiable it is to find support for one's practice in this proposition.

Seventh Proposition *Interpretation and diagnostic conclusions are two relatively discrete parts of test analysis, although the latter are quite dependent on the former.* The important distinction between an *interpretation* and a *diagnostic conclusion* is most readily made by defining the two. An interpretation is a statement that predicts behavior (or thinking). Psychological reports are full of interpretations. A diagnostic conclusion is a statement that an individual's behavior (including thinking) meets the criteria for a classification set forth in a nosological system—such as the DSM-III-R. Clinicians often have difficulty in agreeing on a diagnosis, either because they employ different diagnostic criteria, or use faulty diagnostic reasoning. However, Schafer suggests that the psychological report needn't offer a formal diagnosis.

HOLT ON RAPAPORT-SCHAFER

Holt (1968) summarizes the Rapaport-Schafer tradition in eight propositions that "are applicable to diagnostic work whether carried out by psychiatrist or psychologist, with the aid of social-historical or of test data." A number of these are, expectedly, similar to Schafer's, but in toto, the eight propositions spell out principles that are a source of additional understanding.

First Proposition *Diagnosis is not classification but construction of a verbal model of personality in adaptive difficulty, or suffering from some malfor-*

mation or dilapidation. Holt, in harmony with the practice of those who developed and follow the Rapaport-Schafer tradition, views diagnosis largely in the manner set forth in Schafer's seventh proposition (mentioned previously). He puts distance between his use of the term and its classical, nosological meaning—such as DSM diagnoses are predicated upon. Such diagnosis, in itself, tells relatively little about a person. Holt eschews "sterile categorizing" and mere labeling. However, he regards nosology as of some importance, specifically as providing orienting points (see his third proposition). On this basis, "*a diagnosis is not a sufficient classification but a necessary component of a personality description.*" (emphasis original) Diagnosis is better used as an acceptable expression for a case formulation that describes an individual in words and incorporates an "individual model" or "an organized picture of personality." Such a diagnosis should be capable of generating predictions on how individuals will perform in specified situations—in psychoanalytic therapy, for example. This is a common usage of *diagnosis* and *diagnostic* in Rapaport, Gill, and Schafer's *Diagnostic Psychological Testing*, and also in the widely used terms *psychodiagnosis* and *psychodiagnostic*.

Second Proposition *Such a verbal model must be hierarchically organized, by means of intrapersonal comparisons or quantifications of the variables used.* Rapaport, Gill, and Schafer (1946) stress a need for interpersonal and intrapersonal comparison—a quantitative exercise. Does the clinical tradition, then, embrace the same tenets as the measurement tradition? Not at all. Although Rapaport-Schafer insist that meaningful verbal communication calls for a quantitative means of comparison based on "an exhaustive scoring system," Holt observes that assessment "in the tradition that Rapaport started" is semiquantitative and speaks of the need to make "an effort at ordinal quantification through the use of intensifying and qualifying language." Clinicians recognize how common are such characteristics as passive-aggressiveness, compulsivity, anxiety, and hostility. Adjectives such as "severe," "very," "intense" put these in perspective; for example, "severe anxiety."

Third Proposition *Typological concepts, like diagnoses, are useful as reference points to aid the description of personalities by means of interpersonal comparison.* In this proposition Holt further defines, in a neat metaphor, the role of formal diagnoses in personality description. These are not addresses on buildings, but landmarks. They are more or less approximations to real events and to the real points of interest—they identify the street, if not the address; the church, if not the pew. They help to "point" the clinician in the right direction, and thus are orienting points. Rapaport spoke of the helpfulness of describing a personality in terms of the "next of kind," as a way of providing orientation. A person may be "next of kind" to one with histrionic personality disorder—inasmuch as (s)he is immature, naive, and self-dramatizing. Noting additional features characteristic of, say, dysthymia might help to round out the picture, or a third orienting point might also be helpful. In the same manner, classical types, such as introversion, may be employed.

Fourth Proposition *The central emphasis of diagnosis is structural, using a typology of ego structures based mainly on defenses; dynamic and genetic considerations are important but secondary.* This proposition embodies the ego-psychological basis of the clinical tradition, with its emphasis on personality structure. In a psychopathological setting—such as spawned and nurtured the tradition—the role of defenses and adaptation is obvious, but these features of personality structure are also basic to understanding a broad range of persons in many life situations. While genetic sequences and the strength of motives may indeed be secondary in a pathological context, they can be of relatively more importance elsewhere—such as in research settings.

Fifth Proposition *The diagnostic process begins with the identification and measurement of variables by empathic observation and primary inference directly from clinical data (including tests); the clinician then examines the patterning of these variables, and by reference to empirical knowledge about what goes with what and to relevant theory, he makes secondary inferences of a more constructional kind.* Holt conceptualizes the diagnostic process essentially in two parts. The first step is to make *primary inferences*—which consist of any number of variables that are not particularly related—intelligence level, the ability to anticipate social behaviors, anxiety level, dependency motives. The source of conclusions about such variables come from the clinician's bag of tricks—skill in (empathic) observation, a knowledge of empirically established relations between test variables and personality variables, or personal experience of what test scores or manner of approaching test problems "mean." Thus a high Rorschach F+% may lead a psychologist to conclude that the client has good reality testing, or increased reaction time to Rorschach Card VI may contribute to a hypothesis that the client is sexually conflicted. *Secondary inference* is Holt's term to encompass the clinician's efforts to sift through and organize the primary inferences into a meaningful personality picture.

Sixth Proposition *The clinical usefulness of a personality description is enhanced if it includes both characterological and symptomatic diagnosis.* Character refers to an individual's enduring style of adaptation, and a characterological diagnosis may be made in the absence of a symptomatic picture that merits a recognized diagnosis. The (characterological) adaptational style, however, may to an extent resemble a full-blown symptomatic disorder. Holt points out, for example, that "schizothymic personalities" and "cyclothymic personalities," who function in the normal range, can decompensate to more extreme conditions to the point of schizophrenia and manic-depressive psychosis. This observation, Holt notes, also recognizes that there are adaptive and maladaptive variants of ego structures—the difference between a hard-working, careful, conscientious person, and a "hand washer."

Seventh Proposition *The diagnostician should try to assess the degree to which aspects of personality play an adaptive role and are well compensated, as against being maladaptive (decompensated).* To merely take note of the defensive structure is not sufficient. To simply pronounce that a client's principal defenses are repression and intellectualization tells little about the quality of her or his adaptation. It is of the greatest importance to know how well these defenses "work." A person who resorts rather heavily—but not too heavily—to the defenses of repression and intellectualization—can function well and be a productive member of the community. But when overused or used inappropriately, the individual can be distressed and ineffectual.

Eighth Proposition *The ultimate purpose of diagnosis is to facilitate understanding and individualized predictions about the behavior of uniquely organized persons. Since a broad range of possible predictions may be clinically called for, the diagnostic description must cover most of the important aspects of personality.* Psychological reports should not be written as an exercise to demonstrate knowledge of people in general or of various types of personality. (Many reports read as though they were written this way, though they perhaps were not formulated with this purpose.) "Individualized" and "uniquely organized" are the key terms of this proposition. Holt suggests that usually appropriate topics for the psychological report are aspects of intellectual functioning, defenses and other structural features, motives, affects, object relations, identity, self-esteem, genetic hypotheses and reconstructions, and pathological trends. Issues of content and focus are emphasized in this book in the interest of selecting content that is appropriate to the case under consideration and maximizing the individuality of each client.

THE CURRENT STATUS OF THE CLINICAL TRADITION

Psychological assessment following Rapaport-Schafer merits to be called a tradition inasmuch as it follows a broad conceptualization and approach laid down many years ago. It is not a tradition in the sense of being static, orthodox, or doctrinaire. The tradition was born in research and innovation, and research and innovation continue as a cornerstone of the tradition.

Some observers, however, stress a continuity of practice in the clinical tradition. Thus, Sweeney, Clarkin, and Fitzgibbon (1987) are of the opinion that "there has been a resistance to change in testing practice." The source of this conclusion is cited in findings that "indicated that psychologists typically continue to use the standard test battery developed by Rapaport, Gill, and Schafer in the 1940s."

Lovitt (1988) takes issue with the significance of these quoted survey findings, and builds a contrary thesis to support his impression that the Rapaport-Schafer tradition very much continues to evolve. He criticizes the conclusion of Sweeney et al., who note that "the original standard test battery developed by [Rapaport, Gill, and Schafer] (1946) remains the primary assessment strategy in hospital settings." This statement, Lovitt observes, "is misleading and poorly stated for a number of reasons."

Sweeney et al. equate currently used instruments, such as the Rorschach and the TAT, with tests used in the original battery of Rapaport et al. simply because, Lovitt suggests, they "bear the same test names." But, the tests cannot be considered the same on this point alone. Lovitt points out the following with respect to the Rorschach:

> The test has undergone extraordinary revision. Changes in administration and an exhaustive redefinition of the empirical basis for interpretation have occurred...Theoretical approaches to interpretation and the conceptual manner in which the instrument has been used have been modified...and approaches to validation of Rorschach variables have been significantly altered.

Concerning the overall evaluation of the clinical tradition, Lovitt summarizes:

> Sweeney et al. totally misunderstood the roles of conceptualization, problem solving, and consultation in assessment that have evolved and flourished since 1946. These more recent changes serve as the theoretical basis within which tests are used and have a profound impact on how psychologists practice and use their tests. In 1949 Schafer initiated a major ongoing development when he encouraged psychologists to limit their use of tests solely in a score-dependent role. He encouraged the study of specific personality processes underlying test performance. This helped initiate a tradition whereby the assessor functions as a problem-solving consultant. Since then, a rich literature (Allen, 1981; Cohen, 1980; Kwawer, Lerner, Lerner, & Sugarman, 1980; Maloney & Ward, 1976; Shevrin & Shectman, 1973; Sloves, Docherty, & Schneider, 1979; Tallent, 1983; Towbin, 1964; Weiner, 1959, 1964, 1965, 1966, 1977a, 1977b, 1977c) has developed, significantly modifying and changing the original manner in which testing practice was developed by Rapaport et al. (1946). These studies have demonstrated how psychologists use tests in conjunction with other sources of data to solve clinical dilemmas. These innovations have been responsive to changing clinical practice occurring in psychology and psychiatry and have consistently validated and enriched the psychologist's role as a consultant and assessor. In essence, this is a 40-year refinement of how psychologists have been linking test scores with clinically relevant conceptualizations by using procedures that have been consistently refined.

Part II The Tools of Psychological Assessment

6
PSYCHOLOGICAL TESTING:
Intellectual and Neuropsychological Evaluation

The tools of psychological assessment are many and cover a broad spectrum of techniques. Reviewed in this and the following chapter is a sampling of psychological tests, including tests prominently listed in various surveys of test usage carried out over the years, and particularly that of Lubin, Larsen, Matarazzo, and Seever (1985). The 10 most popular instruments in 1982, as indicated by the psychologist-respondents of Lubin et al., by total-mention rank and weighted-score rank, are included in this and the next chapter.

Their application to problems presumes extensive study in many areas, including conceptual and physical familiarity with the instruments, background test theory and other relevant theory (e.g., personality theory, intelligence theory, neuropsychological theory), knowledge of psychometric properties, administration, scoring, and interpretation. They cannot be used competently or ethically to carry out an assessment by subprofessional persons.

INTELLIGENCE TESTING

The Wechsler Scales
Description

The individual Wechsler Intelligence scales constitute a family of conceptually related instruments, introduced by David Wechsler in 1939 with the publication of the

Wechsler-Bellevue Scale (W-B). A revision, the Wechsler Adult Intelligence Scale (WAIS) appeared in 1955, and a further revision, the Wechsler Adult Intelligence Scale-Revised (WAIS-R) was published in 1981. The Wechsler Intelligence Scale for Children (WISC) was issued in 1949, the Wechsler Intelligence Scale for Children-Revised (WISC-R) was published in 1974, and the Wechsler Intelligence Scale for Children–Third Edition (WISC-III) in 1991. The Wechsler Preschool and Primary Scale of Intelligence (WPPSI) was issued in 1967, and a revised edition (WPPSI-R) was brought out in 1989. A Spanish edition of the WISC-R is also available.

Wechsler published the W-B in response to his belief that a test of intelligence suitable for adults did not exist. He indicated a number of faults with the widely used Stanford-Binet as a measure of adult intelligence. In addition to inadequate standardization with adults, he suggested that the children's level items of the Binet can destroy rapport with older subjects. Adults, he observed, should not be asked to rhyme the words "day," "cat," and "mill," or to compose a sentence with the words "boy," "river," and "ball." Further, Wechsler believed that age norms (mental ages) are unsuitable for adults, as are the IQs derived from their use. *Deviation IQs* (standard scores computed for seven age groups, e.g., 20–24, with the mean set at 100 and the standard deviation at 15) made much more sense to him. Finally, he believed, the emphasis placed on speed in children's tests is less applicable to adults.

All of the Wechsler scales are divided into a verbal part (dealing with cognitive activity such as may be involved in working with words, concepts, or numbers) and a Performance part (composed of tasks that require visual-motor, spatial, and conceptual abilities). Verbal and Performance parts are further divided into a number of subtests. For example, the WAIS-R consists of six Verbal and five Performance subtests.

The Verbal subtests of this scale are: Information (measuring the subject's fund of information), Vocabulary (measuring the subject's vocabulary level), Comprehension (measuring the subject's knowledge of such matters as cultural precepts and understanding), Arithmetic (measuring the subject's quantitative reasoning and skills), Similarities (measuring the subject's ability to identify commonalities, such as in two discrete things, e.g., an orange and a banana), and Digit Span (measuring the subject's ability to repeat digits forward and backward).

The Performance subtests of the WAIS-R consist of: Picture Arrangement (measuring the subject's ability to put related but out-of-order sketches into a picture sequence that makes sense), Picture Completion (measuring the subject's ability to identify what important part is missing from a sketch), Object Assembly (measuring the subject's ability to arrange cardboard cutouts into a familiar form), Block Design (measuring the subject's ability to arrange patterned and colored cubes to match displayed models), and Digit Symbol (measuring the subject's ability to match symbols with numbers according to a code).

All of the Wechsler scales yield three deviation IQs—a Verbal IQ, a Performance IQ, and a Full Scale IQ. This is an approach that abandons the IQ based on the MA/CA ratio, such as used in the early Binet test. This change was introduced because, as Wechsler points out, a linear relationship between age and achievement on intellectual tasks through the life span does not exist. He calculated his IQ tables separately for various age groups.

Administration and Scoring

Each of the Wechsler subtests has its own directions for administration and scoring which are spelled out in the manuals of the various scales. Because the Wechsler scales are standardized instruments, these directions, including the following of time constraints in the case of timed tests, must be scrupulously followed. To insure that this is done, tests should be administered with the manual open in front of the examiner. Some experienced examiners, however, have thoroughly committed the directions to memory and may dispense with this rule.

Not contradictory of the above, various departures from the instructions in the manual are widely practiced, and, with experience, assessors commonly acquire techniques for enhancing the clinical yield of the Wechsler scales. These are carried out without impairing the basic standard administration of the scale. They are brought into play when the assessor notes unusual responses or unexpected failures, or there is any other reason to believe that the test may serve as a vehicle to elicit further information on the client's intelligence, personality, or neuropsychological status. Such practice need not lead to IQs that differ from what would be obtained with fully standard administration.

On the Picture Arrangement subtest, for example, an unusual arrangement may be queried by asking the client what story the sequence of drawings suggests. Even correct arrangements might be queried if there is reason to believe that the client might produce some revealing information, or even disclose that the arrangement was arrived at through guessing. Such querying usually is best done after the entire scale has been administered so as not to alter the client's test-taking set by creating the expectation that responses will have to be defended. Some examiners, however, query after the subtest in question has been completed while the arrangement is still on the table. Spontaneous corrections at this point are not credited, though they should be noted.

Verbal material, similarly, frequently invites query. To the "marriage license" item on the Comprehension subtest, the client might respond that most husbands would leave their wives if they were not bound by a legal contract. On the Information subtest, a client being tested in a clinic in New York indicates that the population of the United States is "about 10,000,000." As a follow-up, she was asked the population of New York City (not a test item), to which she replied "8,000,000." She was then asked to reconcile these figures, and specifically whether about 80 percent of Americans reside in New York City. The response was one of confusion and feeble rationalization: "I think I heard someplace it was 10,000,000."

A particularly dramatic ad hoc illustration of nonquantitative or nonintellectual information that may be elicited by a nonstandard query was provided by the performance of an intelligent young woman on the Object Assembly subtest. In attempting to place the ear pieces in the Feature Profile, she hesitated, placed one component upside down, removed it, did the same with the other component, then placed both pieces correctly, only to remove them, and look away. Time had expired. "You seem to be having a problem," the examiner observed. The client burst into tears and blurted out, "I'm going deaf." She had never complained of such a difficulty. Referred for examination, she was found indeed to have significant hearing loss.

In *testing the limits*, the assessor looks for intellectual potential that is not disclosed in standard administration and therefore cannot be scored, and also for insights into personality and/or neuropsychological functioning. One approach is to administer items that are specifically excluded in standard testing practice by the rule of *minimal testing*...a rule that saves testing time and also may reduce the experience of failure in the client. For example, directions for the administration of the Information subtest call for the examiner to discontinue testing after five consecutive failures are scored. However, if the examiner has reason to believe that the client knows the answer to items beyond this point, they may be administered, though correct answers are not credited.

Testing the limits, without crediting correct answers, may also be carried out by giving hints. Thus, during the Reagan administration, the examiner could suggest to a client who could not name the President that the occupant of the Oval Office had previously been a movie actor; and if unable to name the President previous to Reagan, the client might be told, for example, that he is from Georgia or had been a peanut farmer. Even alerting the client that an incorrect response was given may tap his or her potential. The examiner's response "Are you sure?" to a wrong answer on the Arithmetic subtest may prompt the client to refigure correctly.

The psychological assessor must be resourceful in using the testing-the-limits approach. In addition to yielding useful clinical data, the method also has research applications. Thus, Wielkiewicz (1990) examined Kaufman's (1975) hypothesis that the Third Factor on the WISC-R (Arithmetic, Digit Span, Coding) is a measure of Freedom from Distractibility. Based on his review of the literature, he concluded that low-scoring children on the triad of subtests that constitute the Third Factor suffer from a deficit of complex cognitive processes—*executive processes* and short-term memory. He suggested that testing the limits by modifying administration so as to place either increased or decreased demands on these processes would more readily expose the child's deficits. Some recommended procedures are: (1) to decrease executive and memory demands for performing the Arithmetic problems by presenting them in writing, (2) to increase these demands on the Block Design subtest by reducing the exposure time for the stimuli, and, similarly, (3) to increase them by having the child arrange the Picture Arrangement cards mentally. Such approaches might also lead to increased clinical insights.

To spell out all of the directions for administration, scoring, and use of the IQ tables would essentially amount to reproducing the Wechsler manuals. It will be instructive to note, however, using the WAIS-R as a model, some general instructions, and, for several selected subtests, a few of the specific instructions that apply to them.

The Information subtest ordinarily is administered first, with alternation of Performance and Verbal subtests through the remainder of the scale. All responses are scored on the record form, immediately when possible, and after completion of testing in the case of items where the client's responses must be compared with criterion responses listed in the manual. It may, for example, be unclear to the examiner whether a response to a Vocabulary item merits a score of 2 or 1, or 1 or 0, and ambiguous responses must be queried as indicated in the manual.

All verbal responses for Information, Vocabulary, Comprehension, and Similarities, and incorrect responses to the Arithmetic subtests are recorded verbatim in the spaces provided on the record form, and a supplementary sheet of paper may be used if this limited space is not sufficient. Other significant information is also jotted down on the record form or on a supplementary sheet. Thus, on Digit Span, incorrect number series are written down; on Picture Arrangement incorrect sequences, and perhaps the "stories" that go with them, are recorded; and on Block Design and Object Assembly, incorrect performances may be sketched or described and interesting features of the client's performance noted.

Specific rules for administering the various subtests must also be observed. A number of these need not be memorized, since they are printed on the record form. For example, at a glance the examiner observes that ordinarily he or she should start with the fifth item of the Information subtest and the fourth item in the Vocabulary series. Time limits, minimal testing rules, and special instructions (for the Digit Span subtest) are set down to be readily available when the various subtests are administered.

Interpretation

The Wechsler scales are noted for their versatility and usefulness. The ensuing discussion of the WAIS-R highlights the fact that this instrument is much more than a measure of "intelligence"; it is a complex matter in itself. Just how complex is brought out in Wechsler's (1975) paper, "Intelligence Defined and Undefined: A Relativistic Appraisal," which makes valuable, perhaps essential, reading for the psychological assessor.

Wechsler's value-infused concept of intelligence views this human characteristic as different from mental abilities or aptitudes—which are merely means to an end—namely, understanding the world and having the ability to cope with its challenges. Intelligent behavior, he asserts, involves (1) awareness, (2) meaning, goal-directedness, (3) rationality, and (4) merit or worthwhileness. Further, what may be considered intelligent behavior is defined by context. To the educator, intelligence implies the ability to learn; to the biologist, the ability to adapt; to the psychologist, the ability to educe relationships; and to the computer programmer, the facility to process information. Thus, in the clinical or educational situation, for example, the reason intelligence is being assessed and the meaning of intelligence in the particular case under consideration is obviously of central importance.

In typical use, the Wechsler scales are employed to gain a general estimate of intelligence, as this might be meaningful to some particular situation, and also to delineate specific assets and liabilities. For example, these instruments can help to clarify the need for special or gifted education, and as a basis for making specific recommendations. In a number of settings these instruments are used diagnostically to assist in questions of mental retardation and to establish its scope and characteristics when present. The making of psychiatric diagnoses and the identification of features of personality functioning also can be a useful application of intelligence tests, as proposed by Wechsler on the publication of the Wechsler-Bellevue.

Quantitative Features of the WAIS-R The basic use of the WAIS-R is in the classification of intelligence into seven categories as set forth by Wechsler (1981).

TABLE 6-1 Intelligence Classifications[1]

IQ	Classification	Theoretical Normal Curve	Actual Sample
130 and above	Very superior	2.2	2.6
120–129	Superior	6.7	6.9
110–119	High average	16.1	16.6
90–109	Average	50.0	49.1
80–89	Low average	16.1	16.1
70–79	Borderline	6.7	6.4
69 and below	Mentally retarded	2.2	2.3

[1]From David Wechsler, *Manual for the Wechsler Adult Intelligence Scale-Revised*. Copyright © 1981 by The Psychological Corporation, San Antonio, TX and reproduced by permission of the publisher.

The official psychiatric classification (American Psychiatric Association [1987]) expands on the mentally retarded category. Psychological assessors who work in psychiatric settings or who are in a consultative relationship with a psychiatrist should have a working familiarity with this classification which takes into consideration several features in addition to IQs.

First is flexibility. IQs are not sacrosanct, and the cutoff score for making a diagnosis of mental deficiency is "approximately 70.": "An IQ level of 70 was chosen because most people with IQs below 70 require special services and care, particularly during the school-age years."

Along with the IQ, the adaptive level of the individual should be appraised. To be considered here are such features as social skills, daily living skills, communication ability, independence, and social responsibility.

This position is consistent with earlier psychological views on mental retardation, including that of Wechsler (1944): "There are many individuals with I.Q.'s above 70 whose behaviour is definitely defective. On the other hand there are individuals with I.Q.'s below 60 whose entire life history is that of a nondefective."

A final consideration in making a diagnosis of mental retardation is the age at onset. To qualify as mentally retarded, the onset must be before the age of 18. In the case of later onset the correct diagnosis is dementia.

In the psychiatric classification, mental retardation is considered along a continuum according to the degree of severity, from mild to profound, as follows:

SEVERITY	IQ
Mild	50–55 to approximately 70
Moderate	35–40 to 50–55
Severe	20–25 to 35–40
Profound	Below 20 or 25

Wechsler (1944, 1958, 1975) advanced the concept of "nonintellective factors" of intelligence as a component of what his original (Wechsler-Bellevue) and later scales measure, and indicated that test responses and scores (when considered as a pattern), in addition to making available data on intelligence, provide information concerning the client's personality and other features of interest.

Thus his suggestion that performance on the Information subtest may be an indication of the subject's alertness to the environment. How well a person does on this subtest, he proposed, may also reflect the client's family background, including educational and intellectual level. Performance on the Picture Arrangement subtest may be an indicator of "social intelligence," and "psychopaths" are noted for good performance on this subtest. Such use of a Wechsler scale, and the development of rationales for performance on the various subtests is organic to the approach of Rapaport et al. and the clinical tradition.

Derived largely from empirical studies, working hypotheses concerning the interpretive significance of WAIS scores and relationships among scores are scattered through the literature and have been assembled by Gilbert (1978) and Ogdon (1981). These hypotheses should not be used in isolation or mechanically. They should be considered tentative and used only in relation to other data and with the application of considerable judgment. Note that a number of findings are consistent with various possible interpretations. Some examples follow:

Verbal Scale Higher than Performance Scale
Tendency to neurosis, commonly depression; markedly higher Verbal may be indicative of psychosis or organicity.

Performance Scale Higher than Verbal Scale
Characteristic of "acting out" types—antisocial and narcissistic individuals, adolescent delinquents, histrionics.

Information
High scores may be found in intellectualizers, obsessive-compulsives; Information lower than Comprehension in histrionic personalities; Information lower than Comprehension and Vocabulary in histrionics and others with repression as a characteristic defense; Information lower than Vocabulary in histrionic personality, depression and schizophrenia.

Picture Completion
High PC associated with antisocial personality and possible paranoid trends; PC lower than other subtest scores may be indicative of schizophrenia.

Digit Span
Elevated scores reported in schizophrenia; Digit Span lower than Vocabulary or Information an indicator of anxiety; Digits backward higher than Digits forward an indicator of schizophrenia; total failure on Digits backward an indicator of schizophrenia, chronic undifferentiated type.

Picture Arrangement
A measure of social anticipation and planning; high scores may be associated with antisocial tendencies; low scores with anxiety, depression, intellectualization, paranoia, and schizophrenia.

Vocabulary
High Vocabulary contraindicative of chronic schizophrenia (except paranoid type); low Vocabulary contraindicative of obsessive-compulsive disorder and paranoia.

Block Design
Very high Block Design scores are indicative of proficient visual-motor coordination, creativity, good prognosis with therapy, and are contraindicative of organicity; low scores may be indicative of organicity, anxiety, tension states, depression, impulsivity, compulsivity, hyperactivity, and tendencies to delinquency or paranoia.

Arithmetic
Arithmetic is widely regarded as a measure of concentration or ability to resist distraction; high scorers likely are normal, but may be given to intellectualizing or obsessiveness; low scorers may show antisocial and narcissistic trends, psychotic conditions, or organicity.

Object Assembly
Object Assembly is a test of visual-motor coordination; high scores are associated with creativity and favorable prognosis in therapy; low scores with anxiety and tension (possibly related to castration anxiety), depression, schizophrenia, and hyperactivity.

Comprehension
Comprehension is generally considered a test of practical judgment or common sense, and this quality is often attributed to high scorers; high scorers have a good grasp of cultural precepts and may evidence a strict moral code; Comprehension lower than Information may point up impaired judgment.

Digit Symbol
Digit Symbol, along with Block Design and Object Assembly, is a visual-motor task and also involves learning; individuals with good manual dexterity tend to do well on this test; high scores also suggest relative freedom from distractibility and a good energy level; very low scores may be linked to various pathologies—right-hemisphere damage, anxiety, tension, frustration, depression, abulia, dissociative tendencies, schizoid tendencies, hyperactivity or manic tendencies.

Similarities
Similarities is widely accepted as a test of abstract thinking or concept formation; high scores generally indicate these skills, but may also be indicative of intellectualization or paranoid thinking; low scores may be associated with cultural deprivation or chronic schizophrenia, paranoid type; Similarities lower than Vocabulary may be associated with cerebral pathology, depression, or schizophrenia.

Qualitative features of the WAIS-R The value of individual responses as "qualitative indicators"—"significant items which reveal themselves either in the form or in the content of the subject's responses" was an early contribution of Wechsler (1944) to the broad use of intelligence tests as diagnostic instruments. He provided a number of examples. Thus, on Comprehension, a patient presented with the question of what he would do if he found an envelope that was sealed and addressed and had a new stamp, replied that he would open it to see if it contained money. Further queried as to what he would do if there were no money, he indicated he would tear it up. Wechsler observed that the patient was a "psychopath."

The need to consider such indicators along with additional data is evident when we consider an attractive interpretive hypothesis of this sort found in Rapaport, Gill, and Schafer (1945). This pertained to the "theatre item" on the Comprehension subtest, the hypothetical question of what the test subject would do if the first to discover a fire in the movies. If "yell fire" was offered, this response was considered as evidence that the subject was impulsive. Studies by Tallent (1958) and Thomas (1966) failed to support this impression.

In his 1958 book, Wechsler supplies numerous examples of gaining diagnostic information from qualitative material. Of particular interest is his approach to the study of thinking characteristics as revealed by responses to the Vocabulary subtest. He identifies four categories:

> *Over-elaboration.* The tendency to give alternate meanings and irrelevant details, or to be overly and unnecessarily descriptive. Thus, for "diamond", "A gem; part of jewelry which consists of precious stones; what you give to a girl when you are engaged."
> *Ellipsis.* The omission of one or more words (sometimes only syllables) necessary to complete the meaning in a phrase or sentence. Thus, for "microscope," "Germs" (omitted or implied, an instrument for magnifying small objects, as germs).
> *Self-Reference.* Incorporation into a definition of personalized elements or of details reflecting self-involvement. Thus, for "conceal", "To hide away from peeking eyes."
> *Bizarreness.* Definitions involving markedly idiosyncratic associations or the juxtaposition of disconnected ideas. Thus, for "plural", "A way of thinking in grammar." For "impale", "Not blanched") (im = not, pale = blanch).

A somewhat different approach to the qualitative use of intelligence test responses was presented by Waite (1961). His explication of the Rapaport, Gill, & Schafer (1945) ego-psychological approach asserts that whereas Wechsler tended "'to view data pertaining to personality variables as supplementary and secondary in importance to 'the primary purpose of an intelligence examination'–that is, the obtaining of a 'valid and reliable measure of the subject's global capacity,'" Rapaport and associates considered intelligence test scores "as just one aspect of the test results, and by no means the most important." They viewed "the interpretation of intelligence test material" as "basically no different from their approach to projective test material."

Waite points out, however, that there are a number of important differences between the interpretations that may be made from intelligence test responses as opposed to those that may be made with the usual projective instruments. "One essential difference" is "...in terms of what the ego is required or encouraged to do when faced with the different tests." He illustrates the practical diagnostic value that may be gained by taking into consideration the differences in ego demands made by intelligence tests and projective instruments:

> Because the demands of the WAIS, unlike projective tests, do not contribute to an increase in the permeability of the barriers between conscious and unconscious, the WAIS

provides a setting in which supposedly reality oriented ego functioning can be scrutinized for representations of regressive trends and where this functioning should be free from such trends. Thus the WAIS can be employed as a valuable aid in making detailed and useful diagnostic descriptions of patients whose projective test protocols suggest psychosis or psychotic trends. For example, the WAIS often provides an estimate of a severely regressed schizophrenic patient's adaptive potentials when his projective test responses reflect little else but confusion, indications of primary process thinking, and despair. Put another way, the psychotic patient, supported by the realistic demands imposed by the intelligence test, often is able to remain relatively organized or to "pull himself together" and his WAIS protocol will reflect his ability to avoid and compensate for the psychotic disturbances.

Other contributions are consistent with this observation. Shapiro's (1954) earlier reference to the preservation of ego functions noted in the "clean" Wechsler-Bellevues of some borderline psychotics is an example. Similar observations have been made with patients clinically diagnosed with borderline personality disorder (Singer, 1977a) (p. 280), their Rorschachs typically being primitive, loose, and idiosyncratic while their Wechslers tend to be "clean."

Evaluation

All of the Wechsler scales have been standardized using extensive stratified samples. The WAIS-R standardization sample was a close match to the United States population with respect to race, region, and occupation, and was also controlled for education and urban/rural location. The WISC-R sample took into consideration age, sex, race, region, urban/rural location, and occupation of the head of the household. The WPPSI sample controlled for age, sex, region, urban/rural location, and parental occupation.

The Wechsler scales are well researched and very widely used. The WAIS-R, for example, is currently the most extensively applied individual adult intelligence scale. All of the Wechsler tests are designed to assess intelligence as a multifaceted—*global* is Wechsler's term—group of skills, and are in harmony with Wechsler's definition of intelligence: *the aggregate or global capacity of the individual to act purposefully, to think rationally, and to deal effectively with his environment.*

Typically a Wechsler scale is a valuable component of a battery. The WAIS-R, for example, makes a significant contribution to a neuropsychological battery. The WISC-R and the WPPSI have been incorporated in the SOMPA (System of Multicultural Pluralistic Assessment). Here the measurement of intelligence is used in conjunction with data on health, weight, sensory acuity, and sociocultural status.

The numerous attempts to gain clinical information from the Wechsler scales that involve drawing personality inferences from score discrepancies between the Verbal and Performance parts of the scale, and from the unevenness of intellectual functioning as observed in the variability—or "scatter"—of subtest scores have, in numerous instances, fallen short of success. With respect to Verbal-Performance discrepancies, Kaufman (1979) points out that of the hundreds of investigations carried out in this area, "in general...results have been contradictory with clear-cut findings few and far between." He notes that the same discrepancy in different subjects may arise from different causes. The use of "scatter" as a (psychiatric) diagnostic indicator also lacks adequate support (Guertin et al., 1956, 1962, 1966, 1971; Matarazzo, 1972).

Kaufman considers "subtest scatter" to be a hazy concept, a "probably overused and abused term" associated with irresponsible diagnostic practices. With specific reference to the WISC-R, he cautions: "The rather large amount of inter-subtest variability for normal children should serve as a precaution against over-interpreting peaks and valleys in the scaled score profiles of children suspected of learning disorders, emotional disturbance, and so on." And, "all of the presumptions about scatter in the profiles of learning-disabled children...may be nothing more than clinical speculation that is not borne out by empirical investigation."

Evidence for reliability and validity of the Wechsler scales is quite acceptable. Reliability coefficients of the WPPSI are illustrative. Internal (odd-even) consistencies for the Full Scale, Verbal, and Performance scales exceed .90. Reliabilities for individual subtests range from .77 to .87. Test-retest reliabilities established with a group of 50 kindergarten children, with an average of 11 weeks between testing, were .92, .86, and .89 for Full Scale, Verbal, and Performance scales, respectively. Reliability coefficients for the WAIS-R are of a similar magnitude.

The test manuals for the Wechsler scales do not report on validity. However, they may be used with confidence. Thus, Anastasi (1988) points out that current information on validity of the WAIS-R must be inferred from data accumulated on the W-B and the WAIS: "since all changes introduced in the later revisions represent improvements (in reliability, ceiling, normative sample, and so on) and since the nature of the test remained substantially the same, it is reasonable to suppose that validity data obtained on the earlier editions underestimate rather than overestimate the validity of the WAIS-R." Additionally, Wechsler (1958) and Matarazzo (1972) argue logically for the validity of the Wechsler approach. Numerous correlational studies, such as with work and academic performance, and with other tests, such as the Stanford-Binet, tend to support construct-related validity of the instrument. The same strategy has been used in the interest of establishing validity for the WPPSI, the WISC, and the WISC-R.

SELECTED REFERENCES ON THE WECHSLER SCALES

Glasser, A. J., & Zimmerman, I. L. (1967). *The clinical interpretation of the Wechsler Intelligence Scale for Children.* Orlando, FL: Grune & Stratton.

Kaufman, A. S. (1979). *Intelligent testing with the WISC-R.* New York: Wiley.

Kaufman, A. S. (1990). *Assessing Adolescent and Adult Intelligence.* Boston: Allyn & Bacon.

Matarazzo, J. D. (1972). *Wechsler's measurement and appraisal of adult intelligence* (5th ed.). Baltimore: Williams & Wilkins.

Sattler, J. M. (1988). *Assessment of children* (3rd ed.). San Diego, CA: Jerome M. Sattler, Publisher.

Wechsler, D. (1958). *The measurement and appraisal of adult intelligence* (4th ed.). Baltimore: Williams & Wilkins.

Zimmerman, I. L., Woo-Sam, J. M., & Glasser, A. J. (1973). *The clinical interpretation of the Wechsler Adult Intelligence Scale.* Orlando, FL: Grune & Stratton.

Peabody Picture Vocabulary Test-Revised (PPVT-R)
Description

The Peabody Picture Vocabulary Test-Revised is an instrument designed to provide a quick measure of the (hearing) vocabulary element of intelligence, or, more concretely, of verbal ability or scholastic aptitude. The stimulus materials consist of 175 plates, each displaying four pictures. The plates are presented one at a time, the examiner pronouncing a word and the subject indicating (usually by pointing) the picture that s(he) believes best illustrates the meaning of that word. The test finds such uses as evaluating students for remedial education, speech therapy, screening for mental retardation and giftedness, and evaluating the English vocabulary of non-English speaking persons.

The test is suitable for administration to subjects from the 2 1/2-year to the adult level, and is particularly recommended for young children and for those handicapped adults who would be at a disadvantage with other scales. Administration time is 10–20 minutes. Four kinds of derived scores may be obtained: a standard score with a mean of 100 and a standard deviation of 15, percentile ranks, stanines, and age equivalents. Two parallel forms, L and M, are available. A Spanish edition suitable for the same age range as the English edition, shortened to 125 items, and separately standardized with Puerto Rican and Mexican children, is also available.

Administration, Scoring, and Interpretation

Test administration for most subjects under age eight is slightly different from that for most subjects over age eight. For the younger group, administration starts with training plates, of which there are five (designated A–E). For children in this group, the procedure starts with Plate A. After preliminary instructions, the child is told to place a finger on the picture that corresponds to the word the examiner pronounces. The examiner reacts to the child's performance with such comments, printed in bold type in the manual, as "That's fine. Now put your finger on ..." or, "You made a good try, but this is the correct answer." This training period continues until the child responds correctly to three plates without help. Following the training period, the subject is asked to respond to plates of the test proper.

To avoid unnecessary testing, administration is ordinarily started at a point that is in harmony with the subject's age. This strategy, on average, results in the administration to subjects of only 35 of the 175 items. Adjustments are made from the starting point printed on the record form when the individual is known, or suspected, to deviate from the average range of intelligence.

Basal and ceiling rules must be followed in all cases. The basal is defined as the highest eight consecutive responses, the ceiling as the lowest eight consecutive responses containing six errors. When the ceiling is reached, the last item presented is the ceiling item. The raw score is then found by subtracting from the number of the ceiling item the number of errors made up to that point. Tables for converting raw scores to age norms are furnished in the manual. Grade norms may be obtained from the test publisher.

Evaluation

The standardization sample consisted of 4,200 subjects aged 2 1/2 to 18 years, with 200 persons in each of 21 age groups. The sample, drawn from 25 cities across the United States, was, based on the 1970 census, representative of age and sex, geographic region, occupation, ethnicity, and community size. Reliability coefficients are quite acceptable, with internal consistencies in the .70s and .80s. Alternate-form reliabilities are of a similar order. Concerning validity, the PPVT correlates well with other tests of vocabulary (.71 based on 55 correlations), moderately with other tests of scholastic aptitude, and "to a reasonable degree with measures of school achievement administered concurrently, but it does less well as a predictive measure of school success" (Dunn & Dunn, 1981).

SELECTED REFERENCES ON THE PEABODY PICTURE VOCABULARY TEST-REVISED

Dunn, L. D., & Dunn, L. D. (1981). *Manual for the Peabody Picture Vocabulary Test-Revised*. Circle Pines, MN: American Guidance Service.

McCallum, R. S. (1985). Review of Peabody Picture Vocabulary Test-Revised. *Ninth Mental Measurements Yearbook*, Vol. 2, 1126–1127.

Wiig, E. H. (1985). Review of Peabody Picture Vocabulary Test-Revised. *Ninth Mental Measurements Yearbook*, Vol. 2, 1127–1128.

NEUROPSYCHOLOGICAL ASSESSMENT

Neuropsychological assessment has a long history, though for a number of years its scope and objectives were limited. In part an outgrowth of intelligence testing based on scatter analysis, neuropsychological testing was for many years in widespread use as a test for "organicity," and, in psychiatric settings, psychologists with considerable frequency responded to the request, "Rule Out Organicity." Measures of "organicity" were frequently identified in terms of "deficit" or "deterioration."

The test of Harriet Babcock (1930) stands as a landmark. Her approach was to use the Vocabulary score of the Stanford-Binet as a baseline index of efficiency (that is, not readily impaired as a result of brain damage), and to compare this score with scores on a number of short tests on which performance typically declines in the presence of brain damage. Shipley (1940) presents a neat approach to the development of a "conceptual quotient" (CQ) that is based on the discrepancy of scores on a 10-minute, multiple-choice vocabulary test and a 10-minute test of concept formation or abstract reasoning. A low CQ could be indicative of brain impairment.

Wechsler's (1939) approach is similar. He designated four subtests as "Hold Tests"—tests whose scores tend to hold up in the presence of brain damage—and four subtests as "Don't Hold Tests." His original listing of these subtests was for the Wechsler-Bellevue scale and was subsequently revised for the WAIS, as follows: Hold Tests—Vocabulary, Information, Object Assembly, Picture Completion; Don't Hold Tests—Digit Span, Similarities, Digit Symbol, Block Design. Entering age-scaled score equivalents in the formula $\frac{\text{Hold - Don't Hold}}{\text{Hold}}$ yields a "Deterioration Quotient." Thus, if the subject's Hold score adds up to 50 and the Don't Hold to 40, then the quotient (or loss) is $\frac{50 - 40}{50} = \frac{1}{5}$ or 20 percent. Wechsler provided a method to calculate the normal percentage of loss to be expected at each age level, and postulated possible deterioration when normal decline was exceeded by 10 percent and definite deterioration when this discrepancy exceeded 20 percent.

The modern era of neuropsychological assessment starts with the establishment by Ward Halstead of a laboratory at the University of Chicago in 1935 and his research there on "biological intelligence" (Halstead, 1947). This work was the basis for the Halstead-Reitan Neuropsychological Battery. Particularly since the refinement of Halstead's instrument by his former student Ralph Reitan (Reitan & Davison, 1974), and the publication of Russell, Neuringer, and Goldstein (1970), neuropsychological research and the practice of clinical neuropsychology have burgeoned.

The Halstead-Reitan Neuropsychological Battery (HRB)
Description, Administration, and Scoring

The basics of the Halstead-Reitan Battery are the outcome of the work of Ward Halstead, and it was the intention of Ralph Reitan that the formal name of the battery reflect this fact. However, as a result of Reitan's long and intensive work with Halstead's approach, the battery became identified with him. Informally, many call it "The Reitan."

The HRB, as presently constituted, consists basically of a number of tests of diverse psychological and neurological origin. In addition to the tests specifically developed as neuropsychological tools, a Wechsler scale and the Minnesota Multiphasic Personality Inventory (MMPI) are commonly administered to make for a more comprehensive assessment that includes information on personality and intellectual functioning.

As we have seen, the Wechsler scales contribute data relevant to the issue of brain damage. Wechsler IQs and subtest scores are used in formulas for determining brain damage, and the Digit Symbol subtest is routinely used in arriving at the crucial Average Impairment Rating (pp. 138–139). The MMPI might also have value in contributing to a diagnosis of organicity. Two of the better known scales used for this purpose are listed in Dahlstrom and Welsh (1960). These are the 36-item Caudality scale (Williams, 1952) and the 32-item Parietal-frontal (Friedman, 1950) scale, which purport to differentiate anterior from posterior lesions.

The MMPI has value in delineating a picture of the functioning personality in an individual who has suffered brain damage. What, for example, is the impact on the personality of one who is experiencing the effect of brain pathology? Further, the MMPI can be an aid in the interpretation of the neuropsychological tests. Depression, for example, which can impair performance on a number of these is readily assessed with the MMPI.

Individual clinicians may take a flexible approach to assessment and commonly choose to delete some of the basic tests that make up Reitan's battery. A major consideration is the fact that test administration can be time consuming, on the order of six hours.

Halstead-Reitan Category Test The Halstead Category Test measures the ability to develop and learn abstract principles. Two hundred and eight slides constitute the stimulus material of the test, which is divided into seven subtests. Each subtest is based on a different principle that the subject must deduce and retain in order to respond correctly to the subsequent problems of the subtest.

The test is administered with the subject seated in front of an opaque screen, beneath which are four controls (levers or buttons) numbered 1 to 4. A lighted display appears on the screen and the subject's task is to pick the "right" response— 1, 2, 3, or 4. (It is guesswork at this point, since what is the "right" answer was so designated by the test author.) For example, the first stimulus of a subtest could be a triangle. From this the subject may deduce that the "right" answer is "3," since a triangle has three sides. Or, she or he may be impressed that the triangle is one item, and therefore the "right" answer could be "1." So that the subject may grasp the *principle* or the *concept* of the subtest, each time she or he selects a "wrong" answer a harsh buzzer is sounded, and each "right" selection is reinforced by a pleasant door chime. The score for the Category Test is the number of errors, or

$$\frac{\text{Number of Errors}}{\text{Number of Items Attempted}} \times 208$$

The Category Test is also available in booklet format.

Speech-Sounds Perception Test Sixty nonsense words, divided into six sets of 10 words, all consist of the *ee* sound preceded and followed by a consonant. Thus the nonsense term *theets*. With *theets* presented by tape as a stimulus, the subject must identify this expression from a printed multiple-choice format with the following options: *theeks, zeeks, theets, zeets*. The score is the number of errors.

Seashore Rhythm Test The Seashore Test of Musical Talent is the source of the Seashore Rhythm Test. As adapted by Halstead, the test consists of 30 pairs of rhythmic presentations, and the task of the subject is to record whether the items in each pair are the same or different. Raw scores, which range from 0–30 are converted into scaled scores of 1–10.

Tactual Performance Test Halstead's revision of the Seguin-Goddard Form Board is the basis for the Tactual Performance Test. The equipment for this test consists of a number of wooden blocks in such common shapes as a square, a cross, a star, a triangle, and a circle. A large wooden board, with hollowed out areas to accommodate these shapes, is the other essential component.

To administer the test, the subject is first blindfolded and seated in front of the board, which rests on a stand placed on a table. The examiner familiarizes the subject with the materials by running his or her (the subject's) dominant hand first against each of the shapes and then the hollowed-out spaces that will receive them.

The performance proper consists of three trials. In the first the subject uses the dominant hand only, in the second the nondominant hand only, and in the third both hands. Finally, the test materials are removed from sight, the blindfold is taken off, and the subject is given pencil and paper and asked to produce from memory a drawing of the board with as many shapes as possible arranged in their proper position on the board. When the subject recollects shapes, but not their location, they may simply be drawn on any unused part of the paper.

Six scores are recorded for this test. The first four are for performance time for the trials with the dominant hand, nondominant hand, both hands, and total time for all of the three trials. A localization score is assigned for the accuracy with which the blocks are placed in the drawing. And finally, a memory score is assigned for the number of shapes that are correctly drawn (not necessarily well drawn; difficult to interpret shapes are credited if the subject assigns to them their proper names).

Trail Making Tests There are two parts to the Trail Making Test, Part A ("Trails A") and Part B ("Trails B"). The test material for each part consists of a sheet of white paper (8 1/2" x 11") on which 25 circles are placed. In Part A each circle contains a number, from 1 to 25. The subject's task is to draw a line connecting all of the circles in proper number sequence, starting with Circle 1. Performance is timed. The examiner alerts the subject to errors, which he or she is asked to correct while timing continues. Part B also has 25 circles on a sheet of paper, with numbered circles running from 1 to 13, and 12 circles containing the letters A through L. The task here is to connect the circles in a number to letter sequence, Circle 1 to Circle A, Circle A to Circle 2, Circle 2 to Circle B, and so on. Time is recorded, as in Part A. Time scores for both parts are recorded in seconds, to a maximum of 300. Both parts are also scored for errors, to a maximum of 25.

Reitan-Klove Sensory Perception Examination The Sensory Perception Examination is a neurological examination of tactile, auditory, and visual perception, and consists of numerous procedures to assess these functions.

To evaluate tactile perception, the subject sits with eyes closed and the palms of the hands on a table. The examiner then touches the subject's hands in a random sequence and the subject reports which hand is being touched. Four trials on the left and right hands, and four simultaneous trials on both hands are then carried out. Errors are counted separately for the left and right hand, and suppressions (reporting only one hand being touched when both have been touched) are recorded as another category. Tactile suppression may also be noted for trials of simultaneous touching of right hand and left face and left hand and right face.

In testing for fingertip agnosia (difficulty distinguishing tactual stimuli with the fingers), the subject is asked to report which finger the examiner is touching. In a closely related technique, fingertip number writing, the subject is told that the examiner will write the numbers 3, 4, 5, and 6 on the various fingertips, and she or he must recognize the numbers. Still another closely related test is that for astereognosis (loss or severe decrease in the ability to identify by touch familiar objects, like coins, or familiar shapes), in which the subject is required to identify, by touch alone, various coins—penny, nickel, and dime. With analogous procedures, auditory and visual perceptual abilities, together with suppressions, are examined.

Aphasia Screening Test Testing for aphasia is a straightforward procedure designed to disclose any of the various forms of this disorder that might be present. Tasks include naming objects and designs, spelling, drawing (square, triangle, Greek cross, skeleton key), reading (letters, numbers, words, sentences), pronunciation, discrimination of body parts and right and left, and doing arithmetic problems (with and without pencil and paper). Several approaches to evaluation are available: the number of items on which an error occurs may be identified, a weighted system in which some items are assigned more points than others may be employed, or a qualitative approach to identifying problem areas may be taken.

Lateral Dominance Examination Several tests are used to establish hand, eye, and foot dominance. Hand dominance may be determined by asking the subject to perform such tasks as demonstrating how to throw a ball or writing his or her name. The latter is timed, and the subject is then asked to do the same with the other hand and the time is also recorded. A hand dynamometer, to test grip strength, is also basic to testing hand dominance.

Foot dominance is readily observed by asking the subject to "step on a bug" and to demonstrate how she or he would kick a football. Eye dominance is revealed by asking the subject to demonstrate how he or she looks through a telescope or would aim a rifle. The Miles ABC Test of Ocular Dominance is a more formal procedure that may be employed.

Halstead Finger Tapping Test The apparatus for the Finger Tapping Test is on the order of a telegraph key that automatically counts the number of finger presses. Using both hands, starting with the dominant hand, the subject is instructed to tap the key, release pressure, and tap again–as quickly as possible. Five trials of

10 seconds duration are given for each hand, with a rest period after the third trial and additional rest periods interspersed as necessary. The score is the average number of taps for each hand. If, however, considering each hand separately, the number spread (of taps) is greater than five, additional trials are given until five of these are within the five point spread. These five trials are then averaged.

Interpretation

The tests of the Reitan battery were selected on the basis of their ability to delineate various aspects of brain pathology. Thus, the Category test is highly sensitive to the presence of brain damage with an almost 90 percent hit rate (Wheeler, Burke, & Reitan, 1963). (Cutoff points, beyond which brain damage is presumed to be present have been established [Golden, 1979a]. On the Category Test, for example, more than 50 errors are taken to indicate brain damage; on the Rhythm Test more than 7 errors is the criterion.)

Left hemispheric dysfunction is suggested by inferior performance on Speech Sounds, the verbal items on the Aphasia test, Trails B inferior to Trails A, and a WAIS Performance IQ lower than the Verbal IQ (Golden, 1979a). Subjects with right temporal lobe damage are prone to deficit in nonverbal auditory perception, such as is measured with the Seashore Rhythm Test. (Bogen & Gordon, 1971; Milner, 1962, 1971) Hence an examination of the scores of the various tests administered, in combination with such other variables as the reason for assessment, history, behavioral observations, and social status leads to impressions of the functioning of an individual's brain.

More formal approaches are also used. The neuropsychological key approach of Russell, Neuringer, and Goldstein (1970) offers a particularly systematic and objective way of diagnosing brain damage. Three keys are available: a Localization key, a Degree of Lateralization key, and a Process key (based on the understanding that brain damage is a process in which change occurs due to time and organic processes).

The Localization key is to determine if the subject is brain damaged, and when this is the case whether the damage is lateralized to either of the two hemispheres or is diffuse. If lateralized, the Degree of Lateralization key is used to determine whether the damage is strongly or weakly lateralized. The Process key is applied to identify whether brain damage is acute, static, or congenital.

Use of the keys may be assigned to a technician who does the testing and scoring and arrives at a final diagnostic statement. The first step is to convert raw scores, by means of a table, to a rating from 0 to 5, 0 representing good performance and 5 very poor performance. These ratings are then entered into the keys according to instructions, and diagnostic impressions are reached according to the criteria.

The presence or absence of brain damage is determined with the Average Impairment Rating. This rating is found by averaging the following ratings: Category Test, Tactual Performance Test (Speed), total, Tactual Performance Test (Memory), Tactual Performance Test (Location), Seashore Rhythm Test, Speech Perception Test, Finger Tapping—dominant hand, Trail Making B, WAIS Digit

Symbol, Aphasia Examination (rating), Perceptual Disorders Examination (rating). A rating of 1.55 or greater is considered indicative of brain pathology. If this figure is not reached, the other keys need not be applied.

The Luria-Nebraska Neuropsychological Battery (LNNB) Description, Administration, and Scoring

The Luria-Nebraska Neuropsychological Battery (Golden, 1981a, b; Golden, Purisch, & Hammeke, 1985) is a psychometric adaptation of the clinical neuropsychological examination of the distinguished Russian psychologist A.R. Luria. Luria was a sensitive and intuitive clinician who held the antipsychometric bias of the Russian psychology of his time. The newer 269-item procedure, incorporating his name, thus represents a significant departure from his work and philosophy.

Administration and scoring are specific to each of the tests of the battery. Easy-to-follow instructions are spelled out in the manual (Golden, Purisch, & Hammeke, 1985).

Scale 1: Motor Functions The performance of a variety of simple and complex motor tasks is required for this test. Parts of the body involved in testing include the upper extremities and the mouth area. The test items are divided into eight sections—such as simple movement of the hands (for example, touching fingers with the thumb), hand exercises involving dynamic organization (for example, the subject is asked to tap the right hand twice, then the left hand once, repeating this procedure in rapid sequence), and complex forms of praxis (demonstrating how to pour and stir tea).

Scale 2: Rhythmic and Pitch Skills The pitch skills evaluated have to do with the ability to discriminate tones in terms of whether they have the same pitch (the subject must tell whether two tones that are presented are the same or different). The subject is also asked to judge which of two tones is higher, and to reproduce pitch relationships and melodies (for example, the subject is asked to sing the first line of a well-known song). In testing for rhythmic skills the subject is required to report how many tones (beeps) have been sounded, and on whether rhythmic patterns are the same. The subject is also asked to produce rhythmic patterns, such as two taps, three taps, and two strong and three weak taps.

Scales 3–11: The remaining scales of the LNNB Scale 3—Tactile Functions—is concerned with both tactile and kinesthetic functions. For example, the blindfolded subject must identify and discriminate stimuli on the skin and duplicate flexion of the arm as the examiner manipulates him or her in this manner. Scale 4—Visual (Spatial) Functions—calls for the subject to demonstrate that he or she is able, for example, to recognize simple items like photographs and line drawings, to discern objects grouped with other objects, to tell time, to draw the hands of a clock to times indicated by the examiner, and to name the number of blocks in a stack when some of them are not visible. Scale 5—Receptive Speech—tests the subject's comprehension of phonemes (simple phonemes, combinations, and so on) and word and sentence comprehension, including compound constructions and contradictory statements. Scale 6—Expressive Speech—examines simple and complex speech impairments, as may be evidenced in the pronunciation of simple and complex phonemes, by discussing a story as prompted by a picture, and arranging jumbled words into a logical sequence. Scale 7—Writing—examines such simple writing skills as copying letters and words, and reproducing them from memory and dictation. Scale 8—Reading—measures the ability to reproduce sounds from letters, such as by asking the subject, "What word do these letters make: c-a-t?"—and to read sentences aloud. Scale 9—Arithmetic—asks the subject to do such tasks as identifying arabic and roman numerals and performing addition and subtraction, multiplication and division. Scale 10—Memory—calls on the subject to demonstrate his or her memory in numerous ways, such as repeating lists of words recited by the examiner and drawing a picture on a card after the examiner shows it and then removes it from view. Scale 11—Intelligence—is a short test of intelligence, with many items similar to items that appear on the adult Wechsler scales.

Interpretation

Raw scores for performance on each scale are converted to T-scores. These are plotted on a profile sheet, thus making available for neuropsychological interpretation a quantitative picture that may readily alert the assessor to possible areas of brain dysfunction. Additional scales, including localization and factor scales, may also be scored.

The instrument yields scores on 14 dimensions. Eleven of these bear the names of the scales that measure them, for example "motor," "rhythm," and "tactile," which refer to functions that may be impaired in the presence of brain damage, plus a Right Hemisphere scale (composed of all the motor and tactile functions performed with the left hand only), a Left Hemisphere scale (composed of all the motor and tactile functions performed with the right hand only), and a Pathognomonic scale (made up of 31 items that are especially sensitive to brain damage).

Scores above 60 in a subject who is otherwise normal, and above 70 in a patient with a psychiatric history, are considered by Golden (1979a) to be indicative of brain damage.

Evaluation of the Halstead-Reitan and Luria-Nebraska Neuropsychological Batteries

A string of validation studies (Halstead, 1947; Reitan, 1955; Vega & Parsons, 1967; Russell, Neuringer, & Goldstein, 1970) establishes the Reitan as a diagnostic instrument capable of identifying brain damage. Thus, with respect to the neuropsychological key approach to the assessment of brain damage with the Reitan, Russell, Neuringer, and Goldstein (1970) report a comparison of Key findings with those of the neurological examination:

Overall, 58 of the 104 Ss received a Key diagnosis that agreed with the neurological report (55.8% agreement). With regard to presence or absence of brain damage, there were only seven cases (6.7%) in which the Key predicted brain damage that was not confirmed by neurological examination, and five cases (4.8%) in which the Key did not detect brain damage but the neurological examination did. The other disagreements involved the question of localization...It would appear that there is a high degree of agreement between the Key and neurological examination in terms of localization of brain damage. Most of the disagreements occurred in those cases in which the Key predicted a lateralized lesion, while the neurological finding was that the patient had a diffuse lesion. One possible source for this disagreement is that the neuropsychological battery may be more sensitive than the neurological examination to differences in functioning between the cerebral hemispheres.

In spite of its strengths, as demonstrated in the key approach to the battery, there are also limitations. Goldstein (1990) summarizes them:

1. The Halstead-Reitan Battery is too long and redundant.
2. The tests in the Halstead-Reitan Battery are insufficiently specific, both in regard to the functions they assess and the underlying cerebral correlates of those functions.
3. The Halstead-Reitan Battery is not sufficiently comprehensive, particularly in that it completely neglects the area of memory.
4. The Halstead-Reitan Battery cannot discriminate between brain-damaged and schizophrenic patients.
5. Findings reported from Reitan's laboratory cannot be replicated in other settings.

The present status of the Luria-Nebraska is captured in Goldstein's (1990) characterization of the battery as a "controversial procedure." Evidence for validity is primarily discriminative (Golden, 1980; Golden, Purisch, & Hammeke, 1985; Purisch & Sbordone, 1986), perhaps most significantly with respect to distinguishing brain-damaged subjects from normals and schizophrenics (the latter discrimination being beyond the capability of the Reitan), a finding which Shelly and Goldstein (1983) could replicate only partially. Reported test-retest and interjudge reliabilities are high.

Along with the favorable evidence are sufficient critical publications to induce uneasiness (e.g., Adams, 1980a,b, 1985; Spiers, 1981; Crosson & Warren, 1982; Delis & Kaplan, 1982; Stambrook, 1983; Goodglass & Kaplan, 1983). Goldstein (1990) notes that a number of these point out methodological problems. He concludes that the present state of affairs regarding the merit of the Luria is that some observers are "for it" and some "against it." Stemming from this state of affairs he comments, "I would concur with Stambrook's (1983) view, which essentially is that it is premature to make an evaluation, and that major research programs must be accomplished before an informed opinion can be reached," and he follows this observation with recommendations for research.

Beyond questions of the validity of neuropsychological diagnosis is the issue of how the contributions of neuropsychological assessment compare with other approaches to the diagnosis of brain damage. Can other methods do the job more validly or more efficiently than neuropsychological testing? If so, what is the emerging and best role for neuropsychologists?

Historically, the goals of neuropsychological assessment have been "medically referenced" (Heinrichs, 1990). In the early days of this orientation, the major goal was the identification of "organicity" (a now outmoded and nonfunctional concept [Leonberger, 1989]) or the quantification of "deficit" or "deterioration." Later, medically referenced neuropsychological assessment emphasized concern with such issues as the lateralization and the localization of brain lesions, or diffuseness or generalization of cortical damage, and with answering questions on the status or nature of a lesion, for example, acute brain damage (less than three month's duration), static brain damage (more than one year's duration, chronic), or congenital brain damage. Thus, for example, the neuropsychologist might alert the neurologist that a patient's problem is of recent onset and consistent with neoplastic disease.

"For the most part," Heinrichs observes, "medically referenced assessment is receding in relative importance and utility":

> ...with the development of computerized tomography and now positron emission, cerebral blood flow techniques, and nuclear magnetic resonance imaging, this has changed. In contrast with the exquisite resolving power of the new imaging techniques, neuropsychological testing appears as a rather inefficient, ponderous, and generally less accurate means of tracking down neurological events...In this vein Wedding and Gudeman (1980) indicate: The CAT technique is rapid, noninvasive, and more accurate than traditional neurodiagnostic and neuropsychological measures. It is likely that the ability to isolate the suspected location of brain lesions on the basis of psychological test data will become increasingly an obsolete skill, while the ability to specify precise, functional deficits for purposes of litigation and/or rehabilitation counseling will become increasingly important.

Leonberger's (1989) prophecy of the demise of a significant aspect of an honored enterprise is even more definite: "Psychometric means of detecting structural and physiological changes will gradually be relegated to a place in the medical, psychiatric, and psychological history books." This does not mean that neuropsychological assessment is headed for extinction. Leonberger's words state that it is only a particular aspect of the neuropsychological enterprise that is becoming outmoded.

Bigler and Steinman (1981) do not consider modern technology—exemplified by the CAT scanner—to be in competition with neuropsychological techniques. Rather, they make a case, supported by clinical material, that the two approaches are complementary. They hold that in sound clinical practice, the diagnosis of CNS disorders "is never accomplished through the use of only one technique...Thus, NP data and evidence provided by CAT scanners combine to allow the direct observation of the correlation between verified anatomic pathology [the only information that can be gained through use of the machine] and neuropsychologic deficit."

In place of detection and localization of lesions, clinical neuropsychologists are being asked to make statements regarding brain-behavior relationships (Boll, 1977), patients' functional skills, treatment options, rehabilitation prospects, competence in community living, and so forth (Wedding & Gudeman, 1980). Clearly there is a greater need to deal with the behavioral sequelae of neurological disorders. However, all neuropsychologists do not concur with the view that neuropsychology is obsolete as a means of detecting brain damage. Kane, Goldstein, and Parsons (1989), for example, argue that detecting the presence of brain damage must continue as an important function of neuropsychologists.

Looking to the future, Heinrichs (1990) expects a more clearly defined assessment role for the neuropsychologist:

> It...appears likely that the traditional approach in clinical neuropsychology, which emphasizes analytic methods, will require a more systemic complement. The study of brain and behavior is rooted in methods aimed at isolating individual elements and separating the effects of each variable. Although this approach can be expected to nurture rehabilitation-referenced assessment, it probably will not be effective for ecologically referenced problems. There is more to assessing a brain-injured person's potential adjustment to family and work life than the direct effects of lesions or even premorbid personality...Instead a systemic approach, which emphasizes the interaction of numerous elements—neural, environmental, premorbid, and others—will be required...Incorporating systemic thinking into ecologically referenced assessment offers intriguing possibilities for a new generation of assessment techniques. If this is achieved, then the conventional test battery—and perhaps the conventional neuropsychologist—will go the way of the battleship. *A powerful and problem-oriented assessment practice* will replace aims and methods that are losing their utility (emphasis added).

This prediction calls up the long term problem of the "qualitative vs. quantitative approach" (Goldstein, 1981), which may conceptually be compared with the issues in the clinical-versus-statistical prediction controversy. At one pole, the approach is psychometric (and involves the use of a fixed battery). At the other is an approach customized to the client (and employs a flexible battery), an approach in which the assessor is always cognizant of the presenting problem and of the emerging data of the examination, and which emphasizes clinical judgment.

SELECTED REFERENCES ON NEUROPSYCHOLOGICAL ASSESSMENT

Filskov, S. B., & Boll, T. J. (Eds.) (1981). *Handbook of clinical neuropsychology.* New York: Wiley.

Franzen, M. D., & Berg, R. A. (1989). *Screening children for brain impairment.* New York: Springer.

Golden, C. J. (1979). *Diagnosis and rehabilitation in clinical neuropsychology.* Springfield, IL: C. C. Thomas.

Golden, C. J., Purisch, A. D., & Hammeke, T. A. (1985). *The Luria-Nebraska Neuropsychological Battery: Forms I and II (Manual).* Los Angeles: Western Psychological Services.

Hartlage, L. C., Asken, M. J., & Hornsby, J. L. (1987). *Essentials of neuropsychological assessment.* New York: Springer.

Lezak, M. D. (1983). *Neuropsychological assessment* (2nd ed.). New York: Oxford University Press.

Reitan, R. M., & Davison, L. A. (1974). *Clinical neuropsychology: Current status and applications.* New York: Winston/Wiley.

Reitan, R. M., & Wolfson, D. (1985). *The Halstead-Reitan Neuropsychological Test Battery: Theory and clinical interpretation.* Tucson: Neuropsychology Press.

Russell, E. W., Neuringer, C., & Goldstein, G. (1970). *Assessment of brain damage: A neuropsychological key approach.* New York: Wiley.

7
PSYCHOLOGICAL TESTING:
Personality Inventories and Projective Techniques

PERSONALITY INVENTORIES

Minnesota Multiphasic Personality Inventory
Description, Administration, and Scoring

The Minnesota Multiphasic Personality Inventory (MMPI), a self-report inventory, is the most widely used and researched objective instrument for personality assessment in current use. Published studies on the inventory are in excess of 8,000. Translations have been made into at least 15 languages, and a number of MMPI computer programs for scoring and interpretation enjoy widespread popularity.

The original MMPI The culmination of research beginning in 1939, the MMPI was first published in 1943. It consists of 566 affirmatively worded statements (shorter forms of the instrument may also be administered) to which the test taker responds *True*, *False*, or *Cannot Say*. The original focus of the instrument was on the diagnosis of psychiatric disorders, which was a matter of emphasis in many clinical settings at the time. With experience, however, MMPI use reflected a concern with identifying personality traits and developing a picture of personality functioning.

The scales that constitute the profile were empirically derived at the University of Minnesota. Visitors at the University of Minnesota Hospitals served as a normal group and hospitalized psychiatric patients were the basis of clinical norms pertaining to various psychopathological categories (some of which are not currently recognized or have been redefined in the several versions of the *Diagnostic and Statistical Manual* [American Psychiatric Association, 1987] that were introduced following the publication of the instrument). Ten *clinical scales*, thus derived, are fundamental to MMPI interpretation. They are:

Scale 1   Hypochondriasis (Hs)
Scale 2   Depression (D)
Scale 3   Hysteria (Hy)
Scale 4   Psychopathic Deviate (Pd)
Scale 5   Masculinity-Femininity (Mf)
Scale 6   Paranoia (Pa)
Scale 7   Psychasthenia (Pt)
Scale 8   Schizophrenia (Sc)
Scale 9   Hypomania (Ma)
Scale 10 Social Introversion (Si)

Administration and Scoring

The MMPI may be used as an individual test or a group test, and is generally considered suitable for subjects who are 16 years of age or older and who have completed six years of schooling. The ability to read and understand the items is the crucial factor.

Instructions are simple and easy to follow. However, to complete the lengthy task requires a good deal of motivation and patience. Highly anxious subjects may experience discomfort, and severely depressed persons may require encouragement, perhaps even requiring that the examiner read the items to the subject and record the responses. For some subjects it is appropriate to divide the task into two or three sessions.

Mean administration time with the booklet form is approximately 90 minutes. Responses are scored by hand, placing plastic templates over the answer sheet, or by computer. When hand-scored, the obtained scores are transferred to a profile sheet (a different sheet for males and females) as dots on a score continuum, and when these are connected with lines, a profile is formed. The elevations of the various scales may then be read as T-scores. The time-consuming exercise of scoring and profiling is now largely being done by computers.

Interpretation

In addition to the clinical scales, there are four *validity scales*. These are measures of test-taking attitudes and thus are indicative of the degree of confidence that may be placed in the obtained scores. Beyond this use, scores on the validity scales are interpretable as they have implications for personality.

The Cannot Say (?) Scale score is the number of items that the subject does not answer either True or False (or answers both True and False). There are various reasons why subjects do not respond to items, such as indecisiveness or unwillingness to admit negative information about oneself. In any event, such omissions tend to lower scores, and some psychologists consider a record to be invalid when the ? score exceeds 30.

The L Scale was originally designed as a measure of lying (hence the L). Normal subjects (who show variations related to such factors as insight, education, intelligence, and socioeconomic status) answer False to about 4 of the 15 items of the scale that are blatantly true of most people. However, it also appears that naive or defensive people, or those who may be characterized as highly conventional, moralistic, rigid, repressed and given to denial—also are prone not to recognize in themselves even the benign shortcomings that are true of most people—as indicated in items similar to "Sometimes I feel a little angry."

The F Scale is composed of items that are answered in a statistically infrequent direction, that is, by fewer than 10 percent of normal respondents. By definition, then, F responses are deviant. Whether or not a particular high F score is indicative of pathology is, however, a matter for individual interpretation depending on the degree of scale elevation and other data on the person. Thus, a high F may be the product of a psychotic or a neurotic, a malingerer, or one who is pleading for help. If not reflective of deviance, the test taker's attitude may be one of "faking bad"— deliberately seeking to create a picture of psychological deviance.

Finally, the K Scale is a measure of defensiveness, whose items are more subtle than those on the L scale, suggesting that the subject with a high K score wishes to be seen as psychologically "healthier" than is the case, a matter of "faking good." When this happens, the clinical scales likely would tend to underestimate the extent of psychopathology present. This is guarded against by adding points to some of the clinical scales in accordance with a *K correction.*

As experience with the MMPI increased and research accumulated, clinicians tended to drop scale names—such as the Schizophrenia Scale—in favor of thinking and communicating in terms of scale numbers. Thus, instead of speaking of the Schizophrenia Scale, clinicians now tend to speak of Scale 8, and empirical correlates of Scale 8 are sought out. High Schizophrenia scores do not necessarily identify a person who is suffering with schizophrenia.

Scales additionally are combined into two-point codes (for example, the 49 code—indicating elevations on Scales 4 and 9) and three-point codes (for example, the 139 code) and these are linked with behavior dispositions. For example, people with a 49 code tend to manifestations of superego deficiency, alcoholism, other forms of lessened control, and a history of marital problems. Graham (1987) is a good source of empirical correlates of two-point and three-point codes as well as of the correlates of the clinical scales considered singly.

In addition to the "standard" clinical scales, there are numerous—several hundred—"special scales" or "research scales" that may be used as supplementary scales to tap special areas of interest. These bear such identifying labels as "first factor," "anxiety index," "cynicism factor," "escapism," "obvious hysteria," and "subtle hysteria." Several of the other clinical entities are also measured in terms of subtle and obvious scales, "subtle paranoia" and "obvious paranoia," for example. Many of the special scales were empirically derived, but some were logically assembled on the basis of what the authors believed the diagnostic significance of various items to be. A series of well-accepted subscales for depression, hysteria, psychopathic deviate, paranoia, schizophrenia, and hypomania were developed in this manner by Harris and Lingoes (1955).

Yet another source of personality data may be gained from an inspection of *critical items*. These are items which the subject answers in ways suggestive of various pathological dispositions–such as anxiety, depression, dissociation, thought disorder, or physiological disorders, and may provide a basis for amplifying (or disconfirming) this information in follow-up interview. For example, a True answer to the statement "There is something wrong with my mind" strongly invites inquiry. Several lists of critical items have been published, including lists by Koss and Butcher (1973) and Lachar and Wrobel (1979). Lists are available also in Graham (1987).

A particularly intriguing synthesis of psychometric (MMPI) data and a psychodynamic conceptual system is reported by Trimboli and Kilgore (1983). Clearly an original and challenging approach, it is rooted in longstanding, less-rigorous clinical practice:

> The present writer has heard discussions in case conferences at the University of Minnesota Hospitals which make as "dynamic" use of MMPI patterns as one could reasonably make of any kind of test data without an excessive amount of illegitimate reification. The clinical use of the Strong Vocational Interest Blank is another example (Meehl, 1945).

In the approach set forth by Trimboli and Kilgore, MMPI Scales 3,4,5,6,9, and 0 are identified as "character scales," and, as such, reflective of the test taker's defensive structure. The validity scales—L, F, and K—and their patterning, also disclose the testee's defensive structure. The psychometrically more unstable (less-reliable) scales, 1, 2, 7, and 8 are designated "symptom scales."

In this framework, the following dimensions may be extracted from MMPI score patterns:

Characteristic security and defensive operations

Capacity to manage or tolerate anxiety

Characteristic ways of dealing with aggression and hostility

Stability of reality contact

Quality of object relations

Level of pathology

Though score-based, Trimboli and Kilgore's is a conceptual, not a cookbook, approach. Here is how they hypothesize the defensive significance of the character scales:

Scale 3 (Hysteria) This is suggestive of conversions when elevations are high (T > 80), and the defense mechanisms long identified with this disorder are denial and repression, keeping unpleasantries out of awareness, and channeling conflicts into vague physical complaints. Thus the interpretive significance of Scale 3 is in harmony with commonly accepted clinical understanding.

Scale 4 (Psychopathic Deviate) This scale correlates with hostility, high-scoring males being rated high in hostility and aggressiveness, also in rebelliousness, impulsiveness, hedonism, and antisocial tendencies. Hence the defense mechanisms associated with this syndrome are externalization, acting out, and rationalization or intellectualization.

Scale 5 (Masculinity-Femininity) This scale, when highly deviant for one's gender, suggests the possibility of an identity problem, which in turn might be expected to preclude the crystallization of an effective defensive structure. Impulse control and aggressiveness (or control of aggressiveness) appear to be associated with more moderate deviations from one's gender norm, "feminine" scorers tending to passivity, inhibition of impulses, and suppression, while those who register a high "masculine" are weak on these defenses and prone to greater assertiveness and aggressiveness.

Scale 6 (Paranoia) If not indicative of clinical paranoia—which is likely to be present when the elevation is very high—at more moderate levels is associated with suspiciousness, excessive interpersonal sensitivity, and rigidity. In line with clinical experience, we would expect that elevations on this scale point to the mechanisms of projection and externalization.

Scale 9 (Hypomania) This is associated with various diagnoses that have central features of low impulse-control and low frustration-tolerance characterized by a propensity to aggressive outbursts and episodes of irritability, ineffectual overactivity and perhaps a grandiose self-concept. Hence these are people who discharge tensions directly in psychomotor activity. The authors conceptualize a defensive picture involving distraction maneuvers (psychomotor discharges), denial, and acting out, the latter particularly in the presence of Scale 4 elevation.

Scale 0 (Social Introversion) When high ($T > 70$, and sometimes lower than this), this scale suggests an individual who is uncomfortable in social situations, hence the defenses would be expected to be avoidance and withdrawal.

Evaluation

The reliability and validity status of the MMPI are summarized by Graham (1987). Concerning reliability,

> Several summary statements can be made about the temporal stability of MMPI scores. Individual MMPI scales seem to be as reliable temporally as other personality measures. Code types tend to be more stable when their scales are more elevated and when they are significantly more elevated than other scales in the profile. Although MMPI configurations probably are not as stable as often assumed by clinicians, subjects often produce the same code types on different administrations of the test. When the code types change from one administration to another, they tend to remain in the same diagnostic grouping. When the code types change dramatically, there often are concomitant behavioral changes.

Some instability is of course to be expected in measuring personality, particularly of those features that fluctuate over time, with or without treatment, such as levels of anxiety and depression.

Regarding validity, Graham writes:

> Although research data concerning validity of the MMPI are considerable, differences in subjects, settings, criterion measures, methodologies, and statistical analyses make it difficult to reach precise conclusions concerning the MMPI's validity. Almost all of the research data are concurrent rather than predictive in nature. However, existing data indicate that judgments, inferences, and decisions based on MMPI data are likely to be more accurate than judgments based on no assessment data or on projective data. Accuracy is likely to be enhanced greatly if MMPI data are used in conjunction with social history and interview data.

Despite such a generally encouraging picture, one cannot blithely assume the validity of MMPI scales. Megargee and Mendelsohn (1962) designed a cross-validation study of 10 MMPI scales and two scoring indices that purport to measure hostility and control, using four groups of subjects known to differ on these dimensions on the basis of their past behavior. Most of the significant findings were opposite to what would logically be expected: a group of assaultive criminals was found to be (psychometrically) less hostile and better controlled than a group of nonviolent criminals and a group of normals.

MMPI-2 The MMPI-2, published in 1989, incorporates a number of significant revisions of its predecessor while maintaining the basic features that have made the original instrument popular. Retained are the 10 original clinical scales and the provision for supplementary scales. The body of MMPI research that has been developed over the years, and the instrument's interpretive manuals, continue to be relevant. It will obviously be a matter of years before a similar body of research specific to the new instrument is built up. Although there has been some change in the individual items, and the order of the items has changed, the current item total is virtually the same as in the original, 567.

New scales have been added. The MMPI-2 has measures for such variables as treatment potential, suicidal behavior, Type A and Type B personality, and post-traumatic stress disorder. A new approach to validity, in addition to the standard validity scales, assesses the consistency with which the subject responds. Deleted from the MMPI-2 are those items pertaining to religion and sexual practices which have been a focus of complaints about the earlier version.

The new standardization involves an appreciably larger, more diversified sampling that is more representative of the U.S. population. Approximately equal numbers of males and females were included, and minorities are represented in the proportion in which they appear in the 1980 census.

These improvements notwithstanding, some nine months after introduction of the instrument, Adler (1990) found widespread questioning and discontent among psychologists. The normative sampling is problematic in several respects, and, particularly, the educational level of the normal group presents an obvious target. Thus, 45 percent of the normal sample is made up of college graduates—approximately three times the percentage in the previous U.S. census; and only about 5 percent had less than a high-school education, whereas the census figure is almost seven times greater. W. Grant Dahlstrom of longtime MMPI fame—and one of the four authors of the revision—is quoted in Adler's article to the effect that the normative group will better conform to the 1990 census (not published at the time). Graham (1990) deals with the issue of education by suggesting that the sample "appears to be quite representative of persons who are likely to take the MMPI."

A lack of concordance between the versions has also come in for a good deal of attention. "We're not sure the patterns mean the same thing still," according to Dahlstrom. Clinicians have reported that the two inventories tend not to yield the same results: subjects commonly seem to disclose pathology on one version but not the other. People who are presumably normal have normal profiles, but these tend to differ greatly on the two versions, and the interpretations of these would suggest different personality features in the same individual.

Adler's article casts the issue in the paradigm of the 1980s controversy over "New Coke" versus "Classic Coke." What cannot be disputed is that much more research is in order.

SELECTED REFERENCES ON THE MMPI

Archer, R. P. (1987). *Using the MMPI with adolescents.* Hillsdale, NJ: Lawrence Erlbaum Associates.
Butcher, J. N. (1990). *MMPI-2 in psychological treatment.* New York: Oxford University Press.
Dahlstrom, W. G., Welsh, G. S., & Dahlstrom, L. E. (1972). *An MMPI handbook: Vol. II, Research applications.* Minneapolis: University of Minnesota Press.
Friedman, A. F., Webb, J. T., & Lewak, R. (1989). *Psychological assessment with the MMPI.* Hillsdale, NJ: Lawrence Erlbaum Associates.
Graham, J. R. (1987). *The MMPI: A practical guide.* New York: Oxford University Press.
Graham, J. R. (1990). *MMPI-2: Assessing personality and psychopathology.* New York: Oxford University Press.
Greene, R. L. (1990). *The MMPI/MMPI-2: An interpretive manual.* Boston: Allyn and Bacon.

Millon Clinical Multiphasic Inventory...And Related Inventories
Description

In the broad tradition of the MMPI, the Millon Clinical Multiaxial Inventory (MCMI) was first published in 1977 and was subsequently revised (MCMI-II) (Millon, 1987). There are, however, important differences between the MMPI and the MCMI. Most notably, the MCMI was designed to coordinate with the Axis II personality disorders delineated in the DSM-III-R (Chapter 8), and the personality constructs of Millon's (1981, 1986) biosocial theory.

The MCMI consists of 175 self-report statements in booklet form to be answered True or False, and administration time is 20–30 minutes. The inventory yields scores for 22 personality disorders and clinical syndromes, including scores for 10 personality disorder-related scales grouped together as Clinical Personality Pattern Scales: Schizoid, Avoidant, Dependent, Histrionic, Narcissistic, Antisocial, Aggressive/Sadistic, Compulsive, Passive-Aggressive, and Self-Defeating. Related to the severe personality disorders (Kernberg, 1967, 1970, 1984; Millon, 1969, 1981) are three scales—Schizotypal, Borderline, and Paranoid—grouped as Severe Personality Pathology Scales. There are six Axis I (Chapter 8) Clinical Syndrome Scales—Anxiety Disorder, Somatoform Disorder, Bipolar—Manic Disorder, Dysthymic Disorder—Alcohol Dependence, and Drug Dependence; and three Severe Clinical Syndrome Scales—Thought Disorder, Major Depression, and Delusional Disorder.

In addition to these clinical scales, there are three correction scales called "Modifier Indices." The Disclosure scale is a measure of the subject's frankness and self-revelation in responding, the extent to which he or she was open but not exaggerating. The Desirability scale taps such factors "as putting one's best foot forward, appearing psychologically healthy and socially virtuous, denying unattractive or problematic characteristics, and the like" (Millon, 1987). The Debasement scale evidences the extent to which an individual is prone to self-"put downs," to exaggerate shortcomings, to accentuate the negative.

Administration, Scoring, and Interpretation

A profile of the scores on the 22 scales may be interpreted by the clinician in terms of the characteristics measured by these scales. Computer interpretive reports are available in several ways: with the use of a software program that enables the test user to administer, score, and print a report in the office; through teleprocessing service; and through mail-in service.

The interpretive report is prefaced with several cautions in the interest of ethical considerations (American Psychological Association, 1986) and alerting the test user to the limitations of such a document. Additionally, the report suggests that the printout be evaluated in the context of collateral information, such as the client's history, current life circumstances, observation and interview data, and data and impressions gained with the use of other instruments.

A unique feature of the MCMI-II interpretive narrative is the discussion of Axis I issues in the context of a functioning personality:

> From now on the interpretive narrative will elaborate the meaning of Axis I disorders in light of the patient's basic Axis II personality pattern. "For example, two subjects achieving the same score on Scale D (Dysthymia) may have substantially different descriptive texts characterizing the nature of their depressive symptoms, its meaning, how the patient experiences his or her depression, the dynamics that underlie it, and its likely form of expression" (Fleischauer, 1987, in an interview with Theodore Millon).

Various gauges are built into the computer scoring system that may challenge the validity or reliability of individual records. The rationale of the Validity

Index is particularly clear. This index consists of four items that make assertions that are bizarre or highly improbable as applied to the test taker. When, for example, an individual were to endorse the statement that his or her picture has appeared on the front cover of several magazines in the past year, the accuracy of the record would be suspect, and two such endorsements would trigger the computer to stamp the record INVALID.

Evaluation

The MCMI is suitable for use with subjects 17 years of age and older who are being assessed or are in treatment for emotional or interpersonal problems. It is not recommended for use with "normals" or with persons who present with severe pathology, a caution that is in line with Dana and Cantrell's (1988) review, and false positives and false negatives can be a problem. Its best use is with persons whose psychological problems are in the moderate range of severity.

Additional Millon Scales

Two additional Millon scales, constructed in a format similar to the MCMI, are the Millon Behavioral Health Inventory (MBHI) (Millon, Green, & Meagher, 1982a) and the Millon Adolescent Personality Inventory (MAPI) (Millon, Green, & Meagher, 1982b).

The MBHI has application in the formulation of treatment plans, in predicting the course of chronic illness, and in predicting response to treatment. The instrument may also disclose patients' style of relating to health-care personnel, and psychosocial attitudes and stressors that may pose problems in treatment.

The Millon Adolescent Personality Inventory (MAPI) was designed to assess the overall personality functioning of adolescent subjects rather than to focus on pathology. It has application both in clinical and educational settings, and a clinical and an educational report are available. The instrument may be administered to subjects from 13 to 18 years of age. Items are worded at the sixth-grade reading level.

SELECTED REFERENCES ON THE MILLON INVENTORIES

Millon, T. (1987). *Manual for the MCMI-II* (2nd ed.). Minneapolis: National Computer Systems.
Millon, T., Green, C. J., & Meagher, R. B., Jr. (1982a). *Millon Behavioral Health Inventory manual* (3rd ed.). Minneapolis: National Computer Systems.
Millon, T., Green, C. J., & Meagher, R. B., Jr. (1982b). *Millon Adolescent Personality Inventory manual.* Minneapolis: National Computer Systems.

Personality Inventory For Children
Description

The Personality Inventory for Children (PIC) introduced by Wirt, Lachar, Klinedinst, & Seat (1977) is in the University of Minnesota/MMPI tradition, with overlap of methodology and format. The instrument is primarily for use in assessing children and adolescents, ages 6–16. It may also be used to assess children from 3–5 years of age, although scores at this level are less stable.

There are 600 affirmatively worded statements in the PIC, which are answered True or False, preferably by the child's biological mother, particularly if she has lived continuously with the child. Other possible respondents might be the child's father, stepparents, foster parents, or other adults who have known the child well since the early years.

Inventory scales are in two broad categories, the *profile scales* and the *supplementary scales*. The profile scales, in turn, consist of *validity and screening scales*, and *clinical scales*.

The validity and screening scales are reminiscent of those on the MMPI. They are labeled Lie, Frequency, Defensiveness, and Adjustment. Lie items identify respondents who seek to present the child as unduly virtuous and without the minor failings that are found in most children—statements on the order of "my child always does immediately what I ask him (her) to do." Frequency scale items are items answered in a deviant manner, that is, differently from the way approximately 95 percent of respondents for normal children answer them. Such responses, then, may be due to the presence of deviant behavior in the child or to a deviant response set in the adult who is responding to the inventory items, such as exaggeration of symptoms or random responding. The Defensiveness scale is a measure of the respondent's tendency to deny or fail to recognize negative features in the child. There is also a measure of maladjustment labeled the Adjustment scale, designed to bring to awareness children who should have further psychological evaluation.

There are 12 clinical scales identified as Achievement, Intellectual Screening, Development, Somatic Concern, Depression, Family Relations, Delinquency, Withdrawal, Anxiety, Psychosis, Hyperactivity, and Social Skills. Supplemental scales bear such labels as Aggression, Excitement, Ego Strength, Sex Role, and Somatization. A revised format edition (Lachar, 1982; Wirt, Lachar, Klinedinst, & Seat, 1984) also contains four broad-band factor scales. These are: Undisciplined/Poor Self-Control; Social Incompetence; Internalization/Somatic Symptoms; and Cognitive Development.

Scoring and Interpretation

Inventories may be hand scored and interpreted by the clinician. A guide prepared for this purpose is available (Wirt, Lachar, Klinedinst & Seat, 1990). Presented in the guide are integrated narrative conclusions that correspond with scale elevations. Computer scoring and interpretation are also available.

Evaluation

The standardization sample included almost 2,600 subjects. Nearly 2,400 normal boys and girls were in the 6–16-year-old standardization group and nearly 200 constituted the younger 3–5-year-old age group.

A major strength of the inventory is the time-saving flexibility of use that it permits. Divided into four parts, only as many parts as necessary to respond to the reason for assessment need to be administered. Thus, Part I (131 items) is suitable as a screening instrument. It yields a score for the Lie scale plus scores for the four factor scores derived from Part I: Undisciplined/Poor Self-Control, Social Incompetence, Internalization/Somatic Symptoms, and Cognitive Development. Further Parts may subsequently be administered to obtain a fuller personality picture, if necessary. High reliabilities are reported by the authors for the scales that constitute the personality profile, and correlations of the abbreviated scales of Parts I–II with the complete test are also reported to be very high (.92–.97).

SELECTED REFERENCES ON THE PERSONALITY INVENTORY FOR CHILDREN

Lachar, D. (1982). *Personality Inventory for Children (PIC): Revised format manual supplement.* Los Angeles: Western Psychological Services.

Wirt, R. D., Lachar, D., Klinedinst, J. K., & Seat, P. D. (1990). *Multidimensional description of child personality: A manual for the Personality Inventory for Children.* Los Angeles: Western Psychological Services.

California Psychological Inventory
Description and Administration

Another of the instruments spawned by the MMPI is the California Psychological Inventory (CPI), originally published by Harrison G. Gough in 1957 and revised (CPI-R) in 1987. Intended for use with normal adults (ages 14 and up), approximately half of its 462 True-False items were taken from the MMPI. In reusable booklet format, the inventory may be completed by one individual, or by individuals in a group, in 45–60 minutes.

Scoring and Interpretation

The inventory may be hand-scored or computer-scored, and may be clinician interpreted or computer interpreted. A software system for in-office administration, scoring, and interpretation is available from the publisher, or the clinician may purchase mail-in scoring and interpretation that provides the Gough five-part narrative and the CPI configural analysis supplement by Gough and McAllister.

Evaluation

Scale scores tend to intercorrelate on the order of .50 or greater, indicating overlap in what they measure. Test-retest reliabilities and internal consistency are at an acceptable level.

A strong feature of the CPI is its diversity of application and the breadth of personality data that it yields. The instrument was designed to be particularly applicable to counseling/assessment situations in schools and colleges, to business and industry, and may be used as an aid to counseling, selection, and career guidance. More specifically, in clinics and counseling agencies, and in combination with other instruments, the CPI may yield insights in the case of various maladjustments, including social immaturity, delinquency/criminality, marital problems and substance abuse. In educational use it can be helpful in predicting success in a variety of careers. In business and industry the CPI may be used to identify potential managers and other personnel, and to provide information that may be helpful in counseling employees in exploring vocational goals or dealing with personal problems.

Data derived from the CPI yield three major vectors as the basis for a typological structural view of personality, and are the basis for delineating lifestyles or "ways of living." The five basic scales of the revised CPI are labeled: Interpersonal Style and Manner of Dealing with Others, Internalization and Endorsement of Normative Conventions, Cognitive and Intellectual Functioning, Thinking and Behavior, and Special Scales and Indexes. Each of these in turn measures a number of variables. For example, the Interpersonal Style and Manner of Dealing with Others scale is composed of the subscales Dominance, Capacity for Status, Sociability, Social Presence, Self-Acceptance, Independence, and Empathy.

SELECTED REFERENCES ON THE CALIFORNIA PSYCHOLOGICAL INVENTORY

McAllister, L. W. (1988). *A practical guide to CPI interpretation* (2nd ed.). Palo Alto, CA: Consulting Psychologists Press.

Megargee, E. I. (1972). *The California Psychological Inventory handbook*. Palo, Alto, CA: Consulting Psychologists Press.

PROJECTIVE TECHNIQUES

Rorschach
Description

The Rorschach inkblot method, based on responses to 10 inkblots, 5 in black and gray tones and 5 chromatic, all printed on cards 6 3/4 inches by 9 5/8 inches, is among the most widely used psychological diagnostic instruments, and has been well documented to be so for many years (Lubin et al. [1984, 1985, 1986]). It is also considered by its adherents to be the most penetrating, the most revealing of all instruments that probe the workings of the mind. At the same time there is appreciable consensus that it is among the least valid of instruments when examined by psychometric criteria, an allegation that is acknowledged by many who champion its use. We may also place in this array of extremes the matter of the profitability of the Rorschach to its developer: "During his whole life, Mrs. Rorschach told me, he earned only 25 Swiss francs ($5.00 at that time) with his test" (Ellenberger, 1989).

Hermann Rorschach (1951) conceived of his inkblots as a test of perception (and apperception). In summarizing the use of his "psychological experiment," as he identified the method, he indicated that "There is...no doubt that this experiment can be called a test of the perceptive power of the subject." Perception continues to be afforded a major role in the eyes of many Rorschachers, but in more recent times the instrument has also become increasingly valued and employed to illuminate how individuals construe the meaning of their experiences and their reality, and their inner representations of themselves and others (Blatt, 1986).

More generally, the Rorschach is seen as an approach to appraising personality, with various personality features specified or emphasized by different writers. Thus, Exner (1986) notes:

> When the standard procedures for collecting the data are employed faithfully, the yield is very substantial. It provides information about habits, traits, and styles, and about the presence of states, and about many other variables that can be listed under the broad rubric encompassed by the term *personality*...it is not an x-ray of the mind or soul, but it does afford, in a brief glimpse, a picture of the psychology of the person, as it is, and to some extent as it has been, and to some extent as it will be.

The Longman *Dictionary of Psychology and Psychiatry* (Goldenson, 1984) writes of the Rorschach:

> The object is to interpret the subject's personality structure in terms of such factors as emotionality, cognitive style, creativity, bizarreness, and various defensive patterns.

Administration

The above observations are generalities. They are more or less pertinent to psychological assessment using Rorschach's 10 original inkblots administered according to one of the several more or less widely used procedures. That is, when they are presented to subjects one at a time with a request to interpret them (*Free-Association Phase*), following which the examiner conducts an *Inquiry* primarily to help establish to which part of the blot the subject responded (*Location*) and what features of the blot—shape, color, movement, shading, etc. gave rise to the response (*Determinants*).

More specifically, administration varies among the several Rorschach "systems" (pp. 159–160) and also among individual Rorschach examiners. Some administer the cards face-to-face with the client; other examiners sit side-by-side and slightly behind the subject. Some conduct the Inquiry after the client has responded to all 10 cards; some inquire after the free-association to each card is completed. Some encourage the client to produce more responses when he or she offers only one response per card, but do so only for Cards I and II; some follow this procedure for the first five cards. Probably the most widely followed procedure is the meticulous set of instructions provided by Exner (1986).

Testing the limits with the Rorschach is another individual matter. It is a feature of Rorschach administration that may be brought to bear when the examiner believes that additional useful information may be available through the skillful use of appropriate questions as a follow-up to the administration proper. For example, normal subjects generally see human figures on the Rorschach, most particularly on Card III, and failure to see them may be indicative of pathology.

To determine, then, whether a subject who has reported no humans is capable of this percept, the examiner might spread out all of the cards and say, "Some people see humans on one or more of these cards. Can you see any?" If the answer is negative the examiner might select Card III and say, "People often see humans on this card. Can you see any?" Again, if the answer is negative, the examiner might point out the usual area where humans are seen, and ask, "Do you see them?" If the subject indicates he or she does not, the examiner might finally suggest, "Well, some people see this part as the head, this as the arms..." At this point the subject might concur that the blot area is indeed reminiscent of humans...or demur, with the observation that the figures do not resemble humans because what the examiner pointed out as a head resembles a bird's head, or because what the examiner suggested as torso and legs are separated.

Scoring and Interpretation

Like Rorschach administration, scoring and interpretation varies. Each system has a number of its own notations or prescribed ways of coding responses. For example, while most systems recognize the percept of an animal in motion (scored FM), Beck does not believe that subjects really perceive an animal in motion—that what they really see is the shape of the animal—and the percept should be notated as a Form response (F). Innovations in scoring are scattered through the Rorschach literature, such as Beck's Z (organizational activity) (Beck, 1933), Rapaport and Schafer's (Rapaport, Gill, & Schafer, 1946) deterioration color (Cdet—pure color responses characterized by such expressions as "gory" or "uncanny" or evidencing severely haphazard association), or Exner's (1986) set of "special scores" that identify unique characteristics of a response. *Ag* would be the score for a movement response involving aggression.

There are also numerous similarities of scoring across systems. However, all of them use Rorschach's (1921/1951) scoring as a basic reference point. Human Movement (M), (pure) Color (C), and Form (F) responses are examples of major variables universally recognized by Rorschachers. Exner's (1986) scoring system is currently very popular.

Responsible interpretation of the Rorschach demands extensive and intimate familiarity with the literature on the instrument. There is also consensus that to become competent with the Rorschach a period of instruction and supervised experience is mandatory. Beyond this observation it is hard to be specific. It is not certain whether Bruno Klopfer's (Klopfer & Kelley, 1946) observation during the early days of Rorschach testing would serve well as a prescription today:

Proficiency as a Rorschach administrator can be gained within a few months. However, even those who are able and qualified to proceed to the next step of proficiency as Rorschach interpreters usually will remain in a "learning stage" for two or three years.

Clinical Rorschach interpretation involves finding meaning in research or in clinical lore for (usually) tabulated Rorschach scores (and their frequencies) and relationships among scores, in combination with such matters as sequence and orderliness of responses, response times, manner of responding, emotional responses to the procedure, verbalizations, behaviors of clinical interest, reason for assessment, other inputs of information, intuition, and an indefinite number of other factors.

The Rorschach also lends itself to computer interpretation. In Exner's (1985) Rorschach Interpretation Assistance Program (RIAP), an offspring of Exner's well-known system, coded responses yield a three-section report of about five pages in length. Use of this aid does not obviate the need for a skillful Rorschach clinician, however. The offerings of the computer are best regarded as hypotheses to be considered along with other data.

Evaluation

The basic issue for students of the Rorschach is that of validity—an extremely complex problem. Just what the problem is specifically, however, is not a matter of consensus. Zubin, Eron, and Schumer (1965) consider the difficulty as one of seeking psychometric validity for an instrument that lacks some of the requisite psychometric properties. Exner (1986) acknowledges the psychometric limitations, but indicates that "none have been unresolvable." (see pp. 106–107)

What sort of validity we should seek is yet another difficulty. Is it psychometric validity we are after, or should we seek to validate idiographic findings which may have more credibility (Aronow, Reznikoff, & Rauchway, 1979)? Should we seek empirical validity or conceptual validity which has been reported to hold more promise (Weiner, 1977a, 1986; Atkinson, Quarrington, Alp, & Cyr, 1986)? Are limitations of the single-variable approach sufficiently serious to warrant dismissal of the often negative findings that it yields; is consideration of clusters of scores or dealing with scores in a configuration a more proper approach to Rorschach validation?

Beyond such basic considerations there is no entity that we may properly call *The* Rorschach, though such an expression has become part of our everyday speech. But there can be problems when we lump together data and conclusions from diverse studies that have little more in common than the use of the same 10 blots. Exner (1969) identified the problems for the profession that accompany the side-by-side existence of varying Rorschach *systems*—and advanced his *comprehensive* system (1974, 1978, 1986) by way of an approach to remediation. He identifies five widely used systems of the time—those of Klopfer, Beck, Piotrowski, Hertz, and Rapaport-Schafer.

All of these diverge, to a greater or lesser extent, from Rorschach's Rorschach (1921/1951), and from one another, with respect to such features as seating arrangements of the examiner vis-à-vis the subject, instructions, conduct of the Inquiry, scoring, goals of the examination, and interpretive principles.

Exner and Exner (1972) report on the Rorschach practices of almost 400 clinicians with respect to some of these issues:

> Responses...indicate substantial diversity among Rorschachers in training, preferred Rorschach system, and in general approach to administration, scoring, and interpretation... Most respondents have been trained in either the Beck or Klopfer methods but most alter the method in which they have been trained with other methods or personal experience.

Traditionally, then, there has been no uniform Rorschach approach to arriving at useful personality interpretations or generalizable validity information. Exner's comprehensive system provides a basis for establishing such uniformity and building a meaningful body of data. A computer program incorporating well-defined variables and having applicability to the needs of a broad range of examiners and assessment problems obviously is actuarially sounder than programs based on less systematic attention to data.

In any event, computer-generated Rorschach reports, when used, should be in the context of heavy assessor involvement. The assessor may wish to "compare notes" with the computer, perhaps to examine its report for material that he or she may have overlooked. But the assessor must retain the clinical prerogative, and bring to bear clinical skills and knowledge—information concerning the client's situation and history—and ability to understand the Rorschach idiom (Chapter 12).

SELECTED REFERENCES ON THE RORSCHACH

Aronow, E., & Reznikoff, M. (1976). *Rorschach content interpretation*. Orlando, FL: Grune & Stratton.

Aronow, E., & Reznikoff, M. (1989). *A Rorschach introduction: Content and perceptual approaches*. Boston: Allyn and Bacon.

Exner, J. E., Jr. (1969). *The Rorschach systems*. Orlando, FL: Grune & Stratton.

Exner, J. E., Jr. (1974). *The Rorschach: A comprehensive system, Vol. 1*. New York: Wiley.

Exner, J. E., Jr. (1978). *The Rorschach: A comprehensive system, Vol. 2: Current research and advanced interpretation*. New York: Wiley.

Exner, J. E., Jr. (1986). *The Rorschach: A comprehensive system, Vol. 1: Basic foundations* (2nd ed.). New York: Wiley.

Exner, J. E., Jr., & Weiner, I. B. (1982). *The Rorschach: A comprehensive system, Vol. 3: Assessment of children and adolescents*. New York: Wiley.

Holt, R. R. (Ed.) (1968). *Diagnostic psychological testing* (Rev. ed.). New York: International Universities Press.

Potkay, C. R. (1971). *The Rorschach clinician*. Orlando, FL: Grune & Stratton.

Rickers-Ovsiankina, M. A. (1977). *Rorschach psychology* (2nd ed.). Huntington, NY: Krieger.

Thematic Apperception Test(s)
Description

The Thematic Apperception Test (TAT) is an outgrowth of the personality theory of Henry A. Murray (Murray et al., 1938) that stresses the role of needs (internal tensions) and press (external influences) in the understanding of human functioning.

The TAT materials consist of a series of large cards, each of which bears a black-and-white picture, and one of which is blank white. The subject's task is to make up stories about them. The cards are coded B, for young boys; G, for young girls; M, for males over 14 years; F, for females over 14 years; BM, for males of all ages; GF, for females of all ages; and numbered cards without letters that are suitable for administration to both male and female subjects of all ages.

In telling a story, the subject is said to identify with a (usually same sexed) figure known as the "hero." The hero's fantasies, goals, relationships, conflicts, fears, and so forth are understood to relate to those of the subject. Thus, the hero's needs, such as the need for affiliation, or recognition, or aggression—or the press, such as environmental demands, as the hero experiences them, are believed to reflect these issues in the story teller.

Administration

The examiner selects about 8 to 10 cards that he or she judges might reveal information pertinent to the reason assessment is being done. The TAT is then administered by reading or paraphrasing the instructions in the test manual. Time constraints mentioned in the manual generally are ignored, however. Many examiners also omit Murray's statement to the subject that the TAT is "a test of imagination, one form of intelligence," and also the request to make up as dramatic a story as possible. The essence of the instructions is to ask the subject to make up a story for each card that will be shown, one at a time, and to include in the story a description of what is going on in the present scene, to tell what led up to the scene that is shown, what the characters are thinking and feeling, and what the outcome will be. In the case of the blank card the subject is asked to imagine a picture on the card and then make up a story about that picture.

To obtain diagnostically rich material the examiner must follow the telling of the story very carefully and query when the subject fails to supply requested information, or the examiner sees an opportunity to gain additional useful information. Thus such queries as "How does he feel about that?," "Why did she say that to her?," "How will the story turn out?" "Do you think he will achieve his ambition?," "Why not?" Or the examiner may prod, "Go ahead and make it up." In cases where the subject is intelligent and can communicate well in writing s(he) may be asked to write the story, often a fruitful procedure. The stories obtained in this way may also be queried after the task is completed.

Scoring and Interpretation

Formal scoring, in terms of needs and press, is used by some clinicians, but, for the most part, when scoring is done it is for purposes of research. In clinical practice, interpretation may be described as subjective, intuitive, impressionistic, and qualitative. The TAT is a "clinical" instrument. A formal approach to scoring and interpretation would be forbidding in clinical practice. Scoring in the Murray system is a three-hour proposition (Carlile, 1952) and interpretation a matter of four to five hours (Bellak, 1954)!

Evaluation

Attempts to establish reliability and validity have not been very rewarding. These, generally, involve scores, such as in studies of interscorer reliability or stability of scores over time, but, as just pointed out, most clinical assessment with the TAT is attentive to something other than scores. The study by Megargee and Parker (1968) points up a problem with validity studies. These investigators could find little agreement between TAT need scores and those derived from the Adjective Check List and the Edwards Personal Preference Schedule. The meaning of this finding may be brought into question, however, simply by pointing out that the several instruments may tap the same-labeled needs at different levels.

Another problem with TAT research has been identified by Keiser and Prather (1990):

> The research on the TAT is highly variable, with stimulus cards so varied that generalizations from one study to another or to clinical practice is hardly possible. A large part of this appears to be due to the lack of consistency and specificity of materials and procedures. It has become commonplace to use cards other than Murray's...and few people follow his instructions. However, in most cases, not only were the specific cards or administrative procedures not mentioned, but often Murray's cards were not used.

Karon (1968) introduces perspective to the issue of validity studies. He notes that "There are hundreds of articles on projective techniques which show them to be valid and hundreds of articles demonstrating them to be invalid." He contributes to an understanding of this situation in a discussion of "some of the common misconceptions which have led to confusion, conflicting evidence, and inappropriate conclusions."

These issues aside, surveys such as those cited on pp. 83 and 121 indicate that the TAT enjoys great popularity as an assessment tool. Numerous adaptations of the TAT, both for clinical and research use, have been made. The Children's Apperception Test (CAT) and the Senior Apperception Test (SAT) are well-known examples.

SELECTED REFERENCES ON THE THEMATIC APPERCEPTION TEST

Bellak, L. (1975). *The TAT, CAT, and SAT in clinical use* (3rd ed.). Orlando, FL: Grune & Stratton.

Murray, H. A., et al. (1938). *Explorations in personality*. New York: Oxford University Press.

Murstein, B. I. (1963). *Theory and research in projective techniques (emphasizing the TAT)*. New York: Wiley.

Stein, M. (1981). *The Thematic Apperception Test: An introductory manual for its clinical use with adults* (2nd ed.). Springfield, IL: C. C. Thomas.

Sentence Completion Methods
Description and Administration

The sentence completion method is a popular, simple to use, often fruitful self-report instrument. A number of clinical versions are available, and some assessors assemble their own group of items for clinical or research use. A versatile method, sentence completions may be used to gain information in any number of areas of human functioning.

Sentence completion items consist of sentence roots of one or more words to which the subject is asked to add words to make a sentence. Thus, "I...," "When I think of men...," or "Alcohol is..." Instructions ordinarily call for the subject to complete the items as quickly as possible. The instrument may be administered to one person at a time or to a group.

The task may be structured somewhat as follows: "I am going to start some sentences and I would like you to finish them with the first thought that comes to mind." A sample item or two may then be offered: "For example, if the sentence starts 'I am going..., you could say 'to write a letter', or 'to tell off my boss', or 'to be an engineer.'" The examiner may read the sentence roots to the subject and record the responses. Or, the subject may write the completions.

An inquiry is commonly helpful. The examiner may encourage the subject to try to complete items that were left blank, the omission possibly signaling an area of conflict. Asking the subject to amplify or explain responses ("How do you mean that?") can also reveal much content of interest. Example: The subject makes the completion "My father...sucks." Followed up with a simple "Can you tell me more about that?" may open the floodgates to a torrent of clinically rich material.

Authors of sentence completion forms seek out predefined areas of information usually for target identified groups. Thus, Forer (1957) authored four different forms of his instrument: for men, for women, for adolescent boys, and for adolescent girls. His content focus is on attitude-value systems, individual differences, evasiveness, and defense mechanisms. The Rotter Incomplete Sentences Blank (1950) seeks data in such areas as attitudes, goals, and fears. The Sacks Sentence Completion Test (Sacks & Levy, 1950) is a systematic approach to tapping into 15 areas of personality functioning:

I. Attitude toward Mother
II. Attitude toward Father
III. Attitude toward Family Unit
IV. Attitude toward Women
V. Attitude toward Heterosexual Relationships
VI. Attitude toward Friends and Acquaintances
VII. Attitude toward Superiors at Work or School
VIII. Attitude toward People Supervised
IX. Attitude toward Colleagues at Work or School

X. Fears
XI. Guilt Feelings
XII. Attitude toward Own Abilities
XIII. Attitude toward Past
XIV. Attitude toward Future
XV. Goals

Each of these areas is addressed sequentially every fifteenth item. Thus, in one version of the instrument, Attitude toward Father is addressed by the first item, that reads, "I feel that my father seldom…" and the sixteenth item, that reads, "If my father would only…" Fears are addressed by Item 7, "I know it is silly but I am afraid of…" and Item 22, "Most of my friends don't know that I am afraid of…"

Scoring and Interpretation

The sentence completion method is primarily a clinical technique. Interpretation is commonly impressionistic. Scoring is available, but its use is for the most part in a research context.

Holsopple and Miale (1954) suggest the following approach to interpretation:

> The psychologist should read through the entire record to gain a global impression. Following this, he should go through it again, this time getting the feel for sequence, for response clusters, and responses which have little reference to openings. Finally, he should examine individual sentences, after which he should set down hunches and inferences preparatory to outlining the personality picture.
>
> As one proceeds through the sentences, vague structures and outstanding properties begin to emerge. These clarify themselves gradually with full use of the examiner's insight, empathy, and experience, until a personality picture in terms of handling conflict, limitations and defects, as well as positive resources, has developed.

Evaluation

Complementing the popularity of the method are favorable reports of its reliability, evidently higher in many cases than for all other projective techniques. This observation is especially true of interjudge reliability, which extends to the upper .90s. Test-retest reliabilities tend to be more modest, with reliabilities of .38 to .54 reported when retesting is done at intervals of six months to three years. The Rotter Incomplete Sentences Blank was able to predict freshmen who would subsequently enter counseling, with a biserial correlation of .37 for men and .42 for women. (Churchill & Crandall, 1965)

Impressions of validity also tend to be favorable. Murstein's (1965, p. 777) summary statement is congruent with the impression of a number of psychologists: "The Sentence Completion Test is a valid test, generally speaking, and probably the most valid of all the projective techniques reported in the literature."

SELECTED REFERENCES ON THE SENTENCE COMPLETION METHOD

Forer, B. R. (1957). *Forer Structured Sentence Completion Test–manual.* Los Angeles: Western Psychological Services.

Rohde, A. R. (1957). *The sentence completion method: The diagnostic and clinical application to mental disorders.* New York: Ronald Press.

Rotter, J. B. (1950). *Rotter Incomplete Sentences Blank–manual.* San Antonio, TX: The Psychological Corporation.

Sacks, J. M., & Levy, S. (1950). The sentence completion test. In Abt, L. E., & L. Bellak (Eds.). *Projective psychology: Clinical approaches to the total personality.* New York: Knopf.

Drawing Tests: Draw-a-Person (DAP) (Also Human Figure Drawing); House-Tree-Person (HTP)
Description

The Draw-a-Person Test and the House-Tree-Person Test are overlapping projective techniques of personality assessment introduced about the same time. Both involve the drawing of a person. The HTP (Buck, 1948) was introduced one year before Machover (1949) brought out her monograph on figure drawing. Both soon became, and continue to be, popular instruments.

There is also overlap in their rationales, administration, and interpretation. With reference to the DAP, Machover (1949) offers the view that

> It is safe to assume that all creative activity bears the specific stamp of conflict and needs pressing upon the individual who is creating. The activity elicited in response to "draw a person" is indeed a creative experience, as will be testified by the individual who is drawing. Wide and concentrated experience with drawings of the human figure indicates an intimate tie-up between the figure drawn and the personality of the individual who is doing the drawing.

Administration and Scoring

For the DAP, the subject is supplied with a sheet of paper, 8 1/2" x 11", a medium-soft pencil with an eraser, and instructed to "draw a person." This accomplished, the subject is then asked, "Now draw a man (woman)," depending on the sex of the first-drawn figure. To preclude the possibility that the subject will understand that an adult figure is being called for, some examiners ask for a figure of a male or a female. If the subject draws only a head the subject is asked to complete the drawing. Or, to avoid a head drawing, the examiner may ask for a full-length drawing of a person. For subjects who verbalize uneasiness about their drawing skills (of which there are many), Machover advises the examiner to say, "This has nothing to do with your ability to draw. I am interested in how you *try* to make a person."

A similar interaction between examiner and subject characterizes the administration of the HTP. With this instrument the essential feature is a sequence of instructions to have the subject draw the house, the tree, and the person. In administering both instruments, clinical observations, including verbalizations and manner of performing the task, are recorded. With respect to the DAP Machover recommends noting such features as the approximate time to do the drawings, the sequence of the body parts drawn, and the sex of the first-drawn figure. A scoring system is not used with the Machover technique, though Buck (1948b; 1949) deals with a quantitative use of the HTP in his manual.

The second phase of administration for both instruments, not carried out by some examiners, is the asking of a series of questions. For the DAP, the subject may be introduced to this phase of the examination to make up stories about the figures as if they were characters in a novel or a play. A resistive subject may be eased into the task with such questions as "How old does s(he) appear to be?," and "Does s(he) look married or single?" And so on through a list of printed questions: "Is he strong?," "What is the best part of his body?," "Why?," "What are his good points?," "What are his bad points?," and then such questions as "Does he remind you of anyone?," "Would you like to be like him?," "Would you like to marry someone like him?"

Interpretation

The interpretation of both techniques is essentially impressionistic. Numerous correlates of drawn features of humans, houses and trees have been contributed by Machover (1949) and others, and are reported in Gilbert (1978) and Ogdon (1981) (both of these for humans), and in Ogdon (1981) (for houses and trees).

Thus, subjects who emphasize unessential details are reported to be schizophrenic; who elaborate on details of clothing, to have homosexual trends; who draw a tie, to have masculine striving or to be experiencing sexual inadequacy; who omit feet, to be discouraged or withdrawn; who emphasize the foot, to be assaultive; who emphasize the mouth, to be alcoholic, regressed, or depressed; who draw the opposite sex first, to experience sexual role conflict; who emphasize the breast area to be dependent, emotionally and sexually immature, or to trend to homosexuality; and who draw small breasts, to experience an unnurturing mother figure.

Similar interpretations are made on the basis of how houses and trees are drawn. When a house is drawn to appear as distant the person may feel inaccessible or wish to withdraw, or to be experiencing a home situation with which he or she cannot cope well. Those who draw very small houses may have withdrawal tendencies, feelings of inadequacy, be experiencing rejection at home, have regressive tendencies, or possibly be neurotic or schizophrenic. Women who draw diminutive houses may be controlled, humble, and reserved. Subjects who draw saplings may feel immature or be regressed; those who draw weeping willows may be depressed.

Evaluation

As with other impressionistically interpreted instruments, psychologists may be expected to differ in how acceptable they find drawing techniques. Consider the following statements from Machover (1949):

Wide and concentrated experience with drawings of the human figure indicates an intimate tie-up between the figure drawn and the personality of the individual who is doing the drawing.

Interpretation of symbol values are in line with common psychoanalytic and folklore meanings.

Though some of the assumptions may lack experimental verification, they have proved clinically valid.

We must also note that very many of the interpretations offered are very general (cf. Aunt Fanny statements, pp. 236–240). Further, a number of the interpretations offered are tentative, qualified, or offer several alternatives—it could be this or it could be that.

Nevertheless, these techniques provide a rich source of hypotheses to be responsibly evaluated in the context of the data mix of a battery.

Levy (1950) considers the status of figure drawings in the context of the status of psychology itself. To make his point he quotes Murray (1938) who quotes Samuel Butler:

> "The profession of psychology is much like living, which has been defined by Samuel Butler as 'the art of drawing sufficient conclusions from insufficient premises.' Sufficient premises are not to be found, and he who, lacking them, will not draw tentative conclusions, cannot advance."

SELECTED REFERENCES ON DRAWING TESTS

Buck, J. N. (1948a). The H-T-P test. *Journal of Clinical Psychology, 4*, 154–159.

Buck, J. N. (1848b). The H-T-P technique: A qualitative and quantitative scoring manual. I. *Journal of Clinical Psychology, 4*, 319–396.

Buck, J. N. (1949). The H-T-P technique: A qualitative and quantitative scoring manual. II. *Journal of Clinical Psychology, 5*, 37–76.

Hammer, E. F. (1958) (Ed.). *The clinical application of projective drawings*. Springfield, IL: C. C. Thomas.

Hammer, E. F. (1960). The House-Tree-Person (H-T-P) drawings as a projective technique with children. In A. I. Rabin & M. R. Haworth (Eds.). *Projective techniques with children*. Orlando, FL: Grune & Stratton.

Machover, K. (1949). *Personality projection in the drawing of the human figure: A method of personality investigation*. Springfield, IL: C. C.Thomas.

Vernier, C. M. (1952). *Projective drawings*. Orlando, FL: Grune & Stratton.

Bender Visual Motor Gestalt Test
Description and Administration

The Bender Visual-Motor Gestalt Test (Bender-Gestalt; Bender; B-G), introduced by Lauretta Bender as a developmental test, is employed as a screening device for organic brain damage and also as a projective technique. The physical materials of the Bender consist of nine cards, with the first card labeled A and the remaining eight cards numbered 1 through 8. On each card appears one of the figures used by Wertheimer in his experiments in gestalt psychology. The examiner shows the designs to a subject, one at a time, with instructions to copy them onto an 8 1/2 x 11 inch sheet of unlined white paper "just as they appear to you." Requests by the subject for further instructions (e.g., "Shall I make them the same size?") are parried with a remark like, "Just draw them the way they appear to you."

Scoring and Interpretation

Scoring systems are available for children (Koppitz, 1989) and for adults (Pascal & Suttell, 1951). Using the Bender as a projective technique, however, follows essentially an impressionistic approach. There is the subject who repeatedly asks for instructions and assurances; "Just draw them the way they appear to you" is not sufficient for such a person. There is the tense subject who continuously erases and redraws; the fearful, withdrawn subject who crowds all his tiny figures into the upper left hand corner of the sheet, the expansive subject who covers each sheet with one figure, the subject who anxiously shades his lines, the subject who distorts figures to phallic representations, the undercontrolled subject who "slap-dashes" off the figures, and the compulsive who just can't get his reproductions precise enough. The experienced assessor has seen all of these, and much more.

Evaluation

Murstein (1965, p. 703) summarizes a number of key facts about the Bender in a few, to-the-point observations:

> The B-G has been used...for personality description, as a measure of intelligence, and to diagnose brain damage, Stranger still is the fact that, despite this broad usage, surprisingly few generalizations can be made about the test. Various scoring systems have been employed, with great variability of results from one study to the next. Further, there is no hard core of accepted signs that have proved valid for any of the three tasks mentioned above. Usually a researcher who replicates a study that resulted in one set of signs will reject the majority of these signs and find only a few still valid. He is also apt to discover new signs that, however, will not be validated by his successor, who will find new signs, etc., ad absurdum, ad infinitum.

Clinicians nevertheless like the Bender, as witness its position near the top of the list of most used tests (Lubin, Larsen, & Matarazzo, 1984; Lubin, Larsen, Matarazzo, & Seever, 1985). The Bender is an easy source of inferences and hypotheses, which, if inconclusive in themselves, take on added importance when considered in the context of the data mix gained by use of a battery. Also not to be overlooked is the fact that typical administration time is about five minutes. Further, even psychiatric patients tend not to be intimidated by the Bender task, and using the Bender as the first test administered is commonly a pleasant way to ease a client into a battery.

SELECTED REFERENCES ON THE BENDER GESTALT TEST

Bender, L. (1938). *A visual motor gestalt test and its clinical uses.* Research Monograph No. 3. New York: American Orthopsychiatric Association.

Clawson, A. (1962). *The Bender Visual Motor Gestalt Test for children: A manual.* Los Angeles: Western Psychological Services.

Hutt, M. L. (1985). *The Hutt adaptation of the Bender Gestalt Test: Rapid screening and intensive diagnosis* (4th ed.). Boston: Allyn and Bacon.

Koppitz, E. M. (1989). *The Bender Gestalt Test for young children.* (2 Vols.). Boston: Allyn and Bacon.

Ogdon, D. P. (1981). *Psychodiagnostics and personality assessment: A handbook* (2nd ed.). Los Angeles: Western Psychological Services.

Tolor, A., & Brannigan, G. C. (1980). *Research and clinical applications of the Bender Gestalt Test.* Springfield, IL: C. C. Thomas.

8
ADDITIONAL TOOLS OF PSYCHOLOGICAL ASSESSMENT:
Observing and Interviewing, and A System of Classification

OBSERVING AND INTERVIEWING

Observing and interviewing typically are employed simultaneously and are accordingly discussed under one heading. Both are ancient techniques. Observation of one person by another is recorded as occurring in the Garden of Eden. Interviewing was also practiced in Biblical days, as noted in Chapter 1. Recollect the very brief—and very effective—interview ("Are you an E'phraimite?") that the Gileadites used to ferret out enemy soldiers. Observation and interviewing are used by professionals and nonprofessionals alike, and attention to a few basics can improve the effectiveness of the procedure.

Observation

The well-trained professional should be familiar with the literature of person perception, (such as Taft, 1955, 1956; Allport, 1937, 1961), particularly with respect to the avoidance of commonly made errors. Consider here the halo effect (positive and negative) and the use of stereotypes–that can make our work easier by doing our thinking for us.

Psychoanalysis also alerts us to numerous sources of error. The professional who is prone to the use of projection, in any of its guises, will, according to theory, find his or her features in the client. (But see the discussion on p. 276–297.) Countertransference can lead to gross, unrecognized distortions. For example, an erotic countertransference may be expected to detract from objectivity. Projective identification on the part of the client can compromise objectivity as the assessor becomes entangled with the client. Similarly, the assessor who identifies with the client is too close to be objective. The assessor who has tendencies to rationalize, or is inclined to downplay pathology, may view the client in too positive a light. A similar outcome may occur with observers who are inclined to overuse the defenses of repression and denial.

The skilled observer knows what to look for. In test situations, for example, the clinician establishes informal norms for client behaviors—how clients typically respond when asked to make up stories to TAT stimuli or how most clients go about solving Object Assembly tasks. Deviations from these norms well might have significance. The clinician also makes it a point to be attentive to a myriad of variables, such as affect, speech content and manner of speech, dress and grooming, interpersonal style, sweating, flushing, and hyperventilation, all of which may correlate with personality features of interest or with psychopathology.

Interviewing

Just as everyone is an observer of others, everyone is an interviewer. An apt definition for an interview is "a conversation with a purpose" (Bingham & Moore, 1924). "During the Spanish Inquisition, the accused were interrogated to establish their heresy, and the guide for enticing heretics to admit guilt was formulated as perhaps the first systematic interview" (Zubin, 1989). Currently, psychologists involved in assessment devote 39 percent of their assessment time to interviewing (Norcross, Prochaska, & Gallagher, 1989). "The interview is the cornerstone of psychodiagnosis and has surely been used in diagnosis for thousands of years" (Wiens & Matarazzo, 1983).

The skilled clinical interviewer, like the skilled clinical observer, brings to the task a rich technical background, including training in areas once not considered germane. An example brought to attention by Brown (1990) stresses the need for the interviewer to have an extensive understanding of gender-related issues. She observes:

> Every person has bias related to gender, without an awareness of that bias and its impact on our clinical judgment, and without access to data concerning its sources in our personal experiences and professional training, the assessment that takes place may be socially irresponsible, whereby the assessor acts out her or his unresolved countertransferential responses in the form of inaccurate or incomplete diagnostic inquiry and findings.

She provides as an example the tendency to underassess "well-socialized" men who present with problematic functioning, while battered women are "overpathologized" because of their overt expression of anger at their batterers, behavior that falls outside the range of expected 'womanly' behavior. She proposes a remedy centering about her "gender role analysis" (Brown, 1986).

A clinician must take on a particular mind-set in order to facilitate the process of gender role analysis. This perspective is one in which the assessor continually calls into question her or his taken-for-granted notions about what is usual and "normal" in regard to gendered phenomena and instead attends to several important variables that can influence the expression of gendered attitudes and ways of being. In addition, the assessor must choose to make gender a salient variable by purposefully inquiring about gendered phenomena and experiences that are related to biological sex. Last, gender role analysis requires an awareness of the data regarding gendered high base rate experiences—that is, experiences that occur in very high rates in one gender or another for a variety of reasons relating to the customs of a culture or the position of women or men within a given societal context, or both, that will have an impact on the nature and type of problems presented by clients.

In this era of scientific application, particularly of measurement techniques and methodological rigor, interviewing has not been without its detractors. The variability across interviews and interviewers has been shown to result in low reliability and therefore to rejection of the method of interviewing itself. Endicott and Spitzer (1972) suggest, however, that a remedy exists and not to interview may result in the loss of significant data such as pertain to thought processes, reality testing, interpersonal relations, and subjective content. They report:

> We have found that interviewers of different levels of clinical experience can be trained to make and record accurate judgments about the psychopathology of individuals whom they interview. The level of judgment may range from single observations such as "he cried during the interview" to more complex judgments such as "he has a paranoid delusion."
>
> Interview schedules and guides have been developed in order to combine the advantages of flexibility and rapport that are inherent in clinical interviews with advantages of completeness of coverage and comparability of method of eliciting information.

The purpose of clinical interview, basically, is to obtain information that will be useful in another context, usually therapy. Interviewing also offers an occasion to structure forthcoming therapy; the interviewer gives as well as receives information. And, as with all other assessment activity, such as test administration, the transactions of the interview situation can also be used in a therapeutic manner.

Broadly, interviews are of two types: standardized and informal, and differ in the degree to which they are structured and systematized. Standardized interviews may be *schedule standardized interviews* or *nonschedule standardized interviews*. The first is the most formal, consisting, as it does, of a list of printed items. These may be in the form of questions ("What was the highest grade of school you completed?"), and follow-up items may be included ("Why did you drop out of school?"). A nonschedule standardized interview, by contrast, lists only the items of information the interviewer is to elicit and permits him or her to phrase the questions.

Gunderson's (1982) Diagnostic Interview for Borderline Patients provides an example of a semi-schedule (or semi-structured) standardized interview. Structured items provide the basis for determining the extent, and the ways, in which the interviewee meets the criteria for borderline personality disorder. Examiners are encouraged to probe further, however, when they distrust the information the patient provides or when it appears that additional data would be helpful. Some representative items are:

To assess social activity—
  Do you find it easy to meet new people?
To assess self-destructive behavior—
  Have you ever behaved self-destructively?
    How about overdosing?
    Hurt self other than suicide?
To assess anger—
  Has impatience or demandingness gotten you in trouble?
And concerning other affects—
  Do you suffer chronic feelings of loneliness?
  Do you suffer chronic feelings of boredom?

The Structured Clinical Interview for DSM-III-R (SCID) (Spitzer, Williams, Gibbon, & First, 1990) is a semi-structured instrument to be used as an aid in establishing the major psychiatric diagnoses. Many of the items are open-ended so that the interviewer may determine not only the presence or absence of symptoms, but use the patient's own words to enhance the quality of the judgments to be made. It may be administered by a "clinician" or a "trained mental health professional who is familiar with the DSM-III-R classification and diagnostic criteria." Suitable subjects with whom the instrument may be used are adults (age 18 or over) and, with modification, with adolescents.

A unique feature of the SCID is its division into a number of modules, for example, Psychotic Disorders, Substance Use Disorders, and Personality Disorders. All of the modules may be employed with a given patient, such as may be done as an intake procedure to establish the extent to which indicators of the various disorders are present. In a more economical use of the instrument, it is possible to gain the information needed with the use of only one module. A patient with evident symptoms of bulimia nervosa, for example, can be systematically questioned for the existence of this condition according to DSM-III-R criteria with the Eating Disorders module.

The authors of the SCID have also prepared a "Mini-SCID," a quick computerized DSM-III-R screening interview.

In clinical practice, informal interviews, flexible and open-ended, are commonly employed. Interviewing in this manner clearly is an art. While the interviewer starts out with more or less of an agenda, the interview not infrequently flows in unexpected directions. Leads that the client throws out must be followed up as the interviewer's judgment dictates.

The skilled interviewer can call on a number of specialized techniques. Othmer and Othmer (1989), for example, discuss how to recognize and "handle" the defense mechanisms the client may employ during interview inasmuch as these may damage rapport and cause a problem with history taking. The authors present five "management techniques" for dealing with the client's defenses:

Bypassing The interviewer ignores the client's defensive operations. To tackle the problem, in some instances, can do more harm than good.

Reassurance "Reassurance works by viewing a defense mechanism from the patient's vantage point." This is a supportive approach, primarily by providing an ally to a person who may be lacking in self-confidence, is anxious, and perhaps suspicious.

Distraction Distraction may be used with disturbed persons, individuals with a severe psychiatric disorder or who are in an acute intoxicated state. Here the defense is frontally assaulted by such techniques as shouting, calling the person by name, or physical contact.

Confrontation "Confrontation is used to draw the patient's attention to a particular behavior with the expectation that he will recognize and correct it during the interview." Confrontation may be dissonant and provocative, or empathic.

Interpretation of Defenses Interpretation is used in the interest of getting the client to understand her or his use of maladaptive defenses. The client, of course, is probably not aware of these defenses, so confrontation commonly must precede interpretation.

As an interview progresses, the skilled interviewer narrows the focus of attention and seeks to sharpen the definition of the area of interest. Powers and Rustagi (1989) illustrate with a mnemonic device how they establish the existence of a borderline personality disorder, a matter of clinical importance since they find that patients with this diagnosis are likely to be at the center of transference/countertransference complications. They note that borderline patients are adept at draining the emotional resources of their therapist, thus calling up the word "sap," the full mnemonic being *I'm a sap*, i.e., borderline. With this expression, the interviewer finds it easy to keep in mind and be alert to the eight criteria for the diagnosis as spelled out in DSM-III-R: *I*mpulsiveness, *m*oodiness (affective instability), *a*nger, *s*uicidal threats, *a*bandonment, *p*attern of unstable relationships, *i*dentity disturbance, and *e*mptiness. While the efficacy of this device has not been challenged, it has been criticized as being in poor taste and insulting to the patient that the practitioner is seeking to help. (Larson, 1990; Cannon, 1990).

SELECTED REFERENCES ON OBSERVATION AND INTERVIEWING

Barker, P. (1990). *Clinical interviews with children and adolescents*. New York: Norton.

Craig, R. J. (1989). *Clinical and diagnostic interviewing*. Northvale, NJ: Jason Aronson.

Kahn, R. L., & Cannell, C. F. (1957). *The dynamics of interviewing: Its forms and functions*. New York: Wiley.

Othmer, E., & Othmer, S. C. (1989). *The clinical interview: Using DSM-III-R*. Washington, DC: American Psychiatric Press.

Pascal, G. R. (1983). *The practical art of diagnostic interviewing.* Homewood, IL: Dow Jones-Irwin.

Richardson, S. A., Dohrenwend, B. S., & Klein, D. (1965). *Interviewing: Its forms and functions.* New York: Basic Books.

Shea, S. C., (1988). *Interviewing: The art of understanding.* Philadelphia: W. B. Saunders.

Wiens, A. N., & Matarazzo, J. (1983). Diagnostic interviewing. In M. Hersen, A. E. Kazdin, & A. S. Bellak (Eds.) *The clinical psychology handbook.* New York: Pergamon Press.

The Mental Status Examination

The Mental Status Examination (MSE) is an interview directed to issues of diagnosis and treatment, and may also be used to establish a baseline against which to evaluate change. Its origin is traceable to Adolf Meyer (Lief, 1948). Closely identified with psychiatry, the MSE is also known as the *psychiatric examination.* Psychologists, too, use the MSE, in its entirety, or, more usually, in abbreviated form.

Outlines for doing a mental status examination are available from a number of sources, for example, Graham (1965), and Ginsberg (1985a, b). These are best used in an informal, nonschedule manner. Graham advises "No single outline would serve for all cases," and suggests that his outline is intended only as a guide. The client, the nature of the problem, and the situation in which the examination is done, will determine the specifics of conducting the MSE.

In a chapter titled Psychiatric History and Mental Status Examination, Ginsberg (1985a, b) suggests the following areas for exploration:

PSYCHIATRIC HISTORY

> Identification of The Patient
> Chief Complaint
> History of Present Illness
> Family History
> Past Personal History
> Sexual History
> Medical History

MENTAL STATUS EXAMINATION

> General Description
> Speech and Stream of Talk
> Emotional Reaction and Mood
> Perception
> Thought Content
> Cognition

Consciousness
Orientation
Memory
Intellectual Tasks: Information and Intelligence
Reading and Writing
Judgment
Insight
Other Diagnostic Studies
Diagnosis
Prognosis and Treatment Report

Under each heading are suggestions for kinds of information to seek, what to observe, questions to ask, or tasks for the client to do. Some examiners have favorite items—items that they find particularly productive.

The Mental Status Examination, as generally carried out, is an informal matter. Graham (1965) prefaces his mental status manual with the observation: "The manual is more effective when its items are not structured rigidly but are extended according to the specific aspects of a given situation." Spitzer, Fleiss, Endicott, and Cohen (1967), however, have reported on a factor analytically derived schedule standardized interview, called the Mental Status Schedule (MSS), to serve as a mental status examination. In addition to factor scales, the instrument may be scored in terms of traditional clinical diagnostic considerations. The primary purpose of the MSS is "to increase the research value of data collected during psychiatric interview."

Examples

To study motoric behavior, the examiner observes the client walk for indications of pathological gait-such as ataxia or Parkinsonism. Spontaneous speech is observed. Is it slow, rapid, or dysarthric? Or the client may be asked to repeat "test phrases," such as "rural artillery brigade" or "try three threads."

Affect may be assessed on the basis of responses to such questions as "Are you anxious or tense?" or "What makes you angry?" Suicidal implications may be elicited with questions like "Does life seem worthwhile?" or "Do you have feelings of harming yourself?"

Memory may be assessed with questions like "What is the name of your doctor?," "Do you know the names of any of the nurses on the ward?," or "What did you have for lunch today?" (In an institutional setting gaining access to the daily menu is a simple matter-so you can make sure the client's answer is not fiction). Judgment may be gauged by posing a number of intelligence-test-like questions, such as Similarities, for example: "How are an apple and a banana alike?" Or a hypothetical situation may be presented: "What would you do if you won $100,000 in the lottery?" (How this question is answered might also disclose information concerning depression.)

As a final illustration, we may look at some questions having to do with perception. Questions to elicit evidence concerning hallucinations are commonly asked in some settings, particularly when there is a possibility that the client is psychotic. Typical questions include: "Do you hear voices?," "Do you recognize them?," "What do they say?," "Do you experience strong sensations—like electricity or radar going through your body, or unusual sexual sensations?"

SELECTED REFERENCES ON THE MENTAL STATUS EXAMINATION

Ginsberg, G. L.(1985a, b). Psychiatric history and the mental status examination. In H. I. Kaplan & B. J. Sadock (Eds.) *Comprehensive textbook of psychiatry* (4th ed.). Baltimore, MD: Williams & Wilkins.

Graham, T. F. (1965). *Mental status manual*. Hanover, NJ: Sandoz Pharmaceuticals.

Leon, R. L. Bowden, C. L., & Faber, R. A. (1989). Diagnosis and psychiatry: Examination of the psychiatric patient. In H. I. Kaplan & B. J Sadock (Eds.). *Comprehensive textbook of psychiatry* (Vol. l) (5th ed.). Baltimore, MD: Williams & Wilkins.

THE DIAGNOSTIC AND STATISTICAL MANUAL

Along with those psychological instruments known by such classificatory terms as tests, inventories, projective techniques, questionnaires, and so forth, a system of classifying mental conditions that come to professional attention can be an asset in many contexts. Developed to systematize and advance the efficacy of psychiatric practice, the Diagnostic and Statistical Manual (DSM) is in widespread use in the training and practice of a number of professional groups, including nonpsychiatric physicians, psychological assessors, various nonmedical psychotherapists, and attorneys. The DSM is not without its critics and acknowledged shortcomings, however. It is not a finished document either. Currently in a revision of the third edition (DSM-III-R) (American Psychiatric Association, 1987), observers confidently predict even while DSM-IV is about to join the clinical armamentarium that there will be many editions to follow.

Hundreds of professionals from several disciplines served on various working and advisory committees involved in the development of the DSM-III-R. Among the more obvious values of a well-thought-out system of classification that enjoys a degree of consensus is the opportunity it affords to contribute to improved scientific and clinical communication and to facilitate the comparison of results between various studies. Thus, a schizophrenic subject in Study A is much more likely to be similar to a schizophrenic in Study B than once was the case. We would look askance at the once prevalent situation where patients diagnosed as schizophrenic were in the majority in one hospital while "manic-depressives" predominated in the patient population in a comparable institution servicing the same catchment area. It is no longer acceptable for a clinician to have a "favorite" diagnosis; the agreement of a client's symptoms and behaviors with explicit DSM criteria takes precedence over whatever private insights a diagnostician may claim.

The DSM is useful to the clinician in organizing his or her diagnostic thinking. A formal diagnosis, of course, as DSM-III-R cautions, is but a first step in developing a treatment plan. All clients with the same diagnosis are not alike, just as all items of furniture classified as chairs are not alike in all respects. The DSM is also helpful in placing symptoms into a context that has meaning for therapy. Thus, identifying a prominent symptom of depression does not automatically lead to selecting an efficacious treatment. Depression, for example, exists in various personal-social-biological-situational contexts and occurs as a feature in numerous diagnoses. Different approaches may be appropriate when, to mention several examples that do not begin to exhaust the list, depression occurs in a person with Dysthymic Disorder, with a Major Depressive Episode, with Organic Mood Syndrome (which may have various etiologies), with Amphetamine or Cocaine Withdrawal, with Borderline Personality Disorder, with Adjustment Disorder with Depressed Mood, or in a person who does not have a diagnosable mental disorder (see V Codes, below).

Organization of the DSM-III-R

Unique to the DSM—introduced with the DSM-III in 1980—is the system of *multiaxial classification*. The term *axis*, before being adopted to play a leading role in classifying mental disorders, had no technical psychological or psychiatric meaning. Each axis, in the DSM context, has reference to a class of information that may contribute to case formulation and treatment. Of the five DSM axes, numbered I to V, the first two may incorporate two or more subclasses of information. Following is a guide to their use:

Axes I and II may first be considered together inasmuch as all mental disorders and conditions are classified here. Individuals presenting for treatment of a mental condition (or coming to professional attention for some other reason) will be assigned a diagnosis or diagnoses on one or more of these axes. Many clients present with multiple disorders. All Axis I and Axis II disorders are assigned a code, which is listed in the DSM-III-R. For example, the code for Developmental Arithmetic Disorder is 315.10.

Axis I One or two subclasses of information may be recorded on Axis I. The conditions listed here are (1) the "clinical syndromes," which may include conditions as severe as schizophrenia, disorganized type, or other hallucinatory or delusional conditions; and (2) "conditions not attributable to a mental disorder that are a focus of attention or treatment" Such conditions are listed under "V Codes." Examples are academic and occupational problems, marital problems, phase-of-life problems or other life-circumstance problems, and uncomplicated bereavement.

Axis II Listed on Axis II are (1) the personality disorders, and (2) developmental disorders (specific mental disorders, pervasive mental disorders, and mental retardation). Personality traits or defense mechanisms are also permitted here, although they are not mental disorders. In this respect the pathology model is diluted.

Axis III On Axis III may be listed the client's diagnosed physical disorders and conditions, whether or not related to the client's mental disorder, but which could be pertinent to the understanding or management (including treatment) of the client.

Axis IV Axis IV is for recording the severity of psychosocial stressors, acute (less than 6 months duration) and chronic (more than 6 months duration) that impinged on the client in the previous 12-month period, and which are judged to have precipitated, exacerbated, or reactivated a mental disorder. Severity is rated on a scale ranging from 0 (inadequate information) to 6 (catastrophic event, such as the suicide of a spouse). The rater should think in terms of how stressful a particular event would be for the "average" person. A wide range of stressors should be considered, such as conjugal, financial, and occupational stress. DSM-III-R has two tables to guide the rating of the severity of stressors. One table lists stressful situations that tend to occur mostly with adults (e.g., unemployment), the other with children (e.g., parental divorce).

Axis V Axis V is for recording the results of a global assessment of functioning (psychological, social, occupational) (1) as of the time of assessment, and (2) during the highest level of functioning achieved in the past year. The GAF (Global Assessment of Functioning) Scale, available in the DSM-III-R, guides the clinician who must match his or her information of the client with descriptive statements in the table, for example, "Mild symptoms, but functioning generally well." Scoring is on a scale from 1 (most severe) to 90, representing an absence of symptoms. The level of current functioning may serve as a baseline against which to measure changes with treatment. The highest level of functioning achieved in the past year may be considered a reasonable prognosis.

The DSM-III-R Classification

More than 240 mental disorders and "conditions not attributable to a mental disorder that are a focus of attention or treatment" (V Codes) are listed in the DSM-III-R. Following are the major categories and subcategories of the classification (Axes I and II):[1]

DISORDERS USUALLY FIRST EVIDENT IN INFANCY, CHILDHOOD, OR ADOLESCENCE

Disruptive Behavior Disorders
Representative Disorders: attention-deficit hyperactivity disorder; oppositional defiant disorder
Anxiety Disorders of Childhood or Adolescence
Representative Disorders: separation anxiety disorder; overanxious disorder

---

[1] Adapted from *Diagnostic and Statistical Manual of Mental Disorders* (Third Edition-Revised). Copyright © 1987 by the American Psychiatric Association. Reproduced with the permission of the publisher.

Eating Disorders
Representative Disorders: anorexia nervosa; bulimia nervosa
Gender Identity Disorders
Representative Disorders: gender identity disorder of childhood; transsexualism
Tic Disorders
Representative Disorders: Tourette's disorder; chronic motor or vocal tic disorder
Elimination Disorders
Representative Disorders: functional encopresis; functional enuresis
Speech Disorders Not Elsewhere Classified
Representative Disorders: cluttering, stuttering
Other Disorders of Infancy, Childhood, or Adolescence
Representative Disorders: elective mutism; stereotypy/habit disorder

ORGANIC MENTAL DISORDERS

Dementias Arising in the Senium and Presenium
Representative Disorder: primary degenerative dementia of the Alzheimer type, senile onset
Psychoactive Substance-Induced Organic Mental Disorders
Representative Disorders: alcohol withdrawal delirium; amphetamine delusional disorder; caffeine intoxication; nicotine withdrawal
Organic Mental Disorders associated with Axis III physical disorders or conditions, whose etiology is unknown
Representative Disorders: delirium; organic anxiety disorder
Psychoactive Substance Use Disorders
Representative Disorders: alcohol dependence; alcohol abuse; cocaine dependence; cocaine abuse; nicotine dependence; phencyclidine (PCP) or similarly acting arylcyclohexylamine dependence

SCHIZOPHRENIA

Representative Disorders: schizophrenia, catatonic type; schizophrenia, disorganized type

DELUSIONAL (PARANOID) DISORDER

Representative Disorders: delusional (paranoid) disorder, erotomanic type; delusional (paranoid) disorder, grandiose type

PSYCHOTIC DISORDERS NOT ELSEWHERE CLASSIFIED

Representative Disorders: brief reactive psychosis; schizophreniform disorder; schizoaffective disorder

MOOD DISORDERS

Bipolar Disorders
Representative Disorders: bipolar disorder, depressed; cyclothymia
Depressive Disorders
Representative Disorders: major depression, recurrent; dysthymia (or depressive neurosis)

ANXIETY DISORDERS (or Anxiety and Phobic Neuroses)

Representative Disorders: panic disorder, with agoraphobia; social phobia; obsessive compulsive disorder (or obsessive compulsive neurosis); generalized anxiety disorder

SOMATOFORM DISORDERS

Representative Disorders: conversion disorder (or hysterical neurosis; conversion type); somatization disorder

DISSOCIATIVE DISORDERS (or Hysterical Neuroses, Dissociative Type)

Representative Disorders: multiple personality; psychogenic fugue

SEXUAL DISORDERS

Paraphilias
Representative Disorders: exhibitionism; fetishism; sexual sadism
Sexual Dysfunctions, Sexual Desire Disorders
Representative Disorder: hypoactive sexual desire disorder
Sexual Dysfunctions, Sexual Arousal Disorders
Representative Disorders: female sexual arousal disorder; male erectile disorder; premature ejaculation

SLEEP DISORDERS

Dyssomnias
Representative Disorders: primary insomnia; sleep-wake schedule disorder

Parasomnias
> Representative Disorders: dream anxiety disorder (nightmare disorder); sleepwalking disorder

FACTITIOUS DISORDERS

Representative Disorders: factitious disorder with physical symptoms; factitious disorder with psychological symptoms

IMPULSE CONTROL DISORDERS NOT ELSEWHERE CLASSIFIED

Representative Disorders: intermittent explosive disorder; pathological gambling

ADJUSTMENT DISORDER

Representative Disorders: adjustment disorder with anxious mood; adjustment disorder with withdrawal

PSYCHOLOGICAL FACTORS AFFECTING PHYSICAL CONDITION (Specify physical condition on Axis III)

PERSONALITY DISORDERS

Cluster A (Tending to oddness or eccentricity)
> Representative Disorders: paranoid personality disorder; schizotypal personality disorder

Cluster B (Tending to dramatic, emotional, or erratic behavior)
> Representative Disorders: antisocial personality disorder; histrionic personality disorder

Cluster C (Tending to anxiety and fearfulness)
> Representative Disorders: avoidant personality disorder; dependent personality disorder

CONDITIONS NOT ATTRIBUTABLE TO A MENTAL DISORDER THAT ARE A FOCUS OF ATTENTION OR TREATMENT (V CODES)

Representative Conditions: malingering; parent-child problem

Use Of The DSM-III-R

The user of the DSM-III-R should be thoroughly familiar with its contents and be in command of the clinical skills needed to carry out its instructions. There are rules to guide (not mandate) the making of diagnoses, and decision trees are also available (see Appendix B of DSM-III-R [American Psychiatric Association, 1987]), but these should not be applied mechanically or casually. The user of the manual should be well grounded in personality and psychopathology, as well as in the principles of the DSM, and should seek consultation as necessary. For example, a psychologist may benefit from medical consultation when an Axis III disorder (physical condition) is a pertinent consideration in fully grasping a client's emotional or cognitive disorder, and a psychiatrist may require psychological consultation to properly make a diagnosis of mental retardation, since an intelligence quotient obtained from one or more individual intelligence tests is required to arrive at this diagnosis.

In addition to the above considerations, the framers of the DSM are particularly concerned that several other caveats be adhered to. They make the point that the manual is not sufficiently comprehensive to encompass all of the conditions that may be legitimate objects of treatment or research. Another caution is that DSM diagnoses are not congruent with legal or other nonmedical criteria of disorder, disability, competency, or responsibility (for example, *psychosis* is not synonymous with the legal term *insanity*). The user should also be aware that the manual cannot be validly applied in cultures—particularly non-western cultures—other than the examiner's.

Several considerations are particularly important in the making of Axis I, II, and III diagnoses. Both multiaxial diagnoses, and multiple diagnoses on each of these axes, are legitimate and encouraged, as appropriate. Abstracting from several cases, we note, in the first case, on Axis I the diagnosis cocaine dependence and on Axis II narcissistic personality disorder. As an example of multiple diagnoses on one axis, in the second case we have, on Axis I, (1) organic personality syndrome, and (2) pedophilia. In a third case, we have on Axis II (1) borderline personality disorder and (2) histrionic personality disorder. Finally, we look at a case with Axis III diagnoses of (1) Alzheimer's disease, (2) alcoholic cirrhosis of liver, and (3) essential hypertension.

In the making of diagnoses, and listing them in an order that will make them clinically most useful, attention must be given to the DSM principle of *diagnostic hierarchy*. In accordance with the rules of the hierarchy, the diagnosis of an organic mental disorder preempts other diagnoses that might be associated with a symptom picture similar to that which defines the organic disorder. For example, the diagnosis panic disorder would not be made, even though the criteria for this diagnosis are met, when the diagnostic evidence is also consistent with an organic anxiety disorder. In the presence of a pervasive disorder that encompasses a less-pervasive disorder, only the more pervasive disorder is diagnosed. A frequent occasion for applying this rule is when a client presents with schizophrenia–a condition in which symptoms such as of anxiety and dysthymia may be prominent but do not merit separate diagnoses. When multiple diagnoses are listed, the Axis I or Axis II diagnosis that identifies the primary reason for the client to be in the clinical situation is called the *principal diagnosis*. In the case of the assignment of multiple diagnoses, if one of the diagnoses indicates a need for more immediate treatment than the other, then that diagnosis is listed first. For example, if the diagnoses alcohol-withdrawal delirium and schizophrenia, paranoid type are both applicable, alcohol-withdrawal delirium would be listed first because it is a life-threatening syndrome and obviously in need of acute care.

The making of individual diagnoses involves comparing the client's history and behaviors with systematically set-forth descriptive diagnostic criteria, a process that requires clinical acumen and judgment. In conceptualizing the DSM-III and DSM-III-R, the goal was to be "atheoretical," inasmuch as the etiology of the majority of listings is not understood or in dispute. In Table 8–1 are listed the criteria for making the diagnosis Identity Disorder.

Table 8–1 Diagnostic Criteria for 313.82 Identity Disorder

A. Severe subjective distress regarding uncertainty about a variety of issues relating to identity, including three or more of the following:

   (1) long term goals
   (2) career choice
   (3) friendship patterns
   (4) sexual orientation and behavior
   (5) religious identification
   (6) moral value systems
   (7) group loyalties

B. Impairment in social or occupational (including academic) functioning as a result of the symptoms in A.
C. Duration of the disturbance of at least three months.
D. Occurrence not exclusively during the course of a Mood Disorder or of a psychotic disorder, such as Schizophrenia.
E. The disturbance is not sufficiently pervasive and persistent to warrant the diagnosis of Borderline Personality Disorder.

From *Diagnostic and Statistical Manual of Mental Disorders* (Third Edition - Revised). Copyright © 1987 by the American Psychiatric Association. Reproduced with the permission of the publisher.

Students, and others who are new to the DSM system, will profit from instructional materials designed to promote proficiency. Particularly valuable are the DSM-III-R Training Guides by Reid and Wise (1989) and Rapoport and Ismond (1989) (for childhood disorders).

Spitzer, Skodol, Gibbon, and Williams (1981) pioneered a case-book approach to training that permits self-testing of diagnostic skills by the learner, whose task is to supply DSM diagnoses for patients depicted in a series of case vignettes. Reid and Wise (1989) and Rapoport and Ismond (1989) adopted this case-vignette approach to teaching, and Andersen and Harthorn (1989) constructed a Diagnostic Knowledge Inventory (DKI) consisting of case vignettes and demonstrated its reliability, validity, and applicability to teaching the use of the DSM-III-R.

SELECTED REFERENCES ON THE DIAGNOSTIC AND STATISTICAL MANUAL

American Psychiatric Association (1987). *Diagnostic and statistical manual of mental disorders* (3rd ed., Rev.). Washington, DC: Author.

American Psychiatric Association (1987). *Quick reference to the diagnostic criteria for the DSM-III-R*. Washington, DC: Author.

Rapoport, J. L., & Ismond, D. R. (1989). *DSM-III-R training guide for diagnosis of childhood disorders* (Rev. ed.). New York: Brunner/Mazel.

Reid, W. H., & Wise, M. G. (1989). *DSM-III-R training guide*. New York: Brunner/Mazel.

9

THE ASSESSMENT PROCESS

There probably still are some clinicians who ask (or tell) a psychologist to "Do testing with this patient," or, "Give this patient a Rorschach and see what you get." Would that the gaining of meaningful and helpful psychological information were so simple a matter!

Psychological assessment is a rational, problem-solving process, guided by principles, theories, and empirically established relationships among personality characteristics and between personality characteristics and test variables. It follows a consultation paradigm and involves a high degree of personal commitment on the part of the assessor, which cannot be transferred to tests or scores.

A number of schemas have been developed to portray the assessment process in a form that can serve as a guide to practice.

CONCEPTUALIZING AN ASSESSMENT SCHEMA

The Sloves-Docherty-Schneider Model

Sloves, Docherty, and Schneider (1979), in building their model of psychological assessment, stress the need to distinguish between assessment and testing: "The current state of affairs in psychological assessment is one of confusion, misconception, attack, and counterattack." (See also the opening discussion on psychological assessment and the confusion between assessment and testing, pp. 4-7.)

Following Comtois and Clark (1976), they call their schema a problem-solving model. "The model is called 'scientific' because it is based on the scientific method and reflects the steps of scientific inquiry applied to traditional research and to clinical practice." It is scientific not only in its scientific (logical, defined, systematic) approach to gathering data to solve problems, but also in evaluating and disseminating findings.

Abstracted from the model are the authors' six steps of the problem-solving process. They are presented in sequence, though it is of the essence to the model, in conceptualization and in practice, that it is interactive, dynamic, iterative, and nonlinear.

First Step: Problem Clarification "Give this patient a Rorschach and see what you get" is not a problem the psychological assessor can work with. In every case she or he must question whether there is a legitimate reason for making a referral, reason enough to believe psychological assessment can make sufficient contribution to justify the expense of consultation. Is a diagnosis needed? A differential diagnosis? Recommendations for treatment? Is there a latent reason for referral (p. 35)? Unless, then, the referral question is explicit and it is clear how psychological assessment can *make a difference*, the assessor should meet with the referral source and seek clarification.

Indeed, the authors advise that "the assessor must approach formal and informal requests for help with guarded skepticism to avoid accepting implicit or explicit a priori assumptions inherent in the referral." The compelling reason for this caveat rests on the principle that "The problem-clarification step represents the activity of reframing the presenting problem or reason for referral into a statement of needs. A need is defined as the discrepancy between a current state of affairs and a desired state of affairs." The magnitude of the psychological assessor's task is summarized by Sloves, Docherty, and Schneider (1979) as follows:

> The assessor must take into consideration (a) the object of the referral, (b) the referral process within the social system, (c) the referral agent, (d) the precipitating factors that led to the referral, (e) possible sources and causes of the problem(s), (f) constraints operating against problem definition and resolution, (g) availability of resources to conduct an assessment and plan an intervention strategy, and (h) the social, political, organizational, and structural context in which the problem is embedded.

Watch out for that first step! It's a big one.

Second Step: Planning If the presenting problem is a proper one for assessment, the task is then to frame hypotheses for testing. These may be set forth as answerable questions. The authors offer as an example the case of a child described by his teacher as hyperactive. What changes can be made to bring the child's attention to an appropriate level? Here are some hypotheses that might be helpful:

> Does the child's activity level differ from other children's in the classroom?
> Is the child's hyperactivity situation specific?
> Is the teacher selectively reinforcing hyperactive behavior in this child?
> Is the child organically driven?

The authors propose that multiple methods would be appropriate here. Systematic observation might be the method of choice to test the first hypothesis, neuropsychological assessment the last.

Third Step: Development   The third step involves planning for implementing the previous step; that is, determining what data must be gathered to test the hypotheses and deciding on the tools that will be necessary. Extant instruments or procedures might be quite acceptable to the purpose. Or the assessor may construct new instruments such as might be used in systematic observation or rating, for example. In this stage the assessor might find it necessary to review and become familiar again with the use of instruments with which he or she has become "rusty."

Fourth Step: Implementation   Direct observation and testing–data gathering, in general—is what happens in this step. Necessary "entrance strategies" are used at this time, including the structuring of the assessment situation and informing clients of their legal rights as test takers.

Fifth Step: Outcome Determination   There are various foci of attention at this stage. Most important: Was the necessary information obtained; were the hypotheses adequately tested? Was the level of competence of the assessor commensurate with the task, was supervision adequate (particularly in the case when the assessor is a trainee), was collaboration of a colleague sought, if necessary? How adequate were the instruments to the purpose, were there any problems of validity or reliability of the assessment due to instrument bias or assessor bias? What were the subjective reactions of those assessed?

Sixth Step: Dissemination   The final stage is that of sharing information, specifically of "*useful* information to those concerned with the assessment" (emphasis added). The mode of communication may vary—written psychological report, case conference, or face-to-face consultation. Very important is a follow-up conference with the consumer of the assessment, a situation that enhances both the effectiveness of the original communication and permits the assessor to evaluate its effectiveness.

In addition to the problem-solving process, there are two other components of the model, all three of these components being in interaction. The second component is identified as "levels of organizational action," and the third as "methods."

Levels of organizational action has reference to the unit that is the object of assessment. For example, the traditional unit to be assessed is the individual. The authors, however, identify a number of other units, such as families, therapy groups, school districts, hospital wards, entire hospitals, corporations, and so forth.

Methods has reference to "a hierarchical arrangement of skills, tactics, and strategies. In the area of assessment, methods represents the set of instruments and technical skills that make up psychological testing." In many situations, such as in the assessment of school districts or corporations, the individual psychological instruments that are a mainstay in clinical, school, and counseling psychology obviously have little or no applicability. Methods may properly be considered only after hypotheses have been formulated.

The fact that the formal presentation of the model could be a barrier to its application prompts the following observation from the authors:

> By making the process explicit, of course, it becomes at once laborious to use and a gross simplification of the actual clinical process. However, it need only be used in this unwieldy manner until the model is internalized. The oversimplification of the model is a characteristic of any conceptual model and can actually be considered an advantage for the sake of training. Once the process is internalized, the clinician-trainee can begin to provide his or her own elaboration in practice.

Zins's Problem-Solving Model

A scientific problem-solving approach, stemming in part from the framework of Comtois and Clark (1976), and thus similar to the contribution of Sloves et al., has been advanced by Zins (1984) specifically for application to the functioning of school psychologists. The focus is on developing accountability for practice, including the practice of psychological assessment. Zins abstracts his procedure as follows:

> Steps in the model are (a) problem definition and formulation, (b) generation of alternatives, (c) decision making, (d) implementation and outcome evaluation, (e) dissemination of results, and (f) metaevaluation. These steps are interrelated; what is done at any one step influences what is done at subsequent points in the process.

Lovitt's Conceptual Model

Lovitt's (1987) schema is based on the "conceptual approach" to Rorschach interpretation as developed by Weiner (1966) and Exner and Weiner (1982). In applying this approach to the assessment of hysterical pseudo-seizures—it no doubt can be applied to the assessment of other disorders—Lovitt focuses on the personality processes that contribute to such seizures, recognizing the roles also of constitutional, biological, and environmental variables.

Following the extant literature on hysterical personality processes, Lovitt identifies five dysfunctional areas that may be brought to light through psychological assessment—in this case Rorschach assessment. The processes associated with hysterical processes, and thus may be contributory to hysterical pseudo-seizures are:

(1) Conflict and Anxiety
(2) Pathological Inner Life (cognitive, affective, interpersonal)
(3) Disrupted Ideational Resources

Figure 9–1 A decision-making system for providing school consultation.
From Natalie S. Berger, "Beyond Testing: A Decision-Making System for Providing School Psychological Consultation." *Professional Psychology*, *10*, 275. Copyright © 1979 by the American Psychological Association. Reproduced with the permission of the author and the publisher.

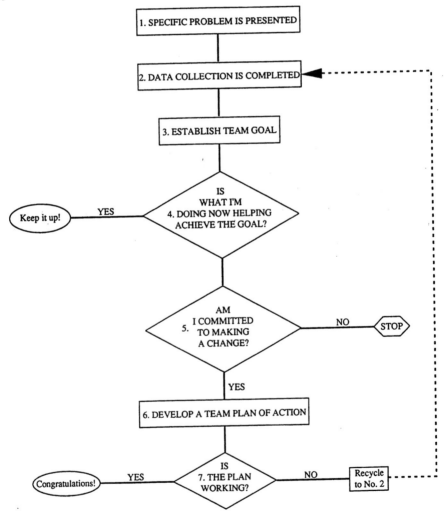

(4) Poorly Controlled Discharge
(5) Lack of Insight

Berger's Decision-Making System

Diagrammatic conceptualization of the psychological assessment process may be useful as a training device, as well as in work with clients in a number of applied areas, particularly school psychology, counseling psychology, clinical psychology, and psychiatry.

Berger (1979) has developed a decision-making system for providing school psychological consultation. The schema shows similarities with the models of Sloves et al., and Zins. Inspection of her flow chart (Figure 9–1) reveals key elements in common with the above, particularly problem definition, data gathering, implementation, and evaluation.

The system differs from the foregoing models, however, and from much extant psychological practice by its stress on team involvement and commitment to successful problem resolution. This is clearly evident in the flow chart, and is also stressed in words: "The team members who will be providing the necessary resources must be involved here [Step 6] in order for this planning to result in an effective program. Plans must not be made *for* another person." Further, "Blanket recommendations are never pronounced and left to the primary caregivers to administer. The *continuing interaction of psychologist and caregiver* around individual cases also provides opportunity for secondary observations, which could become the focus of future consultations" (emphasis added).

Berger contrasts the consultation system she describes with one in which the psychological examiner is detached from the action and aloof. Examiners who assume such a role provide "psychological services that are short-circuited, ending up in black and white, entitled 'Psychological Report.'"

The Hulse-Jennings Visual-Integrative Technique

Hulse and Jennings (1984) introduce "a visual display of nine information categories essential for counseling conceptualization." Emphasis is on "the ability of the individual counselors to not only collect but also integrate case information with theory to formulate conceptualizations that may be used for planning appropriate interventions." Further, the model is also designed to "facilitate the integration of data as a way to consider a case from any theoretical perspective." The authors stress that their scheme is a tool and not a substitute for clinical judgment.

Nine categories of content are considered in case conceptualization. They are shown in Figure 9–2.

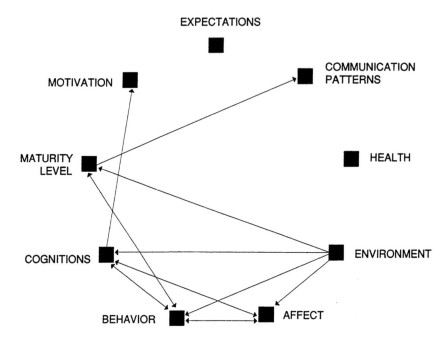

Figure 9–2 Case example category relationships.
From Diana Hulse and Martha Jennings, "Toward Comprehensive Case Conceptualizations in Counseling: A Visual Integrative Technique. *Professional Psychology: Research and Practice*, 15, 257. Copyright © 1984 by the American Psychological Association. Reproduced with the permission of the authors and the publisher.

The BASIC ID

Lazarus (1973) conceptualizes a tight, behavior-therapy-oriented relation between symptoms and treatment. His system, the BASIC ID, is not a psychoanalytic schema, but an acronym that summarizes assessment in seven areas of functioning: Behavior, Affect, Sensation, Imagery, Cognition, Interpersonal Relationships, and Drugs (and Biological). In the following representation, (see Figure 9–3), six of these areas are involved:

MODALITY	PROBLEM	PROPOSED TREATMENT
Behavior	Inappropriate withdrawal responses	Assertive training
	Frequent crying	Nonreinforcement
	Unkempt appearance	Grooming instructions
	Excessive eating	Low-calorie regimen
	Negative self-statements	Positive self-talk assignments
	Poor eye contact	Rehearsal techniques
	Mumbling of words with poor voice projection	Verbal projection exercises
	Avoidance of heterosexual situations	Reeducation and desensitization

MODALITY	PROBLEM	PROPOSED TREATMENT
Affect	Unable to express overt anger	Role playing
	Frequent anxiety	Relaxation training and reassurance
	Absence of enthusiasm and spontaneous joy	Positive imagery procedures
	Panic attacks (usually precipitated by criticism from authority figures)	Desensitization and assertive training
	Suicidal feelings	Time projection techniques
	Emptiness and aloneness	General relationship building
Sensation	Stomach spasms	Abdominal breathing and relaxing
	Out of touch with most sensual pleasures	Sensate focus method
	Tension in jaw and neck	Differential relaxation
	Frequent lower back pains	Orthopedic exercises
	Inner tremors	Gendlin's focusing methods
Imagery	Distressing scenes of sister's funeral	Desensitization
	Mother's angry face shouting, "You fool!"	Empty chair technique
	Performing fellatio on God	Blow up technique (implosion)
	Recurring dreams about airplane bombings	Eidetic imagery invoking feelings of being safe
Cognition	Irrational self-talk: "I am evil." "I must suffer." "Sex is dirty." "I am inferior."	Deliberate rational disputation and corrective self-talk
	Syllogistic reasoning, overgeneralization	Parsing of irrational sentences
	Sexual misinformation	Sexual education
Interpersonal Relationships	Characterized by childlike dependence	Specific self-sufficiency assignments
	Easily exploited/submissive	Assertive training
	Overly suspicious	Exaggerated role taking
	Secondary gains from parental concern	Explain reinforcement principles to parents and try to enlist their help
	Manipulative tendencies	Training in direct and confrontative behaviors

Figure 9–3 The BASIC ID system.
From Arnold A. Lazarus, "Multimodal Behavior Therapy: Treating the BASIC ID." *Journal of Nervous and Mental Disease, 156,* 404–411. Copyright © 1973 by The Williams & Wilkins Co., Baltimore and reproduced by permission of the author and publisher. See also A. A. Lazarus, *The Practice of Multi-Modal Therapy.* Baltimore: Johns Hopkins University Press, 1989.

Clinical Decision Making in Behavior Therapy

Another comprehensive behavioral approach to assessment and treatment is that of Nezu and Nezu (1989). Conceptualized as an idiographic, problem-solving, clinical decision-making process, the authors present a five-part schema:

(1) Problem Orientation
(2) Problem Definition and Formulation
(3) Generation of Alternatives
(4) Decision Making
(5) Solution Implementation and Verification

The schema is applicable to "a wide variety of psychological disorders," such as agoraphobia, sexual dysfunctions, chronic pain, and personality disorders.

Howe's Decision-Making Evaluation Scheme

Howe (1981) has presented a practical, clinically oriented scheme, which he characterizes as dispositional ("a disposition assessment perspective") as opposed to merely descriptive approaches, either one that results in a complex formulation that is inapplicable to the situation at hand or one that produces a formal diagnosis to no evident clinical purpose. His point of view follows that of Cole and Magnussen (1966) who conclude that "traditional diagnostic procedures are only loosely related, if at all, to disposition and treatment." Further, these authors suggest:

> ...the ultimate criteria for a meaningful study of a patient rest with the ability to distinguish between a number of possible dispositions, one disposition which will lead to action resulting in better handling of whatever problem exists, and not necessarily the accuracy with which labels can be applied...

"From the dispositional perspective," Howe suggests, "diagnosis has meaning only insofar as an isomorphic relationship exists between diagnostic categories and treatment." His "evaluation scheme" is based on this point of view:

> In short, the evaluation scheme poses three questions about the total assessment process: (1) Is a meaningful question posed to the assessor? (2) Does the assessment result in an accurate understanding of the client? (3) Is sufficient understanding of the intervention alternatives available to allow useful recommendations to be made?

Studying the evaluations performed on 58 vocational rehabilitation clients, Howe reports "a surprisingly high percentage of cases [nearly one-third] in which *no meaningful referral questions were asked*" (emphasis added). Such referrals were "bureaucratic" referrals made for institutional purposes (in this case to satisfy the institution's recertification requirement) rather than for clinical reasons. The author suggests it would be of value to educate agency staff in the making of meaningful referrals, and particularly in developing a better appreciation of when psychological consultation may be helpful.

The a Priori Approach to Psychological Assessment

Carey, Flasher, Maisto, and Turkat (1984) position their a priori approach to assessment as it contrasts with what they term the "traditional approach":

> The traditional approach to psychological assessment frequently involves the administration of a standard test battery from which a post hoc case formulation is derived. In contrast, the a priori approach advocates the selection of specific tests or the construction of clinical experiments that can serve to validate an a priori case formulation.

The authors present their approach as the more systematic one and the one most clearly linked to a logical and scientific/experimental rationale. Their schema consists of four steps, one more than in what they call the traditional approach to psychological assessment. The additional (third) step, situated in the middle of the sequence of steps, is that of validating the case formulation, the development of which was the task of the previous step.

The four steps of the schema are labeled (1) Initial Interview, (2) Case Formulation, (3) Formulation Validation, and (4) Treatment Plan.

Initial Interview In this step data are collected as a basis for creating a case formulation (Step 2), and for positing a psychiatric diagnosis "for purposes of scientific classification and communication." Answers are sought to these questions:

What are the presenting complaints?
When, how, and why did these problems begin?
How are the various presenting problems related?
What are the aspects of the client's development that are relevant to the presenting problems?
What were the predisposing factors to the problem onset?

Case Formulation The case formulation is an explanatory and predictive hypothesis, a construct. Its purpose is threefold: (1) to explain the origin of the client's problems, (2) to find common meaning among the presenting symptoms, and (3) to predict response to various stimulus conditions; for example, to interventions or to the tests to be used in validating the hypothesis.

Formulation Validation In this phase the hypothesis, or hypotheses, are tested empirically. This may be done with the use of appropriate tests, that is, tests "selected to measure the presence of a particular construct." Thus, if the extent of depression, and the nature of the depressive symptom picture is a matter of concern, the Beck Depression Inventory might be part of the battery; conversely, this instrument might not be considered when depression is not an issue.

In addition to tests, "controlled observation" is part of the validation procedure. Here various physiological and motoric behaviors, such as sweaty palms (evident to the assessor on handshake) or "nervous" tapping with the fingers, may be observed. Simple clinical experiments relevant to the hypothesis may also be designed. For example, certain topics may cautiously be introduced to determine whether they lead to defensiveness, tenseness, or anxiety. Then, taking into account data from all the sources, the test data and observations may be credited if they evidence convergent validity (p. 64).

Treatment Plan The a priori approach of Carey et al. outlines a treatment plan that makes a crucial distinction between the hypothesized mechanisms of a disorder (the case formulation) and the presenting symptom picture:

> The present model of assessment implies that treatment should be designed idiographically only after the hypothesized mechanism(s) of disorder is validated. The modification methodology must specify the independent variables (i.e., treatment features, environmental factors) and the dependent variables (i.e., the specific presenting complaints of the client as well as other problems that were revealed during the assessment process) that are to be monitored throughout treatment. It is important to reiterate that in our approach, *treatment is aimed directly at the hypothesized mechanism of the disorder* and not at the symptoms. Therefore, the success of such a formulation-based treatment is seen as largely dependent on the accuracy of the formulation.

A SCHEMA TO PRESENT THE BASIC CONCEPTS OF THIS BOOK

The final schema of the overall assessment process to be presented is my own and incorporates my present understanding of the assessment process. Accompanying the diagram are definitions of the components of assessment.

Tallent's Interactional Schema of the Psychological Assessment Process

Structure of the Model Psychological assessment is a process of multiple and complex interaction. The psychologist (Ψ) functions at the center of the process, as the chief diagnostic instrument, in continuous interaction with the other elements of the assessment process shown in Figure 9-4. The product is the psychological report, the significant outcome of assessment and the topic of the next chapter.

The Psychologist The person of the psychologist, along with his or her technical skills, is of great importance in contributing to the outcome of psychological assessment. Each clinical assessment, as Hunt (1959) and others have suggested, is an experiment with the capability of contributing to scientific knowledge as well as to immediate clinical application. A stereotypical approach to assessment will not do.

The psychologist is a bundle of life experiences and instructional and professional background. All of these are brought to bear in seeking solutions to an individual's problems. Their use always involves consideration of the clinical, social, and historical context, and the exercise of clinical judgment and flexibility.

Reason for Assessment Next to the psychologist, the reason for assessment is most basic to the initiation and conduct of the assessment. In Figure 9-4, Reason for Assessment is situated at the vertex of the accompanying diagram. Without an explicit and meaningful reason for assessment, there is no reason to carry out an assessment. A problem-solving approach to assessment requires that the problem to be solved be clearly defined.

We have seen, however, that those who refer clients for assessment do not always make referral with a particular goal in mind—or on paper. Experience suggests that the lack of meaningfulness of referral questions reported by Howe (1981) probably is not atypical in clinical settings. The psychological assessor cannot function as a passive recipient of referrals. Frequently it is necessary that he or she meet with the referral source to clarify why an assessment should be carried out–or, at times, not carried out—since assessment procedures carried

Figure 9-4 Psychological Assessment Schema.
From Norman Tallent, *Psychological Report Writing* (2nd ed., 1983; 3rd ed., 1988). Copyright © 1976, 1983, 1988 by Prentice Hall.

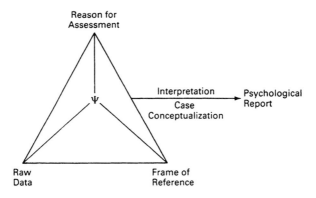

out without a problem to solve may not be particularly contributory to a case, or cost effective. What *use* is contemplated for the outcome of the assessment? Discussion of the reason for referral—rather than just making a referral—is a proper team function.

The reason for referral defines the problem to which the psychological assessor will seek to contribute a solution, and thus provides a guide for developing an assessment strategy. If the problem is to formulate a DSM diagnosis, then the necessary information to do so may be available through the client's history, direct observation and interview (these are the sources that contribute to the sort of information that make up the DSM criteria for diagnosis). Tests can be particularly useful, however, if quantitative and/or qualitative conclusions on the client's intellectual functioning are the topic of concern. Similarly, tests can be highly useful to help illuminate such areas as personality structure and dynamics, or to gain a fuller picture of a client's self and object relations.

Raw Data The gathering of raw data, through testing and interviewing, commonly is demanding of the assessor's time. As such, measures that can be taken to reduce the time expenditure of this phase of the assessment process deserve attention. Interviewing carried out in accordance with a rationale (see the discussion of interviewing in Chapter 8) and with constant attention to the problem to be solved can be more efficient and productive than the meandering discussions that sometimes pass for interviews. Of course, when the problem has not been identified it is not possible to focus the interview on a problem.

Similarly, testing can be better focused when the problem is identified. The goal is to assemble a battery that is most likely to yield answers to the issues raised. This is the flexible battery approach, as opposed to the use of a standard battery with all clients. While many clinicians, stemming from their experience, have developed a basic battery that they find helpful with most of their clients, the use of a standard battery probably is not justified in much clinical work. An assessor, most of whose clients are schizophrenic, might use a different battery than one whose clients suffer with various of the anxiety disorders. In turn, we would expect an assessor who works with head-injury cases to rely on yet a different basic battery.

However, the use of a standard battery might be more justified when the client population is relatively homogeneous with respect to their presenting clinical picture or their needs, for example, when the need is to explore work-relevant abilities. Another exception is when tests are used in research. Thus, the use of a standard battery was basic to the historical research on psychological testing carried out at the Menninger Foundation (Rapaport, Gill, & Schafer, 1945, 1946).

Commonly, test scores, percentages, profiles, relations among test scores, description of test performance, and so forth have been regarded as *test results*. The present writer prefers the term *raw data* for such material, a term that applies also to (nonspecifically test-related) "clinical behaviors" and other observations and to the information gained from interview. Such material does not qualify as *results* in the present orientation. Nor does an interpretation of test data (with or without other raw data) independent of context—namely Reason for Assessment and Frame of Reference—constitute *results*. According to the present schema, by *results* we mean the content of the psychological report.

Content of the psychological report, in turn, conveys the psychologist's interpretations and case conceptualizations, as discussed below. The fatuity of considering raw data to be the results of an assessment is readily illustrated. Consider a test subject for whom an IQ of 110 is obtained. What does this score mean? It may carry the sad message that severe loss of intellectual functioning has occurred, as likely would be the case if the score were representative of the present capacity of a noted scholar or a highly acclaimed novelist. On the other hand, this score might indicate that a patient who had sustained a head injury had suffered less decrement of function than had been feared. Or the 110 may suggest a significant improvement in the emotional status of a problem-ridden child who had scored between 85 and 90 in earlier assessments.

Frame(s) of Reference Frame of reference pertains to the psychological assessor's views on personality, psychopathology, various other clinical variables, and orientations to assessment. The assessor's frame of reference is not necessarily as comprehensive as a formally stated theory of personality. An assessor may consider, for example, that what is important is the identification of target symptoms, while another may stress developmental history. Shall the focus be on overt behaviors or on the unconscious?

However its specifics are conceived, theory is a tool; more a slave than a master, we may hope. A formal theory is a statement of principles or constructs that help to explain our data or predict functioning. A theory, thus, is an aid to developing meaning or making sense out of data. Freudian theory, for example, helps us to predict that a person whose test protocol holds significant indicators of "orality" is more likely to be dependent than compulsive. But theory must not dictate conclusions. A paragraph that reads as if it were reproduced from "Inhibition, Symptom, and Anxiety" very probably does not contribute as accurate a portrayal of the client as might be possible with less uncritical input of Freud's contributions.

Views on the topic being assessed (whether psychopathology, vocational aptitude or school failure) determine the assessor's approach to assessment. If personality is considered to be of basic importance, the assessor might use the Rorschach. If she or he stresses object relations, the Rorschach and the TAT may be employed as possible sources of information. If the actual behavior of a child, as observed by others, is considered to be of significance in formulating a behavioral picture of a child and designing a remedial approach, the Personality Inventory for Children (Wirt, Lachar, Klinedinst, & Seat, 1984) may be selected as an appropriate instrument for assessment.

Interpretation The process of interpretation involves the recasting of information to add meaning. Using the techniques and understandings of the psychometrist and the psychotherapist, it is the translation of data with varying degrees of inherent meaning into statements that make more sense in terms of the problem to be solved. Thus, in the example above, we saw that the knowledge that a subject has an IQ of 110 has little inherent meaning by itself, but when this information is applied to three different problem situations it contributes to three different solutions.

The rationale for making interpretations arises from various sources, not the least of which is experience. Experience in living may alert an observer to "nervous" laughter, betraying anxiety and tension rather than mirth or amusement. Experience with the Rorschach enables an assessor to identify "Card 1 shock," suggesting that the subject tends to be apprehensive on entering novel situations. Negative comments made about the older woman on TAT Card 2 may suggest that the subject holds negative attitudes toward mother figures.

Interpretation may be arbitrary, a matter of definition. Thus, an IQ of 60 obtained on a standardized test of intelligence provides psychometric support for the conclusion that the subject may be placed in the category Mild Mental Retardation. In practice, most interpretations are based on various degrees of such empirical evidence, usually in combination with clinical experience. This is the basis of interpretation of Rorschach and MMPI responses. Cookbook compilations of interpretations for numerous test responses are available in such sources as Gilbert (1978, 1980) and Ogdon (1981). Good practice dictates that these not be applied in the absence of clinical seasoning.

Reasoning added to empiricism is seen in the approach of Trimboli and Kilgore (1983), more fully discussed on pp. 148–149. Whereas in the typical use of the MMPI the interpretation of scores is in terms of their empirical correlates with areas of behavior and symptoms, Trimboli and Kilgore also deduce psychodynamic factors. Particularly, they emphasize the defense mechanisms, inferring these from the behaviors that have been empirically associated with various scale elevations.

A number of the parameters of the interpretive process can be identified, but their precise definition or best manner of use often quite elude us. It is when we seek to spell out what we actually do and why we do it when interpreting data that the fact that we use intuition and practice an art becomes glaringly evident. Interpretation is not a matter of mechanically applying rules. Rather, we make use of interpretive strategies in various combinations, never losing sight of the unique situation of the client or of the problem to be solved. Our judgments must always be informed by a theoretical position, and we should have a compelling rationale for conclusions that fly in the face of this position.

Having said this, we may mention some of the commonly employed strategies of interpretation. The normative approach, particularly, commands respect because it is basically a quantitative technique. An individual's standing may be compared with those in the standardization group. Less exacting are the "personal norms" held by clinicians.

The logic of induction and deduction is commonly used to arrive at conclusions, and, like the normative approach, may be based on formal (empirical) or informal criteria, or a combination of both. Reaching conclusions in a phenomenological frame of reference is now popular in an atmosphere that emphasizes self-representations and object representations. And finally, there is the projective approach that commands so much attention in clinical assessment. The long-understood characteristics of projection are not a simple matter, however, as brought out in Holmes's (1968) discussion of this topic in Chapter 12. Introducing Holmes's position is the research-based conclusion of Exner (1989) concerning projection on the Rorschach, namely that this instrument yields a paucity of projective material.

Case Formulation (Conceptualization) Interpretation and case formulation are sometimes used synonymously. That is, the entire formulation of a case may be called interpretation. In this book, interpretation is used in a more limited sense to refer to the recasting of discrete content, such as behaviors and test responses, into more meaningful terms addressed to the problem to be solved.

Case formulation refers to the integrated conclusions pertinent to this problem. These are the substance of the psychological report. To responsibly and effectively present this material, however, a number of the principles of psychological report writing must be taken into account. (Tallent, 1988). The remainder of this chapter is a discussion of the basics of case formulation, the *sine qua non* of the psychological report, and the next chapter is reserved for discussion of a number of the special issues of psychological report writing.

The content and format of the case formulation varies widely, reflecting the orientation of its author. Inevitably, a behaviorally oriented clinician will prepare a formulation vastly different from that produced by her or his psychodynamically oriented colleagues. Test-using psychologists likely will include in the formulation test-derived material, such as intellectual factors or an evaluation of visual-motor function; while clinicians who do not use tests are likely to omit such material from their formulations, especially an account of the latter. Biologically oriented psychiatrists are likely to emphasize laboratory findings, such as EEG interpretations, other neurological or neuropsychological findings, or the results of a dexamethasone suppression test. When establishing a DSM diagnosis is emphasized, the case formulation may be essentially a build-up in support of a particular classification.

Focusing on the problems that face psychiatrists in making meaningful formulations, Cooper and Michels (1988) are critical of obstacles placed by the DSM itself. They note:

> In our 1981 review of DSM-III...we were concerned that it would prove 'difficult to teach, particularly to students who have had little clinical experience or personal familiarity with psychiatric patients. The absence of comprehensive organizing principles...tends to leave one with confusing masses of data.' We thought that it would be difficult for the student to develop an integrated 'clinical picture' of the individual patient if he or she focused too narrowly on the criteria for establishing a DSM-III diagnosis. This, unfortunately, has turned out to be the case. As Reiser [1988] has described it, medical students and residents today, influenced by the adynamic and relatively nonhistorical characteristics of DSM-III, have tended to approach their patients with the primary goal of establishing diagnostic certainty rather than knowing their patients' clinical life stories,

of which the psychiatric diagnoses are but one part. Establishing the diagnosis is often done at the expense of curiosity about the patient. Some hoped that the multiaxial system would help to provide this broader perspective, but although rating stressors and global functioning may provide quantitative measures they do not contribute importantly toward a richer or more textured understanding either of the patient or the patient's illness.

The consequence of these shortcomings is suggested by Perry, Cooper, and Michels (1987):

> One common misconception is that a psychodynamic formulation is indicated only for those patients in a long-term, expressive psychotherapy. This belief ignores the fact that the success of any treatment may involve supporting, managing, or even modifying aspects of the patient's personality. Therapeutic effectiveness or failure often hinges on how well or poorly the therapist understands the patient's dynamics, predicts what resistances the patient will present, and designs an approach that will circumvent, undermine, or surmount these obstacles.

Improvement could be in the offing as the DSM series continues its march:

> We envision a DSM-IV...that, like American psychiatry itself, will be less preoccupied with the doctrinal schisms that shaped DSM-III and DSM-III-R, will be more accepting of the clinical as well as the research roots of psychiatric knowledge, will be more interested in the *psychological processes* that have always been a central theme of psychiatry, and will continue the evolutionary process that can be traced back through Robert Spitzer to Emil Kraeplin (Cooper & Michels, 1988) (emphasis added).

APPROACHES TO CASE FORMULATION

It is helpful to consider separately the gathering of information from the rationale of organizing it to be meaningful and useful. For many clinicians, it is the latter that is the most difficult aspect of the assessment process. It is far easier to present "test results" (p. 9) and consider the job done.

Millon's Approach to Personality Conceptualization

Various systematic approaches to assessment have been proposed. Millon's (1984, 1986c) taxonomic approach to case formulation (incorporated in the Millon Clinical Multiaxial Inventory, Chapter 7) follows a straightforward logic:

> A critical step toward the goal of sharpening assessment discriminations is *the specification of a distinctive diagnostic criterion on every clinically relevant attribute for each personality disorder* (emphasis added). To illustrate: If the attribute 'interpersonal conduct' is deemed of clinical value in assessing personality, then a specific diagnostic criterion should be identified to represent *the* characteristic or distinctive manner in which *each* personality 'conducts its interpersonal life.'

By composing a taxonomic schema that includes all relevant clinical attributes (e.g. behavior, affect, cognition) *and* specifies a defining feature on every attribute for each of the DSM-III's 11[1] personalities, then the proposed format will be *both* fully comprehensive in its clinical scope and possess directly comparable criteria for its parallel Axis I categories.

Altogether, Millon (1984, 1986c) identifies eight clinical attributes, four *functional* ("dynamic processes that transpire within the intrapsychic world and between the individual and his psychosocial environment"), and four *structural* ("a deeply embedded and relatively enduring template of imprinted memories, attitudes, needs, fears, and so on, which guide the experience and transform the nature of ongoing life events"). These constitute four clinical domains labeled Behavioral, Phenomenological, Intrapsychic, and Biophysical:

FUNCTIONAL CRITERIA

Expressive Acts (Behavioral Domain)
Interpersonal Conduct (Behavioral Domain)
Cognitive Style (Phenomenological Domain)
Regulatory Mechanisms (Intrapsychic Domain)

STRUCTURAL CRITERIA

Object Representations (Phenomenological Domain)
Self-Image (Phenomenological Domain)
Morphological Organization (Intrapsychic Domain)
Mood/Temperament (Biophysical Domain)

Following this scheme, each of the 13 personality disorders may be described prototypically in terms of these variables. Thus, for the schizoid individual, the key feature of interpersonal conduct is the individual's aloofness, which is then spelled out as follows: "Seems indifferent and remote, rarely responsive to the actions or feelings of others, possessing minimal 'human' interests; fades into the background, is unobtrusive, has few close relationships and prefers a peripheral role in social, work and family settings." For the person with borderline personality disorder, interpersonal conduct is described as "Paradoxical: Although needing attention and affection, is unpredictably contrary, manipulative and volatile, frequently eliciting rejection rather than support; reacts to fears of separation and isolation in angry, mercurial and often self-damaging ways." (Millon, 1986b, p. 690). Comparing a person with these features can be a basis both for making a

---

[1]Since updated for the 13 personality disorders of the DSM-III-R (including the sadistic [or aggressive] and self-defeating [or masochistic] personality disorders "proposed as diagnostic categories needing further study").

diagnosis and listing personality features of interest that may then be incorporated in a case formulation. This is the essential logic of the Millon Clinical Multiaxial Inventory (MCMI).

Following Freud (1915) and other early theorists, Millon (1969, 1981, 1986b) has also constructed a "framework of three polarities" which he proposes as a systematic approach to conceptualizing personality—a way of organizing our thinking. Study of an individual's polarities may, for example, suggest areas of imbalance in personality functioning and thus the goals of psychotherapeutic intervention that should be set.

The three polarities are:

Active-passive—"whether the individual takes the initiative in shaping surrounding events or whether behavior is largely reactive to these events."

Pleasure-pain—"motivations are ultimately aimed in one of two directions, toward events which are attractive or positively reinforcing versus away from those which are aversive or negatively reinforcing."

Self-other—"among all objects and things in our environment there are two that most stand out above all others in their power to affect us: our own selves and others" (Millon, 1981, p. 58).

Looking at various personality pictures, Millon illustrates this approach by contrasting individuals who share stylistically similar features in terms of their polarities. Thus, he classifies dependent and histrionic pathology as evidencing "stylistic dependent personalities." Persons in both categories are other-oriented; they look to others for support and "goodies." The dependent person, however, emphasizes a passive approach to acquisition while the histrionic individual actively influences others to give, such as through self-dramatization. Or consider "stylistically independent persons"—the narcissistic personality disorder and the antisocial personality disorder. Both emphasize the self-polarity. But the narcissist is passive, while the antisocial person is active; he takes (by manipulation, force, stealth, or whatever) what he feels he needs or deserves.

Clinical Case Conceptualization (Formulation)

The following discussion and illustrative case material is adapted from Tallent, (1988) (Chapter 5, "Conceptualizing the Psychological Report").[2]

Clinical case conceptualization (formulation), as discussed here, is based on my psychological assessment schema presented above (Figure 9-4, p. 197), which illustrates assessment as an interactive, not a linear process, and that each of the categories of information, schematically placed at the angles of the triangle, enters the interpretation and case conceptualization (formulation), and the psychological report.

[2]Tallent, N. (1988), *Psychological Report Writing* (3rd ed.), Englewood Cliffs, NJ: Prentice Hall.

Organization Effective case formulation requires not only the recording of information for which an assessment was carried out, but also the organization of that information to convey maximum meaning. To merely convey information without rationale falls short of presenting an adequate depiction of a client.

I recollect reviewing a student's case formulation of a client I knew well. He carried on at great length, quite accurately, about the client's abundant hostility, and then went on to another topic. I inquired about the client's severe dependency on a mother who had infantilized him, thus engendering strong and pervasive resentments. "It's in there," the student triumphantly exclaimed. Indeed it was "in there," some five paragraphs after he finished expounding the hostility theme. Suddenly I recollected a TV commercial for spaghetti sauce, something I don't usually think about shortly after lunchtime—which is when this particular transaction with the student took place. "Yes," I agreed, the choice ingredients are "in there," but topics that go together should be presented together; a psychological report is different from spaghetti sauce. Since that day I have had numerous occasions to give free advertising to the spaghetti sauce maker.

Per the discussion that follows, it is my position that following a standard outline (e.g., Bellak, 1965; Carr 1968; Lacks, Horton, and Owen, 1969; Sturm, 1974; vanReken, 1981) detracts from an effective case formulation. Standard outlines tend to result in reports that are overly stereotyped, and therefore detract from the individuality of the person. Most outlines, for example, call for the report to begin with a discussion of intelligence, which in numerous instances (particularly in mental health settings) is not the reason for assessment, and possibly is of no concern at all. Such is likely to be the case when the topic is addressed in terms of IQ or through a recitation of relative areas of strength and weakness. When a client is in treatment for anxiety, is it important to know that her visual-motor coordination is superior to her fund of information?

It makes no sense to address the same topic in every case. This is a Procrustean approach. Yet in seeking to be helpful, some outlines are highly detailed, calling for information that is not pertinent to formulating many individual cases. On the other hand, in a particular case, certain information that is uncovered may have a low base rate of occurrence in the general population. Rosenwald's (1965) illustration is to the point:

> In analyzing test batteries, the tester may one day hit upon a case which leads him to state: 'This subject strikes me as an honest person,' or 'This patient thinks women want to devour him,' or 'This girl has a Cinderella complex.' These characteristics are unusual but they have clinical meaning, and they can be verified independently. Yet the tester who has in one case drawn such a sketch would shudder at the suggestion that henceforth he state for every patient he encounters to what extent he or she has a Cinderella complex, or is honest or deluded in a specific way.

Flexibility is a basic feature of case formulation. We may learn from the more exact field of engineering. Thus, James Souther (1957), writing in *Technical Report Writing*, a guidebook for engineers, observes:

There is, of course, no one way to write a report, just as there is no one form or organization that will always suffice. *Each writer's personal characteristics will determine, in part, how he will attack his problem* (emphasis added).

His approach to the writing of engineering reports is equally applicable to psychological reports:

The point of attack is always identification of the problem and analyzing the writing situation. Material must be gathered and evaluated, and the report must be designed and written. Failure and confusion often result because the writer starts in the middle of the process or overlooks major considerations. Thus the application of the engineering approach to the solution of writing problems is certain to produce more effective reports, for a report, like any other engineering product, must be designed to satisfy a particular industrial function with its own specific set of requirements. If the analysis is accurate and extensive, the investigation complete and thorough, the design detailed and purposeful, and the application careful and ordered, the report will effectively communicate to its audience, play its industrial role, and fulfill its purpose.

Parsimony is also basic to organization in addition to whatever other virtues it may have. Parsimony not only saves the time of the writer and reader, and cuts down on bulk, but also eliminates some possible sources of confusion and misunderstanding. Parsimonious writing tends to emphasize (rather than dilute in words) the central problem(s) and personality issues, whereas shotgun reporting (p. 73) tends to put the main conclusions on a par with matters of minor relevance. For example, for a patient who had been economically and socially successful but was now being evaluated for discharge following hospitalization for a depressive episode, an unneeded recitation of the relations among intellectual skills would probably not increase, and likely would detract from, attention to the main problem. We might similarly judge to be insignificant knowledge about psychosexual development, feelings of inadequacy as a male, fear of heterosexual contacts, or oedipal status in a patient who is being evaluated for protective institutional employment.

In some respects, the psychological assessor can profit from the commonsense approach to describing personality of those without benefit of psychological training. Lay evaluation is organized into functional unities that focus on behaviors. Nonpsychologists concentrate, as the occasion demands, on areas of felt concern, such as an associate's intelligence, sincerity, friendliness, or "personality." They reach conclusions rather directly—come to the point and tell what sort of person someone is. "He's the sort of feller you can trust. You can count on him when you need him. He'll go out of his way to help when you're in a jam." The narrator may then cite some empirical supporting evidence, or perhaps even intuitive knowledge. One can hardly be more succinct than the late president Lyndon Johnson who characterized a political rival as "a man who can't walk and chew gum at the same time." The nonpsychologist never segments a subject into predetermined and fixed discrete areas such as "intellect," "emotions," and "object relations." The lay listener might have difficulty in integrating such segments into a functional whole. Professional people sometimes have similar problems.

A segmented presentation of more or less static personality may appear to be scientific and clinically functional because it suggests the existence of distinct, identifiable personality components that were isolated and measured, or otherwise assessed. However, we believe that personality is a functional interrelated unity, and we concur with those who believe that clinically important traits are largely specific, that a stimulus in a total situation is as relevant as the organism or its responses. Nevertheless, to some workers, segments seem a convenient way of thinking about a person. A report composed of information on various a priori established segments may seem crisp and "scientific." It is crisp, but it is no more scientific than an integrated presentation.

Case-focusing Case-focused reports (1) are composed of interpretive statements clearly related to the reason for assessment, (2) are organized in such a way that conclusions are presented with maximum effectiveness (the major conclusions are highlighted and the minor conclusions are supportive of the central conclusions) and (3) present material parsimoniously and straightforwardly so as not to dilute the message of the report in surplus words and topics of minor relevance. Test manuals and the literature, good as they may be, can suggest interpretations only in the general terms of the accepted meanings of such variables as test responses, scores, or quantitative patterns. The psychological assessor must adapt these general interpretive meanings to the specific case and mission (e.g., treatment planning, discharge planning), determine the central and pertinent topics with which to deal, and develop the interpretations (conclusions) in these topic areas as the mission requires.

Topics around which a case may be conceptualized Based on clinical experience we can draw up a useful list of tentative topics pertaining to general personality and related matters that could provide the basic elements around which the psychological assessor might conceptualize a case. These may be regarded as "handles" with which the psychologist can come to grips with the mission in the presence of the mass of data accumulated about the client. Although something might be written on almost every one of these topics for every person (a systematic approach to shotgun reporting!), usually a person can be meaningfully and effectively described in skeletal form by focusing on just a few of them. In most instances the case can probably be conceptualized around perhaps three to six of these topics. Occasionally seven or eight might be required, but at other times, particularly when a pointed question is asked, even one or two might suffice. The report can then be rounded out with subcategories also taken from the list.

This list of topics is not offered as complete, nor are all of the topics mutually exclusive. Each psychological assessor may wish to add those variables that are pertinent to his or her assessment activities.

EXAMPLES OF GENERAL PERSONALITY TOPICS AROUND WHICH A CASE MAY BE CONCEPTUALIZED

Achievement
Affect
Aggressiveness
Antisocial Tendencies
Anxieties
Aptitudes
Attitudes
Aversions
Background Factors
Behavioral Problems
Biological Factors
Brain Dysfunction
Cognitive Functioning
Cognitive Skills
Cognitive Style
Competency
Conative Factors
Conflicts
Content of Consciousness
Contingency Management
Defenses
Deficits
Developmental Factors
Diagnostic Considerations
Drives, Dynamics
Emotional Cathexes
Emotional Controls
Emotivity
Fears
Fixations
Flexibility
Frustrations
Goals
Hostility
Identity
Imagery
Insight

Intellectual Controls
Intellectual Level
Interests
Interpersonal Relations
Interpersonal Skills
Lifestyle
Molar Surface Behavior
Needs
Outlook
Perception of Environment
Perception of Self
Personal Consequences of Behavior
Placement Prospects
Psychopathology
Rehabilitation Needs
Rehabilitation Prospects
Self-Concept
Sentiments
Sex
Sex Identity
Sex Role
Significant Others
Situational Factors
Social Consequences of Behavior
Social Role
Social Stimulus Value
Social Structure
Special Assets
Subjective Feeling States
Substance Use
Symptoms
Target Behaviors
Thought Processes
Treatment Prospects
Value System
Vocational Topics

The process of case conceptualization In conceptualizing a case, the psychological assessor might imagine being asked to "Tell me about this person—*with regard to reason for assessment.*" This task will be easier if the assessor will recollect the commonly made observation that the various aspects of a person's existence may be understood in terms of some kind of hierarchical order, and that from this structure those traits that are of "central or dominating importance" may reliably be judged (Conrad, 1932). As a result of psychological study of a person, certain features suggest themselves as predominant. We may identify in clients, in addition to overt behavior of interest, organizing centers or central themes, which may relate to tendencies or to modes of expression. Thus we become aware of the basic role of such issues as a faulty self-concept, an attitude of interpersonal hostility, a need for achievement, a rigid control over emotional expression, tendencies to withdrawal, conflicts over sexual goals, or a pattern of achieving self-needs through the manipulation of others. A large number of such issues may be identified in any person, although there is perhaps a relatively smaller number of recurring themes that accounts for many of the topics found to be apparently relevant in case studies.

The organization in a case formulation of the central themes of a person's life involves several different tasks. What the assessor considers most important must be made to stand out, with other material assigned an auxiliary role. Importance may be gauged in terms of consequences, which might mean that the major emphasis is not accorded to the most central and enduring feature of the personality. Thus a hospital psychologist must think in such practical terms as whether the information gathered about the patient will provide the staff with the sort of understanding it needs in order to relate more effectively to the patient. The psychologist may have determined that dependency, hostility, and a poor sex identity are the central themes, and a hierarchy of their centrality to the personality postulated. But if an acute depression with suicidal tendencies were also identified, the imperativeness of this finding would dictate that it be emphasized, at least in the short run, even though sex conflict was basic in undermining the patient's adjustment.

There are as many means of supplying appropriate emphasis to content as literary creativity will permit. For practical use, however, the more common techniques will generally suffice. These include the order of presentation, the skillful and appropriate use of adjectives, and the use of vivid illustrative material. Less often the psychological assessor might resort to underlining, capitalization, or dramatic presentation, such as may be produced by a clipped statement or an exclamation point. Sometimes the central issue can be stated quite directly: "This man is best understood through a description of his deep dependency needs and his manner of attempting to gratify these."

The skillful use of repetition can also make for effective emphasis. This is perhaps best accomplished by weaving the central theme through all or a substantial part of the formulation, relating subsidiary themes to that which has been selected as the main point for emphasis. The dependency theme mentioned in the previous paragraph, for example, can be related to the other prominent and clinically relevant themes of his life. Suppose that a person has strong but inexpressible urges, a tendency to perceive the environment as threatening, feelings of inadequacy and depression, deep anxieties about his core gender identity, and the objective appearance of free anxiety. All of these may be more or less directly related to the crucial dependency problem, and the dependency theme might be presented in a number of contexts.

What this amounts to is that the psychological assessor should practice a mild form of caricature. We are charged with presenting a clinically useful picture, not an exact photograph. Admittedly, by eliminating certain material judged to be nonrelevant to the purpose of assessment, we produce a distortion of the whole person; yet we might as well accept that we cannot present a totally undistorted picture of a person—the full content of the person's life is simply not available, and we may not be entirely accurate in what we think we know. Even the shotgun report might omit information, but its fundamental error is primarily in its bulk that detracts from the reader's ability to recognize the relative importance of the various topics presented, and thus can lead to the development of a distorted image.

Along with formulating a case in terms of its needed emphasis, the psychological assessor must consider the details of the central themes to be spelled out in the formulation. Each basic theme must be seen in terms of its role in the person's economy, its unique components, its social import, and associated personality information (such as the relationship of a central theme of inferiority feelings to a subsidiary theme of deficiencies in sexual functioning). It is these that make the central themes take on the action characteristic of life.

EXEMPLIFICATION OF CASE FORMULATION

I have already offered the opinion that *standard* outlines for case formulation detract from the effectiveness of the endeavor to fashion a meaningful statement of the case. Each individual case, however, should be based on an ad hoc outline. A useful place to start is with the list of topics around which a case may be conceptualized (p. 208) as a source of topic entries for outlining the formulation.

The following Case of Mr. A[3] illustrates the process of case formulation, starting with an outline. The often troubling problem of intraparagraph and interparagraph organization is considered in detail.

The client, a young man in his twenties, twice in recent months had come into difficulties that led to his arrest, the first time for "bookie" activities and the second time for threatening his parents with a gun after consuming "12 or 14 beers." The psychiatrist who examined the client on direction of the court referred the case to us, with the request that we probe the meaning of the antisocial tendencies.

We determined that the client had a basic conflict centering on passivity and dependency, these being associated with what the client perceived as a harsh father, and hence a (now generalized) need to rebel was developed. No fewer than four clinically relevant defenses were erected against this conflict: (1) a denial of

---

[3]From Tallent, *Psychological Report Writing* (3rd ed.), Chapter 5.

personal inadequacy, (2) a denial of real events, which precludes effective or constructive action, (3) a renunciation of personal goals so as to gain support (and thus perhaps to be maneuvered by "bad company"), and (4) a hostile and unrealistic fantasy life. The typical view he presented to others and the difficulties he experienced in cognitive functioning round out this picture.

The core personality topic outline might go like this:

    I. Conflicts
   II. Social Stimulus Value
  III. Cognitive Functioning
  IV. Defenses (1)
   V. Defenses (2)
  VI. Defenses (3)
 VII. Defenses (4)

This preliminary outline form is both general and incomplete. Yet it presents an overall structure for the report, and the topic headings might well form the bases for paragraphs. In practice, we would now simply translate these headings into more specific behavior referents and elaborate on the content to be discussed in these paragraphs by drawing the following additional topics from the same list that supplied the material for the core personality topic outline:

Attitudes	Interpersonal Skills
Awareness	Needs
Cognitive Skills	Outlook
Conative Factors	Perception of Environment
Content of Consciousness	Perception of Self
Deficit	Personal Consequences of Behavior
Drives, Dynamics	Psychopathology
Emotional Cathexes	Subjective Feeling States
Emotional Controls	Social Consequences of Behavior
Frustrations	Social Role
Goals	Value System
Interpersonal Relations	

...the outline then becomes:

    I. Conflicts
       A. Self-Perception
       B. Goals
       C. Frustrations
       D. Interpersonal Relations

    E. Perception of Environment
    F. Drives, Dynamics
    G. Emotional Cathexes
    H. Emotional Controls
 II. Social Stimulus Value
    A. Cognitive Skills
    B. Cognitive Factors
    C. Goals
    D. Social Role
III. Cognitive Functioning
    A. Deficit
    B. Psychopathology
IV. Defenses (1)
    A. Self-Perception
    B. Needs
    C. Conflicts
 V. Defenses (2)
    A. Subjective Feeling States
    B. Attitudes
    C. Deficits
    D. Personal Consequences of Behavior
    E. Insight
    F. Subjective Feeling States
    G. Insight
    H. Social Stimulus Value
    I. Social Consequences of Behavior
VI. Defenses (3)
    A. Interpersonal Relations
    B. Needs
    C. Interpersonal Skills
    D. Emotional Controls
VII. Defenses (4)
    A. Content of Consciousness
    B. Needs
    C. Values
    D. Needs
    E. Social Consequences of Action

...which now, in more lifelike terms, still highly detailed for teaching purposes, becomes:

I. Conflict centering on dependency and passivity
   A. Feelings of inadequacy
   B. Frustrated personal goals (dependency and passivity)
   C. Faulty, unsatisfying relationship with father
   D. Father seen as cold, rejecting, punishing
   E. Rebellious tendencies which are generalized
   F. Control over negative impulses out of fear
II. How others see client
   A. Intellectual level and skills
   B. Lack of will to function at optimum
   C. Fluctuating goal for self-achievement
   D. Social irresponsibility
III. Cognitive functioning
   A. Deficiencies under stress
   B. Psychopathological aspects of deficiencies
IV. Denial of felt inadequacy
   A. Negative view of self
   B. Need to feel "like everybody else"
   C. Conflict over adequacy as a male
V. Denial and nonexperience of pertinent realities
   A. Partial avoidance of depressed feelings
   B. Naive attitude
   C. Inability to assess his behavior adequately
   D. Inability to correct own behavior
   E. Inability to understand problems
   F. Depressive tendencies
   G. Lack of full experience of depression
   H. Social masking of depressed feelings
   I. Relation of inner feelings to negative social behavior
VI. Social maneuvers to gain acceptance
   A. Receptive orientation
   B. Need for support
   C. Techniques for gaining support
   D. Control of negative impulses to retain support

VII. Fantasy as a basic defense
   A. Value of fantasy
   B. Needs as reflected in fantasy
   C. Deficiency of social values
   D. Need to appear in socially favorable light
   E. Fantasy content and deficiency of social values as a basis for unlawful activity

...and then, initiated by an opening summary or overview, is translated into a case formulation:

> This man is most readily understood in terms of his unusually passive, dependent approach to life and his attempts to overcome the deeply unhappy state brought about by this personality limitation.
>
> Mr. A does not feel very adequate as a person, an attitude that is developed through experiencing a continual sense of failure in terms of his own goals, and that apparently is reinforced by others. In fact, his relations with his father very likely are the basic reason for such feeling. This person is seen by the patient as cold, rejecting, punishing, and unapproachable. He has an urge to rebel and fight against this person—an urge that has been generalized to all society, but he is afraid to give vent to his impulses. Whatever emotional support he does get (got) seems to be from the mother.
>
> As others see him, he seems to have the essential capacity to do well if only he would try. He scores at the average level on a test of intelligence (IQ: l06), he is able to learn readily, when he wants to, and on occasion can perform unusually fast and effectively. Yet he does not typically follow through on this advantage. His willingness, sometimes even his desire, to do well fluctuates, so that in the long run he would not be regarded as a constructive or responsible person.
>
> Other personality deficiencies also compromise his functioning. Under stress or when faced with difficult problems he becomes blocked, confused, and indecisive. His thinking does not show sufficient flexibility to meet such situations so that he would be regarded as unadaptable and unspontaneous.
>
> Mr. A's felt inadequacy causes him to feel that he is not as good as others. By way of reassuring himself on this matter he frequently during examination makes remarks that he is "like everybody else." The feeling that he is inferior includes also the sexual area where he is quite confused about his maleness. It is likely that one or more sex problems contribute to his sense of failure, although, quite understandably, he denies this and indicates a satisfactory sex life "like everybody else."
>
> He hardly experiences the full effect of his behaviors, however. He protects himself by denying many events of reality, by keeping many facts about himself and others unconscious, by a general attitude of "not knowing"—an attitude of naiveness. He can hardly take corrective action about himself because he does not understand himself or his actions, or recognize the nature of his problems. Oddly enough, as already stated, this is an unhappy person, but he does not adequately recognize this fact, nor does he appear to others as depressed. Yet on occasion this might be a factor in his behavior that could be personally or socially unfortunate.
>
> This man's insecurity about himself forces him into a receptive orientation to other people. He must have friends to provide support. To achieve this he presents himself in

a positive, correct light, tries to say the "right" things and even to be ingratiating and obsequious. It is important that he create the "right" effect and may resort to dramatic behavior to bring this about. "Friends" are so important to him that he sometimes must take abuse in order to hold them. He must always hold back hostile expression.

But it is perhaps in fantasy where the greatest satisfaction is derived. He dreams of being a "success" (his term)—accumulating enough money by the age of 35 so he can retire and effortlessly enjoy the comforts of the world. In his fantasy he is independent of authority, can openly express the aggression he ordinarily cannot, and flout society. He has no positive feelings about social rules (although he may profess to), but is concerned when apprehended for misconduct, possibly less for the real punishment than for how it "looks" to be known for doing what he is afraid to do. It is little wonder that he is easy prey for an "easy money" scheme.

Arranging Findings in the Formulation

How are the component findings to be arranged in a report? How, for example, was the scheme for the preceding formulation developed?

The reader will note that the sections of the outline and the paragraphs in the formulation contain heterogeneous and occasionally repeated content. This is intentional. A formulation consisting of homogeneous paragraphs would be a form of segmented report (although perhaps not as artificial as the kind of segmented reports commented on in the next chapter and subject to some of the same censure). The psychological assessor should try to relate in the formulation those behaviors that occur together in the functioning context of the person. If sex conflicts hamper intellectual functioning, these related facts should be mentioned as closely together as they are in this sentence, not as unconnected statements occurring in different and possibly widely separated paragraphs. In a good formulation, the beginning of a paragraph commonly announces the integrated theme of the topics that compose it.

Let us look at the intraparagraph organization. The intention was to take the main integrated themes emerging in response to the imaginary request to "Tell me about this person"—the brief statement of the psychologist's findings that precedes the outline (pp. 210–211). Thus each of the four basic methods of defense Mr. A uses has some meaningfully interrelated components. Consider the derivation of the fifth paragraph of the report. That Mr. A feels inadequate was one of the principal conclusions of the psychological assessor. In fact, his repeated statement that he is "like everybody else" strengthens this conclusion and also suggests how he tries to adopt an attitude to deny his feeling of inadequacy. The psychological assessor also had strong reasons to reach the conclusion that Mr. A had several prominent sex conflicts associated with his feelings of inadequacy—a conclusion perhaps strengthened by the client's comment (to a sentence-completion item) that he has a sex life that is "like everybody else." (Notice, incidentally, the emphasis to be gained by repeating this expression closely together in different but related contexts. The topics in the fifth paragraph obviously belong together.)

Or, look at the third paragraph. From observations of samples of Mr. A's intellectual functioning, it was apparent to the psychological assessor that he would impress others well in this respect, at least as regards capacity. Yet it was also clear by Mr. A's performance on a number of tests that there was a fluctuating will and a consequent lack of goal-directedness and responsibility. It was further noted that he meets many of his problems through fantasy, but this possible way of elaborating on the theme of irresponsibility and its social effects was reserved for the emphasis that can be brought about by treating a topic in a final paragraph. In the third paragraph, however, it was thought appropriate to contrast his capacity with his output, since this discrepancy suggests that people would be critical of him, an important finding in view of what rejection means to Mr. A. The theme was not "pushed" more strongly, only because the conclusion was not judged to be sufficiently firm. If it were, it could easily have been developed in this paragraph.

There is one simple rule for deciding on the contents of a paragraph: functional relatedness. (What relatedness is there in the other paragraphs in the formulation of the case of Mr. A?) This criterion permits the intentional repetition of items of content in different paragraphs. Beyond this, the psychological assessor has to decide how to arrange the several items in the paragraph and how to word thoughts for effectiveness. The limiting factor in learning this skill is probably the basic prose style of the assessor. Nevertheless, much of the ingenuity needed for this skill can be acquired. Perhaps most important are the terms in which the psychologist thinks. If the task is conceptualized in terms of communicating "findings"—perhaps that the client has anxiety, hostility, and narcissistic wounds—such content probably is precisely what will be recorded. But if the assessor understands the case in terms of a practical mission, conceptualization of content and the manner in which it is expressed are likely to be more functional.

The novice can learn how to make a paragraph hang together by studying samples of effective clinical writing. Supervisors are often in a position to make relevant suggestions in training conferences based on live case material. There are any number of writing techniques that can be adapted for specific effect. For example, in paragraph three the method of contrast was used. Mr. A's capacity was contrasted with his productivity because of the social meaning and implications such a discrepancy may have. Some of the techniques that aid in interparagraph organization might also be useful.

The organization of paragraphs in a case formulation is possibly more complex than the organization of conclusions within a paragraph, because the formulation is a larger conceptual unit. Moreover, the organization of each formulation must have its own rationale, although certainly other reports may have a similar rationale and be organized along similar lines. How do we arrive at a rationale for organizing a case conceptualization? How, for example, was the rationale for the report on Mr. A reached?

First, Mr. A was understood in terms of an approach to life that is not socially adaptive and leads to some personally unsatisfying results (central personality theme). The ways in which he tries to overcome some of the effects of his basic personality orientation bear rather directly on the reason for his being referred to us. By stating the central problem the client may quickly be introduced to the reader in general terms, with the understanding that the necessary details will follow.

The top priority then became the further development of the theme introduced in the first paragraph, hence the need to know about Mr. A's feelings of inadequacy. This topic led naturally to a discussion of what the client is "really" like in contrast to his misperception of himself. However, he is also objectively seen to have shortcomings, so the deficiencies mentioned in the fourth paragraph supplement those commented on in the third. So far we have presented the logically related topics of Mr. A's perception of himself and an external evaluation of some of his qualities. All of this was thought to be pertinent to the problem for which he was referred.

The next four paragraphs are logically interrelated, since they serially disclose how Mr. A copes with his feelings about himself. First, in paragraph five is a discussion of the basic manner by which he tries not to feel inadequate. The theme is amplified in the sixth paragraph, which suggests a very wide scope of denial and the effect this might have. The seventh paragraph shows a social maneuver he uses as a defense for the same basic problem. The final paragraph suggests an additional defense for this problem, that of a fantasy life that seems to be closely associated with his long-term antisocial activities (being a "bookie").

The overall guiding principle was to present the man in terms of his personality as this pertains to his antisocial activities. Nevertheless, the relationship between what is described in these paragraphs and his social difficulties is not mentioned in every instance. It would be logical enough to do so, but a different scheme was used in preference to cluttering the report with what in this case would be speculations. Instead, the speculations were gathered together as a "speculative note" that was appended to the body of the report. Its purpose was to attempt to relate, more directly than responsible interpretation practices permit, the basic personality of the man to his unwanted behaviors.

Speculative note The client's antisocial behavior appears to be related to the personality problems noted here and to his method of coping with these. His negative attitude to authority (father), of course, would seem to be a basic ingredient. His need for support is another factor, and the support of a group of persons on the other side of the law might be as meaningful as support from another source. As we have seen, he will go out of his way (engaging in illegal activities?) to retain his "friends." His fantasy life of wealth and leisure would also seem to make unlawful activities appealing. Finally, his intellectual inefficiencies and his unadaptability might tend to give trouble in more straightforward enterprises. He does not genuinely feel he is wrong.

Concerning the gun incident, the client seemed to be trying to indicate to the examining physician that the weapon was used to try forcibly to extract sympathy and support that he could not get by passive means. The gun evidently made him feel powerful, and the reasoning was childish and incomplete. Apparently the act was impulsive. The client admits to consuming 12 to 14 beers before the event and this probably loosened his usual tight control over direct hostile expression. Further acts either against himself or against others cannot be ruled out, although no specific or immediate danger is foreseen.

Strategies for Organizing the Case Formulation

There are many possible schemes suitable for organizing reports, The total number is probably limited only by the assessor's ingenuity and the variety of case material. The following suggestions pertain to some elementary organizing strategies. In many instances one of these will not be a sufficient strategy for an entire formulation; several strategies will have to be combined.

Regardless of the presentation scheme employed, an overview statement is commonly in order. In any event, a clear focus and objective must always be established in the light of the available material and its significance. Sometimes it will be most effective to present a major conclusion at the beginning (a purpose often served by an overview) and then make supporting information available. At other times, the psychological assessor may be able to build up to the major conclusion and present it more forcefully at the end of the report. It is difficult to generalize. Most often, when the psychological assessor is asked to contribute a diagnosis, this matter may be dealt with at the conclusion of the formulation after the relevant evidence to support that diagnosis has been presented. However, a diagnosis may be offered at the beginning of the formulation for a good reason: "This is a severely schizophrenic patient whose homicidal fantasies and inability to control her behavior could pose a serious threat to the community."

1. The simplest approach to organizing a case formulation is possible when it is necessary to deal only with a limited segment of behavior, such as might be the situation when dealing with a circumscribed matter. Thus, when dealing with intellectual efficiency, the presentation considers sequentially several pertinent aspects of this problem. Or if the problem is one of cognitive deficit, such as in a brain syndrome, it is necessary to cite the related data contributing to the major conclusion—for example, that the deficit is present. Probably the relative seriousness of the signs, such as memory defect, inability to shift concepts, concreteness, confabulation, loss of mental control, confusion, and loss of orientation, will suggest a meaningful order of presentation and appropriate data groupings—for example, memory defect and confabulation would probably be closely linked.

2. With more complex material a quite simple, yet effective, approach is to present a general opening statement, an overview, or an introductory statement, followed by the necessary elaborations and whatever other pertinent information is required to round out the personality picture. A formulation might start with: "The dominant emphasis in Ms. B's life is manipulating others in order to realize a set of strong ambitions." The nature of these ambitions, why they are important to her, and her techniques of manipulation might then be commented upon. Finally, whatever else is important, such as capacity (for example, intellectual or social), situational frustrations, adaptability, or the effects of failure, could be woven into the theme.

3. Some formulations might be essentially a build-up to a diagnosis or some major conclusion. What is required is that the psychologist present bits of evidence step by step, as these contribute to a final conclusion. A tightly reasoned formulation of this sort might be in order particularly when the conclusion is of far-reaching significance. Examples would occur when a diagnosis is an essential ingredient in a court decision, or when contemplated action–like commitment to or release from a hospital–might hinge on the psychological assessment. Such an organization might be in order when the assessor feels the need to convincingly present findings that are not at all apparent. Quite frequently, for example, clinical diagnosis may point to neurosis or personality disorder while psychological indicators suggest a psychotic process.

4. A cause-and-effect presentation can be useful when concern is with some symptom whose basis needs to be understood. Physical symptoms that are thought by a physician to be psychogenic are a common instance. This approach is also particularly valuable when a social symptom, such as misbehavior in school or criminal behavior, needs to be understood and identified with a set of dynamics or with pathology, such as an organic mental disorder. It may be best at times to first explore the nature of the unwanted symptom and then to deal with its causes. At other times it may be appropriate to deal with the pertinent underlying psychological material and show how this relates to the issue of concern.

5. In many instances, the order of presentation might be from periphery to center or from center to periphery, and the most effective approach can be a subjective matter. Frequently it is helpful to contrast the surface picture with what is not apparent. Reasons for doing this might be (a) to alert others to unsuspected personality features; (b) to contribute understanding as to why a person who is without evident pathology gets into difficulties; or (c) to contrast a superficial picture or facade with what a person is "really" like.

6. Sometimes it is appropriate to emphasize the subjective view of the individual if the writer feels it is important to understand the situation(s) as the client does. Contrasting the subjective picture with the external viewpoint can often contribute valuable perspective to a case. When the fantasy life, orientation, or perception of environment is particularly important, the value of this approach becomes evident.

7. Contrast can be an appropriate organizing focus of a report. The nature of a conflict may be brought out quite effectively by contrasting its elements—for example, incompatible goals. Contrast can also be functional when different layers of behavior need to be understood in relation to one another. An illustration of this might be severely hostile attitudes sublimated in one who fights for social justice. This technique is also called for when the findings of a current examination are compared with those of a previous examination. The writer sets forth the important similarities and differences uncovered in the two examinations and whatever significance these might have.

10

THE ASSESSMENT PROCESS, CONTINUED:
Responsible and Effective Psychological Report Writing

The case formulation is the substance of the psychological report—the organized conclusions of consultation. To present this material as a responsible and effective document that the consumer of the report will look forward to, and whose writing the assessor will not find burdensome, a number of principles of psychological report writing must be attended to.

How to write a good psychological report is here discussed in terms of three foci. First is the matter of the content of the report; for sound reasons the assessor should not seek to tell all he or she knows about the client. Of the masses of data commonly available to the assessor, which content is likely to be useful and which not? The next focus is on the central theme of this chapter, *responsibility* and *effectiveness*, and how these can be enhanced. The final focus is on the many specific practices that detract to various degrees from the quality of psychological reports—the pitfalls in psychological report writing—and how to avoid them.

CONTENT OF THE PSYCHOLOGICAL REPORT

Selection of Content

The psychological assessor, staring at masses of raw data that may be interpreted and incorporated in a case formulation, must face questions about the potential usefulness of the many units of information that are available for recording and transmittal. Which of these might be useful, even vital, in the case under consideration? Which would contribute nothing to the assessment goal, or even detract from an effective presentation? Which, frankly, would not be appreciated? In psychological assessment, a few well-placed items of information, like a well-aimed rifle shot, is much more effective than a shotgun blast that splatters psychological content over the bullseye—and everywhere else.

Multiple Uses for Report Content

There are various ways in which psychological material may be used to advantage. The most obvious purpose of psychological content is as a response to the reason for assessment. The assessor, then, must be well acquainted with the problem to which his or her efforts are addressed. Thus, it may be decided to accent intellectual functioning when poor school performance is the issue, and recently acquired organic deficit in the case of a drop-off in job performance in a previously well-functioning person who had suffered a head injury.

In addition to addressing the immediate reason for assessment, the psychological assessor should also anticipate needs. For example, in the case of an elderly man referred for study of the psychological features of a delirium, the assessor notes some specific ways in which the patient is likely to present problems in nursing care. This finding, along with suggestions for coping with the anticipated difficulty should be passed along. Or, a client may have been referred for clarification of diagnosis. In the assessment process, however, the assessor may uncover some conflicts that might be dealt with to the client's advantage and spells these out along with recommendations for psychotherapy.

The creation of a record, congruent with ethical practice and test standards is an additional purpose of psychological content. A record may have multiple uses. It may be used, for example, to compare a client's psychological status from one assessment period to another, such as before the initiation of psychotherapy and after a number of therapy sessions. Other uses cannot be precisely predicted, but an available record may be consulted as the need arises. Thus, a record may be searched for clues of oppositional tendencies and dyscontrol when an individual without a history of violence commits a destructive act.

The practice of retaining records should be in accord with *Ethical Principles of Psychologists* (American Psychological Association, 1981) and the *Standards for Educational and Psychological Testing* (American Psychological Association, 1985). Concerns with confidentiality of information and obsolescence of records is uppermost:

> Psychologists make provisions for maintaining confidentiality in the storage and disposal of records. (*Principle 5c*) Psychologists recognize that assessment results may become obsolete. They make every effort to avoid and prevent the misuse of obsolete measures. (*Principle 8d*) Organizations that maintain test scores on individuals in data files or in an individual's records should develop a clear set of policy guidelines on the duration of retention in an individual's records, availability, and use over time of such scores (*Standard 15.11*).

Kinds of Report Content

Psychological report content may be *primary* or *secondary*. Primary content is the core content of the report, the original contribution of the psychological assessor. Such content is basic, substantive, and includes conclusions on such topics as intellectual functioning, neuropsychological status, goals, conflicts, and object relations.

Secondary content is of several sorts. First is administrative material, such as the dates the client was seen, the name of the referring person, and a listing of the psychological instruments used. Secondary data include also information that supports, or is an example of, the conclusions that are reported, such as scores, test responses, or client verbalizations. In this vein also are items from the history, or a comparison of the conclusions of the report with those of a colleague who has had contact with the client.

Orienting data are helpful in putting raw findings into meaningful context. Included here may be a client's age, educational level, ethnic background, life experience, and reason for referral. All of these may influence how raw findings are to be understood. Intelligence test scores, for example, do not necessarily have the same meaning for a native-born American and a recent immigrant to the United States.

Illustrative and persuasive content may both be used to good effect, but will backfire if overused. Persuasive writing? Yes. The psychological assessor is responsible for forming conclusions, and to the extent that there is confidence in them the psychological assessor has the *responsibility* to try to be an effective contributor to the clinical process. Such is particularly the case when the assessor's colleagues, who lack the benefit of penetrating psychological tools, cannot "see" what the assessor "sees." In light of this fact, Appelbaum (1970) suggests that a psychologist must also be a sociologist, a politician, a diplomat, a group dynamicist, a salesperson, and an artist. He explains specifically why he includes salesperson in his list. The term "...may denote high pressure, 'activity,' hucksterism, and, indeed, there may be clinical situations that do require some of this. Usually, however, the test report is more akin to institutional advertising, a low key presentation of evident factualness."

It is also in the interest of being convincing to build major conclusions on a substructure of subconclusions. The assessor should not proclaim a person to be a schizophrenic "out of the blue" (which happens). The diagnosis must build on a number of lesser conclusions, such as that the person shows evidence of a thought disorder, bizarre delusions, prominent hallucinations, and continuous presence of such disturbance for at least six months (American Psychiatric Association, 1987).

Appropriateness and Relevance of Report Content

All content that enters psychological reports is not appropriate, not pertinent or relevant to the reason for which assessment was indicated. This is unfortunate at several levels. Most serious, inappropriate content blurs the focus of the report and detracts attention from that which is pertinent. Attending to and recording material that is not pertinent is time consuming for the psychological assessor, and tends to make report writing burdensome. Reports thus padded with unnecessary content are also burdensome to report readers and are a frequent source of complaint. Complaints are also engendered when inappropriate content is experienced by readers as an intrusion in their bailiwick (Tallent & Reiss, 1959c).

As a general rule—there are exceptions—it is well for the psychological report not to duplicate the contribution of others. Following is an excerpt from a psychological report on Frank, an eight-year-old child of concern to his teacher because of perfectionistic strivings and a low threshold for emotional upset when he cannot handle a problem:

> Frank is a neatly dressed, eight-year old boy whose left eye constantly squints. He is courteous, perhaps overly courteous, and is most cooperative. When he doesn't know an answer, he becomes noticeably upset, sometimes appearing to be on the verge of tears.

It is inevitable, even desirable, in a team setting that different clinical workers make a contribution in such areas as psychodynamics and ideas about treatment. It is not appropriate, however, for the psychological assessor to merely duplicate what is best, or traditionally handled by others. It is not uncommon for several team members to report essentially the same content: "This is a 21 year old white male who was born out of wedlock to a teenage drug abusing mother..."

On the other hand, there is occasion to appropriate such information. A psychodynamic formulation, for example, may stress a client's attitudes to mother figures and females in general, and the circumstances of birth and the early years can be highly appropriate content. In such instances the psychological assessor should report such data, even if the material was originally obtained by another team member. *However*, such material should be reported *in the context of a new integration*: for example, the client's hostile attitude to females, his sexual fantasies, and how the conflicts these entail are related to his early life situation.

Consider how much better Frank's situation was presented when the psychological assessor rewrote his report to address and make reference to the information supplied to him by the teacher:

> This child's perfectionistic strivings, if not modified, can become a way of life, crippling spontaneity and ability to relate with warmth and satisfaction. He could develop a very serious breakdown as early as adolescence. He has the feeling that catastrophe awaits him if he does not achieve at an exaggeratedly high level, that somehow such performance is expected of him. Seeking to minimize fear, he sacrifices the positive feelings and true interest in his scholarship, for being correct is what is important to him and not the meaning of the work. This child has need for warmth, kindness, and acceptance—especially when he does not know the answer. He needs to learn that he can be accepted for himself rather than for his performance. He should be involved in play therapy, particularly in contact and rough-and-tumble games where getting dirty is assured. Finger painting might also be helpful.

When the role of the psychological assessor, as institutionally or otherwise defined, goes beyond that of psychological assessment we may see much content in the report that was not developed as psychological information. It is not uncommon to read social history and medical material in psychological reports, references to ulcers and fractures, their treatment, and the patient's medical progress.

The topic of content appropriateness (or relevance) can, therefore, be a slippery one, if only because what is relevant in one situation may be less so, or beside the point, in another. As an extreme contrast, just consider how different is the content in a report written in a psychodynamic treatment center from one written in a school for the mentally retarded. It is not possible to prescribe the content that would be suitable for all psychological reports.

In practice, report content is explicitly, or implicitly, judged to be relevant on the basis of one or more of the following: (1) the orientation of the psychological assessor, (2) the orientation of the referring person or the setting in which assessment is done, (3) the problem under consideration, and (4) the anticipated use(s) to which the report will be put. Perhaps more often than we know, what is considered to be relevant is a matter of habit.

The interests of the client and the goals of the setting that serve the client should be emphasized. What is relevant in a rehabilitation center obviously differs from the central concerns in a school setting. It is unlikely that any sort of content is relevant in *all* cases (other than administrative content such as the client's name and the date). It is also important to note that certain data (such as medical prescription) are *never* appropriate as a *contribution* from a psychological assessor, though there could be a reason to allude to such material.

Also never appropriate is material that is contrary to ethical principles. Thus, the *Ethical Principles of Psychologists* (American Psychological Association, 1981) cautions psychologists not to exceed their limitations. All psychologists are not equally or adequately trained in assessment. Although the Rorschach is well entrenched as a psychological tool, and many consumers of psychological assessment have an interest in what can be gained when it is part of a battery, the assessor who is not well grounded in the Rorschach ought not to develop interpretations based on the use of this instrument. Further, the psychologist should not include as report content statements that are not germane to the assessment or that are an undue invasion of privacy.

THE COMMON CONTENT CATEGORIES IN "TRADITIONAL" PSYCHOLOGICAL REPORTS: A CRITIQUE

Psychological reports, originally closely linked to the Binet examination, and later to other measurement instruments as they were developed, were in fact *test reports*, a report of "test results" or "test findings." Their content emphasized scores, relations among scores, test responses, a description of qualitative features of performance, interpretations to personality functioning—such as relation of test functioning to social functioning in the classroom, and predictions (regarding academic performance, for example), and recommendations. Over the years, additional features were added to reports; for example, with the introduction of the

Wechsler scales, the reporting of three IQs per subject and a stereotyped discussion of the skills and abilities measured by these instruments, and the relations among them, became common. When Freud and projective techniques were introduced, these new approaches were incorporated in psychological reports.

The psychological report, then, evolved in response to the evolution of tests and theories, not on the basis of a rationale incorporating the needs of the individual and the most effective means of gathering and presenting information in response to these needs. Taylor and Teicher (1946), with the test reports of the time in mind, noted that "clinical psychology appears to have given little systematic study to the manner in which test findings are organized and formulated to provide necessary records and to render the data easily and fully understood by professional associates." Their solution to the problem was to offer a report writing outline quite similar to those now in existence.

Test-by-test Reporting

Test orientation favors test-by-test reporting, a means of keeping the conclusions from straying very far from the data to which they are anchored. Indeed, conclusions commonly are anchored to subtests or sections of tests, the report sequentially addressing such matters as vocabulary level, arithmetic skills, or reasoning ability. Apparently most psychological assessors (and the consumers of their reports) now favor an integrated approach.

Reporting in Terms of Part Processes

In a similar approach to presenting a segmented version of personality, presumably more scientific than an integrated presentation, some psychological reports identify, and present singly, various components of personality as if they were distinct, unconnected entities—intelligence, perception, motivation, emotion, and so forth. Such an approach clearly does violence to our understanding of personality. Pruyser (1979) sees merit in examining personality one feature at a time, such as perception, intelligence and memory, thought, and thought organization. But these are various perspectives on the individual. Reality, he notes, exists in "the one process that sustains life...integrative by its very nature, it promotes both personal and social integration and is therefore succinctly called the 'integrative process.'"

Preliminary Part of the Report

Various classes of information commonly appear in the preliminary part of the report. These range in importance from very to doubtful to useless—really less than useless, since, in addition to providing nothing of value, they also require time to write and to read ("The client wore a white blouse, a brown skirt, and brown loafers." If there is something of significance to interpret here, interpret it!) An example of the psychological significance that a client's clothing may have appears in the psychological report on Jim W., starting on page 309.

An accounting, ranging in length from a paragraph to an extended and detailed recapitulation of the client's appearance, conduct, verbalizations, and test performance commonly precedes the psychological report proper. The psychological assessor certainly should be attentive to such material, and as much of it as is pertinent to the reason for assessment should be interpreted and integrated into the case formulation. Here the information on the client's behavior and so forth can be particularly meaningful, since it is interpreted by the assessor in the context of interaction with the client and other available assessment data. The reader of the psychological report, by contrast, lacks the advantages that are available in this context.

For less obvious reasons, Sugarman (1981) objects to the practice, entrenched in many settings, of reporting "clinical behavior" or "test behavior" or "clinical observation." He is concerned over the ease with which the examiner's description of the client's behavior is distorted by countertransference, and by distortion of the picture of the client in the mind-body dualism implied in separating, for discussion, overt behavior from the mental content inferred from test material.

> Many graduate programs and treatment facilities teach testers to begin each test report with a description of the patient's behavior. Although there are many reasons to focus on nontest variables (some legitimate and some suspect), such a format allows the examiner's affective response to the patient to creep into the report in an unintegrated fashion. Such reports usually read as though behavioral attributes and the responses they evoke in others are distinct from internal attributes which have been assessed through the test responses. This separation reflects the mind-body quandary that has plagued psychology since Descartes and that impedes a holistic understanding of the patient.

The reason for assessment commonly is noted in the beginning section of the report. This, of course, is an important item of information since it is an integral part of the assessment. On the other hand, particularly in institutional practice, it also is likely that it is readily available in several places in the client's chart. In a court of law, however, Dillon and Wildman (1979) advise the psychological assessor: "Restate the questions you have been asked to address. This should demonstrate to the officers of the court that you know what the relevant questions are." What is best practice sometimes differs across settings.

Intellectual Aspects

In traditional psychological reports, following the preliminary section is usually a discussion of the "intellectual aspects" of the client. There does not seem to be a current firm rationale for thus accenting intelligence. The practice of presenting an exhaustive accounting of intellectual functioning became entrenched at a time when psychological testing was all but synonymous with intelligence testing. Now that psychological assessment frequently has to do with personality functioning, psychopathology, psychotherapy-related topics, and various adjustment issues, standard outlines continue to call for dealing with matters of intelligence first.

In this section is commonly recorded an IQ—or IQs, sometimes subtest scores, a notation of items passed and failed—perhaps with an accompanying description or a quote of a verbalization, and a discussion of areas of high performance and low performance. "Scatter" of the subtest scores has for many years been a favorite topic here, though research has not been supportive of the practice (e.g., Piedmont, Sokolove, & Fleming, 1989). In this section it has been common to report personality implications of intelligence test performance, such as interests, emotional control, and impulsivity and compulsivity. These are topics that cannot smoothly be divided into intellectual functioning and some other, equally arbitrary segment of personality. In an integrated report there is no need to thus arbitrarily separate findings into categories, to be concerned, for example, with whether a particular conclusion regarding the client's functioning relates to the intellectual or emotional domain.

Appelbaum (1972) discusses how information regarding intellectual functioning can be a rich source of information on personality issues. Indeed, he finds it useful to have two IQs—an alternate IQ in addition to the standard IQ:

> These alternate scores represent the patient's assumed Verbal, Performance, and Full-Scale *capacity* which, alongside the usual *achieved* scores, illustrate quantitatively the clinical recognition that a range is a better indicator of how people are likely to function than is a single score. Included in this section, also, should be extrapolations from intelligence *per se* to other aspects of personality. A person's attitude toward his rightness or wrongness, to the accumulation of knowledge and ideas, how he functions with emotionally stressful subjects as against relatively impersonal and objective tasks, what the development and use of intelligence may mean symbolically to him—all of these provide avenues toward information about his underlying motives, styles, values, conflicts, and adaptive potentialities. Aspects of thought style—such as subjective, objective, direct or allusive, trenchant or fuzzy—may be included here as well, when they are pertinent and not covered elsewhere.

"Personality" or "Emotional Factors"

What appears in this section, generally, is material derived from personality testing. Topics commonly covered here are psychopathology, unconscious drives, attitudes, conflicts, frustrations, guilt, anxiety, defenses, psychosexual development, and interpersonal relationships. Information on intellectual functioning gained through the use of personality instruments commonly does not appear in this section.

Diagnosis

DSM diagnoses are a part of the case study in many settings, and commonly the psychological assessor is asked, or expected, to contribute in this area. A few psychiatrists, however, hold that the making of psychiatric diagnoses is strictly a medical function (Tallent & Reiss, 1959c). Generally, a formal diagnosis is best made in the context of a case formulation. In good practice, when the case formulation is skillfully done, it is but a short step from this contribution to a DSM category. Far less desirable is to merely offer a clipped diagnosis, such as Adjustment Disorder with Depressed Mood, as if this brief communication offered an adequate understanding of the client and an obvious guide to action.

What must scrupulously be avoided by the psychological assessor is a medical diagnosis or an unwarranted intrusion of a psychological diagnostic statement in a medical situation. A discussion by Sarbin, Taft, and Bailey (1960) illustrates how such practice may be hazardous. The following is abstracted from that source:

> The case was of a 17-year-old girl referred to a psychiatric clinic because of "hysterical manifestations" after the examining physician could find no organic basis for her complaints of abdominal pains. As part of the total evaluation process the patient was seen by a psychologist who reported, in part, "the patient's unresolved oedipal conflict is apparent in her responses to the Thematic Apperception Test. The 'abdominal pains' *are* at one and the same time an identification with her departed father and a way of getting love from her mother" (emphasis supplied). The validity of this diagnostic statement was not borne out, however. She was soon found to have a far advanced cancer in the region of complaint and succumbed to this condition the day following its discovery.

The psychologist's psychodynamic explanation was based on a sound understanding of the patient. According to the mother, the young woman had always been given over to dramatizing her problems and had been close to her father, who died as a result of a perforated ulcer. Such collateral information about the girl is similar to what the psychologist concluded with the aid of tests, particularly the TAT, but it should have been regarded in the light of the original medical findings only as *suggestive* of the nature of the ailment, what it *might* be. How much better it would have been if the psychologist had not rendered an unqualified opinion on the nature of a bodily complaint, but had offered the opinion that the findings were *consistent with* a functional complaint, or even, in the light of the medical conclusion, suggested that "hysteria" was a *possible* explanation of the complaint.

Prognosis

Prediction of future events can be important when working with people. What are the expectations for this person without intervention? With intervention? How might the client fare with different kinds of intervention, psychotherapy versus chemotherapy, for example? Prognosis is an old medical term for such forecasting, and, like diagnosis, some medical people believe the term (and the practice) should be reserved for their exclusive use. Using a formal term to announce when one is making a guess about the future is, of course, not necessary. Or, a term like *outlook* will do nicely to alert the reader to when the report narrative switches from present to future concerns.

Recommendations

Most users of psychological assessment reports wish to find recommendations there for dealing with the client (Tallent & Reiss, 1959c). Teachers, clinicians, counselors, judges, and so forth seek assessment precisely because they need help with those for whom they bear some responsibility. To many consumers of psychological assessment, recommendations are the most important part of the report. The body of the report is of interest in and of itself, but also because, if well conceived, it will lead up to the recommendations that are offered.

Summary

The use of a concluding summary is well entrenched in the writing of reports of psychological assessment. It is hard to argue against the use of summary content, particularly because report readers seem to feel the need for such a statement (Tallent & Reiss, 1959a,b). Nevertheless, the use of a summary may often be injudicious, and should be considered for use with discretion.

Too often, the only justification for a summary is that it serves as an antidote to an otherwise inadequate report—particularly a report that is too long, poorly organized, and too difficult to comprehend. As a result, many readers become "trained" to go directly to the summary and perhaps entirely ignore the body of the report. Such is particularly likely to happen when the report is forbiddingly long.

At the opposite extreme are quite short reports whose writers nevertheless feel that a summary is called for (or mandatory?). By actual measurement, I have seen reports of six to eight inches in length to which were appended summaries aggregating five to eight inches! Such disproportion appears ludicrous and difficult to justify on logical grounds.

Hammond and Allen (1953) propose an "opening summary," a suggestion with which I readily concur. Here is a technique long used in journalism, particularly in feature articles, and also with good effect in scientific journals (abstracts) and with book chapters. An *overview*—presenting as it does the essence of the material at the beginning—if interesting, seems to entice the reader to delve further into the main body of the writing. By contrast, many are of the opinion that a summary at the end, when read first, tends against turning back to the text proper.

RESPONSIBILITY AND EFFECTIVENESS

Acceptable writing skills are important to the preparation of responsible and effective psychological reports. Sydney Smith suggests: "*Everything which is written is meant either to please or to instruct. The second object is difficult to effect, without attending to the first.*" If you need to improve your composition, reading a good instructional book like Flesch's *Say What You Mean* (1972) and his earlier *The Art of Readable Writing* (1949/1974) can pay off.

Beyond the commonsensical requirement that composition meet an acceptable standard is the need to develop technically sound data. The psychological assessor must have a good grasp on theory of personality and behavior but not be ruled by it, must know what *can* be interpreted and what *should* be interpreted, and must be able to present the client as an individual—with individual needs and goals—and not travel the easy road of stereotypy. This view of the assessor is consistent with the pervasive theme of social responsibility in the practice of psychology:

> As practitioners, psychologists know that they have a heavy social responsibility because their recommendations and professional actions may alter the lives of others (*Ethical Principles of Psychologists, Principle lf,* American Psychological Association, 1981).

Matarazzo (1981) suggests how intelligence testing, through the work of Binet and Wechsler, has had profound social impact:

> ...the fruit of their creative minds and the simplicity of the practical tools of measurement and assessment produced by Alfred Binet and David Wechsler would touch the lives and influence the careers of the majority of people who were born during the 20th century. Probably the work of no other psychologists, including Freud or Pavlov, has so *directly* impinged upon the lives of so many people.

Ethical and Legal Constraints

The practice of psychological assessment is informed by legal requirements and the ethical codes of professional associations. The guiding principles and constraints of both are necessary. "It is apparent that psychology's codes are insufficient protections against increased scrutiny by the courts," suggests Bersoff (1975). He further points out that "while psychology may permit different interpretations of its ethical guidelines, the courts may not be so benevolent. They do not find it at all difficult to disregard a profession's claim to autonomy when the behavior of its practitioners is perceived to interfere with the rights of individuals or the public at large."

While the ethical codes of professional bodies and community ethics as incorporated into law presumably tend in the same direction, Bersoff indicates that "codes of ethics and the law may present competing demands." His reasons are as follows:

> 1. A basic reason for the failure of ethical codes to provide adequate bases for behavior is their ethnocentrism...codes represent the professional group's point of view and are rarely developed with help from the consumers who receive the professional's services. Psychologists may be living under the false presumption that their ethic is shared by the people they serve.
> 2. Ethical principles are formulated on such an abstract level that they merely provide general guides to actual behavior; practitioners rarely understand how those principles are to be applied in specific situations.
> 3. The value of codes may be perceived solely as a means of providing practitioners with a symbol that they are truly professionals.

While ethical codes of professional bodies hold the potential for confusion and misapplication, they may also have a significant impact on practice. Bersoff, specifically emphasizing the shortcomings of the 1974 ethics code of the National

Association of School Psychologists (NASP), quotes several principles that are sound in their conception, if insufficient in practice.

For example, *Principle II(c)* is consistent with the present thesis concerning responsible and effective report writing: "the emphasis is on the interpretation and organization rather than the simple passing along of test scores," a few words that can make a profound difference in the quality of psychological reports in settings where outmoded test centrism continues. *Principle V(c)* requires that students' parents be involved with the findings of psychological assessment through "frank and prompt reporting...of findings obtained in the evaluation of the student." This principle is an example of congruence between professional ethics and the law...in this case the "Buckley Amendment." (p. 234)

The emphasis in this book that reports be understandable and serviceable is also a matter of law (case law). The case in question is that of *Wyatt* v. *Aderholt* (1974), which was brought in the U.S. District Court for the Middle District of Alabama. The issue centered on the constitutional guarantee of the right to treatment of persons who are committed under civil law. The evidence, based on expert testimony, "established that the hospitals failed to meet the conditions of individualized treatment programs," namely that

> the patient records kept at the hospital were wholly inadequate; that they were written in such a way as to be *incomprehensible* to the aide level staff that had prime responsibility for patient care; and that they were kept where they were not accessible to the direct care staff particularly in need of them" (emphasis supplied).

The creation of an individualized treatment program is also central to the implementation of the Education for All Handicapped Children Act of 1975 (Public Law 94–142). In excess of eight million children are affected by this act at any given time. An individualized, case-focused report, identifying and causing to stand out the key issues in a child's situation, can be a most effective contribution to the preparation of the individualized educational plan called for by the law.

Sharing Reports

For many years it was the conventional wisdom that psychological reports would be hazardous to clients if they were permitted access to their contents. Whatever access was allowed was likely to be in a context of selectivity of material and protective deception. A more casual sharing of data between assessor and client might at one time have been considered a breach of ethics. With particular concern for the potential damage inherent in Rorschach interpretations, B. Klopfer and D. M. Kelley (1946) advised:

> It should be considered an unalterable role of professional conduct *never* to give a written Rorschach interpretation to the subject himself, since psychological terminology is so readily misinterpreted even by persons who should be familiar with it (emphasis supplied).

> [Also,] when the Rorschach expert deals directly with a subject without any professional intermediary, a completely new problem arises. No one should be permitted by his own professional conscience to give to another person as penetrating information about his personality as the Rorschach provides, unless he has specific psychotherapeutic training. Any person who violates this rule of professional conduct uses the Rorschach method in an irresponsible way.

In 1954, W. G. Klopfer (in B. Klopfer et al.) wrote:

> If particular concern is expressed by the patient about test results it is best to give fairly superficial kinds of interpretation, which are apt to be consciously acceptable to the individual and not particularly anxiety provoking. In these cases it usually has been found that an emphasis on the intellectual aspects of the personality, thought contents, characteristic ways of reacting to stressful situations and the like can be discussed most easily. It should be kept in mind that some aspects of the Rorschach are apt to be of an unconscious nature, dealing with repressed material, and should not be brought out except in the context of intensive psychotherapy, and after the establishment of substantial rapport. It need hardly be stated that giving a written report to a patient is an extremely dangerous and harmful thing to do and may cause much grief, both to the patient and to the psychologist.

Such dire allegations do not stem from research, while limited studies on the possible harmfulness to clients of psychological data fail to bear them out. Stein, Furedy, Simonton, and Neuffer (1979) approached the issue by allowing psychiatric patients access to their records. They report that their patients believed they were better informed and more involved in their treatment, and staff became more conscientious in record keeping. Roth, Wolford, and Meisel (1980) allowed *selected* psychiatric patients limited access to their records in the presence of a staff member whose function was to explain the clinical material. The authors report that the outcome was "a generally positive experience for the patients, and harm has not ensued."

In a 1971 American Psychological Association symposium entitled "Shared Results and Open Files with the Client: Professional Irresponsibility or Effective Involvement?," Brodsky (1972) succinctly juxtaposes the traditional view with the position that is current:

> Traditionally the sharing of a client's files with the client himself has been only minimally considered, and when discussed at all, the practice has been seen as unethical, irresponsible, or at least questionable. Contrary to such traditional views, we suggest here that specific ways of sharing results with a client are a means for effective involvement and the assumption of appropriate professional responsibilities and roles.

Many psychological assessors today have shifted from writing reports *about* clients to writing *for* clients. Dorr (1981), for example—see one of his reports reproduced in chapter 13—addresses his reports specifically to clients. Feedback to clients is widely accepted, and has been extensively written about. Noteworthy are papers by Richman (1967), Aronow and Reznikoff (1971), Craddick (1972, 1975), Mosak and Gushurst (1972), Fischer (1970, 1972), Dorr (1981), and Allen (1981). A number of these authors advocate not only making information available to clients, but also having them participate in the interpretation of the raw data they supply—in the context of what Allen (1981) calls a "diagnostic alliance."

Berg (1985) views feedback from a position that goes beyond the ethical and legal concerns that have "established the rights of patients to full disclosure." He holds that such disclosure is of diagnostic advantage to the clinician and of therapeutic value to the client. Both parties gain information in the feedback process and an *exchange* of information permits both to change their view of matters. The client's response to feedback, Berg reports, can provide diagnostic information concerning "the patient's capacity for self-reflection, synthetic functioning, anxiety tolerance, defensive flexibility, and the conditions under which he can accept help."

Appelbaum (1990) tells of his personal experience with sharing data—which initially involved a good deal of trepidation: "I was afraid of having to reveal information that would upset patients, would be too complex for them to understand, or would be revealed as, or seem to be revealed as, wrong, thus humiliating me as the tester, and undermining my position as the therapist.":

> To deal with these fears, when I was to report my test findings to the patient during the interview, and to facilitate the transmission of information, I jotted down three or four salient points from the test report on a small scratch pad and clutched it like a security blanket. My fears proved to be groundless; I almost never consulted the scratch pad. I really knew what I wanted to say, and once I began the words came without prompting. The patients, for the most part, knew what the test findings were...
>
> More importantly, I was forced to find palatable, helpful ways of putting things, focusing more on adaptation than on pathology. Thus, did good practice force good theory, for in truth, the use of "pathology," in word and thought, is barely appropriate for psychological matters no matter how useful it may be in medicine...In sum, the imposition of sharing test results with patients can be responded to as an opportunity, rather than as an intrusion. It provides a chance to mutually clarify goals and at least adumbrate what is to be worked on with what assets.

Sharing of data is not universal, however. A major exception to the tendency to share psychological information exists in the case of computer-generated psychological reports. The reluctance to share such data with the client, at least before it is reviewed and perhaps edited, is more a matter of scientific caution and tentativeness rather than with concern that receiving psychological information, per se, can be damaging to the client. We have already noted the potential for error and inconsistency in computer reports and the possibility for a nonprofessional to misunderstand such reports.

Prefacing the conclusions of a number of computer-generated reports may be statements reminding the test user (such as a psychologist) that what follows in the report are hypotheses rather than firm conclusions, while some computer products caution that the report is a professional consultation between the test service and the test user, and not to be shared with the client. (Cf. *Principle 8e, Ethical*

Principles of Psychologists [American Psychological Association, 1981]: "The public offering of an automated interpretation service is considered a professional-to-professional consultation.") Other computer printouts may include the caveat that the information supplied is inferential and probabilistic.

Error may be the outcome when the test taker does not fit the characteristics of the normative population—a judgment that the client should not make. Further, computer reports are incomplete and best used as a part of a case study which also incorporates data from other sources of information, such as history, interview, clinical observation, and other tests. However, it is proper for the clinician who stands between the computer and the client (pp. 33–34) to make available to the client as much information from the report that in his or her judgment appears accurate and potentially helpful.

A number of computer reports, however, are specifically designed for client use. The well-known Strong-Campbell Interest Inventory (1984) is one such instrument; the Vocational Interest Inventory (Lunneborg, 1981) is another. An MMPI report published by Behaviordyne addresses the client directly in the second person and in nontechnical language.

Practices vary, then. Bringing some unity to the scene are professional ethics and standards, and a number of statutes.

Standards for Educational and Psychological Testing (1985) offers further instruction regarding the sharing of psychological information:

> Those responsible for testing programs should provide appropriate interpretations when test score information is released to students, parents, legal representatives, teachers, or the media. The interpretations should describe in simple language what the test covers, what scores mean, common misinterpretations of test scores, and how scores will be used. (*Standard 15.10*)
>
> In school, clinical, and counseling applications, test users should provide test takers or their legal representative with an appropriate explanation of test results and recommendations made on the basis of test results in a form that they can understand. (*Standard 16.2*)

To be reckoned with along with these various professional and scientific considerations are legal constraints, state and federal, concerning client access to clinical records. Most notable are the *Privacy Act of 1974*, the "Buckley Amendment," and PL 94–142, the Education for All Handicapped Children Act of 1975. These various laws stipulate the terms under which clients and others, such as parents and guardians, may have access to records.

Confidentiality

Confidentiality is a basic consideration for those who are entrusted with personal, often sensitive, information about persons who are assessed in a help providing context. Guidelines for confidentiality are set forth in the *Ethical Principles of Psychologists* (American Psychological Association, 1981) and the *Standards for Educational and Psychological Testing* (1985).

The basic statement on confidentiality is found in *Principle 5a* of the *Ethical Principles*. This principle clearly has to do with respecting the "dignity and worth" of the client.

> Information obtained in clinical or consulting relationships, or evaluative data concerning children, students, employees, and others, is discussed only for professional purposes and only with persons clearly concerned with the case. Written and oral reports present only data germane to the purposes of the evaluation, and every effort is made to avoid undue invasion of privacy.

Principle 16.3 of *Standards* further notes:

> Test results identified by the names of individual test takers should not be released to any person or institution without the informed consent of the test taker or an authorized representative unless otherwise required by law. Scores of individuals identified by name should be made available only to those with a legitimate, professional interest in particular cases.

To seek to maximize confidentiality, the psychological assessor must look beyond her or his personal conduct to the safeguarding of clinical records. Several of the *Standards* are addressed to this topic. *Standard 15.7* speaks to limiting access to test materials to those who have legitimate need for them. *Standard 15.11* expands on *Ethical Principle 8d*, which has to do with preventing the retention (and thus the extended possibility for unauthorized use) of obsolete materials. It suggests that organizations establish guidelines concerning how long records shall be retained, recognizing that in some cases, such as longitudinal assessment, long-term retention is indicated.

Standard 16.5 addresses the topic of protecting data files from improper disclosure. Of special concern are time-sharing networks, data banks, and other electronic data-processing systems. Safeguarding the microcomputer's magnetic media involves a number of technical problems that are discussed by Bongar (1988) and abstracted on pages 91–92.

Another major issue concerning confidentiality is *privileged communication of psychological* records. Privileged communication is a legal privilege extended to certain professionals that exempts them from the requirement that they make available a client's records in legal procedures unless the client specifically consents to such disclosure. Laws regarding privileged communication vary from jurisdiction to jurisdiction, and it is well for the psychological assessor to be familiar with the law as it covers his or her practice. Laws granting privileged communication to psychiatrists (as medical practitioners) do not necessarily apply to psychologists whose records hold content similar to that in the records of psychiatrists.

Individuality versus Stereotypy

People come to clinical attention because in some important way(s) they are different from most of their peers. They are, to select from numerous everyday situations, unable to master school work or to gain insight into egregiously faulty interpersonal relations, distressed by suspicions and interpersonal insecurities, or given to habitual antisocial behaviors. The goal of psychological assessment is to pinpoint and to define the individual parameters of such complaints. It is not to assemble stereotyped statements that are true to some extent, at some level, and in some contexts, about most people, or about most people who present with a certain class of problems, such as pervasive suspiciousness or antisocial behaviors.

Several common practices that defeat the goal of individualizing client descriptions and lead to a distorted personality picture have been described and labeled (Tallent, 1958a). Fortunately they are easily discerned, thus paving the way for individualized reporting. Consider the following forms of stereotypy.

Aunt Fanny The "Aunt Fanny" label was inspired one day when I was listening to the report of a psychology trainee droning on with a theme I had heard too many times before. The client, it seems, was anxious, had sexual conflicts, was hostile, oral, anal, and so forth. I suddenly interrupted this recitation of what the client *is* or *has*, blurting out "So has my Aunt Fanny!" My Aunt Fanny, and everyone else, could be described in these terms, leading to little understanding of what the client under consideration is like.

Barnum "Barnum" stereotypy, like Aunt Fanny stereotypy, relies for its accuracy on using high base rate statements. In conceptualizing the term, the late D. G. Paterson incorporated as the central thesis the idea of deception that is associated with the name of P. T. Barnum, and he used high base-rate statements to accomplish this objective. The idea was to please the reader, to "sell a bill of goods," such as to a client, a psychiatrist or an administrator; to tell such readers "what they want to hear," by, for example, confirming an impression or a bias. Such a commercial technique led Klopfer (1960) to identify the *Madison Avenue Report.*

Paterson used his original Barnum Report as a lesson to business executives on irresponsible personnel evaluation practices. Ostensibly the report was written individually for each executive, most of whom agreed that "their" personality descriptions were accurate. I have, in an informal, and unoriginal, demonstration of this phenomenon, obtained similar results with classes of college students who were told that the reports stemmed from interpretation of samples of their handwriting (cf. Dunlap [1922]).

Here is another early Barnum-type report (Nathan, 1941). How many statements, as applied to you, do you disagree with?

> You have great self-control—when and if you care to exercise it. You sometimes misplace confidence, and regret it. You are impatient of interference in your affairs and of anyone who tries to dictate to you. Although you sometimes affect an air of indifference, you are deeply sensitive. You have a strong will and do not like to confess to a

mistake when you have made one. You are not revengeful or vindictive, but let someone, in your own estimation, wrong you in some way and you are through with him. You are inclined to lay a little too much stress on outward appearances. You cannot tolerate narrow-minded people. You can be taken in, but not often twice by the same person. You are of necessity at times materialistic, to a certain extent. Generally honest and sincere, you can still be very inexact and unreliable in things you say.

The original Barnum Report follows:

Abilities: Above average in intelligence or mental alertness. Also above average in accuracy—rather painstaking at times. Deserves a reputation for neatness—dislikes turning out sloppy work. Has initiative; that is, ability to make suggestions and to get new ideas, open-mindedness.
Emotions: You have a tendency to worry at times but not to excess. You do get depressed at times but you wouldn't be called moody because you are generally cheerful and rather optimistic. You have a good disposition although earlier in life you have had a struggle with yourself to control your impulses and temper.
Interests: You are strongly socially inclined, you like to meet people, especially to mix with those you know well. You appreciate art, painting, and music, but you will never be a success as an artist or as a creator or composer of music. You like sports and athletic events but devote more of your attention to reading about them in the sporting page than in actual participation.
Ambitions: You are ambitious, and deserve credit for wanting to be well thought of by your family, business associates and friends. These ambitions come out most strongly in your tendency to indulge in daydreams, in building air castles, but this does not mean that you fail to get into the game of life actively.
Vocational: You ought to continue to be successful so long as you stay in a social vocation. I mean if you keep at work bringing you in contact with people. Just what work you pick out isn't as important as the fact that it must be work bringing you in touch with people. On the negative side you would never have made a success at strictly theoretical work or in pure research work such as in physics or neurology.

The above prompts the present writer (Tallent, 1958) to view the Barnum report as a method "to describe a personality by using a few mildly negative generalities [e.g. "your tendency to indulge in daydreams, in building air castles"] which are quickly neutralized in a matrix of acceptable, even flattering remarks [e.g. "but this does not mean that you fail to get into the game of life actively"], both types of comments being apparently applicable to almost everybody." The Madison Avenue variant of the Barnum report does not have to flatter the person about whom it is written. Rather, it flatters the consumer of the report by playing to his or her bias, thus making the acceptance of the report likely.

It is cause for concern that some psychological assessors, when they can't, or don't care to, supply meaningful and accurate information might resort to the Barnum technique. It is an approach that seems to have been in use for a long time. M. Brewster Smith (1986) reports on a "phrenological analysis," written by a practitioner he identifies as a "distant relative," that bears the date July 12, 1889. We may presume that the person about whom the report supposedly was written was pleased by such statements as:

> You are friendly but still guarded in making friends but what friends you do make you are very devoted to. You are very fond of pets and animals. Your constructive talent is very good and you have much inventive genius.

Trademarked reports Many psychological assessors, unwittingly, trademark their reports. They routinely include, and often overemphasize, particular aspects of personality that appear to relate to problem areas in their own lives, or to a limited understanding of what are the significant variables in personality. Some assessors are known to their colleagues for their emphasis on such themes as hostility, sexual immaturity, homoerotic impulses, or conflicts centering around mother, father, or authority figures. The existence of such stereotyped writing has been documented by Filer (1952), Hammer and Piotrowski (1953), Robinson (1951), and Robinson and Cohen (1954). Keller (1971) reports on three "types" of Rorschach interpreters: the *optimizers* who emphasize health and minimize pathology, and two "types" (discussed in the next paragraph) that emphasize disorder, the *intrapsychic pathologizers* and the *interpersonal pathologizers*.

Prosecuting attorney briefs Prosecuting attorney briefs are "saturated with...negative dynamics...but give little or no attention to positive features, to commendable conscious strivings, socially valuable compensations, and other well-used defenses. These reports consistently reflect the motto, 'always interpret at the lowest possible level of psychosexual fixation or regression.' They are prepared by psychological simians who hear no good, see no good, and report no good" (Tallent, 1958).

Surely this phenomenon is widespread as noted in what Keller (1971) identifies as *intrapsychic pathologizers* and *interpersonal pathologizers*. Klopfer (1960) also recognizes an overinclusion of pathology in many psychological reports, and refers to psychological reports with this shortcoming as evidencing a *maladjustment bias*. Even staff members in clinical settings, where extensive pathology is to be expected, sometimes complain that some psychological assessors write reports that read like an indictment.

Stereotyped reporting, particularly that depending on Aunt Fanny stereotypy, may readily be adapted to the faking of reports or to portions of reports. For example, when reporting on a schizophrenic patient, it is possible to "fill in" discussion on areas of personality where dependable information is not available with stereotyped content on how schizophrenics are supposed to be.

Sundberg, Tyler, and Taplin (1973) illustrate the technique with a phony report, followed with an explanation of its rationale. It reads not unlike many actual psychological reports written on schizophrenic patients. Note in addition to the Aunt Fanny statements a bit of the Madison Avenue approach—furnishing the reader with a preferred diagnosis. Note also the hedging, and a few other tricks that are readily available to those who would use them. Report writers, supervisors, and report consumers should all beware of these irresponsible practices.

COMPLETELY BLIND ANALYSIS OF THE CASE OF A SCHIZOPHRENIC VETERAN[1]

—Norman D. Sundberg

(Written before knowing *anything* about the patient except that he was a new admission to the Roseburg VAH and was to be worked up for an OPA meeting.)

This veteran approached the testing situation with some reluctance. He was cooperative with the clinician, but was mildly evasive on some of the material. Both the tests and the past history suggest considerable inadequacy in interpersonal relations, particularly with members of his family. Although it is doubtful whether he has ever had very close relationships with anyone, the few apparently close relationships which he has had were tinged with a great deal of ambivalence. He has never been able to sink his roots very deeply. He is immature, egocentric and irritable, and often he misperceives the good intentions of the people around him. Projection is one of his prominent defense mechanisms. He tends to be basically passive and dependent, though there are occasional periods of resistance and rebellion against others. Although he shows some seclusiveness and autistic trends, he is in fair to good contact with reality. Vocationally, his adjustment has been very poor. Mostly he has drifted from one job to another. His interests are shallow and he tends to have poor motivation for his work. Also, he has had a hard time keeping his jobs because of difficulty in getting along with fellow employees. Though he has had some affairs, his sex life has been unsatisfactory to him. At present, he is mildly depressed, although a great deal of affect is not shown. What physical complaints he has appear mainly to have a functional origin. His intelligence is close to average, but he is functioning below his full capacity. In summary, this is a long-time inadequate or borderline adjustment pattern. Test results and case history, though they do not give a strong clear-cut diagnostic picture, suggest the diagnosis of schizophrenia, chronic undifferentiated type. Prognosis for response to treatment appears to be poor.

This completely blind analysis is based on the following assumptions:

1. The veteran being referred for psychological testing is not likely to be an obvious or clear-cut diagnostic case. There is no need for testing unless there is some indecision. Consequently, hedging is to be expected on a report anyway.
2. This is a schizophrenic case. Given the general class of schizophrenia, one can work back to some of the characteristics which belong in that class and have a fair chance of being right.
3. There are some modal characteristics of patients coming to VA hospitals. In placing bets on what the patient is likely to be like, the best guess would be

---

[1]From Sundberg, N. D., Tyler, L. E., & Taplin, J. R., *Clinical Psychology: Expanding Horizons*, (2nd ed.). Copyright © 1973 pp. 577–579 by Prentice Hall and reprinted by permission of the publisher and Dr. Sundberg.

a description of the modal personality. For instance, most of the veterans coming to Roseburg are chronic cases who have not succeeded in jobs or in family life. Also, the best guess on intelligence would obviously be average intelligence, but since the person is a psychiatric patient it is likely that he is not functioning at his best.

4. There are also certain modal behaviors of the clinical staff. They use certain words, certain jargon; they have a preference for certain diagnoses. Oftentimes, a large percentage of the cases wind up with the diagnosis of schizophrenia, chronic undifferentiated type.
5. There are some "universally valid" adjectives which are appropriate for any psychiatric patient, such as "dependent," "immature," "irritable," and "egocentric."
6. In the less clear areas where modal characteristics are not known, it is more safe to write a vague statement or one which can be interpreted in various ways. Readers can be counted on to overlook a few vague misses and to select the descriptions which jibe with their own preconception.
7. All this is intended to say that we have much in common with the old fortune teller, and that what we need is better ways of dealing with individuality. Knowing modal personalities is very useful; it certainly adds to ease of social communication; however, we are sometimes fooled into thinking that we know persons when actually all we know is our own stereotypes.

The Appropriate Use of Raw Psychological Data

Psychological assessors differ in the extent to which they offer raw psychological data to the readers of their reports, and also in the manner in which they use such data. This variation in practice seems to relate to the lack of general understanding on the distinction between assessment and testing, or, in some cases, to lack of awareness that there is a distinction.

At a time when psychologists were testers, it was customary to fill the report with scores, relations among scores, descriptions of "clinical behavior" and "test behavior," verbalizations, and verbatim responses. The meaning of such material was assumed to be self-evident to the reader, hence was routinely reported. Raw data such as the following were once common in psychological reports, but have fallen out of favor (Tallent & Reiss, 1959b):

> On the Object Assembly subtest, the patient seemed at a loss as to where to begin. He picked up pieces at random and attempted to fit the parts together in an unplanned fashion. Finally, he stated his inability to solve the problem and gave up the task.
> This patient's Verbal IQ is 91 and his Performance score is 105. The Comprehension score (11) is five points greater than Information (6). The high subtest score is on Object Assembly, the weighted score being 14, while his lowest is a 3 scored on Arithmetic.

When we consider that consumers of psychological reports vary widely in their level of psychological sophistication, from almost none to a high level of competence, we must question the validity of the test interpretations they might make when supplied with raw data. The validity of having report readers reach their own conclusions from raw data is further brought into question in view of the fact that it is generally not feasible to present the report reader with an entire battery protocol. Of necessity, then, the data that the examiner presents is selective, that is, a biased sample. On the other hand, it would be forbidding to present all of the data. The exception is to present the entire protocol as an appendix to the report, as may be the practice in neuropsychological assessment. This is justifiable when the report consumer has significant knowledge of the psychometrics of neurology.

A workable approach to the question of presenting raw data is for the psychological assessor to review, together with the report consumer, the protocol and the conclusions to which it contributes. This procedure can be particularly effective when the consumer is reasonably well informed about the psychological instruments from which the data were derived.

It is also recommended that the psychological assessor use judiciously selected and forceful or compelling illustrative material. Material that meets these criteria can be incorporated in the report, and also shared on a person-to-person basis. Both options provide an opportunity for the psychological assessor to share logic as well as data, to walk the report consumer through the interpretation process.

Style

We have already noted that for writing to be instructive it must first be pleasing. Good writing style, then, is more than just a nicety; it is a necessity.

Each field must develop its own basic style. The proper style for reporting a psychological assessment is not yet a matter of consensus, and three basic styles have been identified. These are the *clinical style*, the *scientific style*, and the *literary style*.

The *clinical style* focuses upon pathology, maladjustment, deficiency, and equilibrative processes, and some would say that the report more nearly describes a "case" than a person. The orientation is medical and normative. An orientation in this vein might make it hard to account for such psychological variables as attitudes, sentiments, or relationships, unless these are diseased or associated with disease.

The *scientific style* is more closely related to the academic psychologist's discipline. This approach stresses the normative, and sometimes also the pathological. It differs from the clinical style most in its relation to a conceptual scheme of personality or to a theory of assessment. This style would apparently be particularly compatible with approaching a personality through its segments or part processes and dealing with these in some detail. Here the psychological assessor becomes involved with what, for convenience of study, might be regarded as discrete functions–intellection, perception, emotion—or finer divisions of these—much as the physician may be concerned with units of clinical study like the cardiovascular system, the genitourinary system, or the neuropsychiatric system.

Literary style sometimes becomes too dramatic or flowery: "Crushed and defeated by telling setbacks, the patient feels unable to continue to fight what she sees as an oppressive environment." Freud (1895) wrestled with this matter of style. Writing in terms of "human interest" can hardly be wrong when the subject matter is the functioning of a human being.

> It still strikes me myself as strange that the case histories I write should read like short stories and that, as one might say, they lack the serious stamp of science. I must console myself with the reflection that the nature of the subject is evidently responsible for this, rather than for any preference of my own...A detailed description of mental processes such as we are accustomed to find in the works of imaginative writers enables me, with the use of a few psychological formulas, to obtain at least some kind of insight into the course of that affection (Freud, S. [1895], *Studies on hysteria*. S.E. 2).

Speculation

It is not uncommon for the contents of psychological reports to outrun the data that are needed to support them. Apparently some psychological assessors feel constrained to report on certain classes of information that are widely accepted as important in psychological circles. If sexual dynamics are considered crucial to understanding a person, then something about this topic is likely to appear in the report even when the protocol does not hold substantial material bearing on this topic.

Responsible reporting has room for speculation, providing there is sound reason for doing so. An uncertain answer may be better than none in *some* cases, particularly if it is not misleading. Blank (1965) suggests that "waiting for ironclad proof [not an event occurring with great frequency] leads to a sterile report." Speculation, for example, can call attention to previously unsuspected, or potentially crucial issues, like suicidal danger or the possibility of brain dysfunction. Indeed, it would be irresponsible not to report on issues of such gravity where further evidence should be pursued to support or discount low confidence impressions. Always, however, speculation should be properly identified as such.

Transfer of Responsibility

Only the psychological assessor can be responsible for the information presented in the report. Our history of test centrism, however, too often leads the assessor to hide behind tests, to transfer responsibility from oneself to the tests. All too often conclusions are introduced with such dodges as "Psychological testing reveals...," "Stories given to the TAT point up a person who...," "The Rorschach shows...."

A widespread means of avoiding responsibility is to oversupply the report reader with raw data in place of the conclusions that are needed. Test data do not constitute information that can responsibly be used by the consumer. Test data (commonly based on a battery rather than on single tests) must be interpreted in the context of test theory, personality theory, knowledge of the area being assessed, and clinical judgment. In this context, the data take on additional meaning, and become ready for the use of the consumer as they are presented in a case formulation.

The Words We Use

Tennyson has noted that "words, like nature, half reveal and half conceal the soul within," and the words used in many psychological reports have long been criticized as a bar to the communication of psychological information. "Jargon," "gobbledygook," "psychologese," and "psychobabble" are among the many expressions applied to such terminology and the use of such language comes in for a good deal of censure (for example, Tallent & Reiss, 1959c; Della Corte, 1980). Hallenstein (1978) identifies the use of psychological jargon as "a hindrance to the healing process" and thus an ethical matter. He suggests the following problems with its use:

1. It can distort truth and understanding.
2. It can provide a means for avoiding responsibility.
3. It can foster the development of an elitist class.
4. It can lead to the denigration of psychology as a profession.

Does this mean that technical language should be avoided? Opinions vary. Those of Sargent (1951) and Hammond and Allen (1953) continue to be influential. Sargent suggests that, at least in writing for technically trained consumers, in the context of relating "the degree and kind of abnormal psychological functioning...technical terms and concepts are...considered to be more economical and cogent carriers of meaning...than if they were to be translated into everyday language."

Hammond and Allen contend that "technical vocabulary is indispensable for three reasons: first, it is precise; second, it can communicate concepts that are virtually impossible to convey in ordinary language; and third, it is economical." They are of the opinion that terms like *empathy*, *rapport*, and *subliminal* "are virtually impossible to express in plain English: They may by means of a lengthy paraphrase be approximated, but the communication thus achieved is far less complete and *satisfactory* than that produced by use of the terms themselves *when they are fully understood by the reader*" (emphasis supplied).

Such views are difficult to reconcile with the classical findings of Grayson and Tolman (1950). Studying the definition of 20 items that commonly are found in psychological reports, these authors conclude that "the most striking finding of this study is the looseness and ambiguity of the definition of many of these terms." A replication of the Grayson-Tolman study 15 years later (Siskind, 1967) found no decrease in their ambiguity. As a striking illustration, Grayson and Tolman report that the definitions offered for the commonly used clinical term *anxiety* could be classified into seven categories of meaning!

On the basis of having clinical personnel match behavior descriptors with psychologists' definitions of technical terms, Auger (1974) concluded that "either the behavior descriptors lacked specificity, the definitions were ineffective, or both." Technical terms are also noted to create problems in school situations. Rucker

(1967) and Shively and Smith (1969) reported poor agreement on the meaning of terms that are commonly used in psychological reports. In Shively and Smith's study, teachers, counselors, and students, using a four-item multiple-choice format, were asked to select the best definition for terms such as *aphasia, borderline intelligence, cortical involvement, neurological impairment,* and *perseverate.* Counselors tended to disagree significantly with both students and teachers, with more than a third of the latter group failing to understand a number of terms that are presumably related to learning problems. Rucker found poor agreement between school psychologists and teachers when members of each group contributed definitions of educational terms that appear in psychological reports.

One sensible approach to avoiding the problems of technical language is to think and write in a straightforward descriptive and operational manner. Schafer's (1976) *action language* provides a conceptual framework. His basic definitional statement, which follows, introduces the method, which he then amplifies:

> We shall regard each psychological process, event, experience, or behavior as some kind of activity, henceforth to be called action, and shall designate each action by an active verb stating its nature and by an adverb (or adverbial locution), when applicable, stating the mode of this action.

A psychological report written in action language appears on page 272.

Report Length

A final consideration of word usage has to do not with what words we use, but with how many words we use. Many psychological reports are too long, and there is a good deal of consensus on this matter (pp. 257–258). Psychological reports, like any practical writing, gain in effectiveness when consideration is given to the economics of writing and reading them.

"QUICKIE" REPORTS

The writer of case-focused reports, not feeling constrained to comment on all aspects of a client's life that may be explored or that may readily come to his or her attention, zeroes in on what is of importance in each consultation. *Quickie reports* are the strategy of choice when a limited amount of information is required and a global assessment of such issues as personality, of intellectual functioning, or neuropsychological status is quite beside the point. Considerable information can be packed into a few lines or a paragraph.

Quickie reports should particularly be considered when:

1. A fast initial impression is needed.
2. A case is "well documented" and an update is called for.

3. The assessor judges that what he or she needs to communicate can most effectively (as well as most economically) be gotten across in a small number of sharply focused statements.

Here are some examples of quickie reports:[2]
Ellen was referred because of declining effort and grades.

Yes, Ellen's interest in school is diminished because she does not know what she wants to do on graduating high school. Work? What kind of work? College?
We shall administer interest and aptitude tests and discuss possibilities with Ellen.

Debbie is a 12 1/2-year-old girl from a broken home (father deserted six years ago and continues to upset the family by calling to complain to Debbie's mother about his present wife). Debbie is thought to be underachieving in school. Her teachers see her as an angry, troubled child. Debbie herself complains that schoolwork overwhelms her, tires her out. The following report seeks to achieve an understanding of Debbie as a basis for taking further action.

Debbie's intellectual status is above average. Her observations are accurate and there is originality of thought. She is an insecure child who has many fears. She fears the loss of her integrity, attack from others, and her own impulses. Debbie has a great need for acceptance and affection, but is inhibited by an overpowering fear of being rejected and hurt. There seems to be hostility directed to the mother. The relationship has not been mutually satisfying, often leaving Debbie frustrated. It is my impression that the mother's inconsistencies in handling the child may be a source of anger. Now she wants her own way and is conflicted about her dependency. Her attitudes to men also are unwholesome. They are seen as weak and mutilated. And she is confused about herself. She feels inadequate, and having a specific learning disability she requires more guidance and love than most children her age. However, not being able successfully to reach out to others has only left her more frustrated. Since Debbie finds it difficult to relate to people and because her own feelings are threatening to her, she withdraws to an immature fantasy world that provides little refuge. Even her fantasy is fearful, involving aggression and fear of being injured emotionally. Debbie is a very unhappy child.

D.J.H. was hospitalized on the "advice" of a judge after he was charged with assault and battery on his wife for the nth time during one of their battle royals. There is no "curable" condition, and (barring a minor miracle) only separation of the couple can put a stop to the presenting complaint. This report does not do justice to the polished histrionic behaviors of this man—a veritable Hollywood actor as he plays out the scenes that regularly take place at the home. But what if the report, with the investment of great effort and time, did a superb job of capturing the flavor of this actor, surely one of the most colorful people I have ever met? Would it make any difference at all?

[2]From Norman Tallent, (1988). *Psychological report writing* (3rd ed.). Englewood Cliffs, NJ: Prentice Hall.

The patient presents a solid picture of histrionic personality disorder. The dominant defenses are denial and repression, with resultant naiveté, poor respect for reality situations, poor judgment, and a variety of socially immature behaviors. He is remarkably self-centered, employing exaggerated histrionic techniques in a continuous attempt to gain support. He is rigid, demanding, and potentially somewhat paranoid in defending what he regards to be his best interests. He thus finds himself involved in frequent interpersonal problems, particularly with those to whom he relates most closely; and low frustration tolerance, exaggerated and labile emotional response, and acting-out tendencies that he regards as "righteous" make for assaultive behaviors. He is preoccupied with sexual fantasy and somatic problems, seeking to live out the sex material in flirtatious behaviors. Marital problems are a source of stress, albeit he contributes to these problems, most recently through his flirtations. The outlook for significant change is not great.

THE PERENNIAL PITFALLS IN WRITING PSYCHOLOGICAL REPORTS

In a large scale survey of Veterans Administration clinical workers—psychologists, psychiatrists, and social workers—over 700 respondents completed the sentence (or paragraph) root, "The trouble with psychological reports..." (Tallent & Reiss, 1959c). The voluminous data emerging from this exercise were then sorted into five major categories: Problems of Content, Problems of Interpretation, Problems of Psychologist's Attitude and Orientation, Problems of Communication, Problems of Science and Profession, and numerous subcategories.

The pitfalls that were placed in these categories are a hardy breed that seem to exist across professional settings. Lacey and Ross (1964), for example, identified in a poll of workers in child guidance clinics a number of the same issues found in the Veterans Administration study. Olive (1972) found that psychoanalysts experienced similar problems with psychological reports in 1952 and 1970, with numerous criticisms centering on lack of clarity, vagueness, excessive use of jargon, theoretical bias, unreliability, and overgeneralization. The persistence of pitfalls, specifically the faulty use of language, has already been noted in the discussion of Siskind's (1967) replication after 15 years of the Grayson-Tolman (1950) study of semantic confusion in the use of psychological terms.

Each generation of psychological report writers must be taught anew how to identify in their reports the pitfalls they have fallen into, and how to avoid them. The persistence of pitfalls is not unlike that noted by the teacher of rhetoric who finds that each new crop of students makes the same errors in composition as the last. It is my impression that neophyte report writers make the same errors, with the same frequency, as did their mentors in the earlier years of their professional development.

When the pitfalls discussed below find their way into a psychological report the consequences can be serious. Most obvious, a report thus compromised falls short of effectively communicating the material needed to understand the client about whom it is written. Less obvious, perhaps, a pitfall marred report can have the effect of alienating the intended report reader from psychological assessment and psychological assessors, an inescapable conclusion from the numerous gratuitous comments about assessors and assessment incorporated into the sentence completion item, "The trouble with psychological reports..." (Tallent & Reiss, 1959c).

It is particularly instructive to read Ziskin (1981), who directs heavy fire at the pitfalls that may be found in forensic psychological reports, an effective way of putting in question the psychological assessor's expert testimony in the courtroom. "I have almost invariably found the clinician's report to be a gold mine of material with which to challenge his conclusions," he writes. The pitfalls in psychological report writing always create a problem, to say the least, but the hazards they create can be devastating in the courtroom—when pitfalls are downfalls (Tallent, 1988).

A discussion of categories of pitfalls follows. A few of them are particularly controversial (and perhaps not pitfalls) and are offered to stimulate thinking rather than by way of endorsement or disapproval.

Problems of Content (Category I)[3]

The psychological assessor is charged with providing information that will be helpful to a client. Report content frequently falls short of this goal. If the client is to be seen in psychotherapy, for example, does the assessor deliver material that will be useful to the therapist? Or does the report read more like an exercise in the popular theoretical issues of the day? There are a number of ways in which the content conveyed in a report can fall short of its purpose.

Raw data Congruent with a view expressed earlier in this chapter—namely, that raw data should not be used where interpretation clearly is called for (pp. 188–189)—psychological respondents were generally critical that too much raw data appears in reports. Psychiatrists, seemingly believing that they ought to be able to make their own interpretations, complained that there is too little, and social workers were divided on the issue.

A psychologist writes:

They are too often descriptive rather than interpretive, leaving this job to the reader when really the psychologist is in the best position to interpret results.

And an opposing view from a psychiatrist:

They do not contain enough selected raw material to permit the psychiatrist to draw his own conclusions.

Which contrasts with the opinion of two social workers:

Reference to specific psychological material in reports has little meaning to non-psychologists.

---
[3]From Norman Tallent, (1988). *Psychological report writing* (3rd ed.). Englewood Cliffs, NJ: Prentice Hall.

When reference is made to test cards, formulas, etc., the reader is often not familiar enough with the tests to understand what significance they have.

Improper emphasis When a report may accurately be characterized as showing improper emphasis, the report writer is, to a greater or lesser extent, off target. The report is not well case-focused. The report is not written with a clear purpose in mind and an understanding on the part of the writer of what sort of information can be helpful and what is unlikely to be.

They seem to emphasize the personality state of an individual whereas I think more emphasis should be placed on the functioning of an individual in terms of what the person is doing to and with other people. If the patient is to be seen in psychotherapy, the psychological report should include some predictions about how he probably will act toward the therapist, how he will see the therapist, some goals for the therapist, and how the therapist might try to accomplish these goals and why he might do it in the way suggested. If the psychologist knows something about the limitations of the therapist who is to see the patient, then he should take these into consideration before he includes some of the goals of treatment.

Tendency to emphasize the unconscious to the neglect of the conscious goals and values.

And, can you empathize with this one?

Too much pressure on sex. I know, I know, it is important, but, for heaven's sake, the world does not spin around the axis of...genitals.

Minor relevance When statements of minor relevance (or in some cases irrelevance) are written into the report the focus of the report tends to become blurred. The ready availability of such content, however, may be a blessing to the report writer who is at a loss concerning what to write about. Thus,

They include data that I believe are not an essential part of the report, such as clinical description of the patient, social and medical data. This may be necessary to the examiner conducting the tests in evaluating the responses of the patient, but I do not believe this should be included as a routine procedure.

Omission of essential information Readers of psychological reports complain not only when they are subjected to content they do not find useful or enlightening, but also when information they believe they need is not forthcoming.

They do not present specific and essential data which would be helpful to a team conference or individual attempting to formulate a plan of treatment and working diagnosis.

Seldom do they make recommendations regarding treatment goals, nor do they specify areas of strength.

Diagnoses, prognoses, recommendations We have just seen that some report readers complain when psychological reports do not include recommendations.

Now let us note that some clinicians believe such material in a psychological report is misplaced. Diagnoses and prognoses may be equally objectionable to some readers. Clearly, psychological report writers ought to share understanding and consensus with their readers.

> Recommendations should be excluded from psychological reports. It would seem more appropriate a function of a staff decision where other data can be considered.
>
> In my opinion, the recommendation as to plan of treatment, chemotherapy, etc., is not appreciated.

Unnecessary duplication The intentional duplication of content, such as in several different contexts of a report, may sometimes be justifiable as a means of providing emphasis to an important conclusion. Most duplication, however, addresses no useful purpose, and often enters the report without the awareness of the report writer.

Problems of Interpretation (Category II)

Irresponsible interpretation Numerous respondents were critical of the quality of interpretations that find their way into psychological reports. Forty-one percent of the psychiatrists, 27 percent of the psychologists, and 22 percent of the social workers offered criticisms pertaining to a variety of irresponsible interpretation practices. Dana (1966) compared psychological interpretation compromised by such factors as personal bias and incompetence with *eisegesis*—or, misreading (originally, of scripture). Note the variety in the following limited selection of comments.

> Clearly written to please the psychiatrist for whom it is being written, often interpreting data to fit his known pet theories and thus rendered unscientific.
>
> Tending to find more or less schizophrenia in every case.
>
> They sometimes seem to reflect the psychologist's feelings about the patient.
>
> They draw conclusions from insufficient data, lack objectivity.
>
> They are frequently too arbitrary, expressing theory as fact.
>
> They are not sufficiently related to the tests they presumably are derived from.
>
> The referral question is frequently vague, and psychologists frequently hate to admit it when the tests don't give much information, and so overinterpret what they have.
>
> Too much "Barnum effect" (see pp. 236–238).
>
> We read in the reports the examiner's own conflicts. These are usually discernible after seeing a few reports in which certain phrases and ideas repeatedly occur (see the "trademarked report," p. 238).
>
> Sometimes there is more of the psychologist than the patient in the test reports.

Overspeculation Readers of psychological reports commonly criticize them for the excessive speculation that some of them contain. Perhaps one reason for all the speculation is captured in a respondent's impression: "People who write them frequently feel that they have to say something about all areas of the client's life, even those about which they have little or no information." The safest course, however, is perhaps not to speculate on the reason for all the speculation.

The following observations are typical of the comments made about speculation.

> Speculative assertions beyond the realm of the testing results.
> Too theoretical and speculative.
> Too much speculation, reading between the lines, personal interpretation rather than reporting facts as observed.

Unlabeled speculation Speculation, per se, however, appears to be an acceptable report writing practice. If you must speculate, speculate, but let your reader know you are speculating.

> Facts, inferences, speculations are often mixed and not labeled.
> The distinctions between reasonable deductions from the data, speculative extrapolations from the data, and the psychologist's clinical impressions are not clear.
> If some indications were given for the bases for speculation and if clearly labeled as speculation.
> Many speculate and do not so indicate until questioned.
> Data is frequently overinterpreted. One can speculate but should label it as such.

Inadequate differentiation The task of the psychological assessor is to present a workable picture of an individual client. Stereotypy, vagaries, nonfocused presentations, and generalizations about people are defeating of this end.

> Too little individuality of descriptions.
> All too often they don't present a comprehensive, logical picture of a unique individual.
> Very frequently they are made up of too many stock phrases which do not give any real feeling for the individual client.
> They frequently involve too many generalizations about human behavior and fail to describe the specific person who is involved.
> They tend to present generalizations that might apply to anyone rather than to the particular individual.
> Typically, they present a rather stereotyped picture into which any number of patients—or other people—might fit, rather than describing the individual.
> They report in broad generalizations that, although they sound quite profound, really would apply to nearly any patient.
> Too often the generalizations are so great that one could visualize the same report having been made on the preceding dozen persons seen at staff. Reaching for psychoanalytic concepts too often is the reason (and I am psychoanalytically oriented).
> They tend to rely on vague, psychoanalytically-oriented phrases which fail to convey an individualized picture of the client. Their vocabulary is excellent but what is lacking is a feeling for the client's individuality as a troubled human being.

Problems of Psychologist's Attitude and Orientation (Category III)

Technical errors, based perhaps on inadequate or faulty training, are evident in most of the pitfalls in psychological report writing. Some pitfalls of psychological reports, however, are linked to the person of the report writer—to his or her attitude and/or orientation.

Not practical or useful The psychological assessor is expected to address the real problems to which assessment presumably can contribute a solution. The sampling of comments about psychological reports that follows suggests, however, that many psychological assessors do not understand their task this way.

> Our prejudices often lead us to make statements which are of little import to the recipient and to ignore or deal lightly with the objective reason for the referral.
>
> Their lack of function and value to the person.
>
> Often lack of comprehensibility in terms of a real-life treatment program.
>
> They are often written without a clear idea of the practical "users" or "consumers" on the receiving end.
>
> In my view we need to write more in the spirit of an operational approach.
>
> Many writers forget the purpose(s) of their reports and wander all over the psychic range, even when they are asked for a relatively clear-cut opinion.
>
> They're too sophisticated, too impractical for the people who rely upon the information they dispense.
>
> They are not pertinent to the purpose desired.
>
> They seem at times very professional but useless in terms of the personality of the patient.
>
> They are too often written to satisfy the interest of the psychologist rather than for the clinical application and understanding.

Exhibitionism It also detracts from practicality and usefulness when psychological reports are written to compliment and draw admiration to those who write them. Such practice also detracts from the quality of relations among those on the professional team.

> They are written in stilted psychological terms to boost the ego of the psychologist.
>
> They are attempts on the part of the examiner to show what he or she can do rather than what the patient is.
>
> Reports delight in including details of findings which are obviously comprehensible only to one who has made a study of psychological testing or is versed in the finer significance of statistical research expressions. Such reports occasionally produce the feeling that words of less than four to six syllables and sentences with less than two thoughts will convince the reader that the writer is too simple.
>
> It is not necessary to impress the reader with the psychologist's mentality.

Their reports reflect their needs to shine as a psycho-analytic beacon in revealing the dark, deep secrets they have observed.

Reports should be concise and clear without an attempt to impress the reader with the erudition of the person who performed the test.

Too authoritative Reports that read like authoritative pronouncements well may be written to gain admiration for the writer. However, reports that pontificate tend to irritate the reader even more than those that are merely "show-offy." Psychiatrists seemingly take more offense at authoritative reports than do other clinical workers.

They are too positive, confident, assured, as though they were the last word, irrefutable, authoritative.

Many reports are much too opinionated and obviously reflect the author's own biased viewpoints.

They often are too definite in their interpretations and assume to have all the answers.

The psychologist feels too superior and will generally write a short summary of his interpretation forgetting that a psychiatrist reading the report might differ in interpretation. This feeling of superiority on the part of the psychologist has alienated many intelligent psychiatrists.

A lack of humility. I never cease to be amazed by the confidence some psychologists have in their tests and in their own abilities to interpret them. To accept such reports the psychiatrist would have to lose what little intelligence he or she is supposed to have.

I have seen some reports which affected me adversely because of a tendency to sound pompous with the implication "This is the final word!" rather than "This is an opinion which is intended to be helpful in understanding the whole" and to be all-inclusive to the point of excluding the specific contributions of other disciplines—a sort of "I can do everything approach" which sometimes results in the clouding of the most important observations. A second, though no less important result, is the impairment or even destruction of the team function.

Test orientation versus client orientation Nonpsychologist team members are more accepting of raw data in psychological reports than are psychologists. Comments like the following were contributed mostly by psychologists.

They usually talk about tests and test results rather than the client's personality.

Talking about the tests too much and the patient too little.

They often describe responses rather than people.

They are test centered too often rather than containing statements about behavior in the nontest environment.

Often the writers feel it necessary to include scoring and other quantitative detail at the expense of providing a useful and helpful picture of the person evaluated.

Psychological reports should reflect the judgment of the psychologist with all the limitations of maturity and experience. The psychologist should proceed as though he knows something about human behavior and tests are aids in his understanding. He should not act as though he is lost without his tests. I think other disciplines want us to give opinions which are free to open discussion and exchange.

Too theoretical It is evident from the developing context that the ways of compromising the usefulness of psychological reports are many. Discussing theory rather than the client is another one of them.

In general, they are too theoretical.

They concern vague hypothetic properties of people.

They often are too theoretical or academic in language to be comprehensible or meaningful in terms of future treatment goals for the client. They occasionally give us the feeling that no client was present at the time.

At times one has the feeling he is reading a biological dissertation on protoplasm rather than about a flesh and blood person.

Sometimes I come across psychological reports which are loaded with textbook phrases, but giving very little clear picture of the particular individual involved.

We sometimes get bogged down in vague, theoretical terminology which has little direct relation to the actual behavioral dilemmas confronting the individual, Also, we employ theoretical concepts reflective of basic psychological processes (e.g., oral sadistic orientation) which are so general and so removed from the level of behavior that we write more like textbook theoretricians than as psychologists confronted with the task of making some sense out of a client's behavior.

Overabstract There is obvious overlap between the concepts of theory and abstraction. Indeed, many complaints about psychological reports mention that they are both too theoretical and overabstract.

They are sometimes too theoretical and/or abstract; and on the other hand, too concrete—as reports of exact performance on tests as such. Ideally, there should be a happy medium.

They are too often lofty abstractions or concrete banalities. In either case, they fail to offer a meaningful, readily grasped, exposition of the subject's psychological condition. The more abstract and/or intellectual the report is, the more likely the examiner is either defensive or projecting his own conflicts into the report.

Some are unnecessarily involved, technical and abstruse so as to be virtually useless in planning disposition of the subject.

Fischer [1985] suggests that the sort of pitfalls discussed here, at least in some cases, may be the result of other than faulty attitudes and orientation. The following can be good advice to those who rush to draft their reports in the absence of adequate case conceptualization: "Saying what one means, both in speech and in writing, requires one to anchor abstractions in concrete examples. Ask yourself how you would explain what you mean to a 12-year old. If you can't figure out how to do that, then you do not yet know what you mean—what your technical formulations come down to in terms of your client's life."

Miscellaneous deficiencies of attitude and orientation Other of the numerous deficiencies of attitude and orientation brought to our attention do not neatly fit the above categories, though clearly there is overlap. They are included here, however, because we cannot afford to overlook the shortcomings they point out.

> They are too studiously intellectual.
> Too pedantic—obscure to other professions.
> Usually too involved, pedantic.
> In many instances psychological reports have the tendency to be too academic.
> They are often esoteric to the practice of psychological testing.
> Esoteric reference to statistical mechanisms.

The final subcategory in this grouping clearly involves personal rather than technical shortcomings. These have to do with a reluctance of some psychological assessors to take on the consultant role and to write reports—both basic to psychological assessment.

> Psychologists feel it is almost below their dignity to do them.
> [The trouble is] that you've got to write them.
> Psychologists appear to have lost confidence and/or interest in testing.
> I have a strong personal dislike for writing psychological reports, in spite of my recognition of their usefulness. Perhaps part of my feeling is due to the excessive length and detail of reports which are seldom read by anyone else, anyway. To me it is the most distasteful part of my job.

Problems of Communication (Category IV)

Psychological report writing is much more than a matter of rhetoric, as the various preceding issues attest. Nevertheless, rhetoric must be attended to if the technical product of assessment is to be gotten across; and, in fact, comments about faulty communication outnumbered comments about other faulty report-writing practices. This class of pitfalls seems to be most obvious to the consumers of psychological reports, more so than the technical psychological problems that are found in reports.

Word usage The most prevalent criticisms of faulty communication are grouped together here as problems of word usage. Of those making negative comments about psychological reports, 37 percent of psychologists, 45 percent of psychiatrists, and 65 percent of social workers registered one or more complaints in this area. These pertain to a variety of offenses against the King's English. Deficiencies of terminology are mentioned with particularly great frequency, and psychoanalytic terminology is a prevalent offender according to our respondents.

> A good report uses the language of the novelist, not the scientist, unless he's writing for another psychologist. Analytic language is a language of generalities and thus loses the uniqueness we should be striving for.

Too much emphasis is placed on psychological phraseology and such when we could say the same thing quickly, efficiently, and simply.

Often padded with meaningless multisyllable words to lengthen report.

Gobbledygook.

Too much jargon.

They are too often written in a horrible psychologese—so that clients "manifest overt aggressive hostility in an impulsive manner"—when, in fact, they punch you on the nose. They do not take advantage of simplicity and ordinary words. Their value depends on whether the psychologist talks English or a special language of his own.

They are not frequently enough written in lay language. I believe it requires clear thinking to write without use of technical terms.

Semantics have a tendency to creep in, and the phenomenon of "verbal diarrhea" occurs too often.

The appearance of stereotyped phrases.

Vague, unclear, ambiguous There are many techniques for writing reports that are difficult to understand. Violence to the King's English is particularly evident in the next list of criticisms.

They sometimes are vague and unsubstantial.

They tend to rely on vague, psychoanalytically oriented phrases.

New words or new meanings to familiar words are used, leaving the reader confused as to what is meant.

Excessive wordiness which clouds the findings.

Perhaps some are a little "veiled" in meaning, so as to attempt to prove the psychologist is truly a professional.

They contain too many ill phrased, hard-to-understand sentences.

Often lack of comprehensibility in terms of real life treatment programs.

They are intellectual vagaries.

They are not clear enough to be wrong.

They suffer mostly from vagueness, double-talk and universality without enough of an attempt being made to specify more precisely what sets this person off from other people (and what does not).

Scores have little meaning even to the psychologist who understands their rationale, unless he also knows how they fit together in terms of cause and effect regarding behavior. To cover up his ignorance he resorts to the reporting of percentages, ratios, etc., and overwhelms his reader with such technical language that little information is conveyed.

Too technical, too complex Reports that are highly technical and complex can be crystal clear to one who is versed in the words and concepts that go with a particular discipline, but be quite incomprehensible to one who is not.

The more simply the material is presented, the more useful it is.

I have made "Flesch counts" of quite a large number of reports and the level of difficulty tends to be much too high. Psychological reports should not be so difficult to read as our professional papers, but often they are. Many reports of this type are actually meaningless—a kind of polysyllabic illiteracy.

Too technical or too esoteric.

Technical terminology, particularly Freudian or statistical language, where these do not serve as highly specific communications, which implies writing a report for another psychologist or analyst.

I think that it is important that the person write in such a way as to communicate to those who will read the report. In some cases this will require that he write in a much simpler and more descriptive manner.

Documentation makes reports too technical.

It appears that the psychologist prepares the report for one of his own group rather than the benefit of other members of the team.

Style Style, of necessity is an individual matter; nevertheless, effective communication is dependent on certain basic style considerations.

The reports tend to sound very much alike—to represent a personal "style."

Style is a matter of choice, but since we are supposed to be literate people, we should have certain standards of excellence to meet–too often this is not the case.

Too concerned with literary style.

The art of report writing should be akin to caricature.

They become too "flowery."

They all sound too much alike, as though the writers are adhering to a standardized model instead of allowing the form of their reports to be determined by the individual subject and the circumstances.

Too many reports follow a stylized form without due consideration to the real needs of the patient for which psychological testing had been requested.

Too often they seem to satisfy the writer's literary, "expressive" needs rather than communicate adequate description.

They give one more the impression of poetry than of scientific writing.

Under the guise of "capturing the flavor of the patient," appropriate scientific writing is sacrificed for style.

Organization Psychologists, more so than other team members, are critical of the organization of psychological reports.

Often they are not coherently organized in terms of a personality or psychoanalytic theory and hence become meaningless jumbles of bits of data and information. Frequently they are not organized—thought out—before they are dictated.

Too often they are so poorly organized that the reader has a difficult time to get a clear psychological picture of the client.

The analysis is in fragmented form rather than being integrated.

Write-ups frequently are not really organized, but formulations are "faked" in a sense by the use of syntax and grammatical construction.

They are often not organized around a central pattern characteristic of a person. Each paragraph seems a separate, discrete, unrelated part which could be clipped out and inserted in any other report.

When several tests have been administered, many psychologists cannot integrate the findings without giving separate results for each test.

Hedging   A number of respondents were impressed that too many psychologists hedge their reports and that they should commit themselves at one level or another, and not straddle the fence.

Some writers refuse to take a chance and say anything definite. They beat about the bush, include every possible descriptive or diagnostic phrase.

Psychologists seem too often to "play it safe" and include so much in their reports (or so little) that they can never be wrong, refuse to make specific predictions, and therefore can never really be right either.

They too often are riddled with qualifications—"it appears that," "it may well be," "the test reports indicate." This is fine when speculation is being introduced, but many reports merely convey the inadequacy and timidity of the writer.

We seem to be afraid to commit ourselves in a few words, using too many qualifying statements and thus avoid ever being wrong, but never actually predicting anything at all. Can't they be more confident in their findings, i.e., when it might appear from testing that the patient may be homicidal or suicidal and may act this out, to say so clearly? It's better to know before than later—or too late.

Often no definite conclusions are reached and the reader of the report is left as bewildered as he was prior to requesting psychological examination.

Length of reports   There is clear consensus that psychological reports tend to wordiness. Some respondents, however, feel that they are too short, definitely a minority opinion.

They are too lengthy—should be concise and to the point.

Many are too long. This usually teaches the reader to look for a summary and ignore the rest.

Too often the completed report is too long. Often I might go to the summary to get the gist of the examination.

Most of them are too long. Few people, if any, will take the time to read them.

Psychological reports should present specific data and specific interpretation. Too many contain omnibus recommendations and universal statements which apply to most people. I'd rather see brief reports with relatively little said than lengthy stereotyped reports which also say little. A good report should stop when it has run out of useful data.

And finally, a comment by a psychologist who evidently speaks from experience:

They are:

Over-imaginative,

Over-academic,
Over-syllabic,
And not over soon enough!

Making light of what is a patently serious problem tends to add depth to how we understand it. Appelbaum and Siegal (1965) thus deal with the frame of mind of psychological report writers who strive for "completeness" (Read: to write a shotgun report): "For them the weight of the pages seems evidence of ability, so they set themselves the task of including everything, often substituting data for thought."

Problems of Science and Profession (Category V)

Problems of science In taking a hard look at psychological reports, it is well to balance off the allocation of blame to those who write them with some larger issues that the individual report writer cannot escape. Shortcomings of theory, particularly of personality and psychopathology, and of psychological instruments, including their validity and applicability to the situations in which they are applied, were commented upon by many respondents.

There is too little research on effective report writing.

I suggest that a "sociologist from Mars" would find the test reporting behavior of psychologists quite as "weird" as any of the rituals and customs and beliefs of many so-called primitive societies.

There is lack of agreement, even among members of a small staff, as to how they should be written. Clinical psychology doesn't have an adequate basis, either in theory or tools, for writing simple, straightforward, meaningful reports.

Most people, including psychologists, don't know what they are for or how to use them once they are written.

It has never been convincingly shown that the type of information contained in a psychological report contributes information which can improve the validity of decisions beyond that possible on the basis of interview impressions and a good case history. The trouble does not lie so much with psychological reports as with the material we have to report.

Primarily that their utility is unknown and untested. Few encouraging reports of prediction studies have been noted lately. Assuming validity and reliability (mighty big assumptions) psychologists are still in doubt as to the purpose of their own diagnostic efforts—particularly in a team setting.

Interpretation is too often based on theories which are yet poorly validated.

Essentially the same trouble as is found with psychiatric and psychological theory and terminology in general. That is, theories and concepts are vague and of low reliability and validity. We have too many concepts, none of which can be regarded as demonstrably fundamental. Thus we write confused reports which depend on literary excellence more often than scientific knowledge.

The greatest defect is inadequate and unsympathetic personality theory on which to hang our observations.

One of the key modern tools of clinical assessment, and a decided improvement over its predecessors, is the DSM-III, yet it is a tool riddled with shortcomings and the target of many more criticisms than can be considered here (D. W. Goodwin, for example, characterizes the document as a "semireligious work"). Both the assets and the failings are well covered, however, in Millon and Klerman (1986), which points the direction for the next major advance toward a comprehensive diagnostic scheme of mental disorders (DSM-IV):

Two examples of major deficiencies of DSM-III will suffice. The first pertains to its dearth of therapeutic implications (Millon, 1986a). This, despite the fact that "planning, executing, and evaluating therapeutic interventions" is a central purpose of psychological assessment (Korchin & Schuldberg, 1981).

The second deficiency is the inability of the DSM-III to achieve nearly the level of objectivity to which it is dedicated. Faust and Miner (1986) appear to suggest in the title of their paper, "The Empiricist and His New Clothes: DSM-III in Perspective," that the prevailing notion that the DSM is an objective tool is an illusion:

> The methodological doctrine underlying DSM-III—strict empiricism—has not been achieved, and should not be pursued, at least in its extreme form.
>
> DSM-III's appearance of objectivity is largely illusory. Theory and inference have perhaps been reduced somewhat but eliminated nowhere—the document is replete with presuppositions and theoretical assumptions.

While a number of the above pitfalls are remediable, Holtzman (1964) suggests that a number of the pitfalls the assessor faces, mostly the problems of science, pose tenacious challenges. Of six "unresolved issues," five are in this category. (The sixth centers on the "moral dilemmas" arising out of the individual's right to privacy and the investigative probing needed to understand the client's personality.)

(1) Personality assessment is hampered by lack of a clear, adequate, and consensual definition of personality. Looking ahead, Holtzman is of the opinion that "it is likely to become even more difficult to specify clearly what we mean by personality, a dilemma of definition and conception to which I see no good answer in the immediate future."

(2) There is no agreement on what are the units and combinations of units needed to understand a person. "A major dilemma is that in any practical situation one must continually make rather arbitrary choices and exclude all but a small portion of the general model for personality assessment. One is repeatedly haunted by the question, Can we ever really understand a personality?"

(3) Personality variance and method variance are not readily separable. "Such response sets as Tendency to Acquiesce or Social Desirability often overshadow the substantive meaning of items in personality inventories. The interaction between examiner and subject in such projective techniques as the Rorschach or the TAT poses a similar dilemma...." He further comments on how often "the measurement of a given personality trait is really a function of the method used rather than the theoretical construct."

(4) Personality and personality assessment are overly culture-bound. "Given the difficulty of grasping the nuances of a strange vocabulary and the problem of understanding a sharply divergent world view, even a skilled anthropologist intimately acquainted with the culture has difficulty of interpretation while a psychologist would be completely lost."

(5) It is questionable that a systematic, comprehensive personality theory, closely linked with empirical data can be developed. "In their comprehensive review of personality theories, Hall and Lindzey...were notably impressed by the diversities, disagreements, lack of formal clarity, and lack of demonstrated empirical utility characteristic of personality theories. About the best that can be said of most theories is that they stir the imagination, strike a respondent chord here and there, and have a heuristic value in stimulating research. Certainly there is no single widely accepted theoretical position today, nor does it seem likely that one will emerge in the near future. Man is simply too complex an animal to capture so easily.

"Implicitly or explicitly, we all have some kind of theoretical position that we employ as a point of departure in personality assessment. As often as not, however, we are hard-pressed to rationalize our personality theory with assessment techniques. Perhaps it is expecting too much to ask that our practice be in accord with our theory. Perhaps we should be content with theory that is sufficiently vague and general to allow maximum freedom for what we want to do."

Problems of role conduct Placed in this final subcategory of pitfalls are issues pertaining to what commonly are called turf battles. Interestingly, *none* of the psychologists in the sample indicated that psychologists encroach upon the function of other clinical workers—who made abundant complaints that such is the case. All representations of this sort were not merely defensive of ones own turf; quite a few social workers viewed psychologists as intruding in the psychiatrist's domain, as well as in their own. And a number of clinicians, social workers, and psychiatrists believed that many psychologists write reports that encompass the function of the entire clinical team; that is, that their reports include content that is traditionally the primary concern of social workers and psychiatrists.

> Many psychologists tend to digress in other fields. They frequently do not mind their own business and go beyond their ken—invading territory properly allocated to the M.D.
>
> Some reports go to the extreme of becoming a clinical summary of the client, including social and personal history and mental status.
>
> Some even suggest medical and other treatment.
>
> There is a tendency to avoid the very purpose for which psychological testing exists. Namely, to present laboratory data codified in its original terminology so that the physician who has requested such testing for his own purpose of treating the patient may add to his clinical estimate of the patient. In my opinion, the recommendation as to plan of treatment, chemotherapy, etc. is not appreciated. Psychological testing and reporting is certainly a highly specialized and technical field which adds a great deal to the doctor's knowledge of the patient and should confine itself to this area.

They tend to make diagnoses rather than furnish specific data supporting a certain diagnosis. They are requested by the M.D. to help him make the diagnosis, prognosis, etc. The M.D. is not interested in what the psychologist thinks but why he thinks so. History and behavior are already available on the patient. The skilled psychiatrist knows how to interpret the data. If the psychologist feels his M.D. does not know what all this means, he should first give the data and follow it with a polite interpretation beginning such as "The data suggests...etc...."

Some psychologists seem to take offense and think it too menial to perform IQ tests. Their reports reflect their needs to take over the functions of a psychiatrist.

One social-work respondent takes a broad view of the problem of role encroachment. In the view of this clinician it can be difficult for a professional to confine her or his activities to the discipline in which trained:

Our hospital has six psychologists and many student trainees. They have a wide range of duties and responsibilities but can't keep inside their own yard! Our staff has six social workers, one researcher, and an anthropologist.
The social workers all want to be psychologists.
The psychologists anthropologists.
The anthropologists social workers.
And only God knows what direction we are all going in.

11
ASSESSMENT FOR TREATMENT

Assessment has long been assumed to be basic to the practice of therapy. Indeed, as we have seen (p. 45), assessment may be more than an aspect of the therapeutic process; assessment and therapy in a real sense may be synonymous (Schlesinger, 1973; Allen, 1981). An axiomatic relation between the two was evident in the practice of Lightner Witmer as long as a century ago (Brotemarkle, 1947) and in the classical practice of psychology, since: "If diagnosis did not imply treatment, the diagnostic study would be of little pragmatic value" (Watson, 1951). Gough (1971) proclaims matter-of-factly, and with accompanying logic:

> The function of diagnosis is to identify the problem the patient has presented in such a way that an appropriate and restorative treatment may be carried out. It is easiest to think of this formulation in medical terms, and indeed the logic of diagnosis is probably most clearly illustrated in the medical treatment of physical illness. Complaints and symptoms may arise from many different sources, and depending on these sources the same treatment may be helpful, inconsequential, or dangerous. To treat abdominal distress with an aperient would be extremely unwise if the underlying condition was an inflammation of the vermiform appendix. Treatment, to be effective, must be addressed to the underlying condition as this is determined by accurate diagnosis.

In spite of such a firm, time-honored linkage between assessment and therapy, some psychologists seem to find it necessary to affirm anew the logic and the validity of carrying out assessment in the interest of providing better therapy. Thus, responding to recent calls in a professional publication that diagnosis should provide a rational basis for treatment, we read:

I cannot help but wonder why we need to call for the obvious...Rational treatment planning must be based on both a diagnosis and a formulation of the etiology and factors maintaining the disorder (Lipton, 1988).

QUESTIONING THE ASSUMPTION

Perhaps the strength of the relationship between assessment and therapy is not so obvious. Prout (1986) observes, rather paradoxically:

> It appears that the actual utility of assessment (behavioral or traditional) in planning and conducting treatment programs is unclear and has not been empirically demonstrated at this time. Despite this equivocal situation, good clinical practice still dictates that assessment remain an important part of a comprehensive treatment approach.

Clinical Impressions

A number of early papers growing out of clinical experience, some of them supported by case material, argue for the value of assessment in the conduct of therapy. Klopfer's (1964) theme is that psychotherapy without assessment is a matter of "the blind leading the blind." And, "to deliberately blind himself and handicap himself as the psychotherapist by refusing to use the tools of assessment available to him, would seem a practice so questionable as to border on the unethical." DeCourcy (1971) and Lambley (1974) also seek to make the point that therapy without prior assessment can be hazardous. Supported by three case presentations, Cerney (1978) views the psychological report "as an objective measure to assist in understanding the progress of psychotherapy and to alert the therapist of potentially very critical and delicate situations."

Baker (1964) was among the first to report on the sharing of data as a therapeutic technique. Along with a description of her approach, she provides a rationale and a caveat:

> The great advantage in beginning psychotherapy with a discussion of test results seems to be that it reduces defensiveness, perhaps because test data are more observable and tangible than interpretations or inferences offered by the therapist as the result of listening to the data the patient brings to the conventional therapy session. Or perhaps the patient attributes to tests some magical potency he is not willing to allow another individual to have. Certainly, it is true that tests furnish convincing examples of the patient's behavior that can be pointed out to him for illustrative purposes.
>
> It would not be possible to offer a "cook book" for a process that necessarily must be characterized by a good deal of variation, depending on the subject's test protocols and personality and the skill and personality of the psychologist who undertakes the interpretation. This is truly an interaction process, a factor which adds to the complications that are likely to arise. It is probably appropriate to offer the warning that only the experienced and relatively secure psychologist should undertake such a discussion of test results.

A number of other papers based on clinical experience (e.g., Richman, 1967; Fischer, 1970, 1979; Mosak & Gushurst, 1972; Berg, 1985) report a positive linkage between assessment and therapy. Dorr (1981)(see pp. 334–343) performs assessment as an integral part of therapy, as does Fischer (1970). Like Allen (1981), and numerous practicing psychological assessors, she views performance on a test as a microcosm of the client's life. In an interesting example, she employs a test of intelligence, less as a means of assessing the client's intellect than as a therapeutic vehicle to help a client gain insight into his personality functioning. Here is a brief excerpt from a diagnostic/therapeutic interaction between a P(sychologist) and her C(lient):

P: Did you notice you didn't do as well on the arithmetic part and the part where you said numbers back to me? You know, on both those kinds of problems, you had to figure in your head. I wonder if you have trouble with those same things out in life, like on the job?
C: Well, yeah, that's right. But it doesn't matter about numbers—it's doing it in my head. I just always know that I can't get things to work out when I've got to keep numbers in my head, or like those block pictures.
P: I hadn't thought of that. I guess you did do better on the first half of the test where you were telling me answers about everyday things than you did on the last half where you had to quietly figure out the answers to abstract, new kinds of problems, and then tell me the answer.
C: Sure, I'm always at my best when I'm talking to people. It's like I know where I stand. Like in a business conference, I can talk up a really great idea, and everybody's impressed. But I'm sure not the guy to write it out by myself, or figure out a cost analysis. I just know I'm beat before I start—so I don't.
P: So when jobs call for you to work on your own you see that as equivalent to certain failure. Therefore, you never try to do them?
C: That's what I just said.

These varied clinical contributions pertaining to the use of psychological assessment in therapeutic interventions cannot be lumped together to arrive at a general conclusion. They are based on material that is anecdotal, on impressions gained from long experience, on theoretical linkages between assessment and therapy, on case studies, and on combinations of the above. The subjects reported on varied among studies, and included private psychotherapy clients, clients in couples therapy, and clients seeking help for an assortment of other problems.

Empirical Findings

The findings reported below present some similar problems. Additionally, we must ask, what is the significance of the quantitative or quasiquantitative material that is reported? If, for example, psychological reports contribute to clinical decision making in 26 percent of cases, as below, is this a high figure or a low figure, a positive or a negative finding? What is the comparable figure for the utility of, say, clinical tests in medicine? What percentage of urinalyses or blood chemistries or chest auscultations contribute to a successful treatment outcome? Is it meaningful to make such cross-discipline comparisons?

Single-issue studies Dailey (1953) found that psychological reports contributed to decisions in 26 percent of clinical cases. Breger (1968), examining the importance of diagnosis as a prerequisite to treatment, reports "Serious questions are raised about the clinical usefulness, logic, and validity of practice." Hartlage, Freeman, Horine, and Walton (1968) found that psychological reports were "evidently of little value in contributing toward any treatment decisions for the patient." Cole and Magnussen (1966) conclude, "Traditional diagnostic procedures are only loosely related, if at all, to disposition and treatment."

Other studies have yielded more positive results. Dana, Hannifin, Lancaster, Lore, and Nelson (1963), examined the relationship between routine psychological diagnosis and treatment planning in a juvenile probation department. They report, "Predictions of prognosis were made from psychological reports with 80.5% accuracy. When recommendations contained in these reports were followed, 82.5% accuracy of predictions was obtained."

In a more recent study reported by Alpher, Perfetto, Henry, & Strupp (1990), a single instrument—the Rorschach—was found to yield predictor variables, such as texture responses and the lambda ratio, that relate to clients' capacity to engage in short-term dynamic psychotherapy.

Affleck and Strider (1971) found high utility of psychological reports: "About two-thirds of the requested items of information were seen as either providing new and significant information or as providing information which confirmed information previously suspected, but which was not well established." Further, "It was found that 52% of the reports altered management in some manner, 24% had a minimal effect or confirmed current thinking, 22% had no effect, and 2% were felt to have an erroneous or detrimental effect." Hartlage and Merck (1971) conclude that psychological reports often fall short of having their full impact because of lack of reflection on the part of the report writer, or, in blunter terms, because of failure to use common sense. The implications of their conclusion are far reaching:

> Reports can be made more relevant to their prospective users merely by having the psychologists familiarize themselves with the uses to which their reports are to be applied...It appears that merely having the psychologists who write reports to consider the value to users of some of the statements that they commonly make in their reports can have a significant salutary effect on the value of these reports...Psychologists learn to test and write reports in an academic setting and that in the absence of any external stimulation they tend to persevere in a somewhat theoretical, non-decision-oriented approach to handling test data.

They advise that psychologists:

...evaluate their own reports in terms of what these reports contribute to the operation of their unique settings rather than to continue to grind out reports with good theoretical consistency but little decisional value.

Broad-scale reviews Korchin and Schuldberg (1981) acknowledge the value of neuropsychological assessment, but otherwise present an ambivalent view of the relation of assessment to treatment:

> A basic justification for assessment is that it provides information of value to the planning, execution, and evaluation of treatment. It seems self-evident that interventions are more rational, faster, and more effective if based on prior diagnosis of the problem, whether we are talking about repairing a car, the human body, a conflict between nations, or the human problems that bring people into psychotherapy. Few would hold that it is better to proceed from ignorance than from knowledge. However, it can be argued that not all knowledge is equally good or relevant and that clinical assessment may not provide the kind of information needed by therapists. Objective evidence is slim...It is surely true that skilled clinicians, understanding the conceptual framework and therapeutic work of their colleagues and working more in a consultative than in a technical mode, can and do make impressive contributions, it is probably equally true that in many instances the assessment information is less than useful.

Hayes, Nelson, and Jarrett (1987) are impressed that "clinical assessment has not yet proven its value in fostering favorable treatment outcomes." On the basis of an extensive survey of treatment utility studies, including the questions asked and the methods used, they conclude:

> To date, the role of treatment utility has been buried by conceptual confusion, poorly articulated methods, and inappropriate linkage to structural psychometric criteria...Treatment utility research has also been hindered by nonspecific types of therapy, nonspecific types of assessment, unnecessary divisions between the role of assessor and therapist, and an overemphasis on technique over conceptual advancement. The trends in the field all seem positive in these areas.

Large-scale clinical studies A comprehensive scheme, certainly not a quantitative one, linking psychological assessment to intervention has not yet been offered. Some linkage, however, as in the above reported studies by Dana et al. (1963), Affleck and Strider (1971), and Hartlage and Merck (1971), does seem to exist. Following are abstracts from two large-scale studies that provide data and a number of insights relating assessment to therapy. They are also a source of useful guidelines to the conduct of therapy and provide ideas for further research.

The psychotherapy research project of the Menninger Foundation Six findings reported by Appelbaum (1977) are particularly germane to our present concern. Of these, one conclusion is overarching: Therapists who ignore the findings of the psychological assessor do so at peril; they are more inclined to make faulty clinical judgments than their colleagues who incorporate this information in their therapeutic interactions with patients. "The largest source of error was in underestimating the patient's difficulties, thus getting some of the patients into treatment situations of greater intensity and demandingness than they could optimally use" (Appelbaum, 1990).

As to the specific benefits of psychological assessment, Appelbaum lists providing information:

1. Leading to better decisions as to who should get treatment—and who should not. Psychological data on ego strength point up the extent of improvement that can be anticipated and are highly pertinent to this decision.
2. For determining what kind of intervention would benefit different people.
3. Pertaining to the setting of goals and formulating strategies for reaching those goals.
4. Concerning a useful way of organizing data about people—that is, whether they need greater access to, or more control over, their thoughts and feelings.
5. Concerning the meaning of change to a client, whether it is beneficial or harmful in a given personal and social context.

The Penn Psychotherapy Project The studies by Luborsky, Mintz, Auerbach, Christoph, Bachrach, Todd, Johnson, Cohen, and O'Brien (1980) and Luborsky, Crits-Christoph, Mintz, and Auerbach (1988) are highly pertinent to, but also broader than our present concern. Examined in this study are factors in the patient, the therapist, and the patient-therapist interaction in psychodynamic treatment situations. Here we focus attention on pretreatment factors in the patient as these might be established as predictors of outcome, though the interaction of all three factors might influence this all-important concern.

With respect to (the measured) patient factors as pretreatment predictors of outcome, the level of success was "barely significant" or "modest," even for the best predictors, or, to continue with another of the authors' quotes, the results were a "cold bath of limited success." The best of the pretreatment patient factors accounted for approximately 5 to 10 percent of the outcome variance, with correlations ranging from .20 to .30.

More impressive relationships were found between a nonpretreatment variable ("helping alliance") and outcome. Thus, the correlations between helping-alliance questionnaire measures and seven-month outcomes were .72 for drug use, .70 for employment, .51 for legal status, and .58 for psychological function, all significant at p<.01. These results pose a challenge to clinicians to predict both clients' and therapists' ability to enter into a helping alliance in a therapy relationship.

A broader grasp of the factors related to psychotherapy outcome is available through the authors' presentation of the Penn studies in the perspective of the large body of previous studies that have addressed aspects of this problem area. These are compiled in a form that may be helpful for clinical application and as a springboard for further research and theory building. It might be of interest to review the following research findings as confirming or disconfirming the prevalent conviction that the good therapy patient is a YAVIS—Young, Adaptable, Verbal, Intelligent, and Successful. It might, in fact, be helpful to review the listed findings in terms of how consistent they are with clinical lore and practice.

Abstracted from Luborsky et al. (1988) is a categorization of studies of patient pretreatment variables as they suggest factors (A) that trend to more-favorable outcome, (B) that trend to less-favorable outcome, (C) that show no clear-cut trends concerning outcome, and (D) that lack consistency of results or sufficient studies to define a trend. The items of category (A), which include mostly variables that are commonly dealt with in psychological reports, heavily outnumber the items in the other three categories combined, suggesting that the psychological assessor, at least potentially, has much to offer to the practice of psychotherapy. Data on patient characteristics contributed the most to predicting outcome, while information about the therapist and the treatment added little.

(A) *Trending to More-Favorable Outcome*
1. Global Measures of Health-Sickness and Adjustment (Those who are relatively healthy on entering therapy tend to leave therapy relatively healthier.)
2. Healthier Personality Traits/Coping Styles
3. Lesser Severity of Diagnosis (Psychosis, overt and subclinical, and certain personality disorders, such as borderline personality disorder, and antisocial personality disorder, are conditions associated with low therapeutic success.)
4. Lesser Severity of Maladjustment as Gauged by the MMPI (e.g., favorable indicators are low scores on F, D, Pd, Pt, and Sc [Hunt, Ewing, La Forge, & Gilbert 1959], and higher Mf values—in males [Casner, 1950])
5. Higher Barron Ego Strength Scores
6. Adequacy of Functioning on the TAT
7. Greater Problems of Functioning as Reported on the Symptom Check List (SCL)
8. Higher Scores on the Rorschach Prognostic Rating Scale (RPRS)
9. Higher Level of Anxiety
10. Higher Level of Depression
11. Higher Level of Affect (Other Than Anxiety and Depression)
12. Higher Motivation for Treatment
13. Higher Expectation of Improvement
14. Higher Positive Attitude toward Self, Therapist, and Treatment

15. Higher Interest In and Capacity for Human Relations
16. Higher IQ and Higher Estimates of Intellectual Skills (Support for the I in YAVIS; also the V inasmuch as good vocabulary and word fluency were found to be related to symptom reduction [McNair, Lorr, Young, Roth, & Boyd, 1964])
17. Greater Somatic Concern
18. Greater Self-Understanding/Insight
19. Greater Judged Suitability as a Candidate for Therapy
20. Greater Mastery (As opposed to helplessness and passivity. A plus for the A in YAVIS.)
21. "Some Aspects of Rorschach Scoring" (e.g., M, FM, m, and shading are favorable indicators.)
22. Socioeconomic Status (Probably a plus for the S in YAVIS.)
23. Better Occupational Adjustment (More support for the S in YAVIS.)
24. Higher Educational Level (Still more support for the S in YAVIS.)
25. Student Status (Probably also an indicator of successfulness.)

(B) *Trending to Less-Favorable Outcome*
1. Greater Chronicity
2. Higher Ethnocentrism

(C) *No Clear-Cut Trends Concerning Outcome*
1. Age (Indecisive results fail to support the Y in YAVIS.)
2. Sex (Three of eleven reported studies favored females, but the other eight studies failed to find a relationship between gender and outcome.)
3. Race
4. Religion
5. Marital or Sexual Adjustment (We would expect the YAVIS to be successful in this area—S and A.)
6. Social Competence (As above, we would expect this variable to relate to the YAVIS thesis.)
7. Early Home Situation
8. Previous Psychotherapy

(D) *Lack of Consistency of Results or of Sufficient Studies to Suggest a Trend*
1. Performance on Perceptual Tasks (e.g., cube test, concealed figures, flicker-fusion.)
2. Authoritarianism (e.g., California F Scale.)
3. Performance on Figure-Drawing Test
4. Locus of Control

RECONCEPTUALIZING THE RELATIONSHIP OF PSYCHOLOGICAL ASSESSMENT TO THERAPY

Implications of the Measurement Tradition and the Clinical Tradition

The measurement tradition and the clinical tradition each dispose to the production of psychological content that is linked to its concepts and its methods. Information gained in the measurement tradition is heavily quantitative and much of it (particularly if we bypass the technical trait names that are often assigned to measured variables) is generally close to everyday experience—aggressiveness, assertiveness, shyness, dependency, for example. The clinical tradition, by contrast, emphasizes content that is recondite and difficult for many observers, professionals and laypersons, to relate to.

Looking at the variables examined in the Penn study as predictors of therapeutic outcome, we note that they tend to be quite accessible—often surface characteristics—and quantifiable. Thus the foci of attention were on such points of interest as IQ, MMPI and Rorschach scores, educational level and student status, and chronicity of disorder. However, a rigorous approach in the measurement tradition to gathering and processing data employing predictor variables such as those employed in the Menninger Foundation study (Appelbaum, 1977) could pose operational problems and be generally daunting.

In the clinical tradition that prevails at the Menninger Foundation, interest is directed to such variables as defenses, goals, conflicts, fantasies, self- and object-representations, interpersonal strategies, and transference issues, any of which may be a significant factor in some cases and not in others. Consider the hazards to operational definition of a number of the variables used by Appelbaum, such as: patterning of defenses, affect organization, thought organization, psychological-mindedness, and even plain old "honesty."

With reference to his list of 24 variables of this sort, Appelbaum observes:

> Even a cursory reading of this list of variables reveals that, first of all, they are not the sort of discrete factors about which one can say it is or is not there; or, if there, how much of it numerically there is. Second, they are on the face of it unoperational, and can therefore be expected to include surplus meaning, and meanings which vary from person to person and according to methods of investigation. It is not even always possible to tell which is superordinate and which is subordinate to the other. For example, *anxiety tolerance* is obviously related to *ego strength*, but where one leaves off and the other begins, which is a cause or an effect of the other, is difficult to say.

Can the use of terms that carry such admitted baggage be helpful? Kernberg (1977) cites one of Appelbaum's cases, that of a woman psychiatrically diagnosed "as having a hysterical personality and good prognosis for psychoanalysis":

> The initial test report, however, stressed the indications of ego weakness, the predominance of infantile (in contrast to hysterical) features in her character, a certain degree of looseness

in her thought processes, suggesting an occasional breakthrough of autistic paranoid thinking (not in well-structured situations, but in the projective tests), and a predominance of oral-aggressive impulses together with evidence of perverse sexual ideation.

This sample of Kernberg's language reflects the fact that the case is conceptualized in a particular characterologic frame of reference:

> The prognosis for a typical hysterical personality with ordinary neurotic structure undergoing psychoanalysis is different from that of an infantile personality with borderline personality organization. Second, high intelligence and verbal facility may mask severe character pathology in patients with common psychoneurotic symptoms...[therefore] it is always crucial to supplement symptomatic diagnosis with a characterological diagnosis and, more generally speaking, a structural diagnosis, that is, the diagnosis of ego organization and strength.

The following is abstracted from Appelbaum's prediction, in nonoperational terms, of this patient's therapeutic possibilities:

> My overall feeling is that although she has all the requisite characteristics for analysis, that is, intelligence, psychological-mindedness, anxiety tolerance, and a pervasive enough problem, she would be a difficult case. I base this on my feeling that although there are definite neurotic aspects to this, the infantile character structure is very prominent. In my discussion of ego strength, I emphasized that she lacked the flexibility to give up gratifications necessary to succeed in psychoanalysis. I would add to that the strength of secondary gain and the strength of the primary gain she must derive. I am thinking of the oral impulses here and the rather gratifying position she has herself in, in regard to her sexual conflict. That is, in fantasy she seems to feel more powerful and as though she has a bigger phallus than the man. This fantasy is a very important part of her makeup.

Clearly, this approach to linking assessment to prediction of therapeutic outcome is very heavily influenced by theory, and, just as clearly, research in this frame of reference must entail a paradigm shift from neater operational approaches.

The Therapeutic Implications of How the Results of Assessment Are Presented

The meaning of information, together with its implications for therapy, varies with the manner in which it is presented. In the case of the psychological report, to merely present a mass of information does not provide a useful guide to therapeutic intervention. By contrast, case-focused reports written for a psychotherapist clearly point out the relevant issues of the case, such as the problem(s) needing remediation, the specific goals of therapy, the techniques that might be helpful, anticipated therapist-client relationship factors, problem areas that are likely to be encountered, and the amount of change that can be expected.

Harty (1986) illustrates the advantages of action language through contrasting a conventional report on a hypothetical case with a report on the same case written in action language. The first is an all-too-familiar write-up, saturated with theory, stereotypy, and rife with the going jargon.

> The patient's obsessive-compulsive facade is crumbling under the impact of intense oral-aggressive impulses. His preferred defenses of intellectualization, reaction formation, and isolation of affect are badly strained, and more primitive projective mechanisms are now visible, especially under conditions of reduced external structure. There is an occasional intrusion of primary process material into his conscious thinking, and it is likely that occasional outbursts of poorly modulated affect may occur. Although probably a man whose relationships have always been distant, he now shows increasing signs of withdrawal and weakened cathexis of reality. His failing ego functions leave him increasingly vulnerable to sadistic fantasies and panic attacks that may result in impulsive action.[1]

In the action-language version of the case, Harty notes, the purpose "is not to diagnose what the patient is, has, or contains, but rather to understand and convey, as fully as possible what the patient is doing." He further suggests that action-language reports "force the test report writer to address the questions of greatest relevance to the therapist's work." What the person *does* may help to define therapeutic goals, and thus be more closely related to effecting meaningful change than what the person *is* or *has*.

> The patient strives ineffectively to regard each situation as an intellectual puzzle, which he attempts to solve by reasoning out all the possible consequences of anything he or others might do. He approaches situations this way so that he will not interpret them as opportunities for seizing, consuming, and destroying sources of possible satisfaction, only to have punishments of equal savagery inflicted on himself. He does not currently use his preferred approach consistently, and on occasion he thinks consciously of inflicting or receiving violent damage. At such times, he also thinks illogically and inefficiently, in contrast to his more usual accuracy and precision.[2]

A case-focused report, and its application to a practical problem, is presented by Lovitt (1984). Issues of high-flown theory are not involved here; the issue, rather, is one of how to provide nursing care for a medical patient. A sophisticated clinical instrument, the Rorschach, is applied to a down-to-earth problem:

> The patient is undergoing an acute adjustment reaction to the uncertainties of his medical situation. His ability to realistically understand the behavior and intentions of those caring for him is seriously distorted. The patient attempts to deal with his fear by withdrawing from his environment and his contact with other people. The reality of hospital life is that he is not permitted to do this; in fact, he is required to cope with a strange environment and, at times, with novel and invasive diagnostic procedures. His typical way of coping with anxiety and uncertainty runs counter to the demands of hospital life. This person,

---

[1]From Michael K. Harty, "Action Language in the Psychological Test Report," *Bulletin of the Menninger Clinic*, 50 (1986), 456–463. Copyright © 1986 by the Menninger Foundation, Topeka, Kansas, and reproduced by permission of the author and the publisher.

[2]From Harty, "Action Language."

when stimulated by others, has been conditioned to react with activity and emotional output rather than by thoughtful and careful deliberation. He is currently deficient in his ability to control and refine this emotional behavior and responds with strong and poorly controlled feelings with a poor appreciation of the effects of this behavior on others. Because of his past experiences, he is skeptical about being supported, protected, and helped by other people, and he becomes extremely anxious and confused during the administration of normal diagnostic and nursing procedures. The patient's maladaptive behavior, therefore, can be understood as generating from a naturally occurring, self-protective withdrawal in a person who responds with overt behaviors and emotions to situations that puzzle him. He is suspiciously alert to being harmed because of his fears and actively and regularly distorts and misunderstands the motivation and intentions of other people. The quality of his adjustment is a maladaptive one for the social system that he finds himself in.

THE CURRENT STATUS OF PSYCHOLOGICAL ASSESSMENT IN THE PRACTICE OF PSYCHOTHERAPY

The relation of psychological assessment to psychotherapy is in a state of transition. Clinical experience favors the notion that assessment can be helpful to the conduct of therapy while research support lags. On the other hand, the systematic review of the research by Hayes, Nelson, and Jarrett (1987) (see p. 266), finds that studies in this area are flawed by conceptual confusion and methodological shortcomings—though "the trends in the field all seem positive." In the meantime, numerous extant proposals for applying assessment findings to therapy merit attention.

Kissen (1973) summarizes his understanding of the value of assessment to the therapeutic situation:

> A skillful and clinically-focused test report can be of immense practical usefulness to the psychotherapist—if it is appropriately addressed to relevant treatment issues. A good test report ... can alert the therapist to such important clinical factors as the character structure and characteristic defensive maneuvers of his patient, his expressive style, his salient psycho-dynamic conflicts, his psychological-mindedness and motivation for treatment, and perhaps most importantly his typical interpersonal interaction tendencies which may very well be enacted in the form of a transference-countertransference interaction with the therapist. Other factors such as the patient's impulsive potential, possibility for further decompensation, and subjective experience of himself are also useful for the therapist to know at the beginning point of therapy.

It is important to note that information useful to the conduct of therapy draws on sources other than test scores. Kissen (1977) cites the following non-score material:

1. The interpersonal engagement of tester and patient.
2. The way the patient responds to the conditions of testing.
3. Experiential study of self-representations and object-representations.
4. Major transference issues and potential countertransference.

5. Resistance-counterresistance.
6. Important parameters of psychotherapy manifested during the typical testing session.

In gathering such data, Kissen suggests that the psychological assessor uses the self as an instrument, including the employment of ingenuity, special strategies, and subjective reactions:

> A modern approach to psychological testing involves a delicate, essentially measured use by the tester of his own personality reactions in order to gain a more therapeutically relevant understanding of the patient. The ability to note and jot down various personal reactions during the course of the testing session is an essential skill of the sophisticated tester. I ask my supervisees to cultivate the habit of jotting down personal feelings and interactional observations in addition to the more typical process recording during testing sessions. Personal recording of this sort typically may involve statements such as "I feel myself being subtly intimidated by the patient" or "I find myself becoming angered by something about this patient." Other personal observations may involve noting unusual degrees of assertiveness, exhibitionism, or passive withdrawal in response to some aspect of the interaction with the patient. Of course, the tester must be aware of his own personality and typical testing reactions in order to make reliable and valid phenomenological inferences of this sort...since the affective dimension is such an important (and often neglected) aspect of the tester-patient interaction. It is incumbent on the experienced tester to pay careful attention to his various mood states before, during, and after a particular testing session. Over time a sophisticated tester will gain an increasing capacity to discriminate interpersonally generated affects for the purpose of making reliable inferences with regard to the patient's self- and object-representations from intrapsychically motivated feeling states which relate largely to personal self- and object-representations of the tester.

Among the specialized (nonstandard) techniques for gaining non-score data are Appelbaum's (1959) Altered Atmosphere Procedure, described by Appelbaum as follows:

> Directly following the usual test administration, I have come to discard some of the paraphernalia of the testing situation, implying by my behavior that the test is over. While putting down my pen, shuffling response sheets together, leaning back in the chair, adopting a more conventional tone, I hand all the cards back to the patient and suggest that he go through again to see whether he might see something else, something he perhaps did not notice before. These directions might best be taken as conveying the gist of what occurs rather than as an inflexible prescription, for different patients elicit spontaneous alterations in the technique necessary to establish and maintain the desired atmosphere.

This variation of testing the limits—approaches to gain additional material beyond what is gained through standard administration—is used to assess the patient's resistance. The presumption is that a patient who produces rich material under these circumstances is less prone to show resistance in therapy than one who does not.

Yet another of Appelbaum's variations of testing the limits in the interest of understanding resistance issues is:

> The use of the so-called "paradigmatic" techniques... [which] also allows for an exploration of resistance tendencies during the testing session. The experienced examiner, once in touch with induced counterresistance feelings, can sensitively utilize such feelings to explore certain qualities of the patient's object relationships. The delicate use of ironic observations which either nonverbally mirror or verbally confront a given patient's resistances can be effectively utilized to test the limits of that patient's characterological rigidity and defensiveness.

Research on the value of psychological assessment to psychotherapy must take into account such qualitative and subjective material.

Putative Contributions of Psychological Assessment to the Practice of Psychotherapy

The contributions and/or the claimed contributions of psychological assessment to the conduct of psychotherapy are many. However, as the discussion of empirical findings at the beginning of this chapter indicates, conclusive studies in this area are not readily available.

A number of largely theoretical contributions added to accumulated clinical experience point up how assessment can be helpful, even of crucial value, to the selection of candidates for therapy, to the conduct of therapy, and to the evaluation of therapeutic outcome. Against this background it appears that the value of assessment entails more than the instruments that are used and the scores that they yield. Assessor variables are foremost. The assessor's knowledge and insightfulness, ingenuity, orientation to and understanding of the therapy process, flexibility, and the ability to seize and exploit unusual test responses and unique and unexpected events in the assessor-client interaction make a contribution that is otherwise nonavailable.

Among the advantages to therapy offered by the use of psychological instruments is that they present stimuli (actually it is the stimulus picture of the assessor in interaction with the instruments and the client) that are different from those presented by the psychotherapist. They make available to the assessor the opportunity to observe the client in differently structured situations and when confronted with a variety of circumstances and challenges. Further, the various instruments differ in their stimulus value and in the sort of information they are best suited to predict, whether intelligence level, cognitive style, thought disorder, or personality regression—to cite a few examples of common clinical interest. Data on these topics become particularly important in the light of the theoretical and empirical variables that guide the search for material that is applicable to the conduct of therapy.

Appelbaum (1990) also suggests that the helpfulness of psychological assessment goes beyond providing a statement of the client's functioning. The therapist's functioning, as well, including his/her degree of self-confidence and the numerous judgments he or she makes in the course of therapy, can also be enhanced by the availability of a psychological report:

> Sometimes the tests fail to elucidate anything new. They merely confirm what others have thought about the patient. Superficially, that may make the tests seem like a waste of time. Yet, when one looks closely at the reality of psychotherapeutic work one reaches a different conclusion. Probably all psychotherapists, including seasoned veterans, make comments to their patients with more or less anxiety and consequent indecision. They may ask themselves whether the content is right, whether the comment is pitched at the right psychosexual level, whether the patient's defenses at the moment will allow the patient to be receptive to a particular kind of intervention, what words to use, and in what tone of voice. All such judgments can more easily be attended to when the therapist's anxiety is at a minimum. The therapist can be helped to achieve that minimum when inferences made from interviews are independently supported by inferences made from the tests.

Concreteness as a therapeutic variable Concreteness is generally recognized by therapists as a major factor that may affect the outcome of psychotherapy. It has also been a matter of concern to the practice of psychological assessment, at least since the 1930s, and particularly with the landmark contributions on abstract versus concrete thinking by Goldstein and Scheerer (1941) and Hanfmann and Kasanin (1942). Knowledge of how abstractly or concretely a person thinks can determine whether a client is suitable for a particular approach to therapy, or answer the question of what approach might be suitable. Such information can also be helpful when the reason for a client's failure to make progress in psychotherapy needs an answer.

Brown (1985) identifies concreteness in three psychopathological situations: in the thought-disordered patient's pathological ramblings, in the organically impaired individual, and in the depressed patient whose presenting symptom picture is intractable. However,

> The common thread running through these instances is the concrete patient's imprisonment in a current situation (the pressure of an intrusive thought, the desperate grasping to recover a lost thought, the seemingly endless fog of depression) that casts a shadow of narrow meaning across all experiences. The concrete patient cannot lift himself out of the immediacy of the moment and is trapped in a state of mind that cannot see beyond itself.

Josephs (1989) suggests that concreteness is the greatest obstacle to the conduct of psychoanalysis, whose essence he defines as the interpretation of the symbolic meaning of psychic events. He views the concrete mode of thinking thus:

> The most obvious indicators of the concrete attitude are two negative signs, capacities notable in their absence:
> the absence of an abstract attitude and the lack of an imagination. In contrast to the abstract attitude, the concrete attitude involves an immersion in the details of a particular situation with an obliviousness to the larger class or category of which the particular may be an example or a part. The abstract attitude brings a breadth of perspective which is

lacking in the concrete. The concrete attitude also involves a loss of distance from and a stimulus boundedness to the press of current situational events which seem to compel a particular response, in contrast to the free play of the imagination which allows for a transcendence of the immediacy of current events. In treatment, the concrete attitude is most apparent in the patient's viewing each interpersonal dilemma as idiosyncratic without an appreciation of characteristic patterns of relating, a paucity of reported dreams and fantasies, and impersonal, conventional or nondescript language lacking in evocative metaphor. When fantasy life is consciously entertained, fantasy is construed as a literal rather than a symbolic reality; dreams really do predict the future and ghosts and hobgoblins really do exist. The appreciation of the symbolic dimension which psychoanalysis has investigated requires an imagination capable of forming symbols as well as an abstract attitude capable of interpreting symbols.

With a view to its therapeutic implications, psychological assessors review their test protocols for the quantitative and qualitative indicators of concreteness they may hold. When a client's thinking is concrete, this fact is likely to register in response to a broad spectrum of items, from tests specifically designed as measures of abstract-concrete thinking, like the five-test Goldstein-Scheerer battery (the tests may also be used singly) (Goldstein & Scheerer, 1951) to instruments like the TAT that were designed for assessing personality characteristics quite distant from this concern.

The Wechsler intelligence scales, particularly since they are in such widespread use—even more or less routinely in some settings—are a valuable source of information concerning this dimension of functioning. Thus, a low score on the Block Design subtest is suggestive of loss of the "abstract attitude" (Wechsler, 1939). The Similarities subtest is quite useful as a measure of abstraction-concreteness, both in terms of the scores they yield and verbalizations to the items. A person disposed to concrete thinking almost certainly will do poorly on this subtest and the responses are likely to be characteristic: "An orange and a banana are not alike; a banana is long and yellow, an orange is round and orange."

Answers to the proverbs items of the Comprehension subtest also are likely to be characteristic: Question- "What is the meaning of 'Strike while the iron is hot'"? Answer- "You can't shape the iron when it's cold." The assessor, in fact, must be alert to indicators of concreteness wherever they occur.

To the vocabulary item requiring a definition of *winter*, the concrete individual might simply reply, "It's cold," while a less stimulus-bound subject (evidently tending in the direction of another diagnostic consideration) cognizant of a host of factors, some of them distant from the personal experiences of the respondent and placed in a larger scheme of things, might define *winter* as "one of the four seasons, specifically the season of coldest weather between fall and spring and typically associated, in our latitude, with frozen precipitation. It is the season when the sun's rays strike our latitude at an oblique angle."

On the TAT, the concrete person responds with dull and unimaginative stories, or commonly with simple description: "Here's a picture of a girl with books on her arm, an old woman leaning against a tree, and a man with a horse plowing the field." Queried for further information, what the characters are thinking or feeling, what led up to the scene or how the story might turn out, the subject indicates an inability to comply, or protests that the picture does not show these matters. Requests to "Use your imagination" or "Make it up" encounter a brick wall.

Rorschachers have long scanned their client's protocols for quantitative and qualitative indicators, or possible indicators, of concreteness –too much D (large usual Detail), "lazy" W (Whole blot responses that involve little energy in organizing the parts of the blot) (Beck, 1952); poorly organized responses; and W:M (Number of Whole blot responses to human Movement responses) ratio greater than 2:1 (Rapaport, Gill, & Schafer, 1946). Unimaginative stereotyped responses—such as A% (percent of animal percepts} >50, high P (Popular responses, responses seen by at least one out of three persons), Landscape and Geography responses, Anatomy, and perseveration of vague responses all deserve a close look. Loss of distance—is exemplified in the response "This is real scary...a giant...coming right at me." Stimulus-bound responses—are particularly suspect. Inability to see humans on Card III, on free association, and even in the testing the limits phase—because "the heads look like birds' heads" or similar suspicion arises when the client does not accept the human response, even when the assessor suggests such features as the torso and the leg "because [the torso and the leg] wouldn't be separated with a space between if it were a person."

Weiner and Crowder (1986) employed the WAIS-R Similarities subtest and the three proverbs items on the Comprehension subtest as an estimate of concreteness of thinking. The authors report on a sample of hospitalized medical patients whose abstract ability, as judged by these two subtests, was found to be low. Accordingly, they were considered as being deficient in the ability to understand reasoning by analogy, simile, and metaphor. But these, commonly, are prominent vehicles of therapeutic communication in insight therapy, hence this sort of therapy is beyond the grasp of patients who think in the concrete mode. Tragically, therapists rarely assess their patients' ability to think abstractly, according to the authors.

But when concreteness is identified this need not be understood as a bar to effecting therapeutic change. What is needed is a shift to a more appropriate therapeutic strategy, Brown and Crowder advise:

> Inability to think abstractly does not preclude changing attitudes and behaviors by means that do not involve the development of insight and unconscious conflict or motivation. Such techniques include role playing, the giving of concrete advice, and modeling by the therapist.

Regressive personality features as a matter of therapeutic concern–the borderline personality as a case in point of therapeutic challenge Therapeutic interaction, as with psychotics and patients with *severe personality disorders* (Kernberg, 1967, 1970, 1984; Millon, 1969, 1981)—namely, borderline personality disorder, paranoid personality disorder, and schizotypal personality disorder, involves issues different from those presented by clients with more intact ego functioning. The identification of primary process thinking thus can contribute to the formulation of a therapeutic approach and recognition of the problems and limitations that are to be expected.

Schwartz and Lazar (1984) studied contaminated thinking on the Rorschach as "a specimen of the primary process." They point out that condensation and displacement are the two major mechanisms of the primary process manifest in dreams, and, following Holt (1977), they regard contaminated Rorschach responses as a "waking analogue of dream condensation." These are viewed by the authors as a combination of primary and secondary process thinking. Further, such responses imply a "struggle...between a regressive loss of objects, and an effort to remain in contact with reality." The variations of contamination discussed by the authors are *simultaneous percepts, fusion responses*, and *contamination by means of influence*.

> A major hypothesis emerging from this study states: The contaminated response appears to be an indication of an underlying process that assumes different forms. The range of phenomena that are referents of this process include perceptual fluidity, the alternation of images, the simultaneous perception of two or more images, a change in meaning of one image by another, and the interpenetration of images or their attributes. The common denominator in these different varieties is the joint perception of two images, which interact in a manner described in the text. At one extreme, both images retain their identity, as in fluidity, alternation, and simultaneity. At the other extreme, both images lose their identity—this was observed in the rare perceptual fusions, where the perceptual material was recombined in a manner characteristic of dream condensation. Tentatively, then, we conclude that the process of contamination leads in the direction of a complete fusion of images, and thus a loss of object boundaries. This process, however, is typically aborted, in that both images usually can be identified, if only by implication.

The treatment of clients with borderline personality disorder poses a number of characteristic problems associated with regressive attributes. Further, as Kernberg (1967, 1984), Hartocollis (1977), Millon (1981), Gunderson (1984), and others observe, all borderline patients are not alike. Some present with symptom pictures that overlap with the affective disorders, others are at the borderline of a schizophrenic psychosis, while still others, at least periodically, show clinically paranoid features. Borderline personality exists in the context of numerous personality styles, and in the absence of a thoroughgoing diagnosis a clinician may be impressed that the individual is, for example, hysteric, obsessive-compulsive, narcissistic, dissociative, a dependent personality, or suffering with a generalized anxiety disorder.

The borderline person at times can also appear to be quite "normal," sincere, or cooperative, only to unexplainedly fly into a rage, become accusatory, engage in self-mutilation or property destruction, give evidence of identity diffusion, or adopt a stance that is dependent, childlike (ineffectual, weepy, or tantrum-like, for example), or demanding, and so on, through an extended list of pathological behaviors.

Clearly, the potential therapist needs much more information than is evident on the surface. What is the general prognosis, and what sort of improvement can reasonably be expected? What is in the client's Pandora's box, and how should these behaviors be dealt with as they emerge? What is the likelihood of psychotic decompensation? Volkan (1987) is particularly impressed that regression induced by therapy can manifest as further disorganization and increase primitive impulse expression.

A number of psychological studies have investigated borderline functioning. Reviews by Gunderson and Singer (1975) and Singer (1977a) accentuate the finding that borderlines tend to do well on highly structured tasks, such as a Wechsler Adult Intelligence Scale (WAIS), but poorly on unstructured instruments, such as the Rorschach, where primary process thinking may be in distinct contrast to the quality of WAIS responses. Arnow and Cooper (1984) confirm that, in the case of borderline patients, Rorschach testing "actively precipitates the emergence of a host of regressive and primitive processes," and thus is predictive of thinking in psychoanalysis. They point out that the unstructured nature of the Rorschach parallels that of the psychoanalytic situation, as well as various life situations that precipitate regression. They express the hope that "the clinical usefulness of the Rorschach can be enhanced with a deeper understanding of the dynamic interactions between properties of the testing situation and specific developmental vulnerabilities, which together shape the response process." And, "A grasp of the psychological impact of the testing situation provides additional data for clarifying the kinds of situations likely to stimulate regressions or exacerbations of a borderline patient's psychopathology."

Carr, Goldstein, Hunt, and Kernberg (1979) generally support the Rorschach-WAIS discrepancy thesis. Regarding the Rorschach, "It is impressive to note that in all but one case the Rorschach test (administered and scored in the tradition of Rapaport, Gill, and Schafer) revealed the unequivocal presence of scores considered to reflect thinking disturbances in both borderline and psychotic patients." The case for the WAIS not revealing evidence of thought disturbance in borderline patients is less certain, however. Whereas WAIS scores for this group might be quite high, serious qualitative flaws can occur at the same time. By way of example, the authors present a case where the subject scored 131, but nevertheless, produced problematic responses. *Praise* and *punishment*, he indicated, are not alike, but when encouraged to respond, replied that "They both begin with the letter P." He offered another egregiously erroneous response to the "city land" item ("More people are living proportionally in the city"). A further point made in this paper is that "I don't know" responses might conceal questionable responses that the client is able to inhibit while not necessarily damaging the score appreciably.

Berg's (1983) systematic review of the usefulness of psychological tests to the assessment of borderline psychopathology leads him to the conclusion that contributions in this area have been sparse. In his presentation, he looks at the issue from a number of perspectives: *ego functions* (intelligence, cognitive operations, thought and language, and reality testing), *organization of affect, configuration of defenses, structure of the object world, dynamics,* and *interpersonal aspects of the test process.* His orientation is clearly in the clinical tradition. Because of the variation of presentations by which borderline psychopathology is manifested (both between and within individuals who carry this diagnosis), the limitations of quantitative indicators is basic:

> Borderline psychopathology represents a spectrum disorder for which discrete diagnostic markers do not exist and a sign approach is thus of little value. In the absence of

psychometric criteria for nosological exclusion and inclusion, a complex inference process must be pursued to determine the manner in which test behavior reflects enduring patterns of behavior typifying the patient's adaptational efforts.

Berg expands on the findings concerning intelligence tests reported on by Carr et al., such as the often less-than-evident thought pathology that does not surface when "I don't know" responses go unqueried. Inquiry, Berg indicates, is commonly in the interest of clarifying how a response should be scored, while nonstandard inquiry (not necessary to clarify scoring) may yield diagnostically rich data. Further, less-than-complete recording of the client's verbalizations, including asides—judged not necessary for scoring and not worthy of the limited space available on the record form—also keeps out of the psychologist's awareness evidence of thought disorder. To gain the full diagnostic implications for the presence of a borderline disorder, the protocol must be examined microscopically ("milking the data"—p. 111) and the variability of performance—typical of borderlines—must be attended to. Berg, then, like Carr et al., finds that unstructured tests, such as the WAIS, evidence greater impairment in borderline psychopathology than had been suggested in the Gunderson and Singer (1975) and Singer (1975) reviews.

Rather than gross disturbances in thought and language, such as characterize the psychotic, disturbances in the productions of borderlines tend to be less pronounced; which is why, as noted above, the assessor must be closely attuned to the data. Thus, Berg speaks of the borderline protocol as "speckled with lapses in logical thinking," and of "subtle derailments of logic." However, "More extensive pockets of disorganization can be observed on the Arithmetic subtest when the patient is asked to recount the process by which he arrived at an incorrect response; arbitrary logic and magical thinking is often resorted to in the face of stress aroused by these problems." Berg notes also the tendencies to response contamination as explored by Schwartz and Lazar (1984) (p. 279), and the implications of such responses for the blurring of boundaries in object relations "where self and others can merge and in the realm of dynamics where affects can become fused in highly ambivalent amalgams." Also, shading off in the direction of psychosis is seen in language peculiarities, such as the use of neologisms, generally less glaring than those seen in schizophrenia; and fluid thinking, as in "brief interludes of free association-like thought."

Along with Kernberg (1984), Berg notes the relative intactness of the reality testing and perceptual organization of borderlines. Indeed, Kernberg proposes that this observation may serve in making a differential diagnosis between borderline personality and psychosis. This clinical impression is largely consistent with Rorschach performance, with the obvious exception of the occurrence of primary process thinking, as discussed above. Berg points out, however, the rapid recovery of the borderline in the presence of such regressions. He also observes that borderlines may lose distance from test stimuli (pp. 113–114), such as the Rorschach blots.

Berg's discussion of the affect of borderline individuals parallels the clinical observations made repeatedly by those who have significant experience with this class of patients; namely, that their deficiencies of ego organization and reality testing are less impressive than their affective disturbances, and also less impressive than the behavioral descriptions of those discussed in this category in DSM-III-R (American Psychiatric Association, 1987a). Stressed in this discussion are behaviors grouped under the headings *fluctuating affect and need states*, *global and diffuse discharge patterns*, *action potential*, and *primitive drive representations*.

The familiar behavior patterns thus classified have their distinct representations in performance on psychological instruments, and Berg illustrates with reference to performance on the Rorschach and the TAT. On the Rorschach, the borderline may offer the "point and counterpoint" of chromatic and achromatic color responses, and overemphasis of color or shading (often occurring in content suggestive of anger and violence—fire, explosions, blood). Stories told about the TAT cards are more likely to be action-oriented than revealing of inner experience. Berg provides a neat example in this discussion of how the assessor may use the self as a diagnostic tool:

> Without transition, emotions can abruptly give way to each other in quick succession. This flux of emotions, if stirred during the testing process, can evoke in the examiner a vague and anxious sense of anticipation about what will happen next. For example, attempts at ingratiating subservience and cooperation oftentimes are peppered with sudden flares of irritability in response to the stress of challenging tasks.

"The defense configuration of borderline individuals," Berg summarizes, "is a conglomeration of faltering efforts to manage stress characterized by regressive dips followed by demonstrations of higher level functioning...A wide range of defensive tactics are resorted to as none is sufficient to stave off the stress of unbidden impulses, ideas, and narcissistic collapse." He mentions, particularly, three of the principal recognized defenses of the borderline—denial, projection, and splitting. Denial is witnessed on projective tests in the breakdown of the subject's ability to respond. Or, responses of a sexual, aggressive, or dysphoric nature are seemingly taken back by following them with an opposite content, or dysphoric content; for example, being followed up with a happier theme. Paranoid material is seen in threatening content—danger, murder, robbery, and so forth. Splitting may be witnessed on a number of instruments, such as the WAIS, where "the borderline patient reveals patently contradictory and concurrent attitudes and values" reflective of a life of contradictions.

Compared with all the other live presentations of the borderline, the individual's object relations are among the most evident personality features that are revealed in test productions. "Primarily, the test representations of objects and descriptions of people reveal fragmentation and internal contradictions which serve as a hallmark of the borderline individual's failure to resolve discrepant aspects of the self and inability to view others as stable and predictable." Rorschach percepts of human-animal combinations is one way in which such confusion may be represented. "Self and others are experienced in a black and white dichotomous manner indicating inadequate capacity to integrate and resolve conflicting wishes and feelings. Thus, test depictions of people are shallow and superficial, for they remain unidimensional portrayals as either good or bad, gratifying or withholding, deprived or enriched."

The dynamics of the borderline individual are seen as dominated by anxious, dysphoric themes, with derivative high levels of anger and aggressiveness. These are emotionally needy, very dependent people, fearful of the environment that threatens destruction by malevolent forces. They fear that others will withhold gratification of their dependency needs and that they will be abandoned. They fear also nonfulfillment of their "pansexual" needs that hold them in its grip. Corresponding test themes are seen in anger permeated protocols. The TAT evidences dependency themes and also human interactions fraught with tension, opposition, and frustration. The "pansexual" theme is reflected on the Rorschach in intermixed oral, anal, and genital wishes, infantile urges precluding any clear-cut sexual orientation, certainly not genital sexuality. "Stories describing intense and tempestuous romantic involvements often point to a wish to possess and incorporate the beloved object in an infantile, oral mode."

The interactions that take place during the test process may be conceived as an in vivo demonstration of the client's more or less typical interactions with others in the everyday world. As such they are potentially very revealing diagnostically. Insights do not happen automatically, however. The assessor must be observant and cognizant of what is happening, and this is particularly true of the effects the client is having on the assessor: "The examiner may become aware of primitive fantasies, for example, concerning rescue, sexual seduction, withdrawal or retribution which are stimulated by the patient's dramatic behavior." The borderline individual is likely to resort to the use of projective identification, projecting onto the assessor aspects of his or her disowned self. In turn, the assessor may be "left wondering whether the patient had indeed detected an aspect of his personality which is denied or avoided." The assessor must therefore look within himself or herself to gain information about the client. This assessment tactic, basic to the therapeutic use of countertransference—understanding the client through understanding oneself—seems as far from psychometrics as one can get.

A "new set of lenses" for the psychotherapist—and the issue of timeliness of psychological information Berg (1983) presents Kernberg's view on the limitation of interviewing in the diagnosis of borderline patients, juxtaposed with his own observation on the benefit of using psychological instruments to overcome this shortcoming:

> Kernberg (1976) asserted that the standard clinical interview does not provide an accurate picture of a patient's dynamic organization contributing toward a differential diagnosis of borderline pathology. Relying on data consciously filtered by the patient, the interviewer's vision is skewed and constricted by the patient's choice of material. On the other hand, psychological testing is a particularly powerful technique for examining the dynamic organization of motives by virtue of normative standards for the prevalence of specific dynamic themes in the projective tests and the indirect manner of eliciting dynamic concerns which can elude conscious censorship.

Such values of psychological assessment are, of course, not specific to the diagnosis of borderline pathology; they apply, to a greater or lesser extent, to gaining significant information across a spectrum of clinical conditions. Observations of the sort made by Berg have long been the underlying rationale for much of the psychological assessment that is performed.

Kernberg's position on the limitations of the interview would tend also to be pertinent to the psychotherapist's ability to understand—and therefore effectively treat—the client. Such a conclusion appears consistent with the view of Cooper and Witenberg (1985), who consider that information gained by the therapist frequently is inadequate to the task, poorly integrated and unfocused, and thus jeopardizing treatment. As training and supervising psychoanalysts, they observe:

> Most analysts are familiar with what happens when a treatment situation gets bogged down. The same issues are discussed over and over, unrelated issues are raised, and both patient and analyst become repetitively monotonous. An atmosphere of boredom pervades the situation; a feeling of not being understood. The sense of dissatisfaction which characterizes the bogged-down treatment ranges from a vague unease to a marked feeling of despair.

Too often, the therapist works with a collection of "fragments": "The analyst remains essentially disorganized about the patient. He sees only a fragmented person, a collection of diagnostic labels, pieces of transference behavior, and assorted dynamics."

When treatment appears to be bogged down in chaos or inertia, these authors suggest the need for "a new set of lenses through which to view the patient." Such lenses may be gained through an understanding of how the patient perceives his world, his experiences in living, what he is trying to accomplish in life, and central themes of life, such as the "secret plot" as conceived by Fromm (Maccoby, 1972), the "core issue" of Saul (1958), or "the underlying theme in a psychological novel."

A frequent cause of bogged-down treatment, according to Cooper and Witenberg, lies in a failure of the analyst to elicit a coherent overview of the patient *in the beginning of treatment* (emphasis added). Cooper and Witenberg quote Harry Stack Sullivan to the effect that the understanding needed to move therapy forward could be gained in the course of treatment within 7 to 15 sessions. Seven to fifteen sessions, of course, is early in the treatment in a more or less classical psychoanalytic approach. Particularly with less-lengthy therapies, however, 7 to 15 sessions can be a long time to search about for a workable treatment formulation—and costly to the client. Might therapy be committed to a firm direction much earlier with the timely availability of a report of psychological assessment that focuses on a coherent overview of the client?

Mortimer and Smith (1983) and De La Cour (1986) discuss the importance of having, and properly using, a focus in psychotherapy. Establishing a focus is seen as of particular value in conserving time and making for effective therapy. According to De La Cour,

The use of a focus is the single most decisive and active alteration of psychodynamic technique introduced by brief therapists, with the exception of the use of time limits.

Further,

> It may feel premature, omnipotent, intrusive, directive, or rude to set about searching for and suggesting a therapeutic focus during the initial hours of treatment. It may feel controlling, hardhearted, or narrow-minded to stay with, and help the patient to stay with, the focus, at times leaving aside obviously meaningful material. However, relinquishing the focus, or the time limit, for countertransference or other reasons, is probably the most frequent reason for failure of brief therapy.

Mortimer and Smith also consider that focusing therapy is crucial to its successful outcome. They point out that therapists have different ideas of what the focus of therapy should be, some of them emphasizing neurotic conflicts, some defenses, and some overt behaviors and their consequences. They submit that the written psychological report can be of value in setting the focus in individual cases:

> As diagnosticians, we feel a responsibility for helping therapists and other treaters appropriately focus their treatment efforts. Although it is easier to write a test report which sets no priorities, we have sufficient diagnostic and conceptual tools for determining the critical issue to be addressed in treatment for many of the patients we test. In order to use these tools we need to be willing to assess the relative importance of a given set of ego functions, a given pattern of defenses, or a given transference paradigm with reference to its pervasiveness and significance in the life of the patient. When we determine the relative centrality of the different facets which the patient presents to us on testing, we are able to help psychotherapists determine where to focus their efforts and attention.

THE ROAD MAP CONCEPT OF PSYCHOLOGICAL THERAPEUTICS

In harmony with the above, Brown (1965) conceptualizes the psychological report as a "road map.": "It is seldom that the therapist is taught to regard the psychological report as a road map or itinerary of the terrain he is to traverse with the patient." He indicates that those who shun the contribution of psychological assessment "fail to formulate a therapeutic plan, and often embark on 'blind' therapy without psychological charts, compass or sextant." This is Klopfer's (1964) theme of "the blind leading the blind."

Blank's (1965) *Psychological Evaluation in Psychotherapy: Ten Case Histories* is the "first book...to document the direct relationship between a patient's response patterns on a battery of psychological tests and his subsequent behavior in psychotherapy" (Brown, 1965). The road maps that Blank provides consist of both general observations and more or less specific recommendations.

General observations may cover large segments of personality or treatment—the major areas of personality dysfunction, for example, or a broad approach to therapy, including treatment goals and strategies. Such information may be most useful in the beginning phases of therapy, or when a hitch in treatment develops, and a review of the case formulation and the therapeutic approach are in order. Specific recommendations may be of the "Do this" or "Don't do that" sort: "Tell the client she must make her own decisions concerning her marital problem," or "Don't let the client manipulate you to depart from agreed upon rules to govern the therapy situation."

Recommendations, of course, reflect the orientation of the psychological assessor, his or her personality orientation and orientation to therapy. We may contrast the classical symptom-centered approach that prevails in the mental health field with the character-centered approach such as set forth by Everly (1986), which considers that psychopathology is an extension of dysfunctional personality styles: "The real target of intermediate and long term psychotherapeutic efforts becomes the personality dysfunction."

Perusal of Blank's (1965) cases discloses that they present a variety of contents bearing on the therapy process. Different reports address different areas of concern and make different kinds of recommendations. This fact reflects the differences among clients and their situations.

Exemplification by Leonard Blank

In the following samples of psychological report content from Blank's case presentations, there are statements concerning present behaviors and predictions of future behaviors, intrapsychic and objective behaviors. There are predictions of outcome and tips for the conduct of therapy. It is a very important contribution when the psychological assessor alerts the therapist to potential problems. At times the assessor may "warn" the therapist of particular hazards.

Here is some material gleaned from a report whose recommendations alerted the therapist to some impending problem areas that have implications for the conduct and outcome of therapy. They

1. Warned the therapist of the client's morbid distress.
2. Warned of her tendency to test relationships with seduction.
3. Suggested the client's need to focus on her sense of inability to give.
4. Especially underscored her need to make commitments—with respect to relationships in general, and to treatment in particular.

In another case, where the time available for therapy was limited, but a favorable outcome was expected anyway, the assessor recommended that the therapist

1. Focus on reality.
2. Capitalize on the transference relationship.

In a third case, the assessor was of the opinion that the outcome would be poor, and it was. The report focused on morbid processes. Five main conclusions were:

1. A poor prognosis.
2. Poorly integrated defenses with potentiality for regression to severe psychopathology.
3. The possibility of suicide.
4. Markedly distorted perception of self and others.
5. Morbid preoccupation, rage, and helplessness.

Additional therapy-related material from Blank's cases suggests the range of possible therapeutic usefulness of psychological assessment:

1. The need to encourage expressions of anger.
2. The need to foster independent, autonomous behavior.
3. Alerting therapist to a 'stumbling block' posed by the "weaning process."
4. A discussion of defenses.
5. Basic mistrust in the patient.
6. The fear of self-examination.
7. The patient's need to examine family relationships.
8. A neurotic relationship with family members.
9. The need to tap rage that is confused with sexual concepts.
10. Tendencies to somatization.
11. Tendency not to confront conflicts.
12. Discussion of social defenses and related problems.
13. Inaccessible tendency to act out.
14. Need for special effort to promote secure, warm relationship in therapy.
15. Prediction of behavior in therapy.
16. Ego strength.
17. Social needs.
18. Need to understand and work with impulses.
19. Identity issues.
20. Need to proceed cautiously.

Prout's Assessment-Therapeutic Scheme

Prout (1986) presents a seven-part systematic and comprehensive approach to the assessment and treatment of children and adolescents:

1. *Establish a baseline.* In this first step, the assessor records the extent or the severity of the problem in both descriptive and quantitative terms. These data form a basis for initiating treatment and evaluating the efficacy of treatment as it proceeds.

2. *Pinpoint treatment targets.* "Pinpoint," or focus, is the key concept here. Themes or content to be dealt with are sharply defined.
3. *Assess developmental status.* Judgments of normality or abnormality are made relative to a client's age. Cognitive and language levels and social and emotional development must all be considered in treatment planning.
4. *Assess children's view of the problem.* Does the child perceive that he or she has a problem? If so, how does he or she understand the problem? The answers help to determine the nature of treatment or whether treatment is possible at all.
5. *Assess relevant environmental factors.* The impact of environmental factors (school, family, peers) is defined, and plans for dealing with disruptive factors are made.
6. *Select appropriate treatment strategy.* Prout advocates an eclectic approach, the role of assessment being to enable the therapist to tailor treatment to specific identified issues.
7. *Evaluate efficacy.* The purpose of this step is to evaluate program efficacy and/or to conduct research. The goal is to understand the effectiveness of various treatments with different disorders.

Butcher (1990) sets forth the use of the MMPI-2 as a road map which helps the client and therapist to their destination and also identifies the location of "minefields":

> Foremost among the benefits of pretherapy assessment is that psychological testing can provide information about motivation, fears, attitudes, defensive styles, and symptoms of which the client may be unaware...a normative framework from which such problems can be viewed.

Butcher identifies a special role for the validity scales:

> Through the use of the MMPI-2 validity indicators, the individual's openness to treatment can be discerned. It is usually assumed that patients who enter therapy are motivated to seek help and to become engaged in the task of describing and relating their problems to the therapist. It is further assumed that patients, because they want to be understood, are accessible to the therapist's inquiries and will disclose problems appropriately. Unfortunately, the assumption that patients are ready to engage in the treatment process is not always well founded. The MMPI-2 validity indicators provide a direct test of a patient's readiness for treatment. By directly assessing response attitudes, the therapist can evaluate the patient's level of cooperativeness and encourage or reinforce the willingness to engage in the task of self-disclosure. For example, patients who produce defensive, uncooperative test patterns, as reflected in the test validity scores, may likewise be relatively inaccessible to the therapist during sessions. When the therapist has this knowledge early in the treatment process, problems of lack of trust or hesitancy to disclose personal information can be confronted.

Appelbaum's Approach to Assessment for Psychotherapy

Adapted from a list of psychological assessment goals prepared by Schlesinger for training purposes, Appelbaum (1969) lists five categories of psychological information that can be helpful to the psychotherapist.

1. The illness from an adaptive point of view.
    a. Positive and negative consequences of the illness.
    b. The effect of the illness on object relations and transference paradigms.
    c. The identities the illness is modeled on.
2. The possibilities for other "choices," growth, and change.
    a. Strength of drive.
    b. Commitment to infantile patterns, and areas of "openness."
    c. Resiliency, acceptability of substitutes, possibilities for sublimation.
    d. Utilizability of anxiety or pain, and anxiety tolerance.
    e. Ability of the ego to function and grow under frustration.
3. Possibilities of further decompensation.
    a. Likely course of decompensation.
    b. Resiliency, ability to take distance.
    c. Capacity to withstand regression.
    d. Special areas of vulnerability—intolerant "superego," ego-weakness, specific conflicts and their associated trigger words and ideas.
4. Ego capacities.
    a. Psychological-mindedness.
    b. Humor.
    c. Objectivity.
5. Subjective experience.
    a. Moods.
    b. Attitudes.
    c. Emotional quality with which the environment is invested.
    d. Psychosexual level of experience which is most likely under what conditions.
    e. Repertoire of roles and identity fragments.[3]

---

[3] From Stephen A. Appelbaum, "Psychological Testing for the Psychotherapist," *Dynamic Psychiatry* 2, 158–163. Copyright © 1969 by Pinel-Verlags GmbH, Berlin, and reprinted by permission of the author and publisher.

12
THE CASE WORKUP

Following a common orientation, this chapter might have been called "Testing"—since this term is commonly applied to the activities discussed here. What follows, however, is broader than the mere activity of testing: selection and administration of instruments, and scoring and interpreting them. The case workup, by contrast, following the medical usage of the term, means that in addition to "running" tests, there is the larger goal of developing a plan of action. In psychological assessment, as conceptualized in previous chapters, testing occupies a position that is subordinate to fulfilling the consultant role, with the implications this holds for case formulation, and, is also subordinate, to borrow an expression from Meehl (1960), to "the cognitive activity of the clinician."

Of specific concern is the cognitive activity of the assessor who functions in a frame of reference that is in harmony with the clinical tradition as it has evolved and is evolving. In contrast to the standardized procedures upon which the measurement tradition rests, latitude and ad hoc resourcefulness in practice are valued among practitioners in the clinical tradition. Hence the following discussion of assessment in this tradition may approximate the practice of many assessors, but perhaps not entirely reflect what any of them do.

SELECTING A BATTERY

"Tests" are powerful tools of assessment, which, however, tend to overlap in the sort of information that can be gained from their use. Time constraints, therefore, and the need to limit the duplication of information dictate that the tests used in any given case be those judged by the assessor as capable of targeting defined areas of interest. Thus, of the large number of psychological instruments available for clinical assessment, the typical assessor approaches each problem with just a few of these, which he or she selects on the basis both of the characteristics of the instruments and experience.

Allison, Blatt, and Zimet (1988), in their basically Rapaportian (Rapaport, Gill, & Schafer, 1945, 1946), ego-psychological orientation provide explicit rationale for their selection of a basic assessment battery for use with adults—the WAIS, the Rorschach, and the TAT, a mainstay of many assessors that is irreverently dubbed the "holy trinity" in some settings. In addition to these, other instruments commonly included in a basic battery are such old stand-bys as the MMPI, the Bender Gestalt, Figure Drawing, HTP, and a sentence completion test.

It makes sense, according to Allison, Blatt, and Zimet, to include the WAIS in a battery because it taps "highly logical, reality-oriented, secondary process modes of thought." Its basic function, however, "is to assess certain adaptive potentials of the individual, namely, his ability to function effectively in relatively impersonal situations which involve past achievements and current problem solving efforts." Further, these authors stress the role of the WAIS in revealing the "ego processes which [the client] uses to integrate and adapt to reality demands." They remind us that the WAIS, like the Rorschach and TAT, "may contain representations of drive, conflict, defense, and adaptive endeavors."

The TAT taps "less conventionally constrained thinking" than the WAIS. It yields data that are more "personal,"—that is, not merely a recitation of stereotyped cultural material ("Why should we keep away from bad company?"), and also interpersonal. Allison et al. challenge the ego-psychological position that whereas the value of the Rorschach is in disclosing the structure and organization of personality, the rationale for using the TAT lies in its ability to define the content of personality. They advance the proposition, that the TAT also reveals structural features of personality. Through the use of both instruments "one can identify when and how representations of drives are successfully integrated in an adaptive way and when synthesizing ego functions are overwhelmed or fail to operate effectively."

In contrast to this reasoned approach to selecting instruments for inclusion in a battery, most assessors constitute a battery with no such explicit, well-thought-out rationale or attention to validity studies (Reynolds, 1979; Reynolds & Sundberg, 1976; Wade & Baker, 1977). Various reasons have been advanced to explain this fact. Personal experience with tests was the major reason for using them that was offered by clinicians in the Wade and Baker survey.

GATHERING NECESSARY DATA

The reason for which an assessment is carried out guides the collection of data. Information that the assessor judges to be potentially useful in solving the problem at hand is noted and retained for inclusion in a working data mix. Data that are interesting but judged not to be relevant to this purpose are bypassed. Thus, in responding to consultation from a neurologist concerning the competence of a brain-damaged patient to function extramurally, the psychological assessor might become aware of interesting information that might be useful in another, but not the present context. He or she might judge that pursuing further a recorded history of the patient being sexually abused as a child or of psychophysiologic skin disorder would not contribute to dealing with the present problem.

In seeking data that are relevant to the purpose of an assessment, much more than the client's test productions may be fair game. The assessor observes the client's test performance, of course, and also records responses given orally, including exact verbalizations. He or she solicits relevant matters of history, listens to whatever else the patient offers that may be pertinent, and observes overall appearance, bearing, dress, grooming, and anomalies. Speech manner and speech content, spontaneity, and social manner are all of interest. And so on. When you shake the client's hand, are the palms moist, or really wet? Are the hands tremulous? Does "nervousness" become particularly evident when certain topics are broached? Is their a body odor? Does the client walk on a broad base or with a stuttering gait?

The psychological assessor is constrained to appropriate to the assessment whatever pertinent nontest data are available. These include such nontest data as above, and collateral data that may be available through others. The assessor may appropriate data from such sources as the statement of the problem in the request for assessment, members of the client's family, a social history, a mental status examination, a discharge summary, a team conference, or transactions with individual team members.

The most obvious use of data involves determining how they can contribute to solving a problem, a task that generally involves more or less interpretation. A less obvious use of data is their use in developing still more data, or richer data, to be interpreted. Any bit of information given by the client may suggest the need for follow-up. When a client completes the sentence root, "What I want out of life..." with the word "happiness" (as many clients do), the assessor may ask for elaboration and tap into such areas as the client's mood, frustrated goals, self-image, living conditions, interpersonal situation, employment status, and so forth. Inquiry following the client's Rorschach or TAT responses commonly yields meaningful data in excess of the client's original offering. Testing the limits, a specialized means of clarifying and probing for additional data that is closely identified with Rorschach administration, can be successfully used with other instruments.

Clearly, the assessor exercises a role in data gathering that is considerably more active than the "passive" role of administering test items and recording responses (Rosenwald, 1963; p. 37). The assessor's awareness that he or she is in a participant-observer role enhances the data yield by being attuned to the transference-countertransference features of the assessment transaction. The assessor must question what about himself or herself might contribute to certain behaviors on the part of the client—hostility or deference, for example. And the assessor must also look inward to find answers to such questions as why he or she likes a client, or why he or she is unusually impatient for a testing session to come to a close.

THE ROLE OF SCORING

Scoring of responses is variously practiced—or not practiced—in psychological assessment. It would be unthinkable for the assessor to administer certain instruments without fully scoring them, and, as called for by usage of the instrument, working up such matters of interest as percentages, ratios, and profiles. Many assessors dispense with this routine, however, when using certain other instruments.

He or she may forego the assignment of scores to responses, and add them up or put them in configurations that are widely accepted as having interpretive significance. Others—four out of five in the case of those who score Rorschach responses—"personalize" their scoring (Exner & Exner, 1972). "Most alter the method in which they have been trained with other methods or personal experience." With the current availability of the Rorschach *Comprehensive System* (Exner, 1978, 1986), the numbers of those who personalize might be less.

Information concerning norming and validity status should be helpful to practitioners in deciding whether they should score responses or limit their efforts to qualitative evaluation of data.

An MMPI or MCMI would be rather meaningless without scores, and an unscored Wechsler scale surely would have far less meaning than it might have if fully scored. But even before scores are recorded, inspection of the client's responses could yield meaningful data about the client's personality *and* intelligence. Scoring, however, makes available more useful data for estimating the client's intelligence, together with other features of cognitive functioning *and* of personality.

Similarly, we would frequently lose too much valuable information by not scoring scorable neuropsychological data. But qualitative data are also widely regarded to be meaningful in neuropsychological assessment, so much so that to neglect them would be irresponsible. Luria's highly respected, but nonstandardized approach relied heavily on qualitative features of patient performance, while Golden, Hammeke, and Purisch (1985) sought to capture Luria's method in their Luria-Nebraska Neuropsychological Battery, a psychometric instrument.

Whether the standardized battery of Golden et al. should find clinical application seems largely to rest on competing claims and opinions. At the same time, the work of Luria continues to be a subject for review. Neither the selection of a qualitative or a quantitative method, of itself, guarantees success in clinical application. Goldstein's (1984) appraisal is to the point:

> Various opinions have...been raised with regard to whether it is proper to utilize the Luria-Nebraska in clinical situations. My view of the matter would be that it may be so used as long as inferences made from it do not go beyond what can be based on the available research literature. In particular, the test consumer should not be led to believe that administration and interpretation of the Luria-Nebraska Battery provide an assessment of the type that would have been conducted by Luria and his coworkers, or that one is providing an application of Luria's method. The procedure is specifically not Luria's method at all, and the view that it provides valid measures of Luria's constructs and theories has not been verified. Even going beyond that point, attempts to verify some of Luria's hypotheses (e.g. Drewe, 1975; Goldberg

& Tucker, 1979) have not always been completely successful. Therefore clinical interpretations, even when they are based on Luria's actual method of investigation, may be inaccurate because of inaccuracies in the underlying theory.

We have already indicated that practices with respect to Rorschach scoring differ widely (e.g., Exner & Exner, 1972); (p. 106). At one extreme is the closely prescribed practice of scoring and tabulating to create a *structural summary* (Exner, 1986). At the other is the use of the instrument as an *interview tool*, as sanctioned by Zubin, Eron, and Schumer (1965), an endorsement supported both by the demonstrated strengths of the interview method and the dim view that these authors, and many others, take of Rorschach validity.

The continuing woes surrounding the question of the psychometric validity of the Rorschach make it difficult, so far as many psychologists are concerned, to defend scoring on a cost basis as well as on a scientific basis. Were the evidence for psychometric validity more encouraging, Rorschach critics would no doubt agree that the time required to score a protocol would not only be justified, but mandatory.

The Thematic Apperception Test (TAT) is much less involved in controversy over scoring. It "remains today an impressionistic instrument in the eyes of many psychologists, and not a test at all in terms of standardization data, reliability, or validity. Its popularity as a clinical instrument has continued to be high" (Vane, 1981).

INTERPRETIVE STRATEGIES

Although data may be transformed into meaningful conclusions of interest rather instantaneously, as in intuition (pp. 29–31), the interpretation of data involves several components. Reflection commonly is involved in extracting from data the insights that may be brought to bear on the problem that is the reason for carrying out an assessment.

Problem Definition

Several issues underlie the need to generate and interpret data when an assessment is done. First is the need to understand what the problem consists of. The client, herself or himself, simply may not know accurately what the problem is. ("I can't seem to concentrate on my studies and I'm afraid of flunking two courses. I don't know why.") ("I'm 'oversexed'" is the client's complaint. The clinician surmises a sex conflict based on yet-to-be clarified problems.) Or, the client may choose not to disclose what the problem is, for whatever reason. A clinician (or other referring party) may also be uncertain what the problem is, and clinicians may disagree on this issue. There may be a latent and a manifest reason for referral (Cohen, 1980; p. 35). At times the assessor can best define the problem only through the use of his or her data!

Clinical Communication

Matters of clinical communication must always be of concern to the assessor. Deliberately or otherwise, various inaccuracies detract from the communicative efficacy of both everyday and clinical speech. Incomplete and misleading communications are commonplace.

How often do you hear such expressions as "Are you kidding?, Get to the point," or "Stop beating around the bush." Common expressions of clinicians and interviewers include: "Can you tell me more about that?, I'm not sure what you mean," or "Can you put that another way?" Clinicians, and others, also seek to clarify and gain additional information simply by repeating content or reflecting feeling in the manner of Carl Rogers: "So you just told him to 'get lost,' That sure must have been a frightening experience."

Another basic factor is that language is laced with metaphors and idioms: Red stands for danger, and the expression, "He makes me sick" has no reference to the health of the one who speaks these words. The psychological assessor constantly deals with metaphors and idioms in the process of interpreting data—what the client says in conversation and in responding to test items.

The usage here of the term metaphor is more or less in the vein of Duhl (1983): "Metaphor is the linkage of meaning—that which connects any two events, ideas, characteristics, modes." Thus, recollected dreams or TAT stories are metaphorical, as are idiosyncratic modes of reproducing Bender-Gestalt figures. Assessment, in fact, requires that we be attuned to the idiom of each instrument we employ. What leads to understanding a client's intellectual or personality functioning do we gain from an IQ, the relation of the Verbal IQ to the Performance IQ, or the discrepancy between Comprehension and Information subtests? Starting on page 299 is a discussion of test idiom, with specific reference to Bender Gestalt and Rorschach idiom.

Some Basic Interpretive Logic

Normative approach The normative approach, which is basic to nomothetic personality study and highlights individual differences, is, of course, basic to psychometrics. Assessment is basically idiographic; but nevertheless, the assessor values normative data. How an individual compares with others can be highly significant in working up a case. Knowing that a person is too dependent, too angry, too withdrawn; or underassertive, underintelligent, or underimaginative can be a valuable ingredient in the data mix.

Both the assessor and the psychometrician may employ data based on careful measurement. The assessor, however, may employ less-rigorous data when careful measurement is not feasible. Such is ordinarily the case, for example, when the unnormed TAT, or an interview, is used as a data source. In such cases the assessor uses norms based on experience, sometimes called "personal norms."

Inference Also subjective is clinical inference, a manner of processing data by the use of logic (reasoning, judgment), particularly the time-honored methods of deduction and induction. Previous observations and judgments or beliefs are involved in the making of inferences. Thus, Trimboli and Kilgore (1983) exemplify the making of (logical) inferences from objective data, such as from MMPI scale elevations. Rorschachers may regard a client's unrestrained exclamations, such as "Oh, Wow!" in response to blots as suggestive of a deficiency of emotional control, and perhaps further, as suggestive of certain diagnostic categories. Such inferences differ in compellingness and pertinence to the case at hand, and generally need to be weighed and combined with other inferences before possibly including them as a conclusion of the assessment.

Considerations of the client's projections commonly figure prominently in inferential reasoning. Projection evidently is not a single operation, however, and its role in assessment is not firmly established. Thus, Exner (1989) discerns little projection as happening when a subject responds to Rorschach stimuli:

> Unfortunately the Rorschach has erroneously been mislabeled as a *projective test* for too long, and that label has often encouraged interpreters to attempt to derive some meaning from the content of every answer. Many answers are simply the result of classifying the blot areas in ways that are compatible with the stimulus field. They are not projections. In fact, it is possible for a subject to give a reliable, valid protocol without including any projected material in the responses.

A number of concepts of projection have been advanced since Freud's (1894/1962) first use of the term. Holmes (1968) proposes that projection differs in terms of whether the individual "projects his own trait or a different (complementary) trait, and whether the individual is aware or unaware of possessing the trait which results in the projection."

In what Holmes calls *complementary projection*, the person projects a trait that is different from a trait he or she is aware of possessing. The existence of such projection is supported by research. Murray (1933), for example, induced fright in young girls by involving them in a game of "murder." Following the game, the subjects were more likely than previously to see persons in photographs as *frightening*, in contrast to their own *frightened* selves.

In *attributive projection*, the individual projects onto others characteristics which are identical to his or her own and are a matter of full awareness. The person holds the naive belief that we are all alike, that we all have the same hopes, frustrations, and outlook on life. Cattell (1944) coined the acronym "NIPE" (naive inference based on limited personal experience) to describe the phenomenon and account for its existence. Such projection has been substantiated both by research and clinical observation. A client may, for example, comment on giving a story to a TAT card, "This is me," or "This is the story of my life."

Similarity projection involves the attribution to others of certain self-characteristics of which one is unaware. Also called *classical projection*, the term generally has reference to the projection of unacceptable and painful features, such as the projection in paranoia as described by Freud (1911/1949). Although clinicians commonly report experience with such projection, supportive research findings are lacking. The concept should therefore be used with particular caution in assessment.

Panglossian-Cassandran projection refers to the projection of characteristics that are the opposite of one's own and of which the person is not aware. The Panglossian version involves the projection of positive views (in a denial of a negative outlook on life). "This is the best of all possible worlds" is the motto. "Everyone is wonderful." In contrast, the Cassandran projector holds a sour outlook on the world and the people who inhabit it. However, Holmes observes, "There have been no attempts to verify Cassandran projection, and it is suggested that psychologists take a tip from Apollo, who decreed that Cassandra, the prophetess of evil, be ignored."

What implications does Holmes's review hold for the psychological assessor? Obviously, he advises wariness:

> What might be concluded about a male who saw a lone male TAT figure as sexually arousing? The position of similarity projection would indicate that he unconsciously saw himself as a sexually arousing person. On the other hand, complementary projection would suggest that the subject was sexually aroused (not arousing) and that he was using the presence of the male figure as a cause or justification for his arousal. Needless to say, the implications stemming from these two interpretations are radically different. To further complicate the issue, if we use an attributive interpretation we would conclude that the individual consciously thought of himself as sexually arousing. Last, the concept of Panglossian projection would imply that the individual was defending against an unconscious self-perception as a sexually nonarousing person by projecting an image of what he wished were actually the case. *Because the interpretation of almost any response would be changed by employing a different type of projection for the analysis, and because there are no guidelines to indicate what type of projection is being used when, the usefulness of the concept of projection in its usual form is considerably reduced.*
>
> The review of the research literature on various types of projection offered strong support for those types in which the projector is conscious of his projection (i.e., complementary and attributive projection). Further, a number of specific predictions from theories advanced to account for this type of responding have been consistently borne out by experimental data. It can be concluded that individuals do in fact attribute to others either their own characteristics of which they are conscious, or the justification for these characteristics. Valuable and productive advances have been made in understanding this type of responding.
>
> The review revealed no support for the projection of characteristics which stem from a characteristic of which the would-be projector is the unconscious possessor (i.e., similarity and Panglossian-Cassandran projection). This is particularly interesting since the type of projection most frequently referred to or implied is similarity or "classical" projection (emphasis added).

Cookbooks Combinations of empirical data and clinical impressionism have led to the accumulation of lists of what various scores, singly and grouped, and observations of qualitative performance "mean." These are scattered throughout the literature and are available in various compilations, such as

Gilbert (1978, 1980), Ogdon (1981), and deMendonca, Elliott, Goldstein, McNeill, Rodriguez, and Zelkind (1984).

Thus, in Gilbert we find the following interpretive material that may be gained from the manner in which Bender-Gestalt figures are reproduced. From Figure A the assessor may gain information regarding "capacity for integrating conflictual elements." Figure 1 discloses "attitudes toward regularity and importance of detail," Figure 3 reveals the client's "handling of instinctual drives," and Figure 5 is a source of data concerning "basic sexual identification." Looking at line quality, we note that "very heavy, very light, or markedly inconsistent line quality" is an indicator of "neurosis."

Ogdon's (1981) combing of the literature typically yields an assortment of interpretations. For example, for the Rorschach Whole response, a greater-than-average number might have such meanings as "high intelligence with good problem solving or artistic ability, especially if of satisfactory quality," a "high energy level," or "anxiety and stress." In women, however, more than the average number of Whole responses might suggest "tendencies toward sweeping verbalizations, ambitiousness, and masculine strivings."

The goal of deMendonca et al. (1984) was to establish an "MMPI-based behavior descriptor/personality trait list." This was accomplished by searching through 10 works on the MMPI and extracting from them thousands of descriptive terms that were associated with elevations on the validity and clinical scales. Those descriptors that achieved a consensus level of 50 percent or more of the authors were then matched with entries on the Gough adjective check list (1952, 1980). Emerging was a list of descriptors for high scorers on the various scales, and also for low-scorers on most of the scales. A high score on validity Scale F, for example, might indicate that the person who achieved such a score may be restless, unstable, changeable, confused, dissatisfied, moody, and opinionated. A low-scorer may be described as "simple."

These illustrations exemplify the stuff of which cookbooks are made. They may be used by an assessor to translate responses and scores into conclusions. They may also form the basis for the development of algorithms to be written into computer programs for interpreting data.

Drawbacks include the obvious fact that many of the descriptors tend to be vague or general. (What can we do with the information that a person has indicators of "neurosis"—a term that covers such diverse disorders as dysthymia, the various anxiety and phobic disorders, and the several dissociative disorders?) It could be difficult to relate some of these descriptive statements to many of the reasons for which assessment is done.

Specifically with respect to the Rorschach, but having significance for other instruments, Rapaport et al. (Rapaport, Gill, & Schafer, 1946) caution against the "temptation—especially for the beginner"—to resort to "dream-books"— a descriptive term that apparently antedates the psychologist's use of "cookbook." The "temptation" of which they write is "to translate a multitude of highly refined scores into 'psychological' statements with the help of a source book of interpretations, and then to throw these psychological 'dream-book' statements together in an interpretation-hash. Regrettably enough, the literature is replete with interpretations in which 'significance of a score' has replaced clinical psychological thinking and understanding of subjects."

Test idiom Interpretation, of course, does not take place in a vacuum. All interpretation, if it is to be meaningful and have practical value, is done with the reason for assessment in mind. This is true in the interpretive mode discussed on the following pages and also when working with research-derived relationships between responses and scores, on the one hand, and interpretations or descriptive statements on the other.

All approaches to interpretation must actively take into consideration whatever pertinent empirical relations have been (reasonably well) established between test data and conclusions. In addition, it is proposed here, as has long been argued and practiced, that a qualitative analysis of test performance can provide abundant rich data. This is accomplished through the translation of the metaphors that constitute the features of responses that traditionally have been scored, and also the unscorable features of responses. Further, such collateral information as observations, verbalizations that are not related to test responses, history, and information gathered by others is included in the data mix. The idea is not to accumulate material to pad the report. It is to strengthen and better illuminate your own data as presented in the context of a new integration.

Each instrument has an idiomatic slant that is largely peculiar to itself, and the individual idiomatic expressions that are discerned often can be translated into clinically meaningful statements. These can usefully be related to other discrete items of information, and to the reason for assessment. If not relatable to the reason for assessment, however, the information probably is not of practical value. For example, one or a number of responses may lead to the firm conclusion that the client is introverted—which can be useless information if the reason for assessment does not pertain to the client's social adjustment.

Although single responses may hold interpretively very rich data, as a general proposition it is best not to rely on gaining conclusions in isolated responses on a one-to-one basis. Impressionistic conclusions are best derived from an accumulation and patterning of responses.

This reasoning is inherent in the logic of interviewing, an approach to eliciting information, assessing behavior, and formulating a personality picture. Psychological assessment, generally, may rest heavily on interview methods. But because many psychological instruments are commonly labeled as "tests," they are held by many to be in sharp contradistinction to the method of interview.

The interview value of instruments such as the WAIS tends to be underrecognized because its psychometric role is so firmly established. The "Rorschach test," lacking generally accepted psychometric validity, has been a better candidate for alternative conceptualization as an interview. Zubin (1954, 1956b) is among the earliest observers to publicize the Rorschach as psychometrically weak, but of value as an interview technique (pp. 43, 105). Ainsworth (Chapter 14 in B. Klopfer et al., 1954) considered the Rorschach similarly: "It is more productive to view the Rorschach technique as a method of observation and appraisal than to class it as a 'test' of personality."

Zubin, Eron, and Schumer (1965) observe that...

> the words, phrases, and content of the responses are often diagnostic in themselves. Some of the successful inferences made by the Rorschach expert depend not on the Rorschach technique *per se*, but on the interview-like material which the protocols provide. Thus, intellectual level can be estimated from the vocabulary level of the responses, bizarre thinking from the outlandish responses given by S, and perseverative tendencies from the actual perseveration of responses. These are not basically Rorschach factors in the same sense as are W, M, and FC.

The widely accepted approaches of content interpretation and impressionism may be incorporated into a comprehensive system of interviewing, utilizing a variety of psychological instruments. Meaningful scores may be part of the interview data mix, just as they are in some structured interviews.

The translation of metaphors, as they tend to occur in the idioms of various tests, is considered in the ensuing discussion. The approach is consistent with Schafer's (1976) action language, which emphasizes what an individual *does* rather than what she or he *is* or *has*. In the interpretation of content derived with the aid of psychological instruments, characteristics of both the individual and the test stimuli are considered. Examples on the following pages illustrate the translation of responses to, and reproduction of, Bender-Gestalt figures, and responses given to Rorschach cards.

The rationale of this approach rests on the assumption that responses to psychological stimuli are representative of, or samples of, a general disposition. This logic is followed in the interpretation of all transactions in the clinical situation. If the client is rude and surly to the assessor, it is likely that such responses are prominent in the client's interpersonal repertoire, a conclusion that is strengthened if the assessor rarely encounters such behavior and does not relate provocatively.

Similar reasoning is followed in the interpretation of test stimuli. When a client is careless and reckless in responding to questions or performing tasks, we presume that such behavior likely is present in nontest situations. When a client performs better in structured than nonstructured test situations, it is likely that he or she also requires much structure in everyday living. And, the quality of cognition, as measured by intelligence tests, is regarded as a valid indicator of the quality of cognition in nontest situations.

A BRIEF DISCOURSE ON RATIONALE IN PSYCHOLOGICAL INTERPRETATION

Interpretive rationale is a blend of research data and theorizing. Based on the input of scientists and practitioners, material on this topic is scattered throughout the literature and is not uniform. What follows is a sketchy overview of the sort of reasoning that enters a case workup.

Under the headings *Bender-Gestalt* and *Rorschach* is a brief exposure to the sort of understandings that are useful in the interpretation of responses to these instruments. In the workup that concludes this chapter the application of rationale to case material is illustrated.

Bender-Gestalt

The above observations concerning the relation of psychological data to the general disposition of the client are consistent with our understanding of the *projective hypothesis*—which pertains to how the individual structures unstructured material, thus evidencing his or her "private world." Rabin (1968) discusses how this hypothesis pertains to the Bender-Gestalt test, an instrument originally used as a perceptual-motor test of development:

> Almost any kind of standardized testing situation, even the type that employs standard and structured stimuli, may offer the clinician an opportunity for projective interpretation. In such instances the examiner does not focus solely upon the "correctness" of the response to, let us say, an intelligence test question. He is more concerned with the subtler aspects of the response that are beyond formal correctness or incorrectness. The subject's "cognitive style," manner of reasoning, idiosyncratic content, and patterns of successes and failures become grist for the interpretive mill. The subject projects of himself in addition to offering objectively correct or incorrect answers or responses.

Hutt (1968) describes his interpretive approach as a *clinical-intuitive method of analysis.* He explains this method with particular attention to the nonuse of scoring, or to limitations in the use of scoring:

> Any armchair analyst can make "wild analyses" of the data available. The role of the clinician-scientist is much more difficult and much more responsible. Although it may be popular to utilize some objective scoring scheme which others have developed without any particular concern for its rationale, such usage may lead to serious abuse of the "test's" potentialities. Even when some scoring method has been carefully validated, the serious clinician will wish to know the limitations of such validity studies and the hypotheses which generated them. Only then can he properly apply the method to a particular case, for only then will he be aware of the degree to which generalizations about the "scale" have meaning in a given case. The use of objective scoring methods has many advantages, but they also have serious limitations.

Interpretation of the Bender starts while the procedure is being structured. Is the client cooperative, affable, resistive, negativistic, perhaps casting aspersions on the "silliness" of the task? Does the request to reproduce unfamiliar figures cause the client to feel challenged or anxious? Or require additional instructions or support? Although the instructions of most assessors allow considerable freedom, simply giving instructions to the effect of "Copy the designs as well as you can," some clients seek support with such queries as "Is this O.K.?," "Shall I start here?," or "Where should I put them?"

Hutt systematizes his analysis by first classifying clients' reproductions into five categories.

(1) *Organization* is divided into several subcategories. One of these, *Sequence*, which itself is further divided according to whether the position of the reproduced figures is *Overly Methodical, Methodical, Irregular,* or *Confused* or *Symbolic*. An overly methodical sequence tends to correlate with an overly methodical approach to life situations, that is, compulsive or perfectionistic. A confused sequence may parallel the confused thinking of a schizophrenic.

(2) *Size* of the drawn figures commonly reflects variables such as emotional state or effort expended. Highly anxious clients may dramatically reduce the size of figures, while clients in an expansive mood may greatly enlarge the figures, a manic individual perhaps using a sheet of paper for each figure.

(3) *Change in Form of the Gestalt* involves such changes to the stimulus figures as *Closure Difficulty, Curvature Difficulty,* and *Change in Angulation*. Certain behavioral correlates of these have been reported. On the first figure, for example, Figure A (a circle joined to a square that is rotated 45 degrees), the two components of the figure—which may symbolize female and male qualities—when drawn separated from one another frequently leads to the interpretation that the individual has a problem in interpersonal relations (cannot relate closely), or, more specifically, in male-female relations.

(4) Severely distorted figures are classified as *Distortion of the Gestalt*. These reflect the manner in which the individual interacts with life situations. Failure to respect the reality of the forms and to integrate them into a meaningful pattern is paralleled by failure to integrate one's experiences and to deal with them according to commonly accepted standards. This observation pertains both to overt behaviors and to the thought processes. Distortions may, of course, reflect a style of life. Careless or rebellious people may produce slapdash figures.

(5) *Movement and Drawing*, the fifth category, is concerned with the manner in which figures are drawn. Clockwise movement, for example, is most typical in reproducing figures, and individuals who oppose this trend are also inclined to show oppositional personality trends.

In addition to this systematic approach to interpreting Bender reproductions, numerous studies (quite a few of them contributed by Hutt) have been gleaned from the literature by Gilbert (1978). Interpretations are offered for 18 features of Bender reproduction, including such considerations as Arrangement, Distortion, Line Quality, Margin, Perseveration, and Pressure.

Under Distortion, for example, it is noted that distorting dots into dashes is an indicator of impulsivity, and enlargement of the square (but not the circle) of Figure A demonstrates masculinity strivings. Concerning the pressure with which the subject bears down when reproducing figures, light line drawings are reported as an indicator of passivity while heavy pressure reveals externalized anxiety.

Rorschach

The Rorschach is a vastly more complex instrument than many of the other tools in the psychological assessor's armamentarium. Responses to a number of these tend to be more self-evident in their meaning than is the case with many Rorschach variables.

For example, in the above illustrations of performance on the Bender, one can empathize with the greater effort it takes to copy dots that are reasonable facsimiles of the stimulus material than it is to simply dash off short lines. Try it. Hence it is a small step to conclude that those who make dashes rather than dots are evidencing impulsive behavior. In a similar exercise in empathy, you can conclude that those who draw heavy lines are experiencing greater hand tension than those who draw light lines. Again, you can experience the difference by drawing both light and heavy lines. You can also look at the sheet of paper from the back and note how the pressure of the pencil "comes through" when heavy lines are drawn. Other widely used instruments, such as the TAT, also may be a source of useful conclusions in the absence of extensive training, even in the hands of untrained persons, as demonstrated by Bettelheim (1947) and Luborsky (1952) (pp. 333–334).

Attempts to demystify the Rorschach have gained from the development of a logic of responding to the blots. The basic approach to establishing a rationale for the many responses that people offer to these stimuli derives to an appreciable extent from the work of Rapaport, Gill, and Schafer (1946), and is discussed in a number of subsequent works, of which Schafer (1948) and Holt (1967) are landmarks.

Does it follow from the availability of scores for which rationales have been provided that all Rorschachs be scored and tabulated? That depends on the level of credence you place on these rationales, how you understand the pertinent psychometric research on Rorschach validity, and your own experience with the instrument. There are, after all, various problems with the validity concept and its applications, and the Rorschach has validity problems that are peculiar to itself. As with other instruments, there can be no one meaning to be attached to a given Rorschach protocol apart from the reason for obtaining it. As a problem-solving instrument, Rorschach data are differentially applied to different problem situations.

Those who consider the Rorschach as an interview needn't restrict the meaning of interview data to personal information, verbalizations, clinical behaviors, and the like. The production of many Whole responses, or a number of poor Form responses, or a paucity of Popular responses may also be regarded as interview data.

The availability of rationales for such Rorschach variables as these can be very helpful to the psychological assessor in thinking through the meaning of client productions. These rationales, however, do not provide simple formulas for translating responses into conclusions. The relationship between response and interpretation can, in fact, be quite complex. One-to-one relationships, as set forth below by way of offering a preliminary handle on the rationale of some of the major Rorschach variables, are not the rule. Individual scores, rather, take on their full significance in a configural context.

The responses for which rationales are sought are classified into three main categories that account for the elements that are considered in the interpretive process. First, in Rorschach language, is *Location*—the area of the blot where the subject reports a percept—the entire blot, for example, or a large commonly identified detail of the blot. *Determinants* are the features of the blot that help to *determine* the response that is given. Is the subject influenced to report "a bear" because a particular area of the blot recollects the form (or shape) of a bear, or "spilled paint" because the color of a blot area could be the color of paint? The third category is for the classification of *Content*—what the person sees, such as humans, animals, objects, landscapes, sex, disease, and so forth. In addition, scoring systems note if the response is *Popular* or *Original*, the former usually being defined as a response that occurs in at least one of three records and the latter as occurring no more than once in a hundred protocols.

Rationale of the Whole response Consider the significance of the Whole response (W), the designation applied when the client's percept includes the entire blot area. Since Rorschach's (1921/1951) introduction of the instrument, the offering by the client of W responses has been considered an intellectual exercise, specifically one of "abstracting, surveying, and integrating" (Rapaport, Gill, & Schafer, 1946). For example, some subjects "may attempt to cope with all the discrepant features of the inkblot; in these cases we usually have a spectacle of uncertainty, self-doubt, self-criticism, and rejection of response possibilities or actual responses." It is evident that the Rapaport group incorporated qualitative features of Rorschach performance in gaining understanding of features of both the general personality and intellectual functioning.

Beyond this generality, "four major kinds of W response" were identified in the Rapaportian approach. W+ refers to whole responses that are "sharply seen and integrated in a convincing way." These responses are usually combinations of details, such as the response to Card I "two angels carrying a headless woman to heaven." (Rapaport et al.) Subvariations of the W+ response include *integrated* W+ responses (emphasizing associative processes) and *abstract* W+ responses —high quality responses indicating imagination that is in tune with reality.

The Wo, by contrast, is a good response; it is of plus quality, which signifies that by consensus, the shape of the blot is a good match for what the subject calls it. Thus, on Card V, almost everyone sees a bat or a butterfly. It is an ordinary response. By itself it is indicative neither of pathology nor of imagination or high intellect.

Wv is a vague, whole response—such as "a map"—which has no definite shape unless specified as a map of some particular country or region. This is not a high-level intellectual production. It may indicate evasiveness, low involvement with the task, or an offhandish approach to problems. A number of such responses in a record could point to pathology.

W- is a W whole response whose shape does not conform well with the shape of the blot; it is arbitrary and undercritical. The (personal) associations of the subject take precedence over the consensual physical reality of the blot, perhaps parallel with a tendency of the individual to allow personal beliefs and needs to overshadow what most of us regard as reality.

A variation of the W- is the DW, recognized by Rorschach (1921/1951) as occurring "in many unintelligent normals, in morons, in epileptics, in organic cases, and in schizophrenics." Called a *Confabulated Whole*, Rorschach defined DW as the score when "the Whole is arrived at from a detail." To Card I, for example, the subject may accurately (consensually) perceive human feet at the bottom of the blot, and from that generalize that the entire blot resembles a human—which it does not resemble at all (again consensually). This is patently faulty reasoning, and is likely to be indicative of the disordered thinking of schizophrenia or among others with disturbed cognition.

This introduction to the Whole response reflects only part of the significance that this group of responses holds. The Rorschacher will note, for example, if Ws are few or many as a percentage of total responses produced, and in relation to other locations of the blot selected, particularly large usual details (D responses). The cards on which the W responses are seen is also of importance. It is much easier, for example, to produce a W response to Cards I and V than to IX and X.

Exner (1986) includes in his analysis of the W response the subject's efforts in organizing the stimulus field (Zf), the quality of this effort (DQ), and the efficiency displayed in processing the stimuli (Zd). Rorschachers have long valued the significance of the relation of Whole responses to responses that are indicative of Human Movement (M). The rationale rests on understanding that W, as an organized response, indicates striving, and M as indicative of fantasizing, reasoning, contemplating. Is the individual's "push" more or less in balance with capacity?

Many Rorschachers also take cognizance of responses that include most, but not all, of the blot area. These are scored W̶—"Cut-Off W." People who respond in this way are displaying test-taking behavior that involves precision, carefulness, meticulousness, and perhaps rigidity. We would look for this sort of behavior in individuals who produce W̶s, particularly a number of them.

Rationale of the Detail response Most of the responses in a Rorschach record consist of large Detail responses. These are easier than Whole responses for the client to discern. Hence individuals who overemphasize D responses, to the relative neglect of W responses, tend to be concerned with the obvious and not very accepting of challenges. To produce a D requires less involvement with the task, less effort; hence those whose records emphasize D are not likely to be very ambitious. Depressed people, of course, commonly evidence low drive, and many of them produce an excess of D, some of them limiting their productivity to one D per card. We would also expect their thinking to be concrete rather than abstract.

Rationale of the Form response The Form response (F) is generally considered to reflect intellectual activity, particularly reasoning. Emotional response is not evident in F. The subject perceives form and then associates to it: "This looks like a butterfly. Here are wings, body, legs, antennae." There is little in the way of spontaneity or emotionality here. Obviously, the personality trends that F represents must be balanced with less controlled behaviors that are more responsive to instinctual strivings. Civilized living requires what is represented in the F response. However, F significantly in excess of what is seen in most records is indicative of an overcontrolled, underresponsive, emotionally constricted individual.

The quality of the F response, the extent to which the response is consensual or conforming to the contours of the blot, is a major consideration in Rorschach interpretation. F+ responses are in harmony with consensual logic—many others make the same response, or can empathize with it. Hence F+ is regarded as an indicator of respect for reality. Poor Form responses, F-, on the other hand, particularly when present in abundance, may be indicative of poor reality testing and thus may identify psychotic thinking. (See also the more detailed discussion of the development of a rationale for the F response, pp. 110–111)

Rationale of the Human Movement response The Human Movement response (M) is scored when the subject sees a human in actual movement or in a lifelike posture (there is some variation in the definition of this response). To see a human in a lifelike stance, one must perceive the *form* of a human figure, hence "All M is F." Further, M is a relatively mature response associated with intellectual activity, and that tends not to occur in the records of young children.

M is associated with the "inner life," and persons who produce a number of M are sometimes described as having a "rich inner life." An "M person" tends to have an extensive fantasy life, to reflect on matters before taking action. An imaginative life can be gratifying, but, individuals who overemphasize M in their Rorschachs may be handicapped by obsessive thinking and destructive doubting. On the other hand, those who show a paucity of M, no more than one such response, may be inhibited, anxious, or depressed. When M is of poor form (M-), or occurs in small details of the blot, we may suspect autistic trends in the person who produces them. Such trends may alert us to possible severe maladjustment or to schizophrenia. But they may also be found in normals, and particularly in normals who are highly intelligent, imaginative, and creative.

Rationale of the Color response The Color response is associated with emotionality, both with the outward expression of emotion (affect) and with the control, or undercontrol of emotion. Color responses have much to do with the person's interaction with the environment, particularly with social relations. M responses and Color responses, then, reflect somewhat opposite (but not opposing) tendencies, in the sense of being incompatible). Both tendencies, within limits, are desirable and present in well-adjusted persons. A crucial Rorschach feature that is useful in judging the balance between the person's inner and outer experiences is provided by computing the ratio of Movement to Color responses (M:C) to yield an *experience balance.*

Three principal categories of Color response are scored. When the Form is of greater importance than the Color in determining a percept, a score of FC is assigned. ("A bow tie." [query] "It's shaped like one. Also, the color would be appropriate.") When Color is primary and Form secondary, the score is CF. ("Somebody spilled paint." [spilled paint has some—not much–shape].) A response determined entirely by Color ("Fire!" [query] "It's red.") is a "pure Color" response and is scored C. In working up the experience balance, these three responses are assigned differential weights. FC carries a weight of 0.5, CF a weight of 1.0, and C is 1.5. These weighted scores are added to yield the C value in the M:C ratio.

Moderate color usage is to be expected in the records of most people, and absence of color, or little attention to color, can be a negative sign. For example, the person who offers no color may be depressed and/or evidencing a low level of drive or spontaneity. Social withdrawal may characterize such a person. To play on words, some individuals who produce a colorless Rorschach might be described as having a colorless personality.

FC represents a "civilized" response. The qualities of reasoning and control reflected in F are combined with the emotional component of personality that finds expression in a Color response. "FC people" tend to be warm and spontaneous, and seek to develop rapport in their relationships. They are described by such terms as "sociable," "compliant," "conforming," and "adaptable." Their emotionality is "responsible" emotionality. They are spontaneous, but not reckless or undercontrolled. These latter characteristics are more likely to be found in the person who produces CF responses, particularly several of them. Impulsiveness, explosiveness, and irritability tend to be observed in these persons. Further down this road is the "C person", who tends to be self-centered, demanding, and emotionally unstable. Multiple C responses are often found in the records of schizophrenics.

Rationale of Rorschach content Rorschach content can include anything from angels and men from Mars, to bears, sex organs, bacteria, musical notes, and "a presence of evil spirits". Animals, humans, and anatomy are frequent items of content, commonly identified by the symbols A, H, and An , respectively. Parts of animals—for example, a wolf's head–are recorded as Ad (animal detail). An animal object—that is, something made from an animal, such as a bear rug—is recorded as Aobj. And, a *humanoid*—a creature from folklore, mythology, or fiction—like a gremlin, a witch or a devil—is (H) (called "H in parentheses"). Examples of other items of content are blood (Bl), clothing (Cg), explosion (Ex), and Sex (Sx).

As with all Rorschach variables, there is not a one-to-one relationship between items of content and interpretation. Items take on significance in the context of the entire Rorschach protocol, including verbalizations, and, beyond this, in the context of an entire battery including interview, observation, and various other collateral data, such as history. This basic clinical approach works best when combined with a grasp of developments in content interpretation, its strengths and its problems. Aronow and Reznikoff (1976, 1987) provide a comprehensive source of such information.

Significant norms for most of the content variables are lacking. Information scattered through the literature, for the most part, tends to identify content items as occurring mostly in certain diagnostic groups or in persons with certain psychological characteristics. Thus, responses of "bacteria" or "bee" may occur in schizophrenia (Phillips & Smith, 1989), and mutilated anatomy, or anatomy with parts missing, may be indicative of castration anxiety (Rapaport, Gill, & Schafer, 1946).

Such impressions may be weak. Rapaport et al. attenuate the significance of their own findings by noting that "'Castration anxiety' appears to be ubiquitous, although of varying intensity, and its clinical manifestations are in general diffuse." (cf. *Aunt Fanny*, pp. 236–240) Some of the data on content are more convincing, however. Animal responses, for example, tend to predominate in children's records, and to represent immature, stereotyped intelligence. Adult records that are made up of more than 50 percent animal responses tend to lead to conclusions that are consistent with this impression.

Rationale of the Popular response To respond with Popular responses suggests that the individual has had experiences that are similar to those of most other people and currently perceives events in a manner similar to others in the culture. Such commonality of understanding would logically be a factor in socialization and lead to conventional and conformist tendencies. Common sense would also go with the person whose P production is in the usual range.

Production of P beyond the usual range may be indicative of an exaggeration of the above—overconventionality, overconformity, and so forth. Common sense, however, can be too much so—that is, too unoriginal, undercreative, stereotyped. Underproduction of P, on the other hand, can be a malignant sign. A person unable to see what large numbers of others see, and who is low in shared understandings, is "not with it." This is a picture that may be related to social withdrawal, perhaps to serious psychopathology, such as schizophrenia. Various other negative characteristics, such as rebelliousness or elevated levels of anxiety, may go with low P.

Rationale of the Original response Those who produce Original responses are "different," most obviously in the intellectual sphere. Such "differentness" can be "good" or "bad." When the original response is of good quality (scored O+), that is, when the Form component of the response (as in M or FC) is rated plus, the individual may be described as "an original thinker," "creative," "highly intelligent," or "brilliant." But an optimal Rorschach, like an optimal life, must show some balance. Rorschach (1921/1951) referred to normal subjects whose records hold more than 50 percent of (predominantly plus–good Form) original responses as "those apart from the world."

One can also be original in a twisted way. Those who produce Original responses whose Form quality is poor (O-) are likely to be mentally disorganized, and O- responses are commonly seen in the records of schizophrenics. Rorschach (1921/1951) noted that schizophrenics with high percentages (50–70 percent) of (primarily minus Form) Original responses are the most scattered.

ILLUSTRATIVE CASE WORKUP

Psychological assessment was initiated on referral from a hospital psychiatrist. His patient, 26-year-old Jim W., was on his ward for the second time, both admissions prompted by court order following arrests for aggravated assaults on women. The latest incident was particularly serious, the assault victim being hospitalized with multiple knife lacerations, a jaw fracture, and contusions.

The consultation sheet very briefly summarized the patient's history of assaultiveness and requested: (1) Please help to establish a diagnosis; (2) Please make treatment recommendations. A provisional diagnosis of intermittent explosive disorder was noted.

The problem to be solved was thus defined by these two requests. Since intermittent explosive disorder is diagnosed very rarely, it became particularly important to make a differential diagnosis and essentially to rule out other conditions that could account for the patient's pathological behavior (the behaviors that must be observed to diagnose an explosive disorder are formally spelled out in DSM-III-R, the personality structure and dynamics are not). A psychotic disorder, an organic personality syndrome, an antisocial personality disorder, a borderline personality disorder, or a substance-induced disorder could account for the patient's problematic behavior. Hence the two reasons for assessment–diagnosis and treatment recommendations–are related; different diagnoses would call for different treatment strategies. Establishing the correct diagnosis (and particularly the related case formulation) contributes to developing a proper treatment plan.

Data Gathering

The tools employed to gather data to deal with the problem of diagnosis and treatment were: interview and observation, MMPI, Bender-Gestalt, Beck Depression Inventory, Sacks Sentence Completions, and the Rorschach. Analyses of data from these sources are listed sequentially, though in practice there was considerable switching back and forth between data from the several instruments to establish consistencies (which were remarkable in this case) and points of variation or differences in emphasis.

Interview and Observation

The Bender was the only formal instrument used to screen for organicity. The impressions gained from this instrument were also used in conjunction with impressions derived from interview and observation concerning possible indicators of an organic personality syndrome. It was concluded that there was not sufficient evidence to link the patient's problem behaviors to organic factors.

More extensive testing for organicity—more extensive than the screening for organicity accomplished with the Bender–would be indicated, however, (1) if there were clinical signs of an organic personality syndrome or of any other brain syndrome or disorder, (2) if definite or equivocal impressions of organicity were gained from the Bender productions, or (3) if there were not convincing evidence for an attitudinal disposition to the behaviors that define an intermittent explosive disorder.

Particularly since we would be concerned here with the possible existence of the explosive type of the organic personality syndrome, it was necessary to be alert to the possible symptoms of Temporal Lobe Epilepsy listed in DSM-III-R (American Psychiatric Association, 1987)—"a marked tendency toward humorless verbosity in both writing and speech, religiosity, and, occasionally, exaggerated aggressiveness."

The interview further explored the patient's history for indications of possible psychotic thinking or behaviors, and additional questions were directed to the patient's drug history. Results were negative with respect to evidence of loss of reality testing in the past, and his current thinking was orderly and showed no paranoid distortions. The patient readily admitted to a history of polysubstance abuse, but further indicated he had been "clean" for over two years. This would suggest that drugs could not have been involved in the assaultive behaviors that led to his hospitalizations in a more recent time frame.

A convincing history of an antisocial personality disorder, or of an earlier conduct disorder, also was not forthcoming. The patient's recent fighting would not be sufficient to establish such a diagnosis. Similarly, there was not enough evidence for a diagnosis of borderline personality disorder. To some extent, some of his behaviors approximate the criteria for this diagnosis. Particularly, an inappropriate manner of dress (below) suggests an identity disturbance and reaching for a fantasy identity, but an adequate pattern to justify the diagnosis of identity disorder or of borderline personality disorder was not discerned.

The patient obviously took great interest in being noticed, and he was! He was dressed identically both times he arrived for assessment. He wore tan riding pants, paratrooper boots, a wide leather belt studded with rhinestones and with a massive, ornate buckle, a bright red shirt, and a neckerchief.

A mildly depressive cast was observed throughout the interviews, but suicidal ideation or intent were not evident. The patient appeared to be a reliable informant about himself, telling a consistent story critical both of himself and others. He tended to see himself as a victim, helpless and hopeless, and he complained that his life had shown little stability. Asked his occupation, he indicated "carpenter, gas station attendant, lab tech., etc." He emphasized the "etc."

MMPI

The first point of interest on the profile shown in Figure 12–1 is the question of validity that it raises. Specifically, the F is high and the K is low; the F-K index (the difference between the raw scores of the two) is 15—far greater than the 9 points that might be indicative, according to Gough (1950) and Meehl (1951), or the 11 points, according to Carson (1969), of a *faking bad* profile. Is this the response set of an individual who wishes to present himself as pathologically deviant?

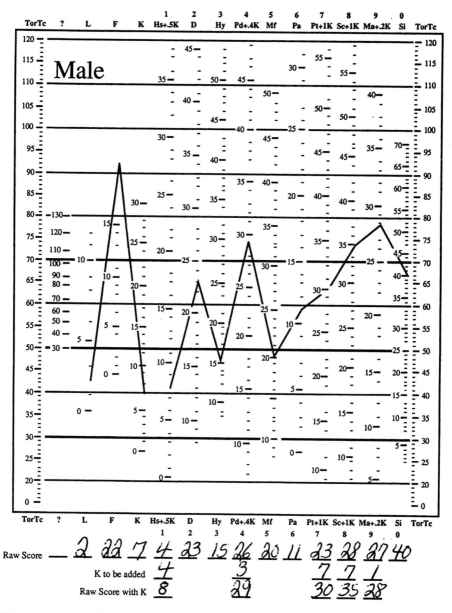

Figure 12–1 From S. R. Hathaway and J. C. McKinley, The Minnesota Multiphasic Personality Inventory. Copyright © The University of Minnesota, 1942, 1943 (renewed 1970). This form 1948, 1966. Reprinted by permission of the University of Minnesota Press.

This conclusion would not appear to be justified. Were the faking bad (attempting to create a pathological picture) hypothesis correct, we would expect significant or more significant elevations on the clinical scales most indicative of severe pathology, including especially scales 6 and 8 (not particularly evident from Scale 6). This is not the case. The profile is consistent, however, with that of a troubled person who is using the inventory to share his troubled feelings. This impression is supported by inspection of the patient's responses to a list of *critical items*, which is notable for his lack of endorsement of items indicative of severe pathology. Instead we find that he assented to items indicating some depressive feelings and a pervasive mistrust and suspiciousness of people, coupled with a negative outlook on the world—the feeling that he has gotten a "raw deal" from life.

To return to the profile, then, we again discern a degree of possible depression that falls short of a clinical depression. He appears to be somewhat withdrawn, perhaps based on faulty self-attitudes (including, speculatively, a questioning of his maleness) and a mistrust of people, though clinical paranoid behaviors are not suggested.

In the context of the attitudinal features observed in interview and in the list of critical items, and his low defensiveness seen in interview and on scales L and K, his elevation on scale 8 (schizophrenia)—a modest elevation in a disturbed population—would not appear to be suggestive of psychosis. Problems of alienation and eccentricity (such as suggested in his manner of dress), negative social and self-attitudes, and questions related to his sexuality would be consistent both with MMPI data and impressions gained from interview and observations. Finally, the 49 pattern, less striking than what is commonly seen in clinically diagnosed character disorders—that is, of the antisocial type and substance abusers—appears consistent with a pattern of alienation and impulse control problems—as seen in his recent incidents of assaultive behaviors and his earlier history of substance abuse.

Beck Depression Inventory

The patient scored 9 on the short form of the Beck, consistent with a mild, possibly moderate level of depression. Qualitative features, however, are of particular importance here. In contrast with so many cases of depression where the individual is unaware of the source of the low mood, or attributes its causes unrealistically, this man relates his depressed feelings to his failures of the past, with resulting disappointment in himself and pessimism about the future.

Bender-Gestalt

The Bender can be interpreted with greater or lesser degrees of research backing and speculation. For example, in item A of Figure 12–2a, the diamond is smaller than the circle, and might be interpreted as evidence of a sense of male inadequacy; and similar sexual conflict might be evidenced in the distortion and separation of the components of item 4 of Figure 12–2a. Certainly evidence that might support these hypotheses should be noted if present in other data—which it is.

A more conservative approach to interpretation of Figure 12–2 might center about conflict and inconsistency. There is a basic carelessness throughout, along

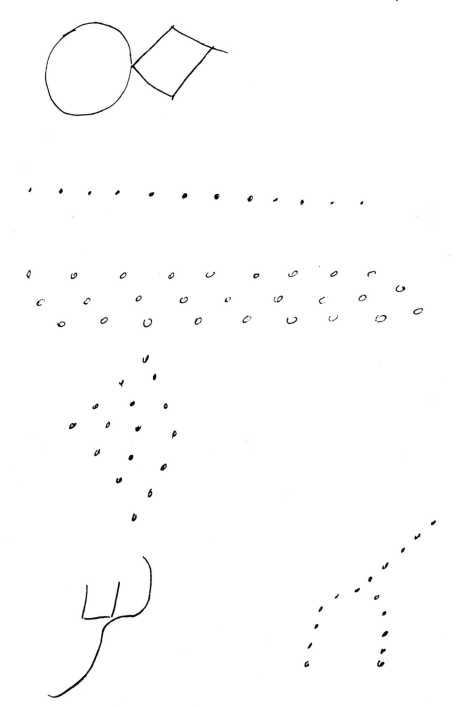

Figure 12-2a Bender-Gestalt (First Page)

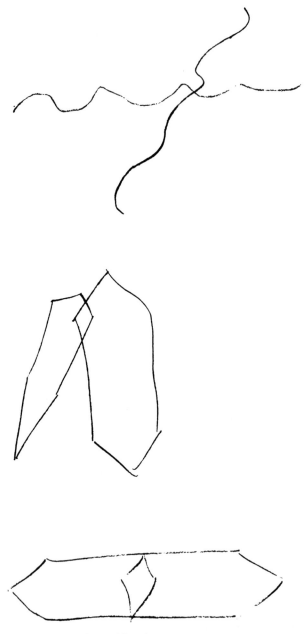

Figure 12–2b Bender-Gestalt (Second Page)

with evidence of genuine effort and concern. Both sides of the sheet are used, there are size and shape distortions, problems in joining components of figures; and, particularly in some instances, the space between figures is greater than that appropriated by most persons. These are suggestive of oppositional tendencies. To comply or not to comply is the question. He starts off item 1 of Figure 12-2a with dots that progressively increase in size and thus require less concentration to produce. Then, in the middle of the figure, he becomes aware and returns to meeting expectations. He performs similarly in item 2 of Figure 12-2a, where several times he finds himself drawing careless, open-ended loops, and then returns to making closed circles whose production is more demanding of attention. Item 5 shows little in the way of dots; the units of the figure are primarily dashes and loops.

Sacks Sentence Completions

The 60 items of the Sacks Sentence Completion Test were perused for items of significance in understanding this man. There were many. The patient was open and his responses were revealing. A picture that is fully consistent with the various components of the battery emerged.

Items of particular clinical interest (26 of the 60), in the order on which they appear on the paper and pencil form, include:

I feel that a real friend...has an alternative motive.
When the odds are against me...I give up.
I would do anything to forget the time...I drank too much alcohol.
If I were in charge...I would be lost.
To me the future looks...bleak.
The men over me...generally are no better than myself.
What I want is a woman who...loves sex.
When I am at home with family...I feel left out of everything.
At work, I get along best with...the females.
I don't like people who...exaggerate.
I believe that I have the ability to... be a great craftsman.
My greatest fault is...lack of self confidence.
If my father would only...give me a break.
Those I work with...are no better than I.
Most people I know...have used me in one way or another.
I failed when...I quit college.
At times, I have felt ashamed...of giving up so easily.
Some day I...hope to get my act together.
When I was younger...I enjoyed life much more.
I believe most women...would enjoy sex with me.
When I'm not around, my friends...must talk about my stupidity.
Compared with others, I...am a failure.

The worst thing I ever did...was rape and cut up a whore.
When I am older...the past will be forgotten.
I remember when...I stayed high for weeks.
What I want out of life...is to succeed in a career goal.

Several significant themes concerning himself and others emerge from these completions. In the simplest terms, he is down on himself and those with whom he relates. He lacks self-confidence, as he states in so many words.

The self-image is that of an inadequate person who struggles with the question of whether he is as deficient as he thinks he is. He is beset with a pattern of failures and remorse, including dropping out of college, failure of vocational achievement, severe substance abuse, and failure to achieve gratifying and supportive interpersonal relationships. Failure with the opposite sex underlines this issue. He sometimes professes that he will overcome his various limitations, but with what inner conviction is questionable. To this observer his efforts thus far appear ineffectual.

Though he cannot help feeling inadequate, he makes a practice of involving others as a cause of his problems. People are unhelpful, exploitive, untrustworthy, and deceptive. Though women are seen as perhaps no more culpable than others in these several respects, for some time now he has experienced them as particularly acute frustrators. He has reacted with aggravated and rationalized violence which at one level he considered to be justified, but which also has become a source of remorse.

Rorschach

The Rorschach consists of 18 responses with a restricted range of content, but holds significant information bearing on the reason for assessment.

The scoring supplied is based on the main Rorschach categories so as to be understandable by all Rorschach workers. The locations indicated are Exner's (1986), but various differentiations such as those indicating whether a response is vague, ordinary, or unusual are not used. Unusualness characterizes the protocol.

The final phase of administration was testing the limits. The goal here was twofold: (1) to determine if when prompted he can see good form human content, and thus disclose something of his object relationships; and (2) to determine whether he is capable of producing good quality, conventional responses. Success with the first would provide evidence for the latter.

All 10 cards were spread out in front of the client. He was instructed, "Some people see human beings on these cards. Can you see any"? After slight hesitation he pointed to Cards VII and III, but added, "Not really." Queried first about VII, he responded, "Yeah, a woman's head and flat-chested bust—an old, old woman, a dried up prune." Asked to tell about the humans on III, he observed, "Yeah, ugly beaks for noses, not real, and the big boobs (shy grin), not real, and those sharp things guarding them. Do you see 'em?"

Clearly, this is not a common Rorschach. We note right off the unusual, perseverative content, the evident lack of connectedness with others seen in the

Figure 12–3 Rorschach

I 11"

1. A giant winged beetle. (E: Some people see more than one thing on these cards.) W F+ A
2. I can also see possibly a 20th century fighter plane. W F+ Fighter Plane

II 4"

1. Wings, tail, whatever they call them in front of their mouths.
2. Yeah, like space ships w/tail, wings, 4 canopies for 4 men to sit in, couple guns (Dd33), and a couple up front (D1).

1. There I definitely see an airplane w/exploding shells or something. DdS CF.FC'. mF Fighter Plane, Ex
2. Or an airplane flying over a battlefield w/lots of bloodshed. W CF Fighter Plane, War, B1 0-

Airplane = DS5, nice design–white, not camouflaged; Exploding shells in mid-air fired at the plane (D2, D3). The color, pushing out, different directions.
The whole thing being a plane flying over a battlefield w/bloodstains of dying men, whatever.

III (33")

I can't see anything there. No (Long pause while looking) –Unh Unh.   Still draws a blank.   Rejection

IV 14"

1. The back blast of a rocket. Dd mF.YF Ex 0-
2. Or the head of a hammerhead shark. DdS F- A 0-

Just tail end of it (D3). Top third of blot = exhaust, condensation, whatever.
W D5 = body of shark, D6 = dorsal fin, D4 = head of shark w/space as eye.

Figure 12-3 Rorschach (cont'd)

(67")

Nothing. (long pause—keeps looking).

1'43"

1. Two fighters of—um—insect species. Clashed head to head.

    W FM- A

V

From the side. Head to head and the antlers are squashed in between going different ways. (What makes them 11 insects?) Just the irregular shape of the body and…somewhat pointed snout on the head. D4 = insect; Dd31 & Dd32 = antlers—or, Dd32 could be tongues; D1 = leg.

VI

41"

1. A Titan missile breaking through an ocean… the surface of an ocean.
2. The tip of a razor gun—or a ray gun rather.

D2 = missle; D1 = surface of ocean; Dd22 = water flying out–or exhaust fumes. Whole thing.

    W Fm.YF Missile
    W F- Im 0-

VII

1. A pair of frogs legs (long pause)
2. A rocket cutting through some clouds, or breaking through some clouds.

D3 = legs; D4 = back part of frog. D6 = rocket; D4 = clouds.

    DdF-Ad,Fd0-
    D YF Rocket, Cl

VIII

6"

1. Foo! A splattered bug on a windshield.
2. A bullet, cutting through some clothes into a body.

Yeah. Whole thing. Just because of the different colors. D4 & D5 = clothing; D2 = body; D1 = blood; center line = bullet. (E: See part of a person? No)

    W CF Ad
    W CF.mF Hd, Cg, B1 0-

Figure 12-3 Rorschach (cont'd)

   3. A geographical aerial map, aerial photograph. I've seen these aerial maps that are different colors and they show heat from the earth or something. It just reminded me of it.   W CF Map

IX (1")

10" We're getting into 3D now, huh?

   1. Again, first impression is a bug splattered. (pause) Whole thing. (?) Because of the different colors.   W CF Ad

   2. I can see a Martian in there. D1 = head; D3 = hair; D9 = shoulders   Dd F- (Hd)

X

9" Seeing stars, woo.

   1. I see a rocket, hitting the earth, exploding w/lots of destruction. Already hit the earth. D11 = tail of rocket; D1 = shrapnel from head of explosion; D9 = people, blood.   Dd CF.mF Ex, H, Bl 0-

   2. A beautiful bouquet of flowers. Whole. Pleasant pastel shades,. Arranged by a floral arranger who knows his stuff. Nice.   W FC Bot

SCORE TABULATION

W	11	FM-	1	Hd, Cg, B1	1	P 0
D	1	YF	1	(Hd)	1	0- 7
Dd	4	F+	2	A	3	Rejection 1
DdS	2	F-	4	Ad, Fd	2	
		FC	1	F. Plane	1	
		CF	4	F. Plane,		
		CF.FC'.mF	1	Ex	1	
		CF.mF	2	F. Plane,		
		Fm.YF	1	War, B1	1	
		mF,YF	1	Ex	1	
				Ex, H, B1	1	
				Missile	1	
				Rocket,C1	1	
				Bot	1	
				Map	1	
				Im	1	
				Fd	1	

absence of Popular responses and the large number of Originals (all minus), and deficiency of human orientation as seen particularly in his rejection of Card III with its prominent human figures that are seen by a majority of subjects, particularly normals. The closest (not very close) he spontaneously gets to reporting human content is the partial humanoid figure—the Martian on Card IX. On testing the limits, however, it appears that his basic perceptual organization is within normal limits. He *can* test reality. His problem is one of the meanings he construes of people, and more particularly of his constructions of cold, denying, and, in a real sense, threatening female people.

He readily entertains hostile fantasy, perhaps seeking to ward off the pervasive dysphoria evidenced both in content and the determinants. His loose color usage, in no way restrained by M, would strongly suggest a person who lives out impulses directly. He is, in fact, without the three basic modes of control postulated by Klopfer and Kelley (1946): M, FC, and good form F— *inner control, outer control*, and *constrictive control*, respectively. Reaction times, we note, are within normal limits, some of them even rather slow, and do not suggest that his typical behaviors are impulsive, but other features of the protocol strongly suggest that he can become so.

Overall, the protocol does not suggest a well-functioning intellect. He emphasizes Whole responses, but almost entirely these are of poor quality, vague, built up, added to, and generally not well perceived as an organized whole. He is readily satisfied with opportunistic findings—projections on the "fighter plane" are guns, the detail above the Martian's head is hair (a *position response* indicative of severe flaws in reasoning–this is hair, regardless of whether or not it looks like hair, because it is on top of a perceived head). His combinations of details (Dd, DdS) have the same lack of meaningful organization.

His last response to Card X is a surprise; it doesn't seem to "belong." In contrast to the thunder, blood, and guts that characterize the protocol as a whole, this is a civilized response, suggestive of a capacity for warmth and hunger for relationship (one gains the same impression from some of his sentence completions). There is conflict between the individual who wants relationship and the individual who too readily lashes out.

Is the man psychotic? Looking at the form level and various other pathological indicators, we ask if he cannot test reality, or merely if he is able to overlook it. His vague responses were given without any particular commitment, self-debate, or self-criticalness. They did, however, appear to faithfully record his fantasies and outlook on life. He also yearns for acceptance and intimacy. This not forthcoming, destructive retaliation holds meaning for him.

The psychological report which follows is addressed to the reasons for which psychological assessment was requested, namely to contribute to a psychiatric diagnosis and to make recommendations for treatment. These goals were accomplished by delineating a sufficient personality picture from which inferences pertinent to these issues could be derived.

A formal diagnostic impression was arrived at essentially by ruling out competing diagnoses that would be consistent with the presenting symptom picture.

Additionally, assessment spelled out the key features of the client's symptomatic behaviors. Treatment recommendations also derive from the personality picture set forth, specifically the delineation of the client's conflicts—what is troubling him and needs therapeutic attention.

PSYCHOLOGICAL REPORT

Pervasive and severely hostile fantasy coupled with inadequate control over impulses are consistent with a direct living out of destructive fantasies and a diagnosis of Intermittent Explosive Disorder. This man is capable of overlooking external reality constraints and becoming responsive to his own primitive urgings, with outbursts followed by both professed remorse and self-justifying rationalizations—a sense of righteous satisfaction (hence, how deep the remorse?). These occur in the context of awareness and with an aware surrender of control; his assaults are not blind rage. He does not present convincing evidence for psychosis, a personality disorder, or an organic syndrome. The history indicates an absence of recent substance abuse that might be associated with the behaviors that led to arrest and admission to this hospital.

A core conflict centers about strong feelings of rejection, by people in general, and, most painfully, by women. These engender exaggerated hostile urges, on the one hand, and ambivalences on the other. Does he want to relate and to love, or does he want to destroy? Are people accepting and lovable, or are they hateful and destructive?

This doubting extends also to the self. What role does he play in courting rejection? What must he do to change? (A highly inappropriate manner of dress, suggesting the affectation of a super-masculine role, defines the direction in which he is groping.) His assaultiveness also suggests that his solution to problems is a "masculine" one. This, then, is a man of very low self-esteem who has failed and regards himself as a failure. And worse, he envisions no constructive solution to his problems.

Jim is a very troubled person, anxious and tense, who needs psychological help and knows it. He also has a degree of insight into his problem areas and his ineffectual and destructive attempts at solution. He needs further insight into his areas of main conflict and the manner in which he seeks new solutions. Coupled with the need for insight and support is a need for guidance and training in social skills and realistic goal setting. A long-term relationship eventually emphasizing guidance and support could be helpful.

13
VARIATIONS AND TRENDS IN PSYCHOLOGICAL ASSESSMENT

The practice of psychological assessment, along with a number of the conceptualizations on which it rests, now differs dramatically from the situation that prevailed when the tenets of the measurement tradition provided the only acceptable basis for the use of psychological diagnostic instruments. The changed picture reflects theoretical advances and a responsiveness to experienced needs and recognized opportunities growing out of practice and a changed clinical climate. Today's psychological assessors are concerned with new and still developing concepts of therapy, with psychopharmacology, and with the *Diagnostic and Statistical Manuals* and their implications for treatment. A key position for neuropsychological assessment replaces an earlier widespread, but generally casual, approach to this specialty.

New and larger roles for the psychological assessor go hand in hand with current views on clinical judgment and with evolving concepts of validity: a fundamental role for clinical judgment and inference is well established (see, for example, *Standards*, 6 and 6.1, and 15 and 15.1; also *Guidelines*' prescription of judgment in computer testing).

Creativity in attending to the individual case is recognized as an important feature of the assessment process, and the ingenuity of individual assessors is shared with colleagues through books and journal articles. Though all of the changes in the assessment field now extant are not universally accepted, the groundwork for greater harmony among the adherents of the measurement and the clinical traditions is in place.

"CREATIVE VARIATIONS" IN PSYCHOLOGICAL ASSESSMENT

For quite a few years, a number of psychological evaluation techniques have been put to work to do tasks in addition to, or other than, the tasks for which they were designed. The position of Zubin, Eron, and Schumer (1965) that the Rorschach should be considered as an interview is a significant example of redefining the function of an instrument. Numerous additional publications—for example, those of Harrower, Vorhaus, Roman, and Bauman (1960), Winter, Ferreira, and Olson (1966), Wynne (1968), Farberow (1968), Cutter and Farberow (1968), Blanchard (1968), Singer (1968, 1977b), Dudek (1969), Klopfer (1969, 1984), Fernald (1970), and Smith (1985)—also discuss the use of widely used instruments in an original way.

What follows is a collection of techniques or ways of doing assessment that may serve as a source of ideas for practitioners and innovators. They are clinical, not psychometric, approaches; not standardized, and not validated in their present form. What worth they have is a matter of clinicians' judgments. Interaction among clients, or between clients and assessors appears to many of them to be a useful variation from more established usages.

In a book by Harrower et al. (1960), several authors present their "creative variations" in the use of projective instruments and psychometric scales. Harrower reports on a psychotherapeutic technique which she calls "projective counseling," a means of imparting insight to relatively normal persons. It is a technique, aspects of which are comparable to methods employed by other clinicians, and is adaptable to various situations:

> As a method it may be described as a re-educational or remedial technique which can be used with individuals, or with couples and groups, and, in essence, it amounts to confronting the person, or persons, with his own productions—with the raw material from the projective tests at those times in the re-educational process when this material can best be used with insight.

Harrower's technique is unusually flexible. In an illustrative case she administered a battery consisting of a Wechsler scale, the Rorschach, Figure Drawing, Sentence Completions, and the Most Unpleasant Concept Test. The "battery," however, can be considerably more limited. Thus, in counseling with a married or engaged couple,

> Understanding of a different "way of looking at the world" can be well presented in projective counseling through the study of a single Rorschach card by both partners simultaneously. Many times one member of the pair will show a holistic approach, the other a more detailed one. It is then possible to assess the holistic approach both in terms of its achievement as an integrated process and as a potential liability in the tendency of such persons to gloss over important aspects of a problem. Similarly, the more pedantic, literal, and detailed orientation can be seen advantageously in terms of its accuracy, yet at the same time its limitations can be noted. No special training is needed for the average

individual to understand this, or to be startled by the realization that the "obvious" things of his own perception are not necessarily the "obvious" objects for some one else. It is not a far cry from this perceptual realization to the understanding that the differences in ideas and concepts may arise from different ways of envisioning the world. The common denominator in many such counseling sessions, in this test and in others, seems to be the removal of the threat that there is implied hostility in the partner's different experiences. The tangible test scores somehow bring reassurance and an understanding of the fact that "this is the way the partner is." This replaces the feeling that differences are somehow a way of showing a critical approach.

Vorhaus's Structured Interview Technique is an adaptation of Machover's (1957) human-figure drawing method (Chapter 7), including the list of questions the assessor asks the subject first about the same-sex drawing, then about himself or herself. Covered by the questions are a wide range of topics that are frequently pertinent to adjustment issues. These include relationships to parents, siblings, health, popularity, marital life, wishes, and ambitions.

Hypothesizing an "individual-group psychological isomorphism," Roman and Bauman resurrect and refurbish the "group mind" concept of William McDougall. Their *interaction testing*, a technique for the psychological evaluation of small groups, is described by the authors as a clinical orientation to the "psychometrics of groups." They consider the technique as an extension of Henry and Guetzkow's (1951) Test of Group Projection, a TAT-type test that employs five cards to which the *group* writes stories.

Various commonly used clinical instruments, such as Wechsler scales, the Rorschach, and the TAT lend themselves to an interaction testing approach. There are two main aspects to the procedure. First, each member of the group is tested individually in the usual manner. Second, with all members of the group assembled, the test—or tests—are readministered, this time with instructions that the responses to be offered reflect the consensus of the group. The manner in which the group arrives at its consensus is also recorded.

Comparison of the responses of the individuals who constitute the group with the group product may provide insight concerning the group's use of the resources of its members. Does, for example, the group interact constructively, as may be seen in group responses that are of better quality than those offered independently by the individuals in the group; or are consensus responses inferior to individual responses?

In an illustration provided by the authors in which two married couples are tested with a Wechsler scale, the data suggest that one couple makes good use of the partners' intellectual resources when husband and wife interact, the other quite the reverse. In the first marriage, the husband's Verbal IQ is 112, the wife's 101, and the "Interaction IQ" 122. In marriage number 2, the husband scores 122, the wife 144+, while their joint score is 133. Looking at the Comprehension subtest alone, in the first marriage the husband scores 9, the wife 8, and together they raise the score to 10. In the second marriage the respective scores are 11, 17, and 15. Roman and Bauman consider that interaction in one marriage enhances social awareness but contributes to decline in this area in the other. Similar patterns of improvement and decline on

Similarities suggest that the partners of one marriage reason well together, while joint intellectual effort by the other couple is counterproductive. Roman and Bauman conclude that the latter is the more disturbed of the two marriages.

Interaction testing is a versatile contribution to psychological assessment. Illustrations of its application provided by Roman and Bauman include its use for making a comparison of two marriages (as above), an engaged couple in conflict, a mother and her schizophrenic son, a homosexual relationship, and a therapy group at two points in treatment. Interaction testing currently is perhaps best known in its application to the Rorschach in the approach to assessment known as the *consensus Rorschach.*

Consensus Rorschach Approaches

The uses of ingenuity are particularly evident in the variations of the consensus Rorschach that have been reported since Blanchard (1959) first described this approach. The consensus Rorschach is adaptable to any number of personality/social issues, and particularly to those where social interaction and situational variables may be of special interest. Dominance-submission, role status, or constructive or destructive contributions to social relations, are examples. Klopfer (1968) recognized the consensus Rorschach as "less of a test" before this term was coined by Korchin and Schuldberg (1981): "The review by this author (Klopfer, 1968) emphasized the emerging importance of content as a major focus in research and practice, having predictive efficiency beyond the formal scoring categories." (He mentioned, specifically, in this regard, psychiatric diagnoses and membership in special groups.) Histories of the consensus Rorschach are available in Blanchard (1968), Cutter and Farberow (1968), and Klopfer (1984a).

Wynne (1968) sums up the strengths and potentials of the method, and related procedures for studying interpersonal patterns, thus:

> The consensus Rorschach provides a potentially relatively standardized situation in which behavior of two or more persons interacting with one another can be observed, recorded, and studied directly without relying upon retrospective reconstructions of behavior patterns. This procedure shares with other techniques the method of asking a group or family to work on a problem together—such as discussing differences in answers to individually administered questionnaires, playing games in which cooperative versus conflictual interests are pitted against one another, etc. In these various procedures, communication and behavior patterns can be compared systematically from group to group, from individual to individual, from role to role, and in relation to a variety of other variables which may impinge upon the procedure and its participants. These procedures open up a whole new area for both clinical interpretations and systematic research investigations. For the latter, a considerable number of methodologic issues will need to be studied and specified.

Singer (1968, 1977b) focuses on the application of the consensus Rorschach—which she conceptualizes as a *transaction*—to family situations. In this usage the Rorschach is viewed "as a bit of reality being looked at by two or more persons in a conversational transaction" (Singer, 1977b). A fuller statement of her position (Singer, 1968) reads:

> The consensus Rorschach offers a standardized way of directly studying interaction within families. It has, as a special advantage, that the individual starting points at which family members begin to communicate are similar for each family member and can be directly observed. Further, the consensus Rorschach is an interpretive transaction in which meanings are attributed to the "reality" of the Rorschach cards. Thus, it can be inferred that this may parallel those repeated times throughout a child's formative years wherein parents interpret, name, label, and instruct children about the world in which they share.

Klopfer (1969) presents two cases to illustrate the application of the consensus Rorschach in the classroom. He proposes that "information gained from the consensus Rorschach, when taken together with observations and school records, can serve as the basis for the consultant's feedback to teachers, parents, and the children themselves."

In a later publication, Klopfer (1984a) reports on the application of the consensus Rorschach to the planning of couple therapy, illustrating with two cases. His rationale for use of this technique is as follows:

> Interviewing techniques oftentimes produce well-rehearsed stories on the part of the couple which may have little to do with the real issues that are causing the difficulty. The use of the Rorschach introduces a game with which the clinical psychologist is more familiar than the clients, and in which information can be gotten which will enable the examiner to learn more rapidly what can be done to help the couple improve their interpersonal exchanges in the direction of better cooperation and greater congeniality.

From his two case illustrations he concludes:

> The Consensus Rorschach is a powerful addition to the individual standardized Rorschach in demonstrating the nature of a relationship. Even though some guesses can be made about how people are likely to get along from individual administration, they are greatly enhanced by actually viewing the interaction *in vivo*...The use of the Consensus Rorschach will reveal rather early in the process what the prognosis for a relationship will be.

Differences in the obtained protocols of the consensus Rorschach under changed conditions have been reported by several investigators. Dudek (1969) reported consensus Rorschachs from two therapy groups obtained at three points during ongoing therapy, and differential response to treatment was interpreted from the groups' psychograms. One group, indeed, was shown to be in a therapeutic stalemate, while the second group evidenced good progress as interpreted from their psychograms. These Rorschach-gained conclusions were in "complete agreement" with independent clinical evaluations of therapeutic progress.

Cutter and Farberow (1968) report on the serial administration of consensus Rorschachs, with one patient participating in several situations. Specifically, the patient participated in responding to the Rorschach with (1) three friends, (2) three roommates, (3) his wife, and (4) one high- and one low-status individual. The results disclosed the different roles that the patient assumes in these several social contexts. The authors indicate that:

a. with friends he expects to be irresponsible,
b. with roommates he expects to maintain affective distance,
c. with his wife he expects to be a victim, [and]
d. with a high-low status group he expects to be inadequate.

Blanchard's (1959) initial use of the consensus Rorschach, which involved two youthful gangs of boys confined in an institution for delinquents as a consequence of having participated in gang rape, demonstrates the potential of the method. Conflict and rivalry were evident in the gangs' response processes and content, similar to what had prevailed in the ordinary relationships of the boys in their gang settings.

An example of parallel roles in Rorschach behavior and behavior in the context of the functioning gang is seen in the interactions and conduct of Pete, the leader of one of the gangs, and Kenny, the gang's "intellectual" (as evidenced by his IQ and the quality of his Rorschach responses as compared with his companions) and relatively most benign member. On two occasions when Pete proposed (homo)sexual content, Kenny resisted and convinced the other members to reject Pete's proposals. Whereas Pete saw two "male homosexuals" on Card III, Kenny convinced the others that the same blot areas represented "two ladies." In the gang rape experience that led to the confinement of the boys, Pete was the initiator and was at first opposed by Kenny who was the last to participate. Further, he did not strike or push the victim as had his peers.

Other Consensus Approaches

The family TAT   The family TAT is another projective consensus approach. In the study of Winter, Ferreira, and Olson (1966), the focus was on hostility themes. One hundred and twenty-six families consisting of a father, a mother, and a child (50 of whom were classified as normal, 44 as emotionally maladjusted — e.g., neurotic—16 as schizophrenic, and 16 as delinquent) were administered a modified TAT. Each family was presented with three TAT cards and instructed to compose a story that all agreed upon and that proceeded in the order in which the cards were presented; for example, 7GF, 5, and 10, a procedure which then was repeated with two additional sets of cards. Two measures of hostility were obtained; weighted hostility (the ratio of total hostility, as measured by the Hafner-Kaplan [1960] scale, to the total number of words in the story x 100), and overt hostility (the ratio of overt hostility themes to total hostility themes). Significant discriminations among the several groups of families were obtained, thus suggesting a clinical diagnostic potential for this approach.

Collaborative Drawing Technique   Smith's (1985) Collaborative Drawing Technique (CDT) was specifically designed to gain information that is meaningful for the family treatment process. Its author notes that "it has often been the case that an identified patient will say little or nothing during a family interview session, but will dramatically communicate through the CDT."

The technique is suitable for use with husband and wife alone, or with entire families (Smith has assessed intact families of up to seven members, and indicates that "Larger families could certainly be assessed, the only modification needed being more paper and more crayons.") In a gamelike atmosphere, each participant selects a colored crayon of her or his choice and takes turns at drawing whatever she or he wishes. Time allotments for drawing are strictly adhered to. In the first round of drawing, each participant has a 30-second turn. In subsequent rounds, the time limit is reduced for each turn, from 30 seconds to 25, 20, 15, 10, 5, and 3 seconds.

Process and *Product* are recorded. Process is concerned with *Adherence* to Instructions—for example, talking in violation of the structured rules of the "game," or exceeding time limits; *Sequence*, for example, how the sequence of participation was arrived at and maintained; and *Involvement*, such as helping and cooperative behavior. The Product has to do with such matters as *Space*—who used the most and who used the least space, for example; *Tone*—Does the drawing suggest conflict, anger, warmth, or love?; and *Theme/Content*, focusing on such matters as unity or disunity of theme, who contributed to this quality and who contradicted or transformed it.

A qualitative technique, Smith illustrates with instructive case examples. Thus, the following brief summary reveals a disjointed, pathologic family situation:

> A mentally gifted adolescent female referred by her family physician after a suicide attempt completed a CDT with her family, including both parents and her younger brother. The final product was four completely separate drawings located in four separate quadrants of the paper.

Consensus intelligence testing Fernald (1970) addresses a topic similar to that investigated by Roman and Bauman (1960) (pp. 325–326). The common concern was how compatibility of group members affects intellectual functioning in the group. Roman and Bauman studied the issue among couples that were married or engaged. Fernald's subjects were male roommates at a private secondary school. In both studies intelligence was assessed with Verbal Wechsler subtests. The procedure was also similar in both studies: First each subject was tested individually, then jointly, to arrive at a consensus.

Fernald's hypothesis was that "Compatible groups make more constructive use of their intellectual resources than incompatible groups." This hypothesis was supported and is in agreement with the findings of the Roman and Bauman study.

Fernald's observations during testing are additionally informative. Concerning compatible roommates,

> When the roommates presented different answers, each roommate seemed to know when his partner's answer was superior to his own, and they were usually able to arrive at the better of their two answers. They spent long periods of time evaluating each other's responses, and they did not give up on a single question until they had arrived at a mutually

acceptable answer. They did not reject a single question. All of their discussions were relatively calm and logical.

Incompatible combinations, on the other hand, were characterized by impatience, arguments and considerable emotionality, and they averaged two rejected questions. Rejections occurred when the two roommates could not agree upon whose answer should be submitted. However, in some instances when one roommate was passive, the consensus answer, either correctly or incorrectly, was the same as or very similar to the dominating roommate's answer.

The approach of Roman and Bauman, and Fernald, may have useful applications beyond the assessment of couples and roommates. Consensus intelligence testing, as well as consensus projective assessment, may also be of value in the workplace, for example. The consensus method has led Fernald to conclude that "two heads are *not* always better than one," but consensus approaches permit us to identify when they are and when they aren't.

FURTHER APPROACHES FOR ENHANCING THE PRODUCTIVITY OF THE ASSESSMENT PROCESS

The above methods were designed to explore areas of functioning that are appreciably less available through conventional assessment approaches. The following represent additional approaches and orientations of current interest to enhance the quantity or usefulness of psychological information.

Jaffe's Selected Response Procedure   Jaffe's (1988) technique is a variation of Appelbaum's (1959) *Altered Atmosphere Procedure* (p. 274), which is an open-ended solicitation for responses. Jaffe requests only a single additional response: "Now that the testing is over, and you are familiar with all of the inkblots, I would like you to look through them again, only this time I would like to see if you can find just one more response, which can be from any card you choose."

Jaffe advances a number of reasons for asking for only one more response. First listed is economy. He rejects a supplementary procedure that might be time-consuming, and indicates that his procedure rarely increases administration time (of the Rorschach) by two or three minutes.

Among the several other advantages that Jaffe advances is that his procedure does not, as a primary focus,

> concern the creation of an atmosphere; it concerns the discovery of another response. This emphasis on the response is preferable, because in order to alter the atmosphere, the examiner must fertilize the interpersonal soil of the patient-examiner relationship at a time when both examiner and patient are likely to feel tired. Also, the idiosyncratic nature of each patient-examiner relationship limits the extent to which the directions for altering the atmosphere can be specified...Although an altered atmosphere is a hoped for consequence of the Selected Response Procedure, the

examiner is not required to establish and maintain "the desired atmosphere" at the end of a standard Rorschach administration.

Yet another technique for gaining additional significant data after completion of the Rorschach administration proper is Cerney's (1984) "One Last Response" procedure. Following administration of the Rorschach in the usual Rapaport-Holt (1968) method, which calls for inquiry after the client's response(s) to each card, and the client completes free association to Card X, the assessor returns the card to the client and asks "Would you please give me one last response." Inquiry is then carried out for all of the responses given to Card X, the original responses, and the "one last response."

The rationale for this procedure stems from Appelbaum (1961), who attaches special significance to the last Rorschach response, particularly when this response differs from the client's previous responses. He further noted a tendency for some of his patients to show a decrease in the defensiveness activated by the Rorschach procedure. Cerney observes:

> With a shift in mental set, they were able to express what hitherto had been unavailable. Other patients saw the end of the test as a "last chance" to reveal the full extent of their disorganization and/or their most troubling preoccupations. Appelbaum found that the greatest number of patients for whom the end of the test was a relevant variable struggled to stave off disorganization or intrusive thoughts in a fashion similar to patients with borderline pathology described by Knight (1954). These patients frequently could handle the more structured tests such as the WAIS even maintaining their equilibrium levels for long periods but were vulnerable to the influence of factors within the response process of the Rorschach.

Indeed, the assessor's request for "one last response" might be viewed as an opportunity (as shown, for example, by the fact that some clients offered more than one additional response).

Thirty-two of the protocols "were judged...to have a 'one last response' that differed significantly in form and/or content from other responses on Card X." Some of the clients showed decompensation: "It is possible that the pressure to give 'one last response' is akin to the pressure a patient experiences in psychotherapy when asked to free associate." Others evidenced an improvement over their earlier responses. Cerney speculates that the procedure identifies clients who will do better in a therapeutic situation that challenges them.

Using the Self as a Diagnostic Tool

All nonmechanical aspects of assessment involve the commitment of the assessor as an instrument to reason, to make judgments, to communicate with clients and colleagues, and to guide and individualize the assessment process. Various ways of using the self have been discussed. Following is a presentation of using the self from a humanistic point of view and from a psychoanalytic point of view; the latter, specifically, being concerned with the phenomenon of countertransference as experienced by the psychological assessor.

Craddick's humanistic practice Craddick (1975) sets forth a basic position held by some, not all, humanistically oriented psychologists. His cornerstone statement reads: "The sharing of oneself with the client in the assessment procedure is a valuable approach to mutual understanding, valuing, and trusting of two persons whose efforts are directed toward a common goal." An attitude of genuine trust and personal investment in the client is incompatible with some outmoded, but not extinct, testing practices—in which the examiner "holds all the cards," and the procedure is characterized by secrecy and deception, and the client is denied access to his or her records.

Test materials, as well as assessor-client interactions, are used to establish the personal involvement and sharing of both parties in the assessment situation:

> At the end of the tests, such as the Rorschach or the Kahn Test of Symbol Arrangement, I ask the client to select a card or an object that he feels best represents himself and other important persons in his life, for example, his wife (her husband), mother, father, siblings, physician, etc., then a card or object that he feels best represents the two of us. Sometimes, the client, after having done the above, will ask me for the card or object that best represents me, and us. At such times, I feel free to select a card or object that I feel best represents me, and us. Since I ask the client for the reasons for his selections, I feel that he should also be given reasons for my selections, and I give these to him if he asks for them. The sharing process is valuable to the client and to me. It makes the assessment situation meaningful, and I often find that it yields rich information about the client's view of the assessment process and of me.

The role of countertransference Countertransference, following Freud, has classically been considered to be counterproductive to clinical process; an unwelcome, uncontrolled intrusion, "a manifestation of the analyst's own pathology" (Sugarman, 1991) and making for a loss of objectivity and distorting the reality of the clinical situation. Whether or not this way of regarding the phenomenon is accurate or helpful, Sugarman (1981) points out that, in fact, "Most sophisticated psychodiagnosticians use their countertransference reactions when arriving at diagnostic formulations." There is, Sugarman indicates, a legitimate role for "the examiner's subjective emotional response to the patient as a data source within testing" that observers of the clinical process may be inclined to overlook. Further, he notes, his "years of testing and supervising have made me aware of the degree to which examiners use countertransference unreflectively."

Sugarman discusses several specific uses of countertransference. He observes that "unusual feelings, thoughts, and behavior can be considered to be reactions to a specific patient and, thus, to impart unique information about the patient." And, there are times when "determination of the particular relational paradigm projected onto the examiner can be gained only through an examination of the tester's emotions and fantasies during the testing." Beyond providing useful data about the client, analyzing countertransference is also advanced as a means of reducing faulty appraisals of clients.

Looking at the far-reaching benefits of using countertransference, Sugarman offers the opinion that

> Attending to such reactions and integrating them with the objective data of the test responses can aid in formulating diagnostic impressions and in guiding the focus of the test report. This process can alert the examiner to particular relational paradigms or self and object representations which otherwise might be underemphasized or neglected...
>
> Such an emphasis can be particularly useful in anticipating the transference-countertransference paradigm that may emerge in the patient's therapy. Forewarned of such potential patterns, the examiner can elaborate the specific psychodynamics that underly these paradigms and alert the therapist to them...By integrating the test response paradigms with his own response to the patient in the test report, the examiner is more likely to validate the therapist's countertransference. Consequently, the therapist will be able to use his countertransference in a therapeutic fashion.
>
> Furthermore, if the examiner is aware of and accepts his countertransference, he can develop an empathic picture of the patient. He will also be able to prevent direct, unanalyzed countertransference reactions and a cold, critical attitude associated with an objective focus from creeping into the test report. Too often the examiner's reaction to the patient "comes through" a test report in an unintegrated fashion. In such cases, the referral source may disregard the report and formulation because of their obvious bias.

Using the Client as a Diagnostic Tool

The psychological assessor is not a mere handler of psychological test materials or a giver of test instructions (p. 37), but is actively involved and invested in the assessment process, as indicated above. Similarly, in the assessment situation the client needn't be a mere follower of instructions, an answerer of questions, a manipulator of articles, a creator of conceptual material, and so forth. The psychological assessor may invite and help her or him to depart from responding to psychological materials in a standardized manner (in both the technical and the general sense) and to produce data that go beyond the typical yield of conventional testing.

Self-interpretation of test protocols   Bettelheim (1947) demonstrates several advantages to self-interpretation of the TAT. He reports this practice as a useful teaching device for students who are learning about the dynamics of human behavior and suggests also that self-interpretation of one's own fantasies may have therapeutic value for the interpreter. Bettelheim considers that exposing the subject to his or her fantasies is analagous to the process of nondirective interviewing. However, he cannot offer other than testimonial to bolster his impression that there is therapeutic value to the method.

Bettelheim sees several advantages to assessment in the process of self-interpretation. Noting that the developer of the TAT (Murray, 1937) cautions that in interpreting the fantasies of others–for example, the assessor interpreting the client's TAT stories–the opportunity presents itself for the assessor to project personal biases into the stories. Self-interpretation does not eliminate this source of misinterpretation, but does, according to Bettelheim, attenuate it.

Two specific advantages are claimed for the method: (1) it offers to the assessor the means to identify the conflictual issues in a person's life that give rise to defensive operations, together with the nature of these defenses, and (2) the depth of repression. An example of repression is seen in the case of an individual who fails to interpret a commonly reported theme, or reports that there is no meaningful story in the stimulus material. According to Bettelheim, the client will interpret stories on the cards that elicit those problem areas of life that he or she recognizes and can face, but will not deal with stimulus material that, were he or she not deeply repressed, would call forth stories that are similar to the client's personal problems.

Luborsky (1952) also studied self-interpretation of the TAT as a possible clinical technique. He reports some encouraging results:

1. The implicit or explicit ability of the patient to recognize the mechanisms that went into the construction of his stories.
2. The many ways in which acceptance or denial of meaningfulness of the story content can be expressed, especially, the dimension of external determination of stories versus internal or psychological determination.
3. Several ways of inferring the patient's capacity for personality growth, and
4. A way of scoring feelings to self and parents.

Dorr's Codiagnostician Model Co-evaluation of psychological protocols can be adapted to various clinical situations. Fischer's (1970) approach to cointerpretation of a protocol to provide insight is illustrated on p. 264. In Dorr's (1981) method, the partners in a marriage work conjointly with Dorr in their role of "codiagnosticians-cotherapists." The highlights of his interactional method are presented below, together with a psychological report that ensued from such an interaction and was designed as a working psychotherapeutic tool. Notice the interesting way in which Dorr hangs his insights on test performance, which in no way detracts from the basic human orientation. The tests are a "handle" the clients can grab onto.

In the first phase of the procedure, the partners are administered a battery consisting of the Duke Psychiatric Intake Booklet, the Edwards Personal Preference Schedule, the MMPI, the Rorschach, and the TAT. The Rorschach is administered first by a psychometrist, following which Dorr administers a consensus Rorschach (pp. 326–328) to the couple in the presence of the psychometrist, who observes and takes notes. As an adjunct to the basic consensus procedure, each partner indicates on separate index cards, unseen by the other; first the best-liked and the least-liked cards, then the cards that the spouse would like the best and which the least. This phase is concluded with a discussion of the results which are placed on a chalkboard: "The consensus procedure usually reveals the way in which the couple resolves differences—their patterns of confrontation, compromise, defenses, and problem-solving strategies."

The second phase, interpretation, is scheduled for the following day. In a three- to six-hour session, the couple, Dorr, and the psychometrist all participate in making sense of the accumulated data as they apply to a troubled marriage.

The Edwards is discussed first. Dorr's explanation of the norming and meaning of the preference schedule profiles is followed with a presentation of the couple's juxtaposed profiles, whereupon the "husband and wife soon begin to comment on the profiles and usually identify sources of conflict."

In the review of the MMPI that follows, Dorr orients the couple to the inventory, and particularly to the meaning of the pathological sounding names of the scales. With help, the couple interprets their profiles, which they frequently relate to earlier impressions gained about themselves from the Edwards.

The Rorschach is reviewed next. The couple's participation here is minimal inasmuch as Rorschach data cannot readily be grasped by those who are not trained in the method.

The TAT is approached with a phenomenological orientation, providing an opportunity for each partner to gain insight into how the other views the world. Each partner reads aloud the stories of the other, and Dorr often makes the first interpretation. He draws the couple into making interpretations with queries such as "I wonder if..." and "Could it be..." which often lead the participants to "brilliantly insightful observations."

In the final step of the process, Dorr writes and mails to the couple a "report letter" that summarizes the insights that emerged during the testing and feedback (interpretive) sessions. He considers that "The follow-up letter" is a crucial aspect of the procedure. The couple cannot possibly absorb all that is said in the feedback session, much less metabolize it effectively.

The following report letter to "John and Mary"[1] was obviously written as a therapeutic tool. Dorr clearly is in the role of a compassionate and understanding teacher. He teaches John and Mary about themselves, including their shortcomings, and tells them what they must do to live better as a couple. Note that he deals with some involved psychological issues in a sympathetic (human) conversational tone that will "get through" to his clients.

```
Mr. and Mrs. John Jones
Street and Number
City, State, Zip


Dear John and Mary:

I hope this letter finds you well. I talked to (my
cotherapists) during and after your work with them in
(another city). They informed me that you did an
enormous amount of work and appeared to be moving in a
positive direction. In this letter, I will summarize
the results of the conjoint psychological testing. I
will report on each test in turn and offer some
concluding remarks.
```

[1]Reproduced with the permission of Dr. Dorr.

The juxtaposed Edwards profiles are appended, together with scale definitions. You will recall that the Edwards is a psychometric instrument that is based on Murray's needs system. The scores are reported in terms of percentiles, hence a score at the 50th percentile is higher than about half of the individuals in the norm group and lower than the other half.

On John's profile we see that the highest need score was for Affiliation; to be associated with other people, to have friends, and this sort of thing. We also see high scores on Abasement which reflects a tendency to accept blame and to take on others' responsibilities. He was relatively high on nurturance which is to give nurturance to others, and his steadfastness is revealed by the high score on Endurance. His Autonomy score was extremely low which in some ways complements the high Affiliation score although these scales are largely independent. He also had a relatively low Dominance score and a low Change score. The Aggressiveness score was very low suggesting that he avoids expression of hostility and aggression. Overall, the profile is consistent with what I observed in the feedback session; a quiet, retiring, gentle man who likes to avoid conflict.

Heterosexuality and Exhibitionism were the two highest scores on Mary's scale which is consistent with the history of fashion modeling. A model who doesn't have exhibitionistic needs probably would not do very well. Further, Mary says that she has gotten along better with men in the past than with women. The high Heterosexuality score reflects this. She had a very low Affiliation need score. Very high or very low need scores usually reflect a transitory emotional state. Mary confirmed that she is very wary of closeness and lives as a psychological "recluse" out of fear of being hurt or betrayed.

In comparing the two profiles I saw some possibility for conflict. For example, the Affiliation scores deviate significantly from the norm and in opposite directions. The absolute difference between the two scores is very large. I am sure this would lead to conflict in marriage. Another factor is that John has fairly high nurturance and succorance needs. Succorance is the need to receive nurturance. Mary is not especially low on nurturance, but in comparison to John's high succorance need, we see that John may feel unsatisfied, unsupported, and generally unnurtured.

The juxtaposed MMPI profiles are appended together with some scale definitions. *Please remember my caution* that these scales were labeled according to the psychiatric norm group and may therefore sound overly pathological.

Mary's profile is that of a woman who hurts very much. This profile reveals a hurt person, a cautious person, who is probably using an enormous amount of psychological energy to protect, defend, and project, leaving little for personal growth or joy. The repressive defenses are not working well and in view of her accomplishments in life, her self-esteem is really quite low. When we are hurt our basic defensive strategies tend to become exaggerated. This is the picture we see before us. One of Mary's defenses is to be angrily impulsive and another is to resort to externalization and projection. Hence, we see an exaggerated elevation of the Paranoia scale. This is not exactly clinical paranoia, but rather a kind of all-seeing, overly sensitive stance toward life. The "feelers" are out just waiting to get stepped on. The problem with paranoia is that it tends to feed on itself. The more sensitive you get the more you find to feed the paranoia. Mary described herself on the Intake Booklet as a very sensitive person. Sensitivity can be a good personal trait. While it is desirable to be sensitive regarding other people's emotions we have to learn to grow some "alligator skin" around our own personalities so that we are not easily hurt ourselves.

John's MMPI profile is "ultranormal." The MMPI does not measure normality except in the statistical sense. Hence, the scores don't mean that he does not have paranoid or impulsive, or other kinds of traits, it merely reveals that these traits are closer to the statistical norm.

When comparing the two profiles, the major problem will be that John might find it hard to empathize with his more emotional, volatile, and sensitive spouse. This is not insurmountable. Furthermore, we know that Mary is in a personal crisis at this time and when the crisis begins to resolve her emotionality will settle considerably.

Now let me turn to the Rorschach. John's Rorschach was that of a man who does his best to keep his life simple, smooth, and relaxed. Obviously, he is extremely bright but he does not choose to exercise his mind in emotional areas. This is not to say that he is not thoughtful. He is very sensitive and thoughtful. However, his major strategy in life is to keep emotional reactions under wrap. The Rorschach was consistent with the Sentence Completion response "When the going gets rough...I get quiet."

The Rorschach suggests that while his "life strategy" helps his stability he may be cutting himself off from psychological growth in certain areas. Is it possible to be too stable? Perhaps. Oversimplification of life's complex problems can lead to as many errors as overreaction. A person can be wrong in either direction. The Rorschach would suggest that in his attempts to maintain psychological equilibrium he may be minimally utilizing certain internal psychological resources such that his problem-solving capability may become stereotyped and ineffective.

Mary's Rorschach reveals a unique mind. She has an extensive associational process and the creativity can lead her in two directions. She can either be very original and clever in perception and problem-solving, or she may be way "off-base." Interestingly, the Rorschach suggests that both of you may at times be way off base in dealing with life's problems but for different reasons; John because he may be overly constricted and Mary because she is overly reactive.

Mary's Rorschach is that of a highly emotional individual. She has a good reservoir of psychological strengths but these strengths are not well organized and may not be particularly accessible to her at this time. With continued work and treatment, of course, these strengths will become more available.

On Mary's Rorschach I see many signs of emotional pain including depression and anxiety. Some of the distress is clearly related to losses in life, but also they may be related to some erroneous assumptions about the way life is to be. I will comment more on this later.

When I look at the Rorschachs together I see two people who are psychologically very different. This is not necessarily a problem, however. I would suggest to Mary that she enjoy her looseness. Looseness is not a weakness. It is a virtue to be built on. I would encourage Mary to think like an artist. Art is disciplined emotion. The artist must risk and then evaluate dispassionately. As a legitimate singer, I am an artist of sorts. I am sure you know the enormous risk of self-esteem that I face every time that I stand up in front of anywhere from 1 to 300 people, and wager that both sides of my brain will work together so that I can get the words and music straight and hope that the small pieces of gristle in my throat will work the way they did in practice. When I go to sing I must think that I am the hottest thing going. I must not doubt myself but when it is all over and I listen to the tape or go back to my teacher, ego must stay outside the door. I must view the performance dispassionately; neither being too harsh on myself (if I don't quite sound like Robert Merrill) or unrealistic in my appraisal of my limitations. John is cautious, guarded, and also stable. While I am encouraging him to explore more the looser side of his nature, I also encourage him to rejoice in his own conservative characteristics as well.

Now let me turn to the TAT. As I mentioned the TAT interpretation is the most speculative aspect of the feedback.

On Card 1 (which shows the boy looking at a violin) John told a story about a little boy who had been scolded by his teacher. He settles down and doggedly goes on and becomes a very accomplished violinist. Is this the discipline that allowed John to excel? In Mary's story the little boy looked at the violin and seemed to be rather overwhelmed by the strangeness and the magnitude of the task. However, little by little he whittled the task down to something that he felt he could deal with and decided that he would at least try. This may be the way Mary views a lot of things in life. At first they are rather overwhelming but as she uses those strong psychological resources within her she begins to regain her self-confidence and go on.

Card 2 is a pastoral scene which shows a young woman in the foreground and a man plowing in the background, and an older woman over on the side. John's story was about the girl in the foreground going on to continue her schooling so that she will hopefully "free her unborn sibling of the farm." The rescue theme is obvious. On the other hand, we see more gloom in Mary's story. The young girl had dreams but now merely becomes "resigned." Accepting life's reality is one thing but, to me, resignation is very depressing. I am enough of a romantic to believe that we can face certain of life's limitations and still reach for magic.

Card 4 depicts a woman clutching the shoulders of a man whose face and body are averted as though pulling away. Ninety percent of the people who respond to this card tell the story about conflict. John, however, chose to project a story in which this man and lady are friends. He is leaving and she is trying to get him to stay. There is no negative affect expressed. When asked what the people feel he responded, "Happy." There is no right answer to these stories but it struck me that John managed to duck out of the potential conflict of this story as he did in response to Card 13 MF (which shows the woman nude to the waist in bed and the man turned away). This card also "pulls" negative emotion. He started a story about a prostitute who overdosed on drugs but after the police were called John focused on the way in which the hero "covers his eyes" because he has never seen anyone dead. Of course, the man is covering his eyes in the picture but almost no one comments on it. Am I overinterpreting in suggesting that this reflects a great reluctance to see hurt in a person. This may be a major dynamic in the marriage. Let me explain.

John met Mary when she was hurting greatly. He could satisfy his nurturance needs in playing the wonderful professional who took care of Mary's mother *and Mary*. He protected her and nurtured her. That sounds like a beautiful way to start a marriage but it really isn't because it starts off confirming Mary's vulnerability and weakness. Perhaps Mary has weakness and vulnerability, but she also has strength and toughness.

On the Intake Booklet John said in response to the sentence completion root "I am...what I am." But this is not really true, at least when he is around Mary. John tiptoes around trying not to get Mary mad, trying not to hurt Mary, to avoid conflict etc., etc. I believe this is done because of a genuine concern for her feelings and welfare. But in so doing he diminishes himself and also diminishes Mary. Mary is no longer a patient. John is not Mary's therapist. John has a right to be who he is and to say what he thinks and feels. As long as he continues to squelch who he is he will lessen both himself and Mary. If Mary is upset over what John is feeling that is Mary's problem, not John's. This is a matter of personal space. Mary can grow only when she is given the space to grow. If she feels that John *must* be this, *must* be that, *should* do this, *should* do that, and he allows her to continue to think that this is true Mary may not grow. He can only genuinely love her when he is honest about who he is. Then she must make a choice whether to love the reality or not love it. But to try to be something else is to be a phony. One cannot love an image very long.

I think Mary's response to the last blank card is the most revealing. I will quote it verbatim.

Variations and Trends in Psychological Assessment

> I had a dream—I dreamed of a world filled with beauty and love. The dream began as it should-or as I had pictured it would. As I grew older the dream began to shatter. Some things I once thought as beautiful were not so. The things I loved became fewer and fewer. Then one day I awoke and found the world could once again be beautiful and I once again could find much of the love I thought forever lost. With each passing year—this time—I clutched dearly the beautiful things and the love I at last had again. But at the last—even with my constant struggle to hold on dearly—the clouds started drifting in one by one covering the beauty and trying to draw up with them—the love. The ending is although I feel like it is time to put the dreams aside and either drift with the clouds or stay behind, I still struggle for my dream.

Mary let me comment on this by quoting from a paper that I am working on.

> Beth's silky black hair tumbles over her honey shoulders in defiance of the paralyzing depression that reigns within her. Her dark brown eyes plead through long, black lashes. The gaze is without malice or strength. Only raw need shows. The concaves of the scrawny body are deepened by the skin's olive hue, and its frailness describes her ego. Hurt Beth, child Beth, pathetic Beth. Her quiet scared eyes scream her loneliness. Though in years an adult, she is very young, vulnerable, dependent; afraid like a new fawn waiting quietly and anxiously in the woods for its mother to return with warm milk.
>
> Carol comes to us differently. She is arrogant, cocky, and aggressive. She doesn't walk, she swaggers. She is cruel, slashing and ripping all that crosses her path. Our reaction is to get away from her as far as possible.
>
> Though different in style, Beth and Carol are very similar. Each is a part person, each is unwhole. Each possesses a personality that is imperfectly integrated, incomplete and static. Each is starving because she cannot drink the milk of love and kindness that is offered. The styles differ. Beth regurgitates nourishment, Carol spits it out petulantly. The reasons are the same and may be understood in the context of

personality structure. Parts are split apart; they do not function in concert, do not speak to each other; thus they are not whole. Carol wrote, "even God didn't deny evil its right to existence—he only split it off."

But did he? John Steinbeck says that "underneath the topmost layers of frailty, men want to be good and want to be loved. Indeed most of their vices are attempted shortcuts to love."

God gave us what we are and it sometimes comes out as evil. Jealousy, hatred, spitefulness, greed are God-given drives, probably set within us to help us survive. To be real we must not deny these parts. Rather they must interact with each other.

Beth and Carol were both patients of mine. Another patient whom I will call Sue once asked me how one attained contentment and a feeling of wholeness in life-how one overcame the horrible feeling of loneliness that she felt all the time. She was a pianist and we discussed music. Together we discovered that a piece of music is only a combination of noise and time. *In its movement it becomes real.*

The parts interact in time and become a new whole. To be of beauty it must have dissonance and resolution. As an art form it must possess and stir emotion, and not always pretty emotion. The emotion may be hate, rage, fear, sorrow, love, or compassion. There can be no body of art that is mere prettiness. It would not be wholly human, thus it would not be art. There is a place for ugliness in art because art is the reflection of the completeness of life.

But what do we do with our own lives? Do we embrace with equal zeal our dullness and our nobleness; our stupidity and our faithfulness; our vileness and our compassion; our goodness and our badness? In my experience we do not. We float the pretty parts to the top but we sequester the not so pretty parts. We rarely know each other and thus we find it so hard to truly love each other. One cannot love a part for very long and when we show to the world only the pretty we live in constant fear that the ugly will be discovered and we will lose those whom we love. So we do not risk revealing ourselves and paradoxically we diminish ourselves and our lovers.

Let me tell you about another patient of mine whom I will call Bret. For five years Bret struggled with the terrible conflict. He wanted so badly to live in a world of beauty and gentleness and he wanted so badly to be this himself. Yet there were other parts about him that he despised. You see, the world he saw was a projection of himself, both beautiful and not so beautiful.

On the fifth anniversary of our work together he brought me a butterfly as a graduation present. He no longer needed me. The black and white butterfly was beautiful. The black symbolized what he thought was the evil—the ugly. The white symbolized what he saw as the pure and the good. What he learned was that when put together true beauty emerged. Life is beautiful in its completeness as he came to accept all parts of himself he also came to rejoice in the fullness of his universe.

Bret was very much like the little girl you told about in the TAT whose mother was reading to her. She was daydreaming about "the way she would like it to be." Bret used to think as you expressed in your response to the last TAT card—"the dream began as it should." He embraced the dream with all of his might. He "shouldered" with the tenacity of a bull dog. But when he finally let go of these myths, the true beauty of life emerged. With the butterfly he gave me a card that said "Thank you for your love, your patience, for believing in me, your friendship...but most of all for helping me become the person I am...for freedom!"

Barbara and I extend to you best wishes in your quest to achieve wholeness and true beauty in life together. If you ever wish to discuss any of this please call.

Sincerely,

Darwin Dorr, Ph.D.
Director of Psychological Services

THE ROLE OF THE PSYCHOLOGICAL TECHNICIAN IN ASSESSMENT

Technicians are widely employed in a number of professions. Medicine, dentistry, and law come readily to mind. Psychology is also a profession where technicians (or assistants) are becoming abundant—a relatively new specialist in a relatively new profession, although the advantages of employing technicians to perform the time-consuming operations of neuropsychological testing were pointed out by Halstead (Boll, 1981) many years ago. The proper role of technicians in the assessment context is a continuing question, however.

In the above case of John and Mary, a technician was employed in both the testing phase and the interpretation phase. Dorr indicates that this technician filled the roles of psychometrist, codiagnostician and cotherapist. In the initial administration of psychological instruments, the technician gathers intake information (with the Duke Psychiatric Intake Booklet) and administers the Edwards Personal Preference Schedule, the MMPI, the Rorschach (using the standard free-association and inquiry procedures), and the TAT. The consensus Rorschach, however, is administered by Dorr, and the technician's role during this procedure is observing and taking notes.

L'Abate (1964) presents a basic position concerning the role of the technician in psychological assessment. He identifies as an issue the demands made upon psychologists "not only in terms of thoroughness and excellence of their work but also in terms of the number of patients tested to satisfy the immediate demands of a clinical setting." He proposes a solution: "By using technicians for routine battery administration, the clinical psychologist has more time to devote to maximal exploitation of professional skills that a technician cannot achieve—complex interpretation of a variety of test results and report writing." He suggests that this approach is not more widely employed because it is recognized that the psychologist must have a first-hand awareness of the client's attitude, verbalizations, and blockings. He is of the opinion, however, that technicians can be taught to make adequate notes on these crucial matters.

Affleck, Strider, and Helper (1968) noted advantages and disadvantages to the employment of technicians in the assessment process. Not the least of the advantages is the comfortable situation that develops when technicians take over the role of tester in which many psychologists are reluctant to function (Holt, 1967). By contrast, Affleck et al. report that technicians attend well to the mechanics of testing, and they tend to be adept in the technical skills of test administration. A further advantage to having testing done by technicians is economic. On the minus side, Affleck et al. found technicians to be deficient in interpersonal sensitivity and skill—a situation that might be improved through training and more careful selection of personnel. Some technicians also were found to be deficient in sensitivity to "the manner in which a patient arrives at a response." The loss of psychologist contact with patients is still another problem frequently mentioned when psychologists are queried concerning the employment of technicians.

Participants at a symposium (Gentry, 1974a) that followed the Affleck, Strider, and Helper study by several years reported conclusions on the work of technicians that are generally consistent with the above. Sloop and Quarrick (1974) summarize: "It has...been noted that faculty and staff supervising technical performance generally regard it to be of high quality, in some cases surpassing their own...It is possible, however, that to some degree the high quality of performance attributed to the technician is biased by the psychologist's need to believe the technician is carrying out her duties well so they in turn will not have to once again take up this somewhat burdensome responsibility."

Musante (1974), basing his conclusions on returns from a questionnaire completed by 21 psychology faculty and staff, reports on the value of the psychological technician in glowing terms: "Overall, the consensus...was that psychology technicians were a welcomed addition to their work settings. They regarded their diagnostic performance as being of extremely high quality..." Of the areas of clinical performance rated, "test administration was regarded as the superior function." Indeed, "Several psychologists indicated that they felt psychological testing was done more efficiently by the technicians than by faculty and staff."

Looking at the broader clinical impact on the assessment function, Musante reports on questionnaire data from three clinical settings:

> Because we are concerned about how the technician might affect the quality of psychologists' work, we asked whether technicians' written observations of patient behavior were used as part of a final report and also whether technician services lessened the psychologists' contact with individual patients. Respondents in the three settings acknowledged considerable use of technicians' behavioral observations in writing their reports, emphasizing that technician notes were often "invaluable" in gaining a complete understanding of the patient's pathological condition. Two of the clinical settings indicated that using technicians had definitely resulted in lessened patient contact, but they regarded this as a positive outcome which in turn led to their being able to see more patients diagnostically...or become more involved in therapeutic and consultation activities. The third setting...differed slightly in that psychologists viewed the availability of technician services as changing the nature of their contacts with patients rather than the amount of time spent with them; they indicate that they now spend more time interviewing each patient than before.

Tallent, Kennedy, Szafir, and Grolimund (1974) report on a variation of this technician model. Situated on an intake psychiatric ward, this approach to assessment has several objectives. The first is to multiply the number of cases a ward psychologist can assess. The second is to make available as soon as possible the psychological assessor's impressions concerning the disorders and indications for treatment of newly admitted patients. Of equal importance to these is the objective of involving the ward nursing team in an experience that will enhance the understanding that nurses and nursing assistants have of their patients' problems and treatment needs. What has evolved, then, is an assessment-treatment model.

Following a period of training, nursing personnel become adequately proficient in administering and scoring a selected group of psychological tests. In this capacity their function goes beyond the role of psychology technician. Rather, they bring to the task their nursing skills, clinical orientation, and interpersonal sensitivity. The RN does not compromise his or her position as a nurse, but functions, rather, in one of the many ways that come under the rubric of "the expanded role of the nurse." Indeed, participation in psychological assessment broadens the nurse's understanding of human nature and psychopathology, knowledge that has multiple professional applications.

The assessment procedure commonly is initiated within a short time after a patient is admitted to the ward, and such rapid involvement in the diagnostic-treatment process is often viewed positively by the patients. Since the ward is staffed at all hours, seven days a week, testing might occur at any time. It is not uncommon for the psychologist to start the week Monday morning by looking over several test protocols of patients who had not yet been admitted at the close of the day the previous Friday.

The mechanics of the method are as follows: As soon after admission as possible, a nursing assistant meets with the patient, and after getting acquainted administers an MMPI, which s(he) scores and profiles as time permits. The nursing assistant then asks the patient to respond in writing to a sentence completion test. S(he) takes notes concerning behaviors, speech content, and impressions. The patient's next contact is with a nurse who administers a Bender, a Rorschach (with inquiry but no scoring), and a TAT. S(he) also records observations and impressions.

In the final phase of this procedure, the nurse, the nursing assistant, and the psychologist meet and review the test material and exchange observations and impressions. The psychologist raises questions concerning the patient's behaviors and verbalizations, including details of the testing, such as the manner of reproducing Bender figures, or facial expressions, or manner of speech. The patient is then called in, interviewed by the team, provided with feedback, and invited to ask questions—at that time or in the future. The psychologist then writes a report and discusses diagnostic and treatment issues with the nursing team and the patient's psychiatrist.

TECHNICIAN-LEVEL VERSUS ASSESSOR-LEVEL FUNCTIONS

Early in this book the distinctions between testing and assessment were discussed. What functions may appropriately be assigned to a technician must have reference to this distinction. These, generally, are testing, or testing-related activities, such as administering tests, scoring and profiling, and recording observations and impressions—what is often referred to as "clinical behavior." The latitude allowed to the technician is essentially within prescribed guidelines. The querying of Wechsler intelligence test responses, for example, is in accordance with instructions to the psychological examiner.

The practice of psychological assessment, by contrast, particularly in the modern application of the clinical tradition, may be flexible and open-ended, attentive to the opportunities offered by unanticipated or developing situations. The watchword is *adaptation*—to whatever the situation might be in the ongoing give and take of the assessment process. The words of Rapaport (Rapaport, Gill, & Schafer, 1945) illustrate this position:

> No attempt was made to proceed with the testing of all patients in the same manner. The requirement of "identity of conditions of testing" was interpreted to be a requirement for the tester to adapt himself to the specific characteristics of the patient. From an "objective" point of view, therefore, the attitude of the examiner varied from individual to individual.

The difference between the function of the diagnostic technician (testing) and that of the assessor is that technical work may be programmatic, rule-following, and standardized; while assessment is fluid, flexible, and both proactive and reactive. The border between assessment and psychotherapy may be blurred (Allen, 1981), or nonexistent (as pointed out by Schlesinger, 1973, in his paper on the interaction of dynamic and reality factors in the diagnostic testing interview; see p. 45). So far as diagnosticians are concerned, "their competence as diagnosticians rests to a significant degree on their skill as treaters" (Smith & Allen, 1984).

Allen (1981) explicates the relationship:

> Just as it should be axiomatic that one cannot treat without diagnosing, it is also true that one cannot diagnose without treating. In the realm of the psychologist's work this statement has two meanings. First, the diagnostic process is hampered if the psychologist is not also a capable therapist. Indeed, the psychologist who has experience in treating a range of patients with a variety of modalities will be most skilled in his diagnostic work with patients and will be most knowledgeable in formulating treatment recommendations. Second, patients tend to experience the process of testing as part of their treatment programs.

PSYCHOLOGICAL ASSESSMENT AS A TRANSACTION

Psychological assessment is more than a procedure; it is a *transaction*. Berg (1985) observes:

> Recent contributions to the theory and technique of psychological testing show that the patient's ego functioning, object relations, and accessibility to treatment can be most clearly highlighted by attending to the vicissitudes of the interpersonal relationship between patient and examiner and by using carefully devised interventions to explore these dimensions...Judicious interventions to determine how the patient responds to various interpersonal approaches can geometrically increase the yield of diagnostic information from the testing...Although such interventions stray from the chimera of rigidly standardized test administration, the experienced examiner knows that the exigencies of the testing relationship necessitate interventions not prescribed in the textbooks, including those virtually forced upon him by the demands of working with a particular patient. The examiner can enrich the diagnostic yield of the assessment by evaluating the significance of such interventions, as well as by making interventions designed to validate specific hypotheses that arise in the course of testing. These latter interventions are pitched toward helping the patient collaborate in diagnostically exploring his psychological functioning. As Breuer and Freud...noted regarding the patient's participation in treatment, "we make him himself into a collaborator [and] induce him to regard himself with the objective interest of an investigator."

The outcome of such transaction is twofold: (1) the therapeutic effect, and (2) the development of useful data—useful particularly in the therapeutic situation—and that goes far beyond the yield of tests employed in accordance with standard testing practice or the intents of their authors. Our present concern is the latter.

Allen (1981) shows how assessment technique may have direct applicability to therapy. Like Berg, above (and also Breuer and Freud) he invites his patient to be a collaborator in assessment. He reports:

> Another means of encouraging the patient's participation throughout the testing process is to engage the patient in exploring the meaning of his responses. For example, when the patient runs into difficulty, his understanding of and feelings about this difficulty can be explored then and there. This kind of exploration can also be built directly into the tests. For example, on the Thematic Apperception Test, the patient is asked to make up stories about a series of pictures; after having completed this task, he can be asked to go back through his stories and provide his own explanation or interpretation of their meaning. This process of engaging the patient in working out the meaning of his test responses and productions is directly analagous to the process of psychotherapy. So conducted, the testing situation becomes a microcosm of the treatment situation, providing the best basis for translating the test findings into the treatment plan.

Smith and Allen (1984) also relate psychological assessment to therapy. The psychologist's understandings of a client will be sought out by therapist colleagues, they suggest, when the psychologist exercises the role of consultant and not that of tester.

> Psychologists will be valuable consultants only if they are knowledgeable about such areas as psychotherapy, personality functioning and development, cognitive processes, and so forth. Moreover, they must be skilled in providing therapy so that they will be able to help their colleagues appreciate the implications of their findings for the treatment process. Although this role is potentially most gratifying to the psychologist, it also carries more of a burden. Specifically, viewing oneself as a consultant implies that the individual psychologist, rather than testing per se, potentially has something to offer. From this vantage point, the psychiatrist is placed in the position of seeking the expertise and opinions of the psychologist rather than the findings of tests.

Transference and countertransference in assessment Insights of the assessor concerning transference and countertransference, and resistance, are seen by a number of authors as having direct implications for therapy. Sugarman (1981), in a critical statement on the neglect of countertransference by some psychological assessors, emphasizes the value of

> the examiner's subjective emotional response to the patient as a data source within testing...[yet] a disciplined examination of countertransference reactions can yield significant information about the patient, assuming that the examiner's ego is relatively unimpaired and resistant to the inroads of neurotic conflict on his work. Given this assumption, a well-trained examiner's unusual feelings, thoughts, and behavior can be considered to be reactions to a specific patient and, thus, to impart unique information about that patient.

Allen (1981) comments:

> Like any clinical encounter, the patient-examiner interaction is enlivened by the feelings, fantasies, and distortions of both the patient and the examiner. These phenomena need to be understood not only because they embody the patient's core conflicts and struggles, but because they also foreshadow major treatment dilemmas. An examiner who is aware of his countertransference is able, for example, to alert those who will treat the patient to the dangers and pitfalls that are likely to emerge in the subsequent treatment process. Thus, the examiner who allows himself to enter into a significant relationship with the patient will be able to provide the richest information.

Berg (1984) alerts us that the issues that are identified when the assessor is tuned in to his or her countertransference may have significant implications for therapy:

> The examiner's emotions may represent a reciprocal response to the patient's feelings and eliciting behaviors that are designed to stir such emotions and related behaviors in the examiner. Observing these responses may disclose the patient's self-images and the corresponding roles he expects others to assume, as well as the emotional responses apt to be stirred in both parties because of the interpersonal exchange arranged by the patient. Such interchanges forecast the transference and countertransference paradigms likely to arise in future treatment.

Though a wealth of data is available in countertransference reactions, all psychological examiners are not capable of mining this wealth. Thus, Sugarman (1981) has observed that many examiners use countertransference unreflectively. Presumably, specialized training would be helpful. Jaffe (1988) advises "In order for the examiner to interpret the meaning of transference and countertransference reactions to psychological testing, the examiner must be thoroughly familiar with the method, intent, and spirit of the assessment procedures." This could be a difficult order to fill for many whose assessment-related training focuses on test administration and scoring.

Resistance to assessment   Resistance, which is so commonly seen in various forms of therapy, and which is a key issue in psychoanalysis, may first be identified in psychological assessment. Berg (1985) observes:

> A patient may, obviously or subtly, undermine the assessment and the examiner's efforts to establish a diagnostic alliance. By remaining attuned to the resistive maneuvers the patient mobilizes during testing, the examiner is privy to a dramatic presentation of the patient's pathological defenses and how they maintain his illness.

Allen (1981) points out, however, that making such observations does not fall within the skill repertoire of the technician:

> Although delegating psychological test administration to a psychometrician is a common practice in some settings, the yield of the data-gathering process would be much enhanced

by the consulting psychologist's skills. For example, skillful intervention in response to a patient's resistances (e.g., constriction, suspiciousness, passivity) not only contribute to an understanding of the patient's functioning but also enhance the validity of the evaluation by enabling the patient to provide a more complete test record.

Maximizing the technician's contribution The experience of numerous assessors, together with limited survey data as cited above (p. 345), indicates that technicians make a valuable contribution to assessment in many settings. At the same time, the (immediately) above discussions of the specialized approaches of the skilled psychological assessor make it clear that much of what assessors do cannot be assigned to technicians.

In the best of all worlds, a well-trained assessor would personally administer all necessary individual psychological tests, and thus be in a position to extract maximum information by virtue of being particularly sensitive to such psychological manifestations as resistance, transference, and countertransference, and any number of subtle but significant communications. Such assessment practice would also permit the framing of numerous nonstandard and opportunistic queries, to depart from standardized test administration as judgment dictates, and to generally structure the transaction to be maximally productive of diagnostic material pertinent to the reason for assessment.

Assessment, like all of life, involves trade-offs. Each assessor may train her or his technicians to best fit into the needs of a particular setting, particularly to be alert to certain behaviors, and to make meaningful notes which the assessor may follow up in subsequent interviews. Additionally, benefits beyond gaining information may be built into the assessment paradigm, such as in the diagnostic-treatment model described on pp. 345–346.

REFERENCES

Abt, L. E., & Bellak, L. (1950). *Projective psychology: Clinical approaches to the total personality.* New York: Knopf.

Adair, F. L. (1978). Review of computerized scoring and interpreting services. In O. K. Buros (Ed.), *The eighth mental measurements yearbook* (pp. 940–942). Lincoln, NE: Buros Institute of Mental Measurements.

Adams, K. M. (1980a). In search of Luria's battery: A false start. *Journal of Consulting and Clinical Psychology, 48,* 511–516.

Adams, K. M. (1980b). An end of innocence for behavioral neurology? *Journal of Consulting and Clinical Psychology, 48,* 522–524.

Adams, R. L. (1985). Review of Luria-Nebraska Neuropsychological Battery, J. V. Mitchell Jr. (Ed.), *The ninth mental measurements yearbook* (Vol. 1, pp. 878–881). Lincoln, NE: Buros Institute of Mental Measurements.

Adler, T. (1990). Does the "new" MMPI beat the "classic?" *APA Monitor,* April 1990, pp. 18–19.

Affleck, D. C., & Strider, F. D. (1971). Contribution of psychological reports to patient management. *Journal of Consulting and Clinical Psychology, 37,* 177–179.

Affleck, D. C., Strider, F. D., & Helper, M. M. (1968). A clinical psychologist-assistant approach to psychodiagnostic testing. *Journal of Projective Techniques and Personality Assessment, 32,* 317–322.

Albert, S., Fox, H. M., & Kahn, M. W. (1980). Faking psychosis on the Rorschach: Can expert judges detect malingering? *Journal of Personality Assessment, 44,* 115–119.

Alexander, I. E., & Basowitz, H. (1965). Current clinical training practices: An overview. In C. N. Zimet, F. M. Throne, & Conference Committee (Eds.), Preconference materials:

Conference on the Professional Preparation of Clinical Psychologists. Washington, DC: American Psychological Association.

Allen, J. G. (1981). The clinical psychologist as a diagnostic consultant. *Bulletin of The Menninger Clinic, 45,* 247–258.

Allison, J., Blatt, S. J., & Zimet, C. N. (1988). *The interpretation of psychological tests.* Washington, DC: Hemisphere Publishing Corporation.

Allport, G. W. (1937). Personality: *A psychological interpretation.* New York: Henry Holt and Company.

Allport, G. W. (1961). *Pattern and growth in personality.* New York: Holt, Rinehart, and Winston.

Allport, G. W., & Odbert, H. S. (1936). Trait-names: A psycho-lexical study. *Psychological Monographs, 47* (No. 211).

Alpher, V. S., Perfetto, G. A., Henry, W. P., & Strupp, H. H. (1990). The relationship between the Rorschach and assessment of the capacity to engage in short-term dynamic psychotherapy. *Psychotherapy, 27,* 224–229.

American Psychiatric Association (1952). *Diagnostic and statistical manual: Mental disorders.* (2nd ed.) (DSM-II) Washington, DC: Author.

American Psychiatric Association (1968). *Diagnostic and statistical manual of mental disorders.* Washington, DC: Author.

American Psychiatric Association (1980). *Diagnostic and statistical manual of mental disorders* (3rd ed.) (DSM-III). Washington, DC: Author.

American Psychiatric Association (1987a). *Diagnostic and statistical manual of mental disorders.* (3rd ed., rev.) (DSM-III-R). Washington, DC: Author.

American Psychiatric Association (1987b). *Diagnostic criteria from DSM-III-R.* Washington, DC: Author.

American Psychological Association (1970). Psychological assessment and public policy. *American Psychologist, 25,* 264–266. Washington, DC: Author.

American Psychological Association (1977). *Standards for Providers of Psychological Services,* Washington, DC: Author.

American Psychological Association (1981). Ethical principles of psychologists. *American Psychologist, 36,* 633–638. Washington, DC: Author.

American Psychological Association (1985) *Directory of the American Psychological Association.* Washington, DC: Author.

American Psychological Association (1985). *Standards for educational and psychological testing.* Washington, DC: Author.

American Psychological Association (1986). *Guidelines for computer-based tests and interpretations.* Washington, DC: Author.

American Psychological Association, Joint Committee on Testing Practices (1988). *Code of fair testing practices in education.* Washington, DC: Author.

Amrine, M. (Ed.). (1965). Testing and testing policy. *American Psychologist, 20,* 857–992.

Anastasi, A. (1988). *Psychological testing* (6th ed.). New York: Macmillan.

Andersen, S. M., & Harthorn, B. H. (1989). The diagnostic knowledge inventory: A measure of knowledge about psychiatric diagnosis. *Journal of Clinical Psychology, 45,* 999–1013.

Appelbaum, S. A. (1959). The effect of altered psychological atmosphere on Rorschach responses: A new supplementary procedure. *Bulletin of the Menninger Clinic, 23,* 179–185.

Appelbaum, S. A.. (1961). The end of the test as a determinant of responses. *Bulletin of the Menninger Clinic, 25,* 120–128.

Appelbaum, S. A. (1969). Psychological testing for the psychotherapist. *Dynamic Psychiatry, 2,* 158–163.

Appelbaum, S. A. (1970). Science and persuasion in the psychological test report. *Journal of Consulting and Clinical Psychology, 35,* 349–355.

Appelbaum, S. A. (1972). A method of reporting psychological test findings. *Bulletin of the Menninger Clinic, 36,* 535–545.

Appelbaum, S. A. (1973). Psychological-mindedness: Word, concept and essence. *International Journal of Psycho-Analysis, 54,* 35–46.

Appelbaum, S. A. (1976). Rapaport revisited: Practice. *Bulletin of the Menninger Clinic, 40,* 229–237.

Appelbaum, S. A. (1977). *The anatomy of change: A Menninger Foundation report on testing the effects of psychotherapy.* New York: Plenum.

Appelbaum, S. A. (1990). The relationship between assessment and psychotherapy. *Journal of Personality Assessment, 54,* 791–801.

Appelbaum, S. A., & Siegal, R. S. (1965). Half-hidden influences on psychological testing and practice. *Journal of Projective Techniques and Personality Assessment, 29,* 128–133.

Archer, R. P. (1987). *Using the MMPI with adolescents.* Hillsdale, NJ: Lawrence Erlbaum Associates.

Arnow, D., & Cooper, S. H. (1984). The borderline patient's regression on the Rorschach test. *Bulletin of the Menninger Clinic, 48,* 25–36.

Aronow, E., & Reznikoff, M. (1971). Application of projective tests to psychotherapy: A case study. *Journal of Personality Assessment, 35,* 379–393.

Aronow, E., & Reznikoff, M. (1973). Attitudes toward the Rorschach Test expressed in book reviews: A historical perspective. *Journal of Personality Assessment, 37,* 309–315.

Aronow, E., & Reznikoff, M. (1976). *Rorschach content interpretation.* Orlando, FL: Grune & Stratton.

Aronow, E., & Reznikoff, M. (1989). *A Rorschach introduction: Content and perceptual approaches.* Boston: Allyn and Bacon.

Aronow, E., Reznikoff, M., & Rauchway, A. (1979). Some old and new directions in Rorschach testing. *Journal of Personality Assessment, 43,* 227–234.

Atkinson, L., Quarrington, B., Alp, I. E., & Cyr, J. J. (1986). Rorschach validity: An empirical approach to the literature. *Journal of Clinical Psychology, 42,* 360–362.

Auger, T. J. (1974). Mental health terminology: A modern tower of Babel. *Journal of Community Psychology, 2,* 113–116.

Babcock, H. (1930). An experiment in the measurement of mental deterioration. *Archives of Psychology,* No. 117, New York.

Baker, G. (1964). A therapeutic application of psychodiagnostic test results. *Journal of Projective Techniques and Personality Assessment, 28,* 3–8.

Bardon, J. I., & Bennett, V. D. C. (1967). Preparation for professional psychology: An example from a school psychology training program. *American Psychologist, 22,* 652–656.

Barker, P. (1990). *Clinical interviews with children and adolescents.* New York: Norton.

Barrios, B., & Hartmann, D. P. (1986). The contributions of traditional assessment: Concepts, issues, and methodologies. In R. O. Nelson & S. C. Hayes (Eds.). *Conceptual foundations of behavioral assessment* (p. 83). New York: Guilford.

Bass, B., & Berg, I. A. (Eds.) (1959). *Objective approaches to personality assessment.* Princeton, NJ: D. Van Nostrand.

Batson, C. D. (1975) Attribution as a mediator of bias in helping. *Journal of Personality and Social Psychology, 32,* 455–466.

Beck, S. J. (1933). Configurational tendencies in Rorschach responses. *American Journal of Psychology, 45,* 433–443.

Beck, S. J. (1952). *Rorschach's Test: III. Advances in interpretation.* Orlando, FL: Grune & Stratton.

Beitman, B. D., Goldfried, M. R., & Norcross, J. C. (1989). The movement toward integrating the psychotherapies: An interview. *American Journal of Psychiatry, 146,* 138–147.

Bellak, L. (1954). *The Thematic Apperception Test and the Children's Apperception Test in clinical use.* Orlando, FL: Grune & Stratton.

Bellak, L. (1965). *Psychodiagnostic test report blank.* Larchmont, NY: C.P.S. Inc.

Bellak, L. (1975). *The TAT, CAT, and SAT in clinical use* (3rd ed.). Orlando, FL: Grune & Stratton.

Bem, D. J., & Allen, A. (1974). On predicting some of the people some of the time: The search for cross-situation consistencies in behavior. *Psychological Review, 81,* 506–520.

Bender, L. (1938). *A visual motor gestalt test and its clinical use.* Research Monograph No. 3. New York: American Orthopsychiatric Association.

Berg, M. R. (1983). Borderline psychopathology as displayed on psychological tests. *Journal of Personality Assessment, 47,* 120–133.

Berg, M. R. (1984a). Expanding the parameters of psychological testing. *Bulletin of the Menninger Clinic, 48,* 10–24.

Berg, M. R. (1984b). Teaching psychological testing to psychiatric residents. *Professional Psychology: Research and Practice, 15,* 343–352.

Berg, M. R. (1985). The feedback process in diagnostic psychological testing. *Bulletin of the Menninger Clinic, 49,* 52–69.

Berg, M. R. (1988). Diagnostic benefits of analyzing the group dynamics of the assessment team. *Bulletin of the Menninger Clinic, 52,* 126–133.

Berger, N. S. (1979). Beyond testing: A decision-making system for providing school psychological consultation. *Professional Psychology, 10,* 273–277.

Berne, E. (1949). The nature of intuition. *Psychiatric Quarterly, 23,* 203–226.

Bersoff, D. N. (1975). Professional ethics and legal responsibilities: On the horns of a dilemma. *Journal of School Psychology, 13,* 359–376.

Bettelheim, B. (1947). Self-interpretation of fantasy: The Thematic Apperception Test as an educational and therapeutic device. *American Journal of Orthopsychiatry, 17,* 80–100.

Beutler, L. E. (1983). *Eclectic psychotherapy: A systematic approach.* New York: Pergamon Press.

Bigler, E. D., & Steinman, D. R. (1981). Neuropsychology and computerized axial tomography: Further comments. *Professional Psychology, 12,* 195–197.

Bingham, W. V. D., & Moore, B. V. (1924). *How to interview.* New York: Harper.

Blanchard, W. H. (1959). The group process in gang rape. *Journal of Social Psychology, 49,* 259–266.

Blanchard, W. H. (1968). The consensus Rorschach: Background and development. *Journal of Projective Techniques and Personality Assessment, 32,* 327–330.

Blank, L. (1965). *Psychological evaluation in psychotherapy: Ten case histories.* Chicago: Aldine.

Blatt, S. J. (1986). Where have we been and where are we going? Reflections on 50 years of personality assessment. *Journal of Personality Assessment, 50,* 343–346.

Block, J. (1961). *The Q-sort method in personality assessment and psychiatric research.* Springfield, IL: Thomas.

Block, J. (1981). Some enduring and consequential structures of personality. In A. I. Rabin (Ed.). *Further explorations in personality.* New York: Wiley.

Board, R. (1958). Intuition in the methodology of psychoanalysis. *Psychiatry, 21,* 233–239.

Bogen, J. E., & Gordon, H. W. (1971). Musical tests for functional lateralization with intracarotid amobarbital. *Nature, 230,* 524.

Boll, T. J. (1977). A rationale for neuropsychological evaluation. *Professional Psychology, 8,* 64–71.

Boll, T. J. (1981). *The Halstead-Reitan neuropsychological battery.* In S. B. Filskov and T. J. Boll (Eds.). *Handbook of clinical neuropsychology.* New York: Wiley.

Bongar, B. (1988). Clinicians, microcomputers, and confidentiality. *Professional Psychology: Research and Practice, 19,* 286–289.

Boring, E. G. (1950). *A history of experimental psychology* (2nd ed.). New York: Appleton-Century-Crofts.

Breger, L. (1968). Psychological testing: Treatment and research implications. *Journal of Consulting and Clinical Psychology, 32,* 178–181.

Brodsky, S. L. (1972). Shared results and open files with the client. *Professional Psychology, 3,* 362–364.

Brotemarkle, R. A. (1947). Clinical psychology: 1896–1946. *Journal of Consulting Psychology, 11,* 1–4.

Brown, E. C. (1972). Assessment from a humanistic perspective. *Psychotherapy: Theory, Research, and Practice, 9,* 103–106.

Brown, F. (1965). Foreword. In L. Blank. *Psychological evaluation in psychotherapy: Ten case histories.* Chicago: Aldine.

Brown, L. J. (1985). Concreteness. *The Psychoanalytic Review, 72,* 379–402.

Brown, L. S. (1986). Gender role analysis: A neglected component of psychological assessment. *Psychotherapy: Theory, Research, Practice, Training, 23,* 243–248.

Brown, L. S. (1990). Taking account of gender in the clinical assessment interview. *Professional Psychology: Research and Practice, 21,* 12–17.

Brown, W. R., & McGuire, J. M. (1976). Current psychological assessment practices. *Professional Psychology, 7,* 475–484.

Buck, J. N. (1948a). The H-T-P test. *Journal of Clinical Psychology, 4,* 154–159.

Buck, J. N. (1948b). The H-T-P technique. A qualitative and quantitative manual, I. *Journal of Clinical Psychology, 4,* 319–396.

Buck, J. N. (1949). The H-T-P technique: A qualitative and quantitative scoring manual, II. *Journal of Clinical Psychology, 5,* 37–76.

Bugental, J. F. T. (1963). Humanistic psychology: A new breakthrough. *American Psychologist, 18,* 563–567.

Bugental, J. F. T. (1964). Psychodiagnostics and the quest for certainty. *Psychiatry, 27*, 73–77.

Butcher, J. N. (1978). Review of Minnesota Multiphasic Personality Inventory: Behaviordyne Psychodiagnostic Laboratory Services. In O. K. Buros (Ed.). *The eighth mental measurements yearbook* (pp. 949–952). Highland Park, NJ: Gryphon.

Butcher, J. N. (1987a). Preface. In J. N. Butcher (Ed.). *Computerized psychological assessment: A practitioner's guide*. New York: Basic Books.

Butcher, J. N. (1987b). The use of computers in psychological assessment: An overview of practices and issues. In J. N. Butcher (Ed.). *Computerized psychological assessment: A practitioner's guide*. New York: Basic Books.

Butcher, J. N. (1990). *MMPI-2 in psychological treatment*. New York: Oxford University Press.

Campbell, D. T. (1960). Recommendations for the APA test standards regarding construct, trait, and discriminant validity. *American Psychologist, 15*, 546–553.

Campbell, D. T., & Fiske, D. W. (1959). Convergent and discriminant validation by the multitrait-multimethod matrix. *Psychological Bulletin, 56*, 81–105.

Cannon, M. (1990). Criticism of mnemonic device. *American Journal of Psychiatry, 147*, 964.

Carey, M. P., Flasher, L. V., Maisto, S. A., & Turkat, I. D. (1984). The a priori approach to psychological assessment. *Professional Psychology: Research & Practice, 15*, 515–527.

Carlile, J. S. (1952). The Thematic Apperception Test applied to neurotic and normal adolescent girls. *British Journal of Medical Psychology, 25*, 244–248.

Carr, A. C. (1968). Psychological testing and reporting. *Journal of Projective Techniques and Personality Assessment, 32*, 513–521.

Carr, A. C., Goldstein, E. G., Hunt, H. F., & Kernberg, O. F. (1979). Psychological tests and borderline patients. *Journal of Personality Assessment, 43*, 582–590.

Carson, R. C. (1969). Interpretive manual to the MMPI. In J. N. Butcher (Ed.). *Research developments and clinical applications*. New York: McGraw-Hill.

Carson, R. C. (1990). Assessment: What role the assessor? *Journal of Personality Assessment, 54*, 435–445.

Casner, D. (1950). Certain factors associated with success and failure in personal adjustment counseling. *The American Psychologist, 5*, 348.

Cattell, R. B. (1944). Projection and the design of projective tests of personality. *Character and Personality, 12*, 177–194.

Cattell, R. B. (1959). *Handbook for the Culture Fair Intelligence Test: A measure of "g."* Champaign, IL: Institute for Personality and Ability Testing.

Cerney, M. S. (1978). Use of the psychological test report in the course of psychotherapy. *Journal of Personality Assessment, 42*, 457–463.

Cerney, M. S. (1984). One last response to the Rorschach test: A second chance to reveal oneself. *Journal of Personality Assessment, 48*, 338–344.

Chambers, G. S., & Hamlin, R. (1957). The validity of judgments based on "blind" Rorschach records. *Journal of Consulting Psychology, 21*, 105–109.

Chapman, L. J., & Chapman, J. P. (1971). Associatively based illusory correlations as a source of psychodiagnostic failure. In L. D. Goodstein & R. I. Lanyon (Eds.) *Readings in personality assessment*. New York: Wiley.

Chodoff, P. (1986). DSM-III and psychotherapy. *American Journal of Psychiatry, 143*, 201–203.

Churchill, R. D., & Crandall, V. J. (1965). The reliability and validity of the Rotter Incomplete Sentences Test. In B. I. Murstein (Ed.). *Handbook of Projective Techniques.* New York: Basic Books.

Clawson, A. (1962). *The Bender Visual Motor Gestalt test for children: A manual.* Los Angeles: Western Psychological Services.

Cleveland, S. E. (1976). Reflections on the rise and fall of psychodiagnosis. *Professional Psychology, 7,* 309–318.

Cohen, L. J. (1980). The unstated problem in a psychological testing referral. *American Journal of Psychiatry, 137,* 1173–1176.

Cohen, M. (1990). Need for clearer thinking about diagnostic criteria. *American Journal of Psychiatry, 147,* 261–262.

Cole, J. K., & Magnussen, M. J. (1966). Where the action is. *Journal of Consulting and Clinical Psychology, 30,* 539–543.

Comtois, R. J., & Clark, W. D. (1976). A framework for scientific practice and practitioner training. *JSAS Catalog of Selected Documents in Psychology, 6* (74), (Ms. No. 1301).

Conrad, H. S. (1932). The validity of personality ratings of preschool children. *Journal of Educational Psychology, 23,* 671–680.

Cooper, A. M., & Michels, R. (1988). DSM-III-R: The view from here and abroad. *American Journal of Psychiatry, 145,* 1300–1301.

Cooper, A., & Witenberg, E. G. (1985). The "bogged down" treatment: A remedy. *Contemporary Psychoanalysis, 21,* 27–41.

Corcoran, K., & Fischer, J. (1987). *Measures for clinical practice: A source book.* New York: Free Press.

Costa, P. T., Jr., & McCrae, R. R. (1985). *The NEO Personality Inventory manual.* Odessa, FL: Psychological Assessment Resources.

Costa, P. T., Jr., & McCrae, R. R. (1986). Personality stability and its implications for clinical psychology. *Clinical Psychology Review, 6,* 407–423.

Craddick, R. A. (1972). Humanistic assessment: A reply to Brown. *Psychotherapy: Theory, Research and Practice, 9,* 107–110.

Craddick, R. A. (1975). Sharing oneself in the assessment procedure. *Professional Psychology, 6,* 279–282.

Craig, R. J. (1989). *Clinical and diagnostic interviewing.* Northvale, NJ: Jason Aronson.

Craig, R. J. & Horowitz, M. (1990). Current utilization of psychological tests at diagnostic practicum sites. *The clinical psychologist, 43,* 29–36.

Cronbach, L. J. (1949). Statistical methods applied to Rorschach scores: A review. *Psychological Bulletin, 46,* 393–429.

Cronbach, L. J. (1951). Coefficient alpha and the internal structure of tests. *Psychometrika, 16,* 297–334.

Cronbach, L. J. (1980). Validity on parole: How can we go straight? In W. B. Schrader (Ed.). *Measuring achievement: Progress over a decade.* Proceedings of the 1979 ETS Invitational Conference, pp. 99–108. San Francisco: Jossey-Bass.

Cronbach, L. J. (1983). What price simplicity? *Educational Measurement: Issues and Practice, 2,* 11–12.

Cronbach, L. J. (1988). Five perspectives on the validity argument. In H. Wainer & H. I. Braun (Eds.). *Test validity*. Hillsdale, NJ: Lawrence Erlbaum Associates.

Crosson, B., & Warren, R. L. (1982). Use of the Luria-Nebraska Neuropsychological Battery in Aphasia: A conceptual critique. *Journal of Consulting and Clinical Psychology, 50*, 22–31.

Cutter, F., & Farberow, N. L. (1968). Serial administration of consensus Rorschachs to one patient. *Journal of Projective Techniques and Personality Assessment, 32*, 358–374.

Dahlstrom, W. G., & Welsh, G. S. (1960). *An MMPI handbook*. Minneapolis: University of Minnesota Press.

Dahlstrom, W. G., Welsh, G. S., & Dahlstrom, L. E. (1972). *An MMPI handbook: Vol. II. Research applications*. Minneapolis: University of Minnesota Press.

Dailey, C. A. (1953). The practical utility of the psychological report. *Journal of Consulting Psychology, 17*, 297–302.

Dana, R. H. (1966). Eisegesis and assessment. *Journal of Projective Techniques, 30*, 215–222.

Dana, R. H. (1988). Culturally diverse groups and MMPI interpretation. *Professional Psychology: Research and Practice, 19*, 490–495.

Dana, R. H., & Cantrell, J. D. (1988). An update on the Millon Clinical Multiaxial Inventory (MCMI). *Journal of Clinical Psychology, 44*, 760–763.

Dana, R. H., Hannifin, P., Lancaster, C., Lore, W., & Nelson, D. (1963). Psychological reports and juvenile probation counseling. *Journal of Clinical Psychology, 19*, 352–355.

DeCourcy, P. (1971). The hazards of short-term psychotherapy without assessment: A case history. *Journal of Personality Assessment, 35*, 285–288.

De La Cour, A. T. (1986). Use of the focus in brief dynamic psychotherapy. *Psychotherapy: Theory, Research and Practice, 23*, 133–139.

Delis, D., & Kaplan, E. (1982). The assessment of aphasia with the Luria-Nebraska Neuropsychological Battery: A case critique. *Journal of Consulting and Clinical Psychology, 50*, 32–39.

Dell, F., & Jordan-Smith, P. (1927). *The anatomy of melancholy by Robert Burton*. New York: Tudor Publishing Company.

Della Corte, M. (1980). Psychobabble: Why do we do it? *Psychotherapy: Theory, Research and Practice, 17*, 281–284.

deMendonca, M., Elliott, L., Goldstein, M., McNeill, J., Rodriguez, R., & Zelkind, I. (1984). An MMPI-based behavior descriptor/personality trait list. *Journal of Personality Assessment, 48*, 483–485.

DeNelsky, G. Y., & Boat, B. W. (1986). A coping skills model of psychological diagnosis and treatment. *Professional Psychology: Research and Practice, 17*, 322–330.

Dillon, C. A., & Wildman, R. W., II (1979). The psychologist in criminal court. *The Clinical Psychologist, 32*, 16–18.

Dorr, D. (1981). Conjoint psychological testing in marriage therapy: New wine in old skins. *Professional Psychology, 12*, 549–555.

Doyle, K. O., Jr. (1974). Theory and practice of ability testing in Ancient Greece. *Journal of the History of the Behavioral Sciences, 10*, 202–212.

Drewe, E. A. (1975). An experimental investigation of Luria's theory on the effects of frontal lobe lesions in man. *Neuropsychologia, 13*, 421–429.

DuBois, P. H. (1966). A test-dominated society: China 1115 B.C.–1905 A.D. In A. Anastasi (Ed.). *Testing problems in perspective*. Washington, DC: American Council on Education.

Dudek, S. Z. (1969). Interaction testing as a measure of therapeutic change in groups. *Journal of Projective Techniques and Personality Assessment, 33,* 127–137.

Duhl, B. S. (1983). *From the inside out and other metaphors*. New York: Brunner/Mazel.

Dumont, F., & Lecomte, C. (1987). Inferential processes in clinical work: Inquiry into logical errors that affect diagnostic judgments. *Professional Psychology: Research and Practice, 18,* 433–438.

Dunlap, K. (1922). The reading of character from external signs. *Scientific Monthly, 15,* 153–165.

Dunn, L. M., & Dunn, L. M. (1981). *Manual for the Peabody Picture Vocabulary Test–Revised (Forms L and M)*. Circle Pines, MN: American Guidance Service.

Durand, V. M., Blanchard, E. B., & Mindell, J. A. (1988). Training in projective testing: Survey of clinical training directors and internship directors. *Professional Psychology: Research and Practice, 19,* 236–238.

Ebel, R. L. (1961). Must all tests be valid? *American Psychologist, 16,* 640–647.

Ebel, R. L. (1983). The practical validation of tests of ability. *Educational Measurement: Issues and Practice, 2,* 7–10.

Eichman, W. J. (1972). Minnesota Multiphasic Personality Inventory: Computerized scoring and interpreting services. In O.K. Buros (Ed.). *Seventh mental measurements yearbook* (pp. 253–255). Highland Park, NJ: Gryphon.

Ellenberger, H. (1989). The life and work of Hermann Rorschach: II. Personality of Hermann Rorschach. *Society for Personality Assessment: Fiftieth Anniversary History and Directory*. Separate Issue Number 1, April, 1989.

Endicott, J., & Spitzer, R. L. (1972). The value of the standardized interview for the evaluation of psychopathology. *Journal of Personality Assessment, 36,* 410–417.

Epstein, S. (1979). The stability of behavior: I. On predicting most of the people much of the time. *Journal of Personality and Social Psychology, 37,* 1097–1126.

Epstein, S. (1980). The stability of behavior: II. Implications for psychological research. *American Psychologist, 35,* 790–806.

Epstein, S. (1987). The relative value of theoretical and empirical approaches for establishing a psychological diagnostic system. *Journal of Personality Disorders, 1,* 100–109.

Erikson, E. H. (1959). *Identity and the life cycle*. New York: International Universities Press.

Evans, B. (1972). *The psychiatry of Robert Burton*. New York: Octagon Books.

Everly, G. S., Jr. (1969/1986). The MCMI in treatment planning. *Responses, 2* (2), 3.

Exner, J. E., Jr. (1969). *The Rorschach systems*. Orlando, FL: Grune & Stratton.

Exner, J. E., Jr. (1974). *The Rorschach: A comprehensive system* (Vol. 1). New York: Wiley.

Exner, J. E., Jr. (1978). *The Rorschach: A comprehensive system* (Vol. 2). New York: Wiley.

Exner, J. E., Jr. (1984). *The Rorschach: A comprehensive system* (Vol. 3). New York: Wiley.

Exner, J. E., Jr. (1985). *Rorschach interpretation assistance program*. San Antonio, TX: The Psychological Corporation.

Exner, J. E., Jr. (1986). *The Rorschach: A comprehensive system* (Vol 1. *Basic foundations*) (2nd ed.). New York: Wiley.

Exner, J. E., Jr. (1989). Searching for projection in the Rorschach. *Journal of Personality Assessment, 53,* 520–536.

Exner, J. E., Jr., & Exner, D. E. (1972). How clinicians use the Rorschach. *Journal of Personality Assessment, 36,* 403–408.

Exner, J. E., Jr., & Weiner, I. B. (1982). *The Rorschach: A comprehensive system* (Vol. 3. Assessment of children and adolescents). New York: Wiley.

Farber, B. (1985). The genesis, development, and implications of psychological-mindedness in psychotherapists. *Psychotherapy, 22,* 170–177.

Farberow, N. L. (1968). Symposium: Consensus Rorschachs in the study of problem behavior. *Journal of Projective Techniques and Personality Assessment, 32,* 326.

Faust, D., & Miner, R. A. (1986). The empiricist and his new clothes: DSM-III in perspective. *American Journal of Psychiatry, 143,* 962–965.

Fee, A. F., Elkins, G. R., & Boyd, L. (1982). Testing and counseling psychologists: Current practices and implications for training. *Journal of Personality Assessment, 46,* 116–118.

Fein, L. G. (Ed.). (1979). Current status of psychological diagnostic testing in university training programs and in delivery of service systems. *Psychological Reports, Monograph Supplement* 2–144.

Fernald, P. S. (1970). Consensus intelligence testing in compatible and incompatible groups. *Journal of Projective Techniques and Personality Assessment, 34,* 238–240.

Filer, R. N. (1952). The clinician's personality and his case reports. *American Psychologist, 7,* 336.

Filskov, S. B., & Boll, T. J. (Eds.). (1981). *Handbook of clinical neuropsychology.* New York: Wiley.

Fischer, C. T. (1970). The testee as co-evaluator. *Journal of Counseling Psychology, 17,* 70–76.

Fischer, C. T. (1972). Paradigm changes which allow sharing of results. *Professional Psychology, 3,* 364–369.

Fischer, C. T. (1979). Individualized assessment and phenomenological psychology. *Journal of Personality Assessment, 43,* 115–122.

Fischer, C. T. (1985). *Individualizing psychological assessment.* Monterey, CA: Brooks/Cole.

Fitzpatrick, A. R. (1983). The meaning of content validity. *Applied Psychological Measurement, 7,* 3–13.

Flanagan, J. C. (1983). A rational rationale. *Educational Measurement: Issues and Practice.* 2 (2), 13.

Fleischauer, A. (1987). *Responses, 3* (1), Winter 1987.

Flesch, R. (1949/1974). *The art of readable writing.* New York: Harper & Row.

Flesch, R. (1972). *Say what you mean.* New York: Harper & Row.

Ford, M. R., & Widiger, T. A. (1989). Sex bias in the diagnosis of histrionic and antisocial disorders. *Journal of Consulting and Clinical Psychology, 57,* 301–305.

Forer, B. R. (1957). *Forer Structured Sentence Completion Test–manual.* Los Angeles: Western Psychological Services.

Fowler, R. D. (1985). Landmarks in computer-assisted psychological assessment. *Journal of Consulting and Clinical Psychology, 53,* 748–759.

Fowler, R. D., & Butcher, J. N. (1986). Critique of Matarazzo's views on computerized testing: All signs and no meaning. *American Psychologist, 41,* 94–96.

Frances, A. (1980). The DSM-III personality disorders: A commentary. *American Journal of Psychiatry, 137*, 1050–1054.

Frances, A., & Widiger, T. (1986). The classification of personality disorders: An overview of problems and solutions. In A. J. Frances & R. E. Hales (Eds.). *American Psychiatric Association Annual Review* (Vol. 5, pp. 240–247). Washington, DC: American Psychiatric Press.

Frances, A., Pincus, H. A., Widiger, T. A., Davis, W. W., & First, M. B. (1990). DSM-IV: Work in progress. *American Journal of Psychiatry, 147*, 1439–1448.

Franzen, M. D., & Berg, R. A. (1989). *Screening children for brain impairment*. New York: Springer.

Frederiksen, N. (1984). The real test bias: Influences of testing on teaching and learning. *American Psychologist, 39*, 193–202.

Freud, S. (1894/1962). The neuro-psychoses of defense. In J. Strachey (Ed. and Trans.). *The standard edition of the complete psychological works of Sigmund Freud* (Vol. 3). London: Hogarth.

Freud, S. (1895/1962). Studies on hysteria. In J. Strachey (Ed. and Trans.). *The standard edition of the complete psychological works of Sigmund Freud* (Vol. 2). London: Hogarth.

Freud, S. (1896/1962). Further remarks on the neuro-psychoses of defense. In J. Strachey (Ed. and Trans.). *The standard edition of the complete psychological works of Sigmund Freud* (Vol. 3). London: Hogarth.

Freud, S. (1911/1949). Psycho-analytic notes upon an autobiographical account of a case of paranoia (dementia paranoides). In E. Jones (Ed.). *Collected Papers* (Vol. 3). London: Hogarth.

Freud, S. (1915/1949). Instincts and their vicissitudes. In E. Jones (Ed.). *Collected papers* (Vol. 4). London: Hogarth.

Friedman, A. F., Webb, J. T., & Lewak, R. (1989). *Psychological assessment with the MMPI*. Hillsdale, NJ: Lawrence Erlbaum Associates.

Friedman, S. H. (1950). Psychometric effects of frontal and parietal lobe brain damage. Ph.D. dissertation, University of Minnesota.

Furth, H., & Milgram, N. (1965). Verbal factors in performance on WISC similarities. *Journal of Clinical Psychology, 21*, 424–427.

Garb, H. N. (1988). Comment on "The study of clinical judgment: An ecological approach." *Clinical Psychology Review, 8*, 441–444.

Garb, H. N. (1989). Clinical judgment, clinical training, and professional experience. *Psychological Bulletin, 105*, 387–396.

Gardner, E. F. (1983). Intrinsic rational validity: Necessary but not sufficient. *Educational Measurement: Issues and Practice, 2*, 13.

Gartner, A. F., Marcus, R. N., Halmi, K., & Loranger, A. W. (1989). DSM-III-R personality disorders in patients with eating disorders. *American Journal of Psychiatry, 146*, 1585–1591.

Gentry, W. D. (Chair) (1974a). Symposium: The emerging profession of psychological technician. *Professional Psychology, 5*, 206.

Gentry, W. D. (1974b). Three models of training and utilization. *Professional Psychology, 5*, 207–214.

Gentry, W. D. (1974c). Technicians' views of training and function. *Professional Psychology, 5*, 219–221.

Giedt, F. H. (1955). Comparison of visual, content and auditory cues in interviewing. *Journal of Consulting Psychology, 19*, 407–416.

Gilbert, J. (1978). *Interpreting psychological test data* (Vol. I. *Test response antecedent*). New York: Van Nostrand Reinhold.

Gilbert, J. (1980). *Interpreting psychological test data* (Vol. II. *Behavioral attribute antecedent*). New York: Van Nostrand Reinhold.

Gilliland, A. B. (1941). Differential functional loss in certain psychoses. *Psychological Bulletin, 38*, 715.

Ginsberg, G. L. (1985). Psychiatric history and mental status examination. In H. I. Kaplan & B. J. Sadock (Eds.). *Comprehensive textbook of psychiatry* (4th ed.). Baltimore: Williams & Wilkins.

Glasser, A. J., & Zimmerman, I. L. (1967). *The clinical interpretation of the Wechsler Intelligence Scale for Children*. Orlando, FL: Grune & Stratton.

Goh, D. S., Teslow, C. J., & Fuller, G. B. (1981). The practice of psychological assessment among school psychologists. *Professional Psychology, 12*, 696–706.

Gold, J. M. (1987). The role of verbalization in the Rorschach response process. *Journal of Personality Assessment, 51*, 489–505.

Goldberg, E., & Tucker, D. (1979). Motor preservation and long-term memory for visual forms. *Journal of Clinical Neuropsychology, 1*, 273–288.

Goldberg, L. R. (1959). The effectiveness of clinicians' judgments: The diagnosis of organic brain damage from the Bender Gestalt. *Journal of Consulting Psychology, 23*, 25–33.

Goldberg, L. R. (1968). Simple models or simple processes? Some research on clinical judgments. *American Psychologist, 23*, 483–496.

Golden, C. J. (1979a). *Clinical interpretation of objective psychological tests*. Orlando, FL: Grune & Stratton.

Golden, C. J. (1979b). *Diagnosis and rehabilitation in clinical neuropsychology*. Springfield, IL: Thomas.

Golden, C. J. (1980). In reply to Adams's "In search of Luria's battery: A false start." *Journal of Consulting and Clinical Psychology, 48*, 517–521.

Golden, C. J. (1981a). The Luria-Nebraska Neuropsychological Battery: Theory and research. In P. McReynolds (Ed.). *Advances in psychological assessment* (Vol. 5). San Francisco: Jossey-Bass.

Golden, C. J. (1981b). A standardized version of Luria's neuropsychological tests: A quantitative and qualitative approach to neuropsychological evaluation. In S. B. Filskov & T. J. Boll (Eds.). *Handbook of clinical neuropsychology*. New York: Wiley.

Golden, C. J., Purisch, A. D., & Hammeke, T. A. (1985). *Luria-Nebraska Neuropsychological Battery: Forms I and II (Manual)*. Los Angeles: Western Psychological Services.

Goldenson, R. M. (Ed.). (1984). *Longman dictionary of psychology and psychiatry*. New York: Longman.

Goldfried, M. R., & Sprafkin, J. N. (1976). Behavioral personality assessment. In J. T. Spence, R. C. Carson, & J. W. Thibaut (Eds.). *Behavioral approaches to therapy* (pp. 295–301). Morristown, NJ: General Learning Press.

Goldstein, G. (1981). Some recent developments in clinical neuropsychology. *Clinical Psychology Review, 1*, 245–268.

Goldstein, G. (1984). Comprehensive neuropsychological batteries. In G. Goldstein & M. Hersen (Eds.). *Handbook of psychological assessment*. New York: Pergamon Press.

Goldstein, G. (1990). Comprehensive neuropsychological assessment batteries. In G. Goldstein & M. Hersen (Eds.). *Handbook of psychological assessment* (2nd ed.). New York: Pergamon Press.

Goldstein, K., & Scheerer, M. (1941). Abstract and concrete behavior. *Psychological Monographs, 53*, No. 2.

Goldstein, K., & Scheerer, M. (1951). *Goldstein-Scheerer Tests of Abstract and Concrete Thinking.* San Antonio, TX: The Psychological Corporation.

Goodglass, H., & Kaplan, E. (1983). *The assessment of aphasia and related disorders* (2nd ed.). Philadelphia: Lea & Febiger.

Gough, H. G. (1950). The F minus K dissimulation index for the MMPI. *Journal of Consulting Psychology, 14*, 408–413.

Gough, H. G. (1952). *The adjective check list.* Palo Alto: Consulting Psychologists Press.

Gough, H. G. (1963). Clinical versus statistical prediction in psychology. In L. Postman (Ed.). *Psychology in the Making.* New York: Knopf.

Gough, H. G., (1971). Some reflections on the meaning of diagnosis. *American Psychologist, 26*, 160–167.

Gough, H. G., & Heilbrun, A. (1980). *The adjective check list manual.* Palo Alto: Consulting Psychologists Press.

Graham, J. R. (1987). *The MMPI: A practical guide* (2nd ed.). New York: Oxford University Press.

Graham, J. R. (1990). *MMPI-2: Assessing personality and psychopathology.* New York: Oxford University Press.

Graham, T. F. (1965). *Mental status manual.* Hanover, NJ: Sandoz Pharmaceuticals.

Grayson, H. M., & Tolman, R. S. (1950). A semantic study of concepts of clinical psychologists and psychiatrists. *Journal of Abnormal and Social Psychology, 45*, 216–231.

Green, B. F., Jr. (1978). In defense of measurement. *American Psychologist, 33*, 664–670.

Greene, R. L. (1990). *The MMPI/MMPI-2: An interpretive manual.* Boston: Allyn and Bacon.

Gross, M. L. (1962). *The brain watchers.* New York: Random House.

Guertin, W. H., French, G. H., & Rabin, A. I. (1956). Research with the Wechsler-Bellevue Intelligence Scale, 1950–1955. *Psychological Bulletin, 53*, 235–257.

Guertin, W. H., Ladd, C. E., Frank, G. H., & Rabin, A. I. (1962). Research with the Wechsler intelligence scales for adults, 1955–1960. *Psychological Bulletin, 59*, 1–26.

Guertin, W. H., Ladd, C. E., Frank, G. H., Rabin, A. I., & Hiester, D. S. (1966), Research with the Wechsler intelligence scales for adults, 1960–1965. *Psychological Bulletin, 66*, 385–409.

Guertin, W. H., Ladd, C. E., Frank, G. H., & Rabin, A. I. (1971). Research with the Wechsler intelligence scales for adults, 1965–1970. *Psychological Record, 21*, 289–339.

Guion, R. M. (1977). Content validity–The source of my discontent. *Applied Psychological Measurement, 1*, 1–10.

Gunderson, J. G. (1982). *Diagnostic interview for borderline patients* (2nd ed.). New York: Roerig Division/Pfizer, Inc.

Gunderson, J. G. (1984). *Borderline personality disorder.* Washington, DC: American Psychiatric Press.

Gunderson, J. G., & Singer, M. T. (1975). Defining borderline patients: An overview. *American Journal of Psychiatry, 132*, 1–10.

Hadley, J. M. (1972). Clinical assessment in mental health facilities. In. R. H. Woody & J. D. Woody (Eds.). *Clinical assessment in counseling and psychotherapy.* New York: Appleton-Century-Crofts.

Hallenstein, C. B. (1978). Ethical problems of psychological jargon. *Professional Psychology, 9,* 111–116.

Halstead, W. C. (1947). *Brain and intelligence: A quantitative study of the frontal lobes.* Chicago: University of Chicago Press.

Hammer, E. F. (Ed.). (1958). *The clinical application of projective drawings.* Springfield, IL: Thomas.

Hammer, E. F. (1960). The House-Tree-Person (H-T-P) drawings as a projective technique with children. In A. I. Rabin & M. R. Haworth (Eds.). *Projective techniques with children.* Orlando, FL: Grune & Stratton.

Hammer, E., & Piotrowski, Z. A. (1953). Hostility as a factor in the clinician's personality as it affects his interpretation of projective drawings (H-T-P). *Journal of Projective Techniques, 17,* 210–216.

Hammond, K. R., & Allen, J. M. (1953). *Writing clinical reports.* Englewood Cliffs, NJ: Prentice Hall.

Hanfmann, E., & Kasanin, J. (1942). Conceptual thinking in schizophrenia. *Nervous and Mental Disease Monographs,* No. 67.

Harris, J. G. (1960). Validity: The search for a constant in a universe of variables. In M. A. Rickers-Ovsiankina (Ed.). *Rorschach psychology.* New York: Wiley.

Harris, R. E., & Lingoes, J. C. (1955). *Subscales for the Minnesota Multiphasic Personality Inventory.* San Francisco: The Langley Porter Clinic.

Harrower, M., Vorhaus, P., Roman, M., & Bauman, G. (1960). *Creative variations in the projective techniques.* Springfield, IL: Thomas.

Hartlage, L. C., Asken, M. J., & Hornsby, J. L. (1987). *Essentials of neuropsychological assessment.* New York: Springer.

Hartlage, L. C., Freeman, W., Horine, L., & Walton, C. (1968). Decisional utility of psychological reports. *Journal of Clinical Psychology, 24,* 481–483.

Hartlage, L. C., & Merck, K. H. (1971). Increasing the relevance of psychological reports. *Journal of Clinical Psychology, 27,* 459–460.

Hartocollis, P. (1977). Treatment approaches. In P. Hartocollis (Ed.). *Borderline personality disorders.* New York: International Universities Press.

Harty, M. K. (1986). Action language in the psychological test report. *Bulletin of the Menninger Clinic, 50,* 456–463.

Hathaway, S. R. (1960). In W. G. Dahlstrom & G. S. Welsh. *An MMPI handbook: A guide to use in clinical practice and research.* Minneapolis: University of Minnesota Press.

Hathaway, S. R., & Meehl, P. E. (1951). *An atlas for the clinical use of the MMPI.* Minneapolis: University of Minnesota Press.

Hayes, S. C., Nelson, R. O., & Jarrett, R. B. (1987). The treatment utility of assessment: A functional approach to evaluating assessment quality. *American Psychologist, 42,* 963–974.

Heinrichs, R. W. (1990). Current and emergent applications of neuropsychological assessment: Problems of validity and utility. *Professional Psychology: Research and Practice, 21,* 171–176.

Henry, W. E., & Guetzkow, H. (1951). Group projective sketches for the study of small groups. *Journal of Social Psychology, 33*, 77–102.

Hertz, M. R. (1970). Projective techniques in crisis. *Journal of Projective Techniques and Personality Assessment, 34*, 445–468.

Hofer, P. J., & Green, B. F. (1985). The challenge of competence and creativity in computerized psychological testing. *Journal of Consulting and Clinical Psychology, 53*, 826–838.

Hoffman, B. (1962). *The tyranny of testing.* New York: Crowell-Collier.

Hogan, R., DeSoto, C. B., & Solano, C. (1977). Traits, tests, and personality research. *American Psychologist, 32*, 255–264.

Holmes, D. S. (1968). Dimensions of projection. *Psychological Bulletin, 68*, 248–268.

Holsopple, J. Q., & Miale, F. R. (1954). *Sentence completions.* Springfield, IL: Thomas.

Holt, R. R. (1958) Clinical and statistical prediction: A reformulation and some new data. *Journal of Abnormal and Social Psychology, 56*, 1–12.

Holt, R. R. (1967). Diagnostic testing: Present status and future prospects. *Journal of Nervous and Mental Disease, 144*, 444–465.

Holt, R. R. (Ed.). (1968). *Diagnostic psychological testing* (rev. ed.). New York: International Universities Press.

Holt, R. R. (1970). Yet another look at clinical and statistical prediction: Or is clinical psychology worthwhile? *American Psychologist, 25*, 337–349.

Holt, R. R. (1977). A method for assessing primary process manifestation and their control in Rorschach responses. In M. A. Rickers-Ovsiankina (Ed.). *Rorschach psychology* (2nd ed.). Huntington, NY: Krieger.

Holt, R. R. (1986). Clinical and statistical prediction: A retrospective and would-be integrative perspective. *Journal of Personality Assessment, 50*, 376–386.

Holtzman, W. H. (1964). Recurring dilemmas in personality assessment. *Journal of Projective Techniques and Personality Assessment, 28*, 144–150.

Holtzman, W. H., & Sells, S. B. (1954). Prediction of flying success by clinical analysis of test protocols. *Journal of Abnormal and Social Psychology, 49*, 485–490.

Holtzman, W. H., Thorpe, J. S., Swartz, J. D., & Herron, E. W. (1961). *Inkblot perception and personality.* Austin, TX: University of Texas Press.

Howe, H. E., Jr. (1981). Description and application of an evaluation scheme for assessment from a decision-making perspective. *Journal of Clinical Psychology, 37*, 110–117.

Hulse, D., & Jennings, M. L. (1984). Toward comprehensive case conceptualizations in counseling: A visual integrative technique. *Professional Psychology: Research and Practice, 15*, 251–259.

Hunt, J. McV., Ewing, T., La Forge, R., & Gilbert, W. (1959). An integrated approach to research on therapeutic counseling with samples of results. *Journal of Counseling Psychology, 6*, 45–54.

Hunt, W. A. (1946). The future of diagnostic testing in clinical psychology. *Journal of Clinical Psychology, 2*, 311–317.

Hunt, W. A. (1951). Clinical psychology–science or superstition. *The American Psychologist, 6*, 683–687.

Hunt, W. A. (1959). An actuarial approach to clinical judgment. In B. Bass & I. A. Berg (Eds.). *Objective approaches to personality assessment.* Princeton, NJ: D. Van Nostrand.

Hutt, M. L. (1968). The projective use of the Bender-Gestalt test. In A. I. Rabin (Ed.). *Projective techniques in personality assessment.* New York: Springer.

Hutt, M. L. (1985). *The Hutt adaptation of the Bender-Gestalt test: Rapid screening and intensive diagnosis* (4th ed.). Orlando, FL: Grune & Stratton.

Ivnik, R. J. (1977). Uncertain status of psychological tests in clinical psychology. *Professional Psychology, 8,* 206–213.

Jackson, C. W., Jr., & Wohl, J. (1966). A survey of Rorschach teaching in the university. *Journal of Projective Techniques and Personality Assessment, 30,* 115–134.

Jaffe, L. (1988). The selected response procedure: A variation on Appelbaum's altered atmosphere procedure for the Rorschach. *Journal of Personality Assessment, 52,* 530–538.

Jampala, V. C., Sierles, F. S., & Taylor, M. A. (1986). Consumers' views of DSM-III: Attitudes and practices of U.S. psychiatrists and 1984 graduating psychiatric residents. *American Journal of Psychiatry, 143,* 148–152.

John, O. P. (1990). The "big five" factor taxonomy: Dimensions of personality in the natural language and in questionnaires. In L. A. Pervin (Ed.). Handbook of personality: Theory and research. New York: The Guilford Press.

Josephs, L. (1989). The world of the concrete: A comparative approach. *Contemporary Psychoanalysis, 25,* 477–500.

Kahn, R. L., & Cannell, C. F. (1957). *The dynamics of interviewing: Theory, technique, and cases.* New York: Wiley.

Kane, R. L., Goldstein, G., & Parsons, O. A. (1989). "Testing to detect brain damage: An alternative to what may no longer be relevant. Response." *Journal of Clinical and Experimental Neuropsychology, 11,* 589–595.

Karasu, T. B., & Skodol, A. E. (1980). Sixth axis for DSM-III? Psychodynamic evaluation. *American Journal of Psychiatry, 137,* 607–610.

Karon, B. P. (1968). Problems of validities. In A. I. Rabin (Ed.). *Projective techniques in personality assessment.* New York: Springer.

Karon, B. P. (1978). Projective tests are valid. *American Psychologist, 33,* 764–765.

Kaufman, A. S. (1975). Factor analysis of the WISC-R at eleven age levels between 6 1/2 and 16 1/2 years. *Journal of Consulting and Clinical Psychology, 43,* 135–147.

Kaufman, A. S. (1979). *Intelligent testing with the WISC-R.* New York: Wiley.

Kaufman, A. S. (1990). *Assessing adolescent and adult intelligence.* Boston: Allyn & Bacon.

Keiser, R. E., & Prather, E. N. (1990). What is the TAT?: A review of ten years of research. *Journal of Personality Assessment, 55,* 800–803.

Keller, C. W. (1971). Characteristics of Rorschach interpreter types: An exploratory study. Unpublished doctoral dissertation, Texas Tech University.

Kelly, G. A. (1955). The clinical setting. In G. A. Kelly, *The psychology of personal constructs* (Vol. 1). New York: Norton.

Kernberg, O. F. (1967). Borderline personality organization. *Journal of the American Psychoanalytic Association, 15,* 641–685.

Kernberg, O. F. (1970). Psychoanalytic classification of character pathology. *Journal of the American Psychoanalytic Association, 18,* 800–822.

Kernberg, O. F. (1976). *Object relations theory and clinical psychoanalysis.* New York: Jason Aronson.

Kernberg, O. F. (1977). Foreword. In S. A. Appelbaum. *The anatomy of change: A Menninger Foundation report on testing the effects of psychotherapy.* New York: Plenum.

Kernberg, O. F. (1984). *Severe personality disorders: Psychotherapeutic strategies.* New Haven: Yale University Press.

Kingsbury, S. J. (1987). Cognitive differences between clinical psychologists and psychiatrists. *American Psychologist, 42,* 152–156.

Kissen, M. (1973). The importance of psychological testing for the psychotherapy process. *The Journal of Clinical Issues in Psychology, 5,* 11–13.

Kissen, M. (1977). Exploration of therapeutic parameters during psychological testing. *Bulletin of the Menninger Clinic, 41,* 266–272.

Kleinmuntz, B. (1990). Why we still use our heads instead of formulas: Toward an integrative approach. *Psychological Bulletin, 197,* 296–310.

Klopfer, B., & Kelley, D. M. (1946). *The Rorschach technique.* Yonkers-on-Hudson, NY: World Book.

Klopfer, B., Ainsworth, M. D., Klopfer, W. G., & Holt, R. R. (Eds.) (1954). *Developments in the Rorschach technique* (Vol. I) *Technique and theory.* Yonkers-on-Hudson, NY: World Book.

Klopfer, W. G. (1960). *The psychological report.* Orlando, FL: Grune & Stratton.

Klopfer, W. G. (1964). The blind leading the blind: Psychotherapy without assessment. *Journal of Projective Techniques and Personality Assessment, 28,* 387–392.

Klopfer, W. G. (1968). In P. McReynolds (Ed.). *Advances in personality assessment* (Vol. I) Palo Alto, CA: Science and Behavior Books.

Klopfer, W. G. (1969). Consensus Rorschach in the primary classroom. *Journal of Projective Techniques and Personality Assessment, 33,* 549–552.

Klopfer, W. G. (1984a). Application of the consensus Rorschach to couples. *Journal of Personality Assessment, 48,* 422–440.

Klopfer, W. G. (1984b). The use of the Rorschach in brief clinical evaluation. *Journal of Personality Assessment, 48,* 654–659.

Knight, R. P. (1954). Borderline states. In R. P. Knight and C. R. Friedman (Eds.). *Psychoanalytic psychiatry and psychology.* New York: International Universities Press.

Koppitz, E. M. (1989). *The Bender-Gestalt Test for young children* (Vols. I & II). Boston: Allyn and Bacon.

Korchin, S. J. (1976). *Modern clinical psychology.* New York: Basic Books.

Korchin, S. J., & Schuldberg, D. (1981), The future of clinical assessment. *American Psychologist, 36,* 1147–1158.

Korman, A. K. (1968). The prediction of managerial performance: A review. *Personnel Psychology, 21,* 295–322.

Koss, M. P., & Butcher, J. N. (1973). A comparison of psychiatric patients' self-report with other sources of clinical information. *Journal of Research in Personality, 7,* 225–236.

Kratochwill, T. R. (1982). School psychology: Dimensions of its dilemmas and future directions. *Professional Psychology, 13,* 977–989.

Kris, E. (1952). *Psychoanalytic explorations in art.* New York: International Universities Press.

Kwawer, J., Lerner, H., Lerner, P., & Sugarman, A. (Eds.). (1980). *Borderline phenomena and the Rorschach test.* New York: International Universities Press.

L'Abate, L. (1964). *Principles of clinical psychology.* Orlando, FL: Grune & Stratton.

Lacey, H. M., & Ross, A. O. (1964). Multidisciplinary views on psychological reports in child guidance clinics. *Journal of Clinical Psychology, 20*, 522–526.

Lachar, D. (1982). *Personality Inventory for Children (PIC): Revised format manual supplement*. Los Angeles: Western Psychological Services.

Lachar, D., & Wrobel, T. A. (1979). Validation of clinicians' hunches: Construction of a new MMPI critical item set. *Journal of Consulting and Clinical Psychology, 47*, 277–284.

Lacks, P. B., Horton, M. M., & Owen, J. D. (1969). A more meaningful and practical approach to psychological reports. *Journal of Clinical Psychology, 25*, 383–386.

Lambert, N. M. (1981). Psychological evidence in Larry P. v. Wilson Riles. *American Psychologist, 36*, 937–952.

Lambert, L. E., & Wertheimer, M. (1988). Is diagnostic ability related to relevant training and experience? *Professional Psychology: Research and Practice, 19*, 50–52.

Lambley, P. (1974). The dangers of therapy without assessment: A case study. *Journal of Personality Assessment, 38*, 263–265.

Lamiell, J. T. (1981). Toward an idiothetic psychology of personality. *American Psychologist, 36*, 276–289.

Landers, S. (1986). DSM by APA? *APA Monitor*, November, 1986.

Lanyon, R. I. (1984). Personality assessment. *Annual review of psychology, 35*, 667–701.

Larson, E. W. (1990). Criticism of mnemonic device. *American Journal of Psychiatry, 147*, 963–964.

Last, C. G., & Hersen, M. (Eds.) (1987). *Issues in diagnostic research*. New York: Plenum.

Lazarus, A. A. (1973). Multimodal behavior therapy: Treating the BASIC ID. *Journal of Nervous and Mental Disease, 156*, 404–411.

Lazarus, A. A. (1989). *The practice of multi-modal therapy*. Baltimore: Johns Hopkins University Press.

Leary, T. (1957). *Interpersonal diagnosis of personality*. New York: Ronald Press.

Lehman, H. E., Ban, T. A., & Donaldson, M. (1965). Rating the rater. *Archives of General Psychiatry, 13*, 67–75.

Leon, R. L., Bowden, C. L., & Faber, R. A. (1989). Diagnosis and psychiatry: Examination of the psychiatric patient. In H. I. Kaplan & B. J. Sadock (Eds.). *Comprehensive textbook of psychiatry* (Vol. I) (5th ed.). Baltimore: Williams & Wilkins.

Leonberger, F. T. (1989). The question of organicity: Is it still functional? *Professional Psychology: Research and Practice, 20*, 411–414.

Lerner, P. M. (1988). Minutes of the meeting of the board of trustees, Society for Personality Assessment, March 11, 1988. *Journal of Personality Assessment, 52*, 743–747.

Leventhal, T., Rosenblatt, B., Gluck, M., & Slepian, H. (1958). The use of the psychological-patient relationship in individual diagnostic testing. *American Psychologist, 13*, 345 (Abstract).

Levinson, D. J., Sharaf, M. R., & Gilbert, D. C. (1966). Intraception: Evolution of a concept. In G. J. DiRenzo (Ed.). *Concepts, theory, and explanation in the behavioral sciences*. New York: Random House.

Levy, L. H. (1963). *Psychological interpretation*. New York: Holt, Rinehart, and Winston.

Levy, M. R., & Fox, H. M. (1975). Psychological testing is alive and well. *Professional Psychology, 6*, 420–423.

Levy, S. (1950). Figure drawing as a projective test. In L. E. Abt & L. Bellak (Eds.). *Projective psychology.* New York: Knopf.

Lewandowski, D. G., & Saccuzzo, D. P. (1976). The decline of psychological testing. *Professional Psychology, 7,* 177–184.

Lezak, M. D. (1983). *Neuropsychological assessment* (2nd ed.). New York: Oxford University Press.

Lief, A. (Ed.). (1948). *The commonsense psychiatry of Dr. Adolf Meyer.* New York: McGraw-Hill.

Lipton, G. (1988). Symptomatic. *APA Monitor,* May, 1988, p. 3.

Loewenstein, R. (1967). In *Indications for psychoanalysis* (Kris Study Group Monograph II). New York: International Universities Press.

Loutitt, C. M. (1939). The nature of clinical psychology. *Psychological Bulletin, 36,* 361–389.

Lovitt, R. (1984). Rorschach interpretation in a multidisciplinary hospital setting. *Professional Psychology: Research and Practice, 15,* 244–250.

Lovitt, R. (1987). A conceptual model and case study for the psychological assessment of hysterical pseudo-seizures with the Rorschach. *Journal of Personality Assessment, 51,* 207–219.

Lovitt, R. (1988). Current practice of psychological assessment: Response to Sweeney, Clarkin, and Fitzgibbon. *Professional Psychology: Research and Practice, 19,* 516–521.

Lubin, B., Larsen, R. M., & Matarazzo, J. D. (1984). Patterns of psychological test usage in the United States: 1935–1982. *American Psychologist, 39,* 451–454.

Lubin, B., Larsen, R. M., Matarazzo, J. D., & Seever, M. F. (1985). Psychological test usage patterns in five professional settings. *American Psychologist, 40,* 857–861.

Lubin, B., Larsen, R. M., Matarazzo, J. D., & Seever, M. F. (1986). Characteristics of psychologists and psychological assessment in five settings: 1959–1982. *Professional Psychology: Research and Practice, 17,* 155–157.

Lubin, B., Wallis, R. R., & Paine, C. (1971). Patterns of psychological test usage in the United States: 1935–1969. *Professional Psychology, 2,* 70–74.

Luborsky, L. (1952). Self-interpretation of the TAT as a clinical technique. *Journal of Projective Techniques, 17,* 217–223.

Luborsky, L., Mintz, J, Auerbach, A., Christoph, P., Bachrach, H., Todd, T., Johnson, M., Cohen, M., & O'Brien, C. P. (1980). Predicting the outcome of psychotherapy. *Archives of General Psychiatry, 37,* 471–481.

Luborsky, L., Crits-Christoph, P., Mintz, J., & Auerbach, A. (1988). *Who will benefit from psychotherapy? Predicting therapeutic outcomes.* New York: Basic Books.

Lundy, A. (1985). The reliability of the Thematic Apperception Test. *Journal of Personality Assessment, 49,* 141–145.

Lundy, A. (1988). Instructional set and Thematic Apperception Test validity. *Journal of Personality Assessment, 52,* 309–320.

Lunneborg, P. W. (1981). *Vocational Interest Inventory (VII), manual.* Los Angeles: Western Psychological Services.

Lyons, J. (1967). Whose experience? Journal of *Projective Techniques and Personality Assessment, 31,* 4, 11–16.

Maccoby, M. (1972). Developments in Erich Fromm's approach to psychoanalysis. Address to William Alanson White Psychiatric Society (Referenced in Cooper & Witenberg, 1985).

Machover, K. (1949). *Personality projection in the drawing of the human figure: A method of personality investigation.* Springfield, IL: Thomas.

Machover, K. (1957). *Draw-A-Person Test.* Springfield, IL: Thomas.

Maloney, M. P., & Ward, M. P. (1976). *Psychological assessment: A conceptual approach.* New York: Oxford University Press.

Martin, R. M. (1967). The role of experiential data in personality assessment: Introduction. *Journal of Projective Techniques and Personality Assessment, 31*, 43.

Masling, J. (1957). The effects of warm and cold interaction on the interpretation of a projective protocol. *Journal of Projective Techniques, 21*, 377–383.

Masling, J. (1960). The influence of situational and interpersonal variables in projective testing. *Psychological Bulletin, 57*, 65–85.

Matarazzo, J. D. (1972). *Wechsler's measurement and appraisal of adult intelligence* (5th ed.). Baltimore: Williams & Wilkins.

Matarazzo, J. D. (1981). Obituary: David Wechsler (1896–1981). *American Psychologist, 36*, 1542–1543.

Matarazzo, J. D. (1983). Computerized psychological testing. *Science, 221*, July 22, p. 363.

Matarazzo, J. D. (1990). Psychological assessment versus psychological testing. *American Psychologist, 45*, 999–1017.

May, R. (1958). Contributions of existential psychotherapy. In R. May, E. Angel, & H. F. Ellenberger (Eds.). *Existence.* New York: Basic Books.

McAllister, L. W. (1988). *A practical guide to CPI interpretation* (2nd ed.). Palo Alto, CA: Consulting Psychologists Press.

McArthur, C. C. (1968). Comment on studies of clinical versus statistical prediction. *Journal of Counseling Psychology, 15*, 172–173.

McArthur, C. C. (1972). Review of the Rorschach. In O. K. Buros (Ed.). *The seventh mental measurements yearbook.* Highland Park, NJ: Gryphon Press.

McCrae, R. R., & Costa, P. T., Jr. (1986). Clinical psychology can benefit from recent advances in personality psychology. *American Psychologist, 41*, 1001–1003.

McCrae, R. R. & Costa, P. T., Jr. (1990). *Personality in adulthood.* New York: The Guilford Press.

McCully, R. S. (1965). Current attitudes about projective techniques in APA approved internship centers. *Journal of Projective Techniques and Personality Assessment, 27*, 271–280.

McNair, D. M., Lorr, M., Young, H. H., Roth, I., & Boyd, R. W. (1964). A three-year follow-up of psychotherapy patients. *Journal of Clinical Psychology, 20*, 258–264.

McReynolds, P. (1975). Historical antecedents of personality assessment. In P. McReynolds. *Advances in personality assessment.* (Vol. 3). San Francisco: Jossey-Bass.

McReynolds, P. (1986). History of assessment in clinical and educational settings. In R. O. Nelson & S. C. Hayes (Eds.). *Conceptual foundations of behavioral assessment.* New York: Guilford.

McReynolds, P. (1989). Diagnosis and clinical assessment: Current status and major issues. In M. R. Rosenzweig & L. W. Porter (Eds.). *Annual review of psychology.* (Vol. 40). Palo Alto, CA: Annual Reviews.

Meehl, P. E. (1945). The dynamics of "structured" personality tests. *Journal of Clinical Psychology, 1*, 296–303.

Meehl, P. E. (1951). *Research results for counselors.* St. Paul, MN: State Department of Education.

Meehl, P. E. (1954). *Clinical vs. statistical prediction: A theoretical analysis and review of the evidence.* Minneapolis: University of Minnesota Press.

Meehl, P. E. (1956). Wanted–A good cookbook. *American Psychologist, 11,* 263–272.

Meehl, P. E. (1957). When shall we use our heads instead of the formula? *Journal of Counseling Psychology, 4,* 268–273.

Meehl, P. E. (1959). What can the clinician do well? Paper read at the symposium "Clinical Skills Revisited," American Psychological Association Convention, September 4, 1959.

Meehl, P. E. (1960). The cognitive activity of the clinician. *American Psychologist, 15,* 19–27.

Meehl, P. E. (1965). Seer over sign: The first good example. *Journal of Experimental Research In Personality, 1,* 27–32.

Meehl, P. E. (1967). What can the clinician do well? In D. N. Jackson & S. Messick (Eds.). *Problems of human assessment.* New York: McGraw-Hill.

Meehl, P. E. (1986). Causes and effects of my disturbing little book. *Journal of Personality Assessment, 50,* 370–375.

Meehl, P. E. (1987). Foreword. In J. N. Butcher (Ed.). *Computerized psychological assessment: A practitioner's guide.* New York: Basic Books.

Megargee, E. I. (1972). *The California Psychological Inventory Handbook.* Palo Alto, CA: Consulting Psychologists Press.

Megargee, E. I., & Mendelsohn, G. A. (1962). A cross-validation of twelve MMPI indices of hostility and control. *Journal of Abnormal and Social Psychology, 65,* 431–438.

Megargee, E. I.., & Parker, G. V. (1968). An exploration of the equivalence of Murray's needs as assessed by the Adjective Check List, the TAT, and the Edwards Personal Preference Schedule. *Journal of Clinical Psychology, 24,* 47–51.

Menninger, W. C. (1950). The relationship of clinical psychology and psychiatry. *Bulletin of the Menninger Clinic, 14,* 1–21.

Mercer, J. R., & Lewis, J. F. (1978). *System of Multicultural Pluralistic Assessment (SOMPA).* San Antonio, TX: The Psychological Corporation.

Messer, S. B. (1986). Behavioral and psychoanalytic perspectives at therapeutic choice points. *American Psychologist, 41,* 1261–1272.

Messick, S. (1975). The standard problem: Meaning and values in measurement and evaluation. *American Psychologist, 30,* 955–966.

Messick, S. (1980). Test validity and the ethics of assessment. *American Psychologist, 35,* 1012–1027.

Messick, S. (1981). Evidence and ethics in the evaluation of tests. *Educational Researcher, 10,* 9–20.

Messick, S. (1988). The once and future issues of validity: Assessing the meaning and consequences of measurement. In H. Wainer & H. I. Braun (Eds.). *Test Validity.* Hillsdale, NJ: Lawrence Erlbaum Associates.

Meyer, J. D., Fink, C. M., & Carey, P. F. (1988). Medical views of psychological consultation. *Professional Psychology: Research and Practice, 19,* 356–358.

Miller-Jones, D. (1989). Culture and testing. *American Psychologist, 44,* 360–366.

Millon, T. (1969). *Modern psychopathology: A biosocial approach to maladaptive learning and functioning.* Philadelphia: Saunders.

Millon, T. (1981). *Disorders of personality–DSM-III: Axis II.* New York: Wiley.

Millon, T. (1983). The DSM-III: An insider's perspective. *American Psychologist, 38,* 804–814.

Millon, T. (1984). On the renaissance of personality assessment and personality theory. *Journal of Personality Assessment, 48,* 450–465.

Millon, T. (1986a). On the past and the future of the DSM-III: Personal recollections and projections. In T. Millon & G. L. Klerman (Eds.), *Contemporary directions in psychopathology: Toward the DSM-IV.* New York: Guilford.

Millon, T. (1986b). A theoretical derivation of pathological personalities. In T. Millon & G. L. Klerman (Eds.), *Contemporary directions in psychopathology: Toward the DSM-IV.* New York: Guilford.

Millon, T. (1986c). Personality prototypes and their diagnostic criteria. In T. Millon & G. L. Klerman (Eds.), *Contemporary directions in psychopathology: Toward the DSM-IV.* New York: Guilford.

Millon, T. (1987). *Manual for the MCMI-II* (2nd ed.). Minneapolis: National Computer Systems.

Millon, T., Green, C. J., & Meagher, R. B., Jr. (1982a). *Millon Behavioral Health Inventory manual* (3rd ed.). Minneapolis: National Computer Systems.

Millon, T., Green, C. J., & Meagher, R. B., Jr. (1982b). *Millon Adolescent Personality Inventory manual.* Minneapolis: National Computer Systems.

Millon, T., & Klerman, G. L. (Eds.). (1986). *Contemporary directions in psychopathology: Toward the DSM-IV.* New York: Guilford.

Milner, B. (1962). Laterality effects in audition. In V. B. Mountcastle (Ed.), *Interhemispheric relations and cerebral dominance.* Baltimore: Johns Hopkins University Press.

Milner, B. (1971). Interhemispheric differences in the localization of psychological processes in man. *British Medical Bulletin, 27,* 272–277.

Mindess, H. (1988). *Makers of psychology: The personal factor.* New York: Human Sciences Press.

Mischel, W. (1968). *Personality and assessment.* New York: Wiley.

Mischel, W. (1969). Continuity and change in personality. *American Psychologist, 24,* 1012–1018.

Mischel, W. (1976). *Introduction to personality* (2nd ed.). New York: Holt, Rinehart and Winston.

Mischel, W. (1984). Consequences and challenges in the search for consistency. *American Psychologist, 39,* 351–364.

Mitchell, J. V., Jr. (1986). Measurement in the larger context: Critical current issues. *Professional Psychology: Research and Practice, 17,* 544–550.

Moreland, K. L. (1985). Validation of computer-based test interpretations: Problems and prospects. *Journal of Consulting and Clinical Psychology, 53,* 816–825.

Morey, L. C. (1988). Personality disorders in DSM-III and DSM-III-R: Consequence, coverage, and internal consistency. *American Journal of Psychiatry, 145,* 573–577.

Mortimer, R. L., & Smith, W. H. (1983). The use of the psychological test report in setting the focus of psychotherapy. *Journal of Personality Assessment, 47,* 134–138.

Mosak, H. H., & Gushurst, R. S. (1972). Some therapeutic uses of psychologic testing. *American Journal of Psychotherapy, 26,* 539–546.

Murray, H. A. (1933). The effect of fear upon estimates of the maliciousness of other personalities. *Journal of Social Psychology, 4,* 310–339.

Murray, H. A. (1937). Techniques for a systematic investigation of fantasy. *Journal of Psychology, 3,* 115–143.

Murray, H. A. (1938). *Explorations in personality*. New York: Oxford University Press.

Murstein, B. I. (1963). *Theory and research in projective techniques (emphasizing the TAT)*. New York: Wiley.

Murstein, B. I. (1965). *Handbook of projective techniques*. New York: Basic Books.

Murstein, B. I. (1968). Discussion for current status of some projective techniques. *Journal of Projective Techniques and Personality Assessment, 32*, 229–232.

Musante, G. J. (1974). Staff evaluations of the technician role. *Professional Psychology, 5*, 214–216.

Nathan, G. J. (1941). *The bachelor life*. New York: Reynal and Hitchcock.

National Association of School Psychologists (1974). *Principles for professional ethics*.

Nelson, R. O. (1983). Behavioral assessment: Past, present, and future. *Behavioral Assessment, 5*, 195–206.

Nelson, R. O. (1987). DSM-III and behavioral assessment. In C. G. Last & M. Hersen (Eds.). *Issues in diagnostic research*. New York: Plenum.

Nelson, R. O., & Hayes S. C. (1979). Some current dimensions of behavioral assessment. *Behavioral Assessment, 1*, 1–16.

Nelson, R. O., and Hayes, S. C. (Eds.) (1986). *Conceptual foundations of behavioral assessment*. New York: Guilford.

Newman, E. B. (1966). Proceedings of the American Psychological Association, Incorporated, for the year 1966. *American Psychologist, 21*, 1125–1153.

Nezu, A. M., & Nezu, C. M. (1989). *Clinical decision making in behavior therapy*. Champaign, IL: Research Press.

Norcross, J. C., Prochaska, J. O., & Gallagher, K. M. (1989). Clinical psychologists in the 1980s: II. Theory, Research, and practice. *The Clinical Psychologist, 42*, 45–53.

Odom, C. L. (1950). A study of the time required to do a Rorschach examination. *Journal of Projective Techniques, 14*, 464–468.

Ogdon, D. P. (1981). *Psychodiagnostics and personality assessment: A handbook* (2nd ed.). Los Angeles: Western Psychological Services.

Olive, H. (1972). Psychoanalysts' opinions of psychologists' reports: 1952 and 1970. *Journal of Clinical Psychology, 28*, 50–54.

Oskamp, S. W. (1962). The relation of clinical experience and training methods to several criteria of clinical prediction. *Psychological Monographs, 76* (28, Whole No. 547).

Oskamp, S. W. (1965). Overconfidence in case-study judgments. *Journal of Consulting Psychology, 29*, 261–265.

Othmer, E., & Othmer, S. C. (1989). *The clinical interview: Using DSM-III-R*. Washington, DC: American Psychiatric Press.

Parker, K. (1983). A meta-analysis of the reliability and validity of the Rorschach. *Journal of Personality Assessment, 47*, 227–231.

Pascal, G. R. (1983). *The practical art of diagnostic interviewing*. Homewood, IL: Dow Jones-Irwin.

Pascal, G. R., & Suttell, B. J. (1951). *The Bender-Gestalt Test: Quantification and validity for adults*. Orlando, FL: Grune & Stratton.

Perry, S., Cooper, A. M., & Michels, R. (1987). The psychodynamic formulation: Its purpose, structure, and clinical application. *American Journal of Psychiatry, 144*, 543–550.

Peterson, D. R. (1968). *The clinical study of social behavior.* New York: Appleton-Century-Crofts.

Phillips, L. & Smith, J. G. (1989). *Rorschach interpretation: Advanced technique.* Boston: Allyn and Bacon.

Piedmont, R. L., Sokolove, R. L., & Fleming, M. Z. (1989). An examination of some diagnostic strategies involving the Wechsler Intelligence Scales. *Psychological Assessment, 1*, 181–185.

Piotrowski, C. (1984). The status of projective techniques: Or "wishing won't make it go away." *Journal of Clinical Psychology, 40*, 1495–1502.

Piotrowski, C. (1985). Clinical assessment: Attitudes of the Society for Personality Assessment membership. *The Southern Psychologist, 2*, 80–83.

Piotrowski, C., & Keller, J. W. (1978). Psychological test usage in southeastern outpatient mental health facilities in 1975. *Professional Psychology, 9*, 63–67.

Piotrowski, C., & Keller, J. W. (1984a). Psychodiagnostic testing in APA-approved clinical psychology programs. *Professional Psychology: Research and Practice, 15*, 450–456.

Piotrowski, C., & Keller, J. W. (1984b). Attitudes toward clinical assessment by members of the AABT. *Psychological Reports, 55*, 831–838.

Piotrowski, C., & Keller, J. W. (1989a). Psychological testing in outpatient mental health facilities: A national study. *Professional Psychology: Research and Practice, 20*, 423–425.

Piotrowski, C., & Keller, J. W. (1989b). Use of assessment in mental health clinics and services. *Psychological Reports, 64*, 1298.

Piotrowski, C., Sherry, D., & Keller, J. W. (1985). Psychodiagnostic test usage: A survey of the Society for Personality Assessment. *Journal of Personality Assessment, 49*, 115–119.

Piotrowski, Z. A. (1965). *Perceptanalysis* (2nd ed.). Philadelphia: Ex Libris.

Polanyi, M. (1958). *Personal knowledge: Toward a post-critical philosophy* (rev. ed.). New York: Harper Torchbooks.

Potkay, C. S. (1971). *The Rorschach clinician.* Orlando, FL: Grune & Stratton.

Powers, A. D., & Rustagi, P. K. (1989). Mnemonic device for criteria for borderline personality disorder. *American Journal of Psychiatry, 146*, 1517.

Powers, W. T., & Hamlin, R. M. (1957). The validity, bases, and process of clinical judgment, using a limited amount of projective test data. *Journal of Projective Techniques, 21*, 286–293.

Privacy and behavioral research (1967). Washington, DC: U.S. Government Printing Office.

Prout, A. T. (1986). Personality assessment and individual therapeutic intervention. In H. M. Knoff (Ed.). *The assessment of child and adolescent personality.* New York: Guilford.

Pruitt, J. A., Smith, M. C., Thelen, M. H., & Lubin, B. (1985). Attitudes of academic clinical psychologists toward projective techniques: 1968–1983. *Professional Psychology: Research and Practice, 16*, 781–788.

Pruyser, P. W. (1979). *The psychological examination: A guide for clinicians.* New York: International Universities Press.

Purisch, A. D., & Sbordone, R. J. (1986). The Luria-Nebraska Neuropsychological Battery. In G. Goldstein & R. E. Tarter (Eds.). *Advances in clinical neuropsychology* (Vol. 3). New York: Plenum Press.

Quigley, J. (1990). *What does Joan say? My seven years as White House astrologer to Nancy and Ronald Reagan.* New York: Birch Lane Press.

Rabin, A. I. (1968). Extensions of the projective hypothesis. In A. I. Rabin (Ed.). *Projective techniques in personality assessment.* New York: Springer.

Rapaport, D. (1950). Theoretical implications of diagnostic testing procedures. *Congres International de Psychiatrie, 2,* 241-247.

Rapaport, D., Gill, M. M., & Schafer, R. (1945). *Diagnostic psychological testing: The Theory, Statistical, Evaluation, and Diagnosis Application of a Battery of Tests.* (Vol. 1). New York: International Universities Press.

Rapaport, D., Gill, M. M., & Schafer, R. (1946). *Diagnostic psychological testing: The Theory, Statistical, Evaluation, and Diagnosis Application of a Battery of Tests.* (Vol. 2). New York: International Universities Press.

Rapoport, J. L., & Ismond, D. R. (1989). *DSM-III-R training guide for diagnosis of childhood disorders* (rev. ed.). New York: Brunner/Mazel.

Reagan, N. (with W. Novak) (1989). *My turn: The memoirs of Nancy Reagan.* New York: Random House.

Reid, W. H., & Wise, M. G. (1989). *DSM-III-R training guide.* New York: Brunner/Mazel.

Reik, T. (1948). *Listening with the third ear.* New York: Farrar, Straus.

Reiser, M. F. (1988). Are psychiatric educators losing the mind? *American Journal of Psychiatry, 145,* 148-153.

Reitan, R. M. (1955). An investigation of the validity of Halstead's measures of biological intelligence. *Archives of Neurology and Psychiatry, 73,* 28-35.

Reitan, R. M., & Davison, L. A. (1974). *Clinical neuropsychology: Current status and applications.* New York: Winston/Wiley.

Reitan, R. M., & Wolfson, D. (1985). *The Halstead-Reitan Neuropsychological Test Battery: Theory and clinical interpretation.* Tucson: Neuropsychology Press.

Reynolds, W. M. (1979). Psychological tests: Clinical usage versus psychometric quality. *Professional Psychology, 10,* 324-329.

Reynolds, W. M., & Sundberg, N. D. (1976). Recent research trends in testing. *Journal of Personality Assessment, 40,* 228-233.

Reznikoff, M. (1972). Rorschach. In O. K. Buros (Ed.). *The seventh mental measurements yearbook* (Vol. 1). Highland Park, NJ: Gryphon Press.

Richardson, S. A., Dohrenwend, B. S., & Klein, D. (1965). *Interviewing: Its forms and functions.* New York: Basic Books.

Richman, J. (1967). Reporting diagnostic test results to patients and their families. *Journal of Projective Techniques and Personality Assessment, 31,* 62-70.

Rickers-Ovsiankina, M. A. (1977). *Rorschach psychology* (2nd ed.). Huntington, NY: Krieger.

Ritzler, B., & Alter, B. (1986). Rorschach teaching in APA-approved clinical graduate programs: Ten years later. *Journal of Personality Assessment, 50,* 44-49.

Robinson, J. T. (1951). *Some indications of personality differences among clinical psychologists as revealed in their reports on patients.* Unpublished master's thesis, Duke University.

Robinson, J. T., & Cohen, L. D. (1954). Individual bias in psychological reports. *Journal of Clinical Psychology, 10,* 333-336.

Rock, D. L., Bransford, J. D., Morey, L. C., & Maisto, S. A. (1988). The study of clinical judgment: Some clarifications. *Clinical Psychology Review, 8,* 411-416.

Rodgers, D. A. (1972). Review of Minnesota Multiphasic Personality Inventory. In O. K. Buros (Ed.). *The seventh mental measurements yearbook* (pp. 243-250). Highland Park, NJ: Gryphon Press.

Rogers, C. R. (1942). *Counseling and psychotherapy.* Boston: Houghton-Mifflin.

Rogers, C. R. (1951). *Client-centered therapy.* Boston: Houghton-Mifflin.

Rogers, C. R. (1955). Persons or science? A philosophical question. *American Psychologist, 10,* 267–278.

Rohde, A. R. (1957). *The sentence completion method: The diagnostic and clinical application to mental disorders.* New York: Ronald.

Roman, M., & Bauman, G. (1960). Interaction testing: A technique for the psychological evaluation of small groups. In Harrower, M., Vorhaus, P., Roman, M. & Bauman, G. *Creative variations in the projective techniques.* Springfield, IL: Thomas.

Rorschach, H. (1921/1951). *Psychodiagnostics: A test of perception.* Orlando, FL: Grune & Stratton.

Rosenwald, G. C. (1963). Psychodiagnostics and its discontents: A contribution to the understanding of professional identity and compromise. *Psychiatry, 26,* 222–240.

Rosenwald, G. C. (1965). Physicalism and psychodiagnosis. *Psychiatric Quarterly, 39,* 16–31.

Roth, L. H., Wolford, J., & Meisel, A. (1980). Patient access to records: Tonic or toxin? *American Journal of Psychiatry, 137,* 592–596.

Rotter, J. B. (1950). *Rotter Incomplete Sentences Blank-manual.* San Antonio, TX: The Psychological Corporation.

Rucker, C. N. (1967). Technical language in the school psychologist's report. *Psychology in the Schools, 4,* 146–150.

Ruebhausen, O. M., & Brim, O. G., Jr. (1966). Privacy and social research. *American Psychologist, 21,* 423–437.

Russ, S. W. (1978). Teaching psychological assessment: Training issues and teaching approaches. *Journal of Personality Assessment, 42,* 452–456.

Russell, E. W., Neuringer, C., & Goldstein, G. (1970). *Assessment of brain damage: A neuropsychological key approach.* New York: Wiley.

Sacks, J. M., & Levy, S. (1950). The sentence completion test. In L. E. Abt & L. Bellak. *Projective psychology. Clinical approaches to the total personality.* New York: Knopf.

Salzinger, K. (1986). Diagnosis: Distinguishing among behaviors. In T. Millon & G. L. Klerman (Eds.). *Contemporary directions in psychopathology: Toward the DSM-IV.* New York: Guilford.

Sarbin, T. R. (1943). A contribution to the study of actuarial and individual methods of prediction. *American Journal of Sociology, 48,* 593–602.

Sarbin, T. R. (1967). On the futility of the proposition that some people be labeled "mentally ill." *Journal of Consulting Psychology, 31,* 447–453.

Sarbin, T. R. (1986). Prediction and clinical inference: Forty years later. *Journal of Personality Assessment, 50,* 362–369.

Sarbin, T. R., Taft, R., & Bailey, D. E. (1960). *Clinical inference and cognitive theory.* New York: Holt, Rinehart and Winston.

Sargent, H. D. (1951). Psychological test reporting: An experiment in technique. *Bulletin of the Menninger Clinic, 15,* 175–186.

Sattler, J. M. (1988). *Assessment of children* (3rd ed.). San Diego, CA: Jerome M. Sattler, Publisher.

Saul, L. (1958). *Technique and practice of psychoanalysis.* Philadelphia: Lippincott.

Sawyer, J. (1966). Measurement and prediction, clinical and statistical. *Psychological Bulletin, 66,* 178–200.

Schachtel, E. G. (1966). *Experiential foundations of Rorschach's test*. New York: Basic Books.

Schachtel, E. G. (1967). Experiential qualities of the Rorschach blots. *Journal of Projective Techniques and Personality Assessment, 31*, 4–10.

Schafer, R. (1949). Psychological tests in clinical research. *Journal of Consulting Psychology, 13*, 328–334.

Schafer, R. (1967). *The clinical application of psychological tests*. New York: International Universities Press.

Schafer, R. (1976). *A new language for psychoanalysis*. New Haven: Yale University Press.

Schafer, R. (1989). *Psychoanalytic interpretation in Rorschach testing*. Boston: Allyn and Bacon.

Schlesinger, H. J. (1973). Interaction of dynamic and reality factors in the diagnostic testing interview. *Bulletin of the Menninger Clinic, 37*, 495–517.

Schwartz, F., & Lazar, Z. (1979). The scientific status of the Rorschach. *Journal of Personality Assessment, 43*, 3–11.

Schwartz, F., & Lazar, Z. (1984). Contaminated thinking: A specimen of the primary process. *Psychoanalytic Psychology, 1*, 319–334.

Seime, R. J., McCauley, R. L., & Madsen, R. K. (1977). Comparing interview impressions and test results: A new test interpretation format and procedure. *Professional Psychology, 8*, 199–205.

Sell, J. M., & Torres-Henry, R. (1979). Testing practices in university and college counseling centers in the United States. *Professional Psychology, 10*, 774–779.

Shakow, D. (1976). What *is* clinical psychology? *American Psychologist, 31*, 553–560.

Shapiro, D. (1954). Special problems in testing borderline psychotics. *Journal of Projective Techniques, 18*, 387–394.

Shea, S. C. (1988). *Interviewing: The art of understanding*. Philadelphia: Saunders.

Shectman, F. (1979). Problems in communicating psychological understanding: Why won't they listen to me? *American Psychologist, 34*, 781–790.

Shelly, C., & Goldstein, G. (1983). Discrimination of chronic schizophrenia and brain damage with the Luria-Nebraska Battery: A partially successful replication. *Clinical Neuropsychology, 5*, 82–85.

Shevrin, H., & Shectman, F. (1973). The diagnostic process in psychiatric evaluation. *Bulletin of the Menninger Clinic, 37*, 451–494.

Shipley, W. C. (1940). A self-administering scale for measuring intellectual impairment and deterioration. *Journal of Psychology, 9*, 371–377.

Shively, J. J., & Smith, A. E. (1969). Understanding the psychological report. *Psychology in the schools, 6*, 272–273.

Simon, J. L. (1990). Overemphasizing diagnostic classification. *American Journal of Psychiatry, 147*, 1699–1700

Singer, M. J. (1978). Projective testing and psychiatric diagnosis: Validity and the future. In R. Spitzer & D. Klein (Eds.). *Critical issues in psychiatric diagnosis*. New York: Raven.

Singer, M. T. (1968). The consensus Rorschach and family transaction. *Journal of Projective Techniques and Personality Assessment, 32*, 348–351.

Singer, M. T. (1977a). The borderline diagnosis and psychological tests: Review and research. In P. Hartocollis (Ed.). *Borderline personality disorders: The concept, the syndrome, the patient*. New York: International Universities Press.

Singer, M. T. (1977b). The Rorschach as a transaction. In M. A. Rickers-Ovsiankina (Ed.). *Rorschach psychology* (2nd ed.). Huntington, NY: Krieger.

Siskind, G. (1967). Fifteen years later: A replication of "a semantic study of clinical psychologists and psychiatrists." *The Journal of Psychology, 65*, 3-7.

Sloop, E. W., & Quarrick, E. (1974). Technician performance: Reliability and validity. *Professional Psychology, 5*, 216-218.

Sloves, R. E., Docherty, E. M., Jr., & Schneider, K. C. (1979). A scientific problem-solving model of psychological assessment. *Professional Psychology, 10*, 28-35.

Smith, M. B. (1986). The plausible assessment report: A phrenological example. *Professional Psychology: Research & Practice, 17*, 294-295.

Smith, D., & Kraft, W. A. (1983). Do psychologists really want an alternative? *American Psychologist, 38*, 777-785.

Smith, G. M. (1985). The collaborative drawing technique. *Journal of Personality Assessment, 49*, 582-585.

Smith, W. H., & Allen, J. G. (1984). Identity conflicts and the decline of psychological testing. *Professional Psychology: Research and Practice, 15*, 49-55.

Snyder, C. R. (1974). Why horoscopes are true: The effects of specificity on acceptance of astrological interpretations. *Journal of Clinical Psychology, 30*, 577-580.

Snyderman, M., & Rothman, S. (1987). Survey of expert opinion on intelligence and aptitude testing. *American Psychologist, 42*, 137-144.

Snyderman, M, & Rothman, S. (1988). *The IQ controversy, the media and public policy*. New Brunswick, NJ: Transaction Books.

Souther, J. W. (1957). *Technical report writing*. New York: Wiley.

Spielberger, C. D., Jacobs, G., Russel, S., & Crane, R. S. (1983). Assessment of anger: The state-trait anger scale. In J. N. Butcher and C. D. Spielberger (Eds.). *Advances in personality assessment* (Vol. 2). Hillsdale, NJ: Lawrence Erlbaum Associates.

Spiers, P. A. (1981). Have they come to praise Luria or to bury him? The Luria-Nebraska controversy. *Journal of Consulting and Clinical Psychology, 49*, 331-341.

Spitzer, R. L., Fleiss, G. I., Endicott, J., & Cohen, J. (1967). Mental status schedule: Properties of factor-analytically derived scales. *Archives of General Psychiatry, 16*, 479-493.

Spitzer, R. L., Skodol, A. E., Gibbon, W., & Williams, J. B. W. (1981). *DSM-III case book*. Washington, DC: American Psychiatric Association.

Spitzer, R. L., & Williams, J. B. W. (1985). Classification in psychiatry. In H. I. Kaplan & B. J. Sadock (Eds.). *Comprehensive textbook of psychiatry* (4th ed.). Baltimore: Williams & Wilkins.

Spitzer, R. L., Williams, J. B. W., Gibbon, M., & First, M. B. (1990). *User's Guide for the Structured Clinical Interview for DSM-III-R (SCID)*. Washington, DC: American Psychiatric Press.

Stambrook, M. (1983). The Luria-Nebraska Neuropsychological Battery: A promise that may be partly fulfilled. *Journal of Clinical Neuropsychology, 5*, 247-269.

Stein, E. J., Furedy, R. L., Simonton, M. J., & Neuffer, C. H. (1979). Patient access to medical records on a psychiatric inpatient unit. *American Journal of Psychiatry, 136*, 327-332.

Stein, M. (1981). *The Thematic Appercention Test: An introductory manual for its clinical use with adults* (2nd ed.). Springfield, IL: Thomas.

Stolorow, R. D. & Attwood, G. (1979). *Faces in a cloud: Subjectivity in personality theory*. Northvale, NJ: Jason Aronson.

Strong, E. K., Jr., & Campbell, D. P. (1974). *Strong Vocational Interest Blank*. Stanford, CA: Stanford University Press.

Sturm, I. E. (1974). Toward a composite psychodiagnostic report outline. *Newsletter for Research in Mental Health and Behavioral Science. 16* (3), 6–7.

Sugarman, A. (1978). Is psychodiagnostic assessment humanistic? *Journal of Personality Assessment, 42*, 11–21.

Sugarman, A. (1981). The diagnostic use of countertransference in psychological testing. *Bulletin of the Menninger Clinic, 45*, 473–490.

Sugarman, A. (1991). Where's the beef? Putting personality back into personality assessment. *Journal of Personality Assessment, 56*, 130–144.

Sundberg, N. D. (1954). A note concerning the history of testing. *The American Psychologist, 9*, 150–151.

Sundberg, N. D. (1961). The practice of psychological testing in clinical services in the United States. *American Psychologist, 16*, 79–83.

Sundberg, N. D., & Tyler, L. E. (1962). *Clinical psychology*. New York: Appleton-Century-Crofts.

Sundberg, N. D., Tyler, L. E., & Taplin, J. R. (1973). *Clinical psychology: Expanding horizons* (2nd ed.). Englewood Cliffs, NJ: Prentice Hall.

Sussman, N. (1989). Factitious disorders. In H. I. Kaplan & B. J. Sadock. *Comprehensive textbook of psychiatry* (5th ed., Vol. 2). Baltimore: Williams & Wilkins.

Sweeney, J. A., Clarkin, J. F., & Fitzgibbon, M. L. (1987). Current practice of psychological assessment. *Professional Psychology: Research and Practice, 18*, 377–380.

Symonds, P. M. (1955). A contribution to our knowledge of the validity of the Rorschach. *Journal of Projective Techniques, 19*, 152–162.

Szasz, T. S. (1960). The myth of mental illness. *American Psychologist, 15*, 113–118.

Szasz, T. S. (1961). *The myth of mental illness*. New York: Hoeber-Harper.

Taft, R. (1955). The ability to judge people. *Psychological Bulletin, 52*, 1–28.

Taft, R. (1956). Some characteristics of good judges of others. *British Journal of Psychology, 47*, 19–29.

Tallent, N. (1958a). Manifest content and interpretive meaning of verbal intelligence test responses. *Journal of Clinical Psychology, 14*, 57–58.

Tallent, N. (1958b). On individualizing the psychologist's clinical evaluation. *Journal of Clinical Psychology, 14*, 243–244.

Tallent, N. (1969). Lightner Witmer's legacy. *American Psychologist, 24*, 473–475.

Tallent, N. (1983). *Psychological report writing* (2nd ed.). Englewood Cliffs, NJ: Prentice Hall.

Tallent, N. (1987). Computer-generated psychological reports: A look at the modern psychometric machine. *Journal of Personality Assessment, 51*, 95–108.

Tallent, N. (1988). *Psychological report writing* (3rd ed.). Englewood Cliffs, NJ: Prentice Hall.

Tallent, N., Kennedy, G., Szafir, A., & Grolimund, B. (1974). An expanded role for psychiatric nursing personnel: Psychological evaluation and interpersonal care. *Journal of Psychiatric Nursing and Mental Health Services, 12*, 19–23.

Tallent, N. & Rafi, A. A. (1965). National and professional factors in psychological consultation. *British Journal of Social and Clinical Psychology, 4*, 149–151.

Tallent, N., & Reiss, W. J. (1959a). Multidisciplinary views on the preparation of written clinical psychological reports: I. Spontaneous suggestions for content. *Journal of Clinical Psychology, 15*, 218–221.

Tallent, N., & Reiss, W. J. (1959b). Multidisciplinary views on the preparation of written clinical psychological reports: II. Acceptability of certain common content variables and styles of expression. *Journal of Clinical Psychology, 15*, 273–274.

Tallent, N., & Reiss, W. J. (1959c). Multidisciplinary views on the preparation of written clinical psychological reports: III. The trouble with psychological reports. *Journal of Clinical Psychology, 15*, 444–446.

Taylor, J. L., & Teicher, A. A. (1946). A clinical approach to reporting psychological test data. *Journal of Clinical Psychology, 2*, 323–332.

Technical manual, cognitive abilities test. Chicago: Riverside Publishing Co.

Tenopyr, M. L. (1977). Content-construct confusion. *Personnel Psychology, 30*, 47–54.

Thelen, M. H., & Ewing, D. R. (1970). Roles, functions, and training in clinical psychology: A survey of academic clinicians. *American Psychologist, 25*, 550–554.

Thelen, M. H., Varble, D. L., & Johnson, J. (1968). Attitudes of academic clinical psychologists toward projective techniques. *American Psychologist, 23*, 517–521.

Thomas, C. A., Jr. (1966). The "yell fire" response as an indicator of impaired impulse control. *Journal of Clinical Psychology, 22*, 221–223.

Thorne, F. C. (1961). *Clinical judgment: A study of clinical errors.* Brandon, VT: Clinical Psychology Publishing Company.

Thurlow, M. L., & Ysseldyke, J. E. (1982). Instructional planning. Information collected by school psychologists vs. information considered useful by teachers. *Journal of School Psychology, 20*, 3–10.

Tittle, C. K. (1982). Use of judgmental methods in item bias studies. In R. A. Berk (Ed.). *Handbook of methods for detecting test bias.* Baltimore: Johns Hopkins University Press.

Tittle, C. K., & Zytowski, D. G. (Eds.) (1978). *Sex-fair interest measurement: Research and implications.* Washington, DC: National Institute of Education.

Tolor, A., & Brannigan, G. C. (1980). *Research and clinical applications of the Bender-Gestalt Test.* Springfield, IL: Thomas.

Towbin, A. P. (1964). Psychological testing from end to means. *Journal of Projective Techniques and Personality Assessment, 28*, 86–91.

Trimboli, F., & Kilgore, R. B. (1983). A psychodynamic approach to MMPI interpretation. *Journal of Personality Assessment, 47*, 614–626.

Tuma, J. M., & Pratt, J. M. (1982). Clinical child psychology practice and training: A survey. *Journal of Clinical Child Psychology, 11*, 27–34.

Turkat, I. D., & Maisto, S. (1983). Functions of and differences between psychiatric diagnosis and case formulation. *The Behavior Therapist, 6*, 184–185.

Turner, S. M., & Turkat, I. D. (1988). Behavior therapy and the personality disorders. *Journal of Personality Disorders, 2*, 342–349.

Tyrer, P. (1988). What's wrong with DSM-III personality disorders? *Journal of Personality Disorders, 2*, 281–291.

Vale, C. D., & Keller, L. S. (1987). Developing expert computer systems to interpret psychological tests. In J. N. Butcher (Ed.). *Computerized psychological assessment.* New York: Basic Books.

Vane, J. R. (1981). The Thematic Apperception Test: A review. *Clinical Psychology Review, 1*, 319–336.

van Reken, M. K. (1981). Psychological assessment and report writing. In C. E. Walker (Ed.). *Clinical practice of psychology*. Elmsford, NY: Pergamon Press.

Vega, A., & Parsons, O. (1967). Cross-validation of the Halstead-Reitan tests for brain damage. *Journal of Consulting Psychology, 31*, 619–625.

Vernier, C. M. (1952). *Projective drawings*. Orlando, FL: Grune & Stratton.

Volkan, V. D. (1987). *Six steps in the treatment of borderline personality organization*. Northvale, NJ: Jason Aronson.

Wade, T. C., & Baker, T. B. (1977). Opinions and use of psychological tests: A survey of clinical psychologists. *American Psychologist, 32*, 874–882.

Wade, T. C., Baker, T. B., Morton, T. L., & Baker, L. J. (1978). The status of psychological testing in clinical psychology: Relationships between test use and professional activities and orientations. *Journal of Personality Assessment, 42*, 3–10.

Wagner, E. E., & Slemboski, C. A. (1969). Construct validation of Piotrowski's interpretation of the Rorschach shading response. *Journal of Projective Techniques and Personality Assessment, 33*, 343–344.

Waite, R. R. (1961). The intelligence test as a psychodiagnostic instrument. *Journal of Projective Techniques, 25*, 90–102.

Waller, N. G., & Ben-Porath, Y. S. (1987). Is it time for clinical psychology to embrace the five-factor model of personality? *American Psychologist, 42*, 887–889.

Waters, R. H. (1948). Mechanomorphism: A new term for an old mode of thought. *Psychological Review, 55*, 139–142.

Watkins, C. E., Jr., & Campbell, V. L. (1989). Personality assessment and counseling psychology. *Journal of Personality Assessment, 53*, 296–307.

Watkins, C. E., Jr., Campbell, V. L., McGregor, P., & Godin, K. (1989). The MMPI: Does it have a place in counseling psychology training? *Journal of Personality Assessment, 53*, 413–417.

Watley, D. J. (1966a). Counselor variability in making accurate predictions. *Journal of Counseling Psychology, 13*, 53–62.

Watley, D. J. (1966b). Counselor confidence in accuracy of predictions. *Journal of Counseling Psychology, 13*, 62–67.

Watley, D. J. (1968a). Do counselors know when to use their heads instead of the formula? *Journal of Counseling Psychology, 15*, 84–88.

Watley, D. J. (1968b). Feedback, training and improvement of clinical forecasting. *Journal of Counseling Psychology, 15*, 167–171.

Watley, D. J. (1968c). Reply to McArthur: Lost by *praeteritio*. *Journal of Counseling Psychology, 15*, 4, 390–392.

Watley, D. J., & Vance, F. L. (1964). *Clinical versus actuarial prediction of college achievement and leadership activity*. Final report, 1964, Project No. 2202, Cooperative Research Program, Office of Education, United States Department of Health, Education and Welfare.

Watson, R. I. (1951). *The clinical method in psychology*. New York: Harper & Brothers.

Wechsler, D. (1939). *The measurement of adult intelligence*. Baltimore: Williams & Wilkins.

Wechsler, D. (1939). *Wechsler-Bellevue Intelligence Scale, Form I*. San Antonio, TX: The Psychological Corporation.

Wechsler, D. (1944). *The assessment of adult intelligence* (3rd ed.). Baltimore: Williams & Wilkins.
Wechsler, D. (1958). *The measurement and appraisal of adult intelligence* (4th ed.). Baltimore: Williams & Wilkins.
Wechsler, D. (1975). Intelligence defined and undefined: A relativistic appraisal. *American Psychologist, 30*, 135–139.
Wechsler, D. (1981). *Manual for the Wechsler Adult Intelligence Scale—Revised*. San Antonio, TX: The Psychological Corporation.
Wedding, D., & Gudeman, H. (1980). Implications of computerized axial tomography for clinical neuropsychology. *Professional Psychology, 11*, 31–35.
Weiner, G. (1957). The effect of distrust on some aspects of intelligence test behavior. *Journal of Consulting Psychology, 21*, 127–130.
Weiner, I. (1959). The role of diagnosis in a university counseling center. *Journal of Counseling Psychology, 6*, 110–115.
Weiner, I. (1964). Differential diagnosis in amphetamine psychosis. *Psychiatric Quarterly, 38*, 707–716.
Weiner, I. (1965). Rorschach color stress as a schizophrenic indicator—A reply. *Journal of Clinical Psychology, 21*, 313–314.
Weiner, I. (1966). *Psychodiagnosis in schizophrenia*. New York: Wiley.
Weiner, I. (1972). Does psychodiagnosis have a future? *Journal of Personality Assessment, 36*, 534–546.
Weiner, I. (1977a). Approaches to Rorschach validity. In M. A. Rickers-Ovsiankina (Ed.). *Rorschach psychology* (2nd ed., pp. 575–608). Huntington, NY: Krieger.
Weiner, I. (1977b). Differential diagnosis. In B. B. Wolman (Ed.). *International encyclopedia of neurology, psychiatry, psychoanalysis, and psychology*. Princeton, NJ: Van Nostrand Reinhold.
Weiner, I. (1986). Conceptual and empirical perspectives on the Rorschach assessment of psychopathology. *Journal of Personality Assessment, 50*, 472–479.
Weiner, I. (1989). On competence and ethicality in psychodiagnostic assessment. *Journal of Personality Assessment, 53*, 827–831.
Weiner, M. F., & Crowder, J. D. (1986). Psychotherapy and cognitive style. *American Journal of Psychotherapy, 40*, 17–25.
Weiss, D. J. (1985). Adaptive testing by computer. *Journal of Consulting and Clinical Psychology, 53*, 774–779.
Weiss, K. M. (1989). Advantages of abandoning symptom-based diagnostic systems of research in schizophrenia. *American Journal of Orthopsychiatry, 59*, 324–330.
Westcott, M. R. (1968). *Psychology of intuition*. New York: Holt, Rinehart and Winston.
Wheeler, L., Burke, C. H., & Reitan, R. M. (1963). An application of discriminant functions to the problems of predicting brain damage using behavioral variables. *Perceptual and Motor Skills, 16*, 417–440 (Monograph Supplement).
Whyte, W. H., Jr. (1956). *The organization man*. New York: Simon & Schuster.
Widiger, T. A., & Frances, A. J. (1985). The DSM-III personality disorders. *Archives of General Psychiatry, 42*, 615–623.
Widiger, T. A., & Kelso, K. (1983). Psychodiagnosis of Axis-II. *Clinical Psychology Review, 3*, 491–510.

Widiger, T. A., & Schilling, K. M. (1980). Toward a construct validation of the Rorschach. *Journal of Personality Assessment, 44*, 450–459.

Wielkiewicz, R. M. (1990). Interpreting low scores on the WISC-R Third Factor: It's more than distractibility. *Psychological Assessment, 2*, 91–97.

Wiens, A. N., & Matarazzo, J. (1983). Diagnostic interviewing. In M. Hersen, A. E. Kazdin, & A. S. Bellack (Eds.), *The clinical psychology handbook*. New York: Pergamon Press.

Wiggins, J. S. (1973). *Personality and prediction: Principles of personality assessment*. Reading, MA: Addison-Wesley.

Williams, H. L. (1952) The development of a caudality scale for the MMPI. *Journal of Clinical Psychology, 8*, 293–297.

Winter, W. D., Ferreira, A. J., & Olson, J. L. (1966). Hostility themes in the family TAT. *Journal of Projective Techniques and Personality Assessment, 30*, 270–274.

Wirt, R. D., Lachar, D., Klinedinst, J. K., & Seat, P. D. (1990). *Multidimensional description of child personality: A manual for the Personality Inventory for Children*. Los Angeles: Western Psychological Services.

Witmer, L. (1925). Psychological diagnosis and the psychonomic orientation of analytic science. *The Psychological Clinic, 16*, 1–18.

Wyatt v. Aderholt (1974). 503 F. 2nd 1305 *Federal Reporter*, 2d Series, 1311–1312.

Wynne, L. C. (1968). Consensus Rorschachs and related procedures for studying interpersonal patterns. *Journal of Projective Techniques and Personality Assessment, 32*, 352–356.

Ysseldyke, J. E., & Weinberg, R. A. (Eds.). The future of psychology in the schools: Proceedings of the Spring Hill symposium. *School Psychology Review, 11*, 113–318 (Special issue).

Zimmerman, I. L., Woo-Sam, J. M., & Glasser, A. J. (1973). *The clinical interpretation of the Wechsler Adult Intelligence Scale*. Orlando, FL: Grune & Stratton.

Zins, J. E. (1984). A scientific problem-solving approach to developing accountability procedures for school psychologists. *Professional Psychology: Research and Practice, 15*, 56–66.

Ziskin, J. (1981). *Coping with psychiatric and psychological testimony* (3rd ed., 2 vols.). Venice, CA: Law and Psychology Press.

Zubin, J. (1954). Failures of the Rorschach technique. *Journal of Projective Techniques, 18*, 303–315.

Zubin, J. (1956a). Clinical vs. actuarial prediction: A pseudo-problem. *Journal of Counseling Psychology, 3*, 107–128.

Zubin, J. (1956b). The non-projective aspects of the Rorschach experiment: I. Introduction. *Journal of Social Psychology, 44*, 179–192.

Zubin, J. (1989). Use of research instruments in psychopathological assessment: Some historical perspectives. In S. Wetzler, *Measuring mental illness: Psychometric assessment for clinicians*. Washington, DC: American Psychiatric Press.

Zubin, J., Eron, L. D., & Schumer, F. (1965). *An experimental approach to projective techniques*. New York: Wiley.

Zytowski, D. G., & Borgen, F. H. (1983). Assessment. In B. Walsh & S. H. Osipow (Eds.), *Handbook of vocational psychology* (Vol. 2: *Applications*). Hillsdale, NJ: Lawrence Erlbaum Associates.

AUTHOR INDEX

A

Adair, F.L., 66
Adams, K.M., 141
Adler, T., 150
Affleck, D.C., 265, 266, 344
Ainsworth, M.D., 299
Albert, S., 40
Alexander, I.E., 20
Allen, A., 51
Allen, J.G., 20, 45, 120, 262, 232, 233, 264, 347, 348, 349
Allen, J.M., Jr., 229, 243
Allison, J., 291
Allport, G.W., 25, 53, 100, 170
Alp, I.E., 64, 159
Alpher, V.S., 265
Alter, B., 3, 21
Amrine, M., 87
Anastasi, A., 63
Andersen, S.M., 184
Appelbaum, S.A., 9, 32, 36, 39, 76, 222, 227, 233, 258, 266, 267, 270, 274, 275, 289, 330, 331
Archer, R.P., 151
Arnow, D., 280
Aronow, E., 105, 159, 160, 232, 307

Asken, M.J., 143
Atkinson, L., 64, 159
Atwood, G.E., 39
Auerbach, A., 267
Auger, T.J., 243

B

Babcock, H., 133
Bachrach, H., 267
Bailey, D.E., 30, 72, 228
Baker, G., 263
Baker, L.J., 3, 20
Baker, T.B., 3, 20, 22, 106, 291
Ban, T.A., 11
Barker, P., 174
Barrios, B., 115
Basowitz, H., 20
Bass, B., 70
Batson, C.D., 13
Bauman, G., 324, 329
Beck, S.J., 158, 278
Beitman, B.D., 49
Bellak, L., 162, 205
Bem, D.J., 51
Ben-Porath, Y.S., 61

Bender, L., 169
Berg, I.A., 70
Berg, M.R., 35, 75, 76, 233, 264, 280, 281, 283, 347, 349
Berg, R.A., 143
Berger, N.S., 190, 191
Berne, E., 30
Bersoff, D.N., 230
Bettelheim, B., 303, 333
Beutler, L.E., 49
Bigler, E.D., 142
Bingham, W.V.D., 171
Blanchard, E.B., 3, 20
Blanchard, W.H., 324, 326, 328
Blank, L., 242, 285, 286
Blatt, S.J., 50, 102, 157, 291
Block, J., 61
Board, R., 30
Boat, B.W., 61
Bogen, J.E., 138
Boll, T.J., 142, 143, 344
Bongar, B., 91
Borgen, F.H., 90
Boring, E.G., 1
Bowden, C.L., 177
Boyd, L., 21
Brannigan, G.C., 169
Bransford, J.D., 12
Breger, L., 265
Brim, O.G., Jr., 90
Brodsky, S.L., 232
Brotemarkle, R.A., 262
Brown, E.C., 16
Brown, F., 285
Brown, L.J., 276
Brown, L.S., 171
Brown, W.R., 3
Buck, J.N., 165, 166, 167
Bugental, J.F.T., 16
Burke, C.H., 138
Butcher, J.N., 34, 68, 92, 95, 96, 113, 148, 151, 288

C

Campbell, D.T., 64
Campbell, V.L., 3, 21, 22
Cannell, C.F., 174
Cannon, M., 174
Cantrell, J.D., 153
Carey, M.P., 195
Carey, P.F., 38
Carlile, J.S., 162

Carr, A.C., 205, 280, 281
Carson, R.C., 95, 96, 310
Cattell, R.B., 88, 296
Cerney, M.S., 263, 331
Chambers, G.S., 12
Chodoff, P., 55
Christoph, P., 267
Churchill, R.D., 164
Clark, W.D., 187, 189
Clarkin, J.F., 108, 119
Clawson, A., 169
Cleveland, S.E., 20
Cohen, J., 176
Cohen, L.D., 238
Cohen, L.J., 35, 120, 294
Cohen, M., 10
Cole, J.K., 194, 265
Comtois, R.J., 187, 189
Conrad, H.S., 209
Cooper, A., 284
Cooper, A.M., 9, 10, 55, 201, 202
Cooper, S.H., 280
Corcoran, K., 85
Craddick, R.A., 16, 232, 332
Craig, R.J., 3, 174
Crandall, 164
Crane, R.S., 63
Crits-Christoph, P., 267
Cronbach, L.J., 64, 65, 107
Crosson, B., 141
Crowder, J.D., 278
Cutter, F., 324, 326, 327
Cyr, J.J., 64, 159

D

Dahlstrom, L.E., 151
Dahlstrom, W.G., 135, 151
Dailey, C.A., 265
Dana, R.H., 89, 153, 249, 265, 266
De La Cour, A.T., 284
DeCourcy, P., 263
Delis, D., 141
Dell, F., 53
Della Corte, M., 243
deMendonca, M., 298
DeNelsky, G.Y., 61
DeSoto, C.B., 65
Dillon, C.A., 226
Docherty, E.M., Jr., 5, 7, 10, 120, 186, 187
Dohrenwend, B.S., 175
Donaldson, M., 11
Dorr, D., 26, 232, 264, 334

Doyle, K.D., Jr., 2
Drewe, E.A., 293
DuBois, P.H., 2
Dudek, S.Z., 324, 327
Duhl, B.S., 295
Dumont, F., 12
Dunlap, K., 236
Dunn, L.M., 133
Dunn, L.M., 133
Durand, V.M., 3, 20

E

Ebel, R.L., 64, 65, 66
Eichman, W.J., 69
Elkins, G.R., 21
Ellenberger, H., 157
Elliot, L., 298
Endicott, J., 172, 176
Epstein, S., 51, 58, 59, 63
Erikson, E.H., 36
Eron, L.D., 43, 105, 159, 294, 300, 324
Evans, B., 54
Everly, G.S., Jr., 53, 286
Ewing, D.R., 3
Exner, D.E., 99, 106, 160, 293, 294
Exner, J.E., Jr., 21, 50, 86, 99, 105, 106, 112, 113, 157, 158, 159, 160, 189, 201, 293, 294, 296, 305

F

Faber, R.A., 177
Farber, B., 32
Farberow, N.L., 324, 326, 327
Faust, D., 55, 259
Fee, A.F., 21
Fein, L.G., 20
Fernald, P.S., 324, 329
Ferreira, A.J., 324, 328
Filer, R.N., 238
Filskov, S.B., 143
Fink, C.M., 38
First, M.B., 173
Fischer, C.T., 16, 232, 253, 264, 334
Fischer, J., 85
Fiske, D.W., 64
Fitzgibbon, M.L., 108, 119
Fitzpatrick, A.R., 65
Flanagan, J.C., 65
Flasher, L.V., 195
Fleischauer, A., 152
Fleiss, G.I., 176

Fleming, M.Z., 110, 227
Flesch, R., 229
Ford, M.R., 90
Forer, B.R., 163, 165
Fowler, R.D., 34, 92, 94, 95
Fox, H.M., 3, 20, 40
Frances, A., 55, 56, 60
Franzen, M.D., 143
Freeman, W., 265
Freud, S., 204, 242, 296, 297
Friedman, A. F., 82, 151
Friedman, S.H., 135
Furedy, R.L., 232
Furth, H., 103, 104

G

Gallagher, K.M., 171
Garb, H.N., 12
Gardner, E.F., 65
Gartner, A.F., 59
Gentry, W.D., 344
Gibbon, M., 173, 184
Giedt, F.H., 11
Gilbert, D.C., 32
Gilbert, J., 127, 166, 200, 298, 302
Gill, M.M., 9, 17, 48, 80, 99, 100, 106, 108, 109, 110, 111, 114, 117, 119, 120, 158, 198, 278, 291, 298, 303, 304, 308, 346
Gilliland, A.B., 17
Ginsberg, G.L., 62, 175, 177
Glasser, A.J., 131, 132
Gluck, M., 104
Godin, K., 22
Gold, J.M., 14
Goldberg, E., 293
Goldberg, L.R., 11, 12, 40
Golden, C.J., 138, 139, 140, 141, 143, 293
Goldenson, R.M., 157
Goldfried, M.R., 15, 49
Goldstein, E.G., 280, 281
Goldstein, G., 134, 140, 141, 143, 144, 293
Goldstein, K., 276, 277
Goldstein, M., 298
Gordon, H.W., 138
Gough, H.G., 71, 72, 262, 310
Graham, J.R., 85, 94, 113, 147, 148, 149, 151
Graham, T.F., 175, 176, 177
Grayson, H.M., 243, 246
Green, B.F., Jr., 68, 89
Green, C.J., 153
Greene, R.L., 151
Grolimund, B., 345

Gross, M.L., 87
Gudeman, H., 143
Guertin, W.H., 131
Guetzkow, H., 325
Guion, R.M., 65, 66
Gunderson, J.G., 172, 279, 280, 281
Gushurst, R.S., 16, 232, 264

H

Hadley, J.M., 62
Hallenstein, C.B., 243
Halstead, W.C., 134
Hamlin, R.M., 12, 106
Hammeke, T.A., 139, 141, 143, 293
Hammer, E.F., 167, 238
Hammond, K.R., 229, 243
Hanfmann, E., 276
Hannifin, P., 265, 266
Harris, R.E., 147
Harrower, M., 324
Harthorn, B.H., 184
Hartlage, L.C., 143, 265, 266
Hartmann, D.P., 15
Hartocollis, P., 279
Harty, M.K., 271, 272
Hathaway, S.R., 82, 93, 311
Hausburg, J., 82
Hayes, S.C., 39, 48, 266, 273
Heinrichs, R.W., 142, 143
Helper, M.M., 344
Henry, W.E., 325
Henry, W.P., 265
Herron, E.W., 105
Hersen, M., 60
Hertz, M.R., 20
Hofer, P.J., 68
Hoffman, B., 37
Hogan, R., 65
Holmes, D.S., 201, 296
Holsopple, J.Q., 164
Holt, R.R., 8, 9, 29, 48, 70, 71, 72, 100, 107,
    108, 109, 112, 114, 160, 279, 303, 344
Holtzman, W.H., 34, 40, 105, 107, 259
Horine, L., 265
Hornsby, J.L., 143
Horowitz, M., 3
Horton, M.M., 205
Howe, H.E., Jr., 5, 10, 194, 197
Hulse, D., 191, 192
Hunt, H.F., 280, 281
Hunt, W.A., 11, 29, 30, 197
Hutt, M.L., 169, 301

I

Ismond, D.R., 184,185
Ivnik, R.J., 20

J

Jackson, C.W., Jr., 3, 19
Jacobs, G., 63
Jaffe, L., 330, 349
Jampala, V.C., 55
Jarrett, R.B., 273
Jennings, M.L., 191, 192
John, O.P., 61
Johnson, J., 3, 19
Johnson, M., 267
Jordan-Smith, P., 53
Josephs, L., 276

K

Kahn, M.W., 40
Kahn, R.L., 174
Kane, R.L., 143
Kaplan, E., 141
Karasu, T.B., 55
Karon, B.P., 162
Kasanin, J., 276
Kaufman, A.S., 124, 130, 131
Keiser, R.E., 162
Keller, C.W., 238
Keller, J.W., 3, 21, 82, 83
Keller, L.S., 95
Kelley, D.M.,158, 231, 321
Kelso, K., 60
Kennedy, G., 345
Kernberg, O.F, 152, 270, 278, 279, 280, 281, 283
Kilgore, R.B., 148, 200, 296
Kingsbury, S.J., 38, 75
Kissen, M., 273
Klein, D., 175
Kleinmuntz, B., 70
Klerman, G.L., 60, 259
Klinedinst, J.K., 153, 154, 155, 199
Klopfer, B., 158, 231, 321
Klopfer, W.G., 104, 236, 238, 259, 263, 285,
    324, 326
Knight, R.P., 331
Koppitz, E.M., 168, 169
Korchin, S.J., 6, 14, 43, 47, 50, 104, 266, 326
Korman, A.K., 71
Koss, M.P., 113, 148
Kraft, W.A., 56

Kris, E., 32
Kwawer, J., 120

L

L'Abate, L., 344
Lacey, H.M., 246
Lachar, D., 148, 153, 154, 155, 199
Lacks, P.B., 205
Lambert, L.E., 12
Lambert, N.M., 89
Lambley, P., 263
Lamiell, J.T., 100
Lancaster, C., 265, 266
Landers, S., 18
Lanyon, R.I., 97
Larsen, R.M., 3, 121, 168
Larson, E.W., 174
Last, C.G., 60
Lazar, Z., 279, 281
Lazarus, A.A., 192, 193
Leary, T., 53, 61
Lecompte, C., 12
Lehman, H.E., 11
Leon, R.L., 177
Leonberger, F.T., 142
Lerner, H., 120
Lerner, P.M., 22, 120
Leventhal, T., 104
Levinson, D.J., 32
Levy, L.H., 8
Levy, M.R., 3, 20
Levy, S., 163, 165, 167
Lewak, R., 82, 151
Lewandowski, D.G., 20
Lewis, J.F., 89
Lezak, M.D., 144
Lief, A., 175
Lingoes, J.C., 147
Lipton, G., 263
Loewenstein, 32
Lore, W., 265, 266
Loutitt, C.M., 99
Lovitt, R., 10, 119, 189, 272
Lubin, B., 3, 19, 121, 168
Luborsky, L., 267, 268, 303, 334
Lunneborg, P.W., 234
Lyons, J., 102

M

Machover, K., 165, 166, 167, 325
Madsen, R.K., 101

Magnussen, M.J., 194, 265
Maisto, S.A., 12, 58, 195
Maloney, M.P., 4, 5, 10, 64, 120
Martin, R.M., 100
Masling, J., 104, 111
Matarazzo, J.D., 3, 5, 8, 11, 68, 69, 96, 121, 168, 171, 175, 230
May, R., 16, 78
McAllister, L.W., 156
McArthur, C.C., 40
McCallum, R.S., 133
McCauley, R.L., 101
McCrae, R.R., 52, 61, 63, 85
McCully, R.S., 19
McGregor, P., 22
McGuire, J.M., 3
McKinley, J.C., 311
McNeill, J., 298
McReynolds, F., 2, 60
Meagher, R.B., 153
Meehl, P.E., 44, 61, 69, 70, 71, 92, 93, 148, 290, 310
Megargee, E.I., 150, 156, 162
Meisel, A., 232
Mendelsohn, G.A., 150
Menninger, W.C., 43
Mercer, J.R., 89
Merck, K.H., 265, 266
Messer, S.B., 48
Messick, S., 54, 65, 66
Meyer, J.D., 38
Miale, F.R., 164
Michels, R., 9, 10, 55, 201, 202
Milgram, N., 103, 104
Miller-Jones, D., 78, 88
Millon, T., 22, 51, 52, 54, 59, 60, 61, 151, 152, 153, 202, 203, 204, 259, 278, 279
Milner, B., 138
Mindell, J.A., 3, 20
Mindess, H., 39
Miner, R.A., 55, 259
Mintz, J., 267
Mischel, W., 51
Mitchell, J.V., Jr., 64, 65, 69, 88
Moore, B.V., 171
Moreland, K.L., 68
Morey, L.C., 12, 59
Mortimer, R.L., 284
Morton, T.L., 3, 20
Mosak, H.H., 16, 232, 264
Murray, H.A., 26, 160, 162, 167, 296, 333
Murstein, B.I., 106, 162, 164, 168
Musante, G.J., 345

N

Nathan, G.J., 236
Nelson, D., 265, 266
Nelson, R.O., 15, 39, 48, 57, 266, 273
Neuffer, C.H., 232
Neuringer, C., 134, 140, 144
Nezu, A.M., 194
Nezu, C.M., 194
Norcross, J.C., 49, 171

O

O'Brien, C.P., 267
Odbert, H.S., 53
Odom, C.L., 73
Ogdon, D.P., 127, 166, 169, 200, 298
Olive, H., 246
Olson, J.L., 324, 328
Oskamp, S.W., 11
Othmer, E., 173, 174
Othmer, S.C., 173, 174
Owen, J.D., 205

P

Paine, C., 3
Parker, G.V., 162
Parsons, O., 140, 143
Pascal, G.R., 168, 175
Perfetto, G.A., 265
Perry, S., 10, 202
Phillips, L., 308
Piedmont, R.L., 110, 227
Piotrowski, C., 3, 21, 82, 83
Piotrowski, Z.A., 238
Potkay, C.R., 105, 160
Powers, A.D., 174
Powers, W.T., 105
Prather, E.N., 162
Pratt, J.M., 3
Prochaska, J.D., 171
Prout, A.T., 263, 287
Pruitt, J.A., 3, 19, 21
Pruyser, P.W., 225
Purisch, A.D., 139, 141, 143, 293

Q

Quarrick, E., 344
Quarrington, B., 64, 159
Quigley, J., 2

R

Rabin, A.I., 301
Rafi, A.A., 17
Rapaport, D., 9, 17, 48, 80, 99, 100, 106, 108, 109, 110, 111, 114, 117, 119, 120, 129, 158, 198, 278, 291, 298, 303, 304, 308, 346
Rapoport, J.L., 184, 185
Rauchway, A., 105, 159
Reagan, N., 2
Reid, W.H., 184, 185
Reik, T., 30
Reiser, M.F., 201
Reiss, W.J., 17, 223, 227, 228, 229, 240, 243, 246, 247
Reitan, R.M., 134, 138, 140, 144
Reynolds, W.M., 3, 22, 23, 291
Reznikoff, M., 43, 105, 159, 160, 232, 307
Richardson, S.A., 175
Richman, J., 232, 264
Rickers-Ovsiankina, M.A., 160
Ritzler, B., 3, 21
Robinson, J.T., 238
Rock, D.L., 12
Rodgers, D.A., 69
Rodriguez, R., 298
Rogers, C.R., 15, 16
Rohde, A.R., 165
Roman, M., 324, 329
Rorschach, H., 157, 158, 159, 304, 305, 308
Rosenblatt, B., 104
Rosenwald, G.C., 6, 9, 37, 43, 45, 77, 79, 103, 205, 292
Ross, A.O., 246
Roth, L.H., 232
Rothman, S., 92
Rotter, J.B., 163, 165
Rucker, C.N., 243
Ruebhausen, O.M., 90
Russ, S.W., 31
Russel, S., 63
Russell, E.W., 134, 140, 144
Rustagi, P.K., 174

S

Saccuzzo, D.P., 20
Sacks, J.M., 163, 165, 167
Salzinger, K., 59
Sarbin, T.R., 18, 30, 72, 228
Sargent, H.D., 243
Sattler, J.M., 131

Sawyer, J., 71, 72
Sbordone, R.J., 141
Schachtel, E.J., 102
Schafer, R., 9, 17, 36, 39, 41, 48, 80, 99, 100, 101, 106, 108, 109, 110, 111, 114, 117, 119, 129, 158, 198, 244, 278, 291, 298, 303, 304, 308, 346
Scheerer, M., 276, 277
Schlesinger, H.J., 45, 262, 347
Schneider, K.C., 5, 7, 10, 120, 186, 187
Schuldberg, D., 6, 14, 43, 47, 50, 104, 259, 266, 326
Schumer, F., 43, 105, 159, 294, 300, 324
Schwartz, F., 279, 281
Seat, P.D., 153, 154, 155, 199
Seever, M.F., 3, 121, 168
Seime, R.J., 101
Sell, J.M., 3
Sells, S.B., 34, 40
Shakow, D., 31
Shapiro, D., 130
Sharaf, M.R., 32
Shea, S.C., 175
Shectman, F., 41, 74, 76, 96, 120
Shelly, C., 141
Sherry, D., 3, 21
Shevrin, H., 120
Shipley, W.C., 134
Shively, J.J., 244
Siegal, R.S., 258
Sierles, F.S., 55
Simon, J.L., 10
Simonton, M.J., 232
Singer, M.T., 43, 104, 130, 280, 281, 324, 326, 327
Siskind, G., 243, 246
Skodol, A.E., 55, 184
Slepian, H., 104
Sloop, E.W., 344
Sloves, R.E., 5, 7 10, 120, 186, 187
Smith, A.E., 244
Smith, D., 56
Smith, G.M., 324, 328
Smith, J.G., 308
Smith, M.B., 237
Smith, M.C., 3, 19
Smith, W.H., 20, 284, 347, 348
Snyder, C.R., 2
Snyderman, M., 92
Sokolove, R.L., 110, 227
Solano, C., 65
Souther, J.W., 205
Spielberger, C.D., 63

Spiers, P.A., 141
Spitzer, R.L., 54, 172, 173, 176, 184
Sprafkin, J.N., 15
Stambrook, M., 141
Stein, E.J., 232
Stein, M., 162
Steinman, D.R., 142
Stolorow, R.D., 39
Strider, F.D., 265, 266, 344
Strupp, H.H., 265
Sturm, I.E., 205
Sugarman, A., 14, 16, 101, 120, 226, 332, 348, 349
Sundberg, N.D., 3, 6, 22, 102, 238, 239, 291
Sussman, N., 57
Suttell, B.J., 168
Swartz, J.D., 105
Sweeney, J.A., 108, 119
Symonds, P.M., 106
Szafir, A., 345
Szasz, T.S., 18

T

Taft, R., 30, 72, 170, 228
Tallent, N., 5, 7, 10, 17, 38, 41, 47, 75, 78, 93, 120, 129, 197, 201, 204, 223, 227, 228, 229, 236, 237, 238, 240, 243, 245 (n), 246, 247, 345
Taplin, J.R., 238, 239
Taylor, J.L., 225
Taylor, M. A., 55
Teicher, A.A., 225
Tenopyr, M.L., 65, 66
Thelen, M.H., 3, 19
Thomas, C.A., Jr., 129
Thorne, F.C., 29
Thorpe, J.S., 105
Tittle, C.K., 90
Todd, T., 267
Tolman, R.S., 243, 246
Tolor, A., 169
Torres-Henry, R., 3
Towbin, A. P., 120
Trimboli, F., 148, 200, 296
Tucker, D., 294
Tuma, J.M., 3
Turkat, I.D., 58, 59, 195
Turner, S.M., 58, 59
Tyler, L.E., 6, 102, 238, 239
Tyrer, P., 60

V

Vale, C.D., 95
Vance, F.L., 40
Vane, J.R., 294
Varble, D.L., 3, 19
Vega, A., 140
Vernier, C.M., 167
Volkan, V.D., 279
Vorhaus, P., 324

W

Wade, T.C., 3, 20, 22, 106, 291
Waite, R.R., 129
Waller, N.G., 61
Wallis, R.R., 3
Walton, C., 265
Ward, M.P., 4, 5, 10, 64, 120
Warren, R.L., 141
Waters, R.H., 78
Watkins, C.E., Jr., 3, 21, 22
Watley, D.J., 40, 41
Watson, R.I., 98, 99, 262
Webb, J.T., 82, 151
Wechsler, D., 6, 85, 125, 126, 127, 128, 129, 131, 132, 134
Wedding, D., 143
Weiner, I., 19, 64, 104, 120, 159, 160, 189
Weiner, M.F., 278
Weiss, D.J., 57, 94
Welsh, G.S., 135, 151
Wertheimer, M., 12
Westcott, M.R., 30
Wheeler, L., 138
Whyte, W.H., Jr., 87
Widiger, T.A., 60, 90
Wielkiewicz, R.M., 124
Wiens, A.N., 171, 175
Wiggins, J.S., 11
Wiig, E.H., 133
Wildman, R.W., 226
Williams, H.L., 135
Williams, J.B.W., 34, 173, 184
Winter, W.D., 324, 328
Wirt, R.D., 153, 154, 155, 199
Wise, M.G., 184, 185
Witenberg, E.G., 284
Witmer, L., 7, 8, 98
Wohl, J., 3, 19
Wolford, J., 232
Wolfson, D., 144
Woo-Sam, J.M., 132
Wrobel, T.A., 148
Wynne, L.C., 324, 326

Z

Zelkind, I., 298
Zimet, C.N., 291
Zimmerman, I.L., 131, 132
Zins, J.E., 189
Ziskin, J., 39, 103, 247
Zubin, J., 43, 72, 105, 159, 171, 294, 299, 300, 324
Zytowski, D.G., 90

SUBJECT INDEX

A

Action language, 244, 271–72, 300
Adaptive testing, 94
Altered atmosphere procedure, 274, 330
Aphasia Screening Test, 137
Army Alpha, 3, 82
Army Beta, 3, 82
Assessment *Zeitgeist*, 4
Average Impairment Rating, 134–35, 138–39

B

Battery approach, 110, 114, 115, 198
Battery, basic, 198, 291
Battery, selection, 35, 290–91
Behavioral assessment
    context of behavior, 15
    as new development, 3
    and psychometric criteria, 15
    and trait conception, 15
Behavior therapy
    changing attitudes, 48–49
    relation to theory, 48–49
Bender Gestalt
    administration, 168
    ambiguous status, 168
    application, 167–168
    brain damage identification, 12, 40, 168
    description, 168
    intelligence measure, 168
    interpretation, 168
    personality description, 168
    scoring, 168
    as test, 9
    use, extent, 168
Binet, Alfred, 81–82
Binet (Binet-Simon) test, 3, 9, 82
    Kuhlman revision, 82
    Stanford-Binet, 82
"Biological intelligence," 134
Brain Watchers, The, 87
"Buckley Amendment," 91, 231, 234

C

California Psychological Inventory (CPI)
    application, 155, 156
    basic scales, 156
    description, 155
    reliability, 155
    scoring and interpretation, 155

California Psychological Inventory (CPI) *(cont.)*
  special scales and indexes, 15
Case conceptualization (formulation) *(see also* Psychological reports)
  in biologically-oriented psychiatry, 75–76
  consultant role, 290
  content, 209
  and diagnosis, coexistence, 9
  and diagnosis, similarities and differences, 10
  organization, 209, 225
  process, 208–10
  taxonomic approach, 202–04
  topics, 207–8
Case-focused approach, 10, 15, 74–75, 271–72
Case workup, definition, 290
Category Test, 134
Cattell, James McKeen, 3, 81
Centralists, 27–28
Character, 115
Children's Apperception Test (CAT), 162
Client as co-evaluator, 16
Clinical assessment theory
  dynamic formulation, 109
  ego psychology, 109
  impulse-defense configurations, 109
  personality organization, 109
  thought processes, 109
Clinical behavior, 198, 225–26
Clinical-intuitive method of analysis, 301
Clinical judgment
  applications, 34–36
  and assessment skills, 24
  centralists and peripheralists, 27–28
  in interpretation, 116
  intuition in, 29–31
  in neuropsychology, 143
  orientations, 28–31
  and psychophysical judgment, 29
  role, 323
  training and experience, 11–14
"Clinical method in psychology," 98
Clinical versus statistical controversy, 40–41, 44–45, 69–72, 93
Clinical versus Statistical Prediction, 69–72
Clinical tradition
  battery approach, 110, 114, 115
  data goals, 101–2
  ego-psychology approach, 100
  flexibility, 100
  goals, 99, 100–103
  idiographic/idiothetic method, 100–101
  interpretive approach, 101

  judgment, inference, and subjectivity, 14
  modern phase, 107
  prediction, 100
  psychological-mindedness, 101
  psychological thinking, 101
  and psychometric doctrine, differences, 108–9
  psychometric use, 99
  scores, role, 101, 115
  statistics, 101, 108
  subjectivity, 101
  test administration, 108
  test role, 108
  theory emphasis, 109
  understanding, 100
  Witmer's contribution, 98
Clinician's personal approach, 99–100
Coaxing data, 111–12
"Cogwheeling," 110
Cointerpretation, 334–35
Collaborative Drawing Technique, 328–29
Communication between assessors and consumers, 41–42
"Computer assessment," 7
Computer-based test interpretation
  characteristics, 33–34
  proper use, 33–34
  qualifications for using, 33–34
Computerized tests, equivalence to conventional tests, 68
Computer reports, different from assessment reports, 7, 75
Computer testing
  acceptability, 96
  adaptive, 94
  administration modes, 94
  algorithms, 68, 69, 94–95
  clinical judgment, 95
  clinician's role, 95–96
  consumer use, 69
  cookbook, 93
  development, 68–69
  Guidelines for Computer-Based Tests and Interpretations, 29, 46, 92
  interactive, 94
  need to monitor, 37
  origin in physicalism and psychometrics, 93
  privacy issues, 91–92, 235
  qualified professional, 93
  records, safeguarding, 91–92
  records, wrongful access, 91–92
  report length, 96
  "second opinion," 97

software taxonomy, 94
subjective input, 68
substitute for clinical judgment, 69
test administrator, 93
test developer, 92–93
test taker, 93
test user, 69, 93
using, 97
validity, 67–69, 96–97
versatility, 94
Conceptualists, 27–28
Conceptual quotient (CQ), 134
Concreteness as a psychotherapeutic variable, 276–78
Confidentiality (see Computer testing, Privacy issues; Testing, privacy issues)
Consensus intelligence testing, 329–30
Consensus Rorschach, 43, 104, 326–28
Consultant role of psychological assessor, 37–38, 290
"Cookbook" (*see also* clinical vs. statistical controversy), 44–45, 93, 148, 297–99
   Bender Gestalt, 298
   drawbacks, 298
   "dream book" interpretation, 106, 298–99
   MMPI, 298
   Rorschach, 298–99
Coping Skills Model (CSM), 61
Counseling psychology
   personality assessment, 21–25
   test use, 21–22
Countertransference, 101, 283, 331–33, 348, 350
Critical items, 113, 148
Cultural factors in tests
   criteria for fairness, 88–89
   cross-cultural tests, 88
   disadvantages based on origin, 88
   documentation of cultural unfairness, 88–89
   culture-common tests, 88
   culture-fair tests, 88
   culture-free tests, 88

D

Data gathering
   collateral data, 292
   nontest data, 292
   reason for assessment, 291–92
   relevance, 292
Defenses, 115, 116, 148–49
Deviant verbalizations, 111–12
Diagnosis

vs. case formulation, 9–10, 58
characteristics, 118
characterologic, 118
defined, 116–17
drawbacks, 9
function, 10
individualized predictions, 119
overemphasized, 10
in psychological assessment, 227–28
symptomatic, 57, 118
underlying dysfunctions, 57
to facilitate understanding, 119
value, 117
Diagnostic alliance, 75, 349
Diagnostic conclusion, defined (Schafer), 116
Diagnostic consultation vs. "prescriptive testing," 43
Diagnosis Related Groups (DRGs), 74
Diagnostic and Statistical Manual of Mental Disorders (DSM)
   acceptance, 54–58, 177
   application, 9, 177–78
   alternatives, 60–61
   atheoretical orientation, 184
   axes, defined, 178–79
   axis code numbers, 178
   behavior therapy view, 57–58
   caution in use, 183
   classification, major categories and subcategories, 179–82
   classification of personality disorders, 55–56
   contrary psychiatric position, 55
   criticisms, 55–58, 259
   decision trees, 183
   development, 177
   diagnostic hierarchy, 183–84
   editions, 54–55
   medical model influence, 18
   multiaxial classification, 178
   multiaxial diagnoses, 183
   multiple diagnoses, 183
   objectivity, deficiency, 259
   and psychodynamic orientation, 55
   and psychological assessment, 57
   and psychological diagnostic methods, 56–57
   psychological view, 56–57
   and psychotherapy, 55–56, 178, 259
   rules for making diagnoses, 182–84
   theoretical rationale, 58
   training guides, 184
   V Codes, 178, 182
Disharmony among professionals, 76
Draw-a-Person test (DAP) (see drawing tests)

Drawing tests
   administration, 165–66
   interpretation, 166, 167
   stereotypy, Aunt Fanny, 167
   Structured Interview Technique, 325

E

Eclecticism, 48–49
Education for All Handicapped Children Act of 1975 (Public Law 94–142), 91, 234
Empathy, 32
Ethical and legal constraints, 230–31
Ethical Principles of Psychologists, 45, 233–35
Experiential data, 102
Extraception, 26–28

F

Fabulized combination, 112
Family TAT, 328
Free association, 157

G

Galton, Sir Francis, 2–3
Gender role analysis, 171–72
Goldstein-Scheerer battery, 277
Guidelines for Computer-based Tests and Interpretations, 29, 46, 323

H

Halo effect in observation, 170
Halstead-Reitan Neuropsychological Battery
   aphasia screening test, 137
   Average Impairment Rating, 134–35, 138–39
   category test, 135
   description, 134–35
   flexibility of use, 135
   Halstead finger tapping test, 137–38
   hit rate, 138
   interpretation, 138–39
   lateral dominance examination, 137
   limitations, 141
   Miles ABC test of ocular dominance, 137
   Minnesota Multiphasic Personality Inventory (MMPI), 134–35
   neuropsychological key approach, 138–39
   Reitan-Klove sensory perception examination, 136–37
   Seashore rhythm test, 135–36
   speech sounds perception test, 134
   tactual performance test, 136
   trail making tests, 136
   validity, 140–41
   Wechsler scales, 134–35
Historical truth, 72
House-Tree-Person Test (HTP) (see Drawing tests)
Human Figure Drawing (see Drawing tests)
Humanistic psychology, 15–16
Hume, David, 77

I

Idiographic/idiothetic method, 100–101
Inference, 14, 30, 118
Information overload, 42, 96
Informed consent, 90–91
Inquiry
   clinical use, 112–13
   illustration, 112–13, 123–24
   MMPI, 113
   nonstandard, 123–24
   psychometric use, 112
   Rorschach, 157, 292
   sentence completions, 112, 163
   strategy, 103
   TAT, 161, 292
   Wechsler, 123–24
Inquiry items, 113
intellectual knowing, 32
Intelligence
   classification, 126
   defined, 125, 130
   nonintellective factors, 85, 127
Intelligence quotient, origin, 82 (*see also* IQ)
Interaction testing, 324–25
Interpersonal pathologizers, 238
Interpretation
   as art, 8
   criticisms,
      inadequate differentiation, 249
      irresponsible interpretation, 249
      overspeculation, 249–50
      unlabeled speculation, 250
   deduction, 200, 296
   defined, 116
   idiom, 295
   induction, 200, 296
   interviewing, 33

intraception, 26–28
introspection, 32
intuitive, 294
logic, 295–300
metaphor, 295
normative approach, 200, 295
personal norms, 200, 295
phenomenological frame of reference, 200–201
problem definition, 294
projective approach, 201, 296
reflection, 294
style, 9
Interviewing
in assessment, extent, 171
defenses, management techniques, 173–74
definition, 171
gender related issues, 171–72
gender role analysis, 171–72
informal, 172
limitations, 283–84
nonschedule standardized interview, 172
reliability, 172
schedule standardized interview, 172
standardized, 172
Structured Clinical Interview for DSM-III-R (SCID), 173
therapeutic use, 172
value, 105
Intrapsychic pathologizers, 238
Intuition
anecdotal accounts, 30
in clinical judgment, 29–31
consensus, 30
definitions, 30
as direct and immediate, 30–31
as inference, 30,
in psychological assessment, 31
IQ
controversy, 92
deviation IQ, 122–23
testers, 36

K

Knowledge *about* psychological matters, 32
Knowledge *of* psychological matters, 32
Kuhlmann, Frederick, 82

L

Language, intensifying and qualifying language, 117

Lateral Dominance Examination, 137
"Less of a test" concept, 43, 50, 326
Luria-Nebraska Neuropsychological Battery (LNNB)
evaluation, 141
interpretation, 140
origin, 139
scales, 140
subtests, 139–40
validity, 141

M

Measurement of psychological variables, 77
Medical model, 18
Medical students, training in psychology, 38
Menninger Foundation Psychotherapy Research Project, 266–67
Menschenkenner, 25
Mental disorder
categorical vs dimensional approach to diagnosis, 58–60
early classification, 54
culinary metaphor for diagnosing, 58–59
empirical vs. theoretical approach to diagnosis, 58–59
Kraeplinian, 54
purpose of classification, 54
Mental illness as metaphor, 18
Mental retardation
classification, 126, 127
diagnosis, 126
Mental Status Examination (MSE)
definition, 62
nonstatistical logic, 33
outlines, 175
purpose, 175
techniques, 175–76
variables observed, 111, 175–76
Mental testers, 36
Merrill, Maud, 82
Metaphor, 295, 300
Miles ABC Test of Ocular Dominance, 137
Millon Adolescent Personality Inventory (MAPI), 153
Millon Behavioral Health Inventory (MBHI), 153
Millon Clinical Multiaxial Inventory (MCMI)
application, 153
Axis I disorders, significance, 152
clinical attributes, 202–4
clinical domains, 203

Millon Clinical Multiaxial Inventory (MCMI) *(cont.)*
  clinical scales, 152–53
  description, 152
  differences from MMPI, 151
  and DSM, Axis II, 151
  false negatives, positives, 153
  interpretive reports, 152
  modifier indices, 152
  polarities, 204
  taxonomic approach, 202–4
  variables measured, 85
Minimal testing rules, 124, 125
Minnesota Multiphasic Personality Inventory (MMPI)
  administration and scoring, 146
  application, 146
  bias, 89
  cannot say score, significance, 146
  caudality scale, 135
  character scales, 148
  clinical scales, 146
  critical items, 148
  description, 145–46
  dynamic interpretation, 148
  "faking bad," 147
  F score, significance, 147
  global measure of personality, 85
  group differences, 89
  history, 145–46
  introduction, 3
  K correction, 147
  K score, significance, 147
  L score, significance, 146–47
  MMPI *Atlas*, 91
  in neuropsychological assessment, 134–35
  parietal-frontal scale, 135
  reliability, 149–50
  research base, 145
  scale numbers, 147
  special or research scales, 147
  standardization, 145–46
  symptom scales, 148
  three-point codes, 147
  two-point codes, 147
  use,
    continuity, 82
    extent, 145
  validity, 150
  validity scales, 146–47, 288
MMPI-2
  additions and deletions, 150
  compared with original MMPI, 150–51
  standardization, 150–51
"More of a test, less of a test" concept, 43

N

Narrative truth, 72
NEO Personality Inventory (NEO-PI), 85
Neuropsychological assessment
  agnosia, 137
  Average Impairment Rating, 134–35, 138–39
  Babcock's approach, 133–34
  "biological intelligence," 134
  brain lesion identification, 142
  conceptual quotient (CQ), 134
  deficit, 133, 142
  "deterioration," 133, 142
  diagnosis of brain pathology, 138
  "don't hold tests," 134
  ecological referencing, 143
  forecasts of future use, 142–43
  Halstead-Reitan Neuropsychological Battery (HRB), 134–39
  history, 133
  "hold tests," 134
  vs. imaging techniques, 142
  medical referencing, 142–43
  "organicity," 133, 142
  problem-oriented practice, 143
  qualitative vs. quantitative approach, 143
  rehabilitation referencing, 143
  Shipley test, 134
  suppressions, 137
  systemic approach, 143
  Wechsler's approach, 134
Nomothetic method, 100–101
Nonpsychometric tools as tests, 9
Nontest factors, significance, 103–4
Nosology, value, 117

O

Objectivity in psychometrics, 81
Observation
  attentiveness to client variables, 171
  countertransference and distortion, 170–71
  denial and overestimation, 171
  halo effect, 170
  identification and loss of objectivity, 171
  informal norms, 171
  person perception literature, 170
  projection and distortion, 170

projective identification and loss of objectivity, 171
rationalization and overestimation, 171
repression and overestimation, 171
stereotypes, 170
One last response procedure, 331
Oracular role of psychologist, 39, 42
Organization Man, The, 87
Overinterpretation (overpathologizing), 8

P

Part-function information, 16
Peabody Picture Vocabulary Test-Revised (PPVT-R)
  administration, 132–33
  basal and ceiling rules, 133
  description, 132
  norms, 133
  reliability, 133
  standardization, 133
  validity, 133
Peculiar verbalizations, 112
Penn Psychotherapy Project, 267–69
Peripheralists, 27
Person perception literature, 170
Personal equation, 24–25, 44
Personal experience, relation to theoretical orientation, 37
Personality
  ability to judge, 25–26
  adaptive role, 118–19
  anticoherency position, 51
  anticonsistency position, 51
  clinical tradition, 102
  holistic views, 51
  stability, 51–52
  style, 53
  structure, 48
  terms, 53–54
  theory
    trait conception, 14, 15
Personality assessment
  cognitive constructions, 50
  representational processes, 50
  in counseling psychology, 21–22
  "renaissance," 22
Personality disorders
  contextual role in diagnosis, 53
  "mixed" or "atypical" diagnoses, 59
  and normal personality, similarities, 52–53
  prognostic significance, 53
  reliability of diagnosis, 59
  symptom coverage, 59
  as target behaviors, 53
Personality Inventory for Children (PIC)
  application, 154
  clinical scales, 154
  description, 154
  profile scales, 154
  reliability, 155
  scoring and interpretation, 154
  screening scales, 154
  standardization, 154
  supplementary scales, 154
  validity scales, 154
Personality theory, subjectivity, 39
Physicalism
  contradiction, law of, 79
  disjunction, 79
  excluded middle, law of, 79
  and humanistic psychologists, 78
  oligotomy, 80
  quantification, 79
  reduction, 80
  traits, 78
Phenomenology, 50
Positivism, 50
Prediction, 72
Privacy Act of 1974, 91, 234
Problem identification, 34–35
Professional disharmony, 76
Prognosis, 228
Projective counseling, 324–25
Projective hypothesis, 109, 301
Projective techniques
  attitudes to, 19–21, 39
  distinguished from tests, 106
  as mirror, 104
  as X ray, 104
Psychiatrists, training in psychology, 38
Psychodiagnosis, 14
Psychological assessment
  a priori approach (Carey, Flasher, Maisto, & Turkat), 195–96
  ancient approaches, 1–2
  armamentarium, 62
  as art, 8, 24
  attitudes to, 19–22
  BASIC ID (Lazarus), 192–93
  behavioral model (Nezu & Nezu), 194
  biblical references, 1–2
  case formulation, 201–2, 204–10
  clinical tradition, 290
  as collaborative effort, 74
  conceptual model (Lovitt), 189–90

Psychological assessment *(cont.)*
  countertransference, 101, 283, 331–33, 348–49, 350
  decision-making evaluation scheme (Howe), 194–95
  decision-making system (Berger), 190–91
  definitions, 4–7
  dispositional perspective, 194–95
  dynamic and conceptual, 7
  disillusionment, 39
  ethical principles, 45–46
  evaluation, 120
  frame(s) of reference, 199
  goals, 1, 47–48, 99
  identification of client variables, 49
  as integrative task, 5
  interactional schema (Tallent), 196–202
  interpersonal variables, 104
  interpretation, 199–201
  and intuition, 31
  modern era, 98
  as multiple and complex interaction, 5, 196–202, 204
  as nonhumanistic, 16–17
  practical use, 34–36
  as problem solving, 4–7, 34–35, 186
  problem solving model (Sloves, Docherty, & Schneider), 186–89
  problem solving model (Zins), 189
  as process, 4–6
  and psychological-mindedness, 32–33
  and psychotherapy, commonalities, 45
  reason for assessment, 197
  resistance, 274, 349–50
  scientific principles, 8
  as "scientific art," 8
  situational variables, 104
  as systems and problem oriented, 7
  team involvement, 190
  and testing, confused with, 4–7
  and testing, different from, 4–7, 186
  and theory-linked personality variables, 49
  therapeutic effect, 347–48
  as transaction, 347–48
  transference, 348–49, 350
  as variable process, 4–5
  visual-integrative technique (Hulse-Jennings), 191–92
Psychological assessor
  active and flexible role, 103
  clinical tradition, 290
  cognitive activity, 290
  consultant role, 37–38, 290, 348
  definition, 36
  instrumental role, 11, 14, 34, 36–38, 39–43, 98, 100, 108, 196–97
  judgment demands, 34
  latitude, 290
  overvaluation and undervaluation, 39
  participant-observer role, 292
  personal factors, 197
  responsibility, 33–34, 37
  vs. tester, 11
  training, 31
  transference-countertransference, 283, 292
Psychological instruments
  ethical injunctions for use, 33–34, 121
  challenges, 39–41
  disillusionment, 39
  judgment in use, 34
  misunderstood, 39–43
Psychological-mindedness
  in clinical tradition, 101
  and psychological assessment, 32–33
  self-analogue, 32
  and self-insight, 26
Psychological reports
  acceptability, 42
  action language, 244, 271–72
  appendix, 241
  assessment outcome, 197
  caricature, 210
  case-focusing, 10, 74–75, 207, 271–72
  central themes, 209, 210
  clinical behavior, 225–26
  communication problems,
    hedging, 257
    length of reports, 257–58
    organization, 256–57
    style, 256
    too technical, too complex, 255–56
    vague, unclear, ambiguous, 255
    word usage, 254–55
  content,
    appropriate emphasis, 206, 209–10
    clinical style, 241
    criticisms,
      diagnoses, prognoses, recommendations, 248–49
      improper emphasis, 248
      minor relevance, 248
      omission of essential information, 248
      raw data, 247–48
      unnecessary duplication, 249
    definition and classification, 222

diagnosis, 227–28
forensic reports, 247
frequently appropriate, 223
illustrative, 222
inappropriate, 222, 224
intellectual aspects, 226–27
length, 244, 257–58
literary style, 241–42
new integration, 223
orienting data, 222
personality, 227
persuasive, 222
primary, 222
prognosis, 228
purposes, 221
raw data, 240–41, 242
recommendations, 228–29
relevance, 222–24
scientific style, 241
secondary, 222
selection, 205–6, 209, 216–17, 220–21
in "traditional reports," 224–29
cost effectiveness, 73–74
effectiveness, 220, 229–30
flexibility, 205–7
information for psychotherapist, 289
intellectual aspects, 226–27
jargon, 73, 243
length, 73, 74, 206, 207, 244
organization, 205–7, 209, 215–19
outline, 205, 210–14
overview, 214, 218
parsimony, 206, 207
personal characteristics of writer, 206
pitfalls, 41, 75, 220, 246–47
"quickie" reports, 75, 244–46
rationale, 73–74
reflecting problems of science and profession
  role conduct, 260–61
  science
    psychological instruments, 258
    theory, 258
    unresolved issues, 259–60
reflecting psychologist's attitude and orientation
  exhibitionism, 251
  not practical or useful, 251
  overabstract, 253
  test orientation vs. client orientation, 252–53
  too authoritative, 252
  too theoretical, 253
repetition, 209–10

responsibility, 220, 222, 229–30, 242
as road map in therapy, 285–86, 288
segmented presentation, 206–7, 225
sharing with clients, 231–34
shotgun reports, 73, 206, 207, 210, 221, 258
speculation, 217–18, 242
stereotypy, 205
summary, 214, 229
technical language, 243–44
writing for clients, 232–33
Psychological testing
  as actuarial, 6
  defined, 6–7
  misidentified as assessment, 7
  as physicalistic, 6
  as psychometric, 6
  teaching to psychiatric residents, 75
Psychological tests (see specific tests by name)
  reliability, 61, 62–63
  standardization, 61
  validity, 61, 63–65
Psychological thinking, 101
Psychological understanding, objective approaches, 33
Psychology, as science of the construction of meaning, 50
Psychometric classification
  five-factor model, 61
  Leary's interpersonal circumplex, 61
  Millon's three-dimensional scheme, 61
Psychometric model, 14
Psychometric instruments, classification, 84
Psychometrics
  heuristic value, 80
  objectivity, 81
  in psychological assessment, 80
  reliability, 81
  standardization, 81
  status, 81
  validity, 81
Psychotherapy
  assessor-client interaction, 275, 283
  assessor-instrument-client interaction, 275
  and assessment
    assumptions, 6, 47, 262–63
    clinical impressions, 263–64, 273–74
    empirical findings, 264–69
    equivocal relationship, 263, 266
  "bogged down," 284
  client variables, 49, 270–71
  commonalities with assessment, 45, 262
  concreteness as psychotherapeutic variable, 276–78

Psychotherapy *(cont.)*
  focus, 284–85
  information for psychotherapist, 289
  Menninger Foundation Psychotherapy Research Project
    benefits of assessment, 267
    hazards of ignoring assessment findings, 266–67
  "new set of lenses," 284
  Penn Psychotherapy Project, 267–69
    "helping alliance" and outcome, 267
    pretreatment patient factors and outcome, general conclusion, 267
    pretreatment patient factors and outcome, specific findings, 268–69
Psychological report as road map, 285–86, 288

Q

Qualified professional, 93
Qualitative analysis, 299

R

"Real test situation," 111
Recommendations, 228–29
Referral questions
  focused, 74
  latent content, 35, 42
  manifest content, 35–42
  meaningfulness, 194–95, 197–98
Regression in the service of the ego, 32–33
Regressive personality features, 278–83
Reitan-Klove sensory perception examination, 136–37
Reliability
  alternate form, 63
  interjudge, 63
  odd-even, 63
  in psychometrics, 81
  split-half, 63
  test-retest, 63
Resistance in clinical communication, 41
Rorschach
  administration, 157–58, 159
  application, 34, 104–6
  in borderline personality disorder, 130, 280–82
  cognitive construction, 50, 102–3
  comprehensive system, 105, 159, 293
  computer interpretation, 50, 86, 159, 160
  concreteness indicators, 278
  consensus Rorschach, 43, 104, 326–28
  construction of meaning and reality, 157
  decrease of distance, 113–14
  description, 156
  determinants of response, 157
  diagnostic effectiveness, 40
  diversity among Rorschachers, 160
  "dream book" interpretation, 106, 298–99
  experience balance, 306
  as experimental procedure, 50
  in formulating diagnoses, 17
  free-association, 157
  identified as test, 9
  increase of distance, 113–14
  inquiry, 157
  interpretation, requisites, 158
  as interview, 104–5, 294, 299–300, 324
  as "less of a test," 43, 50, 104–6
  location of responses, 157
  meaningfulness, 293
  perceptual processes, 102, 157
  personality appraisal, 157
  personality organization, 50
  polymorphous potential, 50
  projection, 296–97
  not a projective test, 296
  psychometric approach, 50
  psychometric properties, 106–7, 108
  rationale, 110–11, 303–8
  representational processes, 50, 102–3
  revisions, 120
  Rorschach idiom, 160
  scores, critique, 106–7
  scoring, as coding, 107
  scoring, misuse, 106
  scoring, personalized, 106, 293
  scoring, across systems, 158
  stimulus-response orientation, 102
  structural summary, 107, 294
  "systems," 157, 158, 159
  survey data, 19–21
  symbolic content, 113
  testing the limits, 158
  thematic content, 113
  time to do, 73, 294
  as transaction, 43, 104, 326
  trendiest use, 50
  use, extent, 3, 156
  validity, conceptual, 159
  validity, empirical, 159
  validity, psychometric, 156, 159, 294

Rorschach Interpretation Assistance Program (RIAP), 50, 86

S

Scatter, 130–31, 227
Science, application to assessment, 50
Scores, contextual interpretation, 116
Seashore Rhythm Test, 135–36
Selected response procedure, 330
Self-analogue, 32
Self-interpretation of test protocols, 333–34
Senior Apperception Test (SAT), 162
Sentence completion methods
  administration, 163
  Forer, 163
  inquiry, 112, 163
  interpretation, 50, 164
  reliability, 164
  Rotter, 163, 164
  Sacks, 163–64
  scoring, 164
  validity, 164
Shipley test, 134
Sophisticated clinical method, 72
Sorting test, 108
Speech Sounds Perception Test, 134
Standards for Educational and Psychological Testing, 14, 29, 33, 37, 46, 85–86, 93–94, 234–35, 323
Standards for Providers of Psychological Services, 46
Statistics, in clinical tradition, 108
Stereotypy
  Aunt Fanny, 2, 167, 235, 238–40, 308
  Barnum, 2, 236–38
  Madison Avenue, 237
  in observation, 170
  prosecuting attorney brief, 238
  test related, 17–18
Stern, Wilhelm, 82
Subjectivity, 101
Sympathy, 32
System of Multicultural Pluralistic Assessment (SOMPA)
  adjusted scores, 89
  compensated scores, 89
  Wechsler scales in, 130

T

Tactual Performance Test, 136

Team members, disparities in training, 38, 75
Technical Report Writing, 205–6
Technician
  in assessment-treatment model, 345–46, 350
  impact of contribution, 345
  quality of work, 344–45
  role, 37–38, 344–45, 347
Temporary inefficiency, 109
Terman, Lewis M., 82
Test administrator, 93
Test bias
  cross-cultural tests, 88
  cultural, 88
  culture-common tests, 88
  culture-fair tests, 88
  culture-free tests, 88
  sex bias, 90
  unintentional bias, 89
Test centrism, 9
Tester
  acceptability of role, 62, 344
  passive role, 37, 103, 292
  as perceived role of psychologist, 38–39
  personality variations, 41
  role, 111
  as technician, 37–38
Test developer, 92–93
Test idiom, 295, 299–300
  Bender-Gestalt, 301–2
  Rorschach, 303–8
Testing
  commercialism, 66–67, 88
  and conformity, 87, 88
  cost-benefit compromises, 86
  in counseling psychology, 21–22
  definition, 290
  ethics, 85–86
  flexibility, 85–86
  industry, 82
  informed consent, 90–91
  interactive, 103
  as moral issue, 88
  movement, 81
  nonstandardized use, 86
  in personnel selection, 87
  privacy issues, 90–92, 234–35
  problematic, 87–92
  professional judgment, 86
  record safeguarding, 91–92
  scientific features, 8
  standards, 86
  validity of hypotheses, 86

Testing *(cont.)*
  validity challenge, 88
Testing the limits, 103, 124, 158, 292
  altered atmosphere procedure (Appelbaum), 274
  one last response procedure, 331
  paradigmatic techniques (Appelbaum), 275
  selected response procedure, 330-31
Test items
  face validity, 88
  post-testing feedback, 91
  privacy invasion, 91
  sex content, 88
Test rationale
  development, 109
  Form response, 110-11
  as hypotheses, 110
  Information subtest (Wechsler), 109
  projective hypothesis, 109
  "real test situation," 111
  research support, 110
  Rorschach, 303-8
    content, 307-8
    Detail response, 305
    Form response, 305-6, 110-11
    Human Movement response, 306
    Original response, 308
    Popular response, 308
    Whole response, 304-5
  Wechsler, 109
Test response process, 103-4
Test results, 9, 10, 33-34, 62, 116, 198-99, 202, 224
Tests
  criterion referenced, 78
  cultural factors, 88-89
  equivalence, conventional and computerized versions, 67-68
  global, 85
  most frequently used, 83 (t)
  as interviews, 299-300
  newly developed, 82
  norm referenced, 78
  as psychometric scales, 78
  single variable, 85
  traditional, 82
Test taker, 93
Test user, 37, 93
Thematic Apperception Test (TAT)
  administration, 161
  concreteness indicators, 277-78
  description, 161
  hero, 161
  as impressionistic instrument, 294
  inquiry, 161
  interpretation, 161-62
  psychometric properties, 108
  reliability, 162
  scoring, 161-62
  as test, 9
  theory, 160-61
  validity, 162
Theoretical orientation, relation to personal experience, 37
Theory
  in behavior therapy, 48
  convergent tendencies, 48-49
  eclecticism, 48-49
  integration, 49
  relation to psychotherapy, 47-49
  and psychotherapy in ego psychology tradition, 48
Therapy (see Psychotherapy)
Thinking style, 115
Thomson, William (Lord Kelvin), 77
Thorndike, Edward Lee, 77
Thought processes, 109
Trail Making Tests, 136
Traits
  isolated with tests, 80
  as part processes, 78
  as physicalistic, 78
Transference in assessment, 348, 350
Typological concepts, usefulness, 117
Tyranny of Testing, The, 87

U

Underinterpretation, 8
Understanding
  definition, 100
  as "empathic sharing," 100
  prediction as means, 72
  in prediction, 100
  in problem resolution, 100

V

Validity
  assessment, 65
  concept, abuse of, 66-67
  conceptualization, 65
  concurrent, 64
  construct-related evidence, 64, 65-66
  content-related evidence, 63-64, 65-66

convergent validation, 64
crisis, 65–66
criterion-related evidence, 64, 65–66
discriminant validation, 64
flawed conceptualization, 64
predictive, 64
psychometric, 65, 81
as social effectiveness, 87
technical, 87

W

Wechsler Adult Intelligence Scale (WAIS), 82, 121–22
Wechsler Adult Intelligence Scale—Revised (WAIS-R), 82, 122
   concreteness indicators, 278
   interpretive significance, 127–30
   in neuropsychological battery, 130
   performance subtests, 122
   qualitative features, 128–30
   verbal subtests, 122
Wechsler-Bellevue Scale (W-B), 82, 121
Wechsler Intelligence Scale for Children (WISC), 82, 122
Wechsler Intelligence Scale for Children—Revised (WISC-R), 82, 122
Wechsler Intelligence Scale for Children—Third Edition (WISC-III), 82, 122
Wechsler Memory Scale (WMS),
Wechsler Preschool and Primary Scale for Children (WPPSI), 82, 122
Wechsler Preschool and Primary Scale of Intelligence—Revised (WPPSI-R), 82, 122
Wechsler scales (see also specific Wechsler scales by name)
   abstraction-concreteness, 277
   administration and scoring, 123–25
   application, 17, 125–26, 130
   in borderline personality disorder, 130, 280
   in borderline psychosis, 130
   and clinical tradition, 127
   description, 121–23
   and diagnosis, 129
   as global measure, 130
   introduction, 3
   in neuropsychological assessment, 134–35
   nonintellective factors, 85, 127
   objectivity, 81
   as projective instruments, 109, 129
   rationale, 109
   reliability, 131
   scatter, 130–31
   standardization, 130
   validity, 131
   verbal-performance discrepancy, 130
Witmer, Lightner, 47, 98, 107